Second Edition

ECONOMICS BY DESIGN
Principles and Issues

ROBERT A. COLLINGE
RONALD M. AYERS

The University of Texas at San Antonio

PRENTICE HALL
Upper Saddle River, New Jersey 07458

Senior Editor: Rod Banister
Associate Editor: Gladys Soto
Editorial Assistant: William Becher
Editor-in-Chief: P J Boardman
Editorial Director/VP   James C. Boyd
Senior Marketing Manager: Lori Braumberger
Production Editor: Carol Samet
Associate Managing Editor: Cynthia Regan
Manufacturing Buyer: Lisa DiMaulo
Senior Manufacturing Supervisor: Paul Smolenski
Manufacturing Manager: Vincent Scelta
Designer: Kevin Kall
Design Manager: Patricia Smythe
Interior Design: David Levy
Cover Design: David Levy
Cover Illustration: Nip Rogers/Stock Illustration Source
Composition: Black Dot

Collinge, Robert A.
    Economics by design : principles and issues / Robert A. Collinge,
Ronald M. Ayers. — 2nd ed.
        p.   cm.
    Includes bibliographical references and index.
    ISBN 0-13-013298-5 (alk. paper)
    1. Economics.   I. Ayers, Ronald M.   II. Title.
HB171.5.C845   1999
    330—dc21   99-28277
                                                                          CIP

Prentice-Hall International (UK) Limited, London
Prentice-Hall of Australia Pty. Limited, Sydney
Prentice-Hall Canada, Inc., Toronto
Prentice-Hall Hispanoamericana, S.A., Mexico
Prentice-Hall of India Private Limited, New Delhi
Prentice-Hall of Japan, Inc., Tokyo
Prentice-Hall (Singapore) Pte. Ltd.
Editora Prentice-Hall do Brasil, Ltda., Rio de Janeiro

Printed in the United States of America

10 9 8 7 6 5 4 3 2 1

To Mary, Mom, Dad, and my students,
for their insights and encouragement.
RAC

To my mother and father, my former professors at the
University of New Orleans and Tulane University, and
the ever-patient Coco and Buddy.
RMA

Contents in Brief

Table of Contents

Preface

Substance, Access, Interest—

These are the goals of *Economics by Design: Principles and Issues.* The second edition, like the first, is appropriate for an issues-oriented course that surveys essential economic principles in one term. *Economics by Design* strives for a clear, crisp, and accurate presentation of the fundamental components of mainstream economic principles, along with issues prominent in today's world.

Economics by Design motivates student learning and promotes retention by systematically combining up-to-date theory and application. The material meets high standards of conceptual rigor, but is easy to grasp because of the intuitive, application-oriented manner in which it is presented. At all times, *Economics by Design* strives to keep the presentation accessible and interesting.

Economics by Design Is Flexible and User-Friendly.

With a conversational style attractive to today's diverse student body, *Economics by Design* motivates readers to learn what they *need* to know and uncover what they might *want* to know. This approach is founded in the age of interactive information—it places the user at the controls.

With an abundance of material and a user-friendly layout, *Economics by Design* allows the instructor to conveniently select what to cover, along with its sequence and degree of depth. *Economics by Design* offers the casual reader an opportunity to get up to speed quickly in the topic areas he or she chooses. While appropriate for a terminal survey or issues course for non-majors, the book also allows the flexibility needed for a one-term principles course. Some chapters offer appendices that allow *Economics by Design* to prepare students for additional economics courses at higher levels, up to and including those of an MBA program and other Masters programs where an economic foundation is required.

Survey Economic Principles . . .

Each chapter is divided into Surveying Economic Principles and Exploring Issues sections. The flexibility of the framework of *Economics by Design* allows the reader or instructor the option to navigate a personally chosen course. The survey section commences with the symbolic icon of car keys. The goal is to provide students with "key" concepts in a concise and engaging manner that allows them to get up to speed quickly in their study of economics. The reader will become familiar with straightforward graphical analysis. However, complex graphs and equations that would slow the reader's progress are avoided. The result will be an ability to analyze and understand the subject when it is encountered in person, on the news, or in other courses. Several Observation Points are set off within each survey section. These extend or apply concepts to show students the relevance of economics beyond the classroom.

Added versatility is provided by appendices to seven chapters, to be assigned at the instructor's option. The appendix to chapter one teaches beginning students the fundamentals of working with economic graphs and data. The remaining appendices succinctly incorporate many topics included in two-term principles courses that are fundamental only to more advanced study in economics or business, and which might be deemed unnecessarily technical for undergraduates in various other disciplines.

. . . and Explore Issues!

Following the survey portion of each chapter is an Exploring Issues section, denoted by the icon of a road that beckons the explorer forward. Two Explorations are offered in this section, each of which examines an important economic issue. These issues can be viewed as case applications of the economic principles learned in the survey section.

Explorations offer an opportunity to examine various dimensions of economic issues, including ethical dimensions currently emphasized by accrediting bodies. These investigations generate student interest in applying economics. Explorations invite students to ponder the application of economic analysis to current issues. Readers will find that economics is not an irrelevant tome of theory, but rather is active and ongoing. The presence of Explorations integrated into their appropriate chapters eliminates the need for instructors to assign a separate readings book or to place articles on reserve, while enhancing students' abilities to retain and apply the theoretical material in the chapter.

To provide greater flexibility to instructors, *Economics by Design* offers more material than many will want to cover in one term. For example, instructors who emphasize the in-depth coverage of the survey materials are unlikely to have time to cover both Explorations along with the rest of each chapter. Instructors might thus exclude one of the Explorations per chapter. Another option is assign only the Explorations from certain chapters, perhaps tying the issues to economic principles from other chapters and providing some supplemental explanation in the process. Alternatively, instructors who wish to expand their coverage of issues might exclude either all or part of the survey sections of certain chapters so as to have more time to devote to the issues.

A Superior Alternative for One-Term Courses

Through concise writing and the elimination of peripheral topics, *Economics by Design* offers ample material for a variety of one-term courses. *Economics by Design* surpasses other texts by simultaneously emphasizing quality in content, writing, and pedagogy. Some one-term texts wander from issue to issue with little apparent organization, offering no more than a scattershot of principles along the way. Although courses using such texts may seem compelling at the time, students leave without a systematic grounding in economic fundamentals. Without a solid foundation in essential economic principles, students do not learn to "think economics" and thus find it difficult to apply economic concepts in the future.

Other one-term texts go to the opposite extreme, with so much emphasis on the dry development of theory that their fragmentary sprinklings of applications do little to captivate student interests. The instructor who seeks to provide this learning stimulus with outside readings is burdened with the task of identifying appropriate readings, tracking them down in the library, complying with copyright laws, and then integrating them with the principles. *Economics by Design* solves this problem by consistently tying in material that engages student interest with the fundamental economic principles that allow for insight and understanding.

With Integrated Coverage of International Topics, . . .

Internationally-oriented material is integrated throughout *Economics by Design*, appearing in every chapter. In recognition that markets are global in scope, a full chapter on the international marketplace is introduced in the first third of the book. This chapter is written so that it can be covered at any point later in the course, if desired. In addition, internationally-oriented issues and principles are brought up in context wherever appropriate. The result is that coverage of issues and principles relating to the global economy recurs throughout the book.

Economics by Design Is Complete and Self-Contained—

Economics by Design offers consistent pedagogical aids to speed the learning process. For example, graphs are captioned with concise, self-contained explanations to reduce back-and-forth page flipping. Especially important thoughts are printed in **bold type,** such as this. In addition, terminology has always been a barrier to entry into the field of economics. In order to surmount this barrier, each significant new term is in color (witness the preceding sentence), as are significant other terms that have been mentioned peripherally in earlier chapters. Where possible, the meaning of terms is made clear in context, so that the pace of conceptual learning is not obstructed. A list of selected terms—those colored in the text—is included at the beginning of each chapter. Definitions of all selected terms are then compiled in a glossary at the end of the book and normally noted in the margin near where the term is first introduced. If a term is of secondary importance, it is italicized and not given a margin note or designated as a selected term.

Each chapter's survey of principles concludes with a set of Questions and Problems, including two Web Exercises that deepen student knowledge of economics through the use of the Internet. In addition, each Exploration is followed by Prospecting for New Insights, two exercises intended to stimulate student thinking about the issue discussed in the Exploration.

With The Finest Ancillaries in the One-Term Market.

Economics by Design offers a full complement of ancillary materials, including a study guide, printed test bank, computerized test bank, instructor's manual with lecture notes, PowerPoint transparencies, the ABC News/Prentice Hall Video Library, and its own Web site offering students an interactive self quiz on the material in each chapter. In contrast to other texts, the authors of *Economics by Design* have personally composed the study guide, the test bank of over 4,100 questions, and the instructor's manual. This commonality of authorship provides consistency in writing style and coverage between the text and the questions, notes, and other materials in these ancillaries.

Advantages: Content that is both Familiar and Current

Economics by Design makes the tasks involved in class preparation and teaching as easy as possible for instructors. Text-based lecture notes are provided in the instructor's manual to ease the transition involved in lecturing from this book. These lecture notes can be used as is, or instructors can add their own favorite examples, data, and other material.

Preparing a course outline using a text with a radically different selection and arrangement of topics can be quite time-consuming. To promote the efficient use of preparation time, topics are both familiar and up-to-date. The chapters are also arranged in the conventional micro-first fashion. Teachers who adopt *Economics by Design* will find that, with minimal rearranging and rewriting of their notes, they can teach in the manner they find comfortable. It is the combination of flexibility, modern content, currency of issues, and an engaging style that comprise the advantages of *Economics by Design*.

New to the Second Edition

In response to feedback from our adopters and reviewers, the second edition exhibits a streamlined and more accessible layout, while retaining the content and manner of presentation that made the first edition a success. Specific changes include:

- **Simplified Chapter Layout, Easier to Use.** The layout of the second edition adheres closely to the theme of a "principles and issues" textbook by concluding each chapter with an in-depth discussion of selected issues. This means that the Challenge modules found in the first edition have been eliminated. In some instances, the substance of those Challenges has been retained, either in appendices or in the main body of the chapter. The result is a smoothly flowing layout that facilitates learning.

- **Fourteen Chapters with More International Content Throughout.** Chapter 15, Global Economic Themes, has been eliminated in the second edition, with much of the material woven throughout the remaining fourteen chapters. This change allows for a shorter book that retains the flexibility of the first edition while more fully integrating international content throughout other chapters. The remaining international chapter has been revised to be more engaging and tied to current issues in international trade and finance. In addition, new sections on the World Bank, the International Monetary Fund, the role of the International Labour Organization, and other international topics have been added in various chapters.

- **Macroeconomics to Promote Student Learning of Today's Topics.** Two significant changes have occurred in the macro coverage. First, the macro presentation has been made more accessible to entry-level students. Second, the order of the presentation has been revised. Specifically, macro analysis is introduced in the context of a chapter on economic growth, followed by a chapter on money, and then by a chapter examining short-run instability. Starting macro analysis with economic growth emphasizes its fundamental importance and is consistent with modern economic thinking. To allow instructors the maximum flexibility in presenting macro topics, however, the chapters on growth, money, and instability can be covered in any order with only minor supplemental input by the instructor.

- **New Explorations with More Economic Content.** Eight completely new Explorations have been added. Other Explorations have been revised and updated where appropriate, some extensively. The educational short stories in the first edition have been replaced by Explorations with greater economic content. The result is a set of twenty-eight Explorations that addresses the central economic issues of our times.

- **Margin Notes.** Definitions of key terms are now provided in nearby margins as well as in the glossary. In addition, numerous Internet addresses are provided in the margin. These addresses refer students to Web sites that relate to the discussion in the text. These Web sites can serve as an instructional resource by instructors who wish to use the Web as a teaching tool.

- **Learning-Focused Chapter Lead-ins.** Each chapter now begins with A Look Ahead that previews the forthcoming material, a set of Destinations that itemize chapter objectives, and a list of important Terms Along the Way. This arrangement was chosen so that students will have a clearer notion of where they are headed and what skills they should master before they begin to read the chapter. The chapter previews have been expanded to discuss both the survey topics and the Explorations.

- **Expanded Use of Other Pedagogical Tools.** More in-chapter QuickCheck items have been added so that students can better test their understanding as they read. Longer, more detailed, bulleted summaries for each chapter replace the relatively terse chapter reviews in the first edition.

- **Added Graphing and Internet Preparation.** The appendix material on graphing in chapter one has been nearly doubled to meet the needs of more instructors. Approximately 100 Web addresses and 28 Web exercises make the book Internet-ready.

- **Fresh Examples, Current Applications.** Drawing from the abundance of economic issues, applications, and statistics found throughout modern life, numerous Observation Points, data, and examples throughout the book have been updated. As always, the goal is to provide applications to engage student interest so they will retain economic concepts and be able to apply them long after their economics course is over.

- **Other Changes.** Numerous, often subtle, changes have been made throughout the textbook. The effect of these changes is to refine the presentation to promote student learning.

A World of Thanks!

Our debts are many. To start, we would like to thank the economics profession, past and present, for putting together the rich body of economic theory from which we draw. In a text of this sort, the vast majority of the individuals responsible for developing these economic ideas must inevitably go uncited. Still, without their anonymous contributions, this text could not have been written.

More personally, our thanks go to the many professional colleagues and students who have shared their thoughts along the way. We have adopted many suggestions at the behest of our students. Their input has been extensive because, in whole or in part, *Economics by Design* has been class-tested at our university for over five years. Class-testing occurred in multiple sections of each of three different courses: the one-term survey/issues course, the two-term principles course, and the one-term principles course for entering MBA students. The text has also been used successfully in a distance-learning environment. Finally, the text has been used in a group-learning context, where the accessibility of the material has allowed the students to teach each other. The group learning has occurred both through in-person meetings, and through synchronous or asynchronous on-line discussion, where the accessibility of the material can promote communication.

We would like to thank the hard-working people at Prentice Hall, including William Becher, Editorial Assistant, Lori Braumberger, Senior Marketing Manager, PJ Boardman, Editor-in-Chief, James Boyd, Editorial Director/VP, Carol Samet, Production Editor, Gladys Soto, Associate Editor, and the many others at Prentice Hall and its affiliates who have taken an active interest in the success of this product. Special thanks go to Rod Banister, Senior Editor, and Leah Jewel, editor of the first edition, who generously shared their insights and gave us room to run with creative ideas on presenting economic principles and issues. We also much appreciate the efforts of Professor Mark Karscig of *Central Missouri State University*, who authored the PowerPoint presentations and On-line Study Guide at the companion Web site for this text. Closer to home, we thank our dean, Dr. James Gaertner, and our division director, Dr. Lila Truett, who have allowed us the time and teaching schedule necessary to class-test and refine our textbook.

We are grateful for the detailed, thought-provoking comments and suggestions of this text's many reviewers. Their input has been incorporated throughout to improve the quality of *Economics by Design*. Any deficiencies that remain are, of course, the responsibility of the other author . . . whichever one of us that may be! The following reviewers have assisted us: George Beardsley, *California Polytechnic State University*; John Conant, *Indiana State University*; Bruce Domazlicky, *Southeast Missouri State University*; Mousumi Duttaray, *Indiana University*; Dan Fuller, *Weber State University*; Anthony Greco, *University of Southwestern Louisiana*; Jan Hansen, *University of Wisconsin*; Matthew Hyle, *Winona State University*; Nicholas Karatjas, *Indiana University of Pennsylvania*; Rose Kilburn, *Modesto Junior College*; Philip King, *San Francisco State University*; Steven Koch, *Georgia Southern University*; Steven Lile, *Western Kentucky University*; Jose Mendez, *Arizona State University*; John Merrifield, *University of Texas–San Antonio*; Wayne Plumly, *Valdosta State University*; David Sollars, *Auburn University at Montgomery*; Darlene Voeltz, *Rochester Community College*; Richard Welch, *University of Texas—San Antonio*; Jim Wheeler, *Vance Granville Community College*; and Larry Wilson, *Sandhills Community College*.

R.A.C.
R.M.A.

PART ONE

THE ECONOMIC JOURNEY

Economics Enjoys a Bull Run at Colleges

—recent headline from *The Wall Street Journal*

Today's growing interest in economics is sparked by the realization that economic principles underlie the choices we make at a personal, business, and societal level. Understanding the scope and central features of this field of study allows us to better understand our own choices and those that form the world around us.

ROADMAP
FOR ECONOMICS

A Look Ahead

ECONOMICS PROVIDES A key to understanding numerous aspects of the world around us. Some are trumpeted in newspaper headlines about the major public policy issues of the day. Others affect us quite personally. For example, economics can explain why the price of textbooks is greater than the price of novels; why some people earn more than others; why some businesses advertise, while others do not; and how countries can all gain through international trade.

This chapter sweeps across the economic landscape. Scarce resources and unlimited wants force us to make economic choices. We will see that these choices can involve the big macroeconomic issues or the more detailed microeconomic issues. The importance of the price system is revealed, and some basic economic questions are examined. The chapter continues by discussing methods of economic analysis. It is seen that economists employ models, which highlight important aspects of the world around us, to explain how the world works. Popular perception to the contrary, the best models are often the simplest—like a roadmap!

Exploration 1–1 looks at the broad-reaching issue of the best economic system, while Exploration 1–2 addresses the pragmatic issue of what an economics education can lead to. Whether the scale is grandiose or personal, though, there is no escaping the power of economic incentives.

Destinations

As you are **Surveying Economic Principles** you will arrive at an ability to

- ❏ describe how scarce resources and unlimited wants lead to the study of economics;
- ❏ distinguish between microeconomics and macroeconomics;
- ❏ identify three basic questions that all economies must answer;
- ❏ recognize the strengths of the marketplace and motivations for government involvement;
- ❏ understand what a model is and why models are best kept simple.

While **Exploring Issues** you will be able to

- ❏ explain how the lack of economic incentives in communism led to its downfall;
- ❏ describe the opportunities for students and professionals in the realm of economics.

Terms Along the Way

- ✔ economics, 4
- ✔ scarcity, 4
- ✔ the margin, 4
- ✔ microeconomics, 6
- ✔ macroeconomics, 7
- ✔ command and control, 8
- ✔ free markets, 8
- ✔ mixed economies, 8
- ✔ equity, 9
- ✔ efficiency, 9
- ✔ technological efficiency, 9
- ✔ allocative efficiency, 9
- ✔ invisible hand, 10
- ✔ market failures, 11
- ✔ public goods, 11
- ✔ externalities, 11
- ✔ market power, 11
- ✔ normative statements, 15
- ✔ positive statements, 15
- ✔ models, 16
- ✔ Occam's razor, 16
- ✔ egalitarianism, 21
- ✔ original position, 24

SURVEYING ECONOMIC PRINCIPLES

Economics studies the allocation of scarce resources in response to unlimited wants.

Scarce Resources, Unlimited Wants

Economics is about choice. Both individually and as a society, we seek to choose wisely. We are forced to choose because resources are scarce, and it takes resources to produce the goods and services we want.

Securing the most value from resources is the objective of economic choice. At a personal level, we each have our own economy. We have limited income to spend on the many things we want. For example, we might forgo the new Jaguar automobile we've long dreamed of in order to pay tuition at Highbrow College. Usually, however, resource scarcity does not force us into all-or-nothing decisions. We might be able to purchase a used Dodge Neon and still afford tuition at Home State University.

When something is scarce, we must choose. We commonly make choices at the margin, meaning incrementally. Decision making at the margin is about the choice of a little more of this and a little less of that. It's about weighing and balancing the benefits and costs of alternatives. Should I eat the last slice of pizza? What is the best use of the next hour of my time? What should I do with the last dollar in my pocket? If we are wise in the use of our money and our time, we get more for them.

Businesses also face alternatives and make decisions at the margin. Should another worker be hired, or should scarce funds instead be used to upgrade the office computer system? Should one more item be added to a restaurant's menu? Should one be deleted? Should the restaurant stay open later, or close earlier? Should it increase overtime, or cut it back? In sum, business decisions are often made one increment at a time.

Many government decisions are also made at the margin. For example, the decision about whether to build more exit ramps on a freeway would weigh the benefits and costs of each incremental ramp one at a time. The decision about how many lanes the freeway should have and how long it should be is also made incrementally. Later in the life span of the freeway more decision making at the margin will be required, as in deciding how many of the inevitable bumps and potholes should be fixed.

Economics looks more broadly at the interactions of households, businesses, and government within the framework of national and international economies. Indeed, most people think of a nation's economy when they think of economics, which brings up some different issues than occur at the personal and business levels. For example, individuals and businesses often focus on spending money wisely. More generally, though, money is just one part of the economic puzzle. From the point of view of a nation's economy, money is little more than grease for the wheels of commerce—a convenience that helps us reach our economic ends. Scarce resources lead to scarce goods, whether or not money is involved.

For example, if everything were declared to be "free," supermarkets, department stores, discount stores, and other retailers would quickly be picked bare. People

A history of the Jaguar can be found at **http://www. car-nection.com/ jagbase**

scarcity: a situation in which there are too few resources to meet all human needs.

More information about the Neon is available at **http://chrysler-direct.com/ neond.htm**

the margin: the cutoff point; decision making at the margin refers to deciding on one more or one less of something.

would complain that they did not take home everything they wanted or that they arrived too late to obtain anything at all. This is often what happens during humanitarian relief efforts, in which food and other aid is distributed from the back of a truck. The result seen in Somalia and other recipient countries is that the fastest and strongest, rather than the neediest, get the goods. Free distribution is not an economical way to allocate scarce resources and the goods and services they produce.

Resource allocation refers to the way in which resources are used. When society makes choices about what goods will be produced, and thus about what to give up, it is making decisions about the allocation of resources. Consider the choices facing the United States in 1957. The Soviet Union had placed the first satellite, *Sputnik*, into orbit around the earth. America panicked—its citizens demanded that the United States catch up. As a consequence, the nation engaged in a deliberate reallocation of educational resources toward greater emphasis on mathematics and science. The space race was on, and by 1969 human footprints marked the surface of the moon.

A Web site that tells the history of Sputnik can be found at **http://www.batnet .com/mfwright/ sputnik.html**

Sometimes the choices about the allocation of resources are literally a matter of life and death. Choices about a nation's health-care system are an example. In wealthier nations, such as the United States, Canada, Japan, and countries in Western Europe, it might seem as if scarcity of resources doesn't apply, and that the maximum amount of health care could be provided for all, rich and poor alike, apparently without giving up anything else. Clearly, more and better health care saves lives. But since more health care requires a greater number of doctors, nurses, and other medical personnel, where would they come from? They would have to come from the ranks of those who otherwise would have sought careers in law, teaching, business, and other fields. Fewer workers in those fields would reduce the output of goods and services there. The consequences of resource scarcity cannot be avoided.

Most decisions about the allocation of resources are less dramatic than the decisions about the space race and health care. The jobs that people hold reflect the allocation of resources. For example, the change in consumer preferences during the 1990s in favor of more cotton and less polyester in clothing created more jobs than otherwise in cotton farming and processing. Similarly, the U.S. housing boom during the latter part of the 1990s created more jobs for skilled construction workers. Workers who assembled appliances and those who manufactured brick, insulation, and the thousands of other inputs going into new homes also benefitted.

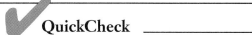

✔ QuickCheck _____

Would $2 million satisfy all of your wants?

Answer: It would be quite difficult to discover someone with $2 million who would decline to accept a third million. Even billionaires would accept another billion, if only to better endow their trust funds. Unless you would actually decline to accept that third million, then $2 million does not satisfy all of your wants. Essentially, your wants are unlimited.

OBSERVATION POINT:
Scavenging, Tinkering, and the Home Workshop—Changing Visions of the American Dream

At the end of World War II, a generation of brave soldiers returned to civilian life. This same generation had grown up in the deprivation of the Great Depression. Adversity breeds resourcefulness. Blemished apples and soft bananas from someone's trash, a piece of tin found in a dump, and a few lengths of lumber that have fallen from a passing truck—each can serve a purpose when you're needy. Later, on foreign fields of battle, the skills developed by scavenging goods and tinkering with balky equipment were highly prized.

Scavenging and tinkering were a way of life, and ways of life influence choices. When the GIs came home to start careers and families, they set their sights on their dream homes, complete with workshops. Builders responded by setting aside a small area in the garage of most new houses built during the postwar construction boom. A man now had a place for his tools, his scrap lumber, his nuts and bolts found in the streets. He had a place to build that bookcase instead of wasting money by buying it at the furniture store. With a spot to work on things that broke down, it was the American dream.

Today? Modern microprocessors can confound the most resolute tinkerers. Even broken toasters are thrown out rather than repaired, because most people are too busy with their jobs to spend their time tinkering. Builders' selling efforts these days focus on high ceilings, fireplaces, and luxury baths, not workshops. The American dream? Each new generation defines it in its own way.

For information about current real estate markets around the United States, visit **http://www. realtor.com**

The Economic Landscape

Microeconomic Issues

microeconomics: concerns the individual components of the economy.

Microeconomics is about the individual components of the economy and includes individuals acting as consumers or as workers. It also includes *firms*, which are businesses that produce goods or services. The industries in which firms operate are also included in the realm of microeconomics; an industry is composed of firms producing similar outputs.

Microeconomics revolves around the interaction of consumers and producers in markets. Markets can take physical, electronic, or other forms. The common characteristic of all markets is that they facilitate the voluntary exchange of resources, goods, and services. Market prices serve as the signals that guide the allocation of resources. Indeed, microeconomics is sometimes called price theory, since participants in the economy make choices based upon *incentives* (motivations) provided by prices.

Microeconomic questions affect our lives each day. Suppose you decide to go on vacation. What will be your destination? Will you use the services of a travel agent? At which hotel will you stay? If you decide to fly, which airline will you choose? Is the fare lower if you purchase tickets in advance? Why do many airlines reduce the fare if you stay over a Saturday night? How are ticket prices related to government regulation of the airlines? Should government regulate airplane noise? If so, how? As you can see from this example, the list of microeconomic questions is long.

Macroeconomic Issues

Macroeconomics looks at the big picture. It concentrates on analysis of economic *aggregates*, total values for the economy as a whole. The most important aggregate is *gross domestic product* (*GDP*), which measures the value of the aggregate output produced by an economy. GDP is obtained by adding up the values of all goods and services produced.

Macroeconomic issues are often raised in the news. Employment, economic growth, interest rates, money, inflation, and the federal budget deficit are examples of macroeconomic issues that will be addressed in this book.

Macroeconomics was first considered a separate field of study following the work of John Maynard Keynes in the 1930s. Keynes suggested macro answers to the problems of the Great Depression, answers that seemed lacking in the microeconomic mainstream of economic thought. The field of macroeconomics became quite popular in the 1950s and 1960s, which led to economics students being served up economic principles in nearly equal doses of micro and macro. However, in recent years, macroeconomics has focused on establishing a solid microeconomic foundation. Thus, the distinction between microeconomics and macroeconomics has been blurring, with more and more micro analysis being applied to macro issues.

> **macroeconomics:** analyzes economic aggregates, such as aggregate employment, output, growth, and inflation.
>
> The latest data on GDP can be found at many government Web sites, including **http://www.bea. doc.gov/**

 QuickCheck _____

The debate over the desirability of free trade among nations has been in the news recently. Can you identify both macroeconomic and microeconomic aspects of this issue?

Answer: The ability of free trade to spur the growth of the economy is one example of a macro issue. A micro issue involves which workers would gain and which would lose jobs. While issues are often pigeonholed as macro or micro, many issues have aspects of both.

What, How, and for Whom?

Every economy must answer three basic economic questions:

1. **What?** What goods and services will be produced and offered for sale and in what quantities? The latest fashions, the newest albums from the hottest rock stars, medical services, fast food, and countless other items are offered for sale in our economy. What is the reason that these things are readily available for purchase, but other items, such as vinyl records and eight-track tapes, are not?

2. **How?** How will goods and services be produced? There are numerous production techniques available to produce most things. Some methods of production

are hundreds of years old, utilizing simple hand tools and much labor. Alternative production methods employ computers, robots, and other high-technology inputs in combination with less labor. For example, a shirt could be sewn with no more than a needle and thread. However, most shirts are sewn with a sewing machine. How are these decisions made, and what motivates the development of new and better ways of doing things?

3. **For whom?** Who will consume the goods and services that are produced? People who live on Poverty Row consume less than those who live on Park Avenue, so income and wealth matter in the distribution of goods. What determines the income and wealth of an individual or family? If a family's income is not large enough to allow family members to consume the necessities of life, should income be redistributed from others who are wealthier?

command and control: government decrees that direct economic activity.

free markets: the collective decisions of individual buyers and sellers that, taken together, determine what outputs are produced, how those outputs are produced, and who receives the outputs; free markets depend on private property and free choice.

mixed economies: the mixture of free-market and command-and-control methods of resource allocation that characterize modern economies.

When it comes to deciding what, how, and for whom, government might make the decisions by decree. If so, the economy is termed **command and control**. Alternatively, government might stay out of the picture and allow economic choices to be made entirely in the marketplace. In that case, the economy is characterized by laissez-faire free markets, also termed laissez-faire capitalism. Laissez faire means "let it be." Freedom of choice in both production and consumption is a defining characteristic of **free markets**. Prices, production, and the distribution of goods and services are determined by markets. Free markets are associated with *capitalism*, in which resources are privately owned.

In practice, countries almost always have **mixed economies**, meaning that countries choose a combination of markets and government. Figure 1-1 illustrates this spectrum of choice. Different countries choose different combinations, perhaps influenced by custom, tradition, religion, political ideology, and other factors.

In the United States, for example, federal, state, and local governments are directly responsible for almost one-fifth of aggregate output and employment. Even when government is not directly involved, it often influences the private marketplace through regulation, taxation, and other means. For example, federal, state, and local

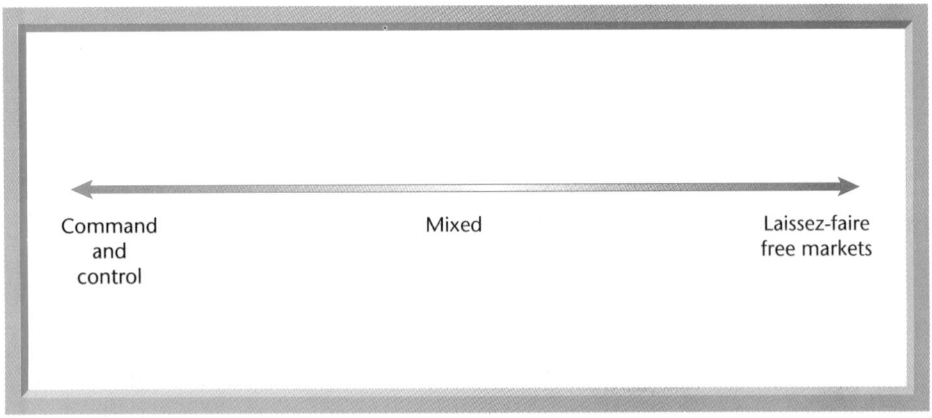

FIGURE 1-1 **The spectrum of economic systems.** Command and control involves government allocation of resources. Laissez faire is characterized by private resource allocation. In reality, all countries have mixed economies, with the mix varying from country to country.

government revenue in the United States totals about one-third of the value of U.S. output, with about half of that revenue going to finance *transfer payments* that transfer income from some citizens to others. For example, Social Security recipients and owners of government-issued bonds both receive transfer payments, the latter in the form of interest payments.

Two primary economic objectives can guide countries in choosing how much government to mix with free markets. The first objective is equity, which refers to fairness. While we often intuitively sense what is fair, the concept of equity is difficult to pin down. There are commonly accepted principles of equity that apply in certain circumstances, such as to taxation (discussed in chapter 10). However, equity is ultimately a matter of personal opinion. Well-meaning people can reasonably disagree about what is equitable, and their views cannot be proved or disproved.

The second economic objective is efficiency, **which means that resources are used in ways that provide the most value, that maximize the size of the economic pie.** Economic efficiency means that no one can be made better off without someone else becoming worse off. Economic efficiency has two components:

- **Technological efficiency,** which implies getting the greatest quantity of output for the resources that are being used. For any given output, then, a least-cost production technique must be chosen.
- **Allocative efficiency,** which involves choosing the most valuable mix of outputs to produce. For example, the economy might be able to produce the greatest possible amount of toothpicks from the resources at its disposal. That choice would be technologically efficient. However, if the economy produces nothing but toothpicks, consumers would not be getting the greatest value from the economy's resources. The economy would be allocatively inefficient, because the wrong mix of goods would have been chosen.

There is frequently a tradeoff between efficiency and equity. More equity may result in less efficiency, and vice versa. For example, many people believe that, for the sake of equity, tax systems should be something like Robin Hood—taxes should take from the rich and give to the poor. However, as tax rates rise, incentives to work and invest tend to fall. Thus the more redistributional is the tax system, the less productive the economy is likely to be. The economic pie may be divided more equitably, but its size would be diminished. The result is inefficiency.

Command and Control—Who Needs Markets?

The marketplace seems cluttered with choices. Aren't all these choices wasteful? Wouldn't it be better to do away with seemingly unnecessary variety, skip all the advertising, and just have government run the economy for the good of us all? Throughout history, many countries have embraced economic systems that promised to eliminate the perceived disorder of the marketplace. Unfortunately, even the most well-meaning *central planners* who make decisions in a command-and-control economy cannot know our desires as well as we can know them ourselves. Moreover, nothing ensures that only the most well-meaning central planners will rise to the top. Even if they do, they face difficulties in motivating actual producers to do their bidding. For example, if the planners assign farmers production quotas measured by the

equity: fairness.

efficiency: means that resources are used in ways that provide the most value; implies that no one can be made better off without someone else becoming worse off.

technological efficiency: the greatest quantity of output for given inputs; likewise, for any given output, requires the least-cost production technique.

allocative efficiency: involves choosing the most valuable mix of outputs to produce.

ton, farmers will seek to maximize the weight of their crops and ignore quality. The result of command-and-control methods is often *inefficiency*, in which resources are squandered on the production of the wrong goods and services or wasted through use of the wrong production techniques.

Governments subscribing to command-and-control methods of resource allocation also must apportion the incomes of workers, thereby determining the distribution of goods and services. If government miscalculates, as shown by the experiences of most of the formerly communist countries, it may well be forced to implement government *rationing* of goods, which permits consumers to buy only limited amounts of essential goods that are in short supply. Rationing by government is inefficient because it wastes resources. While government may attempt to ration equitably, its prospects for success in the long run are doubtful. Nonetheless, in the United States, government rationing has sometimes been adopted, but only on a temporary basis. In World War II, gasoline, tires, sugar, meat, and other essentials were rationed. When the war emergency was over, rationing was quickly ended.

The Invisible Hand and the Price System—Who Needs Government?

A most interesting Web site is maintained by the Adam Smith Institute at **http://www. adamsmith. org.uk/**

invisible hand: the idea that self-interest leads the economy to produce an efficient variety of goods and services, with efficient production methods as well. As described by Adam Smith in *The Wealth of Nations* (1776), the invisible hand of the marketplace motivates producers in search of profit to provide consumers with greater value than even the most well-intentioned of governments could do.

Is it not something of a mystery that goods and services are regularly offered for sale in quantities that satisfy the wants of consumers? After all, there is no commander-in-chief ordering an army of workers to bring those goods to market. In *The Wealth of Nations* (1776), Adam Smith explained this puzzle. Smith described how the invisible hand of the marketplace leads the economy to produce an efficient variety of goods and services, with efficient production methods as well. Guided by this invisible hand, Smith argues that producers acting in their own self-interests provide consumers with greater value than even the most well-intentioned of governments.

The reasoning behind the idea of the invisible hand is straightforward. To prosper in the competitive marketplace, producers must provide customers with things that they value. Those producers who are best at doing so thrive. Those who pick the wrong goods and services to produce, or produce them in an inferior manner, lose out.

Free markets offer people opportunity—the opportunity to get ahead or to fall behind. The market rewards people who use their abilities to satisfy their fellow citizens, so long as that satisfaction is embodied in a good or service that can be sold in the marketplace. "Build a better mousetrap, and the world will beat a path to your door."

All participants in a market economy, including consumers, businesses, investors, and workers, make choices on the basis of information conveyed by market prices. The collection of prices in product and resource markets is termed the *price system*. **Prices provide information about scarcity.** For example, you could probably not afford to hire your friend's favorite rock star to perform at her birthday party. The scarce talents of superstars generally command a price that only a larger audience can pay. Responding to this market price, superstars would skip the birthday party in favor of the concert. More generally, it is the price system that allocates resources in a market economy to their highest-valued uses.

Price changes lead to changes in both consumer and firm behavior. When gasoline prices increased dramatically in the United States in the 1970s, consumers sought to decrease the pain in their pocketbooks when they gassed up by increasing their purchases of smaller cars. The allocation of resources was altered by car makers as a consequence. To increase gas mileage, U.S. auto makers designed and built new, smaller cars and modified existing models by replacing heavy steel with lighter materials.

Guided by market prices, free-market choices lead the economy to allocative efficiency. The preferences of consumers dictate answers to the "what" question. Firms seeking to "make money" choose least-cost production techniques, thus accomplishing technological efficiency in answering the "how" question. The "for whom" question is answered by the market-determined incomes of workers and others who provide economic resources.

The Mix in the Middle—Market Limitations and Government Action

Since markets have such desirable properties in theory and since experience with central planning under communism clearly showed the inefficiency of central planning, why not get rid of government altogether? Let markets reign supreme! Although that may be tempting when it comes time to pay our taxes, getting rid of all government would be neither possible nor efficient. For one thing, any country that abolished its government would soon find itself ruled by gangs, clans, or even the government of another country. Moreover, there are many goods and services that markets fail to provide efficiently. **Market failures occur when markets fail to achieve efficiency.** Market failures include the following:

- Public goods—goods that are jointly consumed by everyone, such as national defense and highways. Although people value these goods, they usually are unwilling to pay for them unless government forces them to do so. The reason is that anyone can consume a public good, whether or not that person has helped pay for it.

- Externalities—side effects of production or consumption that affect third parties who have no say in the matter. The most common form of externality is pollution. For example, drivers of smoky cars are not usually the ones to breathe that smoke; rather, it is the occupants of the vehicles that follow who suffer. Without government action to reduce auto emissions, many drivers wouldn't care if their cars smoked, which would lead to excessive air pollution.

- Market power—when a firm has the ability to avoid competition. The invisible hand of the marketplace leads to efficiency as firms compete with each other to best satisfy consumers. If a firm can find a way to avoid competition, then it can raise prices and produce less output than would be efficient. For example, although more competition might still be desirable, prices, the quality of service, and choices facing telecommunication consumers are much improved from the days when both local and long-distance service were provided by the Bell telephone *monopoly*, a market in which there is only one seller.

- *Imperfect information*—when market participants lack enough information to know what is in their own best interests. For example, it is often difficult for companies who have built a better mousetrap to succeed, because the company and its product are unknown to potential customers. Similarly, government safety standards in the workplace are often justified on the basis that understanding the health effects of alternative workplace practices is too complicated for workers to

market failures: when markets fail to achieve efficiency, as in the case of public goods, externalities, and sometimes, market power.

public goods: goods such as national defense or clean air that are nonexcludable and nonrival, meaning that a person's consumption of the good does not reduce its quantity for others; most public goods are impure, meaning that they are not completely nonexcludable and nonrival.

externalities: side effects of production or consumption that affect third parties who have no say in the matter; these can involve either external costs, such as from pollution, or external benefits, such as from a neighbor maintaining an attractive yard.

market power: when individual sellers have at least a bit of control over the prices of their outputs; arises from barriers to entry.

understand fully and that workers are better off letting government make those decisions for them.

Sometimes market failures are minor, such as the externality experienced by the rest of the class when a student distracts the instructor by showing up late. When market failures are more significant, government action may be needed. However, not all government policies are equally efficient. Many of the most efficient public policies do not abandon markets. Rather, markets can often be steered back on course with public policies that are minimally disruptive to the workings of the invisible hand, while avoiding the inefficiencies of command and control.

Government is also concerned with equity. The distribution of income in the free marketplace rewards those who provide the most value to others. To some extent this arrangement seems fair. To some extent, it does not. For example, through no fault of their own, some people are incapable of providing much of value in the marketplace. This situation could be due to physical impairment or the lack of opportunity to acquire knowledge and skills. The result is poverty. Government may attempt to promote greater equity by redistributing income, by providing social services, and by other means.

Firms and workers pursue their own self-interests in a mixed economy, but within limits placed upon them by government. If consumers demand a particular good or service, the market is free to meet that demand subject to regulations on production techniques, worker pay, product safety, and so forth. Some products may be banned. The sale of heroin and the insecticide DDT are outlawed, the sale of antibiotics and other medicines controlled by prescription, and the use of tobacco discouraged by mandatory warning labels. **The major command-and-control techniques used by government in a mixed economy are the following:**

- **Government production,** such as national defense, highways, public education, postal services, and parks. Government produces about 19 percent of the U.S. output of goods and services.

- **Income redistribution,** such as housing subsidies, food stamps, Medicaid, and other services for the poor. About 15 percent of U.S. income is received from income redistribution programs.

- **Taxation,** which takes about one-third of U.S. income. Major taxes include sales taxes, property taxes, income taxes, Social Security taxes, and other taxes assessed by the various levels of government.

- **Regulations,** such as minimum wage laws, price controls, or any of the various controls over how products are to be produced and what products can be offered for sale. For example, government regulates both workplace and product safety.

- **Mandates,** which are directives for citizens, firms, or lower levels of government to perform specified actions. For example, by law, businesses must provide access for the handicapped.

There is ongoing debate in most countries over how much government is the right amount. For example, when market failures are identified, which, if any, government actions are most promising? As for equity, there is always contention over whether government goes too far or not far enough in trying to correct inequities.

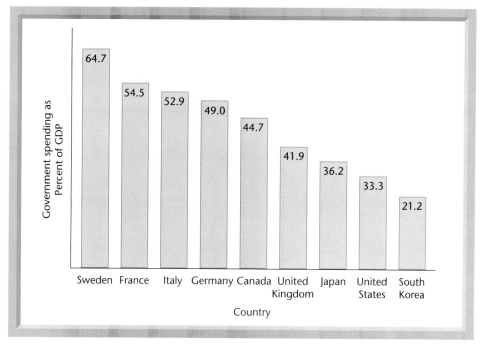

FIGURE 1-2 **Government expenditures as a percentage of gross domestic product (GDP), selected countries, 1996**

Source: 1998 Statistical Abstract of the U.S., Table No. 1364.

The Mix in the United States and around the World

Figure 1-2 shows the fraction of total economic activity directly accounted for by government in selected countries, including the United States. The figure shows that some nations are closer to the command-and-control end of the spectrum of economic systems, while others are closer to laissez-faire free markets. The data in the figure understate the economic significance of government because of the indirect effects of government regulations upon costs in the private sector of the economy.

Unlike in the nineteenth and early twentieth century, the United States can no longer lay claim to having a nearly pure laissez-faire free-market economy. The transition to a larger, activist government has occurred in response to a public perception that government policy provides the only means for correcting inequities and market failures. At the other extreme, few governments still promote central planning because widespread use of command and control in the formerly communist countries caused economic stagnation, leaving their citizens with relatively low living standards.

With the passage of time, more economies have moved toward the middle of the spectrum. In the United States this movement occurred slowly, taking decades. In other countries, such as the former Soviet Union and many of the countries of eastern Europe, the movement occurred swiftly in the early 1990s with the fall of

A large number of links to Web sites that offer data on the mixed economy in many countries is located at **http://www.ntu. edu.sg/library/ statdata.htm**

communism. Vietnam and China, although self-identified as communist countries, have adjusted their centrally planned economies toward greater reliance upon free markets. Since 1985 the People's Republic of China has gone from two-thirds of its production being produced by state-owned enterprises to two-thirds by the private sector. By 1998 Cuba and North Korea were the only well-known adherents to the command-and-control model that characterized the old Soviet Union. Even so, because of the economic distress experienced by those countries, it was not clear how much longer their economic systems would continue unchanged. For example, President Castro of Cuba persisted in denouncing capitalism and the very idea of establishing a market economy in Cuba, while at the same time seeking foreign investment from . . . the market economies of the world!

Some mixed economies, as well as the formerly communist countries, have featured government ownership of large firms and critical resources. In many cases, governments are selling the companies they own to private investors. Until 1994, for example, the large French auto maker Renault was owned by the government of France. In a move bitterly opposed by many Renault workers who valued their secure government jobs, the French government sold shares of stock in Renault.

Privatization occurs when government sells off publicly owned businesses to private investors or contracts with private industry to provide goods or services that had previously been produced by government. Countries turn to privatization to achieve greater efficiency that can ultimately lead to higher living standards for their citizens. The former communist countries are continuing to privatize many formerly state-owned industries, although at an uneven pace. Privatization is contentious because it often leads to mass layoffs of workers in privatized industries as they struggle to become more efficient or because, as in the case of Russian privatizations, the outcome leaves much ownership in the hands of powerful government figures.

OBSERVATION POINT:
Intertwining Economic and Political Philosophies

Economics is concerned with obtaining the most value from society's scarce resources. What is value? Who is to judge? In a democracy, it seems natural that citizens should judge value for themselves. Is this approach best? The philosophical and political issues run deep.

During the eighteenth and nineteenth centuries, economics was called political economy. Prior to that, it was usually referred to as moral philosophy, to emphasize the philosophical nature of seeking human betterment. The term political economy makes clear that politics and economics intertwine. Although the name has been shortened to economics, the link between economics, politics, and philosophy remains as important as ever.

Economic Analysis

The practice of economics often calls for the analysis of complex issues. Sometimes these issues involve value judgments; sometimes they are factual. In either case, economic analysis is improved by following some basic methodologies. It is easy to fall into error when reasoning about economic problems. Fallacious reasoning leads to false conclusions. One example is the *fallacy of composition*. This error in thinking occurs when it is assumed that what is true at the micro level must also be true at the macro level. In other words, the fallacy of composition involves the observation of a truth about some individual component of the economy accompanied by the assumption that this truth will also apply to the economy at large. For example, "Engine Charlie" Wilson, head of General Motors in the 1950s, was widely ridiculed in the press for allegedly saying, "What's good for General Motors is good for the country."

Positive and Normative Economics

Economic pronouncements are in abundant supply from an array of sources. Media commentators, politicians, ordinary citizens, and many economists are often remarkably eager to share their purported insights. How can we make sense of this mishmash of opinions? Is it truly nothing but opinion?

With some sorting, unsupported opinions can be separated from thoughtful analysis. A good start distinguishes between normative and positive economic statements. Normative statements have to do with behavioral norms, which are judgments as to what is good or bad. Examples of normative statements often include "ought" or "should" in them. They imply that something deserves to happen, such as: "The federal government ought to balance its budget."

Positive statements have to do with fact. They may involve current, historical, or even future fact. Positive statements concern what is, was, or will be. The accuracy of positive statements can be checked against facts, although verifying predictions about the future will have to wait until that future arrives. Sometimes it is also hard to judge the accuracy of a statement, although in principle it could be done. For example, "A balanced federal budget will lead to lower interest rates" is a positive statement that would be difficult to verify. Positive economic statements are not necessarily true. However, factual evidence may be introduced to support or refute any positive economic statement. Professional economists generally deal in positive economics, although they might assume some basic normative goals, such as goals of efficiency and equity. Table 1-1 provides examples of positive and normative statements, categorized by whether the subject matter is microeconomics or macroeconomics.

Both positive and normative economics rely upon *theory*, which is organized thought aimed at answering specific questions. Theories can be tested by logic and, for positive economic theories, by data. Theories are first tested for their internal logic. Does a theory make sense? Sometimes the testing stops there. On other occasions, theories are tested by collecting facts to see whether they are consistent with

normative statements: having to do with behavioral norms, which are judgments as to what is good or bad.

positive statements: statements regarding fact, concerning what is, was, or will be. In principle, the accuracy of positive statements can be checked against facts.

TABLE 1-1	Categorizing Economic Statements	
	Macroeconomics	**Microeconomics**
Positive	The unemployment rate is rising.	So many people have switched to eating chicken, I think I'll lose my job at the beef-packing plant.
Normative	The unemployment rate is too high.	People should eat more fish!

the theory. Testing of theories allows us to judge their value, so that the results become more than mere opinion or idle speculation.

Economic Modeling: The Route to Higher-Level Understanding

models: simplified versions of reality that emphasize features central to answering the questions we ask of them.

Economics makes extensive use of **models.** A model is a simplification of reality that emphasizes features essential to answering the questions we ask of it. Different models answer different questions. For example, a roadmap is a model. The wide red lines that designate interstate highways let us know of major high-speed routes. The circles and yellow splotches show us the locations of towns and larger cities. If our goal is high-speed driving, we want the map kept simple, since we need to read it quickly.

Economists are often criticized for using models that omit features of the real world. This criticism is unmerited, unless the omitted features are essential in answering the questions asked. Similarly, a roadmap eliminates many features of the terrain, such as trees, houses, and hills. That lack would be inappropriate if the map is for surveying or hiking. For driving, though, including those details would reduce the map's usefulness. Note also that a good model need not be totally realistic, even in the features it does include. After all, from a helicopter we would not actually find huge red lines connecting black circles and yellow splotches. The roadmap is merely representative, as a good model should be.

An example of a model is shown in Figure 1-3, which uses the notion of a roadmap to represent the layout of chapters in this book. Each chapter in *Economics by Design* is divided into a Surveying Economic Principles section followed by an Exploring Issues section. You can think of the Surveying Economic Principles section as an expressway that allows you to survey prominent features of the economic landscape. The Exploring Issues section offers the option to leave the expressway for an in-depth examination of selected aspects of the surrounding countryside. Alongside the expressway are Observation Points that offer perspectives on the economic terrain and QuickChecks to assess your progress. Note that, while this model illustrates the chapter layout, the actual book looks nothing like the model. Yet, nevertheless, the model conveys the concept, which is its purpose.

Occam's razor: the idea that all nonessential elements should be stripped away from a model.

Keep in mind a guiding principle when producing a model, whether it applies to economics or otherwise. This principle is termed **Occam's razor,** formulated by the English philosopher William of Occam (1300–1349, approximately). Occam argued that reasoning is improved by focusing one's thinking on the most essential elements of an issue. He suggested using a figurative razor to cut away the unnecessary elements from analysis. Occam's razor is a vivid and simple concept. Its use increases the likelihood that modeling will lead to correct conclusions.

Economic models seek to explain the choices people make and the consequences of those choices. Models may explain prices, unemployment, economic growth, and more. Economic models may involve graphs, numbers, or mathematics. Some economic models are quite simple yet amazingly powerful, as we shall see in the following chapters. Other economic models are exceedingly complex, involving advanced mathematics and statistics. Some models consist of hundreds or even thousands of equations stored in computer memory. Even these large, complex models are simplified versions of reality.

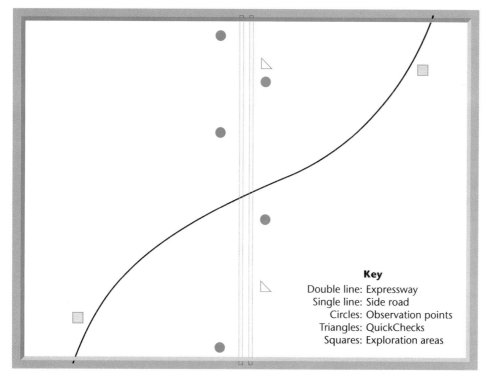

Key
Double line: Expressway
Single line: Side road
Circles: Observation points
Triangles: QuickChecks
Squares: Exploration areas

FIGURE 1-3 **Chapter roadmap.** The Surveying Economic Principles portion of each chapter is analogous to an expressway that zips you through fundamental economic analysis, but which also allows you to pause to take stock of where you've been. The Exploring Issues sections let you journey off the main highway to ponder specific applications of those economic principles. The roadmap analogy serves as a model of the textbook.

OBSERVATION POINT:
Models—From Einstein's Mind to Yours

The renowned physicist Albert Einstein (1879–1955) was in the business of modeling. The most famous model to come from his mind, summarized in the equation $e = mc^2$, provided key insights that led scientists to the ability to split the atom. Is it only economists and physicists that model? No. For example, psychologists say that all of us walk around with models inside our minds of the way the world works.

Take a student's model of learning, for example. How do you perceive the learning process? A simple model is that the job of the instructor is to fill your mind with knowledge. In this model you are a passive recipient of facts, figures, and principles. Students whose internal learning model is similar to this one fail to prosper academically because some important elements of the learning process have been omitted. Remember, Occam's razor tells us to omit only the nonessential elements from models. Quoting Einstein: "Everything should be made as simple as possible, but not simpler." A more sophisticated learning model allows for the student to interact with

QuickCheck

Is there a fallacy in each of the following statements? If not, is the statement normative or positive?

a. The federal government collects more tax revenue than any state government.

b. Because the catering service that I own is profitable, the catering industry must be profitable.

c. After the tornado hit Central City, Uncle Sam moved too slowly in providing aid.

Answers:
a. Positive. The statement can be checked for its factual accuracy.
b. The fallacy of composition.
c. Normative. The statement implies that the government should have moved more quickly, without telling us what is meant by *too slowly*. A positive version of the statement might read as follows: "After the tornado hit Central City, it took two weeks for aid to reach the stricken population. Officials predict a quicker response to future disasters."

the instructor, the material, and other students. Key elements of this model involve setting aside time to reflect on the material, to ask questions, and to work with others such as in groups. Which learning model comes closest to yours?

SUMMARY

- Economics is the study of how to allocate scarce resources to satisfy unlimited wants. Scarcity forces people to make choices, both individually and collectively.

- Economic choices are usually made at the margin, meaning in increments rather than all or nothing. The choices made by individuals, businesses, and government determine the economy's allocation of resources.

- Economic issues can be classified as microeconomics or macroeconomics. Microeconomics deals with the individual parts of the economy, such as consumers or firms. Macroeconomics looks at the big picture, including gross domestic product, unemployment, inflation, money, and interest rates.

- The three basic economic questions are what, how, and for whom.

- To answer the three questions, countries can choose among three types of economic systems: laissez-faire free markets, command and control, and a mixed economy. Most countries have mixed economies.

- In making decisions about the choice of system, countries can be guided by two economic objectives: equity and efficiency. Equity refers to fairness; efficiency to getting the most value from economic resources. Efficiency is of two types: allocative and technological. The first refers to producing the highest-valued output; the second to producing output in the least-costly way.

- In a free market economy resources are allocated as if, in Adam Smith's famous phrase, by an invisible hand. A laissez-faire or hands-off policy by government means that the price system guides the allocation of resources.

- When there are market failures, such as externalities, public goods, and market power, government tends to take action. Government action is also directed toward equity issues. Such government actions include government production of goods and services, income redistribution, taxation, and regulations and mandates.

- Economic analysis can involve normative or positive statements. Normative economics involve value judgments about whether something is good or bad. Positive economics tends toward the factual.

- Economic analysis is practiced using models, often expressed using graphs. Occam's razor suggests that models ought to be stripped down to their necessary elements, that is, that they be as simple as possible, while still conveying the essence of an issue.

QUESTIONS AND PROBLEMS

1. Describe how scarcity affects the following decision makers:
   a. the President of the United States.
   b. a business executive.

2. Think back over the all the decisions you have made in the last 24 hours in your life. Select a few of the clearest examples of how your decision making occurred at the margin.

3. During World War II, sugar, gasoline, meat, and other goods were rationed by the U.S. government. Families were issued ration cards that allowed them to buy a government-determined quantity of rationed goods. Why would the government bypass the price system in time of war? Is government rationing, rather than rationing by price, a good idea? How does government rationing affect the allocation of resources?

4. If farmers stopped farming or transportation workers quit shipping the food that farmers grow, we might wake up one morning to discover our cupboards bare. Why don't we lose sleep over that possibility? What causes the food and other goods to appear in stores?

5. Explain how choices made between government's spending of taxpayer money, or taxpayers spending that money themselves, affect the allocation of society's resources.

6. Suppose on the first day of class that your instructor announces that in the name of equity the final grades of all A and B students will be reduced by enough points to bring each of them down to a C and that the points taken away from the A and B students will be distributed among the D and F students so that they receive a C. Your instructor explains this policy by telling the class, "After all, it is only fair that everyone be treated equally and the only way to do that is to have everyone receive an equal grade." Assume for the sake of argument that the instructor will be allowed to actually implement this policy.

a. Is this policy equitable? What would it depend upon?

b. Why is it likely that there would be no points to distribute to the D and F students?

c. Explain how the instructor's efforts to realize this idea of equity involves a trade-off with efficiency.

d. Would your perception of this situation be different if the instructor announced that everyone would receive the same grade and that grade would be an A?

e. How does accurate grading by professors contribute to the efficiency of the marketplace, especially the job market?

7. Why is the statement "Movies today are too violent" a normative statement? Convert the statement into a positive statement. Is your positive statement true? What sort of evidence could be used to establish the truth or falsity of the statement you wrote?

8. Generally speaking, what is the purpose of an economic model? What guidance does Occam's razor give in creating models?

 Web Exercises

9. a. Using an Internet search engine such as that provided by Yahoo (located at **http://www.yahoo.com**) or Alta Vista (located at **http://www.altavista.com**), perform a separate search for the following terms: **macroeconomics, invisible hand,** and **externalities**. Visit several of the Web sites that your search reveals for each term and observe the context in which each term is used. Explain whether the manner in which the terms are used is consistent with their use in the text.

b. Repeat the above, but this time use a combination of terms that you select from the chapter. To eliminate Web sites that do not contain all terms, place a plus sign in front of each term you enter, such as **+efficiency +economics +equity.**

10. Visit the Resources for Economists Web site maintained by Dr. Bill Goffe of the University of Southern Mississippi: **http://econwpa.wustl.edu/EconFAQ/EconFAQ.html**. Explore a few of the sites offering economics-related material on the Internet by clicking your mouse on several of the highlighted links that look the most interesting to you. Briefly describe the sites and the information you find at each.

 Visit the Web site for *Economics by Design* at
http://www.prenhall.com/collinge for a Self Quiz over
the topics in this chapter.

Exploration 1-1 "From Each According to . . . , to Each According to . . ."?

Choosing the right mix of government and free enterprise involves questions of economics, philosophy, and politics. Economic incentives can lead to the success or downfall of political systems, as illustrated by the demise of the Soviet Union. The philosophical concept of the original position is useful in framing the discussion of the best path for an economy to take.

The *Communist Manifesto* was written by Karl Marx and Friedrich Engels in 1847 as a proclamation for the League of the Just, a secret international organization aimed at overcoming the exploitation of labor. The *Communist Manifesto* was a short book—little more than a pamphlet by today's standards. However, its influence in the field of political economy for a time rivaled Adam Smith's very lengthy *The Wealth of Nations*, first published in 1776. *Political economy* was the term used in the eighteenth and nineteenth centuries to describe the study of what we now call economics. Even today, some use the term to accentuate the close ties between economic analysis and public policy. Nowhere are these ties more apparent than in the two books just mentioned.

On the one hand, *The Wealth of Nations* provided the intellectual basis for the system of free markets found in the U.S. Constitution. James Madison, Thomas Jefferson, and the other founding fathers were well acquainted with Adam Smith's analysis of the virtues of competitive markets. On the other hand, the *Communist Manifesto* served as the intellectual basis for a very different kind of government, one founded on the notion of class warfare between owners of capital and labor resources. This idea was used to justify a strong central government that would allocate resources equitably. Equity was taken to mean, as Karl Marx stated in 1875, "from each according to his abilities, to each according to his needs."

The Communist Philosophy . . .

> *All I ask is a tall ship and a star to steer her by.*
>
> —John Masefield, 1878–1967, poet

What does a person need? A chicken in every pot? Will rice and beans do? A glass of wine and a loaf of bread? Love? Peace and quiet? We each have different ideas when it comes to fulfilling our personal needs. People want more, and yet make do with less. How is a government to know about diverse needs?

Partly because needs are so hard to pin down, the task of following Marx's philosophy has proved difficult in practice. The result is that Marxist governments have tended to expound a philosophy of **egalitarianism,** in which everyone is supposed to get the same access to everything from soap to medical care. If people can make do with what they get, they must be getting what they need, right?

egalitarianism: the idea that an economy's output should be divided equally among all its citizens.

. . . ignores Personal Incentives . . .

The problem with using egalitarianism as the rule to allocate a country's output is that egalitarianism provides no incentive for people to be productive. If a country distributes the same amounts to all, its people are not motivated to do their best. Since the Communist credo requires that each person produce according to that person's abilities, the lack of incentives to do so became a serious problem.

In a communist economy, smart people act stupid. The reason is simple. The smarter you act, the more will be expected of you. To live well, you are well advised to keep your head down and act as if you're no better than anyone else. It used to be said in the former Soviet Union that those whose heads stuck above the crowd got them chopped off!

. . . and Led to Its Own Collapse.

With a central authority attempting to direct the what, how, and for whom of production, bad choices were made and resources were squandered. Everyone had a job, but productivity and purchasing power lagged badly. As put by disgruntled workers in Eastern Europe and the Soviet Union, "We pretend to work, and they pretend to pay us."

Actually, the USSR was quite effective at spurring economic growth when the problem was lack of physical capital, such as tractors. Indeed, the Soviet Union became known for its tractor factories. But a modern economy requires education, training, and the freedom and incentive to express creativity. On this score, communism failed badly.

It was small wonder that, over time, the comparatively free markets of the West led to a dramatically better standard of living than was available in the communist economies of the East. Exposed to this better way of life through the global reach of the media, residents of Eastern Europe and the Soviet Union became disillusioned with communism. Cynicism reigned. When the Communist apparatus was in jeopardy and it seemed safe to do so, there was a groundswell of support for its demise. Communism was not a philosophy worth fighting for, and so it collapsed with only a whimper.

Still, there is nostalgia for the relative order and security that was provided by the Communist State. While living standards were low, life was not crassly commercial. The stress of getting ahead in the job market or business world was absent, since opportunities were confined to the Communist party. Moreover, the advent of comparatively free markets has been rough, with many people finding their paltry living standards declining still further. Then, too, there is the matter of pride. With insufficient conviction to rally to the philosophy of communism, many former Communists have instead turned to the rallying cry of nationalism, risking its attendant danger of war. This risk was fulfilled in the conflict between the Serbs, Croats, and Bosnians in the former communist country of Yugoslavia.

The Marketplace Is Better at "from Each" . . .

Nationalism does not by itself answer the economic questions of resource allocation. Whatever their governmental leanings, nations can choose their own economic system. They are usually well served to allow relatively free markets, if their goal is to get the most value for their citizens from the resources they possess. Even China recognized this fact, leaving behind Mao Tse Tung's castigation of "Capitalist Roaders" in favor of moving in the direction of free markets.

The free market does not work through altruism. Rather, as Adam Smith put it, it is as though producers are guided by an invisible hand. The invisible hand of the marketplace means that people acting in their own self-interests will more effectively serve the public interest than could even the most well-meaning of governments or altruistic of philanthropists. In the marketplace, the myriad of decisions by individual customers determines what is and is not valuable enough to produce. The marketplace rewards those best able to offer goods and services of value to others. The better a person is at providing value to others, the more will be that person's income. In this way, each person has an incentive to develop his or her productive potential.

. . . but Lacks Compassion.

Firms in the private marketplace offer products that people are willing to pay for or they go out of business. The money to pay for successful products comes from incomes that depend upon people's abilities. The marketplace rewards ability with more income. That seems fair, to some extent.

The problem arises that, through no fault of their own, people do not all have the same potential. Furthermore, people may develop their potentials in ways that seem productive at the time, but turn out not to be. For example, elevator operators found their skills obsolete when the ingenuity of manufacturers created automatic elevators. That example reflects the changing opportunities in society, but hardly seems fair to many of the people whose livelihoods are involved.

In other cases people find themselves with disabilities that prevent them from reaching their full potential to provide for others. This situation does not mean that they are worth any less as humans, although the free market tends to pay them less. Again, that does not seem fair. Likewise, situations can arise in most people's lives that prevent them from following their desired paths. The free market appears not to care.

While not immoral, the market is amoral—it seems to turn a blind eye to questions of equity. Sometimes the market seems fair, such as by rewarding those who follow through on ideas that are of benefit to others. However, the free market is fair only by coincidence. Many issues of equity must be addressed through other means.

Attempts by Government to Correct Inequities . . .

Private charities are an attempt to correct inequities. Still, many people think that fairness requires help from all who have the ability. Enter government, with its ability to tax. Specifically, government imposes taxes that take from those who can afford to give and that give to those in need.

There's that word, again—need! What is a need? To the extent that government seeks to take from each in accordance with ability and give to each according to need, it finds itself back in the communist dilemma. Government becomes the arbiter of what people need. Government also becomes a drag on productivity, which leads modern economies to search for the mix in the middle. On the one hand, pure communism shrinks the economic pie badly. On the other hand, laissez-faire capitalism bakes a big pie, but may slice it very unequally.

. . . bring Tough Choices.

How does a government decide where to draw the line on taxes and redistributional spending? In the political process, it may look to voters. Some voters will always want more redistribution; others will desire less. In many cases, the amount of redistribution depends upon the taxes that the individual voters expect to face. Low-income voters tend to want more and high-income voters less. It is the voters in the middle who usually decide elections. Where that middle lies will be affected by the extent to which those voters are paying burdensome taxes. It also depends on perceptions among those voters about whether high income taxes along with generous welfare spending make staying in poverty too easy and escaping it too difficult.

Rawls' Philosophy of the Original Position Can Illuminate . . .

Does political economy offer any help in making these choices? Perhaps economic philosophy can once more shed some light. In particular, imagine that we place ourselves in the original position. As described by twentieth-century political philosopher John Rawls, the original position occurs prior to when we have assumed identities as separate people. We do not know who we will become nor how much of those qualities that help us become wealthy we would have. From that position, we must contemplate the risk of becoming an individual the free market leaves behind. Of course, we could also be someone able to thrive in the marketplace.

. . . the Nature of the Trade-offs We Face . . .

The original position gives us a unique perspective. We might be at either the receiving or giving end of the tax system. What kinds of government policies would we support?

We would not want to be left out in the cold. For this reason, Rawls suggests that we choose a *maxi-min* philosophy, in which government attempts to maximize the well-being of the least well-off person in the economy, the person on the bottom rung of the economic ladder. The focus would be on improving the lot of those who are worst off, whoever they may be.

Alternatively, since the size of the economic pie is generally larger when government keeps taxes low, we might choose to take our chances. After all, while the risk is higher, so is the expected standard of living. We also might doubt government's ability to identify the needy. We might even mistrust government's will to fairly implement a policy to reward the neediest, even if identifying them were possible.

Most likely, we would choose a *safety net* to protect us from some but not all risks. This approach is the basis for such government programs as unemployment insurance and Social Security. We also figure that individuals are better positioned to know their own needs than government could ever be. Thus we want freedom and opportunity to go along with security.

original position: occurs prior to when we have assumed identities as separate people—we do not know who we will become; attributable to philosopher John Rawls.

A look at controversial philosopher John Rawls is available at **http://geocities. com/Athens/ Parthenon/1643/ rawls.html**

. . . but We Will Still Argue.

Exactly how much freedom and opportunity should we mix with exactly how much insurance against life's pitfalls? Debate will continue on and on and on. The issues are important to our lives, and we will have different perspectives. On that we can agree.

■ Prospecting for New Insights

1. JESSE: The values in this country have eroded. Drugs, promiscuous sex, obscenities—you name it, people just do whatever they want. I like the idea of a strong central government that maintains the American way of life. We need freedom and opportunity within limits, where government keeps us from going too far.

   PAUL: I hear you, but you've missed the point. The point of the American way is to be answerable to yourself. Yes, when people harm others or take their property, government needs to intervene. Otherwise, it's just one group imposing its version of morality on everybody else.

   This exchange illustrates that the mix in the middle involves much more than just how high taxes are and how much social insurance there is. What are some of the other points of contention in how "free" free markets should be?

2. Many people think that, the more democratic is a country, the greater reliance it will place upon free markets. Do you think this is true? Explain.

Exploration 1-2 Economics—Out of the Ivory Tower and into Action

Economics is offered as part of the curriculum at most colleges and universities. It is at the heart of many social issues, and is also important at an individual level. How much economics to study is a personal issue for many college students. In this Exploration, some insights into both the opportunities for students studying the subject and into the practice of economics are discussed.

Real World Problems—The Role of Economics

Finding a job, getting a promotion and a raise, the cost of living—problems of everyday life often revolve around economics. As people go about making personal economic choices, they are making *microeconomic* decisions. These decisions affect how content they are with life. Most adults have reflected upon how satisfied they are with their economic progress. These reflections often lead people to make changes designed to improve their lot in life. The performance of the *macroeconomy* affects our contentment, too. For example, the increases in unemployment and poverty associated with *recessions*—economic slowdowns—can make it harder to find a job and get a raise.

Then there are the social economic issues that concern us, both as people who care about society and as voters. Such issues include crime, drugs, health care, Social Security, free trade, education, and tax reform, which are some of the many issues to be discussed in this book.

Clearly, a knowledge of economics can help you make better personal and social decisions. But how much economics should you study? The answer to that question partly depends upon your career plans.

Making a Career Out of Economics

A major in economics can pay well. For example, mid-career men with undergraduate economics degrees earned a median salary of $49,377 in 1993, which was within $4,000 of engineering, the top-paying major for this group.[1] Mid-career women with economics degrees received a median salary of $49,170 that year. That made economics the highest paying undergraduate major for mid-career women. The National Association of Business Economists found that business economists, many with graduate degrees, earned a median salary of roughly $73,000 in 1996. According to a 1998 survey by the National Association of Colleges and Employers, an economics/finance major earned an average starting salary of $35,219. Many other surveys and studies confirm the good pay for economics majors.

Where do economics majors find employment? Some clues are offered in Table 1-2. The table shows the major employers and clients served by economists. As you can see, the employment opportunities for economists are varied.

Of course, not everyone with an economics degree finds work as an economist. Many economics majors find employment as management trainees in banking, retailing, and marketing. Others become sales trainees, research assistants, or administrative assistants. Many economics majors have gone on to eventually take top positions in industry and government. Employers seek economics majors for their analytical abilities and their general grasp of the way the world works. Those qualities also make the economics major the second most common major at the nation's law schools. Table 1-3 shows a few of the career fields that are closely related to economics. People in these careers find a knowledge of economics valuable. They may or may not be economics majors, but they typically will have studied the subject extensively. Furthermore, the study of economics is now recognized to be of value in a number of career fields where traditionally it was not considered very relevant. For example, schools of nursing are increasingly offering training in economics because so much of our health care system has been restructured in response to economic incentives.

The Economics Profession

Students already know at least one economist—their instructor! While teaching is a primary duty of academic economists, the range of duties performed by economics

---

[1] *Source:* Daniel E. Hecker, "Earnings of College Graduates, 1993," *Monthly Labor Review.* December 1995, Table 3, page 6.

TABLE 1-2 Who Needs Economic Analysis?

Lawyers	Accountants
Engineers	Health services administrators
Government	Education administrators
Unions	Environmental scientists
Trade associations	Urban and regional planners
Nonprofit organizations	Bankers
Businesses	

Source: Occupational Outlook Handbook, 1998–1999.

instructors may surprise you. Like other college faculty, economics instructors often apply their expertise to community affairs, provide services related to the operation of their schools, sometimes conduct and publish research on economic issues, and possibly do consulting work for industry and government clients.

Let's consider the lives of academic economists a little more closely, since academia is where most economists work. Typically, the academic economist must have earned at least a master's degree. Many schools require a terminal degree—the Doctor of Philosophy (Ph.D.), which takes at least four years of intense study beyond a bachelor's degree. Full-time instructors often provide services to their school. Some instructors fulfill their service duties by acting as mentors to students and student organizations. Others serve on committees relating to curriculum and university governance. Instructors may also provide their time and talents free of charge to nonprofit community organizations.

Most universities require faculty to publish original research. The phrase "publish or perish" describes the working conditions faced by many academic economists who are early in their careers. Publish or perish means that instructors must publish a significant amount of high-quality research or risk losing their jobs. Those who are successful at publishing are granted tenure, a form of job security, and promotion to a higher rank.

Many schools also encourage their faculty to do paid consulting work for industry. While school policies relating to consulting vary from school to school, it is common to limit faculty consulting to one day a week. Consulting allows faculty to sharpen their skills by applying those skills to real-world problems. It can also provide opportunities to become rich! One well-known academic economist founded a

TABLE 1-3 Related Occupations

Financial analysts	Financial managers	Marketing researchers
Underwriters	Accountants and auditors	Economics teachers
Actuaries	Securities and financial services salespeople	
Credit analysts	Loan officers and budget officers	

Source: Occupational Outlook Handbook, 1998–1999.

consulting business that was so successful that when shares of stock in the firm were sold to the public, the economist found himself $12 million richer!

Some consulting work puts the economist in the witness chair in a courtroom. For example, the practice of "forensic economics" involves applying economic expertise to legal cases. Common applications of forensic economics include estimating the economic damage to an individual who has been illegally fired from a job, and establishing the losses in wrongful death proceedings. The frequent application of economic principles to matters of law makes a comprehensive knowledge of basic economics highly valuable to attorneys and judges. Perhaps that is why economics has been the second leading undergraduate major among U.S. law school students.

A relatively small number of economists are employed full-time in industry in banks, for securities firms, trade associations, and large businesses. In industry the duties of economists are varied. Some forecast the future course of the economy, focusing on interest rates, inflation, wages, and other macroeconomic variables, and then analyze the implications of their forecasts for their employers. Others engage in work related to marketing or to maintaining good company relations with investors or the public. Some economists find work with consulting firms that specialize in supplying economic expertise to companies on a job-by-job basis. Other economists are entrepreneurs who publish newsletters dealing with trends and forecasts. Increasingly, with the globalization of the economy, training in international economics is required of business economists. Salaries in industry tend to be higher than those in academia for individuals with similar levels of training.

Government economists tend to spend their time doing policy-oriented research. New legislation and regulations have economic impacts, which economists attempt to estimate. All levels of government—federal, state, and local—employ economists. In fact, about 40 percent of economists work for government. Salaries in government are similar to those in academia. A number of economists in government, like their brethren in academia, engage in publishing their research in books and journals.

Economics in the Political Arena

It is not surprising that a significant fraction of economists are employed by government. Many of the problems faced by society have an economic dimension to them. Since politics is about how to best go about solving society's problems, economists and economic analysis often take center stage in political disagreements.

The members of the U.S. Congress, in both the House of Representatives and the Senate, seek economic analysis. Economists work with Congress to advise the members on economic matters. Economics is so important that the *Council of Economic Advisors* instructs the President on economic issues and policies. The Council, members of which are appointed by the President, and its staff also author the annual *Economic Report of the President.* This publication, available in printed form and online on the Internet, assesses the state of the economy. The report is written so that it can be understood by readers who have limited training in economics. Each edition highlights the nation's vital economic statistics, economic accomplishments, and remaining economic problems. There are a wide range of problems and issues considered in a typical report. For example, U.S. macroeconomic performance relating to growth, inflation, and unemployment, the economic well-being of children, and economic inequality and poverty are just a few of the issues discussed in recent editions of the report.

Pursuing the Study of Economics

Economics fits the pieces of the world together. For example, many students who choose not to major in economics nonetheless find additional economics courses to be a good fit with their majors. This is especially true of business students, political science majors, history majors, and geography majors among others, since these subjects have a significant economic dimension to them. Applications of economics are found all around, such as in the schoolroom, the corporate boardroom, the courtroom, and even in the Oval Office of the White House!

■ Prospecting for New Insights

1. What are some examples of the economist's job that involve positive economics? Which employer(s) of economists is more likely to require normative economic analysis? Explain.

2. As stated in the exploration, professors at many universities perform their jobs subject to the principle of publish or perish. This means that professors must meet a quota for an amount of creative, published research that is established by university administrators. Those professors who fail to met the quota are subject to penalties and sometimes even lose their jobs.

    a. Does the publish or perish policy change a professor's incentives to allocate more time to research and less to teaching?

    b. What are the advantages and disadvantages of publish or perish from a student's point of view?

    c. How does the policy relate to scarcity?

Appendix
THE ECONOMIST'S TOOLKIT: GRAPHS AND DATA

Economists draw graphs in order to clarify thoughts and show relationships in a way that can be more easily understood. Graphs that present information are often drawn as line graphs, bar charts, and pie charts, all of which are seen in this book.

    Other graphs represent economic models and contain lines that are referred to as curves. As you read this book, you should study each graph and read its caption. Pay attention to the labels on the axes and to the content. Then ask yourself what the graph is saying. When it comes to graphs of models, you will learn the graph better if you can draw it yourself. If you are able to visualize economic relationships graphically, can put an explanation of the graph into your own words, and can draw the graph, you will increase your understanding of economic concepts.

MODELS: DIRECT VERSUS INVERSE RELATIONSHIPS

Each axis of the graph is labeled with the name of a variable, where a *variable* refers to the name of anything that can change. For example, the price of a pound of tomatoes is a variable because the price could be any of several different values. The price will typically vary with the passage of time. Likewise, the quantity of tomatoes sold is a variable because the quantity sold would likely change from one time period to the next.

Within the axes, a relationship between two variables is shown by a curve—a line. Some graphs will have more than one curve in them. For example, in chapter 3 you will see graphs showing a demand and a supply curve.

direct (positive) relationship: when a change in one variable leads to the same direction change in another variable.

inverse (negative) relationship: when a change in one variable leads to the opposite direction change in another variable.

Curves that slope upward to the right show a direct relationship, also termed a positive relationship, between the variables. Curves that slope downward to the right show an inverse relationship, also termed a negative relationship.

An example will help. Suppose we are interested in the relationship between the average yearly sales of umbrellas and the average yearly quantity of rainfall, measured in inches. Hypothetical data for five communities are given in Table 1A-1.

The relationship between rainfall and umbrellas sales is clearly positive, because increases in rainfall are associated with a greater number of umbrellas sold. In Figure 1A-1, the data are plotted with rainfall measured on the horizontal axis (the axis that goes left to right) and umbrella sales on the vertical axis (the axis that goes up and down). A curve is drawn through the plot of points. The curve slopes upward to the right, again confirming the direct relationship between two variables.

In contrast, Figure 1A-2 shows a curve that slopes downward to the right, indicating an inverse relationship between variables. The axes are labeled to show the relationship between the sales of woolen coats and the average January temperature in five cities. A greater quantity of coats are sold when temperatures are lower.

 QuickCheck _____

Use the data in Figure 1A-2 to create a table similar to Table 1A-1. Verify that the numbers in the table show an inverse relationship.

TABLE 1A-1 Hypothetical Data on Rainfall and Umbrella Sales

Data Point	Community	Yearly Rainfall	Umbrella Sales
A	Center City	30 inches	100 units
B	Moose Haven	40 inches	200 units
C	Blountville	50 inches	300 units
D	Houckton	60 inches	400 units
E	Echo Ridge	70 inches	500 units

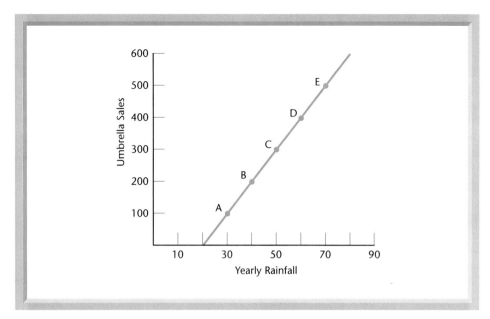

FIGURE 1A-1   **A positive relationship between two variables is represented by a curve that slopes upward to the right.**

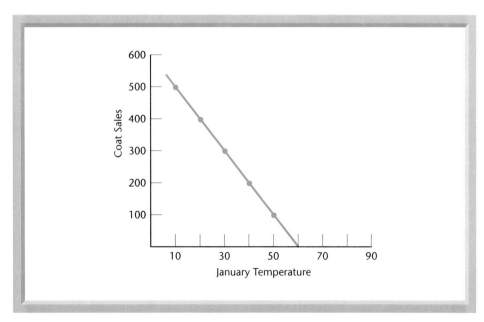

FIGURE 1A-2   **A negative relationship between two variables is represented by a curve that slopes downward.**

THE SLOPE OF A LINE

The *slope* of a line is the change in the variable on the vertical axis divided by the change in the variable on the horizontal axis. The slope is sometimes referred to as the "rise over the run." In Figure 1A-1, the slope of the curve equals 100 (the rise, or vertical change) divided by 10 (the run, or horizontal change), which equals 10. The slope of the curve in Figure 1A-2 equals minus 10, a negative value because the vertical change involves a decrease. Downward sloping curves always have a negative value for the slope.

Straight lines are *linear* and always have a constant slope. This means that if you know the slope between any two points on the line, you know the slope everywhere on the line. Thus, in Figure 1A-1 the slope equals 10 all along the curve and in Figure 1A-2 the slope equals minus 10 everywhere on that curve.

The slope of a *nonlinear* curve changes from one point to the next on the curve. In Figure 1A-3 the upper panels show two graphs with curves that have a positive slope. However, the slope decreases in the left-side graph, but increases in the graph on the right. The lower panels consist of graphs that have curves with negative slopes. In the leftmost graph the slope becomes less negative, while the slope becomes more negative in the graph on the right. Figure 1A-3 illustrates another point about graphs. Notice that these graphs do not have numbers. Graphs of models will often be presented this way when the numbers are less important than the type of relationship between the variables.

Many economic relationships are portrayed as linear. This convention simplifies the analysis, in keeping with the principle of Occam's razor, and allows us to

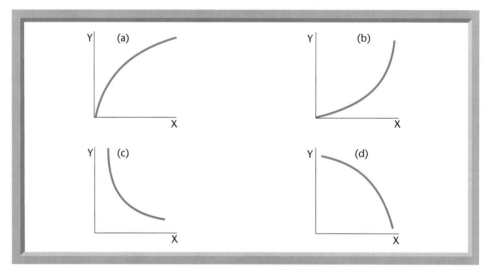

FIGURE 1A-3 The graphs show nonlinear relationships between X and Y, where X and Y can represent any two variables. The slopes are: (a) decreasingly positive; (b) increasingly positive; (c) becoming decreasingly negative; (d) becoming increasingly negative.

focus our attention on the analysis rather than the shape of the curve. When curves are drawn as nonlinear, the nonlinearity will typically be important to the analysis. For example, in the next chapter the curve called the production possibility frontier is shown as nonlinear because the nonlinearity has significant implications.

INTERPRETING SLOPES

Merely glancing at a curve is often revealing. When the curve slopes upward to the right, you know that it has a positive slope and thus shows a direct relationship between the variables on the axes. Likewise, when the curve slopes downward to the right, it has a negative slope that portrays an inverse relationship between the variables.

The slope of a curve is also useful in illustrating decision making at the margin. Recall from the first section of the chapter the question of whether a restaurant should stay open later. To answer the question, a restaurant might experiment with staying open an hour later than normal, then two hours later, three hours later, and so forth. Suppose the experiment revealed that customers can be expected to spend a total of $225 more when the restaurant stays open three additional hours. However, the experiment reveals that spending falls off as the lateness of the hour increases, with $100 in spending the first additional hour the restaurant stays open, $75 the second additional hour, and $50 the third additional hour.

The downward sloping curve in Figure 1A-4 shows the incremental spending by the customers of the restaurant. Note that the slope of the curve equals −25, because additional customer spending decreases by $25 every hour. The managers of the restaurant could use this information, in conjunction with data relating to the cost of staying open, to reach a decision about how long to stay open. For example, if the total expenses arising from staying open exceeded $100 an hour, the restaurant would

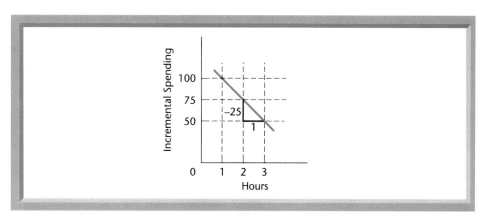

FIGURE 1A-4 **The additional spending by customers at the restaurant decreases as it stays open longer.** The slope of the incremental spending line equals −25, since the amount of money customers spend decreases by $25 with each passing hour.

choose to retain its current hours. If those expenses were to be between $75 and $100, the restaurant would increase earnings by staying open one extra hour. Can you determine what level of expenses would lead to the restaurant remaining open three more hours?

A SHIFT IN A CURVE

A change in the relationship between two variables is indicated by a shift in a curve. For example, suppose that umbrellas become a fashion accessory to be carried even when it is not raining. The curve in Figure 1A-5 would shift up, as shown in Figure 1A-5. In this example, the sales of umbrellas increase by 100 units in each community. If the popularity of umbrellas fades, the curve would shift back down.

When a curve shifts, the student should understand why the shift occurred and in which direction the curve shifts. For example, the production possibility frontier in the next chapter will shift outward from the origin when there is an increase in resources. The student should also be aware **that there is a difference between a shift in a curve and a movement along a curve.** A change in the amount of rainfall will initiate a movement along the curve, as in moving from one point to another in Figure 1A-1. That is different from a shift in the curve, which occurs when the popularity of umbrellas changes.

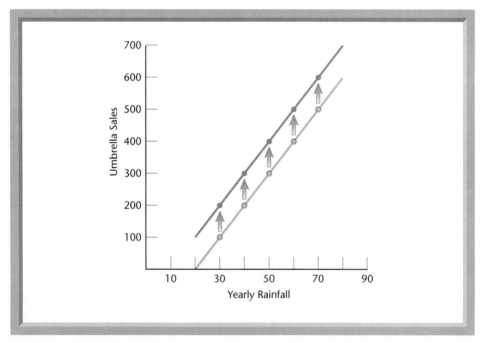

FIGURE 1A-5 A shift in a curve occurs when the curve changes position. A shift represents a new relationship between the variables.

TIME-SERIES AND CROSS-SECTIONAL DATA

As in the preceding example that relates umbrella sales to rainfall, numerical data is important in economics. Time-series data show the values of a variable as time passes. U.S. energy consumption between 1970 and 1997 is an example of time-series data, as shown by the line chart in Figure 1A-6. Cross-sectional data are fixed at a moment in time, but vary in some other way. The 1997 unemployment rate for the United States, Canada, Japan, France, Germany, Italy, and the United Kingdom is an example, shown in Figure 1A-7 as a bar chart. For an example of a pie chart showing cross-sectional data, see chapter 10, Figure 10-2, which illustrates revenue sources for the federal government in 1998.

<aside>
time-series data: the values of a variable over a period of time.

cross-sectional data: the value of a variable at a given moment in time for a number of states, countries, or other separate entities.
</aside>

FINDING ECONOMIC DATA FOR GRAPHS

Much of the numerical data economists use is collected by various levels of government. Important nongovernmental sources of data include industry trade associations, the United Nations, the Organization for European Community Development (OECD), the International Monetary Fund (IMF), Standard and Poor's, Moody's, and Robert Morris Associates.

A short list of useful sources of data follows. If you are interested in finding data on a specific subject, the *American Statistics Index* (ASI), which is found in many

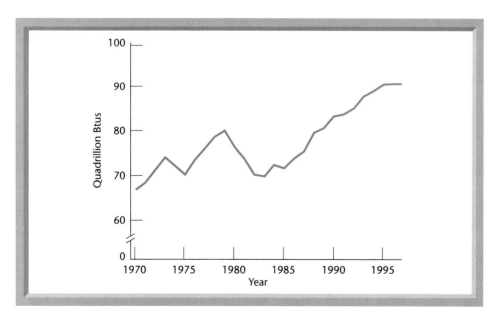

FIGURE 1A-6 U.S. energy consumption by year is an example of time-series data.
Energy usage has risen as energy prices have fallen since the mid-1980s.
Source: 1999 Economic Report of the President, Chart 5-3, p. 208.

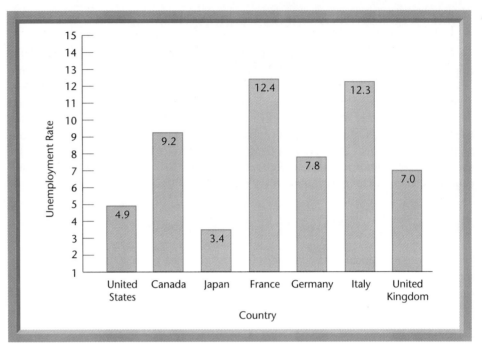

FIGURE 1A-7 **The average unemployment rate in each of several countries is an example of cross-sectional data.** These data are not time series, because they are for a single year, 1997.

Source: 1999 Economic Report of the President, Table B-109. Data for France, Germany, Italy, and United Kingdom are preliminary figures. All figures are for unemployment as a percent of the civilian labor force.

university libraries, is especially useful. It indexes data available in U.S. government publications, by subject.

1. *Economic Report of the President.* Annual. Roughly one-half of the book is a compilation of numerous data tables from among those issued by government agencies. The text is written by the President's Council of Economic Advisers, and provides a professional assessment of the performance of the economy. Written to be understood by the general public, the *Economic Report* is probably the best place for both novices and experts to start a general search for data about the U.S. economy.

2. *International Financial Statistics.* Monthly. Published by the International Monetary Fund in English and other languages, the book presents several hundred large pages of finely printed economic data on the world at large, and on specific countries throughout the world. The focus is on the financial side of economic activity, such as inflation, interest rates, government budgets, and exchange rates. There is also data on a variety of nonfinancial features of world economies, such as the composition of exports and imports. To promote easy access, the IMF also provides a CD-ROM version.

3. **Federal Reserve Bulletin.** Monthly. The user will find extensive data on money, banking, interest rates, and finance, along with news relating to the financial environment. Also featured are articles which analyze economic developments. Articles are written to be accessible to the general reader.

4. **Survey of Current Business.** Quarterly. This publication of the U.S. Department of Commerce offers a rich source of data on business conditions.

5. **City and County Data Book.** Annual. What is the population of your hometown? What is the average age of its residents? Average income? This data source provides information about the economies of U.S. cities and counties.

6. **Statistical Abstract of the U.S.** Annual. This source contains hundreds of data tables, packed full of facts about the United States.

7. **The Internet.** There are numerous sites relating to economics and economic data, many of which are offered by the federal government and by universities. Various Internet locations are presented in the margins throughout this book. In the Questions and Problems section that follows each chapter's survey of principles, a special section called Web Exercises offers activities to do on the Internet.

Applying Concepts

1. Consider the relationship between a college student's grade in a course and the amount of time spent studying. Draw a graph with the vertical axis labeled "grade" and the horizontal axis labeled "time spent studying" that shows the general relationship you would expect between these variables. Do you think the relationship would necessarily be linear? What factors other than study time would affect the grades of college students? How would changes in these other factors shift the curve in the graph you have drawn?

2. Each day *The Wall Street Journal* newspaper publishes stories that focus on the latest economic statistics. Why do business decision makers find this information worthwhile? Why not publish it weekly? Explain.

2

PRODUCTION, GROWTH, AND TRADE

A Look Ahead

WHAT DOES THE word *model* call to mind? A swimsuit model? A model citizen? A model airplane? In this chapter, we will model the essence of economics—scarcity and choice. While designed for different purposes, this economic model shares a common trait with these other models—yes, even the swimsuit model. That trait is simplicity, to highlight the features of greatest significance.

Economics is about common sense. By organizing this common sense systematically, we can shed light on a diverse array of questions that concern our personal lives and our country's choices. For example, the same model that guides us personally to the most promising careers can guide our country to the best trade policy. We will see why economics pervades life on earth and even guides life aboard the starship *Enterprise*.

The basic model of economics developed in this chapter explains the mundane, such as which products a country chooses to produce and how producers respond to prices. It also reveals the sublime, such as the rise and fall of nations. Future chapters investigate the details behind the broad scope of economics that we glimpse here.

Exploration 2-1 explains the role of information and its transmission. The Internet and other advances in communication are seen to increase a country's production possibilities, but leave unresolved numerous other information-related problems. Exploration 2-2 looks at the issue of overpopulation, a topic that once earned economics the nickname of "the dismal science." Dismal or not, economic forces are seen to affect population growth and our planet's future.

As you are **Surveying Economic Principles** you will arrive at an ability to

- ❑ analyze trade-offs facing both individuals and countries;
- ❑ relate entrepreneurship to economic growth;
- ❑ model a country's production possibilities, and how these possibilities respond to technological development;
- ❑ describe how economies can grow faster if they are willing to cut back on current consumption;
- ❑ explain why people and countries gain from trade, even if they do not have an absolute advantage in anything.

While **Exploring Issues** you will be able to

- ❑ identify how the information highway represents capital that solves some but not all information problems in the economy;
- ❑ point out how the incentives for population growth are likely to be inefficient.

Terms Along the Way

- ✔ opportunity costs, 40
- ✔ land, 41
- ✔ labor, 41
- ✔ human capital, 41
- ✔ capital, 41
- ✔ entrepreneurship, 41
- ✔ technology, 41
- ✔ production possibility frontier, 43
- ✔ economic growth, 45
- ✔ depreciation, 49

- ✔ money, 51
- ✔ barter, 51
- ✔ circular flow, 51
- ✔ comparative advantage, 53
- ✔ absolute advantage, 53
- ✔ exports, 53
- ✔ imports, 53
- ✔ asymmetric information, 61
- ✔ "the dismal science," 63

SURVEYING ECONOMIC PRINCIPLES

Scarcity and Choice

There is no such thing as a free lunch.

Economics exists because resources are scarce relative to our wants. Scarcity means we have to make choices. Take lunch for example. Suppose your school cafeteria holds a Student Appreciation Day and offers a free sandwich buffet between noon and 1:00 next Thursday. Would you go? Your decision depends upon opportunity costs.

Opportunity Costs

opportunity cost: the value of the best alternative opportunity forgone.

Opportunity costs represent the value of forgone alternatives. Perhaps you contemplate how good the cafeteria's sandwiches are, relative to other things you could eat. You might also consider how pleasant the surroundings are, relative to other lunch spots. You would also want to check your calendar—your time may be needed for something of higher priority, such as studying for an exam. If you choose to eat the cafeteria's sandwiches, you must give up the value of alternative ways to spend that time. While no money is taken, the lunch is in reality far from free.

The money you pay for an item could have alternatively been spent on something else. The value of the best alternative use of that money is an opportunity cost, but not usually the only opportunity cost. The value of forgone alternative uses of time or other nonmonetary resources must also be included. To compute your own opportunity cost of going to college, for example, you must compute what you would be doing if you were not in school. Would you be working? Then the cost of a semester is tuition plus the forgone earnings from the job you would have had. Maybe you would have been spending all of your time at the beach. That, too, has an opportunity cost. Only you can know how high it is, because only you can know what value you receive from lying in the sun and listening to the surf.

OBSERVATION POINT:
"The Grass is Always Greener . . .

. . . on the other side of the fence," the saying goes. Take marriage, for example. How many married men and women do not catch themselves envying the freedom of their single friends—freedom to meet new people and do what they want, when they want to do it? How many of those single friends do not look back with envy of their own, seeing the warmth and security of sharing one's life with someone special? Oh, those opportunity costs! We cannot have it all!

QuickCheck

The Presidio lies at the southern end of the Golden Gate Bridge in San Francisco. After long service as a military base, the Presidio was donated to San Francisco in 1994 for use as a park. After donating the land, the federal government proceeded to pay rent to San Francisco in order to continue using the Presidio's barracks. The budgetary cost of donating the Presidio to San Francisco is the rent that now must be paid. Is this the true opportunity cost?

Answer: Although the federal budget ignores opportunity costs that do not result in explicit dollar payments, these are also opportunity costs. By converting the land into a park, the federal government gave up the opportunity of selling it. This opportunity cost has been estimated at approximately $1 billion, reflecting that land near the Golden Gate Bridge is quite expensive.

The Chamber of Commerce for San Francisco maintains a Web site with interesting content at **http://www. sfchamber.com/**

Resources

Resources are usually divided into the categories of land, labor, capital, and entrepreneurship. **Land** refers to all natural resources in their natural states. These gifts of nature include such things as minerals, water, soil, and location. For example, neither motor oil nor gasoline would be considered as land. Rather, both are products that make use of land as an input. The crude oil from which the motor oil and gasoline were derived is land.

Labor refers to people's capacity to work. It ignores the increased productivity from acquired skills and abilities, which constitute **human capital**. Human capital is a special case of an economy's third resource, capital. **Capital** is anything that is produced in order to increase productivity in the future. Along with human capital, there is also *physical capital*, which includes buildings, machinery, and other equipment. For example, a college education adds to human capital, and the classroom in which that education was obtained is physical capital. The classroom aids in the production of an education, and the education aids in productivity at the workplace.

Caution: The definition of *capital* used in economics differs from that used in finance. *Financial capital* refers to financial instruments, such as stocks, bonds, and money.

Entrepreneurship is taking personal initiative to combine resources in productive ways. Rather than accepting jobs where orders are handed down from above, entrepreneurs blaze new trails in the world of commerce. If you start your own business, you are an entrepreneur. Entrepreneurs take risks, but have the potential to become the economy's movers and shakers. Countries tap the creative potential of entrepreneurship in order to improve the value they get from other resources. In the process, the entrepreneurs themselves are sometimes handsomely rewarded.

The possibilities for combining an economy's resources depend upon technology. **Technology** refers to possible techniques of production. As technologies change, the

land: all natural resources, in their natural states; gifts of nature.

labor: people's capacity to work, exclusive of any human capital they possess.

human capital: acquired skills and abilities that increase the productivity of labor.

capital: anything that is produced in order to increase productivity in the future; includes human capital and physical capital.

entrepreneurship: personal initiative to combine resources in productive ways; involves risk.

The Entrepreneurship Center can be visited at **http://www. ecenter.org/ ecmain.htm**

technology: possible techniques of production.

relative values of various resources also change. For example, natural harbors declined in significance due to the technology of air transportation. While the value of land around harbors diminished, air travel increased the importance of other resources, such as the human capital needed to pilot the planes.

QuickCheck _____

What economic benefits would enrolling in college offer the prospective student?

Answer: A college education provides students with both capital and goods for current consumption. The capital is human capital, meaning the skills and abilities college imparts, which increase productivity in the workplace. The consumption goods include such things as gaining perspective on life, learning interesting things, meeting interesting people, and having a good time. Such consumption goods have different values to different students, which is one good reason why some people major in ecology, some in education, and others in economics, even when aptitude tests might recommend different choices.

OBSERVATION POINT:
The Entrepreneurial Road to Riches—Sam Walton, Bill Gates, . . . and You?

One in two hundred, they say—the odds of striking it rich as an entrepreneur may not be great, but the potential payoff does motivate people to try. How can a person win at the entrepreneurial gamble?

The answer is to offer a product that fills an unmet need. Former economics major Sam Walton used the concept of one-stop shopping at everyday low prices in cities and towns across America. The success of Wal-Mart catapulted the Walton family to first place among America's wealthy. Bill Gates amassed his fortune by positioning Microsoft to provide the industry-standard interface for the personal computer. The more user-friendly, the more money rolls in.

The home page for Wal-Mart is located at **http://www. wal-mart.com/**

The common theme to the success stories of America's modern entrepreneurs is insight into what the public likes to do and how they could do it better or more conveniently. Talk on the phone? Craig McCaw said "take it with you," and took home $11.5 billion from his sale of McCaw Cellular Communications Corporation. Chat over coffee? Howard Shultze earned his fortune by opening Starbucks Coffee Company as a place to hang out over a steaming brew. FedEx your important papers? That was Fred Smith's idea. Linda Wascher saw The Limited catapult its parent company, Warneco, onto the Fortune 100 list of America's largest companies. It was Domino's that delivered for Tom Monaghan, and Motown that recorded Berry Gordy's profit.

Do you have the next good idea, just waiting to take the world by storm? Are you willing to take the risk to find out? If so, you are ready to join the ranks of the entrepreneurs.

Production Possibilities

Modeling Scarcity and Choice

Recall that a model is a simplified version of reality. Following the principles of Occam's razor discussed in chapter 1, a good model emphasizes only those features pertinent to solving the problem at hand. This section will model the essence of economics—scarcity and choice. An economy's scarce resources limit its options. The economy thus must make choices about what to produce. We can model these options, and the choices among them, with a production possibility frontier.

The production possibility frontier illustrates scarcity and choice by assuming that only two goods can be produced. This simplification is appropriate, because understanding choice between any two goods allows the understanding of choice between each good and any other. It is termed a frontier because it represents the limits of output possibilities, given current resources and technology. Frontiers of knowledge and capability are made to be expanded, and the production possibility frontier is no exception. Over time, as resources are accumulated and new techniques learned, the production possibility frontier will expand outward.

> **production possibility frontier:** model that shows the various combinations of two goods the economy is capable of producing.

Consider the fictional economy of Hermit Island, inhabited exclusively by Herschel the Hermit. Herschel has the island to himself, and it provides for all his material needs. Still, he must spend time to feed himself. His options are to catch fish or harvest coconuts. He values both of these foods in his diet and can spend up to eight hours a day to obtain them. Table 2-1 and Figure 2-1 illustrate a production possibility frontier for Herschel's economy.

The graph reveals the same information as the table, but does so in a manner that, with practice, can be interpreted at a glance. For example, the combination of three fish and sixteen coconuts can be read from the third line of the table or seen as point C on the graph. Point D on the graph shows the combination of two fish and nineteen coconuts.

Relationships among data are more readily apparent in the graph than in the table. For example, a basic message of the production possibility frontier is that, as more fish are caught, fewer coconuts are collected. A glance at the graph reveals this relationship. The inverse relationship between fish and coconuts illustrates the opportunity cost of Herschel using his limited resource, time.

TABLE 2-1   Production Possibility Frontier

Data Point	Fish Caught per Day	Coconuts Collected per Day
A	5	0
B	4	10
C	3	16
D	2	19
E	1	21
F	0	22

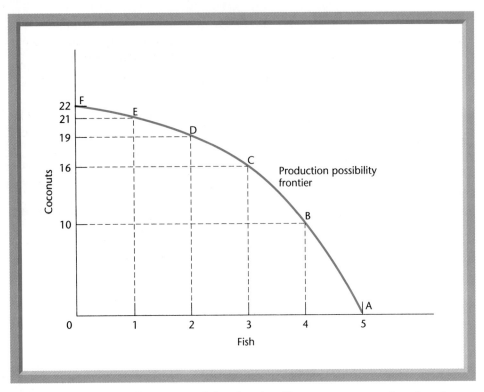

FIGURE 2-1   **The production possibility frontier** illustrates an economy's options from which to choose.

As Herschel increases his catch from zero fish to a maximum of five fish, we see the number of coconuts he collects drop at a nonlinear rate. In other words, the opportunity cost of the first fish is only one coconut. The opportunity cost of two fish is giving up three coconuts. Then opportunity costs really jump. For example, the opportunity cost of four fish is twelve coconuts, which is quadruple the opportunity cost of two fish. These opportunity costs are shown in Table 2-2. Graphing the numbers from this table gives a production possibility frontier that is bowed outward, its typical shape. To understand why this outwardly bowed shape occurs in Herschel's case, consider the choices he must make.

Each working hour of the day, Herschel has to choose between fishing and gathering coconuts. The most productive fishing occurs at certain hours of the day when the fish are biting. While all hours are equally well suited to gathering coconuts, Herschel knows that the number of coconuts gathered per hour declines as he spends more hours per day gathering, because he gathers the most accessible coconuts first. Knocking a few hours off of coconut gathering to fish during feeding time allows him to catch some fish at a cost of relatively few coconuts. Adding more hours to his fishing time leads to less and less incremental productivity in fishing and takes away increasingly more productive hours in gathering.

TABLE 2-2   Opportunity Costs

Data Point	Fish Caught per Day	Opportunity Cost (number of coconuts forgone)
F	0	0
E	1	1
D	2	3
C	3	6
B	4	12
A	5	22

A similar story can be told for all economies. In producing any good X, an economy first uses resources that are best suited to producing X. If the economy keeps adding to the production of good X, it uses resources that are increasingly less well suited to X, but increasingly better suited to other goods, Y. The result is that Y production drops at an increasingly rapid rate as X production increases. The root cause of why the production possibility frontier bows outward is thus that resources are not equally well suited to the production of different goods.

For instance, classrooms are well suited to producing human capital, but not well suited to producing automobiles. Resources are often specialized to perform limited tasks: fish hooks are great for fishing, cooktops for cooking, coal mines for mining coal, and so on. They can sometimes be used for other purposes, but will not be as productive in these uses. For example, coal mines are fine places to grow mushrooms and have led to commercial production under such brand names as Moonlight Mushrooms. However, until the coal seams play out, the coal output is likely to be of higher value.

Figure 2-2 shows the general notion of the production possibility frontier. This idea can be conveyed on a graph without numbers, since the idea transcends any particular numbers. (If you have trouble with a graph without numbers, however, just add some illustrative numbers.) All points within or along the frontier are feasible combinations of goods X and Y. For the economy to be at a point on the production possibility frontier, it must use all of its resources. It must also use these resources efficiently in the technological sense of getting the most output for given inputs.

If the economy acquires more resources, its entire production possibility frontier shifts outward, such as shown in Figure 2-3. **Whenever the production possibility frontier shifts outward, the economy is said to have experienced economic growth,** which allows it to produce more output. In sum,

economic growth: the ability of the economy to produce more output.

- The production possibility frontier shows how much of one good can be produced for any feasible amount of another good.
- If an economy is on its frontier, the opportunity cost of producing more of one good is less of the other good.
- The production possibility frontier is bowed outward.
- Every point along the production possibility frontier is technologically efficient.

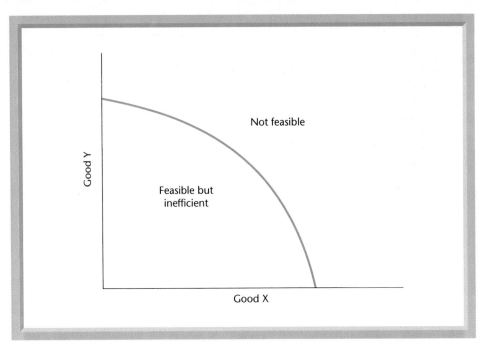

FIGURE 2-2 **All points on the production possibility frontier are technologically effi-cient and feasible.** Points within the production possibility frontier are also feasible, but are not technologically efficient. Points outside the frontier cannot be reached with current resources and technology.

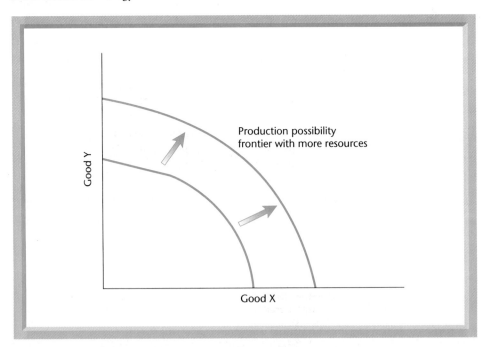

FIGURE 2-3 **Economic growth** can be caused by an increase in resources.

- Points inside the frontier imply some unemployed or misallocated resources and are thus inefficient.
- Points outside the frontier are unattainable with current resources and technology.
- Economies grow by acquiring resources or better technology, which shifts the frontier outward.

 **QuickCheck** _____

Are all points along a production possibility frontier equally efficient? Is an economy indifferent among them?

Answer: All points on the production possibility frontier are technologically efficient, meaning that it is impossible to produce more of one good without giving up some of the other. However, while technological efficiency is necessary for overall economic efficiency, so too is allocative efficiency, which implies a specific point on the production possibility frontier that is the most valuable combination of outputs. People may be quite willing to give up one good for more of another. Thus, not all points on the production possibility frontier are allocatively efficient, and an economy is not indifferent among those points. In response to consumer demand, however, competitive markets will ordinarily choose points that are allocatively efficient.

Technological Change—The General and the Specific

Technological change can increase productivity generally, as has been the case with better information flows made possible by modern computers and telecommunications. Oftentimes, however, technological change is specific to an industry. For example, a biotechnological advance might improve cucumber yields but have no effect on the steel industry.

Figure 2-4 illustrates the difference between general growth and specialized growth, where the economy starts from the original production possibility frontier. In the case of general growth, productivity in both the pretzel and pumpkin industries increases. In the case of specialized growth, productivity increases in only one industry.

The production possibility frontiers labeled Specialized Growth in Figure 2-4 indicate technological improvement in only the pretzel industry. To see why growth occurred in the pretzel industry but not the pumpkin industry, consider the output of each good separately when none of the other is produced. When no pretzels are produced, the technological change has not affected the production possibility for pumpkins, because the point on the vertical axis is the same as before. However, when no pumpkins are produced, the technological change has allowed an increase in the possible output of pretzels. We know this because the intercept on the horizontal axis is to the right of where it was before. Whatever that maximum quantity of pretzels had been, it is now higher. Hence the technological change applied only to the pretzel industry. **Specialized growth thus pivots the production possibility frontier in the direction of more output in the industry affected by the technological change.**

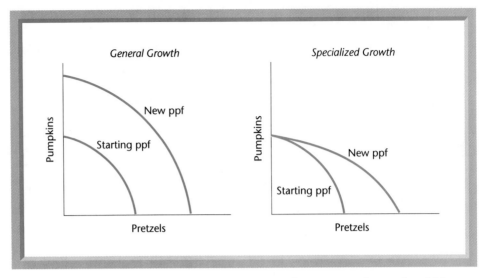

FIGURE 2-4 **Broad-reaching technological change brings general growth,** which shifts the entire production possibility frontier (ppf) outward. **Specialized technological change brings specialized growth,** which causes the production possibility frontier to rotate in the direction of the industry to which the new technology applies.

Modeling Growth—Impoverished Countries Face a Difficult Trade-off

Land, labor, capital, and entrepreneurship—these are the resources the economy has to work with. Production possibilities will depend upon how much of each resource the economy has and upon the technology that is available to make use of those resources. As resources increase or technology improves, production possibilities grow. In the event of natural disasters, the exhaustion of natural resources, or anything else that causes an economy's resource base to shrink, the country's production possibilities will also shrink. This effect would be just opposite to that depicted in Figure 2-3.

For example, suppose we return to the economy of Hermit Island. Herschel might find some netting to use in catching fish and some additional netting to collect the coconuts as they fall to the ground. The nets are capital goods that allow him to catch more fish and collect more coconuts per hour. This shifts Herschel's production possibility frontier outward. Alternatively, were Herschel to overfish, and a coconut blight to strike, too, fewer fish and coconuts would be available. His production possibility frontier would shift inward.

In more complex economies, economic growth does not necessarily mean that standards of living improve in the country. That depends in part on whether the economy measures the right things when it tabulates growth. It also depends upon population. After all, if an economy grows by adding the resource of labor, that also involves more mouths to feed. Thus, economic growth is often measured on a *per capita* basis, meaning output per person.

Economies have relatively little control over how much land and labor they have. They have more influence over capital and entrepreneurship. How much entrepre-

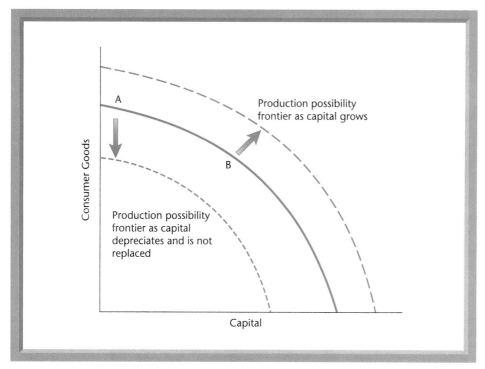

FIGURE 2-5 **Sacrificing current consumption for capital formation hastens economic growth,** but may be painful in the present. For example, choosing point B provides the capital needed to expand production possibilities over time. In contrast, choosing point A allows for more current consumption, but shrinks the production possibility frontier over time. This is because not enough new capital is produced to offset the depreciation of existing capital.

neurship a country possesses will depend upon such things as culture and whether entrepreneurs are well rewarded for their risk-taking. To amass more capital, an economy must also provide incentives for capital creation. Since capital represents output that is produced now for the purpose of increasing productivity later, the creation of capital comes at the expense of current consumption. Figure 2-5 illustrates this choice.

For example, at point A the economy is devoting nearly all of its resources to consumption goods. The result is that its stock of capital decreases over time, because of equipment wearing out, buildings falling into disrepair, and other forms of depreciation. As its stock of capital falls, its production possibility frontier shifts inward. Point B, in contrast, trades off some current consumption for a significant amount of *capital formation*, meaning that it adds to its stock of capital. The result is that its production possibility frontier shifts out over time.

When an economy is characterized by widespread poverty, the route to economic growth involves particularly tough trade-offs. In Herschel's case, if he had to weave his own fishing nets, he would have to subsist on less food until the nets were completed, because time spent weaving means less time to fish and gather coconuts.

depreciation: a decrease in the value of capital, such as from capital wearing out or becoming technologically obsolete.

More generally, for countries to reduce poverty, they must channel resources into amassing capital. Those resources are taken away from the production of goods that meet current needs, such as food and housing.

QuickCheck

Draw three production possibility frontiers: one that rotates, one that shifts inward, and one that shifts outward. Give plausible examples that are consistent with each case. Label the axes in a manner appropriate to your examples.

Answer: Answers will depend upon the stories told. For example, the production possibility frontier between video conferencing and all other goods shows an outward rotation along the video-conferencing axis as video-conferencing technology improves and as capital is added in the telecommunications industry that makes video conferencing easier. The devastation caused by Hurricane Mitch in 1998 caused the production possibility frontiers of Honduras, El Salvador, and Guatemala to shift inward, whichever goods and services appear on the axes of the graph. In contrast, improved technology and added capital in the robust U.S. economy in recent years caused general growth that shifted outward the production possibility frontier between most goods and services.

OBSERVATION POINT:
From the Shah to the Ayatollah—A Slippery Path to Growth

Imagine holding the reins as your country emerges from its long slumber to stand tall and fearless in the new day ahead. Such was the dream of the Shah of Iran, absolute ruler of a country with a fabulous wealth of oil reserves.

With OPEC having dramatically increased the price of oil in the 1970s, Shah Mohammad Reza Pahlavi embarked on a rapid modernization of his country. His goal was for Iran to catch up with the West in prestige, living standards, and culture. Resources were channeled to highways, oil refineries, schools, dams, and other capital infrastructure. Seemingly overnight, Iran's economy was to be transformed from agricultural to industrial.

With all of this change going on, lifestyles were disrupted and animosity seethed among Iran's traditionally oriented Islamic population. Improving living standards remained but a distant promise as change in the here and now was imposed from above. The more discontent simmered, the more its expression was harshly suppressed by SAVAK, the Shah's fearsome secret police.

A bump in the road? A rough spot to traverse before the journey's glorious end? That may have been the idea. The reality was a revolution in 1979, which overthrew the Shah in favor of Islamic fundamentalist Ayatollah Ruholla Khomeini. Rather than join the West, Iran attempted to cut itself off from Western culture. Instead of developing capital infrastructure, Iran poured its resources into more than a decade's worth of warfare with its neighbor, Iraq. As for the Shah's vision, it remained but a shimmering mirage in the Iranian desert.

Circular Flow and the Role of Money

Production possibility frontiers are about possibilities. What a market economy will actually choose to produce is decided through the interaction of consumers and businesses. In effect, consumers vote with their money for the assortment of goods and services that is offered. Money is a medium of exchange. As such, money is used to make purchases. Money also serves other purposes. For example, money can measure the value of things, even if they are not actually bought and sold—"That view is worth a million dollars!" Likewise, money can store value for future spending.

Without money, people would be forced to exchange goods directly, a situation known as barter. Barter is unworkable in a complicated economy. For example, to buy this textbook, you would be forced to provide something the bookstore would want in return. What do you have? Would you offer a chicken? What if the bookstore will only accept Buffalo wings? Yes, the possibilities become convoluted quickly. Money comes to the rescue—it greases the wheels of commerce.

Many things have served as money through the years. In prisoner-of-war camps in World War II, cigarettes served as money. Traditionally, gold, silver, and other scarce metals have been considered money. Such monies are termed *commodity monies*. Unfortunately, the use of commodity money leads to worries over *debasement*, in which people combine less valuable metals with the gold or silver or merely chip or shave off pieces.

Since gold and silver are subject to debasement and are also hard to transport, they were often replaced by paper. The paper money could be nothing more than warehouse receipts for precious metals held in storage. Still, this practice led to a worry about counterfeit receipts and also about the integrity of the warehouse. Paper money was more readily accepted if issued by government and redeemable in precious metals. These days, however, government prints up paper currency without even pretending to back it with gold or silver. Such money is called *fiat money*. People accept these pieces of paper as money, in part because government accepts it as payment, such as for tax payments.

A critical condition for gold, currency, or any other item to be accepted as money is that the quantity of the item must be restricted. Whereas additional gold may be mined, only the mythical King Midas could manufacture gold from other sources. Despite many years of trying, the alchemists in the middle ages never succeeded in turning lead into gold. Likewise, individuals must not be able to print government currencies, or those currencies would lose their value as money. That is why counterfeiting is illegal. Government must also be careful about printing too much currency if it wishes its currency to retain value as money.

Figure 2-6 illustrates the circular flow model of economic activity, which depicts how markets use the medium of money to determine what goods and services are produced and who gets to buy them. The top part of the diagram illustrates the *output market* in which producers sell goods and services to consumers. The actual assortment of goods and services is determined by how much households are willing to pay relative to business firms' production costs.

The bottom part of the diagram shows the *input market*, which illustrates that households supply the resources of land, labor, capital, and entrepreneurship. All of these resources are ultimately owned by people, who make up households. The sale of resources to business provides the income that households use to buy products. Indeed, since it is people who own businesses, business profits also belong to

money: a medium of exchange that removes the need for barter; also a measure of value and a way to store value over time; defined by the Federal Reserve as M1, M2, and M3.

barter: the exchange of goods and services directly for one another, without the use of money.

If you would like to know some interesting facts about U.S. money, visit the Web site maintained by the U.S. Treasury at **http://www.treas.gov/about.html** and click on the links for coins and paper currency.

circular flow: a model of the economy that depicts how the flow of money facilitates a counterflow of resources, goods, and services in the input and output markets.

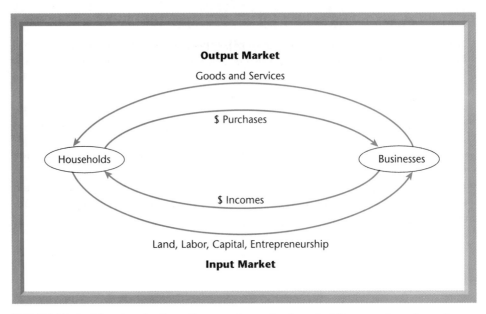

FIGURE 2-6 **The circular flow diagram** shows that household income depends on the sale of resources and that household spending determines outputs and the value of those resources.

households. Hence, the circular flow of inputs and outputs is maintained by a counterflow of dollars.

The circular flow model can be expanded in many respects. For example, it could be expanded to show that government influences the mix of goods that are produced and the manner in which resources are used. Likewise, it can be expanded to include foreign commerce. However, the circular flow model is something like a pictograph on the walls of a prehistoric cave. It is a good picture for conveying the basic essence of economic activity, just as a pictograph can convey the notion of a successful hunt for winter game. More detailed stories are probably better told with more abstract languages. Analytical graphs, of which the production possibility frontier is an example, represent one such language.

Expanding Consumption Possibilities through Trade

Economies are fortunate to have other economies to trade with. This is true for national economies, regional economies, local economies, and even personal economies. For example, we each have our own production possibilities. Yet, if we tried to rely only upon these production possibilities, we would be hard-pressed to live as well as Herschel the Hermit. Thus, we trade. We trade our labor services for income, to allow us to purchase what we want. We trade so that we can consume more quantity and variety than we could produce on our own. Cities, states, and countries trade among themselves for the same reasons individuals trade with one another.

Specialization According to Comparative Advantage—The Basis for Trade

In order to gain from trade, an economy must specialize according to its **comparative advantage.** **An economy has a comparative advantage in producing a good if it can produce that good at a lower opportunity cost than could other economies.** This means the economy chooses to produce those things it does well relative to other things it could be doing. Contrary to popular belief, trade is not based on **absolute advantage,** which refers to the ability to produce something with fewer resources than others could.

For example, Mr. Spock of "Star Trek" is known for his logical mind. He is able to learn new scientific knowledge with little effort. He is a master at chess. Indeed, it is likely that he could clean the passageways of the starship *Enterprise* more effectively than any other crew member. After all, his logical mind would lead him to choose the most effective way to get the job done. Yet, Mr. Spock does not mop the floors and scrub the walls. That would be illogical.

Spock's scarce time could be put to better use than cleaning the starship's passageways, since the opportunity cost of his doing so would be high. Even though Spock has an absolute advantage in almost everything he would choose to undertake, he has a comparative advantage only in things he does relatively well. Spock is many times more efficient than others at scientific research, which is why he holds the post of science officer. He is only slightly more efficient at mopping the floors, which is why he does not hold the post of janitor. Spock does not have a comparative advantage at being a janitor.

In order to gain from trade, it is not necessary to have an absolute advantage at anything. Even if a person cannot do anything well, he or she can still do some things relatively better than other things. For example, it might take Charlie Brown longer to mow yards than it would take other people. Yet, if that is what Charlie were to do best, he would mow yards. Other people would be delighted to hire him because he would charge less than their own time is worth. It is unimportant that it takes him longer.

Thus, both well-endowed and poorly endowed people gain from trade. Likewise, well-endowed and poorly endowed regions and countries also gain from trade. The resulting *consumption possibilities* will be greater for the well-endowed than for the poorly endowed. Still, through trade, both types of economies can consume more than they could produce on their own.

In other words, while a country is constrained to produce along or inside its production possibility frontier, it can exchange some of its own output for the output of other countries. Goods and services a country sells to other countries are termed **exports.** Exports are in effect traded for **imports,** which are goods and services a country buys from other countries. Through this trade, a country can consume a combination of goods and services that lies outside its production possibility frontier.

International trade is more important to small countries than to large countries. This is because, the larger is the country, the more opportunities there are to specialize internally. For example, the United States produces potatoes in Maine and Idaho for sale throughout the other states. Likewise, Michigan specializes in automobile production, Texas in oil and gas production, and so forth. If the United

comparative advantage: the ability to produce a good at a lower opportunity cost (other goods forgone) than others could do.

absolute advantage: the ability to produce a good with fewer resources than other producers.

Numerous Star Trek sites are on the Web. One such site is **http://www. startrek.com**

exports: goods and services a country sells to other countries.

imports: goods and services a country buys from other countries.

Links to trade data are available at **http://www.ntu. edu.sg/library/ statdata.htm**

States were broken into 50 different countries, this trade among states would all be international. As it is, the tremendous diversity of resources found within the United States leads it to have one of the smallest proportions of international trade relative to its output of any country in the world.

Figure 2-7 shows the proportion of various countries' exports relative to their outputs. The smaller the country, typically, the higher that ratio is, and the more it gains from trade.

Economists do not spend a great deal of time attempting to compute the goods in which countries have their comparative advantages. The reason is that markets do that quite effectively on their own. If a country has a comparative advantage in a good, it can produce that good cheaply relative to other goods it could produce. These will be the goods it can offer at the best prices in the international marketplace. Thus, without any economic research, economies engaging in international trade naturally tend to export those goods for which they have a comparative advantage and import the rest.

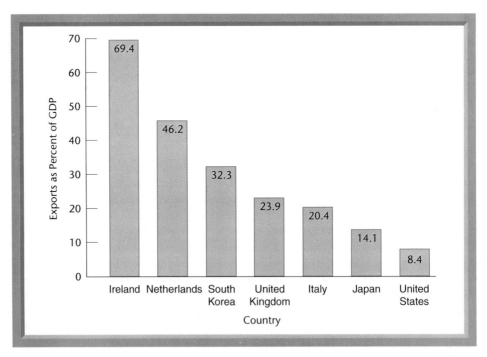

FIGURE 2-7 **Exports as a percentage of gross domestic product (GDP)** are typically smaller for countries with larger economies.

Source: 1998 Statistical Abstract of the U.S. Percentages compiled from 1996 data in Table Nos. 1355 and 1390.

Effects of International Trade on Earnings Opportunities in the United States

Although international trade increases the aggregate value of a country's consumption possibilities, that does not mean that all residents share in those gains. The primary purpose of international trade, like the purpose of market trade within countries, is to promote efficiency. Sometimes the efficiency gains seem unfair, especially to workers who find their jobs and lives disrupted. This is because, while aggregate job totals may not be much affected by foreign commerce, opportunities in specific industries and types of occupations can change markedly. When industries are hit particularly hard by imports, U.S. law allows for various types of *trade adjustment assistance*, designed to ease the transition from industries on the decline to ones with more promise.

Changes in job opportunities caused by trade often seem unfair to workers whose jobs are lost. However, the problem is mainly a function of markets themselves rather than of whether markets are international. Markets typically promote efficiency, not necessarily equity. With or without foreign trade, jobs and lives are disrupted when products decline in popularity, when technological change affects the manner in which products are produced, and when the fortunes of individual companies rise or fall. These changes are brought about by competition in response to consumer demand. While sometimes disruptive to individual lives, the evolving nature of the U.S. market economy has been essential to maintaining America's high standard of living.

The United States has an abundance of both physical and human capital relative to most, but not all, other countries. This means that the United States is likely to have a comparative advantage in goods that are *capital intensive*. In other words, for the United States to gain from international trade, it specializes in exporting goods that use a high proportion of capital in their production. Thus, the United States is known for its exports of airplanes, financial services, and movies. Even U.S. farm exports are capital intensive relative to farm products in other countries. In return, the United States imports goods that use a high proportion of labor and land, such as textiles and crude oil.

There are exceptions. For example, Japan is in some respects more capital intensive than the United States, which explains why Japan exports so many electronic goods to this country. Over all, though, international trade causes the United States to specialize somewhat in capital-intensive goods. Exports thus increase the demand for capital in the United States and increase the prices paid for capital. The prices paid for capital represent income to owners of capital, including human capital.

By increasing the return to human capital in the United States, international trade opens up attractive employment opportunities for those who have acquired skills and abilities. For example, the return to a college education is higher than it would be without international trade. Conversely, job opportunities for unskilled labor are harmed by international trade, as imports of labor-intensive goods lead to lower wages and fewer job openings. The result? Competition among workers to obtain burger-flipping jobs is likely to become increasingly intense. In contrast, it is competition among employers to hire the well-educated and skilled workers that promises to intensify as time goes by.

Protecting Jobs . . . at a Price

"Don't export our good jobs!" "Don't trade with low-wage countries—they'll take our jobs!" We hear the first argument made about U.S. trade with Japan. The second argument comes from opponents of trade with Mexico, China, and other developing countries. Together, the message is simple—don't trade!

While the message may be simple, it is also unsound. For example, should a country prohibit its industries from buying foreign steel? If it does, it is devoting resources to a high-cost industry in which it does not have a comparative advantage. For the sake of transferring a relatively few workers into high-paying jobs, the country would be shrinking the overall value that it gets from its resources. Steel workers are better off, but the country suffers.

The same holds true for protecting low-wage jobs, such as in the textile industry. While it may be a tool for income redistribution, that redistribution is actually a form of make-work project. Better value for the money could be obtained by importing textiles from other countries. For government to change the mix of goods to favor either high-wage or low-wage industries can only reduce possibilities for consumption. The result is a smaller economic pie that is sliced to favor the protected industry.

The United States does protect certain jobs, through restricting imports of textiles, steel, and various other products. For example, protection of the U.S. steel industry in the 1980s was associated with a 20 to 40 percent increase in steel prices from 1984 to 1990. These higher prices decreased the international competitiveness of U.S. steel-using industries. The higher costs from protectionist programs are also felt directly by consumers. For example, protectionist policies in place between 1980 and 1984 were estimated to have added $620 to the price of automobiles sold in the United States. Such cost increases translated into an estimated $160,000 cost of each autoworker's job that was saved.

SUMMARY

- Opportunity costs, which are the value of forgone alternatives, influence the choices people make.
- Resources include land, labor, capital, and entrepreneurship.
- A special kind of capital is human capital, which is different from physical capital because it is embodied within a person.
- The production possibility frontier represents all combinations of two goods that would be technologically efficient.
- The production possibility frontier generally has a bowed outward shape. Points outside the frontier are not now attainable. Points inside the frontier are inefficient. Inefficiency arises from unemployment and/or misallocated resources. Only points on the frontier are both attainable and efficient.
- Opportunity costs are illustrated by the production possibility frontier. Movement from one point to another on the frontier means that more of one good is

produced, but less of the other. The amount by which the production of the other good decreases equals the opportunity cost of the increase in the first good.

- Economic growth expands the frontier by shifting it outward. Such growth can occur if a country adds more capital or other resources, or experiences technological change that enhances its productivity. Specialized growth shifts the frontier outward more for one good than for the other.

- Depreciation shifts the frontier inward because it decreases the amount of capital. The effect of depreciation on the frontier can be overcome by capital formation, increases in the stock of capital at least large enough to offset depreciation.

- The circular flow graph shows how economic activity depends upon markets. Flows of goods and services go toward the household sector as households make purchases. Goods and services are sold in the output market. Households earn the incomes needed to make those purchases by selling the resources they own to businesses. Resources are bought and sold in the input market. Money is used to make it easier for market exchanges to take place.

- Countries specialize according to their comparative advantage, as do people. A comparative advantage in the production of a good requires that a country have a lower opportunity cost of production than other countries. Trade according to comparative advantage allows countries to consume beyond their production possibility frontiers, thus benefitting the countries that trade.

- An absolute advantage is held by a country when it is able to produce something with fewer resources than other countries. It is not necessary to have an absolute advantage in the production of a good to benefit from specialization and trade.

QUESTIONS AND PROBLEMS

1. Do management skills differ from entrepreneurial skills? Explain.

2. What would a straight-line production possibility frontier between coconuts and fish on Hermit Island say about opportunity costs?

3. Draw the original production possibility frontier in Figure 2-4. How does the frontier change when technological change affects only the pumpkin industry?

4. California and France both produce wine.
   a. Without international trade U.S. consumers would be unable to consume French wines, but they would still be able to consume California wines. Would this arrangement be better for the United States as a whole? For any particular groups within the United States?
   b. Do you think France imports U.S. wines? Explain.

5. Succinctly evaluate the validity of the following:
   a. "The United States is losing its competitive edge to other countries with more diligent and skilled workers. The problem is that we are becoming increasingly incapable of producing anything that other countries would want to buy. We are fast on our way to becoming a nation of burger flippers."

b. "The U.S. standard of living has been the envy of the world. Unfortunately, because we have allowed imports from countries where working conditions are dismal and labor is cheap, our own standard of living is rapidly being pulled down to match the competition."

6. Extend the circular flow diagram in the chapter by including the government sector. What flows would go into and out of government? Further extend the diagram by including a foreign sector. What flows would extend to that sector?

7. Since the principle of comparative advantage applies to people as well as economies, perform a self-evaluation designed to identify at least three things you have a comparative advantage in, when compared to your friends.

8. Draw a graph of the production possibility frontier. Then comment on the truth of the following statements, referring to the graph you have drawn:

a. A country that has not been trading with other countries will select a point outside its production possibility frontier as its new production point after trade begins.

b. A country that begins trading will consume at a point inside its production possibility frontier.

Web Exercises

9. a. Using an Internet search engine such as that provided by Web site directory Yahoo (located at **http://www.yahoo.com**) or Alta Vista (located at **http://www.altavista.com**), perform a separate search for the following terms: **entrepreneurship, technology,** and **economic growth**. Visit several of the Web sites that your search reveals for each term and observe the context in which each term is used. Explain whether the manner in which the terms are used is consistent with their use in the text.

b. Repeat the above, but this time use a combination of terms that you select from the chapter. To eliminate Web sites that do not contain all terms, place a plus sign in front of each term you enter, such as **+"comparative advantage" +exports**.

10. Visit the Web site that offers the on-line edition of the latest *Economic Report of the President*: **http://www.gpo.ucop.edu/search/erp.html**. Using the data tables, look up annual federal government spending on national defense for the years 1990 to the present and compare it to spending on nondefense during those years (Table B-20 in the 1998 edition, but may change from edition to edition). Carefully note the size of the year-to-year changes in each category of spending. Then write an essay of approximately one page that discusses how the concept of opportunity cost relates to government choices between defense and nondefense spending.

Visit the Web site for *Economics by Design* at
http://www.prenhall.com/collinge for a Self Quiz
over the topics in this chapter.

Exploration 2-1 Connecting in the Information Economy

The information economy expands our production possibilities. How much depends upon the invest-ment in the capital that facilitates information flows—the information highway. Markets, gov-ernment, and technology all interact to determine the shape this highway takes. No matter these investments, information issues and problems will persist.

"We have entered a new era in which brains count for more than brawn."

—Royal Bank of Canada Newsletter, 1998

Information and its transmittal are taking an ever greater role in the world's economies. For centuries, physical travel was the only way to acquire most information. People would physically go to the store to buy books or would walk or ride to meet people. Travel distances were usually short, because roads were poor and vehicles slow. As roads and vehicles improved over the years, physical travel got easier and lifestyles adjusted. With the advent of the telegraph and telephone, communication even became possible with little or no physical travel. Now, with ongoing advances in telecommunications and computing, many of the physical constraints to information flows are lifted entire-ly. Two-way and multipoint audio, video, and data transfer are changing the way we live and conduct business. In the language of economics, production possibilities are expanded, which can translate into higher living standards. But the increased access to information raises a host of issues, only some of which are addressed below.

Information Highways: Growing the Information Economy

The information highway involves hardware and software infrastructure, such as the wires for telecommunication and the encoding of that information so that it will come across as intended. That infrastructure consists of capital and technology, which expand a country's production possibilities for nearly all types of services and goods, including both new capital and consumer goods. The effect on production possibilities for goods and services is illustrated in Figure 2-8.

Decisions on what shape the information highway takes are driven by a combina-tion of the marketplace, government, and technological possibilities. For example, companies in search of profit have been responsible for stringing billions of dollars worth of fiber-optic, ISDN, and coaxial cables. However, there is also a reluctance to invest in any given technology when new and better technologies are expected soon. There is also a reluctance to invest in new technologies when there is no assurance of their acceptance in the marketplace. This reluctance is sometimes termed the *pioneer problem*, in which the trail-blazing pioneer takes all the risk in opening up fertile new fields that others can exploit. Companies would often prefer to forgo the risk of being a pioneer, waiting to jump in when markets develop. However, this reluctance itself delays the development of new markets based on new technologies.

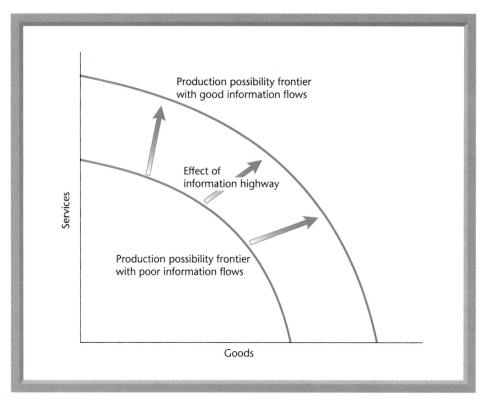

FIGURE 2-8 **The information highway improves information flows,** which has the effect of shifting the production possibility frontier outward for most goods and services, some more than others.

Government can help. For example, to promote the transition from analog television to digital television, government has required broadcasters who use public airways to phase in the offering of digital broadcasts and to phase out analog broadcasts. Since digital signals are superior to analog signals, it is advantageous for broadcasters and viewers alike that the transition be made. But private broadcasters were not making this transition voluntarily because, until most other broadcasters also offered digital signals, few consumers would purchase the television sets or converters needed to receive those signals. This chicken-and-egg problem made it sensible for each private broadcaster to wait for other broadcasters to take the lead. By setting a transition timetable for the broadcast industry to meet a digital standard, government was able to solve the problem.

In other instances, such as in adding video to telecommunications, firms in an industry will set a common standard that they will design their products around, and so preclude the need for government action. Throughout history, standardization has been a natural result of a market economy. The reason is that, whether the application is to industrial, consumer, military, or other outputs, equipment and products that work together are more valuable than those that do not. For example, in the early days of railroading, track and equipment varied from railroad to railroad. Quickly, however, standard gauges for track were developed so as to allow equipment from one railroad to transfer easily to another. Railroad companies voluntarily sought standardization as a way to lower their costs, both of buying equipment and transporting products. In turn, consumers benefitted from lower prices and better transportation. In information-based products today, similar stories abound.

Technology, technology standards, and the physical capital of hardware and software are necessary components of an information highway. In addition, human capital also plays a critical role in making use of the highway's potential. For example, advertisements frequently tout the whiz-bang things that computers can do. Yet, when people go to the expense of actually buying the advertised hardware and software, the purchases often merely take up space—they require an investment in human capital to extract their whiz-bang capabilities. For this reason, people may quite rationally decide to use seemingly obsolete hardware and software. By the same token, if accessing information flows requires too much human capital, the information highway will not be user-friendly, and the information economy will be dominated by a technical elite.

How much effort is put into user-friendliness and other aspects of information systems depends upon consumer willingness to pay. "Build a better mousetrap, and the world will beat a path to your door." How much the world is willing to pay for that better mousetrap determines how much effort will be put into mousetrap innovation. The same holds true for innovation in the hardware and software capital that underlies the information economy.

Asymmetric Information in an Information Economy

Asymmetric information occurs when one person has access to more information than another on a subject of mutual interest. For example, the seller of a used car usually knows more about its condition than the buyer can know, even if the buyer has the car tested. Likewise, the buyer of health insurance knows more about his or her own likelihood of sickness and injury than the insurance company can know. Even easy access to information along the information highway will not resolve such asymmetries.

Asymmetric information is responsible for several puzzling facets of modern life. For example, the value of an automobile drops by a couple of thousand dollars as soon as it is first sold. The reason is that buyers of used cars are aware of asymmetric information. They know what they don't know! Thus, used car buyers figure that there is probably a reason the car is being sold so quickly. The buyer infers that it is likely to have problems, even if the car is actually okay.

In the case of health insurance, the buyer of an individual policy winds up paying a much higher premium than if the same person bought the same policy as a member of an employer group plan. The reason is that the insurance company figures that workers are hired for reasons unrelated to their need for insurance. In contrast, an individual who goes to the trouble of lining up a personal health insurance policy is *signaling*—sending a message to—the insurance company that he or she is more likely to need that coverage. Since insurance claims cost money, the insurance company charges more for the policy, even if the signal is incorrect.

asymmetric information: occurs when one person has access to more information than another on a subject of mutual interest.

There are still other ways that asymmetric information will continue to affect our lives. Are you studying at one of the top ten universities in the country? If you are, you will find that your degree will be worth a great deal more in the job market than degrees held by people who have acquired an equal amount of knowledge at lesser-known schools. This is the problem of *credentialism*. Employers use credentials as a way to ensure that their employees are intelligent and well trained. Since grading standards vary from school to school, and since the job interview process cannot hope to uncover all of an applicant's skills and abilities, employers pay more for degrees from schools they have heard of and trust. It often seems inequitable, but it can be efficient.

Asymmetric information provides at least part of the explanation for another phenomenon observed in the labor market—cronyism. *Cronyism* occurs when employers hire friends, relatives, fellow church members, and so forth. That may be a profitable business practice if these employees are more reliable than strangers. While it seems unfair to applicants outside the group of cronies, cronyism probably does serve to reduce job turnover and minimize false credentials. In short, at a cost of equity, cronyism offers a way to circumvent asymmetric information.

Weighing the Power of Information against the Value of Privacy

http://www. intel.com will bring you to the home page of the Intel Corporation, where its latest technologies are discussed.

In November 1994, an obscure mathematician in Virginia humbled the mighty Intel Corporation by reporting that Intel's Pentium computer chip could not be relied upon to do complex mathematical calculations. The mathematician noted this failing in an Internet forum, which spread the news rapidly through the country. Intel at first made light of the problem. However, in response to an uproar among users, Intel was eventually forced to offer free replacements for the defective chips. Could such a thing have happened a decade ago? Would anyone have listened?

The rapid dissemination of information has changed how the world operates. It offers the potential for much more radical change in the future. For example, the 1930s saw the implementation of banking regulation to protect unwitting investors from losing their money in unsafe banks. With information at everyone's fingertips, however, investors these days could merely call upon data banks provided by government or private ratings companies to determine the bank's reliability. Perhaps information flows can replace government banking insurance.

Increased information flows threaten personal privacy. Can we know too much about each other? At a personal level, they say that knowledge is power. How much of that power do we want to see vested in business and government? After all, if we are to believe the well-known saying, then "power corrupts; absolute power corrupts absolutely." For example, even though collecting each individual's medical records into a single national health database would seem to promote efficient health care, Congress rejected that idea in 1998 because of concerns over privacy. In sum, information flows can promote output and our standard of living. However, modern technology makes it ever tougher to answer the question of how much information is too much.

1. Identify some possible future production possibilities that can be brought about by an information highway. How might readily available information change the role for government in areas other than those discussed in the concluding section?

2. Suppose it requires at least $500 to buy the equipment necessary to connect into the information highway and additional money to access much of the information that is available there. Should government subsidize this access by legislating reduced rates for the poor? Explain, making reference to the benefits and to the problems that can be expected.

Exploration 2-2 Population Growth on a Finite Planet— Must the Outlook Be Dismal?

Economics has been seen as a dismal attempt to temporarily improve living standards, with the inevitable result that population growth will drive them down again. So far, improvements in resources and technology have more than compensated for growing numbers of mouths to feed. Some economic incentives are for lower birthrates. Other incentives push birthrates higher.

Labor is a resource that can increase output—the size of the economic pie. However, increased labor is ordinarily associated with increased population—the number of people sharing that pie. This brings economic problems.

The effects of population growth intrude into our lives. For example, we can relive our nation's history by visiting Civil War battlefields in Northern Virginia . . . if we can make our way through Washington's urban sprawl that has engulfed them. "Grow, grow, grow!" the business and political cheerleaders chant. But do we really want to be surrounded by ever more neighbors? Some people view such questions as beyond the purview of academic disciplines. They might be surprised to learn how central the issue of population growth has been in the history of economics.

The Dismal Science

Most students think they know why economics is called "the dismal science." They envision struggling through an entire term of tough material and tough grading—a dismal prospect!

In truth, the term has very different origins, dating back to the early nineteenth century. At that time, Thomas Robert Malthus popularized the notion that economics could only hope to delay the day of reckoning, in which the world's population finds itself at the brink of starvation. According to this *Malthusian* view, starvation is the only force that can keep population in check. While economics can temporarily improve the world, the inevitability of population growth and the limits of the earth's capacity to produce must inevitably reduce us all to no more than a subsistence existence. A dismal thought indeed!

> **"the dismal science"**: economics, viewed from the perspective of Thomas Robert Malthus, in which population growth must eventually reduce us all to no more than a subsistence existence.

Yet, the world has come a long way since the early 1800s, and both population and living standards have increased dramatically. For the most part, people of the world are much further removed from starvation now than then. Since the earth has not expanded, something else must have happened. That something is technology. Technological change has enabled the world to get much more output for its resources than ever imagined by Malthus.

There is still room for concern. If the world continues to experience the same population growth rate that it has over the course of the twentieth century, it must ultimately fill every nook and cranny with people. There would be no room to produce the food to feed them. Since population grows geometrically, it doubles according to the *rule of 72*, which states that doubling time equals 72 divided by the rate of growth. At a modest growth rate of 3 percent, then, the world's population would double every 24 years. As population keeps doubling, where are those people to go?

Fortunately, there are economic incentives that put a brake on excessive population growth. Specifically, as countries become wealthier, the opportunity cost of people's time rises. Because children take time, people choose to have fewer of them. This is especially true in countries that provide reliable retirement benefits for the elderly. Otherwise, the cost of raising children is offset by the expectation that those children will provide for their parents' retirement.

The Price of Parenting: The Signals Are Distorted

The world has seen its population grow rapidly, from just under 3 billion in 1960 to about 6 billion in 1999. A longer perspective, as seen in Figure 2-9, shows that population has exploded over the last three-and-a-half centuries. Part of the reason for this growth is that advances in medicine and hygiene have lowered death rates, thereby increasing longevity. Birthrates have also been high, however, especially among the segments of the population least able to afford raising children.

To get a handle on why some segments of the population have higher birthrates than others, consider the costs and benefits of having and raising a family. Some of these costs are *private costs*, meaning that the parents pay. Such costs include the time and income the parents must forgo to raise their children, as well as the explicit expenses they incur.

Other costs are *external costs*, meaning that they are borne by others. While some external costs arise from such things as overcrowding, the largest component of external costs involves expenses to other taxpayers, such as to finance the schools that the children attend or to finance the help that government provides to the parents.

To the extent that the costs of rearing children are external, parents face a price of children that does not reflect the full cost of those children to society. *Ceteris paribus* (other things being equal), we can expect the quantity of children demanded to rise because of this inefficiently low price. While few people would choose to have children for the explicit reason of receiving extra welfare benefits, the variety of taxpayer subsidies aimed at rearing children reduces the cost of those children dramatically, especially for people with lower incomes.

The lower cost of children promotes population growth in two ways. First, it affects parents' benefit-cost calculations by increasing the proportion of benefits to costs. Parents will rationally choose larger family sizes than they otherwise would

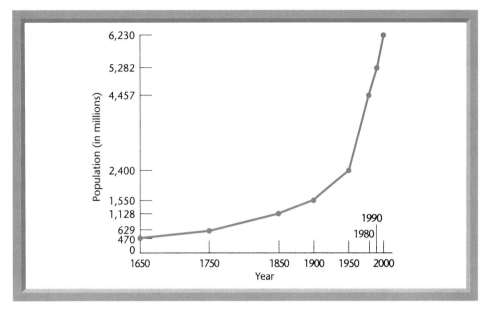

FIGURE 2-9 **The exploding world population.**

Sources: Compiled from Internet Web sites that include Historical Estimates of World Population by the U.S. Census Bureau, the Population Information Network of the U.N., and World Population Since Creation by Lambert Dolphin.

have. Second, it increases the number of unplanned pregnancies. Because the cost of "mistakes" is lower, fewer precautions are taken and more unintended pregnancies occur. For both reasons, the existence of external costs results in a more rapidly growing population.

The children themselves can add both positive and negative externalities, depending on their future contributions in life. Unfortunately, the welfare check to single mothers provides incentives that discourage a cohesive family unit and may thus reduce the quality of child rearing. Specifically, for the mother to receive welfare benefits, it is often necessary for the father to drop out of sight. Sometimes this is done explicitly—the father departs and is not seen again. Other times, it is done fraudulently—the father is still in the family, but keeps out of the sight of the welfare caseworkers. Either way, child rearing is disrupted.

When making the decision as to whether to have children, parents will also consider the benefits. Benefits are received by the parents and the rest of society. Once the children are created, the benefits also go to the children themselves. Benefits to the parents are *private benefits*, because the parents make the choice. Benefits to the children and to the rest of society are mostly external, although the parents may be concerned with some of these benefits, especially those going to their own children. An example of an *external benefit* is that the world is well served by the contributions of many individuals, both famous and obscure. An external cost is that the world is not well served by ever-increasing demands on its scarce natural resources resulting from additional people on the planet.

While taxpayers shoulder many of the costs of additional children, those children do grow up to be taxpayers in their own rights. The children would, on balance, provide an external benefit in terms of taxation if they wind up paying more in taxes than they add in costs. For instance, our current problems with financing Social Security stem in large part from a decline in the birthrate following the post-World War II baby boom. While extra babies in the 1960s would have reduced the stresses on Social Security during their working years now, however, it would also add more recipients later. Thus, the logic of promoting population growth in order to provide external benefits from more taxpayers is rather shaky.

Promoting the Well-Being of Children

When a country seeks to obtain an efficient population growth rate, it faces a fundamental problem. Efficiency calls for parents to face the full costs and benefits of having children. Otherwise, the parents' benefit-cost calculations would not coincide with those of society at large. However, the decision about whether to have children is only one aspect to the issue of population growth. The other is the well-being of the children themselves. The goal of providing the incentive for parents to choose their family size efficiently often conflicts with the goal of equity to children once they are created.

For example, efficiency would suggest that parents should pay all costs of rearing children, including costs of food, shelter, and education. However, equity suggests that children should have comparable opportunities. A child born into poverty does not choose to be there, any more than a child born in more comfortable circumstances does. Thus, from the point of view of equal opportunity in things that matter, it makes sense for taxpayers to subsidize the infant formula, schooling, school lunches, and other elements necessary to bring up the less fortunate child. The trade-off is that those subsidies increase the number of children born into poverty.

This is a dilemma. We wish children to be raised well. A good upbringing does not mean that the children have no hurdles to overcome, but does mean that the hurdles should not be too high. Yet, in well-intentioned efforts to make life easier for existing children, we find ourselves encouraging births into households with the least opportunities in preference to births into more financially secure households. There is no obvious, widely acceptable solution to this dilemma.

Replacing the Resources That Limit Growth

While prices are distorted when it comes to the incentives to have children, prices do come to our rescue in other ways. It has often seemed impossible that the earth could support many more people. However, the world's population keeps growing, and the world keeps supporting that growth. In large part, the saving grace has been technological advancement, spurred on by prices that signal when resources are getting scarce.

Periodically, resources appear to be running out. Well before any resource actually does run out, the perception that it might drives the price higher. For example, when oil supplies dwindled in the 1970s and concerns arose about the world using up this nonrenewable resource, prices surged higher. After all, if you have oil in the ground, and if you think the world's oil is running out, wouldn't you want to forgo pumping now so that you could sell your oil at a lucrative price in the future when the world runs out? Since the same incentives face all owners of a nonrenewable resource, the result is that prices rise in the present because resources are hoarded for the future.

When the price of a nonrenewable resource rises, the market is motivated to do two things. First, it explores for more. In the 1970s, the high price of oil resulted in major new finds in Mexico, Alaska, the North Sea, and elsewhere. The market also develops substitutes. In the case of oil, such substitutes include technology to give motor vehicles more miles per gallon and insulation to reduce the energy costs of homes. Alternative energy sources were also developed, but did not take hold because the search for new supplies was so successful that oil prices dropped back down.

Other examples abound. At one time, copper seemed to provide a limit to growth, since the world's copper supplies seemed to be running out and since copper was needed for electricity and telephone connections. We know what happened. The rising price of copper spurred new technologies, such as fiber optics, that greatly reduced the world's need for copper. In the realm of food, too, technology has so far been very successful at increasing yields per acre more rapidly than necessary to meet the needs of a growing population. As price has risen, technology has responded.

The Options before Us

We know the world cannot sustain an ever-increasing population. Even if we could feed everyone, we might wish to avoid the other stresses of a crowded planet. Unfortunately, prices do not provide the signals necessary for an efficient population growth rate. Moreover, making price signals efficient would not be equitable.

When prices are not used to allocate resources, government turns to command-and-control alternatives. For example, China prohibits a family from having more than one child. The penalty for violating this law can be forced sterilization. Some people have suggested similar options for the United States, although usually only as a condition of receiving extra welfare benefits. Along the same lines, others suggest the less draconian, but still risky, measure of birth control implants. Still, U.S. citizens value their personal freedoms and are uncomfortable with allowing government to be too intimately involved with personal choices. Lacking a consensus for action, we do nothing and watch our population grow.

Despite the high population growth rate, the price system has spurred technological change that has more than kept pace with population growth. After looking for two centuries, people have yet to meet insurmountable limits to growth. Will they ever come? Do we need to take action at all? If so, what should that action be? Population growth is a sensitive issue because it involves people's lives and personal choices. Addressing this issue remains a challenge for our future.

1. Ecosystems have carrying capacities for the species within them. Do you think there is a comparable carrying capacity for humans within the world's ecosystem? If so, how far do you think we are from that capacity, and what would be the consequences of overshooting it?

2. What roles do religious beliefs play in either promoting or hindering a solution to the world's population problems? Explain.

Appendix

SPECIALIZATION ACCORDING TO COMPARATIVE ADVANTAGE—COMPUTATION AND MARKET REVELATION

Economists are not usually called upon to identify the goods for which individuals and countries have comparative advantages. Rather, the marketplace reveals this information automatically. To see why, we can compute comparative advantage in a simple example and then interpret market prices to see why individuals or businesses will choose to produce accordingly, even when they have not done the computation.

Suppose there are two countries: Eastland and Westland. Both countries produce only corn and baseballs. For simplicity, we will assume that all corn is identical and that the baseballs are also interchangeable. The productivity of workers is shown in Table 2A-1. Note that Eastland's workers are more productive at both manufacturing baseballs and harvesting corn. Eastland has an absolute advantage in both corn and baseballs. However, because a worker cannot do two things at one time, countries must allocate each worker to producing either one good or the other. To maximize its gains from trade, each country chooses according to its comparative advantage.

The key to computing comparative advantage is to measure opportunity cost. In this case, the choices are simple. To produce corn, a country must allocate labor away from baseballs and thus forgo baseballs. Likewise, to produce baseballs, a country must forgo corn. Thus, the opportunity cost of corn is in terms of baseballs forgone, and the opportunity cost of baseballs is in terms of corn forgone. Next is some simple algebra to compute the opportunity cost of a single baseball or unit of corn, so as to allow comparison of opportunity costs between countries. Applying this math to

TABLE 2A-1 Productivity per Worker in Eastland and Westland		
Country	**Corn**	**Baseballs**
Eastland	10 units per day	4 per day
Westland	5 units per day	3 per day

Computing Opportunity Cost and Comparative Advantage

Product Location	Opportunity Cost (C is corn and B is baseballs)	Opportunity Cost per Unit
Corn in Eastland	10C = 4B	2/5 baseball (.4B)*
Corn in Westland	5C = 3B	3/5 baseball (.6B)
Baseballs in Eastland	4B = 10C	5/2 corn (2.5C)
Baseballs in Westland	3B = 5C	5/3 corn (1.67C)**

*Lower opportunity cost per unit of corn implies comparative advantage in Eastland.
**Lower opportunity cost per unit of baseballs implies comparative advantage in Westland.

Table 2A-1 yields the results shown in Table 2A-2. By specializing according to this comparative advantage, countries will gain the most from trade.

In the real world, in which products are produced with various types of capital and other resources, computing comparative advantage in this way would be difficult. Fortunately, the market automatically generates specialization according to comparative advantage. This is because the market prices of resources reflect the value of those resources in alternative uses, that is, their opportunity costs. Competition ensures that the prices of goods within a country equal the sum of the opportunity costs of the resources used in their production.

For example, consider Table 2A-3, showing the pretrade prices of corn and baseballs in Eastland and Westland. Prices in Eastland are given in yen (¥) and prices in Westland in pounds (£). The information in that table would lead to the same opportunity costs and comparative advantage figures listed in Table 2A-2, without any computation of labor productivity. The relative prices of corn and baseballs in Eastland imply that a baseball costs the equivalent of 2.5 units of corn. In Westland, a baseball effectively costs 1.67 units of corn. Likewise, corn costs 2/5 of a baseball in Eastland and 3/5 of a baseball in Westland, just as in Table 2A-2.

Were the two countries to trade, the price of a baseball would settle somewhere between these figures, such as at two units of corn per baseball. At such a price, each country would export the good for which it has a comparative advantage and import the other good. Both countries would then see their consumption possibilities expand beyond their production possibilities. Applying this result to the real world, we find countries exporting goods they have comparative advantages in and importing goods for which they do not.

Exceptions can occur when government intervenes, such as by subsidizing selected exports. There are also many goods that are not directly traded. For example, Big

Relative Prices within Countries in the Absence of Trade

Country	Corn	Baseballs
Eastland	¥200	¥500
Westland	£30	£50

Mac hamburgers are always produced locally at McDonald's' restaurants around the world. For goods that are not traded, the reason usually is that transportation, storage, and other costs associated with the trade itself outweigh the gains of comparative advantage.

Applying Concepts

Suppose there are only two countries, A and B. Country A is endowed with abundant resources of all types and a highly intelligent and motivated labor force. Country B has few natural resources and its workers cannot seem to do anything well. Both countries are self-sufficient, each subsisting upon goods X and Y. The price of both X and Y in country A is \$1. In country B, the price of X is £1 and the price of Y is £2. Neither country trades with the other, but both are meeting now to consider removing trade barriers so that trade could occur.

1. If trade were to occur, what would be its pattern; that is, which country would specialize in which product(s)? Why?
2. As Trade Minister for country A, would you recommend free trade? Why or why not? What if you were Trade Minister for country B?

PART TWO

THE POWER OF PRICES

Whether we are consumers or producers, prices motivate us to action. A sale price on CDs spurs CD sales. An increase in the price of cardboard spurs producers to manufacture more. That is the way of the marketplace, a way that keeps our cupboards stocked with the products we want. This section examines market processes and their implications for public policy and international commerce.

3

MARKET PRICES: SUPPLY AND DEMAND

A Look Ahead

"TEACH A PARROT to say 'supply and demand' and you have an economist!" While that venerable quip is not literally true (we hope), it does point out how central supply and demand analysis is to answering economic questions.

Why do college professors get paid more than drugstore clerks? Why do home-run hitters Sammy Sosa and Mark McGwire get paid more than college professors (or just about anyone else)? Polly the parrot knows the answer: "Squawk, supply and demand!" Why do movies contain sex and violence? Why is the air polluted? Why do diamonds cost more than water? The answers? You guessed it . . . "Squawk!"

Of course, you would not be well advised to answer all economic questions with "supply and demand" and leave it at that. Rather, the study of supply and demand analysis must be done with care and precision if it is to reliably answer the economic questions we ask of it. This chapter scrutinizes demand and supply and how they interact in the marketplace to determine the prices we pay and the value we receive. Later chapters make use of this material to answer the previous questions and many more.

Exploration 3-1 examines the issue of school choice. Although government has traditionally provided public schooling directly, there are ways to bring markets into the process with the aim of keeping costs down and quality up. Exploration 3-2 looks at safety, and how both markets and policy actions determine how much of this intangible good we have.

As you are **Surveying Economic Principles** you will arrive at an ability to

❏ distinguish between the general notions of supply and demand used in ordinary conversation and the precise notions employed in the study of economics;

❏ explain what it means to shift demand and supply, and why shifts might occur;

❏ describe how the marketplace settles upon the equilibrium price and quantity;

❏ identify the effects upon equilibrium of shifts in supply and demand;

❏ discuss how the market leads to an efficient quantity of output.

While **Exploring Issues** you will be able to

❏ describe how vouchers can empower consumers in the market for education;

❏ explain how economics determines how safe our lives will be.

Terms Along the Way

✔ demand, 74

✔ quantity demanded, 74

✔ *ceteris paribus*, 74

✔ shift factors, 76

✔ normal goods, 78

✔ inferior goods, 78

✔ substitutes, 78

✔ complements, 78

✔ supply, 80

✔ quantity supplied, 80

✔ market equilibrium, 86

✔ surplus, 86

✔ shortage, 86

✔ consumer surplus, 90

✔ marginal benefit, 91

✔ marginal cost, 91

✔ charter schools, 98

✔ vouchers, 99

✔ statistical life, 106

SURVEYING ECONOMIC PRINCIPLES

The Answer to Economic Questions—Supply and Demand

Supply and demand analysis plays such a central role in answering economic questions that it should come as no surprise that the economics profession attaches very specific definitions to these concepts. The economic definitions of supply and demand are much more precise than the fuzzy notion that demand is something a person wants or needs and supply is what is offered. Rather, supply and demand are both defined as relationships between price and quantity. Supply relates the quantity offered for sale to each of various possible prices. Demand does the same, except now the relationship is between the various possible prices and the associated quantities that would actually be purchased. We start by looking at demand.

Demand

Demand *relates the quantity of a good that consumers will purchase at each of various possible prices, over some period of time,* ceteris paribus.

Demand is a relationship, not a single quantity. For a given price, demand will tell us a specific quantity that consumers will purchase. This quantity is termed the quantity demanded. In other words, demand relates quantity demanded to price over the range of possible prices. To emphasize that demand is a relationship and not just a single point, demand is also sometimes called a *demand schedule* or, more generally, a *demand curve.*

> **quantity demanded:** the quantity that consumers will purchase at a given price.

Demand must be defined for a set period of time. For example, demand for milk will be quite different if the period in question is one day, one week, or one year. Moreover, anything else that might influence the quantity demanded must be held constant. This is termed the *ceteris paribus* condition. It means that we only look at one relationship at a time, where *ceteris paribus* is the Latin for holding all else equal. (It is always either italicized or underlined.)

> ***ceteris paribus:*** holding all else equal.

Suppose we want to know how an increase in water rates will affect the amount of water used to sprinkle lawns. We know that the quantity of water demanded will depend on various things besides the price. To avoid mixing up the effects of price and rainfall, for example, we might estimate one demand curve for times of normal rainfall and another for times of drought. This approach allows us to focus exclusively on the relationship between price and quantity demanded.

By Word, by Table, by Graph

There are various ways to express relationships. One is to provide a table of data. Another is to show that data with a graph. For example, the data in Table 3-1 make up a demand schedule. The data from Table 3-1 can be plotted on a graph to form a demand curve, shown in Figure 3-1, where the horizontal axis is labeled Quantity to denote the quantity demanded at each possible price. Since price is measured in dollars, the dollar sign provides the label for the vertical axis.

TABLE 3-1 Demand

Data Point	Price ($)	Quantity Demanded
A	5	0
B	4	1
C	3	2
E	2	3
F	1	4
G	0	5

Note how the graph pictures an inverse relationship between price and quantity demanded. As price rises, quantity falls. As price falls, quantity rises. This relationship is termed the *law of demand*. It is an empirical law, meaning that no one enforces it, but buyers almost always adhere to it.

You've heard the saying "a picture is worth a thousand words." That saying usually applies to supply and demand analysis. While a table of data can be useful

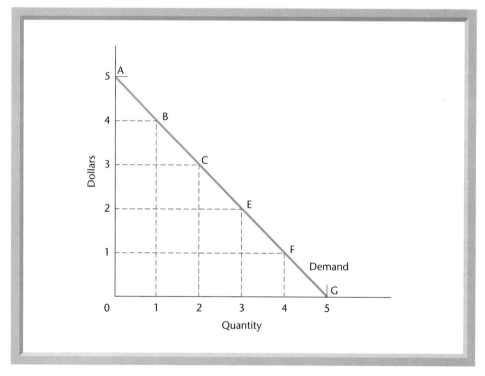

FIGURE 3–1 **Demand** slopes downward, indicating that price and quantity demanded vary inversely to each other.

for applications calling for numerical calculations, a graph is ordinarily better suited for broader messages, such as the inverse relationship between price and quantity demanded. When the specific data are less important than the general nature of the relationship, it is common to draw a graph without attaching any specific numbers to that graph, as is done in many of the graphs in this chapter and the rest of this book.

If you are uncomfortable with a graph without numbers, recall the simple solution mentioned in chapter 2: Add some numbers. Even though the numbers would be artificial, the graphical relationship may then become easier to comprehend. For example, we could have labeled Figure 3–1 with different numbers or with no numbers at all. The graph would still impart the notion that price and quantity vary inversely.

Focusing Thoughts with Ceteris Paribus

Price is not the only factor that influences how much people buy. Quantities purchased are also dictated by income, tastes, the prices of other goods, and various other factors. By holding all but price constant, the *ceteris paribus* assumption lets us focus on one thing at a time. This approach provides order to what otherwise might seem like a jumble of simultaneous changes.

What happens to demand when other things change? Changes in other aspects of the world have the potential to *shift* the entire demand curve, leading to a new relationship between price and quantity. Things that shift demand are termed demand's shift factors. An *increase in demand* occurs when demand shifts to the right. A *decrease in demand* occurs when demand shifts to the left. Figure 3–2 summarizes these shifts. Note that a change in the price of the good neither increases nor decreases demand—demand does not shift. Rather, a price change would change the quantity demanded, which involves moving along the same demand curve.

Consider an example of demand shifting. For instance, a boom in new home construction is generally associated with higher home prices. This association does not mean that consumers buy more homes because the price of homes has risen. Rather, something else has changed. Perhaps a surging economy is responsible for higher consumer income and thus greater home purchases despite higher home prices. In this case, price and quantity rise together, because some other factor is at work—a change in consumer income. To the extent that higher income causes consumers to buy more of a good at any given price, the higher income has increased demand, such as depicted by the rightward pointing arrow in Figure 3–2.

shift factors: anything that would move an entire curve on a graph.

QuickCheck _____

Would an increase in price decrease demand?

Answer: No, a change in the price of a good represents a movement along demand. In contrast, to decrease demand would entail shifting the entire demand curve to the left. Since price is not a shift factor, that shift does not occur.

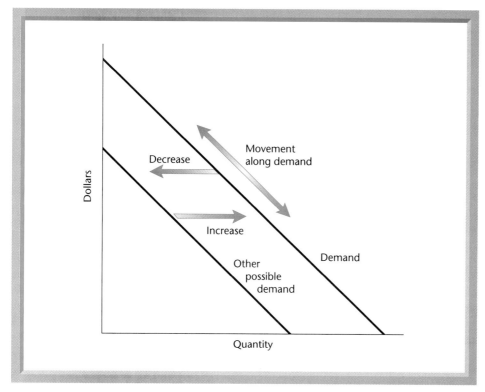

FIGURE 3–2 **Demand shifts** when there is a change in a shift factor. A change in price does not shift demand. Rather, a price change causes a movement along the demand curve to a new quantity demanded.

OBSERVATION POINT:
More Than Nature's Wrath

Whether it be a hurricane's pounding surf that washes away expensive beachfront homes, a swollen river that engulfs entire communities along its course, or sliding mud that obliterates all that stands in its way, the effects of wind and rain cost U.S. citizens billions of dollars annually. Much of this loss is a direct result of expensive structures being built in harm's way. For example, huge amounts of real estate development occur in some of the most at-risk areas, be they California hillsides, Atlantic ocean fronts, or river flood plains.

Is the large amount of building in risky areas proof of people's shortsighted irrationality? More likely, it is evidence of the law of demand in response to government low-interest loans for rebuilding and other assistance that reduce the cost of disasters to their victims. Specifically, disaster assistance lowers the price of taking the risk to build in disaster-prone locations. The lower price leads people to do more building there. Thus, by the law of demand, the unintended consequence of compensating disaster victims for property losses is that there will be a larger amount of property lost when the next disaster strikes.

**http://www.fema.
gov/index.htm** is the Internet address for the Federal Emergency Management Agency, which provides aid to victims of natural disasters.

To reduce the amount of risk-taking by people who have already been victimized by bad weather, it is increasingly common for government aid to be contingent upon the recipients rebuilding in safer spots. Even so, disaster aid lowers the expected price of risk-taking for the rest of us. We respond to this lower price by daring to live closer to our country's scenic but dangerous places.

Things That Shift Demand

Some things are more likely to shift demand than are other things. As mentioned, consumer income is a likely shift factor. *For* **normal goods, an increase in income shifts demand to the right.** However, there are many goods that people buy less of as their incomes rise. These are termed **inferior goods. An increase in income shifts the demand for inferior goods to the left.** Is there anything you would buy less of as your income increases? Perhaps you would eat fewer hot dogs and cans of tuna, and more steak and fresh fish. If so, for you, hot dogs and tuna would be inferior goods, and steak and fresh fish would be normal goods.

Changes in the prices of substitutes and complements also shift demand. A **substitute** is something that takes the place of something else. Different brands of coffee are substitutes. So are coffee and tea. A **complement** is a good that goes with another good, such as ketchup on hot dogs or cream in coffee. The degree to which one good complements or substitutes for another will vary according to each person's tastes and preferences. For example, many coffee drinkers prefer to take their coffee black. For them coffee and cream are not complements. Likewise, to the extent a consumer is loyal to a particular brand of a product, other brands might not be viewed as acceptable substitutes unless the price difference is dramatic.

What would happen to demand for a good if the price of a substitute changes? To answer questions like this one, it often helps to be specific. For example, consider how much Sparkle Beach laundry detergent shoppers purchase at various possible prices. Those quantities would go up or down depending upon the prices of Tide, Surf, All, and other possible substitutes. If the price of the substitutes rises, *ceteris paribus*, shoppers buy more Sparkle Beach. Their demand for Sparkle Beach shifts out. Likewise, should the substitutes be reduced in price, *ceteris paribus*, shoppers would buy less Sparkle Beach—demand shifts in. **Thus, demand shifts directly with a change in the price of a substitute.**

Conversely, **demand shifts inversely to a change in the price of a complement.** Since complements are the opposite of substitutes, a change in the price of a complement shifts demand in the opposite direction from what would occur if there were a change in the price of a substitute. For example, cheese slices are complementary to sandwich meats. An increase in the price of sandwich meats would decrease consumption of those meats and anything that goes with them. Demand for cheese slices would shift to the left. Likewise, a decrease in the price of sandwich meats would shift demand for cheese slices to the right.

Changes in *tastes and preferences* will also shift demand. Over time, as some items become more popular, their demand curves shift out. Other items see their popularity fade and their demand curves shift in. Producers often use advertising in an attempt to influence tastes and preferences toward their particular brand of product.

Changes in population, in expectations about future prices and incomes, or in many other factors can cause demand to shift. Population is a shift factor that

normal goods: demand for these goods varies directly with income.

inferior goods: demand for these goods varies inversely with income.

substitutes: something that takes the place of something else, such as one brand of cola for another.

complements: goods or services that go well with each other, such as cream with coffee.

For some interesting facts about cheese, and the addresses of cheese industry associations, visit the Internet site at **http://www.foodchannel.com/ifc/nutrition/pyramid/dairy/dairy_cheese.html**

TABLE 3–2 Changes in Demand

Demand Shifts to the LEFT When	Demand Shifts to the RIGHT When
The prices of substitutes decrease.	The prices of substitutes increase.
The prices of complements increase.	The prices of complements decrease.
The good is normal and income decreases.	The good is normal and income increases.
The good is inferior and income increases.	The good is inferior and income decreases.
Population decreases.	Population increases.
Consumers expect prices to decrease in the future.	Consumers expect prices to increase in the future.
Tastes and preferences turn against the product.	Tastes and preferences turn in favor of the product.

applies to market demand. Demand will increase or decrease to the extent that population increases or decreases. Interestingly, a change in consumer *expectations* about future prices or income will itself shift demand in the present. For example, if you expect prices to fall in the future, you might put off your purchases now, in effect shifting your current demand curve to the left. You would be treating future purchases as a substitute for current purchases. For some products, other factors could be significant, such as conjectures about future technologies that might make products with current technologies obsolete soon.

Summing up, when consumers buy less of a good at each price, demand shifts to the left. When consumers buy more of a good at each price, demand shifts to the right. Table 3–2 summarizes these shifts. Changing tastes and preferences could shift demand in either direction. **A change in the price of the good causes a change in the quantity demanded, but does not shift demand.** Rather, a change in price causes a movement along the demand curve.

 ## QuickCheck _____

After reaching a low of about 6.75 percent in October of 1993, interest rates on 30-year home mortgages rose to nearly 8 percent by the spring of 1994. In response to this upturn in mortgage interest rates, lenders saw a record number of consumers seek to finance or refinance mortgages in early 1994. In short, the interest rate is the price of a home mortgage, and consumers bought more mortgages when the price started rising. Does this behavior violate the law of demand?

Answer: No, the law of demand is not violated. Rather, there was a change in expectations, which resulted in demand shifting outward. Specifically, consumers observed that rates, which had been falling until October 1993, were starting to rise. Customers began expecting prices to rise rather than fall in the future. With customers anxious to buy sooner rather than later, the entire demand curve for mortgages shifted to the right. As it turned out, consumer expectations were quite correct, as mortgage rates continued to rise throughout that year.

Supply

Supply relates the quantity of a good that will be offered for sale at each of various possible prices, over some period of time, ceteris paribus.

The first thing to note about supply is its symmetry with demand. Supply tells us the quantity that will be offered for sale at various prices. This quantity is termed the **quantity supplied.** Note that supply and quantity supplied are not synonyms. Supply refers to the entire schedule that relates price and quantity and is thus also called a *supply schedule* or *supply curve.* Quantity supplied is the quantity associated with a single point on that schedule. As price changes, quantity supplied changes, but supply does not.

Supply is often referred to as the supply schedule or supply curve in order to emphasize that it is not any single quantity. Like demand, supply must be specified for a set period of time, such as a day, month, or year. The *ceteris paribus* clause makes sure that other things are held constant, so that we can focus clearly on the relationship between price and quantity supplied.

By Word, by Table, by Graph

Just as with demand, supply can be presented as a table or as a graph. An example of supply is listed in Table 3–3 and graphed in Figure 3–3. In contrast to the downward-sloping demand curve, supply nearly always slopes upward to the right. This direct relationship between price and quantity supplied is known as the *law of supply.* As price rises, the quantity offered for sale increases, because the higher revenue per unit sold means that some additional units now become profitable to produce and sell.

Ceteris Paribus–*Same Meaning, Different Shift Factors*

Changes in *ceteris paribus* conditions would shift supply. While changes in *ceteris paribus* conditions also shift demand, the most important shift factors are likely to differ. Remember that, for demand, the most important shift factors are income, prices of substitutes and complements, tastes and preferences, and expectations of future prices and incomes. When it comes to supply, changes in expectations as to future prices are still important. However, the other important shift factors are different. In addition to expectations as to future prices, supply's important shift factors

TABLE 3–3 Supply

Data Point	Price ($)	Quantity (Supplied)
H	5	4
I	4	3
J	3	2
K	2	1
L	1	0
M	0	0

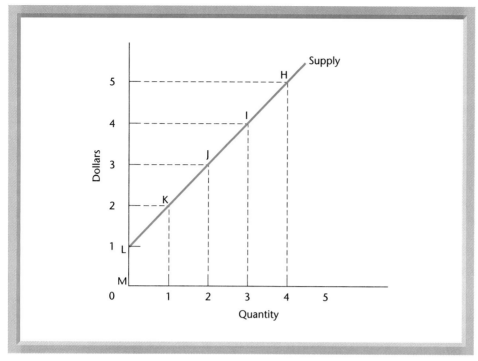

FIGURE 3–3   **Supply** slopes upward because an increase in price leads to a greater quantity supplied.

include: 1) the number of firms; 2) prices of inputs; 3) technological change; 4) government or union restrictions on the manner in which production occurs; 5) prices of substitutes in production; and 6) prices of jointly produced goods.

Why would expectations of future prices be important to a seller? To answer that question, suppose you own an oil field, and that it costs you $1 per barrel to pump your crude oil from the ground. How much oil would you offer for sale if the price were $15? $20? Why wouldn't you pump your oil field dry if the selling price were $1.50?

For each possible current price, you would ask yourself how likely it would be for the price to go higher in the future. If you thought prices were on their way up, you would put off your pumping until later. If you expect prices to remain flat or to drop in the future, you would pump more now. If your expectations change, your entire supply schedule for pumping oil in the present would shift. For example, if you become convinced that the world is about to run out of oil, your supply curve in the present would shift far to the left, so that you would retain plenty of oil to sell at high prices in the future. Thus, **today's supply varies inversely to expected future prices.**

If wages or other input prices fall, firms see their expenses drop, and are willing to produce more at any given price. Hence, a decline in input prices *increases* supply, meaning that supply shifts to the right. Were input prices to increase, supply would *decrease*, meaning that it would shift to the left. In that case, fewer units are offered for sale at any given price. In general, **supply will vary inversely to changes in input prices.**

Firms adopt technological change in order to produce more output per unit of input. This has the same effect as a decrease in input prices. **Technological change in the production of any good shifts its supply to the right.**

When government or labor unions restrict the way that firms do business, the effect is an increase in per-unit production cost. For example, the Environmental Protection Agency requires automobiles to meet exhaust-gas emission standards, such as with catalytic converters. To cover the cost of the catalytic converters, the automakers require a higher price for the autos they sell. For any given price, then, the producers offer fewer units for sale. Thus, the supply curve shifts to the left.

Likewise, if unions succeed in obtaining costly benefits, or in restricting the amount of work firms can expect from any given worker, the result would be a similar increase in expenses per unit of output. This is why **government or union restrictions on the manner in which production occurs have the effect of decreasing supply—supply shifts to the left.**

Other shift factors could also be important in some applications. For example, many farmers have been replacing their traditional crops with different crops that offer more profit. The 1990s saw thousands of acres in the South converted from cotton crops to corn crops because of the relatively high price of corn. As the price of corn rises, *ceteris paribus*, cotton plantings fall and the cotton supply curve shifts to the left. If the price of corn were to fall, conversely, the cotton supply curve would shift to the right. In general, then, **supply varies inversely to the price of a *substitute in production*,** such as in the example above. Be aware that substitutes in production are not the same as the substitutes in consumption that shift demand. After all, would you be willing to trade in your morning corn flakes for a hearty bowl of cotton flakes?

Turning to another agricultural example, some products are produced jointly, such as beef and leather. An increase in the popularity and price of beef would lead to a movement up the supply curve for beef. The greater quantity supplied of beef means that more cattle are raised for slaughter, which has the effect of shifting the supply of leather to the right. In brief, more leather would be offered for sale at each price of leather, in response to people consuming more steak and hamburger. Thus, **supply varies directly with the prices of products that are jointly produced.**

Summing up, when producers offer to sell less of a good at each price, supply decreases. When producers offer to sell more of a good at each price, supply increases. Table 3–4 summarizes these shifts. **Remember that a change in the price of the good causes a change in the quantity supplied, but does not shift supply.** Rather, a change in price causes a movement along the supply curve.

OBSERVATION POINT:
The Livestock Gourmet on a Hot Summer Day

While humans huddle by their air conditioners to escape the sweltering summer sun, life is good for some Iowa pigs and cattle—they enjoy a gourmet feast of tasty wet corn feed. On particularly hot days, farmers in the vicinity of the Cargill corn processing plant in Eddyville, Iowa, can buy this high-quality feed for a very low price. It's not that Cargill pities overheated animals. Rather, it is the availability of electricity that shifts out Cargill's supply of wet feed.

TABLE 3–4 Changes in Supply

Supply Shifts to the LEFT When	Supply Shifts to the RIGHT When
The number of sellers decreases.	The number of sellers increases.
The price of labor or any other input rises.	The price of labor or any other input falls.
Sellers expect price to rise in the future.	Sellers expect price to decline in the future.
Government or union restrictions on production practices increase cost.	Technological change lowers cost.
The price of a substitute in production rises.	The price of a substitute in production falls.
The price of a product produced jointly falls.	The price of a product produced jointly rises.

The many air conditioners that run on exceptionally hot days stress the ability of the local electric company to provide power. The ensuing power shortage leads to electricity cutbacks for industry, including Cargill. Cargill is left with huge piles of perishable wet feed, because there isn't enough electricity to dry and store it. The result is that, although power curtailment is not one of the more common things that shift supply, it's one that leaves some cows very contented.

Equilibrium—Demand Meets Supply and the Market Clears

Market Demand and Supply

Demand can be one individual's or the market's as a whole. Likewise, supply can be from one firm or all firms in the market. The market is the bringing together of buyers and sellers. While most people think of a market as a physical location, markets usually extend well beyond any single place. Markets can be local, regional, national, or multinational in scale. For example, gold, crude oil, and many other commodities are sold in global markets, with only minor variations in price throughout the world.

Market demand is the summation of all the individuals' demands in that market. Summing individuals' demands is straightforward if you remember to add quantities, not prices. For each price, the quantity demanded in the marketplace is the sum of the quantities demanded by all consumers. An example will demonstrate this process.

For our example, we will consider a market with two consumers, Jack and Jill. Jack and Jill are both interested in purchasing—what else?—pails of water. Jack is a laid-back sort of fellow who has no interest in climbing the hill to get water for himself. He is quite willing to pay for at least some of the water he uses. Jill, in contrast, sees climbing the hill as good aerobic exercise, but is worried about tumbling down. The different demands of Jack and Jill can be combined into a market demand, as shown in Table 3–5 and Figure 3–4. In each case, it is quantities that are added, not prices.

Market supply is the schedule depicting the total quantity offered for sale in the market at each price. To obtain market supply, merely add the quantities offered for sale by all sellers at each price. Graphically, market supply is the horizontal summation of each seller's supply curve. Continuing with the example, Table 3–6 and Figure 3–5 show the supplies of two sellers of pails of water—Wally and Wanda—and how their supplies sum to market supply.

Price ($)	Jack's Quantity Demanded	Jill's Quantity Demanded	Market Quantity Demanded
5	1	0	1
4	2	1	3
3	3	2	5
2	4	3	7
1	5	4	9
0	6	5	11

TABLE 3–5   Market Demand Sums the Quantities Demanded by Each Buyer

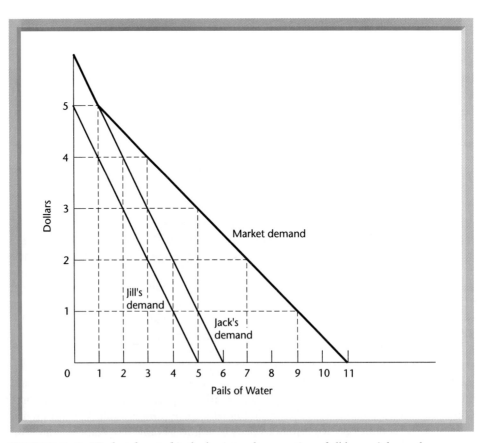

FIGURE 3–4   **Market demand** is the horizontal summation of all buyers' demands.

TABLE 3-6 Market Supply Sums the Quantities Supplied by Each Seller

Price ($)	Wally's Quantity Supplied	Wanda's Quantity Supplied	Market Quantity Supplied
5	4	5	9
4	3	4	7
3	2	3	5
2	1	2	3
1	0	1	1
0	0	0	0

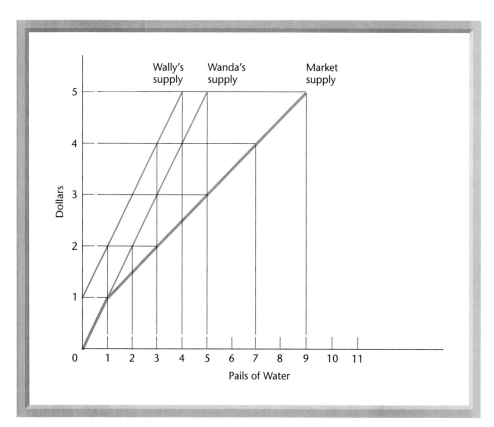

FIGURE 3–5 **Market supply** is the horizontal summation of all sellers' supplies.

Arriving at an Equilibrium

When supply and demand meet in the marketplace, a market price is created. While individual sellers are free to price their products however they wish, there will be only one price that *clears the market*, such that the quantity supplied equals the quantity demanded. **The market-clearing price and the resulting quantity traded comprise what is known as the market equilibrium, meaning that there is no tendency for either price or quantity to change,** *ceteris paribus.*

market equilibrium: a situation in which there is no tendency for either price or quantity to change.

Market equilibrium is determined by the intersection of supply and demand, as shown in Table 3–7 and Figure 3–6. This price and quantity combination is labeled P* and Q*, respectively, at a price of $3 and a quantity of five pails.

surplus: the excess of quantity supplied over quantity demanded, which occurs when price is above equilibrium.

At any price above P*, there would be a surplus, representing the excess of quantity supplied over quantity demanded. For example, a price of $4 would be too high, resulting in a surplus of four pails. In that case, Wally and Wanda would compete with each other for sales by lowering price. More generally, in any market in which a surplus occurs, some sellers would cut their prices slightly so as to be the ones that make the sales. Other suppliers would then be without customers, and would consequently lower their own prices enough to capture customers from their competitors. This leapfrogging process would continue until the quantity demanded and supplied are equal, which occurs at the equilibrium price of P*.

shortage: the excess of quantity demanded over quantity supplied, which occurs when price is below equilibrium.

A price that is too low results in a shortage, equal to the amount by which quantity demanded exceeds quantity supplied. For example, a price of $2 would result in a shortage of four pails. Because there is not enough water to meet demand at that price, Jack and Jill would scramble to be first to buy. More generally, whenever there is a shortage in any market, buyers compete against each other for the limited quantities of the goods that are offered for sale at that price. For sellers, shortages provide an opportunity both to raise prices and to increase sales, a doubly appealing prospect. Price would thus rise to P*, the point at which the shortage disappears. Thus, without any guidance, the invisible hand of the free market eliminates either surpluses or shortages, and leads to the equilibrium at which the market clears.

Suppose one of the shift factors for either supply or demand were to change. For example, suppose an increase in consumer income or a decrease in the price of a complement shifts demand to the right. One of the most common mistakes students make is to think this shift in demand would also shift supply. It would not, because demand

TABLE 3–7 Market Equilibrium at a Price of $3

Price ($)	Quantity Demanded	Quantity Supplied	Surplus (or (Shortage)
5	1	9	8
4	3	7	4
3	5	5	0
2	7	3	(4)
1	9	1	(8)
0	11	0	(11)

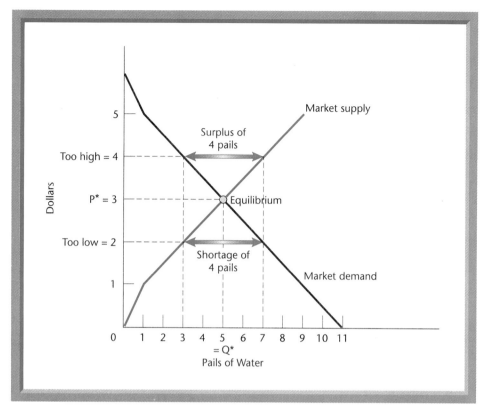

FIGURE 3–6 **Market equilibrium** occurs at a price of $3 and a quantity of five pails. Any price above $3 would lead to a surplus. Any price below $3 would cause a shortage. Neither surpluses nor shortages will persist in a free market.

is not a shift factor for supply. Rather, the rightward shift in demand leads to a movement up the supply curve and results in a new, higher equilibrium price and quantity.

For practice, you might draw the basic supply and demand diagram, and then sketch a few shifts in either demand or supply. Note the effect on the equilibrium price and quantity. Note also that **shifting demand does not cause a shift in supply or vice versa.**

 **QuickCheck** _____

In the example represented by Figure 3–6, how much would be sold if the price is $4? If the price is $2?

Answer: Remember that each sale requires both a buyer and a seller. Thus, if the price is $4, three pails of water would be sold. If the price is $2, again three pails of water would be sold.

Changes in the Market Equilibrium

The market equilibrium will change whenever supply or demand shift. There are only four shifts possible, as follows:

1. an increase in supply, which shifts supply to the right;
2. a decrease in supply, which shifts supply to the left;
3. an increase in demand, which shifts demand to the right;
4. a decrease in demand, which shifts demand to the left.

These shifts and their effects on equilibrium price and quantity, denoted P* and Q* respectively, are shown in Figure 3–7 and summarized in Table 3–8. The four rows of the table, labeled case 1 through case 4, match the four graphs in the figure.

Whether it be in the market for meals, metals, or memory chips, both supply and demand can be expected to shift over time. To understand the effects on price and quantity when there are simultaneous shifts in supply and demand, all that is needed is to look at each shift separately. In other words, we would combine two of the four cases listed in Table 3–8.

For example, if supply shifts to the right and demand shifts to the right also, we would look at the combination of cases 1 and 3 in Table 3–8. That combination of cases tells us that equilibrium quantity will definitely rise, but that equilibrium price might rise, fall, or remain unchanged. Specifically, when we look at them separately, both the demand and supply shifts result in a higher equilibrium quantity. However, case 1 pulls price lower while case 3 pulls price higher. Whether price rises, falls, or stays the same thus depends upon the relative strengths of those pulls.

To truly master all the possible shifts in demand and supply, try working backwards. For example, suppose price rises and quantity falls. What could have caused this situation? One possibility is that supply shifts to the left, *ceteris paribus*, as listed in case 2. But that is not the only possibility. For instance, both demand and supply could have shifted to the left, with the supply shift the more dominant of the two. A higher price and smaller quantity could also be caused so long as the leftward shift in supply is stronger than the rightward shift in demand. Table 3–9 summarizes the results from simultaneous shifts in supply and demand. Notice that in each of the cases in Table 3–9, either equilibrium price or quantity is listed as Unknown to indicate that the direction in which the equilibrium price or quantity will move cannot be known without further information. **The price or quantity change will be unknown when the shifts in demand and supply pull in opposite directions.**

TABLE 3-8	The Four Basic Cases of Shifting Demand and Supply			
Case	**Demand**	**Supply**	**P***	**Q***
1	No change	Right	Fall	Rise
2	No change	Left	Rise	Fall
3	Right	No change	Rise	Rise
4	Left	No change	Fall	Fall

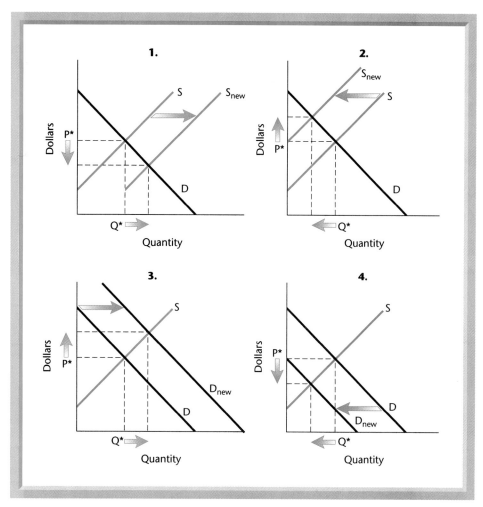

FIGURE 3–7 **The effects on market equilibrium price (P*) and quantity (Q*)** can be explained by a shift in either demand (D) or supply (S), as shown in these four cases. When demand and supply shift simultaneously, the result can be analyzed by combining the pertinent two of the four cases shown.

TABLE 3–9 Cases 5 through 8 Combine Cases 1 through 4

Case	Demand	Supply	P*	Q*
5: 1 and 3	Right	Right	Unknown	Rise
6: 2 and 4	Left	Left	Unknown	Fall
7: 2 and 3	Right	Left	Rise	Unknown
8: 1 and 4	Left	Right	Fall	Unknown

Can you apply this analysis? For example, how would you interpret the observation that the price of video camcorders has fallen in the last 10 years, and people are now buying more? Analytically, it could be case 1, in which demand stays constant while supply shifts right. More likely, however, case 5 applies, in which both demand and supply shift to the right. Demand shifted as camcorders became an increasingly popular addition to the gadgets of modern life. However, the increase in supply has been even more pronounced, which explains why prices have fallen.

 **QuickCheck** _____

List the shifts in demand and/or supply that would result in a lower price and a greater quantity.

Answer: 1. A rightward shift in supply (case 1). 2. A rightward shift in supply that is stronger than a rightward shift in demand that occurs at the same time (case 5). 3. A leftward shift in demand that is weaker than a rightward shift in supply that occurs at the same time (case 8).

OBSERVATION POINT:
Oprah, the Cattlemen, and Mad Cow Disease

An inward shift in demand and the resulting fall in market price hardly sounds likely to attract the attention of a famous talk show host. Yet Oprah Winfrey found out the hard way how important such matters can be.

In the winter of '97, Oprah was summoned to a Lubbock, Texas, courtroom to defend herself. According to some Texas cattlemen, Oprah made too much of the issue of mad cow disease, which had been a problem in England, but not in the U.S. Oprah thus deterred millions of listeners from buying beef, the cattlemen said. That shifted demand to the left, which thus caused a fall in cattle prices and rancher profits, they claimed.

Oprah was vindicated in the courtroom, basing her defense partly upon testimony that demand for beef had shifted in for other reasons. Some in the cattle industry wondered whether the publicity surrounding the trial caused consumers to be even more concerned about mad cow disease, with the result being further weakness in both demand and the market price.

Efficiency of the Market Equilibrium

consumer surplus: the difference between the maximum amount that a good or service is worth to consumers and what they actually pay for it; in brief, demand minus market price.

For a market economy to be efficient implies that it produces the most value from the resources at its disposal. Since goods are produced in order to be consumed, the value of output is ultimately measured by its value to consumers, which is given by its consumer surplus. **Consumer surplus** is how much the good is worth to the consumer in the abstract, minus what the consumer actually paid for it. Thus, **consumer surplus equals demand minus the market price.**

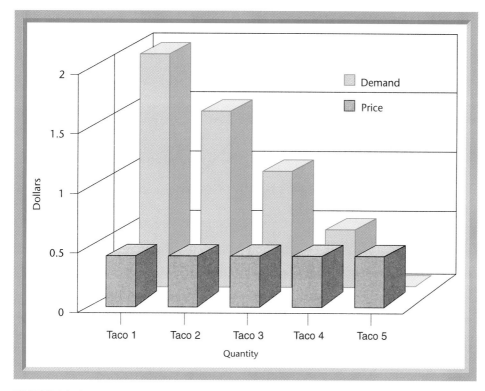

FIGURE 3–8   **Consumer surplus is the difference between demand and market price.**

Figure 3–8 illustrates this concept. In this figure, we suppose that Tina stops for crispy tacos at Taco Bell, and is pleased to see them on sale for 49 cents each. She decides to buy four tacos. Why? What value has she gained? Answering those questions involves computing Tina's consumer surplus.

Tina's first taco was worth $2 to her, her second $1.50, her third $1, and her fourth 50 cents. A fifth taco would have been worthless to her, because she would have been too full to eat it. Unfortunately for Tina, Taco Bell made her pay the 49 cent price per taco, leaving Tina with a consumer surplus of $1.51 for the first taco, $1.01 for the second, 51 cents for the third, and only 1 cent for the fourth. Adding up these values, Tina is seen to have total consumer surplus of $3.04. That consumer surplus is what Tina gained by eating Taco Bell tacos that day. Note that, if the price were 99 cents per taco, she would have only bought three tacos and gained only $1.53 of consumer surplus instead of the $3.04 value that she actually gained.

Turning to the marketplace as a whole, efficiency requires that a good be produced only so long as long as the marginal benefit to consumers, the value of each additional unit of the good, exceeds the marginal cost to producers, the cost of the resources used to produce each additional unit. Just as Tina's demand for tacos that day represented the marginal benefit of tacos to her, so too **market demand for a good represents the marginal benefit of that good** to consumers. Likewise, **market**

marginal benefit: the value obtained by consuming one additional unit of a good.

marginal cost: the cost of producing one more unit of output; change in total cost per unit of additional output.

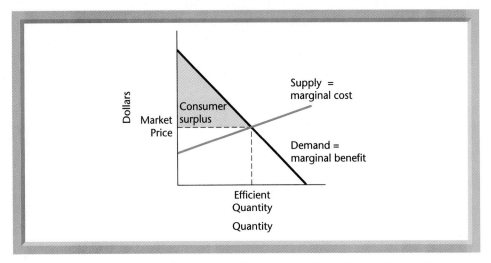

FIGURE 3–9   **By producing to the point where marginal benefit equals marginal cost, the competitive market is efficient.**

supply represents the marginal cost to producers. The efficient quantity is thus given by the intersection of supply and demand, which is exactly the quantity that the market produces. Thus, the free market is efficient, as shown in Figure 3–9, which labels both the efficient quantity and the amount of consumer surplus that it generates. As noted in chapter 1 and discussed more fully in chapter 9, the presence of externalities or other market failures causes exceptions to the rule of free market efficiency.

Note that benefits and costs are defined by the measuring rod of money. Yet, the amount of money that a person is willing to pay for a good depends upon that person's financial situation in addition to how much intrinsic satisfaction—*utility*—that the person receives. Yet utility cannot be measured directly and, even if it could, concerns over some people having more wealth than others is mainly a matter of equity rather than efficiency. While both efficiency and equity are valid economic goals, they are best analyzed separately.

✔ QuickCheck _____

Suppose coffee costs $1 per cup at Handy Stop Shop and $1.05 per cup at Gas'n N Goin' next door. If you buy coffee at Handy Stop Shop, does this mean your consumer surplus from coffee is only 5 cents?

Answer: No, consumer surplus does not depend upon alternative prices for the same product. Rather, it asks you what is the most you would be willing to pay to avoid doing without the product altogether and then subtracts the price you actually pay. Thus, whatever your consumer surplus from a cup of coffee may be, it is 5 cents more if you buy your coffee at Handy Stop Shop than at Gas'n N Goin'.

OBSERVATION POINT:
The Paradox of Diamonds and Water

Some necessities that have a great deal of intrinsic worth are priced lower than luxuries we could easily do without. For example, people pay much more for a diamond than for a glass of water, which seems paradoxical.

The paradox disappears when we realize that a price tells the value of a good at *the margin*. Sure, the last bit of water is not worth much when water is plentiful. But the prospect of losing access to water altogether reveals just how valuable water can be. Witness the costly network of dams and aqueducts serving the burgeoning metropolises of Southern California. Witness also the billions of dollars spent on desalinization plants in the deserts of Saudi Arabia. At a personal level, imagine yourself stranded without water in Death Valley. Which would seem the better bargain—a diamond for a nickel or a glass of water for a one hundred-dollar bill?

In short, as seen in Figure 3–10 on the following page, the consumer surplus from water purchases is vastly greater than the consumer surplus from diamond purchases. It is consumer surplus that truly measures the total value consumers receive from the things they buy.

SUMMARY

- Supply and demand analysis captures the essential role of competition in the free marketplace.
- Market demand curves slope downward, indicating an inverse relationship between price and quantity demanded.
- Demand will shift with changes in the price of a substitute or complement, a change in income, a change in population, changes in expectations and changes in tastes or preferences. An increase in the price of a substitute will reduce demand; an increase in the price of a complement will increase demand. An increase in income will increase the demand for a normal good, but reduce the demand for an inferior good.
- There is a distinction between a change in demand and a change in quantity demanded. A change in demand means the demand curve shifts. A price change causes a movement from one point to another on a demand curve and results in a change in quantity demanded.
- Supply slopes upward, indicating a direct relationship between price and quantity supplied. A price change causes a change in quantity supplied.
- Supply will shift with a change in the price of a substitute or complement in production, changes in union work rules or government regulations that change costs, a change in technology, changes in input prices, and changes in seller expectations.
- A shift in supply causes a change in quantity demanded, a movement along the demand curve.
- The interaction of supply and demand leads to a market equilibrium price and quantity, from which there is no tendency to change. A price less than the market

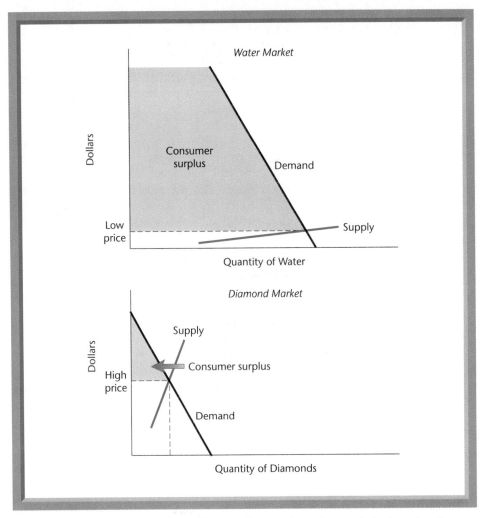

FIGURE 3–10 While the marginal benefit from a glass of water is far less than from a diamond, as revealed by the relatively low price of water, the total benefit from all water as measured by its consumer surplus is immensely larger than it would be for all diamonds.

equilibrium price will cause a shortage; a price above the market equilibrium price will cause a surplus.

- When supply or demand shift, price and quantity adjust to a new market equilibrium. There are four cases involving a shift in either demand or supply: an increase in demand, a decrease in demand, an increase in supply, and a decrease in supply. More complicated cases involve shifts in both demand and supply at the same time. Either the direction of change in equilibrium price or in equilibrium quantity will be unknown in each of these cases.

- Consumer surplus is the difference between demand and the market price. Consumers seek to maximize the consumer surplus from their purchases.
- Demand represents marginal benefit and supply represents marginal cost.
- The efficient quantity of a good is the amount where the marginal benefit curve intersects the marginal cost curve. Markets have proven to be an efficient way to maximize the value that an economy receives from its resources.

QUESTIONS AND PROBLEMS

1. Draw a single graph indicating someone's demand curve for hot dogs (D). Be sure to label the axes of your graph. On this graph, indicate what market demand would be if there were only two people willing to buy hot dogs, and if each had a demand curve identical to the one you just drew. Label this curve Market D.

2. As in the text, suppose Jack and Jill are the only two consumers in the market for pails of water. However, suppose that their demand curves change over time to the following:

Price	Jack's Quantity	Jill's Quantity
$1	10	15
2	5	10
3	0	5
4	0	0

a. Compute market demand.
b. Compute the quantities purchased in total and by Jack and Jill individually if the price per unit is $2.
c. Graph Jack's demand and Jill's demand on separate graphs. Note that, if you connect the data points you are given, you are actually inferring additional data. For example, connecting the data points on Jack's demand implies that Jack would be willing to purchase 2.5 pails of water at a price of $2.50 per pail.

3. Fill in the surplus or shortage in the table below. In each case identify whether the number is a surplus, shortage, or neither. Identify the equilibrium price, and explain why a price above equilibrium would not last.

Price	Quantity Demanded	Quantity Supplied	Surplus or Shortage
$7	12	30	————
$6	15	25	————
$5	19	19	————
$4	23	10	————

4. Using a graph of supply and demand, demonstrate how a leftward shift in demand, accompanied by a rightward shift in supply, can result in the equilibrium quantity rising. On a separate graph, demonstrate how the equilibrium could alternatively have fallen.

5. Compute consumer surplus in the market for pails of water, described in Figure 3–6.

6. Which single purchase of the purchases you have made in the last three months has given you the largest amount of consumer surplus? State the amount of consumer surplus by subtracting what you paid for the item from the amount you would have been willing to pay.

7. List at least five substitutes for your favorite soft drink, in order, starting with the best substitute, second best, and so on. Comment on whether the products on your list are good substitutes. How much would the price have to increase before you would begin to purchase the best substitute?

8. Using the economic definition of inferior goods, list several products that would be inferior goods for you personally. Do you think that these would also be inferior goods for most other people? What information would you need to have to find out?

Web Exercises

9. a. Using an Internet search engine such as that provided by Yahoo (located at **http://www.yahoo.com**) or Alta Vista (located at **http://www.altavista.com**), perform a separate search for the following terms: **demand, supply,** and **consumer surplus**. Visit several of the Web sites that your search reveals for each term and observe the context in which each term is used. Explain whether the manner in which the terms are used is consistent with their use in the text.

b. Repeat the above, but this time use a combination of terms that you select from the chapter. To eliminate sites that do not contain all terms, place a plus sign in front of each term you enter, such as **+substitutes +complements +income.**

10. Visit the Web site maintained by the National Association of Realtors at **http://www.realtor.com**. Follow the link to Find A Home and follow the instructions to view homes for sale in Los Angeles, California, and then in New Orleans, Louisiana. Record a sample of about 20 asking prices for a typical suburban 3-bedroom, 2-bath home in each city. In which city are asking prices higher? Using demand and supply analysis, list any factors that might explain the price differences.

Visit the Web site for *Economics by Design* at
http://www.prenhall.com/collinge for a Self Quiz
over the topics in this chapter.

Exploration 3-1   School Choice—Bringing in the Marketplace

This Exploration uses the principles of supply and demand to analyze the special issues that surround the market for education. Proposals to encourage competition and efficiency in this market are examined.

> *Some people know the importance of education because they have it. I know the importance of education because I didn't.*
>
> —Frederick Douglass, ex-slave and abolitionist

With nearly everyone spending many years in school, the market for education is huge and important. Education expands people's opportunities. Education also benefits society by promoting economic productivity and informed voting. The importance of education helps explain the many strong opinions on how to keep costs down and best improve school quality in grades K–12 (kindergarten through twelfth grade in high school). There is less discussion about improving colleges. The reasons have to do with supply and demand.

College students are painfully aware of the tuition, fees, and other expenses of college, with these costs playing a big part in college choice. In keeping with the law of demand, the lower the price of college, *ceteris paribus*, the more students will seek to attend and the more education will be purchased. That is why government offers tax deductions, subsidies, and financial aid that in effect lower the price of higher education. However, price is far from the only factor influencing school choice. Some students look for a college with a winning tradition in sports, others for one with a personal atmosphere. Location is also a major criterion for most students. These and other nonprice variables translate demand for education as a whole into demands for enrollments at particular colleges. Nevertheless, to the extent that colleges of similar nonacademic characteristics must still compete against each other, colleges have the incentive to supply the best education for the money.

College students usually choose for themselves from among many colleges. However, the large majority of students at the K–12 level of education are enrolled in government-run public schools, where a child's school is determined by where that child resides. Parents may have the option of selecting private schools, although this choice is discouraged by the high cost differential between free public schooling and costly private schooling. Of course public schooling is not free to taxpayers, but it is free in the sense that no family's choice of whether to send a child to public school will influence that family's tax bill.

Free public schooling is a tradition based on the notion of equal opportunity—an equal start in life. However, public schools are not equal. Some are very bureaucratic and inefficient, while others have reputations for high academic achievement. To some degree, this is because some school districts have more money to spend than others. However, to a large degree, less efficiently run schools continue to exist because parents have no alternative way of schooling their children short of moving, which is costly in many ways. Although parents could in principle vote into office school board members who would weed out inefficiencies, parents are rarely experts at how to run schools and thus do not know which candidates would be good at doing so. Moreover, just as one type of college does not fit all college students, neither does one model of school fit all students at the K–12 level.

Policies for Competition

A number of economists and others have argued that what is needed at the K–12 level is school choice, with the invisible hand of the marketplace guiding students to schools that offer the best values, as perceived by parents. Competition would then weed out ineffective schools. Many educators disagree, arguing that, just as parents are not experts when it comes to running schools and picking school board candidates, they would be poor judges of which schools are best, and that public schools would be harmed by competition. Nevertheless, with school choice, parents could choose a K–12 school based on its reputation and accreditation, just as college students pick. This process removes politics from the picture.

For example, as superintendent of El Paso's Ysleta School District, one of the nation's poorest, Anthony Trujillo raised test scores from among the lowest to among the highest of schools across the country. Parents were pleased. However, by a vote of 4 to 3 in the fall of 1998, the school board fired him. Carlos Sandoval, one of his supporters on the board, described the action as nothing more than "a personal dislike by four members." Were the schools market-dependent like other businesses, it is unlikely that personal likes or dislikes would prevail over the pursuit of profit, which dictates providing the parents what they want.

Similarly, if a government-run public school does badly, it often receives more funding, perhaps justified by the argument that more money is needed to solve the difficult educational challenges that school faces. The argument may or may not be correct, since there is no competitive market mechanism to check it. In contrast, if the school is in a competitive environment and is truly doing the best that could be done with its budget, then customers would have no better alternative than to either accept its product as is or provide more money for a better one. However, if the school in this competitive environment were not making the best use of its budget, then it would lose out in competition to a more efficient school, one that provides a better education for the same money.

charter schools: public schools operated under contract to a private, nonprofit organization.

Some advocates of limited competition argue in favor of **charter schools**, public schools in which a nonprofit group receives a contract called a charter to operate a school for a limited period of time, usually 5 years, after which time the charter is renewed if the school meets educational standards. By 1998, the U.S. saw over 170,000 children enrolled in about 800 charter schools. These schools are allowed to operate free from many of the regulations that inhibit innovation in the regular public schools. Charter schools offer an alternative to regular public schools, thus expanding school choice. They must, however, meet specified educational goals, or else risk losing their charter. In that sense, they are more accountable to parents than are traditional schools. About two-thirds of the states allow charter schools.

Unfortunately, most charter schools are new start-ups that cannot take full advantage of past experiences in education. To truly bring in the forces of supply and demand, education consumers should not have to be education producers, too. Rather, consumer demand should elicit competition from among many potential suppliers with specialized skills in running schools. That is where proposals for voucher plans come in.

Vouchers provide an amount that the recipient can spend, but restrict that spending to a certain category of goods. For example, Food Stamps are vouchers that low-income recipients are allowed to use toward food purchases. In the context of K–12 education, the vouchers would be for schooling, and are usually called school vouchers. These school vouchers would be issued by government free of charge to parents, and would be spendable only on the education of their children at a school to be chosen by the parents.

The value of school vouchers could vary, but might best be set equal to the estimated cost of providing a basic level of education for the appropriate grade level. Alternatively, vouchers sometimes offer a percentage, perhaps 80 percent, of what would alternatively have been spent on public-school education. Some parents, such as those of physically challenged children, would receive larger vouchers to compensate for their children's special needs. Vouchers could then be spent for education at the specified grade level in any accredited school. Parents would probably be free to supplement vouchers with extra money of their own. In this way, schools would compete to receive parents' vouchers. Schools could no longer count on politically defined school districts to provide them with a captive group of customers.

With a voucher plan in place, government would not necessarily own any schools. Rather, the location, design, and operation of schools could all be driven by market demand. Despite its advantages, however, such a radical change from the *status quo* is difficult to get through the political process. Thus, most actual legislative proposals for school vouchers retain support for publicly owned schools.

What of religion? Would allowing parents to spend their vouchers on church-run schools violate the separation of church and state that Americans cherish? To answer this question, consider where the voucher money comes from. Under the present system, taxpayers finance the public schools, and get services in return if they send their children there. In other words, the government takes taxpayers' money, and offers to spend it on the taxpayers' children, but only if the children are kept out of religious or other private schools. That policy can be viewed as actively discouraging religion.

The basic notion of vouchers is much more even-handed. With a pure voucher system, taxpayers are offered the opportunity to use their collective tax money if they send children to any school, whether public or private. It would no longer be relevant whether the school is religious or sectarian. The U.S. Supreme Court has let stand a ruling allowing this choice, so long as the voucher program is not targeted toward promoting religion. Even so, local politics has often caused the communities that currently have voucher programs in place to restrict voucher spending to government-owned public schools, thereby missing out on many of the efficiencies that the program is intended to provide. In contrast, financial aid to college students is available to them even if they attend a college operated by a religious denomination.

Florida has followed the college model in constructing its K-12 voucher program, passed into law in 1999. This program offers $4,000 vouchers to students who attend schools that, in the state's judgment, fail to provide an adequate education. Florida's program permits students to use their vouchers to attend a school of their choice, whether it be private or public, and whether or not it has a religious affiliation.

The Spectrum of Control

Some people worry that vouchers would lead to segregated, unequal schools. These critics imagine a collection of elitist schools filled with the most gifted. Alongside would be other schools for the so-called leftovers—those whose parents don't care, those with learning disabilities, immigrants with language difficulties, and so forth. Must vouchers lead to such a grim outcome?

The answer is that vouchers are very flexible, and could be designed to meet a wide variety of objectives. For example, vouchers could be limited only to schools meeting certain educational standards. Those standards need not be restricted to academics, but could also include admission policies and actions to promote diversity. Indeed, anything required of our current system of public and private schools can be incorporated into vouchers, too.

While it is necessary to tie vouchers to some legitimate criteria of what schooling should consist of, there is a danger in going too far toward command and control. If government rigidly specifies exactly what a school must do to qualify for voucher expenditures, then we lose the invisible hand of the marketplace that provides products consumers want. Choice has value to consumers. That value would be lost if the educational products must by law be identical.

As an example, consider mainstreaming, a philosophy that is currently popular among educators. It consists of placing physically challenged students in the same classes as everyone else, rather than isolating them in separate classes. Interpreters or other aides then provide special assistance as necessary. The idea is to promote tolerance and prevent stigmatization. Opponents claim that physically challenged students are often better able to advance if grouped according to their special needs. Those holding this view argue that the deaf and hard-of-hearing, for instance, perform better and feel better about themselves in classes designed exclusively for them.

Should we all debate this issue, and then mandate one philosophy over another? The alternative is to let the marketplace make the decision. Some schools would offer one approach. Others would offer the other. Parents, gauging their own children's experiences, would over time move their children to the schools offering what they perceive as the better way. This is what the marketplace does well, if allowed the opportunity.

Businesses in the marketplace are motivated to make efficient decisions at every turn. Where to locate? How often to empty the trash? How many secretaries? How much paperwork? All these questions are answered with an eye toward being able to compete against other companies producing the same product. This competition keeps choices efficient, meaning that costs are kept to a minimum in providing products that consumers will choose. Similarly, there are all kinds of decisions to make in schooling, including the seemingly mundane decisions of where to build the school and how to operate and maintain it. By bringing in the marketplace, vouchers motivate schools to try to be efficient in these and all other decisions.

For example, consider school location and busing. Schools might locate near one another at relatively central locations to share the same bus routes. In short, rather than locate schools on the basis of politics, the competition spawned by vouchers would position schools in areas that provide the most net value to their customers.

The strongest, most vocal objections to vouchers come from those educators, politicians, and parents who fervently believe that vouchers would ultimately destroy the public schools. This would be true if private schools consistently offered a better quality of education for the same money because parents would voluntarily abandon public schools. Voucher critics have another story in mind, however. They believe that private, for-profit schools, in scrambling for their share of voucher dollars, would aim schooling at the lowest level they could get by with. Their motivation would be to increase enrollments and thus profits by making the children feel good about their school, while skipping the unpopular activities that increase learning and intellectual development. It might be a long time before parents realized that the children were not learning much.

Furthermore, the critics predict that for-profit schools would phase out the social mission of the public schools in promoting good citizenship and replace this worthwhile mission with lowbrow commercial pursuits. For example, schools seeking profit might recruit corporate sponsors such as fast-food chains. A corporate sponsor would pay for the right to put commercials and advertisements in school learning materials, thus distracting from the learning process. These sponsorships would give private schools more money and a financial advantage over public schools. This commercialization might even be attractive to cash-poor parents because private schools with corporate sponsors could lower their tuition rates. Voucher critics want to see schooling remain in the hands of educational professionals whose motives are unsullied by the search for profit.

What Choice to Make?

Voucher plans are making inroads in various communities around the United States. A number of separate ventures have been initiated, such as voucher programs in Milwaukee, Indianapolis, and Cleveland. The private CEO Foundation has even gotten into the act, setting aside $40 million to provide vouchers to low-income students in an underperforming San Antonio school district. States have also gotten into the act. Fundamentally, the motivation is that, by enlisting the forces of demand and supply, vouchers hold the promise of keeping schooling costs down and quality up. But vouchers rely upon parental demand. Do parents know enough to demand well? Do the educational professionals know best? Is competition really workable in education? Time will surely tell.

Prospecting for New Insights

1. **KIM:** Choice is okay for some things, but not for education. We should all learn the same things so we can get started on an equal footing. Anyway, parents often either don't know or don't care about what gets taught at school!

PAUL: That puts too much power in the hands of the educational elite, telling us what and how to learn. Anyway, "different strokes for different folks." Kids have different needs and aspirations, and nobody is in a better position to judge that than the parents and kids themselves.

Should educational opportunities be different? If so, how different? Is it better to leave choice to parents and children, or to the experts? Is there a happy medium?

2. MYRA: I think voucher amounts should vary with household income. The more income, the less help—it's only fair. Still, most people should pay something out of their own pockets to educate the kids they chose to have. Keeps our taxes down!

FRED: Free education for only the needy gives everybody an incentive to hold down family size except the poor. I think education should be free for everyone. Your income shouldn't have anything to do with how much voucher power you have.

Evaluate Myra's and Fred's ideas. If a voucher plan is to be used, should the voucher amount depend upon a person's income?

Exploration 3-2   Buying Safety—At Home, in the Workplace, and on the Road

Our jobs, our homes, and our highways can all be made safer. Safety costs money, however. The higher is the price, the less is the quantity we demand. Sometimes demand is for goods and services sold in the marketplace. Other times, our actions in the marketplace can guide government to make choices for us.

How many of these protective devices do you or your family benefit from: smoke detector, hard hat, orange safety vest, steel-toed boots, fire extinguisher, seat belts, dead-bolt lock, burglar bars, or alarm system? Your life and property probably could be made at least a little safer if you owned all of these. Yet the odds are that you don't. Those orange safety vests are not exactly high fashion, but if all pedestrians were made to wear them, lives would be saved. The market for safety is imbued with certain complications for consumers that are not present in many other markets. A look at these complications will help us understand why we only go so far in seeking safety.

The Market for Safety in the Home

Safety-related products are different from many of the products we buy in the sense that they provide us with a form of insurance. For example, when purchasing a fire extinguisher, it is with the hope that we never have to use it! Nonetheless, we buy the fire extinguisher for the feeling of security it provides. Thus, the intangible benefit of freedom from fear spurs demand onward.

There is another way that safety-related products differ from many other products. Many products are *experience goods* that are familiar to us because we purchase them often. What they do, their quality, how to use them, are apparent from previous experience. Soap, toothpaste, candy, and cola drinks are just a few of the many examples of experience goods. We know from experience what the benefits are from our purchases of these products.

With safety-related goods, in contrast, we typically do not know what the benefits will be. Do we really "need" a smoke detector in our home, for example? That need partially depends upon the risk of fire, and that risk is difficult to estimate. In addition, the feeling of security that a person gets from having a smoke detector in the home is subjective. It depends upon how *risk averse* the person is. People who are extremely risk averse will purchase a smoke detector even if there is a tiny risk of fire. They just feel better, even though they might sometimes wonder if they have merely wasted their money on the purchase. Risk takers, on the other hand, will not purchase a smoke detector even in the face of a high fire risk. Of course, even a risk taker would want a smoke detector if fire was a sure thing. Also, first-hand experience with the risks of fire can increase risk aversion, which in turn would cause a rightward shift of the demand for safety-enhancing goods, such as the smoke detectors shown in Figure 3-11.

In theory, there is a way to arrive at an estimate of the monetary benefits from the purchase of a safety-related product. This method starts with an estimate of the risk of an event that imposes a loss on the consumer. For example, suppose that on average one out of every 100 homes will be hit by a fire every year. If homeowners have no reason to suppose that their risk of fire is any different from the average, then the risk per home is $1/100 = 0.01$. Is the purchase of a smoke detector worth the price? We need to know what damage to expect if a fire occurs.

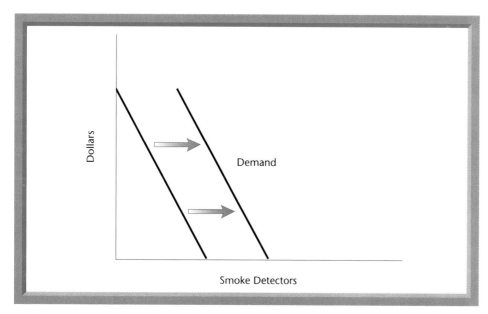

FIGURE 3-11   **The effect of increased risk aversion is to increase the demand for smoke detectors** and other safety-related goods.

Suppose that an average fire causes $10,000 of damage in homes without smoke detectors, but that in homes with smoke detectors, fire damage is reduced to only $1,000. Thus, in the event of fire, a smoke detector will provide the average homeowner with $9,000 in benefits. The benefit of $9,000 must be multiplied by the risk of fire to obtain the *expected benefit* from the purchase of a fire extinguisher: 0.01 multiplied by $9,000 equals $90.

If a smoke detector can be purchased for $30, then the $90 of expected benefits means that a homeowner would obtain $60 of *expected consumer surplus* ($90 of expected benefit minus the $30 price). If the homeowner is a gambling sort and likes some risk in life, that homeowner might experience somewhat less benefit and consumer surplus from buying a smoke detector. However, most people don't like risk, and thus would have somewhat more benefit and consumer surplus from the purchase.

Now, if a consumer has decided to buy one smoke detector, how about a second one? Recall from the Economics Expressway in this chapter that the demand curve is also the marginal benefit curve. Why would the benefit from a second smoke detector likely be less than the benefit from the first? The first smoke detector would be installed in the room most likely to see a fire break out, which is usually the kitchen. Since the second smoke detector would be installed in a room with a lower risk of fire, the expected benefit would be less. Depending upon the price of smoke detectors, the consumer surplus from a second one might be zero or negative, in which case it would not be purchased.

Consumer incentives relating to safety can be influenced by related products. For instance, smoke alarms can sometimes earn homeowners a discount on their homeowners insurance. The lower price on insurance will increase the demand for smoke detectors, just as was illustrated in Figure 3–11 for a different cause.

Governments are not always willing to let homeowners' preferences prevail. In part, the reason is that many homes are occupied by children, who are unable to comprehend safety issues. Also, fires endanger neighboring people and property. Moreover, putting out fires costs public money. For these and other reasons, many localities have ordinances requiring that all homes have smoke detectors installed. Laws requiring homes to be equipped with smoke detectors increase the demand for smoke detectors in the same manner that heightened risk aversion was shown in Figure 3–11 to also increase the demand for smoke detectors.

Safety on the Job—From One Side of the Atlantic to the Other

Safety in the workplace is arguably just as important as safety at home. Just how dangerous the U.S. workplace is can be gauged by referring to Figure 3-12. The data show that the on-the-job death rate has been falling for some 30 or more years. Even so, in 1996, the death rate reveals an average of four of every 100,000 workers were killed on the job. On top of those 4,800 deaths, 3.9 million workers suffered disabling injuries. Some jobs are clearly more dangerous than others, with the highest accident rate found in construction. There is also wide variation from country to country, with the United Kingdom having the lowest rate of fatal accidents and Portugal the highest.

While the workplace can never be made perfectly safe, the risk of injury and death can be reduced if employers spend more money on safety equipment and procedures. Alternatively, employers can offer higher wages to compensate workers for workplace dangers. Employers will be forced to pay higher wages when jobs are dan-

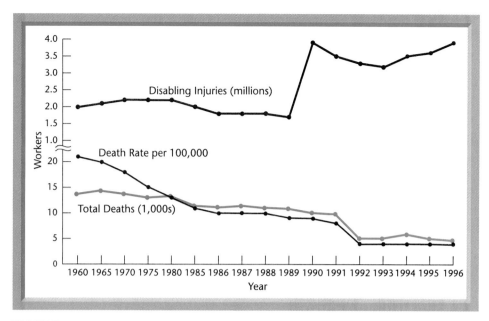

FIGURE 3-12 **Workers killed or disabled on the job, 1960–1996.**

Source: 1998 Statistical Abstract of the U.S., Table No. 705.

gerous because higher wages are necessary to attract a sufficient supply of workers who take more risks. In deciding how much safety to provide, employers compare the marginal cost of making the workplace safer with the marginal benefit of being able to pay lower wages. Indirectly, then, the demand for safety by workers costs those workers lower wages.

In some cases, workers are poorly informed about or choose to ignore the riskiness of their jobs. This can lead to the demand by workers for workplace safety to understate the true benefits of that safety, and thus cause firms to undertake too few safety measures. If so, government regulators might step in to estimate the efficient amount of safety and force firms to achieve that amount. However, it is difficult to estimate these marginal costs and benefits of extra safety, especially since different workers have different preferences when it comes to how much risk they are willing to accept in exchange for extra income.

The Occupational Safety and Health Administration (OSHA) provides an extensive set of safety regulations for America's workplaces. Unfortunately, it is impractical for government safety regulations to be tailored to the wants of different groups of workers. The result is that both firms and workers often complain about rigid work rules and safety measures. However, throwing the rules out risks that the marketplace might surprise workers with just how unsafe their jobs can be.

There is an ongoing controversy over whether government should cut back its regulation of workplace safety. If it did, government could still make information on workplace safety available to workers so that they could choose more efficiently. On the other hand, backers of government safety regulation point out that their workers and firms may not have the expertise necessary to evaluate information about safety.

OSHA's Web site is at **http://www.osha.gov**

The idea is that experts in government would evaluate the information and make choices more efficiently than most workers could do themselves. Whether that ideal is adequately translated into practice is a source of much argument.

Valuing the Chances We Are Willing to Take

Government must also make choices about our safety in many of the other things it does. For example, lowering speed limits saves lives but costs time. As individuals, we accept some risk to our lives by getting on high-speed roadways. We want government to allow us to risk life and limb in this manner, but within limits. We don't want everyone driving 90 mph because that would be too dangerous. So government must estimate what speed limit below 90 mph we most prefer. To do so, it finds guidance in market prices. Prices in the marketplace allow government to infer how much it's worth to us to avoid the risk of death.

One way for government to proceed is to look at data from the workplace that show how much extra wages we require to accept extra risk, and then extrapolate that to estimate the value of a *statistical life*, which is no one's life in particular, but which can let us know how much it's worth to lower the odds that a person will be killed. For example, suppose that the risk of death among police officers is increased by one in one hundred over the risk of death among security guards. Also suppose that police officers are paid $10,000 in additional income to accept that risk. What value do police officers place on their lives in this example? An approximate answer can be had by dividing the additional income by the additional risk. The value that officers themselves place on their lives is $1,000,000 (10,000/.01).

Another way of looking at this calculation is to note that each group of 100 police officers employed costs $1,000,000 in extra wages ($10,000 multiplied by 100 police). That $1,000,000 in wage costs "pays" for the death of one police officer. Since no individual officer knows for sure who will die, the $1,000,000 reflects the value of a statistical life.

Let's use this concept of a statistical life in our speed-limit example. Specifically, imagine increasing the speed limit to the point that one additional traffic fatality can be expected per year. If the value to the time that we save by that increased speed limit is more than $1 million per year, we'd want it done. Otherwise, we wouldn't. This same type of process can be used to decide how safe to make building codes, pharmaceuticals, air traffic control, and a host of other things that government produces or regulates.

In essence, the idea is for government to infer the value of safety to us based on our market choices about safety, and then to apply that information in choosing for us in instances in which markets either do not exist or fail to function efficiently. Government does not always do this process well, with some regulations implying a value of life that is many times higher than the value implied by other regulations. But the presence of market prices at least helps to guide policy in the right direction.

Public or Private Routes to Safety?

In closing, we note that there is often controversy over when safety should be ensured by government regulation and when it should be left to the marketplace. Few people would question that government must be involved in some safety decisions, such as in the specifications to which highway bridges are constructed. However, when it comes to products bought and sold in the private marketplace for private usage, opinions differ.

For example, have you ever noticed the ever-present seal of approval from Underwriter's Laboratories (UL) on electrical products? The UL seal does not come from the federal government, but from a private organization created to verify safety. Manufacturers of products have an incentive to obtain the UL seal because consumers value safe wiring, and expect that electrical products passed by Underwriter's Laboratories are safe.

The marketplace would provide similar means of assuring the quality of meat and other food products were government inspectors to abandon their jobs. Before there were government meat inspections, for example, people would rely upon the reputation of the butcher shop or grocery store to ensure safe meats. Stores that could not maintain a reputation for quality would lose customers and go out of business. In the process, though, some customers would get sick. Thus, customers would usually prefer to see a stamp of approval by inspectors they trust. Laws that require government food inspections mean that customers don't even have to look. Thus, unless government inspectors cost too much, don't do a good job, or intrude into places that they are not needed, inspection laws usually seem like a pretty smooth way to go.

Prospecting for New Insights

1. One of the safest vehicles for vehicle occupants is the Chevrolet Suburban sport utility vehicle. Although popular, many people drive something other than a Suburban. Is this fact evidence that people do not care about safety? Explain.

2. Conduct a personal safety audit. List the safety-related products you see in your home, car, and workplace. Can you justify additional purchases of safety equipment for your home and car? If you think more safety equipment is needed at your workplace, how would you convince your boss to spend more money on safety?

PRICE CHANGES: POLITICAL PRICES AND ELASTICITY

A Look Ahead

IF YOU'VE EVER poured milk over cereal or held a minimum wage job, you have experience with political prices. The price of the milk, the cost of the grain to make the cereal, and your hourly wage were changed from their market levels because of government action. In other words, not all price changes come about because of changes in supply and demand, as seen in chapter 3. In some cases political prices—those that are changed because of government action—replace market prices. This chapter first looks at laws that move prices away from their market equilibrium values. Sometimes the effect is to harm the very people that are intended to be helped. The chapter also looks at elasticity, which is the responsiveness of consumers and producers to price changes. The relationship between elasticity and revenue changes is discussed.

The first Exploration shows how insurance distorts incentives by changing the price of health care to patients, but not the costs to providers. The results have made health care a political issue that has been revisited over and over by legislators. In the second Exploration you will see how the drug war raises prices and spending in markets for illegal drugs, and thus brings about an increase in crime.

As you are **Surveying Economic Principles** you will arrive at an ability to

❏ interpret why rent controls that are designed to help tenants can hurt them over time;

❏ explain how minimum wage laws raise wages but make finding a job harder;

❏ identify the advantages of reducing agricultural subsidies;

❏ discuss how elasticity is used to measure the responsiveness of quantity to changes in price;

❏ describe the conditions under which a price change would increase, decrease, or not change a firm's revenues.

While **Exploring Issues** you will be able to

❏ explain why people both desire and fear government involvement in health care;

❏ discuss how the war on drugs increases crime associated with drug use.

Terms Along the Way

Surveying Economic Principles

Political Prices—Holding Prices Down

To learn more about the OPEC countries' economies, visit a U.S. Department of Energy Web site featuring an OPEC fact sheet at **http://www.eia.doe.gov/emeu/cabs/opec.html**

price ceiling: a law that restricts price from rising above a certain level.

price freeze: a law that restricts a wide array of prices from rising above their current levels.

rent controls: a price ceiling on apartment rents.

Among the many Web sites referring to rent controls are two Web sites that feature opposing views of the effects. These are located at **http://www.nycrgb.com/Collins.html** and **http://www.ncpa.org/pd/regulat/pdreg/pdreg9.html**

In 1973, the Organization of Petroleum Exporting Countries (OPEC) succeeded in restricting oil supplies to Western countries. The OPEC action caused a dramatic spike upward in energy prices. In response, Congress enacted temporary gasoline price controls, which capped price increases. This action caused fuel shortages, with drivers losing much time and patience in long lines at the gas pumps. While sometimes ignored in the political process, economic analysis can be used to forestall such problems.

The problem of gasoline shortages and wasteful gas lines has little to do with gasoline and much to do with the economics of holding prices below the market equilibrium. A law that restricts price from rising above a certain level is called a price ceiling. Price ceilings cause numerous problems, which are magnified when ceilings are imposed broadly under price freezes, where price freezes prohibit a wide array of prices from rising. The transition back to market prices is often quite difficult. For example, consider a policy that continues in effect today in some U.S. cities and many others worldwide. That is the policy of rent controls, which limit rent increases to below what the market would bear.

Promoting Affordable Housing—Are Rent Controls the Answer?

With rising populations in competition for scarce land, major cities sometimes choose rent controls as a way to insulate tenants from higher housing costs. Rent controls hold the monthly price of rental housing to below its equilibrium level. Price tries to rise, but bumps up against the rent control ceiling.

Figure 4-1 illustrates a housing market with a rent control law. For rent controls to be meaningful, the ceiling price must be set below the market equilibrium price, P^*. The result is a housing shortage, as labeled, in which less housing is offered, Q_S, but more housing is demanded, Q_D, than would have been the case at the market equilibrium quantity of Q^*. The amount of housing actually rented will be the lesser of the two, Q_S, with the difference between that amount and the quantity demanded equaling the shortage.

The demand for rental housing slopes downward. As rents rise, young adults become more hesitant about leaving home to set out on their own. Other people choose to share rental homes and apartments with roommates. How many roommates they choose depends on how high rents go. Still others live on their own, but rent smaller and less desirable quarters than they would have preferred.

The supply of rental housing slopes upward, even in the short run before new construction has a chance to occur. Do you believe this? If your town has a special event that attracts an unusually large number of tourists, look around to see what happens. Perhaps the special event is when the leaves change color in the fall. Perhaps it is winter ski season. In New Orleans, it is Mardi Gras; in Louisville, Derby Week. During these events, some permanent residents move out and lease their

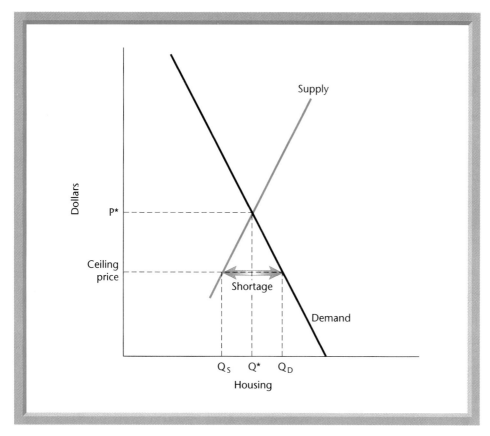

FIGURE 4-1   **Rent controls create housing shortages. The lower the ceiling price, the greater the shortage.**

homes to out-of-town visitors. Others partition off their homes or rent out extra rooms. In Atlanta, for example, some homeowners picked up an extra $500 per day per bedroom during the 1996 Olympics. In these ways, even without new construction, the quantity of rental housing supplied rises in response to higher prices.

Rent controls sound good to tenants. They do benefit tenants first, but not all and not for long. Initially, tenants see no noticeable change except lower rents. Later they see deterioration in the quality of their apartments. After all, with below-market prices, landlords have every incentive to skimp on maintenance and no incentive to build new rental housing. New York City has seen rent-controlled housing crumble for decades. Taking first prize, though, is Paris, France. Paris has had some rent controls in place for over 200 years. The rent-controlled apartment houses in Paris have seen little modernization in that time, with few apartment units containing their own plumbing facilities. In the rent-controlled period between 1914 and 1948, almost no new rental housing was constructed in all of France.

Tenants often have few alternatives. When a significant portion of a city's residential land is taken up with rent-controlled housing, that makes other land more scarce and able to command higher rents. This effect shows up in a dramatic difference between cheap controlled rents and expensive uncontrolled rents. Tenants are stuck—they can't afford to move.

Rent controls also promote discrimination. Landlords can pick and choose among a great many applicants and need not rent to the first person in line. The law allows landlords to discriminate on the basis of such factors as reliability, responsibility, and references. They are legally entitled to reject poor credit risks, as many students are perceived to be. Who can prove differently if landlords also discriminate on the illegal basis of race, creed, gender, or handicap?

With all the problems of rent controls, why are they enacted in the first place? In short, the answer is that there are many more tenants than landlords and that many tenants are ignorant of the long-term consequences of rent control. Others plan on buying houses or moving out of town before the consequences of rent controls get serious. In the meantime, tenants gain lower rents.

Although rent controls do great damage over time, they are always hard to remove, and for good reason. The longer rent controls are in place, the more the housing supply shrinks, as lack of maintenance leads some apartments to deteriorate beyond repair. This is reflected by a leftward shift in supply. Likewise, demand shifts to the right as populations increase over time. The result is an increasing shortage of rent-controlled housing, as shown in Figure 4-2.

Unfortunately, were rent controls to be removed, rents would initially skyrocket to far above where they would have been had rent controls never been imposed. Such an equilibrium is labeled P** in Figure 4-2.

Builders must be convinced that rent controls are a thing of the past before they will invest in much new construction. New construction would cause supply to shift to the right and rents to fall. In the interim, however, sensible tenants would not vote for immediate draconian rent increases. Hopes that rents will drop and housing quality will improve somewhere down the line hardly seem persuasive to someone struggling to meet next month's rent.

Government need not resort to rent controls to accomplish its housing goal. One way for government to ensure affordable housing and avoid the problems brought about by rent controls is to identify the needy and assign them housing vouchers. Housing vouchers are government grants that the recipient can spend only on housing. Thus, even though the price of rental housing may be high, housing vouchers can bring it within reach of impoverished tenants.

housing vouchers: government grants that the recipient can spend only on housing.

In contrast to rent controls, housing vouchers cost the government money. Rent controls also cost money, but the cost is borne by landlords, and by tenants in the form of lower quality housing that is hard to find. The budgetary cost of housing vouchers has kept them from being more widely adopted.

QuickCheck _____

Using supply and demand analysis, explain the effect of housing vouchers in the market for rental housing.

Answer: Housing vouchers represent an increase in income that can be spent only on housing. This shifts the demand for rental housing to the right, which increases both equilibrium rent and the equilibrium amount of housing rented. Over time, the increase in rents attracts new construction. As this new construction shifts supply to the right, rents fall. If the increased construction causes higher land prices, however, equilibrium apartment rents will not return to their prevoucher levels.

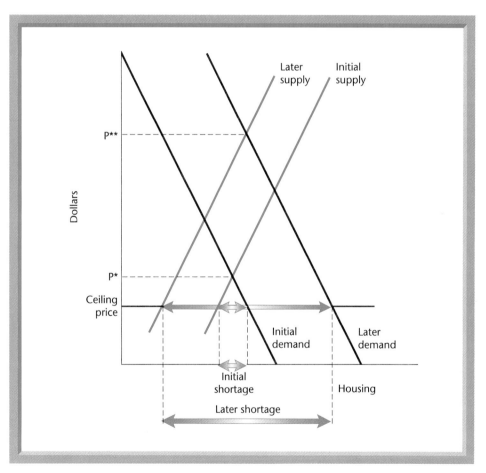

FIGURE 4-2   **Rent controls increase housing shortages over time because of the combination of the increase in demand and the decrease in supply.**

OBSERVATION POINT:
Trump Tower—Shelter for the Homeless?

To see 10 tips from Donald Trump on making a comeback, visit the Web site at **http://www. geocities.com/ Eureka/2949/ donaldcomeback. html**

From the lavish heights of Trump Tower, pedestrians strolling through Central Park and midtown Manhattan seem little more than tiny specks. It would be easy to forget that these are human beings with dreams and problems of their own—some even without homes. Donald Trump did not forget.

To build Trump Tower, the preexisting rent-controlled apartment building on the site had to be demolished. It would violate the law to simply evict the tenants in order to make way for higher-priced housing. Instead, tenants were presented with generous buyout offers which most, but not all, accepted. This left a building that was partially occupied and thus could not be torn down.

What was "The Donald" to do? Rather than let the precious apartment space go to waste while so many New Yorkers roamed the streets, Donald Trump generously planned to open the building's doors to the homeless. No charge! Perhaps not surprisingly, the remaining paying tenants were not well disposed toward their prospective neighbors. Negotiations progressed quickly. The renters agreed to Donald's buyout offers, and the building was demolished. Trump Tower was born.

Anti-gouging Laws, Ticket Scalping, and Price Freezes

price gouging: the practice of raising prices to exploit temporary surges in demand; often illegal.

Price gouging is the practice of hiking up prices to exploit temporary surges in demand. Many municipalities prohibit this behavior with anti-gouging laws, designed to hold prices down in the event of disasters. This practice can cause problems, though, because high prices prevent shortages and allocate sought-after goods to those who value them the most. Profitably high prices also motivate rapid restocking, which means that prices do not stay high for long.

For example, when hurricanes threaten the coastline, oceanfront homeowners seek out plywood to board up their windows. If stores are allowed to raise prices, they have an incentive to send out extra trucks for new supplies. Otherwise, homeowners must scramble to snatch up supplies before the shelves go bare. If homeowners are lucky, stores might use the occasion to generate good will and restock promptly despite the extra costs.

Many municipalities have similar laws prohibiting *ticket scalping*—the practice of buying tickets at the price set by concert promoters and then reselling at whatever the market will bear. In principle, ticket scalping directs goods to their highest-valued uses, thus efficiently allocating seats at concerts, ball games, and other events. As for equity, however, try asking fans of the Rolling Stones or other groups with sold-out performances. Good seats are snared quickly by scalpers, many of whom hire numerous stand-ins to buy up blocks of tickets and then turn a tidy profit.

Price freezes that prohibit increases in most prices are sometimes imposed as a seemingly obvious way to control inflation. However, to the extent that price freezes prevent prices from rising, they result in shortages. The problems with price freezes are merely a wider manifestation of the problems of price ceilings, such as rent controls. Unfortunately, because the coverage of a price freeze is greater, so too are its problems.

Price freezes are difficult to enforce and not widely used. For example, suppose we freeze the price of candy bars. If candy-bar manufacturers desire to raise prices without breaking the law, all they need do is come out with a variation on their price-controlled products. For example, they might keep price constant, but lower the number of ounces per unit. Alternatively, they might introduce slightly different products to replace the ones that are controlled.

Such strategies are widely adopted whenever price controls take hold. To outlaw those practices would not only freeze prices, but also freeze the mix of products available to the consumer. It would be a bureaucratic nightmare for government to try to distinguish new products that are worth producing from those that merely serve to defeat the price freeze.

OBSERVATION POINT:
A Squeeze on Charmin

In 1971, in an attempt to combat inflation, President Nixon signed a price freeze into law, the last time such action was taken in the United States. Shortly afterward, Canadian paper companies increased the price of wood fiber, which eroded the profits of tissue manufacturers. Johnny Carson, true to his form as host of the "Tonight Show," could not pass up this touchy subject.

In his opening monologue, Johnny joked about toilet paper shortages in New Jersey. Guess what? Even though it had not really been very difficult to find toilet paper in New Jersey, a shortage quickly developed. People rushed to the stores to snatch up all brands of tissue. Manufacturers had no special incentive to restock, so the shelves stayed bare. Thus was the start of the Great Toilet Paper Squeeze of 1971!

Black Markets as a Safety Valve

Any time government tries to hold prices below market equilibrium, it provides profit opportunities to those willing to take advantage of them. **Black market** activity is said to occur when goods are bought and sold illegally. Under rent controls, for example, it is not uncommon to hear of prospective tenants bribing landlords for an apartment. Sometimes this black market may seem somewhat gray, as when the bribes are merely offers of gifts, or agreements to "fix up the place."

The black market is nothing more than the free market trying to assert itself when government has attempted to influence that market through taxes or regulation. Regulation could take the form of price controls or the outright ban of market activities. In either case, it is hard to keep willing buyers and sellers from negotiating mutually beneficial deals.

Governments often owe a debt of gratitude to black markets that temper destructive policies. For example, Cubans rely heavily on their black markets. If they had to depend upon government rations, they could not obtain enough food to survive. Similarly, the shelves were often bare in the formerly communist countries of Asia and Eastern Europe. These countries relied in large measure on the industriousness of merchants in the black market to keep their economies going.

black market: an illegal market, which could be for illegal goods or for legal goods when buyers and sellers seek to avoid government taxes or regulations.

The Better Business Bureau warns against black market Freon at **http://www.bbb. org/library/freon. html**

For example, the government of the former Soviet Union legalized private for-profit agricultural production on approximately 3 percent of its arable land. Despite that tiny acreage, this market-driven component of agriculture produced almost one quarter of the country's entire agricultural output.

Political Prices—Propping Prices Up

Although consumers are better off when prices are low, producers prefer them high. Both groups often turn to government for help. If politics dictates propping up prices, government can establish a **price floor**, also termed a **price support**, which sets a minimum price that producers are guaranteed to receive. One way to implement a price floor is for government to agree to buy at that floor price. This approach, used in agricultural price supports, means that taxpayers buy the surplus production that the price floor causes.

Alternatively, government can support prices without buying up any surplus quantity. Rather, it can simply forbid buyers from paying less than some price minimum. Minimum wage laws exemplify this approach. Both methods are discussed in the sections that follow.

Agricultural Price Supports—Economics and Politics in Conflict

The U.S. Department of Agriculture maintains a Web site at **http://www. usda.gov/**

Only 2 percent of the U. S. labor force currently derives a living from agriculture. It is therefore surprising that agricultural price supports have been in place in the United States from the Great Depression through most of the 1990s. With passage of the *Freedom to Farm Act* in the spring of 1996, the stage was set for the possible permanent elimination of U.S. agricultural price supports.

The Freedom to Farm Act phases out agricultural price supports over time, with the timetable varying from one agricultural commodity to another. Instead, farmers are to receive subsidies based on need, rather than on crop prices. The Freedom to Farm Act is an experiment that is scheduled to expire by 2003, when agricultural price supports will be reestablished unless additional legislation is passed. There is good reason for this experiment, as this section reveals.

Agricultural price supports have often been justified on two counts. One is that they sustain the lifestyle of the family farm, an American tradition. However, even with price supports, family farming continued to decline. Also, a disproportionate amount of price support payments went to large farms and agribusiness. The second justification is that price supports are needed to ensure a plentiful supply of food for American consumers. However, this argument does not withstand the logic of economic analysis.

Figure 4-3 shows the effects of an agricultural price support, such as for milk, corn, or wheat. By holding price above the equilibrium, there will be more agricultural production. In other words, the quantity supplied, Q_S, is higher than the market equilibrium quantity of Q^*. However, the quantity demanded, Q_D, is lower, leading to a surplus as shown in Figure 4-3. Thus, while more is produced, less is purchased.

Agricultural surpluses have cost U.S. taxpayers an average of several billion dollars annually. In 1998, for example, the federal government spent $12 billion on agri-

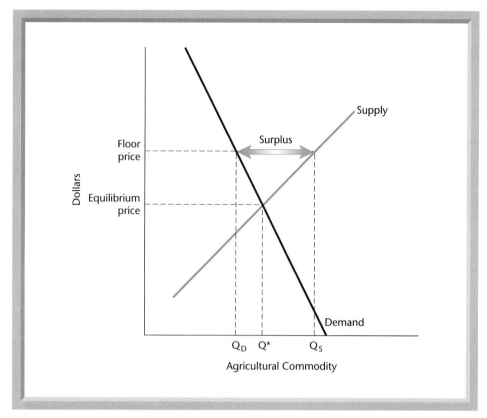

FIGURE 4-3 **Price supports create costly surpluses.** The more elastic are supply and demand, the greater the surpluses will be.

culture, most of which went toward price support programs. In short, eliminating agricultural price supports saves tax dollars and can be expected to cause American consumers to pay less and buy more.

Government must prevent the surplus commodities it buys from being distributed to people who would otherwise purchase that product in the marketplace. To do otherwise would merely mean more of a surplus that government would be forced to buy, because those who received from government would buy less from farmers.

One option is to give the surplus quantity away in a relatively unpalatable form, such as by turning excess milk into powdered milk. Another option is to export the surplus in a manner that does not compete with other agricultural exports. For example, foreign aid to impoverished countries might work, to the extent that the aid does not supplant other food imports from the donor country. However, recipient countries often fear becoming too dependent upon food aid based on unpredictable agricultural surpluses. The dependency arises when farmers in those countries are driven out of business by the low food prices that years of plentiful food aid brings.

There are other options. To rid itself of surplus butter, for example, Denmark offers it for a reduced price if the buyer agrees to export that butter by baking it into

Danish butter cookies. Still another common practice is to store surplus commodities until they are no longer edible and then discard them. It's like the fate of leftover food in a refrigerator!

However government disposes of agricultural surpluses, it has paid much more for these goods than they are worth in the uses to which they are put. It would be significantly cheaper merely to identify needy farmers and write them checks, as pointed out by backers of the Freedom to Farm Act. To some extent, government had indeed written checks to needy farmers. Government has actually paid some farmers not to produce—to put aside some acreage in order to eliminate the need for government to buy the output. In response, until government officials caught on, clever farmers employed such strategies as reducing acreage by planting every other row. The extra sunlight led to higher crop yields, which partially defeated the purpose of leaving aside acreage.

It makes more economic sense to pay farmers not to produce than to squander resources on production that will be wasted. Still, such direct payments may seem too *transparent*, meaning that it becomes obvious to voters what is going on. Agricultural lobbyists would prefer that voters not focus on this aspect of the program and thus do not advocate the mere writing of checks to farmers. The 1996 Freedom to Farm Act took a middle approach by allowing payments to needy farmers, but without restricting acreage. Whether U.S. agricultural price supports will be reestablished in the future remains an open question.

The Minimum Wage

The U.S. Department of Labor oversees the administration of the minimum wage. Its home page is located at **http://www. dol.gov/**

Since its enactment in the 1930s, the minimum wage has established itself as an American tradition. We all remember that first job. We remember how hard we worked to find it, and how we deserved no less than that minimum wage for the work we did. For many, the job served as a springboard toward great success in life. Backing for the minimum wage also arises out of American compassion for the downtrodden. Americans cherish the notion that no one should be exploited and, on the face of it, the minimum wage seems like a good protection against such exploitation. However, there are problems.

People support the minimum wage because it increases the price of relatively unskilled labor. That is also the source of its problems. The higher wage means that more people are willing to work. These extra workers include many college and college-bound students already on the road to success. However, the higher wage also means that fewer jobs are offered. Fast food restaurants, car washes, and other businesses get by with fewer people, but train and work them harder. They also may replace some labor with capital, such as automated dishwashers and car-washing equipment.

The result is a surplus of labor, or shortage of jobs, depending upon how you look at it. The least employable—those with poor language, computational, or social skills—are out of luck. They cannot get that first job they need to start climbing the ladder of success. They cannot join the so-called jobs club—it has become too exclusive. For example, a recent survey of labor economists showed that they predict a 2 percent fall in teenage employment for every 10 percent increase in the minimum wage. In addition, the teens who are employed may also be different, less needy people than before.

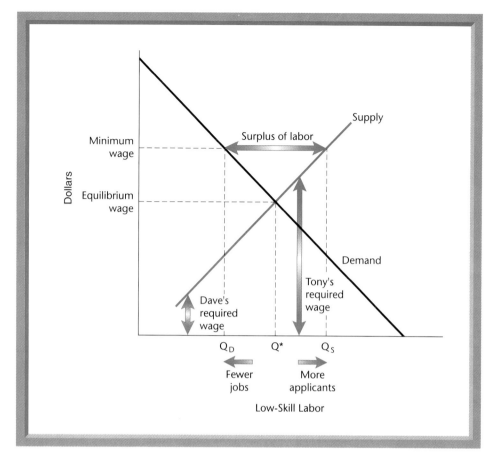

FIGURE 4-4 **Minimum wage laws make it tough to find a job,** especially for the least-experienced and least-skilled job seekers. The higher wage causes fewer jobs and more applicants. Some of the new applicants (such as Tony) take jobs from others who need the jobs more desperately (such as Dave).

Figure 4-4 illustrates these effects, showing how minimum wage laws increase the number of people seeking low-skill work while decreasing the number of jobs available. For example, Tony would not have worked for the equilibrium wage. With a minimum wage, however, Tony might wind up taking Dave's job, even though Dave would have been willing to work for less.

Interestingly, as was the case with rent controls, minimum wage requirements promote discrimination, because they remove the economic cost of that discrimination. With numerous applicants for each job opening, each coming at the same wage, employers can pick and choose as they wish. It would be quite difficult to prove if they choose to discriminate.

For example, is it a coincidence that unemployment rates are so high among African-American teenagers in America's inner cities? In 1998, the unemployment rate for black male teenagers was 30.1 percent, more than six times the rate for the general population, and more than twice the rate for white male teenagers. Perhaps a number of minimum-wage employers chose to locate in areas in which the labor force was more in keeping with their ethnic preferences or perhaps it was merely that inner city neighborhoods are too risky. Either way, the minimum wage law prevents these employers from being attracted to inner city neighborhoods by lower wages and prevents numerous African-American youth from getting their first job.

There are alternatives to the minimum wage that target the problem of low wages without controlling price. One alternative is to subsidize the earnings of low-income workers. Indeed, such a subsidy, called the earned income tax credit, is already embedded in the U.S. personal income tax. The drawback is that earnings subsidies come at a high budgetary cost, because they reduce government tax collections. Minimum wage laws also have high costs, but these costs are borne by businesses, consumers, and those unable to find a job. However, the costs of minimum wage laws do not show up on the government budget.

OBSERVATION POINT:
Snatching Hope from the Homeless

The homeless often carry a disturbing sign—"Will Work for Food." While the claim is often fraudulent, many of the homeless are indeed eager to find steady work. More often than not, however, there are no steady jobs offered to them.

Lack of a home is itself an impediment to finding a job. For example, employers may worry about the employee's personal health and hygiene, and about whether or not the employee is a drifter. For these reasons, potential employers are usually unwilling to pay the minimum wage to the homeless. There are too many other applicants with fewer problems. While employers would be willing to offer jobs at lower wages, that would be illegal.

The homeless are thus caught in the grips of a political vise. Minimum wages are one side of this vise. On the other side, many of the "flophouses" that once offered cheap nightly lodging have closed down. The residents could not afford rent increases that would be needed to pay the expense of renovation. The law demands such renovation to provide accessibility for the handicapped. It also requires security from hazards, such as fires, lead in pipes and paint, and asbestos. Together with minimum wages, however, those well-intentioned policies block access to housing for the very people who need it most, the homeless.

Political Prices Around the World

Both price ceilings and supports are an international phenomena. While price controls and price freezes have never been in place for very long in the United States, such is not the case in many other countries. For instance, government-set prices were a key feature of the central planning practiced under communism. That fact explains the bare shelves and rationing in the communist countries that was referred to in the preceding paragraphs.

In spite of the problems with price controls, many governments persist in setting prices for political reasons. Generally, these actions apply only to basic necessities. For example, in Mexico the price of tortillas is set by the government under the "tortibono" program that seeks to ensure that tortillas remain affordable to the poor. Tortilla makers are subsidized by the government to keep the tortillas coming off the presses. Many other prices were controlled by the Mexican government in the past, but those controls were removed as Mexico sought the efficiency offered by free markets. Nonetheless, tortilla prices were not freed up because of fears of a political backlash.

Other countries also show a history of price controls at one time or another. For example, in Taiwan the Statute for Salt Administration applies price controls to salt. The price of oil is also regulated in order to provide Taiwanese companies with stable prices on what is an important input in manufacturing. Venezuela pledged to lift its price controls in 1996 as a condition for receiving aid supplied by the International Monetary Fund (IMF). Belarus, a country that once was part of the Soviet Union, made a similar pledge to the IMF for comparable reasons after news reports in 1995 indicated that the country planned to return to price controls on "socially significant" products. Many other instances of flirtations with price controls in various countries could be cited.

The IMF maintains a Web site at **http://www. imf.org/**

Price supports are also prevalent internationally. For example, many countries have had price support programs in place for agriculture. As in the United States, the countries of Western Europe are cutting their price support programs. By contrast, in the countries of Eastern Europe, systems of price supports appear to be emerging as the twentieth century draws to a close and these economies seek to join the ranks of the mixed economies that emphasize markets. Price supports in Eastern Europe appear to be seen as a logical step in the transition from a system of government-owned collective farms to privately owned farms.

Turning toward the minimum wage law, in the United States many states have laws of their own. These laws sometimes set state minimums higher than that set by the federal government. Looking abroad, Canada has a minimum wage law at the federal level that mirrors the minimum wages set by law in each province. Mexico also sets a minimum wage, although it is modest by U.S. and Canadian standards. Many other countries in both the developing and developed worlds have minimum wage laws, including New Zealand, France, and Indonesia. However, not all countries have such laws, preferring to deal with poverty through other more direct government programs. Germany and England are notable in this regard.

Elasticity—Quantity and Revenue Effects of Price Changes

In both the public and private sectors, questions often arise over how significant quantity responses are to price changes. For example, we saw in the previous section that increasing the minimum wage decreased hiring. That raises a number of important issues: First, will hiring decrease a little or a lot? A small decrease in hiring could mean that minimum wage workers as a group receive more income because of the higher wage. However, a large enough decrease in hiring would mean that the group of minimum wage workers would receive less income, since the higher wage can be offset by the reduction in the number hired. Issues such as these can be addressed by considering the concept of elasticity.

elasticity: measures the responsiveness of one thing (Y) to another (X), specifically, the percentage change in Y divided by the percentage change in X.

Elasticity measures the responsiveness of one thing to another. Elasticity is defined with respect to any two variables. Although the names of the variables may change, the formula remains the same, as follows:

$$\frac{\text{Percentage change in one variable}}{\text{Percentage change in other variable}}$$

For example, if the one variable changes by 20 percent in response to a 10 percent change in the other variable, the elasticity equals 2, obtained by dividing 20 percent by 10 percent.

Elasticity has a broad range of application. Farmers might be interested in the elasticity of plant growth with respect to fertilizer application. Perhaps you would be interested in the elasticity of your class grade with respect to study time. If that elasticity is high, a small percentage increase in your study time would lead to a large percentage increase in your grade. You would be well rewarded to study more. In contrast, if the elasticity is low, the two variables are not much related.

The Elasticity of Demand

elasticity of demand: measures the responsiveness of quantity demanded to price, specifically, the percentage change in quantity demanded divided by the percentage change in price, expressed as an absolute value.

inelastic: refers to either demand or supply, where the value of the elasticity is less than 1.

In economics, some elasticities are more significant than others. The most significant is the price elasticity of demand, which is often abbreviated as simply elasticity of demand. The elasticity of demand measures the responsiveness of quantity demanded to price. Its formula is given by the percentage change in quantity demanded, divided by the percentage change in price. Since price and quantity demanded are inversely related, the computation of the elasticity of demand will always be negative. For convenience, economists often refer to the elasticity of demand by its absolute value, meaning that the negative sign is dropped.

In absolute value, the elasticity of demand can fall within three ranges. These ranges, summarized in Figure 4-5, are as follows:

1. **Inelastic demand:** Elasticity of demand lies between 0 and 1; in this range, the quantity demanded is relatively unresponsive to price.

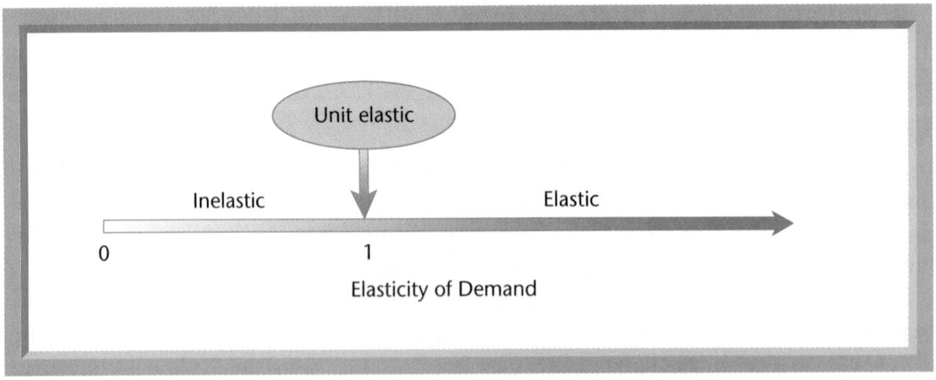

FIGURE 4-5 **Price elasticity of demand** can range from zero to infinity (in absolute value).

2. **Unit elastic demand:** Elasticity of demand = 1; in this range, the quantity demanded changes proportionally to changes in price.

3. **Elastic demand:** Elasticity of demand is greater than 1; in this range, the quantity demanded is relatively responsive to changes in price.

unit elastic: refers to either demand or supply, where the value of the elasticity equals 1.

elastic: refers to either demand or supply, where the value of the elasticity exceeds 1.

In general, the more substitutes there are for a product, or the greater the fraction of a person's budget it takes to buy the product, the greater will be its elasticity of demand. Thus, demand for Domino's Pizza is quite elastic, because there are many close substitutes, including other brands of pizza and other types of fast food. Demand for drinking water is quite inelastic, because it takes a tiny fraction of the budget and there are no close substitutes.

Demand for college textbooks is inelastic, meaning that even significant increases in the price of a textbook will not deter students from buying copies. The reason is that textbooks are tied to courses. Once students register for the courses, there are no longer any close substitute for the courses' texts. Moreover, since a bad text can conflict with good teaching, instructors who assign texts give first priority to their contents rather than to their prices.

Consumer spending translates into revenue for sellers. That revenue equals the quantity sold multiplied by the price received. In other words

$$\text{Total revenue} = \text{price} \times \text{quantity}$$

Most people assume that when price increases, sellers earn more revenue. However, this assumption is often not true, because quantity demanded falls any time price rises. An increase in price will bring in more revenue only if demand is inelastic, meaning that the fall in quantity demanded is less significant than the rise in price. In contrast, were demand to be elastic, the quantity demanded would be quite responsive to price. Any increase in price would cause a proportionally greater fall in the quantity sold and thus would lower total revenue. Table 4-1 summarizes the effects on total revenue of a price change.

For example, if demand is elastic, the quantity demanded is very responsive to price changes. The effect of lower prices is to increase purchases so much that revenues actually rise. This result has occurred in many industries, ranging from air travel to computing. When computing power was very expensive 20 years ago, the revenues of the computer industry were a mere fraction of current revenues, now that computing power is cheap. This illustrates another point as follows: **The longer the time period involved, the greater will be the elasticity of demand.** Time lets

TABLE 4-1   The Effect of a Change in Price Upon Revenues

Change in Price	Effect upon Sales Revenues
Higher Price	If demand is inelastic, revenue rises.
	If demand is unit elastic, revenue remains constant.
	If demand is elastic, revenue falls.
Lower Price	If demand is inelastic, revenue falls.
	If demand is unit elastic, revenue remains constant.
	If demand is elastic, revenue rises.

people adjust, to substitute toward goods that become relatively less expensive and away from those that become relatively more expensive.

The elasticity of demand will vary along most demand curves. Along a downward-sloping, straight-line demand curve, the rule is that demand is unit elastic at the midpoint, elastic above the midpoint, and inelastic below the midpoint. Remember, the lower is the point on a straight-line demand curve, the lower will be its elasticity. The reason is that, when we move down the demand curve, any **percentage** change in price becomes larger relative to the corresponding **percentage** change in quantity. This relationship is shown in Figure 4-6.

 QuickCheck _____

Wally's Water Works sells water. Wally has set the price of water at $5 per pail, but wonders if he should charge less. If Wally faces an elasticity of demand equal to 1/3, why would he regret lowering his price? What if the elasticity is 3?

Answer: An elasticity of demand equal to 1/3 means that demand is inelastic. If Wally lowers his price, his increase in sales will not be enough to make up for the loss of revenue per unit. In other words, keeping the price at $5 per pail means that he sells fewer pails but makes more total revenue than if the price is lower. In contrast, an elasticity of demand equal to 3 would mean that Wally faces an elastic demand for his water. In that case, a price reduction would lead to such a large percentage increase in sales that Wally's revenues would rise.

OBSERVATION POINT:
Sin Taxes—Is It Morality We're After?

Cigarettes and alcohol are taxed at much higher rates than virtually any other good. The reason is partly because these "goods" are seen as bad. Just as important, it is because the elasticity of demand is low relative to that of other goods.

If the elasticity were high, people could more easily switch to other goods with lower tax rates. That would cut into tax revenues, which is exactly what happened after Congress passed five luxury taxes in 1990. Higher tax rates on yachts and other luxuries actually brought in less revenue, because so many people refused to buy these items at the higher prices the tax implied. Four of the five luxury taxes were repealed for this reason—demand was too elastic. Because elasticity is higher at higher prices, the amount of extra revenue government could collect by raising alcohol and tobacco taxes is also limited. Proposals to finance health care through taxes on alcohol and tobacco overlook this fact of economic life.

Cigarettes and alcoholic beverages are not the only goods with low elasticities of demand. Milk has a low elasticity of demand, and yet milk is not taxed at all in most places. It seems that the so-called sin aspect of smoking and drinking means that the public, even smokers and drinkers, are less willing to fight higher taxes on those

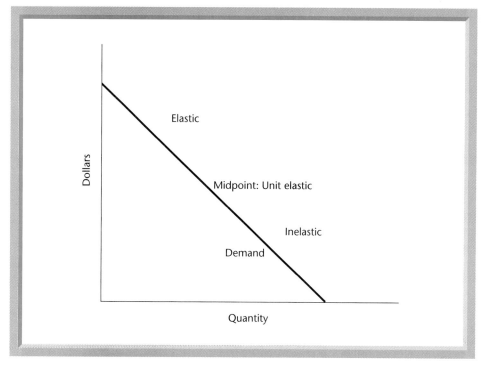

FIGURE 4-6 **Along a straight-line demand curve, the elasticity of demand equals 1 at the midpoint, is higher above that point, and lower below it.**

items. Moreover, smoking and drinking can have some harmful effects on others, whereas what could be more wholesome than milk?

A caution is in order about taxing sin. If goods are singled out for high taxes because they are bad, it is important to figure out just how bad. Let the punishment fit the crime.

The Extremes of Demand Elasticity

There are three extreme cases in which elasticity is constant throughout the demand curve. These are shown as cases 1 through 3 in Figure 4-7. Case 1 depicts a demand that is *perfectly inelastic*, meaning that the quantity demanded will not depend upon price and so the elasticity equals zero. While demand for some goods is highly inelastic, there aren't any goods that do not show at least some respon-siveness to price. For example, demand for insulin or certain pharmaceutical drugs is highly inelastic. However, to the extent that patients must actually pay more when price increases for these necessities, they will skimp on their dosages and thus buy less.

Case 2 depicts a demand that is unit elastic throughout. This shape is referred to as a rectangular hyperbola, because any rectangle drawn under that demand curve will have the same area. Because demand relates price and quantity, when price is multiplied by quantity, the result is a rectangle. The area of the rectangle equals total

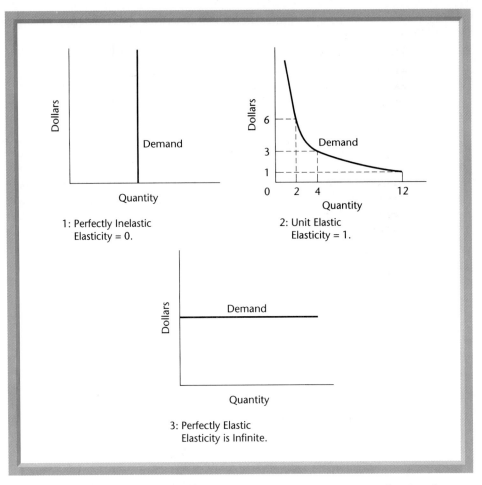

FIGURE 4-7 **These three special cases hold elasticity constant at each point along demand.**

revenue. Thus total revenue does not change in response to changes in price, as is necessary for demand to be unit elastic. In this example, whether the price is $1, $3, or $6, the total revenue is $12, which is the area of either the 1×12, 3×4, or 6×2 rectangle.

For demand to be unit elastic throughout, the same amount will be spent, no matter the price. This scenario occurs only if the buyers have a preset budget that must be fully spent. For example, Congress authorizes a certain amount of money to be spent filling the strategic petroleum reserve each year. The total amount authorized is always spent, without regard to the price of oil.

Case 3 depicts a horizontal demand curve that is *perfectly elastic* throughout. In other words, the slightest increase in price over some threshold price leads to a complete loss of sales. At any price at or below this threshold, unlimited quantities could be sold. This demand is a close approximation to demand facing the firm in the competitive marketplace, in which there is a very large number of other firms. **The**

firm's demand curve in the competitive marketplace is perfectly elastic at the market price.

For example, if you are a Nebraska wheat farmer, you would sell none of your grain if you price it at even one penny more than the market price set by the interaction of buyers and sellers in the commodity exchanges of Chicago. At or below that market price, however, you could sell all you could produce, no matter how large your farm. A firm with perfectly elastic demand like this is called a *price taker.*

The Elasticity of Supply

The elasticity of supply measures the responsiveness of quantity supplied to price. Its formula is given by the percentage change in quantity supplied divided by the percentage change in price. Since price and quantity supplied are directly related to each other, the elasticity of supply will always be positive. The elasticity of supply can fall within the following three ranges:

1. **Inelastic supply:** Elasticity of supply lies between 0 and 1; in this range, the quantity supplied is relatively unresponsive to price.
2. **Unit elastic supply:** Elasticity of supply equals 1; in this range, the quantity supplied changes proportionally to changes in price.
3. **Elastic supply:** Elasticity of supply is greater than 1; in this range, the quantity supplied is relatively responsive to changes in price.

Contrast the description of elasticity of supply and that of elasticity of demand. Note that, with the exception of substituting supply for demand, the definitions are identical.

SUMMARY

- For the sake of equity, government often seeks to change free-market prices. Unfortunately, because price signals are basic to how markets operate, changing these signals sacrifices market efficiency.
- Price ceilings hold price below the market equilibrium, resulting in shortages. The lower the price ceiling is set by government, the greater the shortage that results.
- Rent controls are one example of price ceilings. Whenever rent controls are present, the incentive to provide new rental housing is reduced. Other examples of price ceilings are price freezes and antigouging laws.
- When a price is kept higher than the market equilibrium price because of a government price floor, production rises and consumption falls, resulting in a surplus. The higher the price floor, the greater the surplus.
- Agriculture has traditionally benefitted from price floors, although these are scheduled to be phased out by the Freedom to Farm Act. Minimum wage laws are another example of price floors.
- When surpluses or shortages are present, markets are not efficient.
- Elasticity measures responsiveness, such as of quantity supplied or demanded to price changes.

- The elasticity of demand is particularly important for its insight into revenue effects of price changes.
- Inelastic demand, an elasticity less than one, leads to a revenue change in the opposite direction to the price change; elastic demand, an elasticity greater than one, leads to a revenue change in the same direction as the price change; unit elastic demand, an elasticity equal to one, leads to no change in revenue.
- Along a straight-line demand curve, the elasticity changes from one point to the next. The upper half of the demand curve is the elastic range, the lower half, the inelastic range, and the midpoint is the unit elastic point. A vertical demand curve is perfectly inelastic, a horizontal demand curve perfectly elastic.

QUESTIONS AND PROBLEMS

1. Rent controls lower rents for those lucky enough to have apartments. However, there are several problems.

    a. List several problems with rent controls, and briefly note why each occurs.

    b. Given all the problems with rent controls, why are they ever enacted in a democratic society?

2. Goals of efficiency and equity are often in conflict. Using the issue of price gouging as an illustration, explain why it is so difficult to agree on what is equitable.

3. Draw a graph representing the market for unskilled labor. Label the axes of this graph. Suppose that there is a minimum wage in this market that prevents price from reaching equilibrium. Depict the following:

    a. supply;

    b. demand;

    c. price (wage) in the presence of the minimum wage law;

    d. amount of any surplus or shortage (indicate which);

    e. quantity of labor actually employed.

4. Minimum wage laws are an American tradition. Although the laws seem caring and do raise wages for minimum wage labor, there are many problems. List five problems caused by minimum wage laws and briefly indicate why each occurs. Why are minimum wage laws so popular?

5. Suppose price changes by 10 percent. Provide examples of percentage changes in quantity demanded for elastic, inelastic, and unit elastic demand. Draw a graph to go with each case.

6. Comment on the efficiency and equity aspects of ticket scalping.

7. Draw a graph for the case of perfectly elastic demand and another for perfectly inelastic demand. In the case of perfectly inelastic demand, the elasticity equals _____. A firm that has perfectly elastic demand is called a _____ _____.

8. Contrast housing vouchers to rent control as a means of making rental housing more affordable.

Web Exercises

9. a. Using an Internet search engine such as that provided by Yahoo (located at **http://www.yahoo.com**) or Alta Vista (located at **http://www.altavista.com**), perform a separate search for the following terms: **price freeze, price supports,** and **elasticity**. Visit several of the Web sites that your search reveals for each term and observe the context in which each term is used. Explain whether the manner in which the terms are used is consistent with their use in the text.

2. Repeat the above, but this time use a combination of terms that you select from the chapter. To eliminate sites that do not contain all terms, place a plus sign in front of each term you enter, such as +**"rent controls"** +**"housing vouchers"**.

10. Visit the Web site at the U.S. Department of Agriculture [**http://www.usda. gov/**]. Browse the variety of programs offered by following links that interest you. When you have finished exploring, write a short essay entitled: "The USDA: Purposes and Functions."

Visit the Web site for *Economics by Design* at
http://www.prenhall.com/collinge for a Self Quiz over
the topics in this chapter.

EXPLORING ISSUES

Exploration 4-1 Health Care—Issues of Insurance and Its Coverage

Inefficient pricing incentives under health insurance can distort the choices of both patients and providers. Government efforts to widen health care coverage while reining in costs solve some problems but make others worse.

"Is there something wrong here?" you wonder after whiling away the afternoon waiting for your oh-so-brief visit with your doctor. Yet, you know that health care is expensive and that the plan you selected was the cheapest you could find. Somehow, this healthcare market is quite unlike the markets for most goods and services. The big difference is health insurance, which drives a wedge between the prices you pay and those received by healthcare providers. This price wedge affects the incentives facing both you and your doctor, as we will see.

Health Insurance: From Traditional to Managed Care

For both physicians and patients, health insurance alters incentives. This is true of traditional plans in which the patient pays a *copayment*—a percentage of costs over some *deductible* amount. For example, a patient might pay 20 percent of yearly health care expenses after paying a $300 deductible out-of-pocket. Incentives are also altered by other recently popular forms of health insurance.

managed care: patient care with cost control emphasized.

For example, *health maintenance organizations* (HMOs) assign each patient to a primary care physician, who refers the patient to specialists as needed. The patient pays a flat fee of $10 or so per visit. HMOs are the most common form of managed care, so-called because HMOs aim to lower the cost of health care through efficient management practices, with the patient's primary care physician guarding against the insured overusing specialty care. Patients or their employers often select HMOs because they cost less and do not involve the paperwork and reimbursement delays common to the more traditional plans. Health care is provided by the insurance company in exchange for annual premiums, usually paid for by a person's employer. Because the per unit price of health care is reduced to the patient, patients seek more of it, just as the law of demand would suggest. However, this lower price to patients does not mean the price paid to the health providers has fallen. The result is the problem of moral hazard in which the insurance has led to the overconsumption of healthcare services. Figure 4-8 illustrates how moral hazard leads patients to consume too much medical care.

moral hazard: the temptation for consumers to increase their consumption of an insured good or service, such as health care, if insurance covers part of the cost; more generally, a distortion of price signals under insurance plans, resulting in inefficient behavior.

Examples provided by the 50-year-old National Health Service in Great Britain offer clear evidence of moral hazard. Health care in Great Britain is free at the point of service. For that reason, a large proportion of those who make appointments with their family doctors have no good medical reason to do so, resulting in less care for those who really need it. So-called free medical care also delays treatment, sometimes for years if the ailment is placed in a nonurgent category.

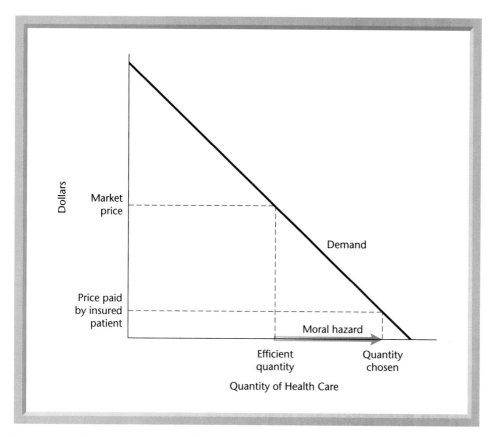

FIGURE 4-8 **Moral hazard results when insurance lowers the price of health care for the recipient, thus causing an increase in the quantity of services demanded.** This figure illustrates moral hazard facing a patient who must pay only 20 percent of actual costs. The result is an increase in consumption of healthcare services relative to what would occur if the patient faced an efficient market price.

The problem of moral hazard also faces healthcare professionals, to the extent that insurance changes their incentives to treat patients. Under the traditional copayment/deductible plan, for example, the incentive is to overtreat patients, because insurance will reimburse for the time and other expenses involved in that treatment. However, an HMO plan primarily rewards its primary care physicians according to how many patients have selected them. The physician has an incentive to sign up as many patients as possible, but treat each one as little as possible. In this case, moral hazard can lead physicians to skimp on the amount of service they provide. For example, a full waiting room minimizes unplanned downtime from canceled appointments.

HMOs require patients to go to their primary care physicians in order to get medical services directly, or through referral to a specialist. The list of approved specialists may also be small, since HMOs usually pay rock-bottom rates for their services. An alternative that allows for greater patient choice is the *preferred provider organization*, or *PPO* for short. The PPO is form of managed care that offers greater flexibility to the patient in terms of what physicians to see and services to seek. Medical providers under a PPO offer discounted rates for members of that PPO. The patient is then responsible for a deductible and copayment, as in traditional insurance. The discounted rate structure keeps down the cost of the PPO to employers and patients alike. However, there are concerns that physicians may respond to the discounted PPO rates by skimping on services.

Worries over the Quality of Care

In general, because managed care providers seek to lower costs in order to cut insurance premiums, they may cut back on the quantity and quality of care. A 1998 NBC News-*Wall Street Journal* survey shows that about half of respondents are of the opinion that HMOs have:

- hurt the patient-doctor long-term relationship;
- lowered the quality of care by putting treatment decisions in the hands of insurance administrators instead of doctors;
- cut patient access to specialists;
- caused doctors to cut short the time spent with patients;
- caused doctors to fail to inform patients about all treatment options;
- reduced patient access to all treatments available.

In short, 86 percent accused HMOs of being more concerned with costs than with quality care.

These concerns with managed care have led to calls for legislation that would reform managed care by establishing a patients' bill of rights. The proposals vary in their details, but their purpose is to allow members of HMOs greater choice in their selection of physicians, along with increased access to specialists and treatments. Although such legislation has not been signed into law as of this writing, the concept is hugely popular and is expected to be enacted soon. This popularity is in spite of predictions that it will drive up costs, and thus premiums.

There is already legislation that addresses some of the problems that have plagued health care in the past. For example, the 1996 Kennedy-Kassebaum law limits exclusions of preexisting conditions, whereby insurers do not cover previously diagnosed conditions for some period of time for new customers. The effect of this law is to force insurers to cover preexisting conditions, although the law does not limit the premiums that they can charge. To further increase access to health care, the act also reduces the ability of insurers to deny coverage or renewal on the basis of health status or claims experience.

Obtaining Health Coverage

Forty-one million people were without health insurance in 1998, one-sixth the population of the United States. A good part of the reason why is a combination of low incomes and high premiums. To understand why individual premiums are high, consider the incentives facing insurance companies. These companies are in business to provide a positive return to their investors, not to give away services that cost more than the value of the premiums they receive. Consequently, they try to distinguish between *ex ante* (before the fact) and *ex post* (after the fact) conditions. The laws of probability allow insurers to cover conditions ex ante.

For example, suppose you have the same chance as everybody else of coming down with some medical condition. By covering many people, most of whom will have no cause to file claims, the insurer can profitably offer you coverage at a fraction of treatment costs. Ex post is another story altogether. If you already have a condition, the insurance company could make money only if they charged you at least the full cost of treatment. That would be no insurance at all! In other words, once you come down with a condition, you lose your option of initiating insurance coverage at an affordable rate.

Even if you do not have any particular medical problems, you still cannot get an individual policy at a price approaching that of a group insurance plan. For example, if you attempt to purchase insurance with coverage identical to that offered by employers, you would be charged a great deal more. The reason revolves around information. Even if you do not have any particular condition yet, you probably know much better than the insurance company which conditions you would be most susceptible to. This is the problem of **adverse selection**—those who seek out insurance coverage are the most likely to need it.

Because of adverse selection, the expected cost to the insurance company of writing an individual policy is much higher than the expected cost per person under a group policy. Insurance companies that survive in the marketplace must know this, and thus charge individuals a higher price to reflect the higher costs. The lowest rates go to groups that are likely to be healthier than average, such as pools of employees at large businesses.

Universal Coverage and Price Controls

Health care expenses can vary dramatically and unpredictably from person to person. This uncertainty motivates us to want insurance. We want others to be covered, too, including the sick and injured who cannot help themselves. Indeed, the healthcare survey shows that about two-thirds of those polled want the government to guarantee everyone access to the best health care available. This is a motivation for **universal coverage,** equal access to health care for everyone, which requires government action to achieve.

Universal coverage would overcome the problem of adverse selection—we would all be in the same group. By forcing everyone to participate, universal coverage would also avoid the free-rider problem. This problem occurs if people figure that some safety net level of coverage will be available to them whether they contribute insurance premiums or not. However, universal coverage raises a new set of issues. For example, if everyone is to be covered, what should that coverage consist of? Should we eliminate all choice? Who should pay? What about malpractice? Indeed, by expanding use of the healthcare system and bureaucratic incentives within that system, universal coverage would probably make the problem of moral hazard worse.

In 1993 President Clinton submitted to Congress a sweeping 1,342 page proposal that called for all Americans to be provided with national health insurance, giving citizens complete freedom to chose their own doctors. However, doctors would have been forced to charge the same "community standard" price, a form of price controls.

adverse selection: those who seek out insurance coverage are the most likely to need it; makes it difficult for individuals to get affordable health insurance and thus promotes employer group insurance.

universal coverage: a situation in which everyone has equal access to health insurance; eliminates the problem of adverse selection.

That prospect frightened many people, and for good reason. Doctors with the best reputations would be flooded with potential patients. The competitive response would have these superior doctors turn many patients away and keep others waiting. There would be long waits prior to scheduled appointments, and then long waits in the office before patients would be seen. The patients wind up paying extra, but the payments are in time, not money.

Likewise, doctors with good reputations cannot be expected to spend time on tricky cases when they could process the easy ones much faster for more money. The result is inefficiency. The best doctors would take the easy cases, leaving the tough ones for the less highly skilled. Yet, even though price controls under universal coverage do not work well, the issue of costly care needs to be addressed in some manner.

Good Care Is Costly

Spending on health care accounts for roughly 14 percent of U.S. spending, compared to about 10 percent of spending in Canada and 7 percent of spending in Japan, as shown in Figure 4-9. One reason that the popularity of managed care soared in the 1990s is the promise by HMOs that healthcare costs could be brought under control. Indeed, the managed care revolution did bring soaring inflation in healthcare costs under control for awhile, although U.S. healthcare expenditures are again on the rise. This effect is seen in Figure 4-9 in the leveling off of the line representing the percent of U.S. spending on health care.

A big part of health care's high cost lies in what we buy. Over time, health care has come to include increasingly elaborate techniques, some of which other countries view as unnecessary luxuries or frivolities. Healthcare charges in the United States must also cover malpractice insurance premiums and the associated overkill of *defensive medicine*, which is extra treatment motivated by a desire to avoid lawsuits. Although estimates differ, we know that these lawsuit-related expenses have added additional tens of billions of dollars to U.S. medical bills.

Looking for Solutions

Many proposed solutions to the healthcare problem involve more government control. However, there is at least one proposal that would place more control in the hands of consumers. **Medical savings accounts,** which allow families to put aside money tax free to apply toward future medical expenses, have been debated in Congress and could become law.

To the extent that patients pay their medical expenses from medical savings accounts, the patients have the incentive to shop around for both high quality and low price, and will use health care only when the benefits of doing so outweigh the costs. The result is no moral hazard and an efficient, market-based allocation of healthcare resources. However, the problem is that it takes money to contribute to these accounts, and there is no assurance that the money in the accounts would be enough to cover necessary healthcare expenses.

Because proposals to reform health care each have their own advantages and disadvantages, the recent actions taken by Congress have been targeted toward solving

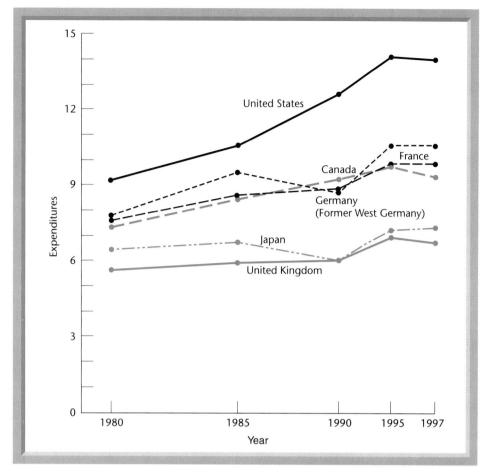

FIGURE 4-9 **Health care expenditures as a percentage of gross domestic product (GDP), selected countries, 1980–1997.**

Source: 1998 Statistical Abstract of the U.S., Table No. 1349.

specific problems. This incremental, piecemeal strategy indicates that Washington has adopted a cautious approach to healthcare reform. How much reform and its impacts are questions to which the ultimate answers are as yet unknown.

■ Prospecting for New Insights

1. JUAN: Government's got it backwards. We need less health insurance, not more. We already waste too much time and money on that bureaucratic mess. People should learn to accept a little risk in their lives. Government could do some real good by outlawing insurance coverage of health expenses below $2,500 per year per person. Anybody who can't scrounge that up would qualify for welfare, anyway. Result? No more health insurance fiasco.

PAUL: Let's not forget to abolish the Food and Drug Administration, while we're at it. If it weren't for their multiyear "worthless until proven otherwise" testing processes, we could actually afford medications. Then, if we could abolish prescriptions, we wouldn't need to pay all those doctors.

Have Juan and Paul simply gone off the deep end, or is there some economic basis for their proposals? Is it economic to prohibit consumption of insurance for people's own good? If government were to enact universal coverage with $2,500 deductibles, do you think the program would get more generous over time? Why?

2. a. Should government pursue the goal of universal health insurance coverage?
    b. During the debate over healthcare reform, strong opposition arose to having employer mandates to fund health insurance. What drawbacks would arise from using this funding method?
    c. If mandates are not to be used, what alternative would you find preferable?

Exploration 4-2 Crime and the Market for Drugs

The war on drugs causes expenditures on drugs to increase. Increased spending on drugs increases the crime and violence that the war on drugs is intended to fight.

The United States has the highest proportion of its citizens behind bars of any "first-world" country. Sixty percent of those prisoners are convicted on drug-related charges. It sometimes appears that recreational drugs are ripping apart our social fabric. Yet, the more we fight the problem, the worse it seems. How can this be?

Many images come to mind when the word drugs is mentioned. There are the wonder drugs that have helped the sick. There is the contrasting image of eggs in the frying pan—"your brain on drugs." The violence of the drug cartels involved in the production and sale of cocaine corruption among public officials who are paid to "look the other way," and the pathos of the cocaine babies born to addicted mothers each come to mind. There are the AIDS patients who have shared dirty needles and the thieves stealing to support their habits. Also woven in are the counterculture of the 1960s and the creativity of such classic writers and poets as Edgar Allen Poe and Samuel Coleridge.

We need to do some sorting. Suppose we put aside questions of whether drug use is moral and of where to draw the line on drug laws. Instead, let's employ economic analysis to solve the dilemma of why toughening up our enforcement of drug laws seems to make drug-related problems worse. Then we will examine the implications of changing the direction of public policy away from the so-called drug war.

The Market for Drugs . . .

Illegal drugs are sold in markets, in many ways much like the markets for other goods. One difference is that information is not readily available about sources of supply, since this information could be used by law enforcement agencies. Nor is product quality ensured by government regulation or legal recourse. In the drug market, it is truly *caveat emptor*—let the buyer beware!

One consequence is that drug users tend to connect with only one or two dealers, who then have an interest in maintaining quality standards to ensure the customer comes back. In turn, most dealers are connected to only one or two wholesalers. Since competition keeps prices down, this reduction of competition causes higher prices.

. . . Sees Violent Crime on the Supply Side . . .

On the supply side of the marketplace, government enforcement of drug laws pushes prices up even more dramatically by increasing the risk associated with dealing drugs. This will drive out the most risk-averse suppliers and add a *risk premium* to prices. Who will remain? Some remaining suppliers will be those who shrug off the risk, perhaps because they enjoy it or have become accustomed to the lifestyle. For the most part, however, competition will select those suppliers who are best at circumventing the law. Usually that involves the insurance of hooking up with a powerful criminal organization.

From street gangs on up to the reputed drug Mafia, organized crime flourishes under tough drug law enforcement. These organizations offer both connections and firepower to the dealers. In addition, because the drug dealer cannot turn to the police for protection, that dealer becomes easy prey for organized criminals. Here is one source of crime associated with drugs—turf battles in which criminal organizations seek to dominate the sales of drugs in an area.

While having criminals killing criminals could be the subject of an intriguing debate, there are also unintended third parties who get caught in the crossfire. Furthermore, the survivors are those criminals who are best at violence. We see this in the violence of the drug trade along the U.S. border with Mexico and within Colombia, the major source of cocaine.

—Witness Colombia—

In Colombia, the dominance of the Medellin drug cartel came to an end with the gunning down of Pablo Escobar, the drug king. Although the dominance of the Medellin cartel merely gave way to dominance by the rival Cali cartel, most people breathed a sigh of relief. After all, the Cali cartel was known to be less violent.

Quickly after the Cali cartel came to prominence, the bosses of that cartel sought government clemency. After all, life had become dangerous for them, and they were already rich. Was this the end of drug violence in Colombia?

Unfortunately, a new generation of brutal, gun-toting drug lords has replaced the old guard of the Cali cartel. The harsh law enforcement had driven out all but the most violence-prone from the top ranks of the leading cartel. Thus, while the new drug lords have learned to avoid directing the wrath of the world at any one of them personally, the overall climate of violence in Colombia's drug-producing areas continues unabated.

. . . Crime for Cash to Buy Drugs, . . .

Why is there drug-related crime by drug users? Perhaps a small fraction has to do with the drugs impairing the user's judgment. Far and away the primary cause, however, is money. Tough enforcement of the drug laws makes it much more expensive to support a drug habit.

Drug users are often addicted to the drugs they use and would go to great lengths to avoid doing without. In other words, the demand for drugs is inelastic because the quantity purchased does not drop proportionally to increases in price. This means that, the tougher we enforce our drug laws, the more money drug users need. Moreover, the tougher we punish a convicted drug offender for the drug use itself, the less the user cares about adding other crimes to the list. Thus, while many addicts can support their habits with legally earned income, others think little of resorting to robberies, burglaries, and other crimes.

. . . and More Addictive Drugs

Tough enforcement of our drug laws has also had the perverse effect of increasing the popularity of the most highly addictive drugs. This effect occurs as users substitute more addictive drugs for less addictive ones. Why would users want to do this?

The answer has to do with bulk. The bulkier the drug, the more likely it is to be intercepted. This is why marijuana grown in the United States today is likely to be much more potent than that grown in the 1960s. More potent drugs cut down on bulk. Unfortunately, the least bulky drugs also tend to be the most addictive. For instance, "cracking" cocaine to form crack requires only a small amount of cocaine, a drug with very little bulk. The relatively lower cost and highly addictive nature of crack has led it to pervade the cities of our country.

Tough enforcement of drug laws causes more violence on the supply side, more money-related crime by addicts, and substitution of more addictive drugs. What about the alternative route of backing off on law enforcement efforts, or even of legalizing some or all drugs altogether?

There are Alternatives to the Current War on Drugs . . .

There are numerous possible drug control policies between the current war on drugs and a laissez faire hands-off strategy. At the extreme, if all drugs were legalized, that would seem to suggest including prescription pharmaceuticals. Should drugstores allow the customer to point and buy "three of those green ones, one of those big red capsules, and twelve of the yellow ones with dots?" In this portion of the Exploration, we look at the implications of moving away from the current war on drugs without specifying the details of how far that movement goes.

Figure 4-10 depicts the market for drugs, where the model is deliberately nonspecific as to exactly what sort of drugs these are. The addictive nature of drugs leads to an inelastic demand curve. The market price and quantity of drugs in the free market is determined by the intersection of free market supply and demand. The drug war causes the price to be higher and the quantity to be lower, *ceteris paribus*.

. . . that Might or Might Not Increase Usage.

Relative to the outcome under the drug war, the free market would appear to offer both good news and bad news. The good news is that the quantity of spending, given by P multiplied by Q, would be lower without the drug war. This means less crime to raise money to buy drugs. Since drugs would be sold by legitimate businesses in the

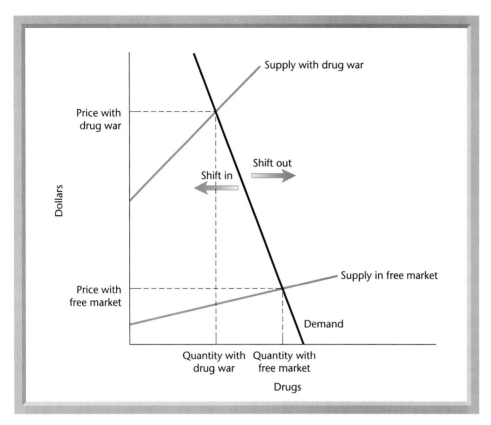

Dollars

Supply with drug war

Price with
drug war

Shift out

Shift in

Supply in free market

Price with
free market

Demand

Quantity with   Quantity with
drug war   free market

Drugs

FIGURE 4-10   **Law enforcement affects the market for drugs.**

free market, the violent territorial crime of the drug rings would also largely disappear. The bad news is that drug use would rise, *ceteris paribus*, because demand always shows an inverse relationship between price and quantity.

Keep in mind that the demand curve keeps constant everything but price. But moving away from the drug war entails more than just a drop in price. For example, the entire demand curve would shift outward to the extent that users no longer fear being arrested, which would lead to greater usage. Alternatively, the demand curve might shift inward to the extent that drug usage constitutes less of an antiauthority rebellion and is seen more as a matter of responsible personal behavior. Nonlegalistic public policy, such as the current DARE programs that attempt to lead students away from drugs, could contribute to this inward shift.

Drug Pushers Would Lose Their Jobs at School . . .

There is another factor that would shift demand inward, one that obliterates one of the most disreputable groups in our society. Specifically, without the risk premium on prices to pay for their fancy cars and lavish lifestyles, drug pushers would be out of business. There would be no incentive to lure schoolchildren to drug use, because there would be no money in it. Without their wads of cash and the power it buys, pushers would lose their ill-bought status as role models for many of our children. Free from the pressure of pushers, and without drugs exemplifying rebellion against authority, fewer kids would turn to drugs. How far this change would shift the demand curve in, though, is anybody's guess.

Some people suggest legalization of many drugs, but only if we impose high sales taxes to discourage purchases and pay for drug-related problems. This policy would be akin to taxing cigarettes in proportion to their *external costs*—those not captured in the marketplace. While taxes can be reasonable, a prohibitively high tax would reopen the doors to criminal pushers and modern-day bootleggers.

Interestingly, some of the biggest unseen proponents of tough drug laws are the drug pushers and their suppliers. Do you know why? Without tough drug laws, these dealers would be out of business. Of course proponents include others with much purer intentions. As the saying goes, "Politics makes strange bedfellows."

. . . and Free Markets Would Keep Usage Down in the Workplace . . .

Moving away from the drug war toward legalization does raise many questions. Some people are concerned about whether quality would diminish in the workplace, especially when that quality involves personal safety. For example, with drug use legal, what would prevent aircraft maintenance and flight crews from being so "stoned" that it would be unsafe to fly in their planes?

The answer is that, without government prohibitions, the free market would provide its own incentives for a clear-headed workforce. The incredibly high cost of a plane crash in terms of replacing the equipment and settling lawsuits would give airlines strong incentives to screen their personnel for drugs, alcohol, or other judgment-impairing problems. In general, companies that employ workers with impaired judgment would lose out in the competitive marketplace to those firms that are more effective at screening out problem workers.

. . . but Problems of Addiction Will Persist.

Legal or illegal, drugs do cause problems for both users and innocent victims. For example, driving-under-the-influence laws have reduced but not eliminated problems of drunk driving. Would a similar approach provide pedestrians and other drivers adequate protection from drivers hallucinating under the influence of LSD?

Questions of law aside, recreational drugs are the source of serious problems. For example, everyone's heart goes out to babies born addicted to cocaine. Viewing addicted babies and other heart-wrenching consequences of addiction can evoke a rage in which drug abuse becomes something to be wiped out at all costs. Should we act on that rage and escalate the current war on drugs? Alternatively, would backing off on the drug war lead to less addiction, more voluntary treatment, and a safer society? You be the judge.

1. TERRI: Drug users are wasting away their lives and not being productive members of society.

PAUL: That's their choice. People should be free to do as they please.

What do you think? Should a person have the right to be unproductive? Who will determine which lifestyles are unproductive?

2. PAUL: Government should not be trying to make personal decisions for us. It would make good economic sense to decriminalize recreational drugs and treat them like alcohol and tobacco. But no one can talk about that, you know.

TERRI: Recreational drugs need to stay illegal, because they're bad for the both users and society. Government shouldn't condone the use of harmful substances. What's more, drug laws give people the incentive to avoid doing wrong.

Find elements in both Paul's and Terri's arguments that make good economic sense. Why would Paul suggest that people are afraid to talk about decriminalizing drugs? Explain why debate on drug-related issues is often heated, and why well-meaning people disagree.

Appendix
COMPUTING ELASTICITY AND REVENUE ALONG A DEMAND CURVE COMPUTING ELASTICITY

All elasticities have the same basic formula, that being the percentage change in one variable divided by the percentage change in another as follows: $\%\Delta Y/\%\Delta X$. Different elasticities merely name the variables differently. Therefore, if you know how to compute one elasticity, you can merely substitute variables to compute any other elasticity. Hence the challenge of computing an elasticity is in being able to compute a percentage change.

In common usage, a percentage change is defined as the change in something divided by what it started out as. For example, if a person's weight rises from 100 pounds to 150 pounds, we say that their weight has risen by 50 percent, that is, by 50/100. Curiously, if the person's weight were to drop to 100 pounds after being at 150 pounds, the percentage change would be -33 percent, that is, $-50/150 = -1/3$. In other words, weight rose by half but fell by one-third.

This type of measure will not do for the computation of elasticities. Rather, a measure is needed that is independent of the direction in which the variables are changing. That measure of percentage change is provided by the *midpoint formula*, which computes percentage change as the change in the variable divided by an amount halfway between the starting and ending amount. Consider the variable Y, which changes from an initial value of Y_0 to a value of Y_1. Symbolically, the midpoint formula to compute the percentage change in Y is as follows:

$$\%\Delta Y = \frac{\Delta Y}{base}$$

where ΔY equals $Y_1 - Y_0$, and the base equals $(Y_0 + Y_1)/2$. Likewise, the percentage change in variable X would be computed as follows:

$$\%\Delta X = \frac{\Delta X}{base}$$

where ΔX equals $X_1 - X_0$, and the base equals $(X_0 + X_1)/2$. To compute the elasticity of Y with respect to X, simply divide $\%\Delta Y$ by the $\%\Delta X$ as follows:

$$\frac{\Delta Y}{(Y_0 + Y_1)/2} \div \frac{\Delta X}{(X_0 + X_1)/2}$$

This is equivalent to the following shortcut formula, which gives the same result:

$$\frac{\Delta Y}{Y_0 + Y_1} \div \frac{\Delta X}{X_0 + X_1}$$

RELATING DEMAND ELASTICITY TO REVENUE

This section focuses on the elasticity of demand and its relationship to revenue. Recall that the elasticity of demand is defined as the percentage change in quantity demanded divided by the percentage change in price. Data from Table 3–1 in chapter 3 are repeated in the first three columns of Table 4A–1. The final two columns of this table contain the revenue implications of demand. *Total revenue*

TABLE 4A-1 Demand and Revenue

Data Point	Price ($)	Quantity Demanded	Total Revenue ($) = P × Q	Marginal Revenue ($) = Δ(P × Q)/ΔQ
A	5	0	0	undefined
B	4	1	4	4
C	3	2	6	2
E	2	3	6	0
F	1	4	4	−2
G	0	5	0	−4

TABLE 4A-2 Computing the Elasticity of Demand, Shortcut Method

(a) Between Points	(b) $\dfrac{\Delta P}{P_0 + P_1}$	(c) $\dfrac{\Delta Q}{Q_0 + Q_1}$	(d) Elasticity of Demand = (c)/(b)
A and B	1/9	1/1 = 1	9
B and C	1/7	1/3	7/3
C and E	1/5	1/5	1
E and F	1/3	1/7	3/7
F and G	1/1 = 1	1/9	1/9

equals price multiplied by quantity: $P \times Q$. *Marginal revenue* is defined as the change in total revenue associated with one additional unit of output, as follows:

$$\text{Marginal revenue} = \frac{\Delta \text{total revenue}}{\Delta \text{quantity of output}}$$

Table 4A–2 uses the shortcut formula described above to compute elasticity between each pair of data points in Table 4A–1. Because the application is to the price elasticity of demand, variable Y is quantity and X is price:

$$\frac{\Delta Q}{Q_0 + Q_1} \div \frac{\Delta P}{P_0 + P_1}.$$

Equivalently, the price elasticity of demand can be computed as

$$\frac{P_0 + P_1}{Q_0 + Q_1} \times \frac{\Delta Q}{\Delta P}$$

because dividing one fraction by a second is the same as multiplying the first fraction by the reciprocal of the second.* For example, in computing the elasticity between points B and C, $(1/3)/(1/7) = 1/3 \times 7/1 = 7/3$. For convenience, the elasticity of demand is expressed in terms of its absolute value, meaning that negative signs are dropped. Otherwise the elasticity of demand would always be negative, because price and quantity demanded always move opposite to each other.

Figure 4A–1 plots the relationships between demand, marginal revenue, and elasticity we derived earlier. Figure 4A–2 on page 145 shows the more general relationships between these variables. Note the following:

- Marginal revenue is positive and total revenue is rising when demand is elastic.
- Marginal revenue is zero and total revenue is at a maximum when demand is unit elastic.
- Marginal revenue is negative and total revenue is declining when demand is inelastic.

---

*Calculus can be used to compute elasticity at a single point on a demand curve with a known functional form. The formula is $P/Q \times dQ/dP$.

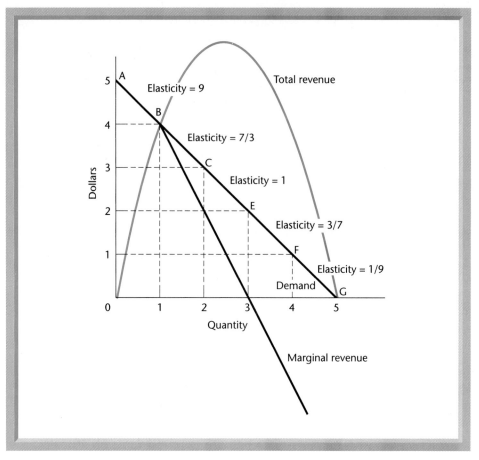

FIGURE 4A–1 The data from Table 4A–1 show the relationship between demand, elasticity, total revenue, and marginal revenue.

 QuickCheck _____

Elasticities and the relationship between demand and revenue usually strike students as difficult until they have engaged in hands-on computation. Work through Tables 4A–1 and 4A–2 to verify that all the information is correct.

Applying Concepts

Durango Bob, owner of Durango Danceland, must decide if he should offer a Saturday night happy hour and drink specials. He knows that, even without special promotions, Saturday night is his busiest night. Being reluctant to experiment with promotions on such a successful night, he decided to experiment on Wednes-

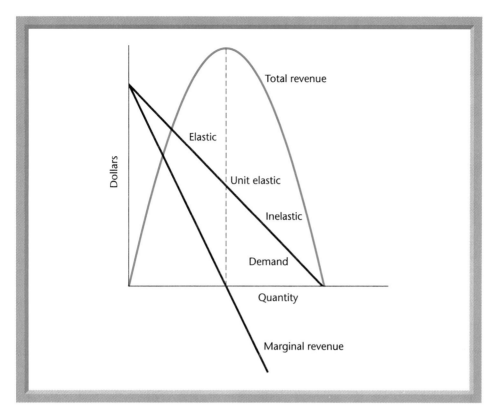

FIGURE 4A–2 When quantities are large, the relationships between demand, revenue, and elasticity will appear as shown. Note that marginal revenue starts where the demand curve intersects the vertical axis, slopes down twice as fast as demand, and thus intersects the horizontal axis below the midpoint of demand, where elasticity equals 1.

day nights, when business is slower. After counting up his receipts for a few weeks with Wednesday promotions in place, he concludes that revenues rise when his prices fall.

1. Is demand at Durango Danceland elastic on Wednesday nights?
2. To determine whether it is profitable to permanently lower prices on Wednesday nights, it is not enough to know that revenues rise. What else must be considered?

5

INTO THE INTERNATIONAL MARKETPLACE

A Look Ahead

COUNTRIES RELY UPON each other more than ever before in history. Yet, no field of economics is more controversial and less understood by the public than international trade. This fact comes as no surprise, since international trade involves all of the elements associated with the economy within a country's borders—its *domestic* economy. In addition, international trade must also take into account foreign currencies and conflicting interests among countries. Nevertheless, a little systematic analysis based on the principles of supply and demand sheds a huge amount of light on this area that at first seems so murky.

Because trade involves foreign currencies, this chapter first uses supply and demand analysis to interpret exchange rates, the price of each country's currency in terms of other currencies. The chapter proceeds to examine imports and exports, along with related issues of jobs and investments. The chapter goes on to discuss some common instruments of trade policy and why they are used. To some extent, countries of the world have recognized the folly of "beggar-thy-neighbor" restrictions on trade. This perspective has led to regional trading blocs, a major multilateral trade accord termed the GATT, and the establishment of the World Trade Organization to enforce the GATT.

The Explorations in this chapter examine issues of trade and immigration. Exploration 5-1 discusses the many special cases for trade restrictions. Arguments for and against these special cases are presented. Exploration 5-2 discusses the effects of immigration on trade patterns and wages. The choice of immigration policy is discussed.

As you are **Surveying Economic Principles** you will arrive at an ability to

- ❏ interpret exchange rates and explain how forces of supply and demand determine their values;
- ❏ describe why an appreciating dollar helps U.S. consumers, but hurts U.S. producers;
- ❏ analyze how trade costs jobs in some industries, but not in the aggregate;
- ❏ predict the effects of tariffs, quotas, and other nontariff barriers to trade;
- ❏ explain the difference between the effects of the World Trade Organization and regional trading blocs.

While **Exploring Issues** you will be able to

- ❏ discuss how the many arguments against free trade apply selectively, if at all;
- ❏ explain how immigration affects wage rates and international trade.

Terms Along the Way

- ✔ exchange rate, 148
- ✔ appreciation, 150
- ✔ depreciation, 150
- ✔ floating exchange rates, 151
- ✔ current account, 156
- ✔ balance of trade, 157
- ✔ capital account, 158
- ✔ tariff, 160
- ✔ General Agreement on Tariffs and Trade (GATT), 161
- ✔ nontariff barriers, 161

- ✔ quota, 161
- ✔ voluntary export restraints, 164
- ✔ trading blocs, 165
- ✔ World Trade Organization, 166
- ✔ North American Free Trade Agreement, 167
- ✔ trade creation effect, 167
- ✔ trade diversion effect, 167
- ✔ infant industries, 170
- ✔ dumping, 173

SURVEYING ECONOMIC PRINCIPLES

The European Community is breaking down the economic barriers among its member countries. The Chinese have embraced international trade as a key to their economic growth. The Brazilians have granted foreign investors huge stakes in that country's railroad and telecommunications infrastructure. Chrysler Corporation, one of the big three U.S. automakers, has combined operations with Daimler-Benz, the huge German automaker. The message is clear. Countries around the world are going global. Those that do not are relegated to the backwaters of economic prosperity. Yet, as countries of the Far East have found in recent years, going global exposes countries to problems created by currency fluctuations and global shifts in trade and investment. Since differences in currencies among different countries is a fundamental feature of international trade, this chapter starts by looking at that issue, and then proceeds to examine trade and investment flows and trade policy.

Foreign Exchange

Each country usually has its own currency. There are pesos, yen, euros, the baht, and many more. Even countries that use the same name for their currencies usually do not actually share a common currency. For example, even though Canada and the United States both use dollars, Canadian dollars are not the same as American dollars. These differences among currencies give rise to *exchange rates* between the currencies, where an exchange rate tells the price of one currency in terms of another. For example, the exchange rate between U.S. and Canadian dollars as of this writing is that one U.S. dollar would buy 1.5 Canadian dollars. What determines these exchange rates? Why do they matter? The answer lies in the *foreign exchange market*, in which currencies are bought and sold for one another.

exchange rate: price of one currency in terms of another.

Market Equilibrium Exchange Rates—How Many Yen Can a Dollar Buy?

Figure 5-1 illustrates a market for Japanese yen in exchange for U.S. dollars. The horseshoe-shaped arrow indicates that, with minor exceptions, U.S. paper dollars never physically make it to Japan. Likewise, paper yen from Japan never make it to the United States. Rather, currencies are exchanged electronically through banks in major financial centers, such as New York, Tokyo, and London. Although global in nature, the basic operation of this market is easily understood using supply and demand analysis, as depicted in the center of Figure 5-1.

As usual with supply and demand analysis, the horizontal axis represents quantity, and the vertical axis represents price. Quantity is the total amount of one currency, and price is its value per unit in terms of the other. That price is termed an exchange rate. In our example, we look at the quantity of yen and see its price in terms of dollars per yen. The market equilibrium exchange rate is labeled XR* in Figure 5-1. In early 1999, that exchange rate was roughly \$.007/yen, meaning that each Japanese yen cost only a fraction of one U.S. penny.

At the market equilibrium exchange rate, the total quantity of yen offered for sale, Q*, is just equal to the total quantity of yen purchased. Moreover, the total number of dollars being spent for yen is just equal to the total number of dollars being received by those selling yen. In other words, all dollars that U.S. residents

Yesterday's exchange rates for numerous currencies can be found at **http://www.trustnet.co.uk/general/rates.asp**

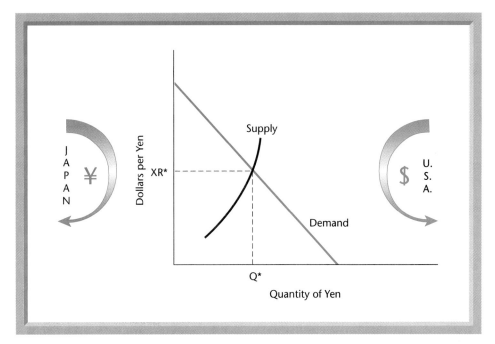

FIGURE 5-1 **The foreign exchange market—buying yen with dollars.** All dollars spent on yen are bought by others spending yen for dollars. In essence, the dollars bounce back to be spent in the United States, and the yen bounce back to be spent in Japan.

spend on Japanese imports are received by sellers of yen. Those sellers would not agree to the sale unless they had something to spend those dollars on.

Those on the demand side for yen include U.S. buyers of imported goods and services from Japan. They also include U.S. investors interested in such things as Japanese property, stocks, and bonds. Those supplying yen have the same sort of interests, except now the roles are reversed. They may be wanting U.S. goods or services, or U.S. investments. The exchange of currencies thus represents the exchange of goods, services, and investments—both buyers and sellers have a use for each other's currencies.

Return flows of dollars may be indirect. For example, a U.S. importer of Japanese fax machines would enter the foreign exchange market to buy yen with dollars. The sellers of the yen may need dollars in order to pay for oil from Iran, because Iran prices its oil in dollars. Iranian oil sellers have no use for dollars in their own country, but might deposit them in a dollar-denominated account in a European or other foreign bank. The bank, in turn, may spend these dollars to buy U.S. investments. Finally, the dollars have returned to the United States. Although it sounds like a long process, all these transactions are likely to occur in such rapid-fire progression that the dollars may be considered to travel directly from the importer back to the U.S. economy.

Exchange rates can greatly affect the prices we see at our local stores. For example, imported products will seem cheaper if the dollar is strong. A *strong dollar* buys relatively more of other currencies than a *weak dollar*, although just how much purchasing power is needed to make the dollar strong or how little to make it weak is a normative issue—a matter of subjective opinion. U.S. consumers and U.S. tourists abroad both like a strong dollar. For example, suppose a ceramic vase costs 30 pesos in Mexico. If the exchange rate is 3 pesos per dollar, the vase costs the U.S. tourist $10. On the other hand, if the exchange rate is 6 pesos per dollar the vase costs only $5. Moreover, not only does a stronger dollar mean that the price of imports is lower to U.S. citizens, it also means that U.S. firms must keep their own prices lower to the extent that their products and the products of other countries are substitutes.

Although U.S. consumers benefit from a strong dollar, U.S. producers of products that compete with imports and foreign tourists in the U.S. prefer a weak dollar. A weak dollar means that U.S. goods and services seem cheap to foreigners, and foreign goods and services seem expensive to U.S. citizens. For example, the exchange rate in 1995 was about 100 yen per dollar (1 yen for a penny). However, it was well over 200 yen per dollar 10 years earlier (2 yen for a penny). The Japanese tourist in 1995 thus had about double the spending power in the U.S. of that same tourist in 1985. Conversely, it seemed to the U.S. tourist visiting Japan in 1995 that everything was twice as expensive as it had been on a previous trip 10 years earlier. Between 1995 and 1998 the annual average exchange rate between the dollar and yen has bounced around within the range of 93 to 131 yen per dollar.

Currency Appreciation and Depreciation

appreciation: when a currency buys more of other currencies than previously; makes imports cheaper and exports more expensive.

depreciation: a decline in the purchasing power of a currency when it is exchanged for other currencies, which makes imports more expensive and exports cheaper.

Currency appreciation occurs when a currency gets stronger. Depreciation occurs when the currency becomes weaker. In the previous paragraph, the yen appreciated against the dollar, and the dollar depreciated against the yen. Although the dollar has regained some of its strength against the yen in recent years, the depreciation of the dollar against the yen from the early 1980s through the mid-1990s can be traced to an increase in U.S. demand for yen, which drove the dollar price of those yen higher. A dominant force behind the strong yen during this period was the demand by American importers for yen to buy the Japanese electronics and automobiles that they sold to U.S. consumers.

Figure 5-2 illustrates currency appreciation and depreciation. In order to illustrate the basic concepts of appreciation and depreciation, the figure is kept simple. In practice, because of the many influences on currency supply and demand, both shift frequently, which means that market exchange rates rarely stay the same for long.

Governments often intervene in the foreign exchange markets in an attempt to maintain exchange rates within *target zones*. In terms of supply and demand analysis, this means that governments seek to support the price of a currency to keep it from depreciating too much, or place a ceiling on the price of a currency to keep it from appreciating too much. Since governments have no ability to enforce price ceilings and supports in international currency markets, they may resort to buying up weak currencies and selling strong currencies.

Governments also take actions to cause private-sector currency demand and supply curves to shift. For example, a government might adopt policies that increase its country's interest rates. Since higher interest rates attract foreign investors who must first buy the country's currency, increasing interest rates in turn increases demand for the country's currency, which causes it to appreciate. However, because of the huge volume of currencies being exchanged, government attempts to influence exchange rates are often futile. For example, **the value of currencies exchanged worldwide in a single week exceeds the value of an entire year's worth of U.S. output.**

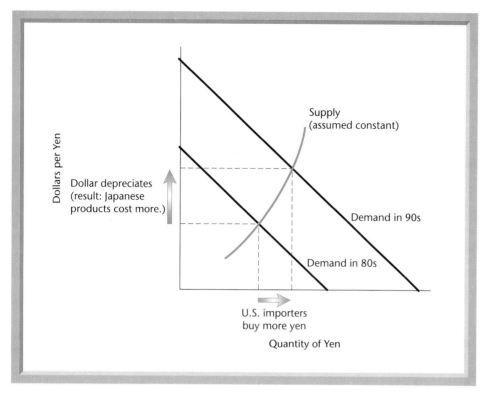

FIGURE 5-2 **The dollar depreciates and the yen appreciates** as U.S. consumers desire more Japanese products.

This was not always the case. In the period after World War II, governments from around the world adhered to the *Bretton Woods agreement.* The Bretton Woods agreement was a treaty signed in 1944 at Bretton Woods, New Hampshire, by most of the world's major trading countries. This agreement *pegged* the dollar to gold ($35/ounce) and all other currencies to the dollar, thereby implying *fixed exchange rates.* Governments agreed to take whatever actions would be necessary to maintain these rates.

As world commerce grew over the next 30 years, however, the size of currency transactions overwhelmed the ability of governments to follow through on that agreement. The system of fixed exchange rates was modified in stages and ultimately abandoned as unworkable during a run on the dollar in 1971. This run consisted of dollar selling that overwhelmed governments' abilities to maintain the agreement, thereby precipitating a financial crisis. American tourists abroad felt this crisis personally, as many tourists were stranded, unable to find anyone willing to risk accepting their rapidly depreciating currency. Since then, exchange rates have been allowed to adjust to whatever level the market dictates, a regime known as floating exchange rates. However, **because governments still take actions intended to affect market exchange rates, the system is often referred to as a** *managed float.*

floating exchange rates: when currency prices are determined by market forces, without intervention by governments.

Some governments try harder than others to manage their exchange rates. For example, the Mexican government supported the peso at a rate of roughly 3.5 pesos per dollar throughout most of 1994. In late December of that year, however, Mexico was forced to let its currency float freely until the rate adjusted to market equilibrium. The Mexican government did not own enough dollars to keep buying pesos, which would have been required to keep the value of the peso up. In November and December, 1994, the exchange rate surged to about 6 pesos per dollar, nearly double its previous value. Mexico was forced to abandon its policy of supporting the peso because it had nearly exhausted its holdings of foreign currencies, termed *foreign reserves*. The Mexican government had spent nearly $10 billion worth of these foreign reserves to buy back its own pesos.

The inability of governments to maintain the values of their currencies in foreign exchange markets was highlighted by the precipitous tumble of Asia's currencies in recent years. By late July, 1998, for example, the Indonesian rupiah had dropped to 14,000 per dollar from 2,600 one year earlier, which means that the rupiah that could have been exchanged for one dollar in July 1997 would buy only 18 cents 1 year later. U.S. goods imported into Indonesia thus cost over five times as much in the local currency in the summer of 1998 than in the summer of 1997.

This abrupt depreciation of the rupiah dramatically increased the purchasing power of dollars in Indonesia and decreased the purchasing power of rupiah in the United States. When the rupiah fell, U.S. investors saw the value of their investments in Indonesia drop. However, many U.S. investors viewed the drop as a buying opportunity, since Indonesian investments seemed available at what looked like bargain-basement prices. However, the precipitous drop also sparked rioting and political unrest, which scared potential foreign investors worried about the security of their investments. These concerns also kept down foreign tourism, even though prices in Indonesia would seem very cheap to those who made the trip.

OBSERVATION POINT:
Doubling the Wrong Money Won't Make You Rich

Interest rates among countries often vary quite dramatically. Yet, it's not a good idea to merely invest your money in countries with the highest interest rates. The value of those high interest rates can be eaten up by the cost of a depreciating currency. Indeed, the highest interest rates are in countries with the highest inflation rates, meaning that the country's currency loses its purchasing power over time. That loss of purchasing power is not just for goods and services, either. It applies equally strongly in the foreign exchange markets.

When you go to convert that foreign currency back to your own, reality hits! You'd find that the lavish gains you'd made are eaten away by the higher price you must pay for your own currency. That reality is called *interest rate parity*, meaning that expected returns on investments will be equal across countries, after accounting for expected inflation, risk, and exchange rate adjustments. The foreign exchange markets make it so.

QuickCheck

1. If you were planning a vacation in France, would your meals and hotel cost you more if the U.S. dollar depreciated or appreciated against the French franc just as you embarked upon your trip? 2. If the reason for your trip was to find customers in France for a product you make in the United States, which event, depreciation or appreciation of the dollar, would benefit your business?

Answer: 1. Recall that when a currency depreciates it loses value. If the dollar depreciated against the franc, then it would take more dollars to buy the same number of francs. For this reason, as a tourist you would be better off financially if the dollar appreciated. It would take fewer dollars to buy the same number of francs. Thus, U.S. travelers going abroad prefer an appreciating dollar. 2. As a producer of a product, the reasoning is different. An appreciating dollar means that the franc depreciates. As the franc loses value, it means that a citizen of France must spend more francs to get the same number of dollars. As a consequence, U.S. products sold in France carry higher price tags. U.S. producers prefer a depreciating dollar because it makes U.S. goods cheaper when they are sold in other countries.

International Trade

Imports and Exports

Chapter 2 showed how countries gain by specializing according to comparative advantage and then trading with other countries. In this way, countries experience consumption possibilities that are greater than their production possibilities. Here, we look at that general concept as it applies to markets for imports and exports. We proceed by imagining a country that embraces free trade after previously allowing no foreign commerce at all. Before free trade, that country's prices would have been based solely on its own domestic supply and demand. However, free trade means that its producers must accept world market prices, which would entail a higher price for some goods and a lower price for others.

Figure 5-3 shows the case of a world price of a good that would lead a country to import that good. The supply and demand for the good within the country, labeled "Domestic Supply" and "Domestic Demand" in the figure intersect at the price that prevails when the country chooses not to trade, labeled "Price, if no trade." However, the world price is less than this domestic price. Since domestic consumers will not pay any more than the world price, and since producers will refuse to sell for less than the world price, it is the intersection of the world price with supply and demand that determines the domestic quantity supplied and demanded, respectively. Because the domestic quantity supplied is less than the quantity demanded, consumers make up the difference with imports, as shown in Figure 5-3.

Opening a country up to trade creates winners and losers. Since domestic producers are forced to sell at a lower price, they lose. They also lose because they produce and sell less. The combination of a lower price and smaller quantity supplied domestically could mean some domestic producers make less money or even go out of business. However, domestic consumers gain by paying a lower price. They also gain by consuming more of the good. Note that when domestic producers cut back output

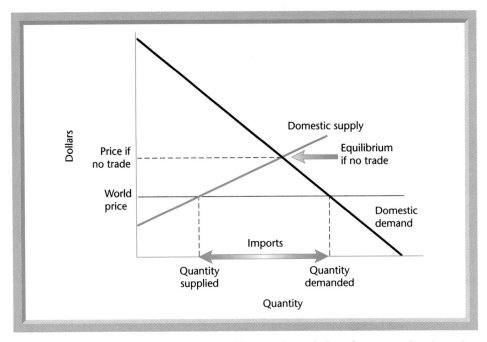

FIGURE 5-3   **Imports result from a world price that is below the country's price prior to trade.** The lower price causes the country's consumption to rise and production to fall, with the difference being the amount imported.

and sell at a lower price, domestic consumers get the benefit of that lower price and merely substitute imports for the amount by which producers cut back. To that extent, then, all of the loss to domestic producers is gained by domestic consumers.

Imports also create extra value for consumers, since the lower world price causes them to move down their demand curves and consume more than they did before. This increased consumption is of value to them, or they would not do it. It increases their consumer surplus, as discussed in chapter 3. Thus, **there is a positive net gain from imports.** It is this fact that makes it desirable for a country to open its borders to trade.

Figure 5-4 is similar to Figure 5-3 except the world price is above the domestic price. In this case, the price difference causes the domestic quantity supplied to be greater than the domestic quantity demanded. This difference between quantity supplied and the quantity demanded results in an excess quantity of the product. This excess is exported, as shown in Figure 5-4.

In the case of exports, it is producers who win and consumers who lose. Producers gain because they sell more at a higher price. Consumers lose because they must pay the higher world price, and thus consume less. To the extent that producers continue to produce as much as before, all of the losses to consumers because of the higher price become gains to producers who get to receive that higher price. In addition, because the export market allows producers to sell even more at that higher

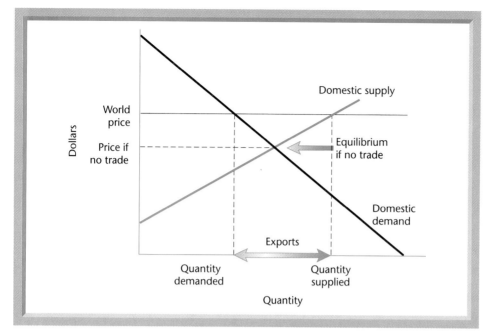

FIGURE 5-4 Exports result from a world price that is above the country's price prior to trade. The higher price causes the country's consumption to fall and production to rise, with the difference being the amount exported.

price, producers gain again. Thus, the gains to producers from exports outweigh the losses to consumers, meaning that **there is a positive net gain from exports.**

In short, **both imports and exports lead to more gains than losses.** Even so, specific consumer and producer groups are hurt in each case. Sometimes those groups have powerful political lobbies and advertising campaigns. Since the American public at large has a somewhat vague understanding of international trade issues, these groups are often able to get their ways.

✔ **QuickCheck** _____

Since consumers gain from imports, but domestic producers lose, isn't a country just as well off to do without imports altogether? Similarly, since consumers lose from exports, but domestic producers gain, isn't a country just as well off to do without exports? Explain.

Answer: No, consumers gain more from imports than producers lose. Likewise, producers gain more from exports than consumers lose. Thus, both imports and exports bring net gains to the country.

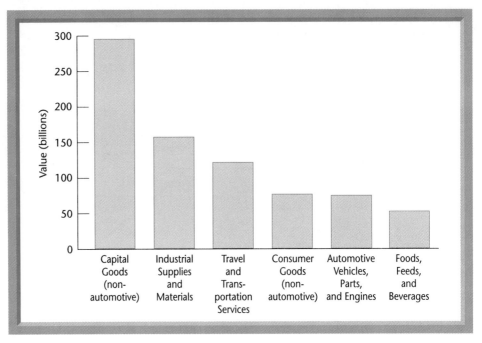

FIGURE 5-5   **Major exports of the United States, 1997.**

Source: U.S. Department of Commerce, *Survey of Current Business,* February 1999, Table F.1.

U.S. Trade with the World

current account: records the monetary value of imports and exports of goods and services.

Recent data on the current account will be found in the on-line edition of *Economic Trends,* published by the Federal Reserve Bank of Cleveland. The Internet address that will allow you to access these data is **http://www.clev. frb.org/research/ index.htm**

Like most countries, the U.S. keeps *balance of payments accounts* that track its interactions with the rest of the world. For example, the U.S. current account measures the value of exports and imports and certain other international transactions. Exports are U.S. goods and services sold to foreigners, and imports are foreign goods and services brought into the United States. Figures 5-5 and 5-6 show the major exports and imports of the United States.

Note that the U.S. imports the same categories of goods that it exports. One reason is that the specific goods within these categories can differ significantly. For example, the imported Honda CR-V is quite different from the exported Ford Mustang, even though they are both automotive, and since the merger of Chrysler and Daimler-Benz, are even produced by the same company. Another reason is that many subcategories of goods are included in the broad categories shown. For example, within the category of capital goods, the U.S. exports far more in aircraft and related equipment than it imports. However, also within the category of capital goods, the U.S. exports far less in computers and related equipment than it imports. Likewise, petroleum and related products comprise about a quarter of U.S. imports in the category of industrial supplies and materials. While the United States is also a major exporter within this category, the fraction of those exports that are petroleum related is relatively insignificant.

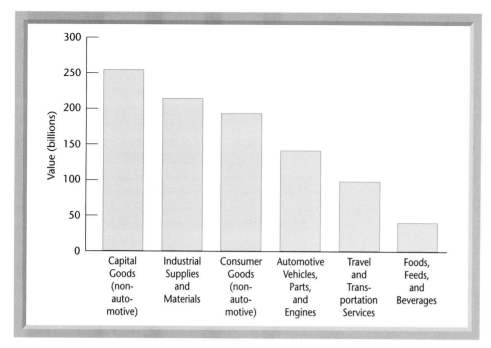

FIGURE 5-6 **Major imports of the United States, 1997.**

Source: U.S. Department of Commerce, *Survey of Current Business*, February 1999, Table F.1; Table 4.3.

The balance on the current account is the dollar value of exported goods and services minus the dollar value of imported goods and services, adjusted for certain other international transactions. This balance has been negative since 1982. Figure 5-7 depicts the U.S. current account balance since 1979. Figure 5-8 shows a time series of exports and imports as a percentage of total U.S. output.

The United States exports more services than it imports. Services encompass a diverse array of activities, including the U.S. schooling of foreign citizens, the leasing of rights to broadcast U.S. television shows and movies, and even haircuts for foreign tourists. A wide range of financial and consulting services is also included. Thus, if only services were included in the current account, the United States would show a surplus. However, public discussions often focus on the balance of trade, which is the dollar value of imported goods minus the dollar value of exported goods, where trade in services is ignored. The balance of trade has a large deficit, called the *trade deficit*. In 1997, that deficit stood at $198 billion, which represented 2.4 percent of the $8.1 trillion U.S. gross domestic product.

balance of trade: the monetary value of exported goods minus the monetary value of imported goods.

Although the figures for the United States show a significant degree of foreign involvement, the figures for other countries show much more. The reason is straightforward. The larger and more diverse is a country, the more possibilities there are to specialize and trade within that country's borders. For example, the United States engages in a large amount of trade across state borders. Were the

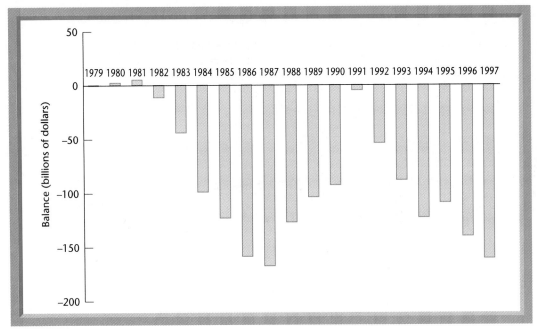

FIGURE 5-7   Balance on the U.S. current account, 1979–1997.

Source: 1999 Economic Report of the President, Table B-103.

states of the United States to become 50 separate countries, the selling of Idaho potatoes in Utah would show up as international trade in goods. Likewise, the Harvard education of the Idaho potato farmer would be international trade in services. Thus, as a percentage of their outputs, smaller countries engage in much more international trade than do large countries.

International flows of investments play a prominent role in modern foreign commerce, as they have throughout history. For example, decaying ruins of European aqueducts and roads attest to Roman foreign investments in centuries gone by. British investment in the New World sewed the seeds that sprouted into the United States of America. These days, foreign investments are likely to be in factories, real estate, and stocks and bonds. Investment flows are recorded in the capital account.

capital account: component of U.S. balance of payment accounts that records the monetary value of foreign investment in the U.S. and U.S. investment abroad.

Investments can be divided into *direct investments* or *financial investments.* Direct investments imply foreign control, such as Japanese ownership of U.S. golf courses and manufacturing plants. Financial investments include foreign purchases of stocks and bonds, such as the purchase of U.S. government Treasury bonds by an Italian bank. In recent years, the country with the most foreign investment in the United States is Japan, followed by the United Kingdom and the Netherlands. In 1997, $254.9 billion more investment money flowed into the United States than went in the other direction. Some of this inflow represented the return on past U.S. investments abroad. The rest was foreign direct and financial investment in the United States.

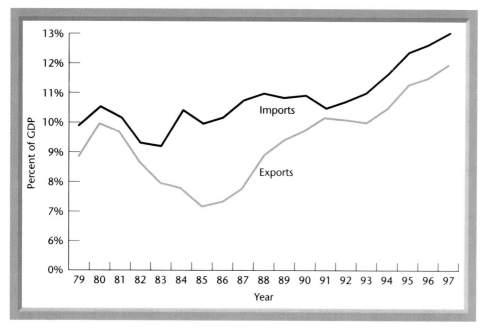

FIGURE 5-8 **U.S. exports and imports as a percentage of gross domestic product, 1979–1997.**

Source: Calculated from data in the *1999 Economic Report of the President*, Table B-1.

OBSERVATION POINT:

Multinational Business—Buying $90 Billion Worth of Oil and Automobiles

That tidy sum of money is about the value of what British Petroleum and Daimler-Benz spent in 1998 to buy, respectively, the Amoco and Chrysler corporations. The deal is indicative of a trend in which companies find themselves forced to compete in markets that are no longer defined by country borders. These markets are global and huge, and are served by giant *multinational firms*, firms that produce and distribute their products in more than one country.

To compete against other giants, firms become giants themselves. While U.S.-based companies in telecommunications, oil, electronics, and a host of other industries remain mighty players in this multinational world and do their share of buying foreign companies, more and more U.S. companies are being merged with or bought out by foreign suitors. Other multinationals build production facilities in the U.S., as has been done by Japanese automakers and many others.

Where do these foreign-based multinational companies get the dollars to spend? From your purchases of imports, in part. Thanks to the trade deficit, your next purchase of a Jeep Cherokee might come with a touch of Mercedes!

The Fallacy of Lost Jobs

The effects of trade on jobs and income opportunities is perhaps the most controversial aspect of international trade. We are frequently assaulted with claims that it is somehow unpatriotic to buy imports. The reasoning is that every dollar spent on an imported product provides jobs abroad to make that product. Using the United States as our case in point, we are told that imports take jobs from American workers who could otherwise have provided an American-made version of the same product. However, it is incorrect to use this line of reasoning to infer that the country's unemployment rate rises as a result of imports. Rather, jobs lost in some areas are gained in others, no matter whether or not the country experiences a trade deficit.

While the argument that imports cost jobs is true in the sense that international trade reallocates jobs and that the transition could lead to a transitory increase in unemployment, neither logic nor data support the claim that imports increase a country's unemployment rate. For example, unemployment in the late 1990s hovered near its 20-year low, even as the United States maintained a very large trade deficit. Rather, imports cost jobs in specific industries—those that produce products in competition with the imports. However, the vast majority of dollars that are spent on products abroad bump up against the currency market and are immediately bounced right back into the U.S. economy, either to buy goods, services, or investments.

These return flows are sometimes ignored by policymakers, but with unfortunate results. For example, the *Smoot-Hawley Act* was passed in 1930 as a means to fight the unemployment of the Great Depression. The Act raised import **tariffs**—taxes on imports—to an average rate of 52 percent on over 20,000 products, a level that was so prohibitively high that imports nearly ceased. Not surprisingly, so did export and foreign investment flows. Rather than lower U.S. unemployment, the Smoot-Hawley Act was followed by even higher unemployment rates.

> **tariff:** tax on imports.

Some U.S. dollars leave the country and do not return. The amount of this U.S. currency in circulation abroad is impressive. About $250 billion of genuine U.S. cash is currently estimated to circulate outside the United States. For example, although Russian merchants violate Russian law if they accept U.S. dollars as payment for their products sold within Russia, it is nevertheless estimated that the value of U.S. dollars circulating there approximately equals the value of Russia's own currency, the ruble. Apparently many Russians have greater confidence in the enduring value of the U.S. currency than they do in their own. Abrupt exchange rate changes, such as the fluctuation of the ruble from 6 per dollar to 20 per dollar and back to 10 per dollar in the span of a couple of weeks in September, 1998, indicate both a cause and effect of this lack of confidence.

Rather than being a drain on the U.S. economy, however, U.S. currency that stays abroad improves the U.S. standard of living. In effect, the U.S. has exported small pieces of colored paper—dollars—in exchange for valuable goods and services. To the extent that those dollars stay abroad, the U.S. government can and does print and spend additional currency to offset that loss. Thus, there is no loss of purchasing power within the U.S. economy.

In short, buying imports reallocates jobs away from domestic producers of substitute products. However, because most of the currency spent on imports bounces right back into the U.S. economy and because any that does not is replaced by government, there is no reason to think that whether there is a balance of trade surplus or deficit has any bearing on the total number of jobs in the economy. Instead, as discussed in chapter 2 and the next section, trade with other countries allows a country to specialize according to its comparative advantage. The result is that the country's production possibilities will generate greater consumption possibilities, thereby increasing the overall standard of living.

QuickCheck _____

Many people worry about the size of the U.S. trade deficit. Are such worries justified?

Answer: When people worry about a trade deficit they probably have in mind that U.S. workers will lose their jobs. This effect will occur in the industries that compete with imports, but not in the aggregate. Thus, if the concern is over the U.S. unemployment rate, worrying about the trade deficit is not justified.

Trade Policy Options

Despite free trade offering countries economic advantages, all major countries have some restrictions on trade. For better or worse, countries often seek to protect individual industries or sectors of their economies from foreign competition. Policies that accomplish this goal are termed *protectionist*, even though these policies usually harm rather than protect the economy as a whole. American humorist Mark Twain recognized the allure of protectionism when he wrote that free traders win all the arguments, but protectionists win all the votes. However, today, most of the major trading countries of the world have recognized the dangers of *trade wars*, situations in which countries punish each other and themselves through retaliatory trade restrictions. To avoid these situations and promote free trade, most countries have signed the **General Agreement on Tariffs and Trade (GATT),** which limits the use of protectionist policies.

Protectionist policies come in two basic forms: tariffs and nontariff barriers. **Nontariff barriers** can be either **quotas,**—quantity restrictions on imports—or any of a variety of other actions that make importing more difficult. Consider the tariff.

Tariffs

Demand for an imported product tells the quantities of the product consumers would purchase from foreign sources at each possible price. This demand is sometimes called *residual demand*, since it represents demand that is left over after consumers have bought from domestic suppliers. Because buyers have the ability to

The text of the GATT agreement can be found at **http://cerebalaw. com/gatttext.htm**

General Agreement on Tariffs and Trade (GATT): an agreement signed by most of the major trading countries of the world, which limits the use of protectionist policies; enforced by the World Trade Organization.

nontariff barriers: any of a variety of actions other than tariffs that make importing more expensive or difficult.

quota: quantity limit on imports.

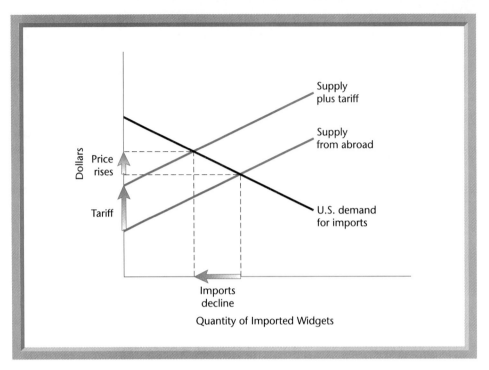

FIGURE 5-9 An import tariff raises prices and reduces imports. Import tariffs help American producers of import-competing products at the expense of consumers of those products.

substitute domestically made products for foreign-made products, the demand for imports is typically more elastic than market demand as a whole. Likewise, because suppliers have many countries to sell in, import supply to any one country is also relatively elastic.

Tariffs increase the cost of selling imported products. This increase in turn increases the prices of those products in the domestic market and, by the law of demand discussed in chapter 3, reduces the quantity that will be sold. That is how a tariff restricts imports. Figure 5-9 illustrates how a tariff raises the price and decreases the quantity of imports, relative to what would have occurred in the free market. Note that the increase in price is less than the amount of the tariff, indicating that importers are often not able merely to pass along the entire tariff to consumers.

By raising barriers to the entry of foreign products, **tariffs can be viewed as a form of price support for domestic producers.** The higher price of imports causes the demand curve to shift to the right for domestic products that are close substitutes. For example, an import tariff on Toshiba laptop computers increases demand for Dell, Compaq, and IBM laptop computers, which in turn causes a new, higher equilibrium price and quantity for those products. The higher price and quantity sold by domestic producers are why an import tariff is said to protect those producers from foreign competition.

Tariffs are said to be *transparent*, meaning that their effects upon prices are clear for all to see. The United States has an extensive array of tariffs, most of which are

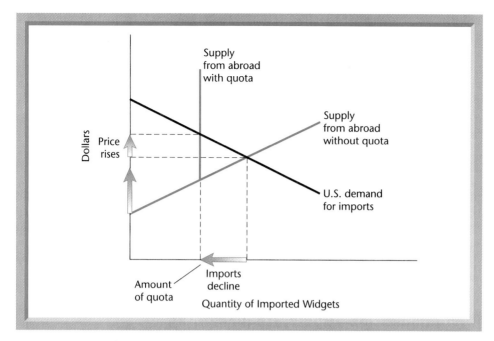

FIGURE 5-10 Like an import tariff, **a quota also raises prices and reduces imports.**

currently below 6 percent and falling. Most other major trading countries also have similar tariffs. With some exceptions, tariff rates are kept low by the GATT.

Quotas

Import quotas are an alternative to import tariffs and can accomplish the same goals as a tariff. Unlike an import tariff, an import quota restricts the quantity of imports directly and thus cuts off supply from abroad at the quota quantity. Figure 5-10 illustrates how the truncated supply from abroad under a quota leads to an increase in prices at home.

GATT limits the extent to which countries can impose import quotas, but does allow quotas for agricultural products and to avoid disruption to countries' domestic economies. While not as widespread as tariffs, most countries have some import quotas.

For example, the U.S. restricts the import of sugar through a set of country-by-country quotas. These sugar import quotas increase the cost of sugar in the United States to about double what it is in the rest of the world. Consumers feel the effects when they buy sugar and sweetened products. Indeed, a primary reason for the use of corn sweetener in U.S. soft drinks is the high price of sugar in the United States. Even so, because U.S. sugar prices are increased indirectly through quotas, rather than directly through a corresponding tariff that would exceed 100 percent, U.S. consumers tend to be unaware of how much extra the quota forces them to pay for sugar. In other words, quotas are not as transparent as tariffs.

In an attempt to increase transparency, sugar import quotas are scheduled to be replaced by tariffs by the year 2004. Agricultural interests oppose converting sugar import quotas to tariffs. They worry that consumers will object to protecting U.S. sugar interests if the effect of the protectionist policy upon the price of sugar becomes too obvious.

As an alternative to import quotas, the United States and some other countries have chosen to negotiate **voluntary export restraints,** in which individual exporting countries agree to limit the quantities they export. For example, the *multifiber agreement,* currently also scheduled for elimination by 2004, sets country-by-country quotas on clothing exports to the United States and some other countries. The alternative would be for the United States or other importing countries to impose import quotas.

The United States offers to forgo quotas in favor of voluntary export restraints in order to maintain good relations with the governments of the other countries involved. Exporting countries know that if they do not agree to the voluntary export restraints, they may face either quotas or some other retaliatory action. Exporting countries can also charge higher prices per unit under a voluntary export restraint than they could if they face import quotas. Exporting countries charge more because they are not competing against each other—they each have their preassigned export restraints and are not allowed to fill those of other exporting countries.

voluntary export restraints: an alternative to import quotas in which exporting countries agree voluntarily to limit their exports to the target country; has an effect similar to an export cartel, such as OPEC.

 QuickCheck _____

Why are exporting countries better off to agree to a voluntary export restraint than to have the importing country restrict imports with an import quota?

Answer: If the importing country imposes an import quota, exporting countries compete to fill that quota, which drives the prices they receive lower. In contrast, by accepting a voluntary export restraint, the countries are not in competition with one another and can thus receive higher prices for their exports.

An Assortment of Nontariff Barriers to Trade

Quotas and voluntary export restraints are examples of nontariff barriers to trade, which include all ways that countries inhibit imports without resorting to tariffs. Most nontariff barriers do not restrict imports explicitly; their effects are even less transparent than quotas. For example, paperwork and red tape delays can inhibit trade. Under the administration of President Salinas, for example, Mexico established a clever system to fight some of its hidden nontariff barriers. The policy was that any application for importing a product into Mexico would be automatically approved, if not acted upon within 90 days. Prior to that time, in the absence of illegal bribery, applications were often delayed so long that the market opportunity to sell the product had long since vanished.

Sometimes, nontariff barriers are incidental to accomplishing other objectives. For example, the United States inspects the manufacturing processes of some products made domestically. It cannot do that for most imports, and so resorts to sampling. For this reason, entire lots of such things as canned foods from China have been discarded because sampling revealed some to be contaminated, labeled improperly, or otherwise not up to U.S. standards. While sampling does increase the cost of importing and is thus a nontariff barrier, its primary purpose is to protect public safety.

At other times, the effects on trade are intentional, but hard to prove. For example, Japan made it difficult to sell Louisville Slugger baseball bats in its country for many years, because the bats did not meet Japan's guidelines for use in baseball games. Since the Louisville Slugger was the best-selling bat in the world market, U.S. trade negotiators asserted that the Japanese regulators set their standards for bats with an eye toward restricting competition from U.S. imports.

The home page for the Louisville Slugger is at **http://www. slugger.com/ home.htm**

Still other times, motives conflict. In the early 1990s, Europe would not allow the import or sale of beef from cattle fed the bovine growth hormone. While illegal in Europe, use of bovine growth hormone was allowed in the United States. Since the U.S. government would not certify its beef exports as hormone-free, the U.S. was barred from exporting beef to Europe. That ban was lifted after the U.S. restricted imports of some minor European products and threatened to go much further if the Europeans did not back down. Since buyers in either the United States or Europe could always contract with cattle ranchers for whatever sort of animals they desire, U.S. negotiators argued that no government certification would be necessary.

OBSERVATION POINT:
Made in Mexico, Brick by Brick

Americans have no legal right to know which state is responsible for producing the goods they buy. By law, however, they do have a right to know the country of origin for imports. This information must be labeled on each imported item. The law applies to all products, including bricks from Mexico. No big deal, perhaps, except when you realize that brick kilns in Mexico are rarely high-tech. The cost of imprinting *Mexico* into each brick bound for El Norté is a significant fraction of the entire cost of producing that brick. If that labeling requirement forms a nontariff barrier that reduces Mexican brick exports, U.S. brick makers don't complain!

Trade Agreements

Countries design their trade policies with an eye toward their own self interests. Since governments are by nature political, trade strategies usually contain a mix of political and economic objectives. However, most countries recognize that their interests are usually best served by freeing up trade with other countries. Countries thus are motivated to sign onto the worldwide General Agreement of Tariffs and Trade. They also may join regional trade agreements, thereby creating what is known as a trading bloc. Both routes toward freer trade are discussed in this section.

trading blocs: agreement among a group of countries that provides for lower trade barriers among its members than to the rest of the world.

The GATT and the World Trade Organization

The broadest trade strategy is embodied in the multilateral General Agreement on Tariffs and Trade. This agreement is termed *multilateral* because multiple nations have joined in. Specifically, the GATT was initially signed in 1947 by the major trading countries of the world at that time. Over the intervening years, the agreement

The World Trade Organization maintains a Web site at **http://www. wto.org/**

has been updated and new countries have been added. Since 1995, the GATT has been administered by the **World Trade Organization,** an arm of the GATT created to settle trade disputes among GATT members and monitor compliance with provisions of the GATT.

The initial impetus for the GATT agreement was the prohibitively high tariffs imposed by the United States and some other countries during the Great Depression of the 1930s. The GATT required significant tariff reductions. The high tariffs were deemed to have harmed the world economically. Furthermore, the high tariffs promoted political animosity and isolationism among countries and led to economic tensions that contributed to World War II.

The GATT agreement has been strengthened through rounds of trade negotiations that have achieved further reductions in tariffs, and also restrictions upon quotas and other nontariff barriers. For example, the *Uruguay round* of negotiations took eight years of often contentious bargaining before being ratified by the United States and other countries in late 1994.

The Uruguay round established the World Trade Organization to enforce the GATT. Prior to the World Trade Organization, the GATT had been administered through a bureaucracy headquartered in Geneva. This bureaucracy had limited enforcement power, however, since individual member countries could veto many of its actions. The World Trade Organization, also based in Geneva, has greater enforcement authority and cannot have its actions vetoed by any single country. This point was contentious in the Uruguay round, since the United States and other countries worried about losing national sovereignty.

The Uruguay round addressed a number of other thorny issues. These issues include the following:

- Tariffs: Tariffs have been cut by an average of about 40 percent worldwide on thousands of products and eliminated altogether on others, such as beer, toys, and paper. After a phase-in period, the percentage of products that can be imported *duty-free* into industrialized countries will more than double to 44 percent of all imported goods.

- Agricultural subsidies: *Subsidies* represent financial assistance to domestic producers. This assistance can lead to inefficient patterns of trade. After particularly heated debate, countries agreed to reduce trade-distorting subsidies to agriculture. Agricultural subsidies have been estimated to cost consumers $160 billion per year.

- Services: For the first time, global trade rules will be interpreted to cover services. To reach agreement, many of the details were left vague, especially in regard to banking and other financial services.

- *Intellectual property rights:* New rules were enacted to better protect patents and copyrights, including rights to copy computer software.

OBSERVATION POINT:
The Trade Game—No Imported Pickup Trucks from Europe

Buy a pickup truck imported into the United States from Europe recently? It's not likely, in part because of a decades-old 25 percent tariff that the United States imposed in response to a threatened trade war long since forgotten. The pickup tariff was merely a shot across the bow, so to speak, because Europeans never had been known for pickup truck exports. The tariff was enacted by the United States as part of strategic maneuvering—a trade game—in which both the United States and Europe were each seeking to both restrict and free up trade in ways that would be of most benefit to their own political constituencies.

In playing the trade game, as in other games, there are strategies and bluffs. Sometimes there are actions. The danger is that actions can lead to counteractions and a full-blown trade war, such as occurred prior to World War II, when beggar-thy-neighbor trade policies brought most world trade to a screeching halt. Threats of trade wars continue. In 1995, for example, only a last-minute concession by Japan prevented the United States from slapping a tariff on luxury Japanese auto imports in order to protest a U.S. belief that Japan wasn't allowing U.S. automakers a fair chance to sell U.S.-built cars in the Japanese market. Had the United States followed through with that tariff, it is likely that Japan would have responded in kind, since Japan thought that its markets were not the problem. That kind of trade policy sparring could easily lead to a useless and dangerous trade war, just the sort that arbitrators at the World Trade Organization seek to prevent.

Regional Trading Blocs

In addition to joining the GATT, most countries have also gone the route of forming regional trading blocs. For example, the European Economic Community is considered a trading bloc, because it has lower trade barriers among its member countries than to the rest of the world. By signing the **North American Free Trade Agreement,** commonly known as NAFTA, the United States, Canada, and Mexico also formed a trading bloc. This bloc is envisioned to someday expand southward to include countries of Central and South America. ASEAN, the Association of Southeast Asian Nations, is yet another trading bloc.

To the extent that regional trading blocs reduce tariffs and other trade restrictions, the trading blocs promote trade among their members. This trade can come from two sources. First is the **trade creation effect,** which involves an increase in world trade. The trade creation effect is efficient, since it allows countries to specialize according to comparative advantage.

The second is the **trade diversion effect,** which represents trade that would have occurred with countries outside the trading bloc, but that is diverted to countries within a trading bloc in response to lower tariff rates. An example of trade diversion would be if the North American Free Trade Agreement induced IBM to assemble its laptop computers in Mexico instead of Taiwan. Trade diversion is inefficient, since it causes trade to respond to price signals from government—relative tariff rates— rather than to comparative advantage.

Economists generally support regional trading blocs as a step toward free trade. However, even supporters of regional agreements have reservations about trade-diversion effects. There are also concerns that regional trading blocs may turn inward and erect higher barriers to the rest of the world. Not only would contentious trading blocs jeopardize gains from trade, they could also be a threat to world peace.

North American Free Trade Agreement (NAFTA): trading bloc that includes the United States, Canada, and Mexico.

Links to various information relating to NAFTA can be found at **http://www.nafta. net/naftagre.htm**

trade creation effect: efficient specialization and trade caused by lower trade barriers among members of a trading bloc; implies a greater amount of world trade.

trade diversion effect: when the lower trade barriers within a trading bloc cause trade to occur among member countries instead of with countries outside the bloc; inefficient.

SUMMARY

- The price of a country's currency, in terms of another country's currency, is an exchange rate.
- Exchange rates vary over time. A currency appreciates or gets stronger when its value in the foreign exchange market rises. A currency depreciates or weakens when its value falls in the foreign exchange market. As a country's currency appreciates it buys more of other currencies, thus resulting in lower prices for its imports but higher prices for its exports. As a country's currency depreciates, its exports become cheaper, but the price of its imports rises.
- The Bretton Woods Agreement (1944) established a system of fixed exchange rates that lasted until 1971. Currencies were pegged to the U.S. dollar, which was pegged to gold.
- When government adopts a hands off policy toward exchange rates, the system is one of floating exchange rates. Today, the world currency system is a managed float, with both government and the market affecting currency values.
- Countries gain from trade. Imports result from a world price that is lower than a country's domestic price. When the world price is higher than the domestic price, exports result.
- The current account records the value of imports and exports of goods and services. Since U.S. imports exceed U.S. exports, the current account is in deficit.
- The current account includes the services account and the merchandise trade account, the balance on which is currently quite negative and is called the trade deficit.
- The capital account measures international investment flows, which currently are characterized by more foreign investment in the U.S. than U.S. investment abroad.
- Trade barriers include tariffs, quotas, voluntary export restraints, and other non-tariff barriers. The GATT limits the extent of trade barriers and protectionist policies.
- Regional trading blocs promote trade among their members. NAFTA is an example.

QUESTIONS AND PROBLEMS

1. Suppose Japanese investors decide to cash in their U.S. investments. What would be the effect upon the exchange rate between the dollar and yen? Why would Japanese investors be unlikely to follow this course of action?

2. At one time the Arts & Entertainment Cable Network advertised its monthly magazine at a price of $18 U.S., or $23 Canadian. Which was stronger, the U.S. dollar or the Canadian dollar? Why?

3. a. The United States runs a trade deficit. Specifically, what does this mean? Briefly distinguish the trade deficit from the current account deficit.

b. Suppose the United States decides to eliminate the current account deficit by prohibiting all imports and exports. Would this approach reduce unemployment in the United States? Explain.

4. Suppose the federal government adopts the policy of "What's good for General Motors is good for the country." To this end, the government decides to prohibit the import of all motor vehicles from other counties. Assuming other countries do not change their own trade policies, what would be the impact on the value of the dollar relative to other currencies? What would be the effect on the quantity of other items imported? What would be the effect on jobs in U.S. industries that did not participate in the making of autos?

5. What purposes would be served by converting quotas or other nontariff barriers into tariffs?

6. In 1998 the new Volkswagen Beetle and Mercedes-Benz M-class sport utility vehicles were unveiled. Explain, using the concepts in this chapter, why Mercedes-Benz chose to produce its new sport utility vehicle in Alabama rather than in Germany. Why would Volkswagen have decided at about the same time to make the new Beetle in Mexico rather than the United States?

7. Find a recent issue of *The Wall Street Journal* newspaper and check on the exchange rates between several currencies of your choice and the U.S. dollar. Has the dollar strengthened or weakened within the last year relative to these currencies?

8. Explain the trade creation and trade diversion effects of a trading bloc. Which of these is considered beneficial and which not? Why?

Web Exercises

9. a. Using an Internet search engine such as that provided by Yahoo (located at **http://www.yahoo.com**) or Alta Vista (located at **http://www.altavista.com**), perform a separate search for the following terms: **exchange rate, current account,** and **General Agreement on Tariffs and Trade (GATT)**. Visit several of the Web sites that your search reveals for each term and observe the context in which each term is used. Explain whether the manner in which the terms are used is consistent with their use in the text.

   b. Repeat the above, but this time use a combination of terms that you select from the chapter. To eliminate sites that do not contain all terms, place a plus sign in front of each term you enter, such as **+quota +"World Trade Organization" +"trading bloc"**.

10. Visit the Cable News Network (CNN) Web site at **http://www.cnn.com**. Use the search feature to browse recent news stories about the global economy. After reading several of the stories that have been posted by CNN reporters, write a short essay focusing on a single theme that ties these stories together. Use several of the terms in this chapter in the writing of your essay.

Visit the Web site for *Economics by Design* at
http://www.prenhall.com/collinge for a Self Quiz over
the topics in this chapter.

EXPLORING ISSUES

Exploration 5-1 Point/Counterpoint—So Many Reasons Not to Trade!

There are many possible exceptions to the rule that free trade is desirable because it increases a country's consumption possibilities. However, objections to free trade frequently have limited applicability or are based on shaky assumptions.

Individuals, regions, and countries can specialize according to their respective comparative advantages and gain from trading with each other. We each do that—no one in modern society is self-sufficient. When we earn incomes that allow us to buy the things we want, we are specializing and gaining from trade. Regions specialize and trade with other regions within a country. Countries do the same with other countries. A country that specializes and trades with other countries will be able to consume more than it could produce on its own. As a general rule, then, restricting trade to protect either high-wage jobs or low-wage jobs is inefficient—it cuts down on the size of the economic pie.

Since the purpose of economic activity is to consume, not to produce for the sake of keeping busy, why restrict imports? Yet countries do impose restrictions on trade, especially on imports. Sometimes the reasons make economic sense. More often, the reasons have much more to do with politics than with sound economics. This Exploration examines some of the special circumstances under which trade restrictions have been justified. In each case, caution is in order.

Infant Industries—Where Are Investors?

infant industries: start-up industries that might be unable to survive the rigors of competition in their formative years.

Developing countries often try to nurture new industries they hope will one day become a source of export earnings. These infant industries are thought to need protection in the rough world marketplace. The infant industry argument claims that government must first identify promising industries and then erect import barriers to protect them. When the infants grow strong enough to fend for themselves, government should remove the barriers.

The infant industry argument is unconvincing if markets function efficiently. In the free marketplace, *venture capitalists* and other private investors will often support firms through many years of losses. They will do so if they expect that the firms will eventually become profitable and reward their patience. If private investors do not foresee profits down the road, they will withhold their funds, and the businesses will fail.

Unfortunately, there is much less assurance that government will pick industries that are likely to survive on their own. Governments often use political considerations to select "infant" industries. Even if governments do attempt careful economic analysis, such analyses are unlikely to match those of investors with their own money at risk. The result is that governments around the world have protected industries that never grew strong enough to withstand foreign competition. By requiring government subsidies to stay afloat, and by charging prices above prices in the rest of the world, such industries have proven to be expensive for governments and consumers alike.

National Defense—Valid but Overused

If imports or exports seriously threaten national defense, it makes sense to restrict them. No one denies this fact. However, translating national defense interests into policy is often not easy. When is the threat serious? For example, the U.S. Department of Defense has advocated restrictions on the export of computers and technology. However, if the United States is an unreliable supplier to other countries, will new technologies evolve elsewhere in places where the government allows producers to reap the profits from exports? Also, what weight should be put on civilian uses for products that could also be used in war?

The judgments are often difficult and the source of debate. In 1998, for example, the President's decision to allow China to launch U.S. companies' satellites sparked a heated debate in Congress about the role of satellite and satellite launch technology in the production of intercontinental missiles, which the United States does not want aimed at it from China.

On occasion, the judgments are easy. For example, is it necessary to protect the jobs of uniform makers and shoemakers in order to preserve the national security of the United States? If you work in or earn investment income from those industries, self-interest might prompt you to argue "yes!" That argument was indeed made to the U.S. International Trade Commission in the mid-1980s.

U.S. leather footwear manufacturing was in trouble, due to inexpensive imports from Brazil and Italy. It looked as if the leather footwear industry might follow the same route as the athletic shoe industry. With few exceptions, the athletic shoe industry had already abandoned the United States in favor of manufacturing facilities in the Far East. The argument to protect remaining U.S. shoemakers went along the following lines:

Without any shoe industry within its borders, what would the U.S. do in wartime if it were to run short of combat boots? Look what happened to the armies of Napoleon in Russia and to the Confederate armies in the U.S. Civil War. The soldiers of these armies marched so much that they wore out their boots. Unable to provide replacements, France and the Confederacy went down in defeat.

Yes, this argument is far-fetched. Few people envision that a modern war would pit the United States against Brazil, Italy, and countries of the Far East in years of ground warfare. Even if that were likely, a simple solution would be to stockpile extra boots. Nevertheless, when the security of an industry's profits and its workers' livelihoods are at stake, the more ammunition the better!

Promoting Values or a Shot in the Foot?

The United States often sees actions in foreign countries that do not meet with U.S. perceptions of what is right and just. The United States has seen many such actions when looking toward China, for example, including the suppression of the democracy movement in the massacre at Tiananmen Square and thus use of prisoner labor to make cheap products for export. To express our disapproval, some people advocate that we should invoke trade sanctions against China, rather than just say "tsk, tsk" and continue business as usual, which is their view of diplomatic responses.

The objection to basing trade policy on the morality of other country's political actions is twofold. One objection is based on philosophy and the other on practicality. The philosophical objection revolves around whether the United States should set itself up as the judge of whether a country's internal policies are moral. For example, other countries could look to the United States and object to various of our internal policies, perhaps claiming that it is immoral to allow any citizens to go without health care, for example. The United States might like to argue the point, but would find no forum. Indeed, citizens of the United States would probably resent the nosiness of the other country.

Perhaps Chinese officials feel this way about our concerns over their prison labor, and would like to point out that the United States uses prison labor, too. Does the use of convicts to pick up litter, chop weeds, and do other maintenance tasks along America's highways not free up American labor to produce goods for export? Is it wrong to have convicts produce auto license plates, such as is done in many states? However you would answer these questions personally, the issues that they raise are legitimate to talk about. Moreover, if the United States is to use similar concerns in other countries as a basis for unilaterally restricting our trade with them, it should be prepared for like-minded retaliation. Whether such trade sniping leads to greater morality in countries' policies is an open question.

The second facet of the objection is that the United States could become known as an unreliable source of goods and services if buyers of our products must fear that their governments might do something that would irritate us and cause us to impose trade sanctions. Given the multinational nature of business today, why not locate new businesses in countries that are more reliable? Thus, U.S. threats of trade sanctions can backfire and cause U.S. companies to be at a competitive disadvantage to similar companies located elsewhere in the world.

Environmental, Health, and Safety Standards— A Level Playing Field without a Game

Some U.S. industries cannot produce products as cheaply as products from abroad, because companies abroad do not have to pay for protecting the environment or the health and safety of their workers. Should the United States attempt to estimate the extra costs of producing in the United States, and then add that cost to imports by imposing an appropriate set of tariffs? Some critics of current trade policy suggest that this approach is the only way to achieve a *level playing field*.

There is merit to this argument, insofar as the environmental or other damages reach U.S. territory or otherwise affect U.S. citizens. For example, the effect of chlorofluorocarbons—chemicals named by scientists as the culprit in creating a hole in the world's ozone layer—does not depend upon which country is the source of chlorofluorocarbon emissions. Likewise, the United States may have an interest in ensuring that the tuna it imports has been caught in a dolphin-friendly manner.

If carried to an extreme, leveling the playing field would remove the very basis for trade itself, comparative advantage. After all, if all firms have identical costs, there is much less reason to trade. For the U.S. to impose its own environmental standards upon other countries, when environmental effects are localized, would benefit neither the United States nor those countries. Such action could easily be interpreted by those countries' citizens as an act of U.S. arrogance or imperialism.

For example, environmental costs of production in poor countries are often less than in the United States because of weaker laws or law enforcement. Higher levels of pollution are likely to be efficient for these countries, because environmental quality is a normal good—as incomes rise, people demand more. Poor countries value extra income to spend on food, shelter, and other goods more highly than extra environmental quality. Thus, poor countries have a higher opportunity cost of environmental quality and might efficiently specialize in industries with a higher pollution content. In contrast, by valuing environmental quality highly, U.S. citizens are better off when those industries go elsewhere.

Dumping—Rarely Strategic

Dumping is defined as the selling of a good for less than its cost of production. A company may engage in dumping for various reasons. One common reason is that the company overestimates demand and produces too much. It then seeks to salvage what revenues it can from its bloated inventories.

A second common reason is that a company may be selling output at a price that covers wages, materials, and other operating expenses of production, but does not cover the cost of its capital and other *fixed costs* that it must pay whether it produces or not. Even though the company loses money, it would lose more by not selling.

A third reason, related to the second, revolves around different elasticities of demand in different markets. A company may dump a product in a country where its elasticity of demand is high, perhaps caused by intense competition from other companies in its industry. The company covers its capital costs by charging a higher price in markets where it faces less competition. Lower prices where competition is heavy are familiar occurrences within a country, as well as internationally. This is one reason why the same brand of gasoline sold along an interstate highway at the edge of a city is often priced much higher than when sold in the city itself.

Dumping for each of the above reasons occurs within a country, as well as in international trade. However, it is only in international trade that dumping is illegal, according to the GATT. If a company is charging a lower price in a foreign market than it does at home, and if that lower price does not cover its fixed costs, the company is guilty of dumping. Indeed, since a foreign company's capital costs are often hard to measure, the United States presumes dumping whenever a foreign company charges less in the United States than it does at home, irrespective of its costs. U.S. law allows for the imposition of antidumping tariffs, such as those imposed in the early 1990s on Japanese computer chips.

Why worry about dumping? After all, aren't U.S. consumers being offered a bargain? In most cases, the U.S. would be better off to accept the low prices and spend the savings on other products. The only time to worry is when there is *strategic dumping*—dumping that is intended to drive the competition out of business, so that the firms doing the dumping can monopolize output and drive prices up in the future. However, in most industries, the prospects for successful strategic dumping are highly questionable. After all, in a world marketplace, there are many potential

dumping: the selling of a good for less than its cost of production; prohibited by the General Agreement on Tariffs and Trade.

The Federal Reserve Bank of New York offers an article on dumping and fair trade via their on-line publication *Current Issues in Economics and Finance* at **http://www. ny.frb.org/ rmaghome/ curr_iss/ci4-8.htm**

competitors lurking in the wings. Even companies that have been driven out of a particular line of business can often reenter it in the future, should an increase in price make it profitable to do so.

Why All the Argument?

Objections to free trade are often well-intentioned, and occasionally these objections are valid. However, mixed in with valid arguments to restrict trade are many arguments that can best be described as self-serving. It is in the interests of U.S. producers to restrict trade if the goods and services they offer are in competition with imports. After all, this competition keeps prices and profits lower than they would otherwise be. Competition forces businesses to find ways to economize and become more efficient. They do not like this competitive pressure.

Of course, many U.S. companies have no interest in restricting imports, especially companies that use imported components or produce products for the export market. U.S. consumers are also poorly served by import restrictions, since these restrictions drive up consumer prices and thus reduce purchasing power. Curiously, consumers often seem unaware of their own interests. They may believe that importing products is somehow unpatriotic, since they perceive that importing products is equivalent to exporting jobs and neglect to consider that dollars return to the U.S. to buy exports and investments, thus creating other jobs.

If the arguments for and against free trade were to be counted, free trade would come up very short. However, the number of objections is not important. It is the validity of those objections that matters. In that respect, with minor exception, free trade offers the best chance of maintaining and improving the standard of living the world now enjoys.

■ Prospecting for New Insights

1. a. One way that the dollars spent by U.S. citizens on imports return to this country is through investment. Is foreign investment in the U.S. good for the country?

   b. Some people claim that allowing the Japanese to own U.S. assets is comparable to a U.S. surrender to Japan in World War II. Others contend that foreign ownership of U.S. assets, subject to U.S. law, is very different from a foreign power conquering the United States and establishing its own laws. What do you think? Explain.

2. What would be the effect on trade and U.S. output if the United States required all other countries to meet U.S. labor and environmental standards pertaining to production bound for the United States? Would this approach be good for the United States? Explain.

Exploration 5-2 Immigration—Implications for Growth and Trade

Countries interact through immigration as well as trade. Focusing mainly on the United States, this Exploration looks at the effects of immigration on trade patterns and on wages. Questions are raised in regard to a country's choice of immigration policy.

We came over on different ships, but we're all in the same boat now.

Traditionally, the United States has been called the melting pot of the world. U.S. citizens are proud of their diverse ancestries and the symbolism of the welcoming arms of the Statue of Liberty. Today immigrants account for about 8 percent of the U.S. population.

The United States is not alone in its role as melting pot. People of different races, religions, languages, and customs have come to live together in more and more nations. Jamaicans, Hindus, and others from countries within the old British Empire fill the sidewalks of London, Algerians those of Paris, and Turks those of Berlin. Immigration touches many nations, either because many of their citizens would like to immigrate to another country, or because their country is a favorite destination for immigrants.

Can Immigration Substitute for Trade?

Immigration can affect a country's trade patterns. In the modern world, both capital and labor can move among countries, although there are usually some barriers to this migration. The barriers to the movement of labor are obvious. In many cases, governments limit the number of immigrants from a particular country. Those who want to immigrate must have sufficient money to at least pay for transportation to their new home. Immigrants might face difficulties of language and culture, and perhaps, discrimination. For these reasons and more, many people remain citizens of the country in which they were born.

The barriers to capital movements arise from diverse sources. Investors often lack information about the risks involved in setting up shop in another country. Many of these risks are referred to as *political risks* because they involve instabilities associated with government. For example, investors in a foreign land might worry that government would confiscate their property without paying them for it. Or they might worry that the citizens of a foreign country, egged on by their government, will develop anger toward the country the investors are from, and burn, loot, bomb, or otherwise destroy their investments. These kinds of political risks are on top of the normal risks associated with investing, and help slow down the flow of capital from one country to another. A further barrier to capital movements occurs when a government refuses to allow foreign investors into their country, or when government limits the amount of foreign investment.

In spite of the barriers to the migration of labor and capital, people move across international borders; so does money in the form of capital investment. Migration of either resource affects patterns of international trade. If this migration were carried to the extreme in which all countries have identical proportions of capital and labor, world trade would be greatly diminished, because differences in the relative abundance of resources provide a major basis for specialization and trade.

If a country has abundant capital relative to labor, it tends to have lower prices than other countries on capital-intensive goods. That country then tends to export goods that are produced with a relatively high proportion of capital and import goods that employ more labor. Likewise, labor-abundant countries tend to export goods that require a lot of labor to produce and import goods that require a lot of capital. Immigration provides countries that have relatively less labor an opportunity to increase their amount of labor. The increase in labor would allow the country the chance to produce within its borders some products that it would previously have imported.

For example, a capital-abundant country could allow free immigration of labor and greatly reduce its need for the imports from labor-abundant countries. However, free immigration involves decreasing the country's average income level, which would occur because of increased supplies of labor. Those already living in the country may object to that effect of immigration. On the other hand, it is often argued that immigrants will do the dirty, low-paying jobs that the rest of the population does not want to do.

There are other ways that immigrants affect trade patterns. One way is by changing the buying habits of consumers in the host country. Foreign products have often become popular after being introduced by immigrants. For example, without Chinese immigrants and their descendants, would Chinese food have become the lunch and dinner staple that it is in the United States today?

Another way that immigration can affect trade patterns is through the skills that immigrants bring to their new country. Suppose a group of immigrants with rug weaving skills arrive in a country that has traditionally imported rugs. These immigrants might well be able to start a rug weaving industry in their new country. At the least, that country would import fewer rugs. It might even be possible for that country to begin exporting rugs at some point.

The intelligence that immigrants bring to a country can also alter trade patterns. For example, opportunities for success in a country encourages particularly inventive and entrepreneurial immigrants. The entrepreneurship and development of technology arising from the efforts of these immigrants expands the country's production possibilities and in the process changes its patterns of trade.

Why Immigration Is a Concern

Increasingly, many countries, including the United States, are ambivalent about the ideal of the national melting pot. This was not the case when John F. Kennedy, the great-grandson of an Irish immigrant, published *A Nation of Immigrants* in 1958. The future President of the United States struck a reverent stance toward immigration in his book, respectfully praising the economic and cultural contributions to the nation from immigrants. Subsequently, the Immigration Act of 1965 opened the door to a new wave of mass immigration into the United States, totaling about 800,000 persons per year. Today, in many other countries as well as the United States, governments are witnessing challenges by the public to open-door immigration policies.

There are numerous reasons for this opposition to further immigration, but not because of the effects of immigration on trade patterns. Instead, opposition arises from the following two root causes:

- Ethnic tensions emanating from issues relating to the assimilation of the newcomers into the existing culture;
- A backlash stemming from concerns that immigration has high economic costs.

The U.S. Census Bureau estimates that by the year 2050, the immigration rates established by the 1965 act will result in a U.S. population of up to 500 million people, which is about twice the population counted in the 1990 census. The nation wonders how the economy can absorb that much population growth without social and environmental stress and reduced standards of living.

If the melting pot is not to boil over into ethnic warfare on our streets, as has happened in other countries, can a role model for immigrants of the future be identified? It could be Albert Einstein, whose development of the theory of relativity made him a household name, or Werner von Braun, whose knowledge of rocketry played a key role in enabling the U.S. space program to reach the moon.

But superstar immigrants are few and far between. Perhaps the country seeks immigrants of the sort profiled in a series of *Saturday Evening Post* and *Country Gentlemen* articles in the 1940s: the Chinese-American Wongs of San Francisco, the Mexican-American Gonzalezes of San Antonio, the Norwegian-American Offerdahls of Wisconsin, and the half-dozen otherwise anonymous families able to succeed with their individual visions of the American Dream.

If it is success that we ask of immigrants, then the economy of today leaves little room for the unskilled. Economist George Borjas' research shows that it takes 100 years, or four generations, for immigrant families to achieve an economic status equal to that of native-born Americans. This research is based upon evidence accumulated over a period earlier in this century when education was significantly less important to labor market success than it is today. The implication of Borjas' research is striking: immigration of low-skilled and relatively uneducated workers is likely to create a nearly permanent underclass.

Permanent Immigrants or Just Guests?

Whether or not a country allows easy immigration has a lot to do with the ownership of resources and the distribution of income within that country. For example, immigration can decrease the incomes and job opportunities for workers who find themselves in competition with the immigrants. Also, if immigrants can claim property rights or subsidies from longer-term citizens, the well-being of those citizens could easily fall, even as the country's output goes up. Thus, whether a country wants to allow easy immigration depends on its objective. If the country seeks to maximize the well-being of its longer-term citizens, it has to consider immigration's effects upon those citizens' incomes and tax burdens, and might choose a relatively tight immigration policy.

As a middle ground, many countries make special provisions for guest workers. *Guest workers* are temporary immigrants, granted limited rights to work and live in a country. For example, Switzerland depends upon its Italian guest workers. Saudi Arabia depends on guests from the Philippines and numerous other countries. For years the United States depended upon guest farm workers from Mexico under the *Bracero* program that ended in 1964. As the U.S. unemployment rate dropped to 4.5 percent in 1998, shortages of cheap labor revived interest in the program. Thus, a new Bracero program may be implemented in the future.

Sometimes, guests become permanent, as with many of the Turkish workers invited into Germany. The same is true of the many temporary immigrants into the United States who make their way into the ranks of those with full citizenship. It is well to remember that, without the entrepreneurial drive of yesteryear's immigrants, the United States would not have produced the economy that beckons to so many more immigrants today.

 ■ **Prospecting for New Insights**

1. If a nation such as China makes it difficult for U.S. firms to sells goods there, should the United States retaliate by barring immigrants from China? More generally, should trade policies and immigration policies be linked?

2. The aging of the U.S. population is predicted to lead to a large increase in the number or retirees relative to the number of workers who will be called upon to support them with their Social Security tax payments. To help with the burden of Social Security, some people suggest that we "import the young to care for the old." The idea is that the U.S. would offer foreigners a stake in America in exchange for their tax contributions. Is this a good idea? Discuss.

PART THREE

THE ENERGY OF THE MARKETPLACE

Markets come in all shapes and sizes. Some have many producers; some have few. Some markets are for products; others are for labor. This section examines the varied types of markets and their effects upon products, prices, and incomes. Underlying the vibrancy of markets is a search for profit. Whether a company produces corn chips or computer chips, the same fundamental economic principles are seen to apply.

6

THE FIRM

A Look Ahead

GATES, ROCKEFELLER, FORD, Walton, Trump: the names are familiar. We read about them in the history books and in newspapers. They were, or are, just a few of the best known of the world's business leaders. Our familiarity with them illustrates the central role of business in the economy and in our lives.

Business firms can be small, large, or somewhere in between. They range from the neighborhood newspaper carrier to billion-dollar multinational corporations. As diverse as firms are, they share the common goal of profit. Investors see to it that management adheres to this goal of profit maximization. To do so, management must think in terms of production relationships, costs, and revenues, as this chapter will describe.

In starting and operating a large business, the entrepreneur usually brings in additional owners and delegates responsibilities to management. In the process, as discussed in Exploration 6-1, businesses encounter the stock market, the need to maintain incentives for employees to be productive, and questions of social obligation. Exploration 6-2 examines agriculture, one of mankind's most enduring industries, but also an industry that has changed dramatically over time in response to changes in production techniques and government programs.

As you are **Surveying Economic Principles** you will arrive at an ability to

❑ identify the legal forms and methods of financing a business;

❑ relate the significance of the law of diminishing returns;

❑ explain the rule of profit maximization;

❑ distinguish between economies and diseconomies of scale;

❑ analyze the effects of technological change and innovation.

While **Exploring Issues** you will be able to

❑ recount some of the hurdles new businesses must overcome;

❑ describe the factors that motivate U.S. farm policy.

Terms Along the Way

SURVEYING ECONOMIC PRINCIPLES

Firms take *inputs* of resources and produce *outputs* of goods and services to be sold in the marketplace. The desire for profit motivates firms to produce. This profit objective guides the legal, financial, and economic decisions firms must make.

Legal Form: Proprietorship, Partnership, and Corporation

A firm can choose to operate in one of the following three legal forms: sole proprietorship, partnership, or corporation. Which should it be?

Consider the personal implications if you open a business. If you commence in a less than formal fashion, you'll become a *sole proprietorship*—a business with a single owner. You may want to visit City Hall and file a dba (doing business as), which lets the public know that you are the operator of a business recognizable by the name you select for your firm. Or you might just print business cards and go. You can hire employees if you wish, but remember that you'll be legally liable for injuries caused to or by the employees acting in the course of their duties. You'll also be personally liable for all debts and taxes of the business. If your firm doesn't earn enough income from sales, you will have to tap into your personal resources to pay off your creditors and the tax collector. You'll report the business' profits or losses on your personal tax return.

If you can find one or more people with whom to start your business, you can form a partnership. *Partnerships* are similar to proprietorships. Each partner can hire employees. Each partner is also liable for business debts that the business is unable to pay. What if you don't wish to be responsible for the debts of your partner? Are you sure your partner is honest and trustworthy? If not, then form a *limited partnership*. Limited partners are liable only for the amount of their investment in the firm. Profits or losses of the firm are reported on each partner's personal tax return, along with a tax filing that provides information on the partnership.

To avoid the disadvantages of proprietorships and partnerships, many firms are formed as corporations. A corporation is a legal entity, a thing separate from the people who own, manage, and otherwise direct its affairs. Unlike other forms of business, corporations can issue shares of *stock*, which are shares of ownership in the company that can be traded on a stock exchange. The market value of the company's stock will depend in large part upon:

corporation: a type of firm that is a legal entity separate from the people who own, manage, and otherwise direct its affairs.

- the company's expected profits over time, which in turn depends not only on the company's decisions, but also upon the expected state of the macroeconomy;
- the value of the company's assets if liquidated or sold;
- the amount of *dividends*, which are cash payments to stockholders;
- opportunity costs to investors, which depend upon the expected returns from alternative investments.

As the owners of the company, stockholders elect a board of directors to oversee the company's management. Corporations tend to be big business. While they account for only about 10 percent of businesses in the United States, they earn over 80 percent of the revenues.

In addition to being able to issue stock, two major advantages of the corporate form of business are *limited liability* and *perpetual existence*. Limited liability means that the owners are not personally liable for the debts of the business. In practical terms, if you choose to incorporate and the business fails, creditors cannot lay claim to your personal assets, such as your house or car. Perpetual existence means the corporation can outlive its owners, providing that it avoids dissolution through bankruptcy.

The major disadvantage to the corporate form of business is the need to pay a corporation income tax, which takes about one-third of profits. There are also reporting and procedural requirements that other forms of business do not face. These disadvantages explain why few small businesses choose to incorporate.

OBSERVATION POINT:
Franchising—Teaming Small Businesses with Giant Corporations

You see them everywhere. The names include McDonald's, Holiday Inn, Pizza Hut, Computerland, Radio Shack, and many others. They are *franchises*, arrangements that let a person or group start a business that uses the name and standards of a parent corporation. The advantage to becoming a franchisee, the holder of a franchise, is the chance to achieve success by putting a well-known name on your business. Franchise holders also receive training in how to operate their businesses. In return, franchisees pay fees and a percentage of their income or profit to the parent company.

Franchising thus pairs the advantages of the corporation with those of the sole proprietor or partnership in the hope of forming a winning team. This teamwork is sometimes contentious, however, as evidenced by the difficulties of many Boston Market franchisees in covering their franchise fees and the complaints of Subway franchisees that the parent corporation was franchising so much that franchisees wound up taking each other's customers and profits.

Alternative Methods of Finance

Firms have three basic sources of *financial capital*, the money needed to start or grow a business. Firms can

- **Use retained earnings**—funds the firm has saved;
- **Borrow**—by taking out bank loans or issuing **bonds,** promises to repay borrowed funds with interest at a specified future date;
- **Issue shares of stock**—but only if the firm is a corporation.

bond: legally binding promise to repay borrowed funds with interest at a specified future date.

Internal versus External Financing

For most small firms, even if they should decide to incorporate, access to the stock market is probably not an option. It is difficult for them to raise financial capital through the issuance of stock, because the costs of going public are high and the firms might have trouble getting listed on a stock exchange. Startup firms with the prospect of large profits in the future may turn to *venture capitalists*, persons or firms that specialize in providing money and advice to promising undercapitalized companies. However, most small firms must initially rely on the personal savings of their owners and their owners' friends and relatives.

More information about the bond market can be obtained by visiting the Bond Market Association at **http://www.bondmarket.org/**

There are also differences in the availability of borrowed funds between large and small firms. Small firms have little hope of raising money by issuing bonds because investors would fear *default*, a situation in which a firm is unable to repay its debts. Large firms have easier access to the bond market, with the interest rates they pay on their bonds dependent in large part upon their bonds' risk ratings by Moody's, Standard and Poor's, or other independent ratings services.

Businesses also seek loans from *financial intermediaries*, including banks, pension funds, insurance companies, credit unions, mutual funds, and finance companies. Many firms find bank credit to be essential, but sometimes hard to come by. For the most part, bank loans to businesses are short-term. As such their primary function is to provide operating funds rather than investment dollars. Banks are sometimes willing to help finance small firms, especially when the firms can offer collateral for their loans. *Collateral* is something of value, such as real estate or equipment, which a firm pledges to turn over to the bank in the event of default.

The New York Stock Exchange can be visited at **http://nyse.com**

When firms look to sources outside themselves for financing, they are said to be seeking *external funds*. Stocks, bonds, and loans provide external funds. Historically, loans have provided about 60 percent of external funds for U.S. business, with bonds providing about 30 percent and stocks about 2 percent. (Other sources of external funds, such as government, provided the remainder.) External funds are not, however, the primary source of funds for firms. All the external sources of funds—including stocks, bonds, and loans—provide only about 25 percent of the funds that firms use. Where then do firms obtain most of their funds?

Internal funds, also called *retained earnings*, are the monies that firms earn and have left after paying all expenses, including taxes and dividends. Retained earnings make up the bulk of funds that finance U.S. firms. While most firms use a combination of retained earnings and external funds to finance growth, there are exceptions. For example, White Castle Hamburgers started in the 1930s as a single store in Columbus, Ohio. True to its depression-era upbringing, it financed its growth into a multistate chain of frugal eating using only retained earnings, avoiding all debt or other external funds.

Global Financial Markets

Unlike in the past, U.S. firms of today, especially corporations, that seek external financing are not restricted to this country in their search for financial capital. Financial markets have gone global as financial capital flows relatively freely across international borders. Large pools of savings have developed in other industrial countries—money that can flow to any firm anywhere that offers the greatest expected rewards.

Both stock and bond markets have become internationalized. Banks also take advantage of opportunities to raise financial capital overseas. These activities are a two-way street. Just as U.S. firms and banks can look overseas for capital, so foreign firms, those based in other countries, can look outside their borders for funds, too.

The *Eurobond market* involves the sale of bonds in one country whose value is stated in terms of the currency of another country. Many Eurobonds are sold in London and stated in terms of U.S. dollars. This market, a fairly recent development, provides U.S. firms with a huge volume of new funds, that in some cases surpasses the amount of funds they are able to raise at home. Foreign stock markets have also been growing in importance. Foreigners, especially the Japanese, have provided a large volume of financial capital to U.S. businesses in recent years, thus allowing these firms and the U.S. economy to grow more rapidly than otherwise.

Production and the Law of Diminishing Returns

The relationship between the amounts of inputs and the quantities of output a firm produces is called its production function. Firms employ numerous inputs. However, in modeling the firm's decisions, economists adhere to the principle of Occam's razor, which suggests stripping away all but the bare essentials. Thus, economists usually model the firm as if it employs only two inputs: labor and capital. Capital is in the physical sense, such as buildings, tools, equipment, and machines. Economists often refer to the quantities of labor, capital, and output as unspecified units. It may be helpful to think of a unit of labor as an hour of work and a unit of capital as an hour's use of machinery.

> **production function:** the relationship between the amounts of inputs and the quantities of output a firm produces.

The Long Run and the Short Run

Production and employment decisions are made by firms in either a long-run or a short-run context. In the long run, all inputs are *variable*, meaning that their quantities can be changed. For this reason, the long run is sometimes called the *planning horizon*. Actual production occurs in the short run, where at least one input is fixed. The quantity of a *fixed* input cannot be adjusted. Capital is assumed to be fixed in the short run, while labor is variable. Capital is fixed since it is difficult to vary many types of capital with any speed. Labor is variable because a change in the amount of labor employed can typically be accomplished relatively quickly.

> **long run:** period of time sufficiently long that all inputs are variable.

> **short run:** period of time in which at least one input is fixed.

Modeling production with only two inputs highlights the distinction between variable and fixed inputs. The implications pertaining to labor apply in the real world to any variable input, including variable capital inputs such as pencils and light bulbs. Likewise, the connotations for capital apply to any fixed input, including long-term employment contracts.

Short-run decision making by the firm focuses only upon the variable input. For instance, in your favorite supermarket, another cashier can quickly be put to work when long lines build up, assuming an idle cash register is available. The number of cashiers to put on duty is an example of a short-run decision about a variable input.

While the number of cash registers is fixed in the short run, the long run offers enough time to make adjustments. With a sufficiently long period of time available, a supermarket is able to add checkout lanes or even build a larger store. Hence, in the long run, both labor and capital are variable for a supermarket, factory, or any other firm.

Marginal Product and Diminishing Returns

When labor is combined with a fixed amount of capital, the additional output from additional units of labor is termed the *marginal product of labor*, or marginal product for short.

> **marginal product (of labor):** additional output produced by the addition of one more unit of labor; Δoutput/Δlabor.

$$\text{Marginal product} = \frac{\Delta\text{output}}{\Delta\text{labor}}$$

where the triangle (Greek delta) represents difference. For example, consider a firm that increases its employment of labor from 100 workers to 101 workers and experiences an increase in total output from 50,000 units to 51,000 units. Marginal product equals 1,000 units of output.

Marginal product is subject to the law of diminishing returns, which states that, **when additional units of labor or any other variable input are added to a fixed input, the marginal product of the variable input must eventually decrease.**

Because the statement of the law involves a fixed input, the law applies in the short run. Once a firm reaches the point of diminishing returns, each successive unit of labor will add less and less to total production. The law assumes that all labor is of equal quality, which signifies that diminishing returns occur for reasons other than those relating to labor quality. For example, although the one hundred and first worker in the previous example has a marginal product equal to 1,000 units of output, the law suggests that a one hundred and second worker, who is just as intelligent, skilled, and energetic as the one hundred and first, will nonetheless exhibit a marginal product of less than 1,000 units.

The explanation for the law of diminishing returns is found in the commonsense proposition that adding more and more labor to a fixed amount of capital reduces the amount of capital each unit of labor has to work with. Eventually, the effect of less capital per worker reveals itself in the form of diminishing returns.

The principle of diminishing returns applies to all types of businesses. Table 6-1 illustrates the behavior of marginal product for Ali's King-of-Ribs Restaurant. Ali has a relatively small building. At first, marginal product rises because his employees can specialize. In Ali's case, the major specializations are the tasks of taking orders, cooking, and cleaning up.

After the third worker, there are fewer possibilities for specialization. Ali's restaurant has reached the point of diminishing returns. For example, the next three workers might "float," relieving the cashier of tending the drive-through window, helping with cleanup, or doing whatever other tasks seem most important at the time. These workers increase Ali's total production, as shown in the output column, but the marginal product column shows that the increments to output decline.

TABLE 6-1   Marginal and Average Product

Labor	Output (Q of meals/hour)	Marginal Product ($\Delta Q/\Delta L$)
0	0	Undefined
1	3	3
2	10	7
3	20	10
4	27	7
5	31	4
6	32	1
7	30	−2

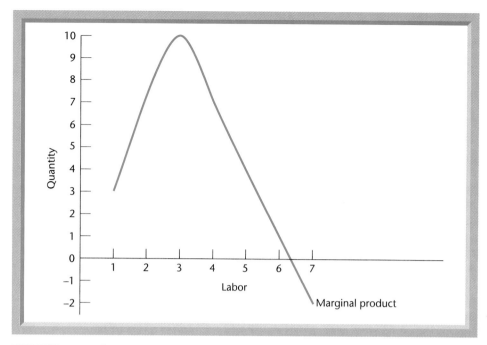

FIGURE 6-1   **The marginal product of labor** is shown with its typical shape.

There is a danger from hiring too many employees. "Too many cooks spoil the ribs," Ali always says, as he imagines excess employees with little to do, chatting and getting in each other's way instead of attending to customers. Suppose Ali mistakenly continues to increase employment to seven workers while keeping his capital constant. In that event, he will reach *negative returns*, in which marginal product is negative. Because output is higher with fewer employees, firms seek to avoid negative returns. Figure 6-1 shows graphically Ali's marginal product curve. Diminishing returns are associated with the downward-sloping part of the curve; negative returns are illustrated by the part of the curve that falls below the horizontal axis.

QuickCheck

Explain how a student faces the law of diminishing returns.

Answer: A student combines ability—an input that is fixed in the short-run—with the variable input of time. The output is knowledge as measured by an examination grade. When studying, a point is reached at which each succeeding minute of study time adds less and less to the student's knowledge. Sometimes students press their studying beyond diminishing returns and into negative returns, which start when an additional minute of continuous studying begins to result in mental confusion. Such a student will lament: "I studied too much for the exam."

The Goal: Profit Maximization

What do firms hope to achieve? The answer, "Make money!" is too vague. Certainly revenue, the income from sales, is necessary. But revenue is only part of the equation. Costs, the expenses a firm incurs, are also important. **Profit** is the difference between total revenue and total cost, as follows:

$$\text{Profit} = \text{total revenue} - \text{total cost}$$

profit: total revenue minus total cost; unlike accounting profit, economic profit defines cost to include implicit opportunity costs.

Economists usually assume that firms seek to maximize profit. Profits are an important source of funds for modernization and expansion that can keep a firm competitive. While a firm's managers might have motivations other than profit, firms that do not maximize profit are likely to be deserted by investors and find themselves in financial trouble. Managers that fail to maximize profit must also fear losing their jobs to shareholder revolts or takeovers by other firms.

The profit figures stated in corporate reports and in the news media are collected by accountants. Firms sometimes pull out of a particular business or operation even when it is profitable according to accounting data. When a copper mining company shut down its profitable mines in Bisbee, Arizona, in the 1970s, for example, its workers were outraged. They protested that the firm should not take away their jobs, especially since the mine was profitable. Clearly, the concept of accounting profit was not adequate to explain the company's decision. To explain this and other facets of business behavior, economists need a different method to measure profit than that used by accountants.

Economic Profit and Opportunity Cost

The key to understanding why reportedly profitable firms sometimes close operations is to recognize the distinction between accounting profit and economic profit. All costs measured by accountants are termed *explicit costs*. However, there are other costs, which accountants do not measure. Specifically, there are **implicit opportunity costs** associated with the value that the capital investments and entrepreneur's time would have in their best alternative uses.

implicit opportunity costs: the monetary value that capital investments and the entrepreneur's time would have in their best alternative uses; also, the value of any best forgone alternative.

General Electric maintains a Web site at **http://www.ge.com/**

Successful companies are well aware of their implicit costs. To judge whether it is allocating its investments wisely, for example, the General Electric Company requires each of its divisions to compute imputed interest on the factories, machines, and other physical capital that they possess. *Imputed interest* is an implicit cost because it measures the return the investment would have had elsewhere. When capital is found to have imputed interest that exceeds the value of its current productivity, then economic profit would be higher if the capital is reassigned to another task. Imputed interest and other implicit costs are added to explicit costs to obtain total economic costs.

Consider an implicit cost at Ali's restaurant. Ali finished paying off the restaurant's mortgage on its building years ago. Although there is no monthly mortgage or other explicit cost associated with Ali's use of the building, implicit opportunity costs could be substantial. Suppose Ali receives an offer from another restaurant operator to rent the building for $1,000 per month. By turning down this sum of money and using the restaurant for his own operations, Ali incurs an implicit cost of $1,000 per month. If this offer is the best alternative use of the restaurant, its opportunity cost is $1,000. In practice, measuring implicit cost is difficult because alternatives are not always known with certainty.

Economic cost also includes economic *depreciation* over time, which is the loss of market value of capital caused by wear and tear, obsolescence, or other events. For example, if Ali originally paid $100,000 for his restaurant, but it could be sold today for only $70,000, then it has depreciated by $30,000. Accounting measures of depreciation are formulas meant to approximate economic depreciation. Approximations are needed because separately estimating the economic depreciation of a firm's every asset would be an extraordinarily difficult and expensive task.

Economic Profit versus Normal Profit

The difference between total revenue and total economic cost is *economic profit*, or simply *profit* throughout this book. When total revenue just equals total cost, including all implicit opportunity costs, the firm is said to be earning a **normal profit, which implies zero economic profit.** From an economic perspective, normal profit provides just enough revenue to compensate the firm's owners for the time, money, and other resources they have invested in the firm. Thus, **normal profit is the cost of keeping the firm's resources in their current use,** which is why it is treated as a cost in the computation of economic profit, as follows:

normal profit: the accounting profit just sufficient to cover implicit opportunity costs.

$$\text{Profit} = \text{total revenue} - \text{explicit costs} - \text{normal profit}.$$

Economic profits are sometimes termed excess profits, to indicate that they are accounting profits in excess of normal profit. Conversely, when a firm earns less than a normal profit, it incurs an *economic loss*, or just *loss* from here on. If losses are expected to continue, the firm's resources eventually will be allocated to more profitable uses.

 QuickCheck _____

Can you explain why the owners of the Arizona copper mine decided to close it?

Answer: Although the firm earned an accounting profit, it incurred economic losses. The firm's opportunity cost of keeping its capital tied up in the copper mine was the return that it could earn by selling those assets and investing the proceeds elsewhere. After closing the U.S. mine, the company invested in an overseas mine that offered a higher return on its investment.

OBSERVATION POINT:
How to Sink a Business

Some people mistakenly believe that the market value of business capital is equal to the cost of producing it. In truth, the value depends upon the capital's ability to produce future profits. For example, the value of a shopping mall will rise as its expected future profitability increases, perhaps because of population growth. Similarly, its value will decline with the rise of e-commerce and other forms of shopping from home. The result is a market value that could be much more or much less than the mall's cost of construction.

Once the mall is built, its cost is a *sunk cost*, an expense that cannot be undone. The search for profit motivates firms to avoid sinking their money into unproductive projects. Excessive sunk costs without revenues to offset them are a sure-fire way to sink a business!

Profit Maximization in the Short Run

total revenue: price × quantity.

A firm receives revenue by selling its output. Total revenue is calculated by multiplying the quantity sold by the unit price. For example, suppose that Ali's King-of-Ribs Restaurant sells an average of 5,000 of its honey-glazed baby back rib dinners each month and that customers pay $10 for each dinner. Ali thus earns an average of $50,000 ($10 × 5,000) a month of total revenue from that menu item. Costs arise when Ali pays expenses, such as for labor and meat.

A Closer Look at Costs

fixed cost: the cost of fixed inputs, which are those that cannot be changed in the short run.

In the short run, firms have both fixed and variable costs. A firm's fixed cost is associated with its fixed inputs. Total fixed cost remains constant regardless of the amount of production. For example, a firm will pay the same amount of property taxes, property insurance, rent, and executive salaries whatever the firm's output.

variable cost: the cost of variable inputs; in the long run, all costs are variable.

Variable cost increases as output rises and declines as output falls, because a firm's use of variable inputs varies directly with production. Raw materials costs, the wages of hourly labor, and shipping expenses are examples of variable costs. Total cost includes *total fixed cost* and *total variable cost*.

total cost: total fixed cost + total variable cost.

$$\text{Total cost} = \text{total fixed cost} + \text{total variable cost}$$

Observe some cost calculations performed by Wendy Webster, owner of WW Wholesale Flour. Wendy has calculated her total fixed cost to equal $200. If she produces six tons of flour, she will incur an additional $460 of total variable cost. Her total cost of producing six tons of flour would thus equal $660. By dividing total expenses by total output, Wendy calculates the per unit cost of a ton of flour to be $110. Per unit cost is call average cost, which equals total cost divided by the quantity of output.

average cost: per-unit cost; total cost/quantity of output.

$$\text{Average cost} = \frac{\text{total cost}}{\text{quantity}}$$

It may be that Wendy will produce and sell additional flour sometime soon. In that case she ought to be thinking about the amount by which total expenses will grow when she increases her output. In the short run, the amount of capital—the amount of floor space and the number of machines—is fixed. When Wendy spends more on labor and raw materials in order to increase output, the total variable cost of production will increase. Marginal cost is the additional cost of an additional unit of output. Note that as quantity is altered the change in total cost must equal the change in total variable cost. The reason is that total fixed cost does not change.

marginal cost: the cost of producing one more unit of output; Δtotal cost/Δquantity, or, equivalently, Δtotal variable cost/Δquantity.

$$\text{Marginal cost} = \frac{\Delta\text{total cost}}{\Delta\text{quantity}} = \frac{\Delta\text{total variable cost}}{\Delta\text{quantity}}$$

Marginal cost must eventually rise, because it is inversely related to marginal product, which must eventually fall according to the law of diminishing returns. The

TABLE 6-2 Selected Costs for WW Wholesale Flour

Output (Q per day)	Total Cost (TC)	Marginal Cost (ΔTC/ΔQ)
4	$400	?
5	$500	$100
6	$660	$160
7	$910	$250

marginal cost of producing additional output will rise when the marginal product of labor falls because the firm must use more and more labor to obtain the same increase in output, which increases the cost per unit of that output.

Because WW Wholesale Flour operates in the region of diminishing returns, the additional cost of increasing production from six tons to seven tons will be greater than encountered when output was expanded from five tons to six tons. Table 6-2 shows the effects on cost of marginal changes in output around six tons. Production increases by a constant one ton per row, while total cost increases by a greater increment as output increases, shown by the rising figure for marginal cost.

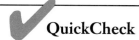 **QuickCheck** _____

Explain why marginal cost must eventually rise.

Answer: The law of diminishing returns means that a firm has to add a greater amount of variable input to expand production by one more unit, which means that input requirements rise for marginal units of output. Because inputs are costly, the marginal cost of output rises. For example, refer back to Table 6-1. When Ali's King-of-Ribs Restaurant employs a fifth worker, total meals served rise by four. If we suppose that Ali pays workers $10 each, then there is $2.50 in marginal labor cost connected with each additional meal. When Ali employs a sixth worker, total meals rise by only one. That one additional meal is connected to $10 of marginal labor cost.

Decision Making at the Margin: Price Takers

WW Wholesale Flour is a type of firm called a price taker, which means that the firm has no choice but to sell its output for the going market price. Every additional ton of flour sold adds an amount of revenue equal to the market price of a ton of flour. This additional income is termed marginal revenue.

$$\text{Marginal revenue} = \frac{\Delta \text{total revenue}}{\Delta \text{quantity}}$$

Any time another ton is sold that has a marginal revenue greater than marginal cost, Wendy's profit will rise. When the marginal cost, seen in Table 6-2, is greater than the marginal revenue, profit will fall. For example, if the market price is $160 per ton, the fifth ton increases profit by $60 because the additional revenue equals the

price taker: an individual, firm, or country with no influence over the market price.

marginal revenue: the increase in revenue to the firm from selling one more unit of output.

TABLE 6-3	Current Economic Data for WW Wholesale Flour, a Price Taker
(1) Price per ton (market price)	$160
(2) Quantity (per day)	6 tons
(3) Total revenue	$960
(4) Total variable cost	$460
(5) Total fixed cost	$200
(6) Total cost	$660
(7) Total economic profit	$300
(8) Profit per unit	$ 50

price of $160, while the offsetting additional cost is the marginal cost of $100. By a similar calculation, the seventh ton subtracts $90 from profit. Wendy can do no better than to produce six tons, exactly. This reasoning allows Wendy to identify the profit-maximizing quantity of flour to produce by following the following general rule:

Rule of profit maximization:

Produce to the point where marginal revenue = marginal cost

Table 6-3 summarizes the maximization of profit at WW Wholesale Flour, using the cost data in Table 6-2.

The rule of profit maximization reveals the most preferred output at any firm, whether a price taker or not and along whatever dimension output might take. For example, in determining what items to offer on the menu and the manner in which they are served, Ali follows this rule at his King-of-Ribs Restaurant. Ali will do anything he can think of for which marginal revenue exceeds marginal cost, and cease doing anything for which marginal cost exceeds marginal revenue. If Ali thinks that offering diners barbecued chicken will add more revenue than it adds cost, he will offer it. He will even provide heated, moist after-dinner napkins if he thinks that the marginal revenue from doing so would exceed the marginal cost. When he is finished, Ali will find that, to a close approximation, marginal revenue will equal marginal cost along all dimensions of his output.

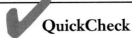 QuickCheck _____

Why would a price taker expand production if the last unit it produced could be sold at a price that exceeded marginal cost?

Answer: Every additional unit of production would add more to revenue than to cost (marginal revenue greater than marginal cost). The firm should keep producing until the equality stated in the rule of profit maximization is reached. These additional units would increase profit.

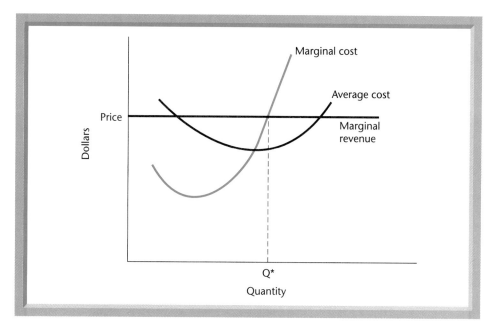

FIGURE 6-2 **The profit-maximizing output,** Q*, occurs when marginal cost equals marginal revenue. For a price-taking firm, marginal revenue is identical to the market price. This firm is profitable, because price exceeds average cost at Q*.

Figure 6-2 illustrates the rule of profit maximization. Because of the effect of diminishing returns on marginal cost, the general appearance of the marginal cost curve is opposite to the corresponding marginal product curve shown in Figure 6-1. The result is that marginal cost is shaped like the letter *J*. **Marginal revenue to a price-taking firm equals the going market price and is illustrated in Figure 6-2 by a horizontal line.** Equating marginal revenue to marginal cost leads to a profit-maximizing quantity of Q*.

If changes in demand and supply alter the wholesale price of flour, WW's output will change. By referring back to the data in Table 6-2, it should be clear that an increase in market price to $250 or more would cause WW to expand production to seven tons. Wendy's total profit would then rise to $840. Verify this result by performing the required calculation in response to the rule of profit maximization. The effect of higher prices on the firm's output is shown in Figure 6-3. **Higher prices lead profit-maximizing firms to produce more output; lower prices lead to less output.**

When price decreases and profit-making firms then respond by cutting back production, there are several possible outcomes, some more desirable than others. One is that the lower price and quantity leads to lower profit. Another is that profit drops to zero because total revenue and total cost are equal, a condition called *break even*. Recall that a firm with zero economic profit is said to earn a normal profit. The least desirable outcome for the firm involves a loss. **When a firm operates at a loss, it will seek to minimize the loss.**

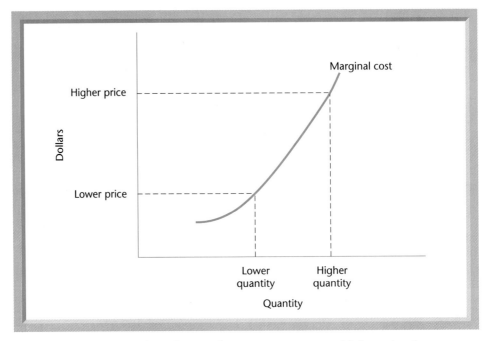

FIGURE 6-3 **A price-taking firm produces more output at a higher price than at a lower price,** as it equates marginal revenue (the price) with marginal cost. Thus, the firm's short-run supply curve is given by its marginal cost curve. The only exception is if the price drops so low that the firm cannot cover its variable costs, in which case it will shut down and hope for higher prices later.

In short, whether or not the firm is profitable, the price-taking firm produces to the point at which price equals marginal cost. For this reason, **the firm's marginal cost curve is also its supply curve**—at any given price, the marginal cost curve says what quantity will be produced. The only exception is if the price drops so low that the firm cannot cover its variable costs, in which case it will lose less money by producing nothing at all. That concept will be covered more fully after the next section.

Decision Making at the Margin: The Price Searcher

price searcher: a firm that faces a downward sloping demand curve.

A firm that is not a price taker is called a price searcher. This type of firm has a downward sloping demand curve because, unlike for a price taker, there is no single market price for its product. It must search for the best price to charge—the price that maximizes profit. If such a firm wants another sale, it will have to offer potential buyers a lower price. The lower price would then apply to every unit of output that it offers for sale. For this reason, the marginal revenue from an extra unit of output would equal the price of that unit minus the price reduction on every other unit sold. Thus, **for a firm with a downward-sloping demand curve, marginal revenue is less than price.**

Suppose that demand for a price searcher is as shown in the price and quantity columns of Table 6-4. Note that, as quantity increases for a price searcher, marginal revenue drops faster than price. In contrast, recall that for a price taker, price and mar-

TABLE 6-4 Demand, Total Revenue, and Marginal Revenue for a Price Searcher

Price	Quantity	Total Revenue (price × quantity)	Marginal Revenue (Δprice/Δquantity)
$12	0	$0	Undefined
11	1	11	$11
10	2	20	9
9	3	27	7
8	4	32	5

ginal revenue are equal. To see why marginal revenue drops faster than price, consider the price reduction from $10 to $9. This price cut allows the firm to sell three units, but also causes the revenue from the sale of the first two units, which would have been $20 at the $10 price, to drop to $18. This drop of $2 means that total revenue will not rise by less than the $9 price of the third unit. Specifically, total revenue rises by $7, which equals the price of $9 minus the decrease of $2 on the first two units.

To find the profit-maximizing price and quantity, the firm will calculate the marginal revenue at various quantities. It will then compare marginal revenue to marginal cost at each quantity. At some point the two must be equal, because marginal revenue declines as more output is produced and sold, while marginal cost rises because of the law of diminishing returns. Once the profit-maximizing quantity is determined, the firm will charge as high a price as possible to sell that output. That price is given by the point on the demand curve that corresponds to the output that the firm has chosen. Note that the price is higher than either marginal cost or marginal revenue at that output. This two-step process is illustrated in Figure 6-4.

For example, suppose the price searcher observes that marginal revenue and marginal cost are both $3 at a quantity of four units. Table 6-4 shows that four units command a price of $8 and that total revenue is $32. Also suppose that checking expenses reveals that total cost equals $15 at this quantity. The firm's total profit is hence $17, the difference between total revenue and total cost. Table 6-5 summarizes the cost, revenue, and profit data for the firm's profit-maximizing output.

QuickCheck

What is the value of marginal revenue at four units of output? Is marginal cost equal to that value?

Answer: Marginal revenue equals $5. Since four units is said to be the profit-maximizing output, marginal cost must also equal $5 by the rule of profit maximization.

When to Shut Down

Whether the firm is profitable or operates at a loss, it will determine its quantity by equating marginal revenue to marginal cost. However, when price drops so low that revenues are insufficient to pay variable costs, the firm can avoid those costs by

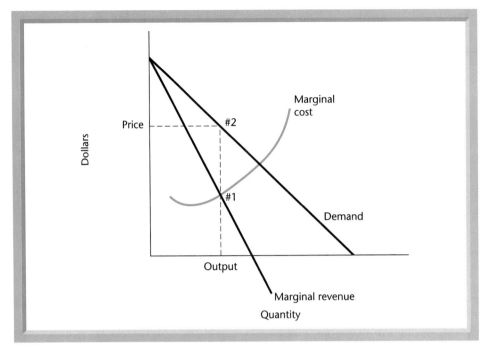

FIGURE 6-4   **The price-searching firm selects output and price in two steps.** In step 1, the firm produces until marginal cost equals marginal revenue (point #1 above). In step 2, the firm charges the highest price that will sell that output, as given by demand (point #2 above).

shutdown: when a firm ceases operations in the short run, but still incurs fixed costs; occurs when price is less than average variable cost.

ceasing production altogether. This decision is called shutdown. To shut down means to cease production temporarily, leaving the firm with no output and hence no revenue. Since fixed costs must be paid even if the firm produces nothing, shutdown results in a loss that is equal to the firm's fixed cost. The *shutdown rule* is as follows:

Shut down when total revenue is less than total variable cost.

exit: when a firm goes out of business; the firm no longer has either fixed or variable costs.

The shutdown rule identifies the *only* exception to the rule of equating marginal cost to marginal revenue. **Shutdown occurs in the short run.** If a firm incurs continuing losses over the long run, it will exit the industry, meaning that it will go out of business. This action is the opposite to the *entry* of new firms, which would occur if the industry appears profitable. **Entry and exit occur in the long run.**

TABLE 6-5	Maximum Profit for a Price Searcher
Price	$8
Quantity	4 units
Total revenue	$32
Total cost	$15
Total profit	$17

QuickCheck

Referring back to the section on the price-taking firm, what is WW's profit if price equals $100? What if the price falls to $70? What if the price continues to fall?

Answer: If the price is $100, output would be cut to five units. Total revenue and total cost both equal $500. Profit would be zero, causing WW to break even. If price fell to $70, the profit-maximizing quantity would fall to four tons. This quantity would minimize the loss, which would equal $120. If price continued to fall, WW would lose more money, but not over $200, which is the point at which Wendy's firm would shut down.

OBSERVATION POINT:
Beg, Borrow, or Steal?

"Crime doesn't pay!" Law enforcement officials everywhere seek to drill that message into the heads of potential criminals. The problem is that, in all too many cases, crime does pay. For example, like any other business enterprise in search of profit, the thief compares the expected revenue from thievery with the expected cost. The thief also factors in risk, treating it as a cost. Other businesses also seek to avoid risk where possible.

To maximize their ill-gotten profits, thieves will steal only until marginal revenue equals marginal cost. The more likely the expected probability of being caught and the harsher the expected punishment if apprehended, the higher is the expected marginal cost of thievery and the less thievery is likely to occur. The difference between legitimate business and thievery is quite simply that businesses are not thieves, some popular complaints notwithstanding. Businesses can only get you money if you voluntarily turn it over. Thieves ignore that nicety.

To look over the FBI's crime statistics, follow the link at **http://fbi.gov**

long-run average cost: cost per unit of output when all inputs are variable.

Economies of Scale and Long-Run Average Cost

The production characteristics of a firm in the short run are determined by decisions made in the long run, before the *scale*—size—of the firm is selected. Changing the firm's scale can change its long-run average cost—cost per unit of output when all inputs are variable. When the long-run average cost drops as the firm proportionally expands its use of all its inputs, then economies of scale are present. For example, doubling the size of a firm might allow it to more than double the amount of output. That benefit would occur if the greater scale allowed more efficient use of inputs. Conversely, diseconomies of scale, which result in increasing per unit cost of output as firm size increases, might occur if the organization grows beyond a size that can easily be managed.

When all economies of scale have been achieved and diseconomies averted, the firm is said to experience constant returns to scale. There is usually a range of possible firm sizes that exhibit constant returns to scale. Within this range, a proportional change in all inputs leads to the same proportional change in output. For

economies of scale: when the long-run average cost declines as the firm proportionally expands its use of all its inputs.

diseconomies of scale: when the long-run average cost rises as the firm proportionally expands its use of all its inputs.

constant returns to scale: when the long-run average cost remains constant as the firm proportionally expands its use of all its inputs.

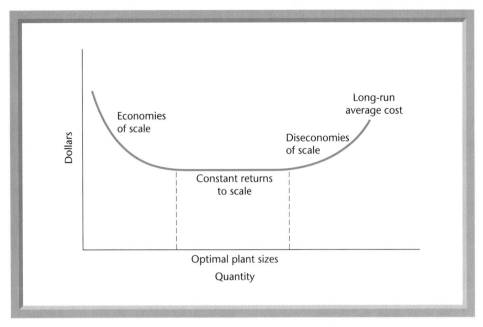

FIGURE 6-5 **In choosing the scale of production, firms seek to minimize average costs** and thus prefer to build plants of a size consistent with constant returns to scale.

example, if this region of constant returns to scale is sufficiently large, doubling the amount of inputs will double the amount of output. The relationship between the scale of production and possible economies, diseconomies, or constant returns to scale is illustrated in Figure 6-5. Businesses can often identify any possible economies of scale by asking some commonsense questions as the firm grows in size. Economies of scale would be associated with affirmative answers to any of these questions:

- Would a larger plant allow a more productive layout of machines?
- Can larger-scale machines be found that produce the output more cheaply than current machines?
- Can jobs be broken down into a narrower range of tasks so that greater specialization of labor can be achieved?
- Will suppliers give discounts for the larger orders that will be placed in the future?

Technological change can shift the long-run average cost curve downward. Innovations in production techniques often arise from technological change. For example, office work today is done on personal computers rather than typewriters and adding machines. That allows either more output of work or fewer resources to be used, shifting down the long-run average cost curve relative to where it would be if the older technology were still in use.

Battling Economies of Scale—the $2 Billion Strike at General Motors

If being big was all it took to attain economies of scale, the General Motors Corporation ought to be the lowest cost producer in the U.S. automobile industry. GM is the biggest car company, but its costs are reportedly the highest of the big three automakers. Has GM reached the region of diseconomies of scale, being just too big to manage, or has it merely been sluggish about capturing the efficiencies that economies of scale offer?

The General Motors Web site is at **http://www.gm.com/**

GM management has spent much of the last decade working to implement the efficiencies that should come with GM's size. However, GM's unions have staunchly resisted these efforts, rightly seeing them as threatening to their jobs and lifestyles. For example, in the summer of 1998, the unions struck GM over its attempts to expand *outsourcing*, the practice of buying parts from other companies when it is cheaper to do so. That strike cost GM at least $2 billion before it was settled.

Reaching the efficiencies offered by economies of scale can save companies huge amounts of money. Owners and customers urge management to deliver these savings. Sometimes, as General Motors knows, the workers have other ideas.

SUMMARY

- A firm will exist in one of the following legal forms: sole proprietorship, partnership, and corporation. The corporation offers the advantages of limited liability and perpetual existence.

- Financial capital includes retained earnings, borrowings, and funds raised by issuing stock.

- The law of diminishing returns states that marginal product must eventually decline. The law applies in the short run.

- The goal of the firm is to maximize profit. Profit equals total revenue minus total cost, where total costs include both explicit and implicit opportunity costs.

- Short-run costs include fixed and variable costs. Marginal cost is especially important in profit maximization.

- The rule of profit maximization: produce the output where marginal revenue equals marginal cost.

- A firm may produce output and earn a profit. Alternatively, in spite of efforts to maximize profit, production may lead to a loss, which the firm should minimize. The firm may also break even, where total revenue equals total cost.

- If the firm loses so much money that it cannot cover all variable costs, it minimizes its loss by shutting down, producing a quantity of zero.

- Long-run costs depend upon whether the firm experiences economies of scale, constant returns to scale, or diseconomies of scale. Per-unit cost decreases when economies of scale are present, remains constant when there are constant returns to scale, and increases when diseconomies of scale are present.

QUESTIONS AND PROBLEMS

1. In light of the advantages that corporations possess, why do you think the proprietorship and partnership forms still exist? In your answer, consider the costs and benefits of each form, including the means of financing.

2. Provide examples of plausible opportunity costs in each of the following instances:
   a. $10,000 cash invested in a firm by its owner.
   b. an extra 15 hours of work per week performed for no monetary payment by a business owner.
   c. a business owner's personal automobile used for business purposes.

3. Categorize each of the following expenses incurred by Alonzo's Big Time Chocolate Factory as either fixed or variable:
   a. the monthly payment Alonzo makes to the local telephone company;
   b. payments to his insurance company for automobile insurance on the company car;
   c. payments to the local utility for electricity to operate the candy-mixing machines;
   d. Alonzo's salary as chief executive officer of the company;
   e. payroll expenses.

4. Explain why it would make no sense for a price taker to set a selling price that differs from the market price.

5. Price scanning by bar code is common in supermarkets today. Not too many years ago, however, the price of every item purchased was entered by hand. Explain in practical terms how scanners lower costs. Must every supermarket install scanners in order to compete? Is this a long-run or a short-run issue? Explain.

6. A price taking firm, Garcia Wholesale Milk and Butterfat, is currently producing 1,000 gallons of milk and butterfat per day. The market price of this output equals $1.50 per unit. Its total fixed cost equals $200 per day, while its total variable cost is $150 per day.
   a. Is this firm earning a profit? Show the calculations that lead to your answer.
   b. If it is earning a profit, is it maximizing profit? Explain.

7. Within the context of production, explain the difference between the long run and the short run. Repeat your explanation, this time within the context of cost. When does the law of diminishing returns apply, in the short run or the long run? When are economies of scale found, in the long run or the short run?

8. RM Motors has the following schedule for total cost:

Quantity	Total Cost
0	$100
1	150
2	175
3	205
4	245
5	290

a. What is the marginal cost of a fourth vehicle?

b. What additional information would be necessary to calculate profit?

Web Exercises

9. a. Using an Internet search engine such as that provided by Web site directory Yahoo (located at **http://www.yahoo.com**) or Alta Vista (located at **http://www.altavista.com**), perform a separate search for the following terms: **profit, price taker,** and **economies of scale**. Visit several of the Web sites that your search reveals for each term and observe the context in which each term is used. Explain whether the manner in which the terms are used is consistent with their use in the text.

b. Repeat the above, but this time use a combination of terms that you select from the chapter. To eliminate Web sites that do not contain all terms, place a plus sign in front of each term you enter, such as **+corporation +bond**.

10. Visit the Web site maintained by the U.S. Department of Commerce at **http://www.doc.gov**. Explore the Web site by following links that appeal to your curiosity. Summarize what you find by writing a series of 10–15 bullet points that describe the purposes and functions of the Department of Commerce.

Visit the Web site for *Economics by Design* at http://www.prenhall.com/collinge for a Self Quiz over the topics in this chapter.

EXPLORING ISSUES

Exploration 6-1 Successful and Ethical Business—From the Entrepreneur to Investors, Employees, and the Community

Entrepreneurs have a vision of success. The stock market can draw individual and institutional investors into that vision. Bringing the vision to reality requires making many choices, one of the most basic of which is how to provide profit-maximizing incentives to employees at all levels. There are also issues of business ethics, such as over investors' obligations to their businesses and business obligations to their communities.

In 1997, about 800,000 new business incorporations occurred in the United States, while almost 72,000 businesses failed. Such business starts and failures are part of the dynamic of the market economy, in which firms in search of profit are in constant competition to satisfy consumers. Often, the motivation for starting a business is the opportunity for financial gain beyond that found in other jobs, as well as the freedom that comes with "controlling the show." Many of the worlds' wealthiest people are business owners, with many others inheriting their wealth from business owners of yesteryear. These prospects might explain why, as estimated by the Entrepreneurial Research Consortium, over seven million people per year consider starting a business.

Success requires a vision of what consumers want, of what niche the business can fill. Incorrect visions can and often do lead to business failures, with the highest rate of failures concentrated among the latest start ups. Before risking all in the start-up of a new business, many people have tried their hands at investing in the stocks of other companies. With stocks, the amount of initial investment needed is less and, by diversifying investments across multiple companies, the risk is less. In addition, the stock market provides these would-be entrepreneurs with lessons on what makes companies successful. In turn, the stock market provides companies with the investors that can help achieve their visions of success.

The Stock Market

Investors in the stock market have one thing in mind—to make money. This explains the fascination with companies's quarterly reports that record their financial performance and discuss their future prospects. If a company fails to meet the profit expectations of stock analysts, even if only by a few cents, that company's stock price can be in for a sharp decline. The reason is that investors use the current information on profits to predict profits down the road. A shortfall below profit expectations today suggests that expectations for future profits must be revised downward as well.

In forming their expectations as to the firm's future profitability, investors incorporate as much information as they can reasonably obtain. For example, the currency crisis of 1997 and 1998 meant that imports into the United States became cheaper. Companies competing head-to-head against cheaper imports or that sold heavily in depressed overseas markets saw their stock prices decline. U.S. companies that could make use of cheaper imported components saw their stock prices rise.

In the same period, political instability gripped Russia, the old nemesis of the United States. In the United States, talk of impeaching President Clinton added uncertainty to economic policy. Investors do not like uncertainty. While it is hard to pin down exactly what moves the stock market, it is probably no coincidence that in that time of uncertainty, stock market averages tumbled. For example, the Dow-Jones Industrials Average—an index of the stock prices of thirty large companies with stocks that trade on New York Stock Exchange—at one point had fallen about 20 percent from its high point a few months earlier.

Companies benefit from the stock market to the extent that they can sell ownership shares—stock—for cash to expand the business. Companies value high stock prices for this reason and because the owners of the company—the shareholders—want to have the option of selling shares of stock for as much money as possible. However, a decline in a company's stock price has no immediate impact on day-to-day operations, because companies sell new shares of stock only infrequently. Almost all stock trading on the stock exchanges is between individuals or institutions and other individuals and institutions. For example, if a Fidelity mutual fund buys 10,000 shares of 3M Corporation, the sellers might include a Dreyfus mutual fund and Charles Thurston, an individual investor with a brokerage account. Except for changing ownership of a small fraction of the company, the company itself is unaffected.

Making the Company a United Team

It's not enough for a firm to have finances and a vision. Success in the business world also takes an efficient execution of that vision. To achieve success in operations, large companies must employ managers and staff. The bigger the company, the more layers of management. This brings about a principal-agent problem, which refers to the difficulties of making employees and managers, who are called agents, act in perfect accord with the will of the owners, who are called principals. As the saying goes, "If you want something done right, do it yourself." However, businesses must find another route.

There are several ways in which the principal-agent problem reveals itself. For example, there could be miscommunications when the owners or management *delegates* a job, which means to assign it to an employee. Also, the abilities of that employee might not be properly known to the owner or manager who assigns the task.

Probably the most significant source of the principal-agent problem arises from differences in the interests of agents and principals. It is not hard to see how profit, the major interest of the principal, might conflict with an agent's personal agenda. For example, as readers of Dilbert know well, managers may use the firm's resources in ways that contribute little to the revenue of the business. Employees are also frequently caught *shirking*, which is usually known on the job as "goofing off."

Owners and managers are well aware of the principal-agent problem and seek ways to fight it. In addition to keeping an eye on agents' activities, principals look for ways to maintain profit-maximizing behavior when direct monitoring is not feasible. A very popular choice in recent years is for the principals to share ownership of the company with the agent. Specifically, it is very common now for executives to receive part of their compensation in the form of the company's stock or options to buy that stock at a fixed price—a *stock option plan*. Such plans have proven so motivational that

principal-agent problem: the difficulty of making agents, such as managers or public servants, act in the interests of principals, such as shareholders or voters.

they are often extended to nearly all employees of the company. The theory behind stock option plans is that the harder and more effectively agents work, the more everyone's stock in the company will be worth, including their own. In this way, rather than competing to see who can get away with shirking the most, workers have an incentive both to work diligently and also to keep an eye upon each other to see that co-workers work with equal diligence.

Fighting the principal-agent problem is also the aim of incentive pay systems that let employees share in the profitability of the firm. For example, many salespeople work on commission, which spurs them to do their part toward increasing profit. There are also bonuses that are based upon performance standards. Whatever the nature of the scheme, its purpose is to more closely align the interests of both principals and agents.

Sometimes designing a proper system of incentives is problematic and can itself pit the interests of agents against principals. For example, the executives of many companies have been accused by shareholders of devising stock option plans that are too generous to themselves. Also, if your businesses faced the task of devising a scheme of incentive pay as a reward for exemplary performance, how would you measure such performance? If sales doubled in the previous year, would your managers deserve bonuses? Not if your competitors' sales tripled! Only with carefully selected benchmarks is it possible to interpret performance.

Issues of Ethical Business at Each Step of the Way

Issues of business ethics arise at each step of the business' way. For example, the management of companies values long-term investors for the stability that they bring to the company's stock price. Indeed, the U.S. tax code punishes short-term investors—those selling stock within 1 year of its purchase—by charging a higher capital gains tax on any increase in value of that stock. Yet, many people out for a quick buck buy and sell stock quickly, sometimes even within the same day. Stock brokerages and some investors will sometimes make money by buying and selling a stock based only on the spread between the price for sellers (the *bid* price) and the higher price for buyers (the *ask* price). Some investors of this sort don't even know or care what the company does! Is this unethical?

Often people resent those who make money in the stock market, especially when they don't care about the companies they invest in and have no long-term commitments. However, having "players" in the market increases its *liquidity*—the ease with which stocks can be bought and sold—and reduces volatility. Moreover, stockholders who have a commitment to profit but not to any particular company facilitate rapid changes in a stock's value. While such rapid changes can be unsettling, they also reflect the speedy and efficient manner in which information is now processed. If new information suggests that a company's future does not look promising relative to other companies, the stock market quickly reduces the ability of that first company to raise money from investors, thus channeling investments into companies that offer products of greater value. In this manner, investors' money follows the invisible hand of the marketplace toward promoting greater efficiency.

The forgoing should not suggest that all is ethical in the stock market. For example, a number of NASDAQ (National Association of Security Dealers Automatic Quotations) brokers increased their profits on "playing the spread" between the bid and ask prices by colluding to keep this spread artificially high. In effect, they were rigging the rules in their favor. When confronted with a class-action lawsuit over these practices, these dealers agreed to stop colluding and to pay over $1 billion into a settlement fund that would cover the costs of the lawsuit and finance payments to investors who had been harmed.

The owners of companies must decide whether to seek managers who only maximize profit, or those who also provide charitable contributions to the communities in which they do business. For example, some firms donate money or employee time to nonprofit organizations whose interests may focus on the environment or the homeless, for example. Yet shareholders often focus on profits alone. Is this ethical?

If firms give to charity, it is the managers who are in effect giving away the money of the owners. Some would argue that to do so is itself not quite ethical. Others might respond that businesses are in a leadership position and are able to be better informed about social problems than are individual owners. Either way, the question of ethics comes down to whether it is more ethical for business management to make charitable decisions for the owners or leave the matter of charitable giving to each owner's individual judgment. A common response to this dilemma is for firms to encourage employees to give to the United Way campaign or to make other individual charitable donations.

Issues of business ethics crop up in many other facets of operations. For example, since monitoring within the firm is imperfect, it is often up to employees to be ethical enough to not take credit for other people's work. Also, it is up to firms to be ethical enough not to engage in *industrial espionage* in which they try to steal their competitors' secrets. Other ethical challenges include government regulations that can sometimes be eluded, such as illicit dumping of toxic wastes, or legal but repugnant behavior, such as the employment of criminal labor in politically repressive countries as a way to lower costs. How well firms face up to these challenges is a matter of personal ethics on behalf of the employees, managers, and owners.

Yet, the basic nature of business is highly ethical. Rather than being a zero-sum game in which the winner wins only what the loser loses, business is a *positive-sum game* that can bring benefits to all involved. The reward of profit goes to firms that are best at responding to consumer wishes. The reward of a high standard of living goes to us all.

zero-sum game: a situation in which the winner wins only what the loser loses; in contrast to voluntary economic transactions, in which both parties gain.

■ Prospecting for New Insights

1. How would you go about deciding what kind of business to start? Where would your start-up financial capital come from?

2. What is your attitude toward the social responsibility of business? For example, should businesses contribute to charity, or is that a personal decision?

Exploration 6-2 Adjusting to Technological Change—Lessons from the Family Farm

Despite costly subsidies paid to farmers, family farming has continued its steady decline. Government farm policies not only affect farmers, but also the public, in the form of higher taxes and higher food prices.

The U.S. Department of Agriculture Economic Research Service can be visited on the Web at **http://www. econ.ag.gov/**

The country, indeed much of the world, is fed by crops grown on American farms. You might think that farmers would be handsomely rewarded for keeping the rest of us from starvation. Some farmers are wealthy. They are the survivors of an exodus from farming that has seen the farm population dwindle from 30 percent of the U.S. population in 1920 to less than 2 percent today. Even so, we have seen various events organized to raise money to ease the financial pain felt by the many smaller farmers who must struggle to stay afloat.

Competitive pressures in the marketplace have brought about this disturbing state of affairs. Have government policies helped or merely compounded the problems? There are lessons to be learned down on the farm, lessons that concern the adjustments of markets to technological change. Change is necessary, but disruptive. The sturdy farmer has faced it directly. Government, too, has learned from those experiences.

Farm Aid—Willie Nelson and Company Didn't Get There First

In recent years, singer Willie Nelson assembled the major stars of country music to perform concerts under the Farm Aid banner. The purpose of these shows was to raise money to promote family farming. It would seem that everyone admires such activities. Only the heartless could ignore the sight of farmers and their families packing up their belongings and moving from foreclosed farms. It's more than a job that is lost; it's a way of life, one that lots of city folks admire.

There is a puzzle, though. Aid for American farmers has been around for many decades. Franklin Delano Roosevelt's New Deal of the 1930s aimed to solve some of the same problems that continue to plague the farm sector today. Other farm programs even predate the New Deal era. Despite government farm aid, though, problems continue to plague the family farmer.

Fewer Farm Families, More Food

Sometimes markets work so well that old problems are replaced by new ones that are just as troublesome as the old. In farming the problem is too much good land. It is easy, but not quite correct, to think of land as a fixed resource. After all, there are only so many acres of land. Unless the United States follows the example of the Netherlands and reclaims land from the sea, there is no possibility of adding more land. Although it might seem as if the supply of land cannot be increased, this reasoning ignores possible improvements to the quality of the land, its ability to produce crops. Achieving this improvement is what agricultural research, much of it sponsored by the federal government, is often about. In this way, the amount of highly productive farmland can be increased.

Such government-sponsored research has proven quite successful at raising crop yields. Crop yields can also be increased through the scientific application of modern fertilizers and through crop rotation practices. But technological change on the farm embodies much more.

Industry has also provided for the farmer. A generation or two ago it was the faithful mule that supplied the power to prepare soil for planting. Today, mules have largely been replaced by tractors. Other kinds of more specialized mechanical planting and harvesting equipment have also been introduced over the long run. The effect has been to increase the productivity of the farmer. The same number of hours spent farming result in more farm output as productivity rises.

Technological change has also included the development of new crop varieties. Better seeds mean more food even if nothing else changes on the farm. Every technological improvement shifts the supply curve of food to the right, *ceteris paribus.*

In farming, all firms must sell at the same market price, despite some of them having cost advantages over others. For example, some farms spread across wide, flat expanses, while others are nestled in river valleys. The result of differences in the physical characteristics of farms is that technological change increases the profit of some farmers while harming others—farmers who cannot adapt to these changes but nevertheless experience the consequent declines in farm output prices. Farmers who are unable to sell their crops at the market price without suffering economic losses will, in the long run, be forced to leave their farms.

For example, farmers in the choppy hills of Tennessee are at a disadvantage to their counterparts in the Kansas plains when it comes to employing the modern technology of huge combines and other types of farm equipment. Yet, if they produce the same product, they must sell it for the same price. As technological change takes hold, that price drops. Farmers must adopt the changes or exit the industry.

Corporate Farming—Can Government Fight Economies of Scale?

Tragedy for one family can be opportunity for another. When one family stops farming or moves off the farm, an opportunity is created for another to expand its operations by buying or leasing the land. As evidence, the average number of acres per farm has been increasing steadily during the twentieth century, rising from 146 acres in 1900 to 461 acres in 1990. Other aspects of the farm problem can be understood by referring to data on farm income, population, and productivity, as shown in Table 6-6. Note the ups and downs in farm income. These fluctuations make it difficult for small farms to keep going. Also note the uptrend in productivity, reflecting technological improvements.

Even though farms disappear, farmland is usually not abandoned. Rather, it becomes part of someone else's farm. When one farmer loses money working a particular piece of acreage, why should another farmer be able to take it over and earn a profit?

An important reason is economies of scale in farming, such as those associated with the use of large-scale equipment, which causes the average cost of farm output to decrease as farms grow larger. For example, farmers waste less time maneuvering their combines when their fields are large. This means that a bushel of corn, wheat, or other commodity can be produced at a lower per unit cost on large farms. Economies of scale are identified with the downward sloping part of the U-shaped long-run average cost curve. Economies of scale do have limits, though. Since bringing in the crop

TABLE 6-6 Farm Income, Population, and Productivity, 1979–98

Year	Net Farm Income (billions of dollars)	Farm Population (millions of persons)	Productivity Index—Farm Output per Unit of Farm Labor
1979	$27.4	6.2	64
1980	16.1	6.1	64
1981	26.9	5.9	70
1982	23.8	5.6	72
1983	14.2	5.8	64
1984	26.0	5.7	74
1985	28.6	5.4	82
1986	30.9	5.2	86
1987	37.4	5.0	87
1988	38.0	5.0	80
1989	45.3	4.8	86
1990	44.7	4.6	92
1991	38.6	4.6	89
1992	47.5	NA	100
1993	43.6	NA	98
1994	48.3	NA	111
1995	36.0	NA	110
1996	53.4	NA	106
1997	49.8	NA	NA
1998	48.0	NA	111

Source: 1999 Economic Report of the President, Tables B-97, B-99, and B-100, NA = not available.

and equipment uses time and fuel, fields that extend too far can lead to diseconomies of scale, in which average costs rise.

Then there is government aid to consider. Government programs to help farmers have had a triple focus. To put more income into the hands of farmers, government has (1) restricted the supply of farm output to drive up crop prices; (2) increased demand by seeking out new markets for agricultural commodities, especially overseas markets, to increase prices of those goods; and (3) set prices of farm outputs above market equilibriums through agricultural price supports (discussed in chapter 4), which are maintained through *deficiency payments* that compensate farmers for the difference between the support price and any lower market price.

To use agricultural price supports to keep every farmer in business would require a price of output that would provide even the highest cost producer with at least a normal profit. Consider the three graphs in Figure 6-6. Farmer A is the low-cost producer, farmer B the medium-cost producer, and farmer C the high-cost producer. Don't forget that each cost curve includes an allowance for the farmer's implicit opportunity cost.

Farmer C may be the high-cost producer because he or she has higher explicit costs arising from poorer quality of land or poor management skills. Farmer C might also have excellent opportunities for earning income off the farm. In that case, farmer C's higher costs result from higher implicit opportunity costs. To keep farmer C farming, the government would have to manipulate prices so that all of farmer C's costs are covered by price. In the process, farmers A and B would grow wealthy on excess profits.

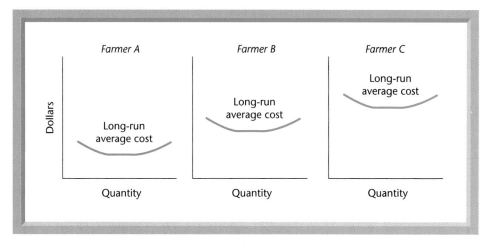

FIGURE 6-6   **Low-cost, medium-cost, and high-cost farmers**

There are several objections to crop prices that keep all farmers farming. For one thing, consumers have to pay the higher prices. Since food is a necessity, high food prices hit the poor the hardest. For example, according to an analysis by Public Voice for Food and Health Policy, agricultural price supports added 33 cents to the price of a jar of peanut butter and 18 cents to the price of a gallon of milk in 1995. In total, price supports are estimated to have cost consumers an extra $4.5 billion dollars per year, most of which went to large operations rather than to small family farms.

Another problem concerns where to draw the line at government efforts to help people whose incomes are not enough to keep them in their present line of work. For example, many college professors find it difficult to support a family on their earnings. Should the government institute policies to increase college tuitions so that professors can be paid more? College students would be well aware of the costs. In general, the incomes of any category of producers cannot be raised without costs to others in society.

Since agricultural price supports are so expensive, why doesn't the government simply eliminate price supports, and replace them with subsidies to needy farmers? Actually, the Freedom to Farm Act of 1996 does just that. After 63 years, government has chosen to abandon most efforts to support prices and restrict supply. Farmers can grow what is most profitable and plant as much acreage as they wish, unlike under the system of price supports. However, supports for peanuts, sugar, and dairy products were left in place by the act. Furthermore, when the act expires in 2002, price supports are scheduled to be reimplemented, unless additional action is taken in the interim.

What Washington Has Learned from the Heartland

Over six decades of price supports failed to stop the exodus from the farm. For this, we should be grateful. If 30 percent of Americans were still to live on farms, as was true in 1920, many goods and services that we enjoy consuming would simply not be available. People would be growing food instead of, for example, assembling cars, building houses, and making movies. Besides, people frequently prefer to live in cities, suburbs, and small towns rather than on farms. We can take comfort that many of those who left farming did so because of attractive job opportunities elsewhere.

The history of government farm policy has been to fight the market, which has been telling us there are too many farmers. Until 1996, government chose to ignore the market's message. If government truly had wished to keep farmers on the farm, it would have been better served to outlaw all technological change in farming. If farmers were forced to stick with the farming techniques of a century ago, the country would need many more farmers today. That policy alternative is, of course, ridiculous. Still, government policies have prolonged the pain of market adjustment, and in the process forced us all to pay more for breakfast, lunch, and dinner.

In farm policy, as in the case of many other government policies, Washington has a choice to make. It can fight the market or work with it. Fighting the market means trying to stop or slow down the changes that occur as markets evolve. Working with the market means accepting change, but trying to ease the pain experienced by those who are adversely affected by that change. When to back off is a lesson learned the hard way by many onetime farmers. The recent changes in farm policy suggest that government lent an ear.

■ Prospecting for New Insights

1. Identify some technological advances that have changed the face of farming. Were these good for farmers? Why did they adopt them? Explain.

2. Do you view government's long-term efforts to help farmers as more a failure or more a success? What policies toward farming would be best? Should these policies be applied to other occupations also? Explain.

Appendix
PRODUCTION, COST, AND PROFIT

RELATING PRODUCTION TO COST

A firm uses a combination of resource inputs to produce an output. Specifically, output is a function of the quantities of capital and labor employed. This production function will vary among firms, depending upon the types of outputs they produce.

In the short run, the firm can vary only its labor input. This special case of the production function is known as the firm's *product curve*, because it can be shown easily by a two-dimensional curve that relates total labor input to the quantity of output produced. This marginal product curve discussed earlier implies a total product curve similar to that shown in Figure 6A-1. The slope of the total product curve equals marginal product. For example, the ranges of increasing, decreasing, and negative marginal product are each noted in this figure. *Average product* can also be calculated by dividing total product by quantity.

Figure 6A-2, on page 212, reverses the axes of Figure 6A-1 to show the labor requirements for any given level of output. The relationship between labor and output

total product: the total quantity of output produced by a firm's labor.

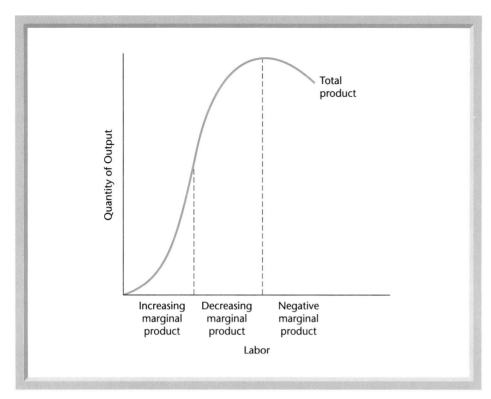

FIGURE 6A-1 **The total product of labor** shows output as a function of labor inputs, holding capital fixed.

in these two figures is identical. The labor required to produce any particular amount of output, when multiplied by the cost per unit of that labor, reveals total variable cost. When the price per unit of labor is the wage rate, then total variable cost is the wage rate multiplied by the quantity of labor. As seen in Figure 6A-3, the shape of total variable cost is identical to that of the labor requirements curve in the prior figure. The only difference is that the vertical axis is now denominated in dollars rather than units of labor.

Figure 6A-3 also shows total cost and total fixed cost. Total fixed cost is constant at all outputs. Thus, when total fixed and variable costs are added, the total cost curve appears as nothing more than a vertical displacement of total variable cost. This means that **the slopes of both total cost and total variable cost are identical. These slopes equal marginal cost.** Marginal cost first falls and then rises, as shown in Figure 6A-3.

Figure 6A-4 shows typical marginal cost, average cost, and average variable cost curves, where *average cost* equals total cost divided by output, and *average variable cost* equals total variable cost divided by output. Marginal cost intersects both average cost and average variable cost at their respective minimum points. The reason these minimums do not occur at the same outputs is that *average fixed cost*, equal to total fixed cost divided by output, declines as output increases.

$$\text{Average cost} = \text{average fixed cost} + \text{average variable cost}$$

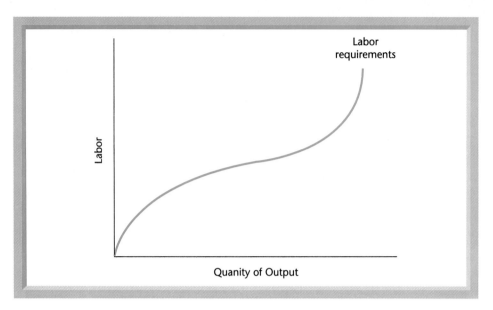

FIGURE 6A-2 **Total labor requirements** for each level of output are revealed by looking at the total product curve from a different perspective.

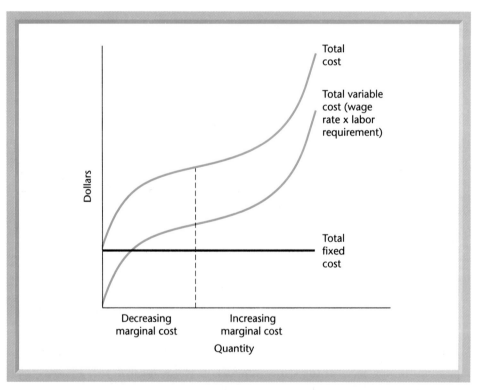

FIGURE 6A-3 **The total cost curve adds total fixed and total variable costs.** Marginal cost is the slope of either total cost or total variable cost.

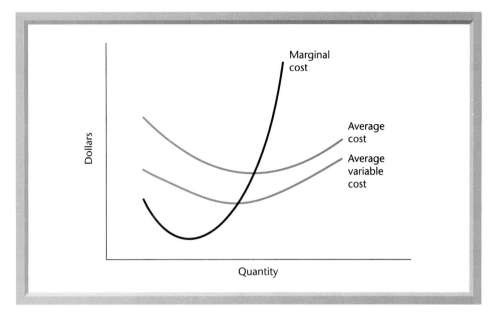

FIGURE 6A-4 **Typical shapes of marginal cost, average cost, and average variable cost** will be as shown. Average fixed cost is the difference between average cost and average variable cost.

Table 6A-1 expands Table 6-2 to illustrate how to compute the various cost measures. Notice that average variable cost starts to rise before average cost, because average fixed cost is constantly declining as output increases.

A little more algebra reveals the inverse relationship between marginal cost and marginal product and between average variable cost and average product. Whatever wage is being paid for the marginal unit of labor, when divided by the output of that labor, reveals the marginal cost per unit of output. Thus, the lower is marginal productivity, the higher is marginal cost.

For example, if a firm pays $10 for an extra hour of work and the worker produces five widgets in that hour, the marginal labor cost per widget is $2. If marginal product falls to four widgets per hour, marginal labor cost rises to $2.50.

$$\text{Marginal cost} = \frac{\text{wage rate}}{\text{marginal product}}$$

TABLE 6A-1 WW's Costs in Detail (all costs stated in dollars)

Output (Q)	Total Cost (TC)	Total Fixed Cost (TFC)	Total Variable Cost (TVC)	Marginal Cost (ΔTVC/ΔQ)	Average Cost (TC/Q)	Average Variable Cost (TVC/Q)	Average Fixed Cost (TFC/Q)
4	400	200	200	?	100	50	50
5	500	200	300	100	100	60	40
6	660	200	460	160	110	76.67	33.33
7	910	200	710	250	130	101.43	28.57

Dividing the wage rate by average product reveals the average variable cost of output. If the wage rate is $10 and the average product is six widgets, for example, the average variable cost of producing a widget would be $1.67. Average variable cost varies inversely with average product.

$$\text{Average variable cost} = \frac{\text{wage rate}}{\text{average product}}$$

DEPICTING PROFIT AND LOSS

A firm seeks to maximize profit, where profit equals total revenue minus total cost. Profit is driven by costs and by price. It is useful to express profit in terms of price, since price is the most widely reported feature of the marketplace. *Ceteris paribus*, profits and prices move in the same direction.

If a firm sells all of its output at a single price, that price is the firm's revenue per unit of that output, otherwise known as **average revenue.**

average revenue: revenue per unit of output; total revenue/quantity; equals price for firms that charge a single price.

$$\text{Average revenue} = \frac{\text{total revenue}}{\text{quantity}} = \text{price}$$

Multiplying average revenue by quantity thus equals total revenue. By the same token, multiplying average cost by quantity would yield total cost. Thus, a firm's profits can be expressed as

$$\text{Profit} = \text{quantity} \times (\text{average revenue} - \text{average cost})$$

or equivalently,

$$\text{Profit} = \text{quantity} \times (\text{price - average cost}).$$

Figure 6A-5 illustrates a profitable firm producing the profit-maximizing output given by the intersection of marginal cost and marginal revenue. The vertical difference between price and average cost at the quantity of output the firm produces is the average profit per unit of output. When this average profit is multiplied by the quantity produced, the result equals total profit, as shown by the shaded box.

Figure 6A-6 depicts the same firm as in Figure 6A-5. The only difference is that the firm is now facing a loss due to a drop in the market price. While the firm still produces the quantity for which marginal cost equals marginal revenue, that quantity is now lower. The firm has minimized its loss, the shaded rectangle.

If the price drops below average variable cost, the firm should immediately shut down, which corresponds to the shutdown rule stated in the chapter. That rule is that the firm should shut down if its total revenue does not cover total variable cost. By dividing both total revenue and total variable cost by the quantity of output, the shutdown rule can equivalently be stated as follows in terms of average revenue (price) and per unit costs: Shut down if price is less than average variable cost. When price falls that low, shutting down minimizes the loss, which is limited to fixed costs.

Like the price taker, the price searcher—a firm that faces a downward-sloping demand curve—chooses quantity and price according to the profit maximizing rule of producing until marginal revenue equals marginal cost. Recall that, unlike the price

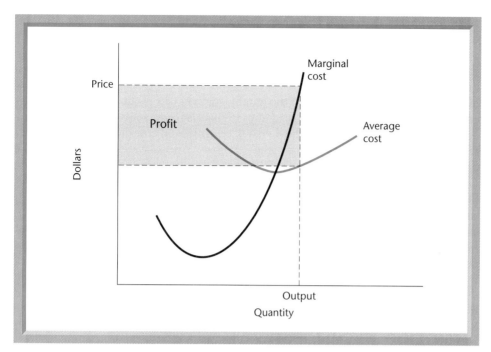

FIGURE 6A-5 **A profitable firm.** The profits are maximized, because the firm produces to the point where marginal cost equals marginal revenue.

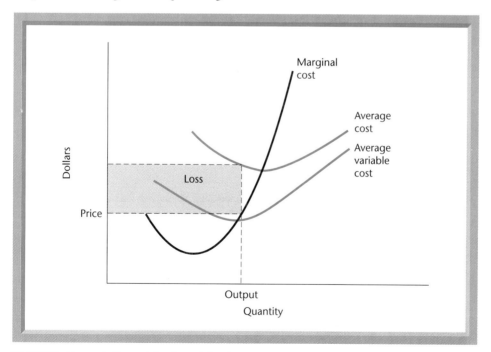

FIGURE 6A-6 **A firm with a loss.** This firm minimizes its loss by producing to where marginal cost equals marginal revenue. If price dropped below the minimum point on average variable cost, the firm would cease production and lose its total fixed cost.

taker, the price searcher will set a price above marginal revenue at this quantity. This is seen in Figure 6A-7, where quantity (Q*) is set at the point where marginal revenue equals marginal cost and price (P*) is set according to the demand curve. The average cost at quantity Q* is labeled AC*. Total profit is represented graphically as the area of the rectangle labeled Profit. This is a simple application of the length times width formula for the area of a rectangle. In the graph, length equals profit per unit, the difference between price and average cost, and width equals the quantity produced.

Table 6A-2 on p. 217 shows the demand, revenue, and cost data required to master the logic of profit maximization. The data is for a price-searching firm, since the firm is seen to vary its price in order to vary the quantity it sells. For the price taker, in contrast, price would remain constant and equal marginal revenue at each point. Otherwise, the analysis of the two cases is identical.

Revenue data make up the first four columns. The price (P) and quantity (Q) columns show the firm's demand. Total revenue (TR) is price multiplied by quantity. Marginal revenue (MR) equals the change in total revenue divided by the change in quantity. The fifth column shows total cost (TC); the sixth shows marginal cost (MC); the seventh shows average cost (AC). The final column shows profit. Sighting down the final column reveals that maximum profit equals $24.50, which occurs at five units of output and a price of $7.00.

The firm's decision to produce five units can also be reached by comparing marginal revenue to marginal cost. The firm will produce the next unit of output so long as marginal revenue equals or exceeds marginal cost, which again leads to the output of five units. The firm would not produce the sixth unit since marginal cost exceeds marginal revenue.

Applying Concepts

1. a. Using the data below, compute total cost, average fixed cost, average variable cost, average cost, and marginal cost for each output. Total fixed cost is $100.

Output	Total Variable Cost
0	$0
1	50
2	90
3	140
4	200
5	300
6	500

   b. Using the data above, calculate profit at each level of output when the output can be sold for $75 per unit. Which output maximizes profit? How much is the profit?
2. Illustrate graphically a price-searching firm that maximizes profit but earns only a zero profit.

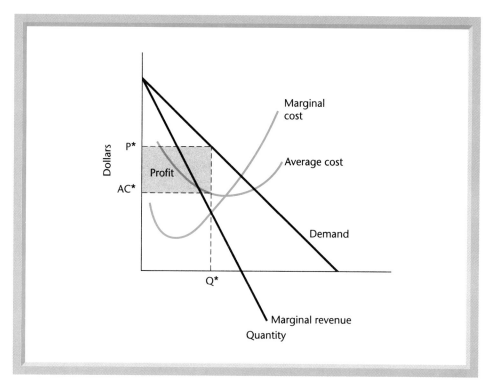

FIGURE 6A-7 **Total profit equals profit per unit (shown as P* − AC*) multiplied by quantity (shown as Q*).** Total profit is illustrated graphically as the shaded area of the rectangle labeled *Profit*.

TABLE 6A-2 Revenue and Costs for a Firm with Market Power (Average cost rounded to the nearest penny)

P	Q	TR	MR	TC	MC	AC	Profit
$12.00	0	$0.00	Undefined	$3.00	Undefined	Undefined	$−3.00
11.00	1	11.00	$11.00	4.00	$1.00	$4.00	+7.00
10.00	2	20.00	9.00	4.50	0.50	2.25	+15.50
9.00	3	27.00	7.00	5.50	1.00	1.83	+21.50
8.00	4	32.00	5.00	7.50	2.00	1.88	+24.50
7.00	5	35.00	3.00	10.50	3.00	2.10	+24.50
6.00	6	36.00	1.00	15.50	5.00	2.58	+20.50
5.00	7	35.00	−1.00	24.00	8.50	3.43	+11.00
4.00	8	32.00	−3.00	36.00	12.00	4.50	−4.00
3.00	9	27.00	−5.00	52.00	16.00	5.78	−25.00
2.00	10	20.00	−7.00	70.00	18.00	7.00	−50.00
1.00	11	11.00	−9.00	92.00	22.00	8.36	−81.00
0.00	12	0.00	−11.00	120.00	28.00	10.00	−120.00

7

MARKET MODELS

A Look Ahead

NORTH, SOUTH, EAST, west—every scout learns to navigate by the four points of the compass. In economics, too, there are four directions to take in the study of market models: pure competition, monopoly, monopolistic competition, and oligopoly. Just as the North Star provided a shining reference for ancient travelers, the model of pure competition offers a benchmark of economic efficiency against which real world markets can be measured.

An examination of the four market models permits greater understanding of various business behaviors and strategies and the manner in which prices are established. This chapter investigates pricing, output, profit, product differentiation, and other forms of business conduct.

Exploration 7-1 examines the market structure possibilities for first-class mail delivery, including the possibility of privatizing the U.S. Postal Service. The second Exploration scrutinizes the historical practice of antitrust with an eye toward understanding current and future antitrust issues.

As you are **Surveying Economic Principles** you will arrive at an ability to

❏ characterize the range of market types;

❏ explain why the model of pure competition is somewhat unrealistic, but still quite useful;

❏ state the meaning and significance of mutual interdependence;

❏ describe product differentiation and its implications;

❏ relate how and why firms charge some consumers more than others for the same products.

While **Exploring Issues** you will be able to

❏ assess the merits of protecting the U.S. Postal Service from competition;

❏ discuss antitrust laws and their application.

Terms Along the Way

✔ pure competition, 220
✔ market power, 220
✔ barriers to entry, 220
✔ monopoly, 220
✔ oligopoly, 220
✔ monopolistic competition, 220
✔ natural monopoly, 226
✔ limit pricing, 228
✔ deregulation, 230

✔ mutually interdependent, 230
✔ cartel, 231
✔ game theory, 232
✔ contestable markets, 233
✔ horizontal integration, 234
✔ vertical integration, 234
✔ conglomerate merger, 235
✔ price discrimination, 236
✔ cross-subsidization, 242

SURVEYING ECONOMIC PRINCIPLES

pure competition: a market in which there are numerous firms, all of which are price takers.

market power: when individual sellers have at least a bit of control over the prices of their outputs; arises from barriers to entry.

barriers to entry: when investors or entrepreneurs find obstacles to joining a profitable industry.

monopoly: a market with only one seller of a good without close substitutes.

oligopoly: a market with a few significant sellers.

monopolistic competition: a market with many firms, each with slight market power.

The interaction of supply and demand in the marketplace creates a single market price. The simplest model of this interaction is called pure competition, which assumes the existence of many price-taking firms selling at the market price. However, pure competition is only one type of *market structure*, the way a market operates.

Individual sellers often have at least a bit of control over the prices of their outputs. When this occurs, firms are said to possess market power. Market power arises from barriers to entry. Barriers to entry exist when investors or entrepreneurs find obstacles to joining a profitable industry. Barriers to entry include anything that makes producing and selling output more difficult for a new firm than for an existing firm.

Market power can lead to monopoly, which is a market with only one seller of a good without close substitutes. Alternatively, if market power is weaker, the market structure will be *imperfect competition*, which takes one of two forms:

- Oligopoly—a market with more than one seller, where at least one of those sellers can significantly influence price; usually characterized by a few significant sellers;
- Monopolistic competition—a market with numerous firms, each of which has only a slight ability to control price.

Market power is greatest for monopoly firms, less for oligopoly firms, and slight for firms in monopolistic competition. *Price searching* behavior is found in these three other forms of market structure. Because these firms are not price takers, they must figure out the selling price that maximizes their profit. Figure 7-1 arranges the market models from left to right according to increasing market power.

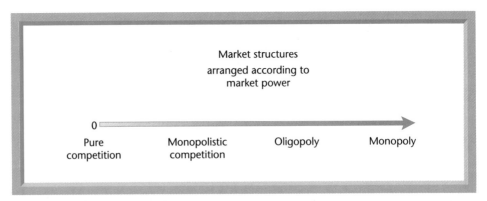

FIGURE 7-1 **Market models can be arranged according to the amounts of market power that firms possess.**

Pure Competition

Pure competition is characterized by the following:

- **Numerous buyers and sellers,** implying that each firm is a price taker and each buyer pays the market price.
- **A homogeneous product.** *Homogeneous products* are identical across all firms in an industry; the output of any single firm is identical to that of any other. For example, the #2 grade yellow corn produced by Farmer Brown, Farmer Jones, and other farmers is homogeneous because there are no differences between their crops. Because products are identical, individual firms reap no benefits from advertising. Thus individual firms do no advertising in pure competition.
- **No barriers to the entry and exit of firms.** It is easy for firms to start up or leave the industry.

The result of these assumptions is that, **in pure competition, firms are price takers,** where that price is set by the intersection of supply and demand in the marketplace. Although market demand slopes down, **the demand facing each firm is horizontal (perfectly elastic) at the market price.** The firm is able to sell as much as it wishes at that price, but cannot sell anything if it charges more. This concept is shown in Figure 7-2.

The firm's demand will shift up or down as market price rises or falls, caused by shifts in market demand or supply. In the short run, the market price could be

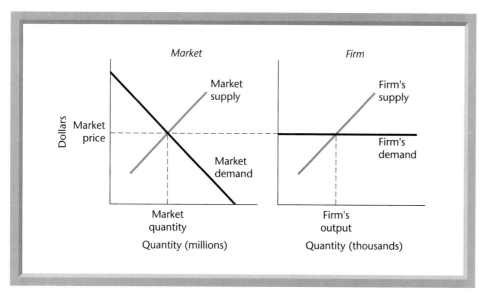

FIGURE 7-2 The firm in pure competition faces a demand that is horizontal at the market price, because each firm is a price taker. The intersection of market demand and market supply sets market price.

sufficiently high that the firm earns economic profits, or it could be so low that the firm loses money. However, the **long-run equilibrium market price results in the expectation of zero economic profits for a firm considering entering the industry.**

Expected profit is zero in the long run because economic profit would attract new entrants that shift the market supply to the right. Entry would continue to occur, driving market price down until expected profit fell to zero. Likewise, loss would prompt exit that shifts the market supply curve to the left. That process would continue until price rises to the level of zero expected profit for firms contemplating entry or exit. Even so, some firms will remain profitable in the long run, such as farms with exceptionally fertile and tillable soil. Figure 7-3 illustrates the effect upon price of entry and exit.

Students wanting to learn more about commodities can visit the Chicago Mercantile Exchange on-line at **http://www.cme.com/**

Examples of businesses that can be understood with the purely competitive model include farms, ranches, dealers in gold and silver bullion, copper mines, steel producers, aluminum refiners, and lumber producers. Outputs are roughly homogeneous within each of these markets. Within a particular grade, all wheat is alike, beef is beef, aluminum ingots vary negligibly from one refinery to another, and so forth. Information about the market prices of these items is widely available in media reports on *commodities,* a term used to describe homogeneous goods.

Pure competition illuminates how markets allocate resources efficiently. Purely competitive firms maximize profit by producing output up to the point where price equals marginal cost. At that point, every unit produced is valued by consumers as greater than or equal to marginal cost. The next unit of output would increase cost more than the value placed upon it by consumers. It should not and will not be pro-

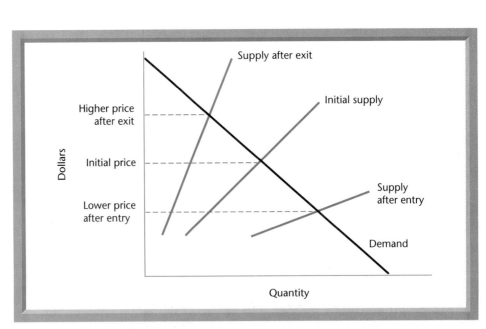

FIGURE 7-3 **Profit attracts new entrants,** which lowers price until entry stops. **Losses cause firms to exit** the industry, which raises price until exit stops.

duced if the market is competitive. Since competition also forces firms to keep costs to a minimum, pure competition is both allocatively and technologically efficient.

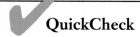

QuickCheck

If you owned a gold coin of known weight and purity, but without collector value, how would you learn what price to ask if you were selling it?

Answer: You would be a price taker who would sell at the going market price for gold. This price changes often as supply and demand shift. The price at any given moment is determined by supply and demand in the commodity exchanges, such as the Chicago Mercantile Exchange, and can be accessed through various online quote services.

OBSERVATION POINT:
Old McDonald Farms Again!

Old McDonald had a farm. Like so many others in the competitive agricultural industry, lack of profit drove him out of business. Exit was painful and distressing. Still, it was also easy, given the well-developed markets for land and used farm equipment. Now he wants back in, eager to sell chickens to health-conscious consumers. Entry is easy, too, although it may take time and effort. The necessary skills can be acquired in an agricultural program at college or, as in the case of old McDonald, by experience.

Entry also takes land, equipment, and other inputs, depending on the type of farming involved. For Old McDonald to raise more chickens, he will need a chicken house. Although land and chicken houses are expensive, this is not much of a barrier to entry in today's world. The reason is that farmers have access to borrowed funds through the banking system. They are also able to lease land and equipment. So, keep your ears open for an "ee-yi-ee-yi-oh" hollered in gratitude for the easy exit and entry in his competitive industry. It lets Old McDonald farm again.

Barriers to Entry

When there are barriers to entry, the "come on in" signal sent by economic profit cannot be acted upon. By impeding the invisible hand, barriers to entry call into question the efficiency of resource allocation in the free market.

Barriers can take a multitude of forms. Some are created by government. For example, tariffs and import quotas limit the ability of foreign competitors to challenge domestic firms. Government licensing of occupations and businesses is a form of barrier. Government-issued patents and copyrights can also be a barrier to the entry of new businesses into a market. Such barriers may be economically justified because they help promote research, development, and other creative activity by ensuring that inventors, authors, and others are rewarded for their efforts.

Firms often attempt to erect barriers in order to protect themselves from new competitors. Research and development conducted in search of patentable outputs is one avenue toward market power. Advertising expenditures provide another. If advertising creates customer loyalty for existing firms, new entry is made more difficult. Still another barrier occurs when a firm gains control of an essential input. Lack of that essential input deprives other firms of the opportunity to produce the output. The Aluminum Company of America (ALCOA) pursued this strategy during the early decades of the twentieth century.

OBSERVATION POINT:
Is the American Medical Association Hazardous to Your Health?

http://ama-assn.org/home.htm will take you to the Web site of the American Medical Association.

The American Medical Association (AMA) is not a government agency. Nevertheless, this professional association has much to say about the availability of health care. Not only does it have power over the standards for licensing physicians, but it also has considerable input into setting standards for medical schools. Some critics of the current U.S. health care system accuse the AMA of setting unnecessarily high standards, which serve as barriers to entry into the medical profession. The purpose? Critics contend that the motivation is more income for physicians. The AMA responds that medicine is a life or death proposition, and that only the best physicians should be allowed to serve the public.

Assessing Market Power

Market power can be measured by the *four-firm concentration ratio*, which is the fraction of total sales in an industry accounted for by the four largest firms. Larger concentration ratios show that the four largest firms sell a larger fraction of total industry sales. In a pure monopoly market, the monopolist accounts for 100 percent of sales. Therefore, the four-firm concentration ratio equals 100. The ratio for oligopolies with only two, three, or four firms will also always equal 100, standing for 100 percent.

Table 7-1 shows four-firm concentration ratios for a selection of industries. The interpretation of each concentration ratio is straightforward. Larger numbers show greater market power and less competition. The four-firm concentration ratio is not a perfect means of assessing market power. For example, the concentration ratios in Table 7-1 ignore the presence of foreign competition. The concentration ratios also fail to capture the effects of market power arising from differences in the size of the top four firms. When one of them is much larger than the others, that one firm may dominate the market. This case would be fundamentally different than the case where a concentration ratio represents four firms of equal size. Also, there is nothing magical about four firms. Indeed, the government also calculates eight-firm concentration ratios and other more complex measures of concentration.

The ability of a firm to choose the selling price of its output depends upon its demand curve. Price takers have horizontal demand curves. They have no choice but to sell at the market price. Firms that possess market power have downward-sloping demand curves. The steeper the demand curve, the more market power the firm has, and the greater its ability to raise price.

TABLE 7-1 Four-Firm Concentration Ratios for Selected U.S. Manufacturing Industries, 1992

Industry	Concentration Ratio (Percent)
Meat packing plants	50
Cigarettes	93
Knit outerwear mills	46
Wood household furniture	20
Paper mills	29
Book publishing	23
Petroleum refining	30
Luggage	43
Electronic computers	45
Aircraft	79

Source: 1992 Census of Manufactures report MC92-5-2.

Figure 7-4 shows three firms with varying degrees of market power. The first firm is a price taker in a competitive market and thus has no market power. The second firm's demand curve barely deviates from the horizontal. Therefore, its market power is negligible. It can raise its selling price only slightly, because there are many close substitutes for its product. The third firm has more market power, because it faces little or no competition. Its demand curve is rather steep, and its ability to set price is substantial.

No firm's market power is absolute, because no firm can raise prices without reducing the quantity that consumers will buy. Observe the third firm in Figure 7-4. If it raises price enough, it will reach the point where the demand curve intersects

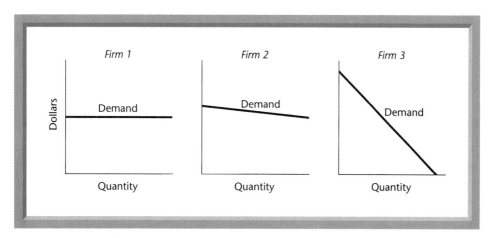

FIGURE 7-4 **Market power is seen in the slope of the demand curve facing the firm.** Judging from the steep slope of its demand, firm 3 has the most market power. Firm 1 is a price taker and has no market power.

the price axis. At that point the quantity demanded equals zero. The firm would never want to raise price that high.

QuickCheck

State the four-firm concentration ratio in each of the following scenarios: (a) Five firms of equal size make up the industry, (b) 100 firms of equal size make up the industry. In which scenario is there more competition?

Answer: (a) 80. Each firm will have a 20 percent market share. Therefore, four of the five firms will sell 80 percent of industry output. (b) 4. Any one firm will have a 1 percent market share; four firms will have a 4 percent share. In scenario (b) there is more competition.

Monopoly—Are There No Good Substitutes?

A monopoly is characterized by a single firm selling an output for which there are no close substitutes. Whether there are close substitutes for a good or service is often not obvious. Consider your local electric company. It is not feasible for most people to install windmills or solar panels in their backyards to generate their own power. The electric cable that serves you is owned by a single firm, a *local monopoly*. What about cable television? Usually only one cable company provides service in an area. However, if satellite dishes, network television, theaters, and other recreation are good substitutes, then local cable companies are not truly monopolists.

Monopolies occur for two reasons. One involves government restrictions on entry. For example, some cities grant a single taxicab company an *exclusive franchise*, a type of government-licensed monopoly that allows no one else to legally provide taxi service. To keep prices down, franchises can be awarded at auction to the firm that promises the lowest price for the franchised good or service. Franchise monopolies are not to be confused with private sector franchise arrangements, such as between the McDonald's Corporation and its restaurant franchisees.

natural monopoly: when one firm can supply the entire market at a lower per unit cost than could two or more separate firms; associated with economies of scale.

Monopoly can also arise naturally in the marketplace. Natural monopoly occurs when one firm can supply the entire market at a lower per unit cost than could two or more separate firms. This situation can happen if there are substantial economies of scale. A potential entrant will think twice about challenging a natural monopolist. To realize economies of scale, the entrant would need to start large, so large that the entrant and the established firm could not both survive. Few investors would be willing to finance such a challenge. For example, imagine three or four water suppliers each burying water mains along a street, with each seller competing for the business of the nearby residents. A single firm could eliminate this wasteful duplication of effort and in the process lower the average costs of providing service. Water companies and local gas and electric companies are examples of *public utilities*, which are usually natural monopolies.

OBSERVATION POINT:
Finding Monopoly—The Case of Cellophane

The existence of substitutes was the central issue in one famous court case involving the alleged monopoly held by DuPont, the producer of cellophane. While monopoly itself is not illegal, anticompetitive behavior to create one can be. The court considered evidence regarding the numerous substitutes for cellophane, a clear packaging material. These substitutes included wax paper and aluminum foil. The final decision reasoned that cellophane was one of many packaging materials produced by a number of firms. The availability of substitutes and the relatively low market share for cellophane relative to the market for packaging materials were facts that influenced the court to exonerate DuPont. The court reasoned that DuPont did not have a monopoly, because the market was for packaging materials, not just cellophane.

The Inefficiencies of Monopoly

A monopoly faces the market demand curve because it is the only firm in the market. Because monopoly demand is downward sloping, **a monopolist is a *price searcher*.** As shown in chapter 6, in maximizing short-run profit a price-searcher will set its price higher than marginal cost. Thus, the marginal cost of additional output in monopoly is less than the marginal benefit to consumers, as measured by the demand curve. **The monopolist produces an output that is inefficiently small because its price is inefficiently high.**

Figure 7-5 compares the efficient quantity to the quantity produced by a monopoly. The efficient quantity occurs where marginal cost intersects the demand curve. At that quantity, the marginal value of the last unit equals its marginal cost. All units of output produced up to that point are characterized by a marginal benefit that is greater than marginal cost. This point can be seen by observing that the demand curve, which was seen in chapter 3 to also measure marginal benefits, lies above the marginal cost curve up to the point where the two curves intersect.

Monopolies can sometimes be quite profitable, since there are no other competitors to undercut its prices. Firms will go to great lengths to obtain or retain monopoly status. However, resources devoted by firms to obtaining monopoly are wasted from society's point of view. For example, AT&T waged a long and bitter legal fight against MCI in the 1970s to retain its decades old monopoly in long distance service. Similarly, MCI expended costly resources for the right to compete. From society's point of view, it is better for firms to engage in activities that increase wealth, rather than fight to transfer wealth.

In a similar vein, a firm might lobby government for quota or tariff protection from foreign competition. This was the route taken by Harley-Davidson in the 1980s. The venerable motorcycle manufacturer was the sole remaining U.S. firm producing motorcycles. Harley was not truly a monopolist, however, because good substitutes for its product were available from foreign manufacturers. Facing stiff competition from Japanese firms such as Honda and Yamaha, Harley was successful in obtaining government protection. That protection transferred wealth from

The Harley-Davidson firm maintains an interesting Web site at **http://www. harley-davidson. com/**

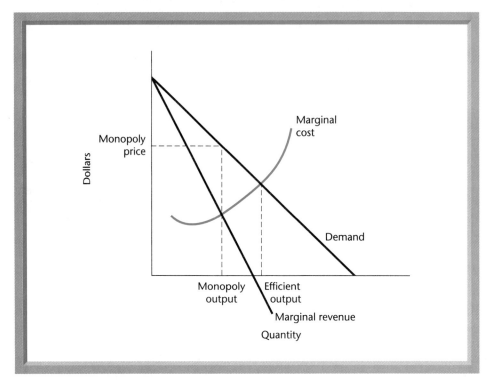

FIGURE 7-5 **The efficient quantity of output exceeds that produced by the unregulated monopoly** because the marginal benefit of additional output (given by demand) exceeds its marginal cost at that output.

motorcycle enthusiasts to Harley by raising the price of imported motorcycles. This effect allowed Harley to increase its prices too.

The invisible hand of the competitive marketplace means that deviations from efficient resource allocation are self-correcting. **In monopoly, inefficiencies can persist indefinitely.** However, although an unregulated monopoly will not produce an efficient quantity at each point in time, it does generate profits that allow it the wherewithal to invest in research and development to enhance its monopoly status. Competitive firms have neither the incentive nor financial ability to pursue this course. Thus, while producing too little and charging too much in the short run, a monopoly that earns excess profits might offer the consumer improved products in the long run.

While the monopolist does not face competition directly, it does face the threat of *potential competition* from new producers or new products. If a monopolist prices its product too high, new substitutes may be developed that draw away the monopolist's customers. Alternatively, a new firm may take the risk of challenging the monopolist's turf. To avoid these possibilities, a monopolist might practice limit pricing, which is charging the highest price customers will pay, subject to the limit that the price not be so high that it attracts potential competitors. **The limit price will be lower than the short-run profit-maximizing price.** Although short-run profit is

limit pricing:
charging the highest price customers will pay, subject to the limit that the price not be so high that potential competitors enter the industry.

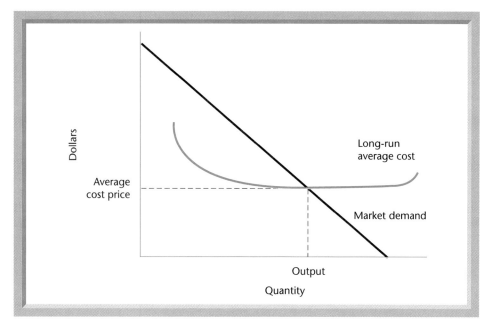

FIGURE 7-6 **In the case of public utilities, regulators commonly attempt to limit monopoly pricing to no more than long-run average production costs,** which would cause the output shown. However, regulators may tend to overestimate these costs because they do not know all of the ways that the regulated firm could economize and because the regulated firm has no incentive to reveal these cost-saving possibilities.

reduced, limit pricing allows the monopolist to earn more profit in the long run by keeping competitors away.

Regulation and Deregulation of Monopoly

Government may hold down the price a monopolist can charge. Most commonly, government employs *rate-of-return regulation*, which prevents the monopolist from charging a price that would generate economic profit. This means that the monopolist's price per unit must equal its average cost per unit, as shown in Figure 7-6. **At the lower price that results under regulation, more output is sold, and the monopolist comes closer to the allocatively efficient ideal** denoted in Figure 7-5. Typically, public utilities are subject to this kind of regulation, with both the federal and state governments participating in the regulatory process.

The regulation of industry by the federal government, undertaken to ensure "fair prices," has a long history. The Interstate Commerce Commission (ICC), dating from 1887, was created by Congress to regulate the railroads, which were the primary means of transporting many kinds of goods at the time. In the 1920s and 1930s, as trucking took a larger share of the transportation market, it seemed natural to extend regulation to that industry as well. Airline regulation was also established as regularly scheduled passenger service took hold in the 1930s. Note that regulation was instituted even though these industries were not characterized by monopoly. Rather, they were imperfectly competitive.

A problem with rate-of-return regulation is that the regulated monopolist has little incentive to control costs or to provide innovative services. Thus, over time, regulation can impede change in production techniques and in the development of new products. Regulation also had the effect of stifling new competition. This effect occurred because regulation often favored existing firms at the expense of potential competitors. For example, during the more than 30-year period that the airlines were regulated, start-ups of new airlines were few.

deregulation: the scaling back of government regulation of industry.

The concern that regulation breeds inefficiencies over time and sets up barriers to entry has led to the **deregulation** of some industries. To a great extent, the trucking and airline industries have been deregulated, beginning in the 1970s. This action was motivated by government recognition that a policy of promoting competition could benefit consumers. The effects of deregulation were quickly felt by consumers as competition forced fares downward among existing airlines. Fares fell even more as many new airlines were created because of the easier entry in a deregulated environment.

In spite of the advantages offered by deregulation, at least some regulation at both the state and federal levels remains the norm for local public utilities. Regulation has greater appeal when the item offered for sale is a necessity, such as water, gas, or electricity. Even promarket Nobel-prize winning economist Milton Friedman, who for the most part opposes government regulation of business, has reluctantly accepted the need for regulation when competition does not seem feasible and the good produced is a necessity.

Attitudes toward regulation and deregulation change as time goes by. For example, the initial success of airline deregulation has been called into question as many of the upstart airlines have since gone out of business or merged with larger airlines. However, deregulation has clearly increased the technological efficiency of airlines. For example, the hub-and-spoke route system is quite cost-effective, but would probably not have developed under regulation. Deregulation of electricity is also on the horizon or a reality in many areas. While the transmission lines that connect homes and businesses to the electric power grid would remain monopolized, deregulation would allow power providers the freedom to compete to feed electricity into that grid, thereby keeping electricity prices as low as possible.

The Tennessee Valley Authority Web site is located at **http://fedgate.org /fg_tva.htm**

As an alternative to regulation, the federal government has also engaged in government ownership of industry. The giant electric utility, the Tennessee Valley Authority (TVA), is a familiar example to those living in the southeastern states of the United States. The U.S. Postal Service, discussed in Exploration 7-1 in this chapter, is familiar to even more people. Government ownership is beset with severe enough problems that it is seen as a policy of last resort, at least in the United States. As noted in chapter 1, many countries with a history of widespread government ownership have begun to abandon that policy in favor of privatization.

Oligopoly—Domination by a Few Large Firms

mutually interdependent: when the individual actions of firms in an industry have direct effects on market conditions facing other firms in that industry.

Numerous markets are characterized by oligopoly, in which there are a few significant firms. In oligopoly, each significant firm's actions affect the other firms in the industry. Oligopoly firms are **mutually interdependent,** with the actions taken by one firm inducing other firms to take counteractions. Thus strategy and counter-strategy is the norm in oligopolistic markets. Mutual interdependence frequently revolves around the pricing decisions of oligopoly firms. The example afforded by the cut in the price of Marlboro cigarettes in 1995 is instructive. The price of Marlboros was lowered in response to the growing market share of generic brands. Rival cigarette manufacturers were then also forced to immediately lower the prices of their leading brands in order to avoid losing sales to Marlboro. Later, when Marlboro prices were increased, the prices of other leading brands increased in lockstep.

Mutual interdependence can also involve product design. For instance, when Ford and Chrysler added a well-received fourth door to their popular extended-cab pickup trucks in 1998, mutual interdependence forced GM to scurry to do the same with its Chevy and GMC models, although GM's response occurred with a time lag that may have cost the giant automaker some sales.

Oligopoly products may be differentiated or homogeneous. The cigarette and automobile industries are examples of oligopolies that produce *differentiated products*—products that vary from one producer to the next. Each brand of cigarette offers smokers unique flavor, packaging, image, and other features. Each vehicle differs from competing models. Styling, colors offered, horsepower, and interior design are just a few of the ways that cars are differentiated. Output of oligopolies is not always differentiated, however. Steel, aluminum, and copper are homogeneous commodities produced by oligopolistic firms.

OBSERVATION POINT:
Theme Parks—The Theme is Competition

Where once stood miles of sleepy back roads crisscrossing orange groves whose bountiful crops helped satisfy the world's thirst for juice, today stand theme parks that satisfy the thirst for fun and adventure.

The place is Orlando, Florida, a world-class tourist destination and home to Disney's Magic Kingdom, Animal Kingdom, Epcot Center, Disney MGM Studios, Sea World, and Universal Studios. The competition among these giant oligopoly theme parks to increase attendance and entice the customers to spend illustrates competition under mutual interdependence. To attract additional dollars from their visitors, both Disney and Universal offer their own hotels, restaurants, and shops. And when the customers grow weary of the parks, give them nightclubs, more shopping, and theater. The strategy is to tie other profit-making activities to the operation of the theme parks. Such is the nature of competition among these oligopolists.

Cartels

If firms would stop competing with each other, they could raise prices and earn greater joint profits. **Oligopoly firms that agree to stop competing are said to form a cartel,** a form of oligopoly characterized by collusion. The objective of a cartel is to increase price to the profit-maximizing monopoly price. The higher price implies a smaller output, which must then be allocated among the members of the cartel.

cartel: a form of oligopoly characterized by collusion; intended to increase profits, but illegal in the United States.

Cartels are likely to exist only in oligopoly industries, because large numbers of firms would be unlikely to agree on a selling price. However, cartels are difficult to keep together for several reasons:

- They are **illegal in the United States** according to the antitrust statutes. Cartels in the United States operate in secrecy.
- Any member firm has an **incentive to cheat,** by undercutting the monopoly price established by the cartel. By secretly selling at a lower price than other cartel members, a member could increase its sales and hence profits at the expense of its partners.
- **A cartel member can drop out** if it becomes unhappy with any aspect of the cartel agreement. Cartel prices are sustained by limits on production for each member. Production quotas also limit the profits of each member.
- If barriers to entry are not absolute, **high cartel profits could induce competition** from new entrants or existing firms who are not members of the cartel.
- Over time, **higher prices can lead to the development of substitutes** for the cartel's product.

In the case of the Organization of Petroleum Exporting Countries (OPEC), the best known cartel, high oil prices spurred exploration, which in turn led to major oil finds in Alaska, Mexico, and the North Sea. Because OPEC did not control these new oil fields, the added oil supplies negatively affected OPEC's ability to set price. Likewise, the higher prices prompted the development of energy-efficient homes and automobiles that reduced demand for OPEC oil.

Game Theory

game theory: the notion that market participants use strategies to play economic "games," similar to strategies used in winning at bridge, poker, chess, and other games.

The mathematics of game theory can be employed to deepen the understanding of oligopoly markets. The method analyzes the behavior of parties whose interests conflict. The tool of analysis is the *payoff matrix,* showing the gains or losses from making a decision when mutual interdependence is present.

In game theory, as in life, the outcome of one player's decision will also depend on a decision made by another. For example, a firm cannot reason out the effect of a price cut on its profits unless it considers what competitors will do. If competitors leave their price untouched, the effects on the price-cutting firm will be very different than if competitors cut their price to match or outdo the price cut of the first price cutter. As in poker, chess, and other games, many additional strategies also provide insights into oligopoly behavior. Some strategies are quite complex and involve the use of advanced mathematics.

An example of a game is illustrated by the *prisoner's dilemma.* Two persons, A and B, who are suspected by police of being partners in the commission of a crime, are arrested. Interrogation takes place in separate rooms, where each prisoner is told the following:

> If your partner confesses, while you keep your mouth shut, we'll throw the book at you. Your partner will get off with 1 year in jail, but you'll do 20 years of hard time. On the other hand, if you confess while your partner keeps quiet, you will get 1 year of jail time, while your partner gets 20. If you both confess, you'll both get 5 years in the

TABLE 7-2 Payoff Matrix—Prisoner's Dilemma

	A confesses	A keeps quiet
B confesses	A get 5 years B gets 5 years	A gets 20 years B gets 1 year
B keeps quiet	A gets 1 year B gets 20 years	A gets 3 years B gets 3 years

slammer. If you both clam up, we've still got the evidence to send you away for 3 years in the pokey.

Table 7-2 summarizes the situation. Studying the payoff matrix reveals that whatever A does, B is better off confessing. Whatever B does, A is better off confessing. Guilt or innocence makes no difference. Collusion between A and B, in the form an oath by both to keep quiet, offers a lighter sentence than the 5 years they both receive by confessing. However, the police have separated them for the very purpose of preventing collusion. The police have in effect stacked the deck, preventing the pursuit by A and B of their joint interests.

The predicament faced in the game applies to the members of a cartel. By cooperating among themselves and raising price while cutting quantity, the member firms making up the cartel can achieve the greatest profit. But reasoned self-interest says that it pays to cheat on the arrangement by increasing sales through secret price cuts. If a member cheats while other members do not, the cheater is better off. If a member does not cheat while other members do, the honest member suffers. No matter what the other members do, a particular member of the cartel is better off by cheating. Cheating is a major reason that OPEC's power has dwindled over time.

Other Models

Oligopoly is the only market structure that includes a collection of separate models. The reason is that different oligopoly industries behave differently. Three of these models—contestable markets, price leadership, and the dominant firm with a competitive fringe—are discussed below.

Contestable markets occur when new rivals can enter or exit the market quickly and cheaply. Contestability can characterize either oligopoly or monopoly. The "quick in and quick out" characteristic of contestable markets limits the ability of the firm or firms already in the market to raise prices. If prices become too high in a contestable market, entry of new firms will occur since entry is easy. Congressional deregulation of the airline industry in the 1970s has brought contestable markets to life in the airports of our major cities, as large carriers can enter or exit a city's market with relative ease. In contrast, the automobile industry is costly and difficult to enter and thus does not meet the criteria of a contestable market.

contestable markets: when new rivals can enter or exit the market quickly and cheaply; could characterize either oligopoly or monopoly.

The *price leadership* model observes that in some oligopolistic industries, when one firm changes its selling price, the remaining firms in the industry copy that change. The firm initiating the price change is called the price leader; the copycats are termed followers. At one time or another the cigarette, automobile, and steel industries have exhibited the pattern of price leadership. In effect, the followers in a price-leadership oligopoly have voluntarily placed themselves in the role of price takers. They count on their leader to set a good price without resorting to illegal collusion.

The *dominant firm with a competitive fringe* is a combination of the competitive and monopoly models. The dominant firm, typically the largest in the industry, has a cost advantage over many smaller fringe firms. The dominant firm has no control over other producers, and thus allows them to produce as much as they want at the market price. However, the production decisions of the dominant firm force that price to below what it would be if the competitive fringe firms were the only suppliers. This lower price allows the dominant firm a significant share of the market.

The dominant-firm-with-a-competitive-fringe model describes the worldwide crude oil market, in which the OPEC cartel takes the role of the dominant firm and the many smaller non-OPEC producers are the competitive fringe. OPEC has no choice but to allow non-OPEC oil producers to sell as much as they want at the world price of oil. However, OPEC has no problem selling its own oil because it sets the world oil price at a level that ensures that quantity demanded far exceeds the quantity supplied by the competitive fringe. OPEC production makes up the difference. Of course, if OPEC were to withhold its oil from the market, the market-clearing price of oil would be dramatically higher.

Mergers

Mergers have the potential to reduce competition in an industry. If enough firms in an industry merge, the industry will inch closer toward oligopoly or even monopoly. This explains why the Antitrust Division of the Justice Department has developed merger guidelines that describe the kinds of mergers that are likely to be met by government-initiated legal challenges. This topic is discussed in more detail in Exploration 7-2 in this chapter.

horizontal integration: when a firm merges with another in the same line of business.

Horizontal integration occurs when a firm merges with another in the same line of business. When a supermarket chain buys another supermarket chain, a bank buys another bank, or a shoe manufacturer buys one of its competitors in shoemaking, horizontal integration has taken place. The acquisition of Gulf Oil by Chevron in the 1980s is an example. Economies of scale can arise from horizontal mergers. To achieve economies, Chevron converted Gulf's chain of gas stations to the Chevron brand. Thus the historic orange disc that was once a fixture along America's roadsides is now rarely sighted except in memorabilia shops and on restaurant walls. More recently, the search for economies of scale has prompted huge mergers among telecommunication companies, among banks, and among oil companies.

vertical integration: when a firm acquires another firm that supplies it with an input, or acquires another firm which can sell the first firm's output.

A firm might acquire another firm that supplies it with an input, or it might acquire another firm that retails its output to consumers. Either case is termed vertical integration. The objective in the first instance is to secure reliable delivery of the input. In the second, it is to ensure a ready market for the firm's output. An example of vertical integration occurred in 1995 when the Walt Disney Company and the ABC television network joined forces to become a powerful producer and distributor of television programming.

A third type of merger is termed conglomerate merger. This variety of merger brings together firms whose lines of business have no obvious relationship to each other. The acquisition of Columbia Pictures by Coca-Cola fell into this category.

Although conglomerate mergers were hot in the 1960s and 1970s, the trend has been away from the conglomerate merger, with many former conglomerates splitting into separate firms. For example, Coca-Cola ultimately came to recognize that a soft-drink maker has no special expertise in film making and sold its Columbia Pictures unit to Sony. In 1995, AT&T proceeded to split itself into three separate firms. Even the ITT Corporation, which once epitomized conglomerates, has now divided itself into separate companies. Under one corporate aegis, ITT's holdings had ranged from the New York Knicks basketball team, to Hartford Insurance, to the manufacture of high-tech military equipment. These firms were worth more to investors as separate companies than as parts of conglomerates.

conglomerate merger: brings together firms whose lines of business have no obvious relationship to each other.

Monopolistic Competition—All Around Us

The diary of a college student: "Walked to Blue and Green to purchase *Economics by Design* and my other textbooks. Picked up my designer jeans at Rubi's Dry Cleaners. Dropped in to House of Burgers for lunch. After class, had to drive to CompuWiz to buy more DataSave computer disks. Gassed up at Gas'n N Go'n, and got some Purr-fection cat food for Kitty while I was there. Haircut at The Hair Team. Later, pizza at Piece-A-Da-Pie. Topped off the day with dancing and snacks at City Limits."

This college student has certainly had an active day. Much of it was spent dealing with firms operating in markets characterized by monopolistic competition, a market structure with many firms, product differentiation, and relatively easy entry of new firms. Many retailers operate in monopolistically competitive markets. In addition, many of the products they sell are also produced by firms in monopolistic competition.

Monopolistically competitive firms face demand curves that slope down somewhat, because although they are the only providers of their version of the product, other firms offer close substitutes. They thus set their output and price in the same manner as a monopoly. However, monopolistically competitive firms also face a great deal of competition from other firms that offer close substitutes. Thus, each firm's demand is highly elastic, meaning that it slopes downward only slightly, such as the demand facing firm 2 in Figure 7-4. This limits the market power of these firms.

Monopolistic competition is exciting, because easy entry and exit make it possible for entrepreneurs to test out their good ideas. If your version of an industry product is particularly appealing to the public, for example, you can open up shop and possibly grow rich. The downside is that your vision of the market could be clouded. For example, it seems that new restaurants are constantly opening. A few will catch on and grow, possibly even into national chains. Many more will allow their owners to scrape by. Others go out of business.

Advertising and Product Differentiation

The key to riches in monopolistic competition is successful product differentiation in such things as style, taste, shape, size, color, texture, quality, location, packaging, advertising, and service. For example, McDonald's has struggled in recent years to develop menu items that appeal to adults. The powerful lure of the trademarked golden arches is just one of many features that attract customers by differentiating McDonald's from its competitors, just as the 31 flavors help differentiate Baskin-Robbins from other purveyors of ice cream.

Monopolistically competitive markets are typically characterized by advertising and sales promotions. Some ads focus on facts, such as Yellow Pages ads with addresses, phone numbers, and hours of operation. On the other hand, much advertising is designed to work on consumers' imaginations and stick in their memories. Advertising slogans permeate our language. Successful advertising, slogans, and sales promotions increase the demand for a firm's version of the industry's output.

When advertising or otherwise differentiating its product, the profit-maximizing firm is still guided by the same principle that guides its choice of quantity of output: marginal cost equals marginal revenue. If the marginal revenue generated by advertising exceeds the marginal cost, advertising raises profits. Otherwise it does not. Similarly, the profit-maximizing firm will adjust its hours of operation, selection of merchandise, and every other aspect of product differentiation with this same principle in mind. For example, if a store's marginal revenue from staying open an extra hour in the evening exceeds the marginal cost of staying open the extra hour, the store will choose to stay open that extra hour.

When Do the Details Matter?

Monopolistic competition accurately describes many more markets than does pure competition. On that basis, it appears that monopolistic competition ought to be the model of choice for analyzing markets. Appearances are deceiving.

The model of pure competition is to be preferred over monopolistic competition when the details of product differentiation do not matter. Remember, the best model is the simplest model, so long as, in simplifying, we do not exclude details relevant to answering the questions we ask. The model of monopolistic competition is usually more useful than pure competition only when analyzing questions specifically relating to the effects of product differentiation and advertising.

Price Discrimination

price discrimination: the selling of a good or service at different prices to various buyers when such differences are not justified by cost differences.

Price discrimination is the selling of a good or service at different prices to various buyers, when such differences are not justified by cost differences. Examples include senior citizen and student discounts, differential rates for business customers for telephone and power, airline super saver fares, and prices that require the use of coupons. These examples of price discrimination are generally legal in the United States, as long as they do not create monopoly or lessen competition.

Price discrimination is feasible when different prices can be charged to different market segments. For example, it costs no less to screen a movie in a theater filled with children than to show it to adults. Yet adult ticket prices are usually twice those of children's, because adults are less deterred by higher prices—demand for adult tickets is less elastic than demand for children's tickets. That's one way that theaters practice price discrimination. Another is to offer cut-rate tickets for afternoon show-ings of a film.

Price discrimination is not an act of charity; it maximizes profits. If theaters can fill otherwise empty seats, the revenue earned is all profit, because the cost of showing a movie in a theater packed with movie goers and in an empty theater is the same.

Price discrimination cannot be practiced if there can be *arbitrage*, in which buyers who are offered goods at a low price can resell those goods to other buyers. Every-one would then wind up buying at or near the same low price. For example, pricing adult movie tickets higher than children's would accomplish nothing if adults could see a movie with a child's ticket. The only tickets that a theater could sell would be child's tickets, purchased by children and then profitably resold to adults at a price less than the regular adult price.

 QuickCheck _____

Differences between in-state and out-of-state tuition at public colleges and universities are usually substantial. Is this price discrimination? How can it be justified?

Answer: It is no more costly to serve a student from one location than from another. Therefore, the custom of charging higher tuition to out-of-state students fits the definition of price discrimination. It is justified by the logic that those whose tax dollars have built the schools deserve a lower price. Thus, this price discrimination is intended to satisfy the goal of equity.

SUMMARY

- Four kinds of markets are: pure competition, monopolistic competition, oligop-oly, and monopoly.
- Markets can be arranged by the degree to which firms possess market power.
- The purely competitive firm is a price taker and thus has no market power. Because entry and exit are free in pure competition, in the long run firms will enter or exit until there is no expectation of either a profit or loss, that is, until expected economic profit is zero. Pure competition leads to an efficient quantity of output.
- Barriers to entry create monopoly, oligopoly, and monopolistic competition. These three kinds of firms are price searchers rather than price takers—they have some control over their price.
- Monopoly firms include natural monopolies, such as the public utilities. The short-run profit-maximizing output for a monopoly firm will be inefficiently small, while the price will be inefficiently high. However, the threat of potential

competition counters to some extent the tendency for monopoly to be inefficient. Monopolies are commonly either owned or regulated by government. Rate-of-return regulation focuses upon bringing down the monopoly price and increasing the monopoly quantity.

- Oligopoly is characterized by mutual interdependence. Since mutual interdependence can manifest itself in several ways, there are several models of oligopoly.

- Cartels are formed when firms band together to limit competition. Game theory can identify strategies for interdependent firms. Other oligopoly models include price leadership and contestable markets.

- Monopolistic competition is a model characterized by many firms producing an output that is slightly differentiated. Because good substitutes are available, the monopolistically competitive firm has slight control over its price.

- Imperfectly competitive firms may practice price discrimination. They may charge different customers different prices for the same product when there are no cost differences to justify the price differences. Price discrimination is motivated by the desire for greater profit. It requires that the firm be able to segment the market, such as into children and adult customers.

QUESTIONS AND PROBLEMS

1. List the four forms of market structure and their characteristics. If you owned a firm, in which market structure would you prefer to operate? Why?

2. You've decided you're going to live the simple life, which requires selling off your belongings. In which of the following instances, if any, would you be a price taker?
   a. For sale: 1984 Escort.
   b. For sale: 100 shares of General Motors common stock.
   c. For sale: Panasonic 19-inch color television.
   d. For sale: apartment full of furniture.

   Does it appear from this exercise that the classified for sale ads are populated with price takers?

3. Does the mere fact of monopoly guarantee that a firm will earn economic profits? Explain.

4. Product differentiation is found in oligopoly and monopolistic competition. What purpose does product differentiation serve from a firm's perspective? From society's perspective?

5. Why is the model of pure competition usually preferable to the model of monopolistic competition?

6. Write a short essay on cartels. Discuss why cartels are unlikely to be found in pure competition or monopolistic competition. Also discuss why firms might want to form a cartel, but have trouble keeping the cartel together.

7. List the three kinds of mergers. Make up an example of each.

8. Discuss the market conditions required for price discrimination to occur. Generally speaking, is price discrimination illegal? Provide at least one example of price discrimination not mentioned in the text.

Web Exercises

9. a. Using an Internet search engine such as that provided by Yahoo (located at **http://www.yahoo.com**) or Alta Vista (located at **http://www.altavista.com**), perform a separate search for the following terms: **oligopoly, cartel,** and **price discrimination.** Visit several of the Web sites that your search reveals for each term and observe the context in which each term is used. Explain whether the manner in which the terms are used is consistent with their use in the text.

   b. Repeat the above, but this time use a combination of terms that you select from the chapter. To eliminate Web sites that do not contain all terms, place a plus sign in front of each term you enter, such as +**"barriers to entry"** +**"limit pricing"**.

10. Visit the Web site maintained by the U.S. Department Commerce at **http://www.doc.gov/**. Seek out information about market structure in the United States by performing a search of that Web site. Summarize what you find by writing a series of 10–15 bullet points that describe key points of information.

> Visit the Web site for *Economics by Design* at
> http://www.prenhall.com/collinge for a Self Quiz over
> the topics in this chapter.

EXPLORING ISSUES

Exploration 7-1 The United States Postal Service—
A Monopoly in the Public Interest?

The United States Postal Service holds a special place in U.S. history, helping bind the nation together from the country's beginnings. Although this government monopoly's mission is to operate in the public interest, economic analysis is as applicable as in the case of private sector monopoly. This Exploration considers whether the delivery of first-class mail is a natural monopoly, and whether privatization and competition would better serve the public.

Neither snow, nor rain, nor heat, nor gloom of night stays these couriers from the swift completion of their appointed rounds.

—Inscription on Manhattan Post Office, adapted from "The Histories of Herodotus"

The U.S. Postal Service Web site can be found at **http://www. usps.gov/**

No Madison Avenue advertising agency could think up a better slogan for the Post Office than the motto adapted from the centuries-old writings of Herodotus. The mails must go through. That principle has inspired the Post Office since it was established on September 22, 1789. What is probably the oldest monopoly in America is rich in tradition. For instance, the first postmaster general was Benjamin Franklin, given the title by the Continental Congress in 1775, even before the creation of the Post Office itself.

For more than two centuries the Post Office has grown along with the country. The Postal Reorganization Act of 1970 established the U.S. Postal Service from what had formerly been the Department of the Post Office. The Postal Service is overseen by a Board of Governors appointed by the President and approved by the Senate. It is intended to pay for itself. By 1998 the Post Office generated about $60 billion in revenue, had approximately 800,000 career employees, and had delivered 190 billion pieces of mail in the prior year, about 40 percent of the world's mail. That is big business—so big that if it were in the private sector, it would be the 10th largest company in the country, according to *Fortune* magazine. Nonetheless, the following questions can be asked: Do we still need a monopoly Post Office? What could replace it? Is there a better way?

Barriers to Entry

Some countries, such as New Zealand and Sweden, have abolished their postal monopolies, with Germany scheduled to follow suit in 2002. Even though the trend is toward greater competition in postal services, entrusting delivery of the mail to a governmental postal monopoly is still the norm in countries around the globe.

The U.S. Postal Service is such a monopoly, guaranteed by the postal monopoly statutes and, according to some interpretations, even by the U.S. Constitution. Rivals are allowed to deliver packages and urgent correspondence, but must charge at least $3 per item or twice the Postal Service rate. Thus, the law is a barrier to entry that prohibits the rise of competition in postal services. The postal monopoly includes at least two elements of law that act as barriers: 1) control over household mailboxes, and 2) a monopoly on the delivery of first-class mail, which includes personal correspondence, post cards, and many business transactions. These restrictions explain why private companies do not deliver to household mailboxes, nor do they deliver your bills, or your letters from friends and family.

In spite of the legal foundations underpinning its monopoly status, private sector competition comes from companies such as FedEx and UPS. Because of this competition, to the extent allowed by the postal statutes, the Postal Service is not a monopoly in all of its markets. Even in the market for first-class mail, the Postal Service faces competition from relatively new technological alternatives, such as e-mail, the fax machine, electronic data exchange, automated bill payments, and automatic transfer of funds. For example, as states and the federal government continue to replace benefit checks with electronic transfers of funds, business for the Postal Service is diminished. Although the Postal Service is unable to accurately say how much the demand for its services has been reduced by new technologies, its $60 billion in revenues indicates that the technological alternatives are far from perfect substitutes for the Post Office's core product—delivery of the mail.

FedEx offers a Web site at **http://www. fedex.com**

Full postal services at the same price to all communities is mandated by law. This mandate facilitates the flow of information and ideas across geographical boundaries and helps support economic growth in rural areas. However, there is debate over whether using money from urban areas to subsidize rural areas in this way is worthwhile or even understood by the average urban postal customer. If companies like FedEx and UPS were allowed to deliver first-class mail, it is likely that they would vary their prices to cover cost differences created by differences in the cost of delivery.

Even if the postal monopoly laws did not provide barriers to entry, the presence of both implicit and explicit government subsidies to the United States Postal Service gives it a leg up on its competitors. Specifically, the Postal Service pays no federal income taxes, no state income taxes, and no property taxes. It can also violate certain government regulations with impunity. For example, delivery drivers know that on the busy urban streets with few parking places, traffic cops will walk right past double-parked Postal Service trucks to issue tickets to the similarly double-parked truck of the UPS or other private delivery service. The reason is that the Post Office is exempt from paying traffic fines.

In recent years, the Postal Service has experienced surprisingly healthy financial results. For example, it earned over a billion dollars a year in net income each year between 1994 and 1997. The lure of obtaining a share of a billion-dollar-per-year profit might entice many potential entrants. On the other hand, the investment required to duplicate the fleet of vehicles, post offices, and equipment, and the recruiting and training of a work force, would mitigate against new competition. All things considered, private companies have shown themselves willing to compete against the Postal Service where competition has been allowed.

Pondering Privatization

Privatization involves government turning over to private enterprise functions that previously were performed by government. The reason to do so is to take advantage of the efficiency of the marketplace in which companies succeed by providing what gives customers the most value for their money. Various examples show that providing services through the private sector rather than through government can pay off. Take weather forecasting, for example. The U.S. government's National Weather Service provides weather forecasts to farmers, seafarers, pilots, and others for whom accurate weather forecasts are a matter of life, death, and livelihood. But many businesses find it is worth the cost to subscribe to one of the many private forecasting services, such as Accuweather.

Dozens of government-provided goods and services have been turned over to the private sector in one place or another. Private sector provision of services such as garbage collection, towing of illegally parked cars, tree trimming along city streets, housekeeping and custodial services, forest management, police protection, education, social services, family planning, and many more provide ample evidence of the widespread acceptance of privatization. Yet there is often resistance to privatization. Partly this is because private firms aim to earn profits from providing public services. To some critics, profiting from providing public services seems wrong. To other critics, the question is why not let government provide the services and save having to pay the profits. This criticism of privatization ignores the possibility that profit is the payment to firms for figuring out how to do things better and cheaper so that customers and taxpayers can both gain.

Suppose that Congress repealed the postal statutes, eliminated subsidies and special treatment, and privatized postal services. If one buyer were to purchase all of the assets of the Postal Service, that buyer would then face potential competition from other companies that wish to enter the market for first-class mail. In that case, the Postal Service would compete against other companies in this market just as it competes now against UPS, FedEx, Airborne, and other private companies that offer urgent mail and package delivery services. Companies would compete on a relatively level playing field.

One of the first effects might be confusion, as a jumble of companies would vie against each other for customers. Companies would find themselves on overlapping routes, and realize that combining operations would be more efficient by eliminating that overlap. If the postal services are a natural monopoly, only the one most efficient company would survive. However, we see more than one survivor in the package delivery business, so perhaps two or even more companies might be able to profitably coexist. Which companies would they be?

Firms that pay their workers an excessive amount or hire on the basis of politics, cronyism, or anything other than productivity would lose out. Firms that offer poor quality delivery, high prices, and poor hours would also lose. The winners would be those firms that figure out what customers think is worth paying for. Competition would force firms to seek to understand and follow the wishes of postal customers.

Currently, postal authorities engage in **cross-subsidization** in which prices on some services are set high enough to offset losses on other services. For example, postal authorities provide *universal access*, in which mail service is offered at equal rates to everyone, despite some people being more expensive to serve than others. In this way, local urban delivery of first-class mail subsidizes cross-country delivery and most delivery of first-class mail to rural areas. A more competitive marketplace would price on the basis of cost and eliminate these examples of cross-subsidization. Specifically, competitors would lower prices of the more profitable services and raise prices of the others.

cross-subsidization: when prices on some goods or services are set high enough to offset losses on other goods or services; may be required by government, such as for postal services.

Innovation—Creating a Postal Service for the Next Century

The Postal Service can choose to innovate or to maintain the status quo. Actually, it chooses both. For example, in efforts to defend the status quo and to preserve its monopoly, the Postal Service aggressively goes after violators of the current postal statutes. Fines have been imposed on businesses that have illegally mailed documents with its competitors. In one recent year, the Postal Service collected $500,000 this way. For example, one company that was sending its regular billings by way of a private urgent mail service agreed to pay the Postal Service the price of one first-class stamp for each of the bills delivered in this manner and to use the Postal Service for all future billings. You see, the bills were not due immediately and thus did not fall under the category of urgent. It is illegal to use a private urgent mail service for non-urgent mail.

Competition spurs innovation. Even though it only faces indirect competition to its first-class mail services, the Postal Service has achieved impressive efficiencies. For example, 93 percent of local first-class mail was delivered the next day, according to a PricewaterhouseCoopers survey of delivers in late 1998. New products and services have also been successfully offered. For example, credit cards are now accepted at over 32,000 post offices and special issue stamps like the Elvis stamps have been quite successful.

Like some private-sector monopolists, the Postal Service advertises its new products and services. A major cost control program has been implemented that helped the Postal Service to earn the billion dollar a year profit referred to earlier. The Postal Service has even entered into side businesses, such as the sale of phone cards. Competing companies complain that the $84.7 million that the General Accounting Office (GAO) reports the Postal Service to have lost on nonpostal businesses between 1995 and 1997 makes it hard for some competitors in those lines of business to stay afloat.

The Politics of Postal Privatization

Postal workers are some of the nation's highest-paid, low-skilled workers. Privatization that increases the efficiency of delivery might involve layoffs, which would be opposed by the postal workers' union. Competition might lead to nonunion workers, which would also be opposed by the union. For these reasons and because of the public's high regard for mail carriers, Congress might find itself embroiled in controversy if it were to pass legislation to privatize postal services.

With unrestricted privatization, prices of each type of service would tend toward the marginal cost of that service. Prices would be efficient, but whether they would seem fair might depend upon the personal impact of the price changes. Politicians often worry about equity as well as efficiency, with equity commonly carrying the most weight in the political process. That process of choice is called democracy!

■ Prospecting for New Insights

1. Do you believe that universal access is a legitimate philosophy to underpin the Postal Service? Should the rural population pay the full cost of providing service to the hinterlands?

2. If the post office is privatized, how should the government go about picking a new owner? What conditions, if any, do you think should be placed upon ownership? Would you prefer to see a privately owned, regulated postal service? If so, why? If not, why not?

Exploration 7-2 Busting the Trusts of Yesterday, Today, and Tomorrow

The antitrust laws aim to rein in monopolies and prohibit unfair business practices. Although the Sherman Act dates to 1890, the application of this and the other antitrust laws is unsettled even after more than 100 years. This Exploration traces antitrust from its origins to controversies over its application in the information age. The insights of economist Joseph Schumpeter are highlighted.

> *" . . . the best of all monopoly profits is a quiet life."*
> —British economist Sir John Hicks

The futurists tell us that a new golden age of the consumer is just over the horizon. The microprocessor and other electronic miracles will revolutionize our lifestyles, or so they say. Free your imagination to contemplate the marvels that await us in the year 2025. You are shopping for a computer, one equipped with the new Millenium XII chip and the long-awaited new operating system from Microsoft. There is only one problem: the government has won an injunction from the courts that forbids computer makers from shipping their machines with the latest operating system installed. "Something about antitrust," the store clerk mumbles. You leave the store without your computer, disappointed that the government's on and off legal wrangling with Microsoft has dragged on since the 1990s.

No one can say for sure whether events similar to those just described will occur. However, Microsoft's antitrust-related legal skirmishes began when the software giant included its Internet browser with Windows 95. In 1998, more legal trouble awaited the software giant, as the federal government and 20 state governments filed a joint antitrust lawsuit against Microsoft. This case was also browser-related. Clearly, when a firm becomes the target of the Antitrust Division of the U.S. Justice Department, the targeted firm can be in for a long, bumpy ride through the legal system. Just ask IBM, which was targeted by the antitrust authorities for years, even as it was losing ground to competing firms. AT&T was in the same boat, before settling with the government by agreeing to divest itself of its affiliated Bell telephone companies. In an earlier era, it was Alcoa, the Aluminum Company of America, that spent decades defending itself against charges brought under the antitrust laws. In the Microsoft case, an appeal could be made by Microsoft, if it were found to be guilty. Appeals can drag on for years.

What are these laws that are the basis for legal action against dozens of well-known firms, including Microsoft, Intel, Coca-Cola, AT&T, and many more? The purpose of the antitrust laws is to protect consumers against unfairly high prices and other abuses that arise from market power. Unfortunately, in practice the issue of market power is seldom clear-cut. Thus, the enforcement of the antitrust laws varies

Two Web sites devoted to coverage of antitrust issues are **http://www.antitrust.org** and **http://www.stolaf.edu/people/becker/antitrust/antitrust.html.** The Antitrust Division of the Justice Department maintains a Web site at **http://usdoj.gov/atr/index.html.**

over time, from one presidential administration to the next, and with new developments in antitrust theory.

Trustbusting Yesterday

Toward the late nineteenth century, large businesses, called *trusts*, began to dominate and even monopolize various industries. By 1890, public outrage over various alleged abuses of the marketplace by the trusts led to calls for action. Congress responded by passing the Sherman Act by the overwhelming vote of 52 to 1 in the Senate and 242 to 0 in the House. This act is the foundation of antitrust policy and is enforced by the Justice Department. The focus of the act is on the conduct of a business, although specific illegal actions are not spelled out. In general, it prohibits contracts, combinations, and conspiracies in restraint of trade. It also forbids attempts to monopolize markets, but does not make monopoly itself illegal.

Because of the failure of Congress to write specific provisions into the Sherman Act, it initially proved ineffective at curbing the power of the trusts. Thus, additional legislation was drafted, aimed at spelling out particular anticompetitive behaviors and making them illegal. The *Federal Trade Commission Act* and the *Clayton Act* were signed into law in 1914, thus completing the job of laying the foundation for today's antitrust enforcement. The Clayton Act supplements the Sherman Act by listing specific illegal actions, such as acquiring stock in a competing firm when that action would lessen competition. The Federal Trade Commission (FTC) was created to oversee markets, with the goal of eliminating so-called unfair trade practices. Additional antitrust legislation includes the *Robinson-Patman Act* of 1936 and the *Celler-Kefauver Antimerger Act* of 1950. The purpose of these two laws is to augment the earlier laws by preventing firms from taking anticompetitive actions that would give them excessive market power.

Table 7-3 summarizes the key features of the statutes that provide the foundations of antitrust. Also be aware that both government and competing firms can file antitrust complaints. A violator of the antitrust laws can be forced to pay up to three times the damages it inflicts on other firms. It can also be fined, broken into competing parts, and its employees imprisoned. Sometimes accused firms will sign a consent decree, in which they agree to change their behavior without admitting guilt. The next section looks at some applications of the antitrust laws.

TABLE 7-3 Key Features of the Major Antitrust Laws

Legislation	Summary of Features
Sherman Act of 1890	Bans monopolization and price-fixing agreements. Provides for criminal and civil penalties.
Clayton Antitrust Act of 1914	Bans certain forms of price discrimination, tie-in sales and other actions, including mergers that reduce competition or encourage monopolization.
Federal Trade Commission Act of 1914	Created by the Federal Trade Commission, a government agency that investigates allegations of unfair trade practices.

Trustbusting Today

Periodically throughout its history, the United States has experienced waves of merger mania. The explanations for why firms merge are varied and include the desire to exploit economies of scale. But firms may also seek to acquire market power through merging with their competitors. In addition, merger activity tends to pick up when the stock market is doing well.

The United States and indeed the world, found itself in the middle of such a wave of mergers in the 1990s. Not only were there more mergers, but the mergers involved bigger companies spread across numerous industries. The number of merger filings with the antitrust agencies is illustrated in Figure 7-7.

Against this backdrop of frenzied merger activity, the difficult—critics would say impossible—task facing the FTC and the Antitrust Division is to identify which mergers will increase economic efficiency through economies of scale and thus benefit consumers. Mergers that are beneficial in the eyes of the antitrust authorities are allowed to take place. Other mergers increase *concentration* too much. Concentration refers to the decrease in the number of firms when mergers occur. **Increasing concentration can increase market power and thus lead to higher prices.** It can also give bigger firms an advantage in the marketplace over their smaller rivals.

Mergers that increase concentration beyond acceptable limits will face legal challenges. The government can oppose a particular merger and the parties to the merger can drop their plans if they wish. Alternatively, prospective merger partners can go

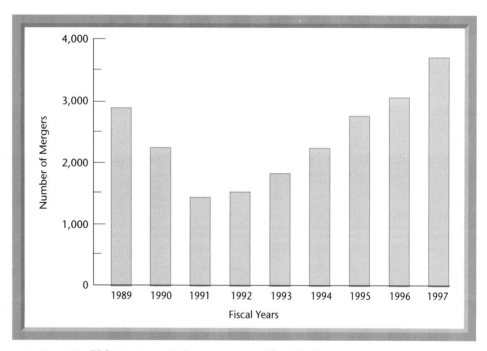

FIGURE 7-7 **U.S. merger activity** rose to record high levels in the 1990s.
Source: 1999 Economic Report of the President, p. 197.

to court for a determination of whether they would be violating the law. For example, when Staples and Office Depot proposed to merge, the Clinton trustbusters at the FTC opposed the merger. The merger was disallowed when statistical evidence was offered that showed higher prices for office supplies when only one office supply superstore was present in a market, as would have been the case in many markets had the merger been allowed.

Government challenges to mergers have been much more common during the 1990s than in the 1980s. This difference primarily reflects a difference in philosophy toward the marketplace. In the 1980s, the presidency was in the hands of Ronald Reagan, who espoused a relatively laissez-faire philosophy. In contrast, the administration of Bill Clinton that dominated the 1990s espoused more governmental oversight of markets. Economists see value in both approaches, fearing both heavy-handed regulators and market dominance that inhibits competition.

The traditional application of the Sherman Act against price-fixing conspiracies continues to be important. Greater concentration in the marketplace increases the likelihood of price fixing by making it easier for firms to communicate their illegal intentions to each other. When there are a few firms it is easier for firms to signal their aims to each other than when there are a few hundred firms. Computerization can also increase the likelihood of price fixing. One important case, settled by the Justice Department in 1994, involved *collusion* among eight major airlines to fix ticket prices. The fact that the airlines relied upon a central computer to issue tickets made it easier for them to conspire to increase ticket prices. Estimates of the cost to consumers of the airlines' collusion ranged up to several billion dollars a year.

Trustbusting Tomorrow

Although today's technologies change rapidly, technological change has been an ever-present component of life for centuries. As observed by Joseph Schumpeter in his book, *Capitalism, Socialism, and Democracy* (1942), new technology provides the impetus for economic growth and higher living standards. However, technological change also has antitrust implications that are sometimes hard to fathom exactly.

For example, the "perennial gale of creative destruction," as Schumpeter termed it, has supplanted the state-of-the-art personal calculating power of the slide rule with first the pocket calculator and then the laptop computer. This progression took a mere 20 years or so. Numerous firms ceased to exist because of an inability to adapt to this technological change. Slide rule makers had no expertise in the electronics required to manufacture calculators. The destruction of existing firms and industries occurred concurrently with the emergence of new industries and firms that possessed or acquired electronics expertise.

Schumpeter hypothesized that a prerequisite to innovation is the market power conferred upon firms by oligopolistic market structures. Pure monopoly and competition are not well suited to initiate innovation, in his view. He perceived monopoly firms as possessing the wherewithal, but not the motivation, to conduct research, because monopolists lack the competitive pressures felt by firms in oligopoly markets. The result is that monopolists can lead the "quiet life" as referred to by Sir John

Hicks in the quote that opens this Exploration. Schumpeter also thought that firms in pure competition and monopolistic competition lack the pool of economic profits required to finance research and development.

The implications of Schumpeter's insights of more than 50 years ago are still of significance in the antitrust area. Antitrust policy is about ensuring effective competition. The question then arises as to how antitrust policy should be applied to markets in which innovation reduces competition. On the one hand, innovation brings higher living standards. On the other, innovation may reduce competition, at least in the short run. Do the benefits of innovation outweigh the costs to society associated with the reduction of competition? The antitrust problem is to answer this question by weighing benefits and costs.

Difficulties in striking the proper balance are illustrated by antitrust concerns about Microsoft, referred to earlier in this Exploration. Microsoft's history shows that it adds innovative features to each new-generation operating system to further consolidate its powerful position in the marketplace. This practice potentially squeezes out makers of competing software. For example, prompted by worries expressed by on-line services such as CompuServe, the Justice Department pondered the potential anticompetitive effects prior to the August 1995 introduction of Windows 95, with its easy access to the Internet via Microsoft Network. They feared that Microsoft would eventually monopolize access to the Internet. Should Microsoft have been barred from providing an easy, albeit Microsoft-controlled, route to the Internet? Are consumers better off with the ease of access now or worse off over time should Microsoft succeed in extending its dominance over computer operating systems to dominance over Internet access as well? The problem in answering questions of this sort is that the immediate gains are clear, while we cannot know what cost diminished competition will bring in the future, whether it be in higher prices, diminished service, or merely forgone future innovations.

There are additional difficulties with the Schumpeter model. For example, the early development of the personal computer was inconsistent with the predictions of the model. Much of the original innovation in PCs came from small start-up firms, of which the most notable survivor is Apple. The personal computer also appears to have partially leveled the playing field between large firms and small ones. Small businesses today have access to information and other computer-related inputs that allow them better to compete with larger rivals. This change means that innovation may occur in more competitive markets, in addition to the oligopolies that Schumpeter had in mind.

At the other extreme, from cable TV to local telephone service, once stalwart monopolies find themselves challenged by newly arisen competition. Even Microsoft is beset by actual and potential competitors to its operating systems, including some that are very well financed. In contrast to the thoughts of Schumpeter, the threat of potential competition may motivate monopolies to innovate. The bottom line is that firms today must concern themselves with innovation, regardless of which type of market they operate in.

Antitrust in the Era of Global Business

Globalization of the economy has eroded the importance of national boundaries in assessing antitrust issues and forced governments to rethink beliefs about the significance of bigness of firms in the marketplace. Is it likely that the Schumpeter model still applies? New technologies quickly become available worldwide, aided by modern information technology. Oligopoly industries within a country are often no longer protected against foreign competition, as was once true. Increasingly, economists believe that U.S. antitrust policy should take a global, rather than national, perspective. That perspective means that foreign competition as well as domestic competition should be acknowledged when antitrust issues arise.

For example, the consideration of global market conditions has been a major factor in the FTC allowing so many large telecommunication mergers in recent years. Telecommunications is a global marketplace in which size matters. Allowing U.S. telecommunications companies the freedom to grow into some of the largest companies in the world is seen as merely a way to keep them competitive in the world marketplace.

In sum, an important job of the antitrust authorities is to allow that innovation to take place, while preserving competition. The choice of growth and greater future prosperity or lower prices and greater choice in the present is the fundamental trade-off facing the antitrust authorities.

■ Prospecting for New Insights

1. Schumpeter suggested that oligopoly promotes innovation more than do other market structures. Explain both his reasoning and alternative reasoning that might explain why much innovation comes from individuals and smaller businesses.

2. Provide economic arguments for both stronger and weaker enforcement of antitrust laws.

8

INCOME FROM LABOR AND HUMAN CAPITAL

A Look Ahead

LABOR MATTERS AFFECT people personally in their daily lives. Numerous stories spring to mind: Ralph, an unskilled worker, seizes the opportunity to enroll in skills training classes; Ethel, a factory worker, ponders joining a labor union in hopes of higher wages; Juanita, a middle manager, frets over the possibility of being laid off; Sam, who has been unemployed for two years, is so discouraged that he is ready to stop looking for work; Jane feels outrage at the wage gap between herself and male co-workers; and college students on the verge of graduation worry about finding their first real jobs in an overcrowded job market. These examples show that labor issues surely enter the everyday thoughts of millions of people. This chapter examines the labor market, with wages, employment, and earnings differentials between individuals and among groups as the primary focus.

The first Exploration in this chapter concerns the role that talent plays in determining income and then proceeds to look at inequality income. Exploration 8-2 looks at discrimination. In general, the market forces those who discriminate to pay a price for their behavior.

As you are **Surveying Economic Principles** you will arrive at an ability to

- ❏ state why the demand for labor is a derived demand;
- ❏ explain the link between the reservation wage and labor force participation;
- ❏ describe the roles of competitive and noncompetitive influences in labor markets;
- ❏ explain why earnings differ among workers and relate this explanation to the earnings gap experienced by women and minorities;
- ❏ identify the extent and significance of poverty in the U.S. economy.

While **Exploring Issues** you will be able to

- ❏ discuss recent trends in the U.S. distribution of income and their significance;
- ❏ distinguish when it is appropriate to place a dollar value on human life.

Terms Along the Way

- ✔ derived demand, 253
- ✔ civilian labor force, 254
- ✔ labor force participation rate, 254
- ✔ reservation wage, 254
- ✔ substitution effect, 254
- ✔ income effect, 254
- ✔ purely competitive labor market, 258
- ✔ marginal cost of labor, 258
- ✔ monopsony, 259
- ✔ monopoly, 259

- ✔ bilateral monopoly, 259
- ✔ compensating wage differentials, 261
- ✔ collective bargaining, 262
- ✔ signaling, 264
- ✔ poverty line, 265
- ✔ occupational segregation, 267
- ✔ comparable worth, 267
- ✔ economic rent, 274
- ✔ affirmative action, 280

SURVEYING ECONOMIC PRINCIPLES

Anyone who has ever had a job or tried to get one has been a part of the labor market. In 1998, of a U.S. civilian, noninstitutional population of 205.2 million people above the age of 16, approximately 131.5 million received income from employment. About 6.2 million labor-market participants were unemployed. The rest of the population did not participate in the labor market.

The labor market comprises firms and individuals. **Unlike the product market, in which firms are sellers and individuals are buyers, individuals sell their labor services to firms in the labor market.** The size of their incomes depends upon two variables: the quantity of labor they supply and the amount they are paid. The quantity of labor supplied is usually measured in hours. The price of labor is the *wage rate*—the amount an individual is paid per hour. When the wage rate is multiplied by hours worked, the result is *earnings*, the income from labor. For example, in 1998 average hourly earnings of private sector workers was $12.77, which when multiplied by average weekly hours of 34.6 resulted in average weekly earnings of $441.84.

Most hourly wage workers who work more than 40 hours a week receive pay for time-and-a-half for all hours over 40. Hours in excess of 40 are called *overtime* hours. Overtime wage rates are 50 percent greater than the *straight-time* rate that a worker receives for the first 40 hours worked. The Department of Labor enforces these rules, which arise from the *Fair Labor Standards Act*, enacted by Congress in 1938.

Workers who are paid a *salary* receive a fixed amount of income, no matter how many hours they work. Employers expect salaried employees to work a minimum number of hours per week, typically corresponding to the regular operating hours of the business. If such employees work additional hours, they are not paid for those hours. Labor Department rules govern what types of jobs pay salaries versus hourly wages.

An employer's *total labor costs* are the sum of wages and salaries plus fringe benefits. Some benefits are voluntarily offered by employers; others are required by government. Typical benefits received by workers include paid vacations, sick leave, employer contributions to Social Security, *workers' compensation* coverage, which provides workers who are injured on the job with a stipend while they recuperate from their injuries, paid time off for lunch, and health benefits. Benefits account for about 28 percent of labor costs for the typical U.S. employer.

The Web site for the U.S. Department of Labor can be visited at **http://www.dol.gov/**

Labor Demand

A market demand curve for labor shows the quantity of labor that all employers in a labor market will employ at various wage rates. The quantity of labor is usually measured in hours rather than number of workers, because employers may increase or decrease the number of hours their employees work rather than hire or fire workers.

Market labor demand curves are downward sloping, as illustrated in Figure 8-1. Higher wage rates decrease the quantity of labor demanded, whereas lower wage rates increase the quantity of labor demanded. Labor demand typically shifts to the

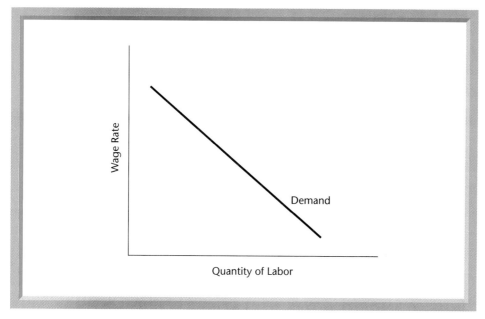

FIGURE 8-1 **Market demand for labor** shows the relationship between the wage rate and the quantity of labor employed. For simplicity, the wage rate is assumed to include fringe benefits.

left when business activity slows down, but shifts to the right when the economy improves. The demand for labor varies by the following:

- **occupation:** The demand for accountants is distinct from the demand for attorneys, which is distinct from the demand for welders, which is distinct . . . well, you get the idea. Occupational demands are distinct for dissimilar occupations because labor is associated with human capital that is specific to the occupation—*specific human capital.* That makes it difficult to transfer skills from one occupation to another.

- **geography:** For instance, the demand curve for labor in your hometown would differ from the demand curves in most other towns.

- **industry:** An industry demand curve for labor shows the quantity of labor employed by all firms in an industry at various wage rates. Various industries may compete for the same pool of workers. The concept of industry demand for labor is especially useful when the mix of occupations in an industry is taken into account. Growing industries create new employment opportunities for workers who are trained in the occupations useful to those industries.

Labor demand is a **derived demand,** which means the demand for labor exists only because there is a demand for the firm's output. If a furniture maker suddenly receives more orders because of an increase in new home construction, the firm will increase its demand for labor. It will either hire new workers or offer current employees the opportunity to work additional hours.

derived demand: the demand for labor; exists only because there is a demand for the firm's output.

OBSERVATION POINT:
Job Entrepreneurship—Finding What's Hot

The "hot" jobs of the future—jobs with openings and high pay—what are they and how do you get one? The U.S. Department of Labor publishes the *Occupational Outlook Handbook*, which projects future labor demand and supply for numerous occupations. Recent projections show that most hot jobs, such as in medicine or computers, require advanced education or training. Unfortunately, projections of labor demand and supply in specific fields can easily become as dated as yesterday's newspaper.

When "everybody" agrees on what will be hot, it may be best to bet on something else. By the time you acquire the needed skills, so have a host of other people. Labor supply shifts out, and lucrative job opportunities become relatively scarce. Instead, the secret to success may lie in being one of the first to identify hot job prospects of the future. There is risk in taking initiative. You might be wrong. If you follow that lonesome road, you may rightfully dub yourself a "job entrepreneur."

Labor Supply

civilian labor force: the population age 16 or over who are either employed or actively seeking employment.

Labor force participation concerns the decisions of individuals to offer their services in the labor market. To be counted as a member of the civilian labor force, a person must be 16 years of age or older and either have paid employment or be actively looking for it. Examples of nonparticipants include full-time students and retirees. The labor force participation rate is the number of labor force participants divided by the population age 16 and over. In 1998 the overall labor force participation rate was 67 percent in the United States. The rate for men was almost 75 percent, for women nearly 60 percent, for whites 67.3 percent, and for African-Americans 66 percent.

labor force participation rate: the ratio of the civilian labor force to the population age 16 and over.

reservation wage: the lowest wage at which an individual will offer labor services.

Individual preferences play a central role in explaining labor force participation. These preferences are evidenced in the individual's labor supply curve. Figure 8-2 illustrates a typical labor supply curve. Below the reservation wage, individuals "reserve" their labor—they choose not to work at all. Note that, unlike supply curves for other things, the individual's supply curve of labor services has a *backward-bending* portion. This shape can be understood by considering the substitution effect and the income effect of increasing wage rates.

substitution effect (of a wage increase): when wage rates rise, the opportunity cost of leisure rises, thus causing the quantity of labor supplied to rise, *ceteris paribus*; the actual change in the quantity of labor supplied will also depend on the substitution effect.

As wage rates rise, the substitution effect of the change in wage rates causes individuals to work more—they substitute away from leisure, because the opportunity cost of leisure becomes higher as wage rates rise. The result is that people offer more hours in response to higher wages, causing the supply curve to slope upward. In place of leisure, workers consume goods and services with their increased earnings.

income effect: when wages rise, real income also rises, thus causing workers to choose more leisure and offer less labor, *ceteris paribus*.

As wage rates rise, the income effect of the wage change tugs the worker in the opposite direction relative to the substitution effect. Higher wages bring higher incomes, which prompt workers to demand more of all normal goods. *Leisure*, time away from work, is a normal good. To buy more leisure, workers pay the opportunity cost of giving up the income from some work hours. The result is that, as wage rates rise, the income effect prompts workers to offer fewer hours of work.

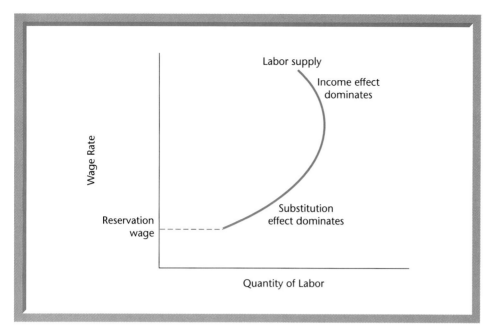

FIGURE 8-2 **The backward bending supply curve** of an individual's labor services is explained by the tug of war between the income and substitution effects of a wage change.

The supply curve bends backward when the income effect outweighs the substitution effect. This accounts for the huge decline in yearly hours of work for the average American worker during the twentieth century. The standard eight-hour work-day and annual paid vacations have permitted workers to partake of more leisure as real incomes have risen this century. Self-employed workers, such as physicians and accountants with private practices, can increase their vacation time to enjoy their substantial income. As seen in Figure 8-2, the substitution effect tends to be stronger at lower wage rates, and the income effect stronger at higher wage rates. The result is a supply curve that first slopes upward and then bends backward.

Individuals' labor supply curves will vary depending on whether they are *primary workers*, the main source of income in households, or *secondary workers*, whose incomes are not as critical to their households' well-being. The labor supply curves of primary workers are nearly vertical, meaning that they will choose to work about the same number of hours, no matter the wages they are able to receive. The quantity of labor supplied by a primary worker is typically in the range of 35 to 45 hours per week. In contrast, secondary workers have a much more pronounced upward slope and backward-bend to their supply curves. Secondary workers are more likely to hold part-time jobs than primary workers.

As an example of an individual's labor supply decisions, consider Elena, a full-time college student. Earning good grades is her highest priority. The $7 an hour paid by the Burger Barn is below her reservation wage. She could earn $7 an hour by occasionally modeling hair styles for Hair Trends, but even that amount is not enough to induce her to participate in the labor force.

If an employer were willing to pay Elena $10 an hour, she would go to work, but not for a penny less—$10 is her reservation wage. She figures that a few hours on the job each week would cause little harm to her grade point average. Elena would work even more hours if she was offered an even higher wage rate. If the wage she was offered soared to $50 an hour, the opportunity cost of her leisure time would be too great to ignore; every hour of leisure time would cost her $50 in lost earnings. She would then be willing to work 20 hours a week, which would still allow her to maintain passing grades.

Because of her commitment to her studies, Elena would not work more than 20 hours. That is the point where her personal labor supply curve bends back. For example, if she could earn a wage of $75 per hour, she would reduce her hours of work because at that wage the income effect outweighs the substitution effect for her.

Elena's reservation wage could change. If she found herself short of tuition funds, she might even be willing to work at the Burger Barn for $7 an hour, if that was the only choice she had. When she graduates with a bachelor's degree, her reservation wage is likely to go up because of her perception that the value of her labor services has been increased by her degree. If she doesn't receive a job offer in a reasonable period of time that meets that higher reservation wage, she might eventually lower her reservation wage. Reservation wages can change as individuals are unable to find work and as they learn more about the job market.

Labor supply curves may shift. Many persons receive *nonlabor income* from investments, pension funds, government transfer payments, interest on bank deposits, gifts from relatives, and so forth. The amount of nonlabor income received can affect labor market choices. Generally, a greater amount of nonlabor income will reduce the labor a worker supplies. When people have sufficient income from other sources, such as from Social Security, they often take early retirement, for example. If Elena did not receive income from home, it is likely that her labor supply curve would shift to the right and her reservation wage would decline.

The *market labor supply* sums the quantity of labor supplied at various wage rates for all the individuals in a labor market. Market supply curves of labor are upward sloping in the range of income that is usually relevant to employers.

An *industry labor supply* sums the quantity of labor supplied to a particular industry at various wage rates. Because higher wage rates in one industry attract workers from other industries, any particular industry supply curve of labor is nearly always upward sloping. It is also usually quite elastic, meaning that a small increase in the wage rate would attract a very large increase in the quantity of labor supplied. For example, as wages rise in the trucking industry, some truckers might work less because of the income effect. However, it is likely that the reduction in worktime by individual truckers will be more than offset by an inflow of would-be truckers from other occupations.

QuickCheck

Compare the outcome of an increase in labor demand if there is: a) an upward-sloping labor supply curve; b) a backward-bending labor supply curve; and c) a vertical labor supply curve.

Answer: When the labor supply curve slopes upward, an increase in labor demand will increase the quantity of labor supplied. If demand intersects the backward-bending portion of the labor supply curve, the quantity of labor supplied would decrease as demand increases. With a vertical supply curve, the quantity of labor supplied would not change. Drawing the appropriate graphs would show these outcomes.

Labor Markets

The exchange of labor services for wages occurs in *labor markets.* To some extent, each occupation, industry, and geographic area has its own labor market. Some labor markets are national in scope; others are local. For instance, the matching of professors to college and university employers typically occurs at national professional meetings. Professors and college administrators come from around the country to participate in job interviews at a central meeting place. Contacts made at these meetings lead to job placements. In contrast, colleges looking for clerical workers tap into their local labor markets for help. In the local area, colleges are likely to find clerks available for employment but few professors with specialized skills.

Labor market analysis may also highlight a geographic area. A particular area's labor market may be robust, providing its residents with good wages and job opportunities. At the same time, the labor market elsewhere could be characterized by low wages and high unemployment. This scenario was played out in the western United States during the early 1990s. California's economy was in recession because of layoffs in defense industries, while neighboring Nevada's unemployment rate was significantly lower because of rapid growth in tourism there.

Differences in labor demand and supply across geographic areas create differences in wages and unemployment rates. Such differences arise because many jobs are filled using labor from a limited geographic area. Common sense says that the unemployed who live in areas where jobs are scarce ought to move to areas where labor shortages exist. Although some workers migrate, labor *immobility* also exists. Workers find that family ties, home ownership, and a preference for their present location inhibits their movement to places where job openings exist. In the 1970s work was plentiful and wages were high along the Alaska pipeline, but relatively few workers were willing to endure the harsh Alaskan winters.

OBSERVATION POINT:
Build It and They Shall Come

The Web site for Branson, Missouri can be visited at **http://www.bransonmo.com/**

In the late 1980s, America began to hear of the small town of Branson, Missouri. For seemingly inexplicable reasons, Branson was developing into a mini-Las Vegas, Ozark-style. Stars of country and middle-of-the-road music had found their home away from home. Theaters, gas stations, convenience stores, and fast-food restaurants sprang up rapidly to service the hordes of tourists who came to see and hear their favorite stars. Even Elvis was rumored to be hiding out there.

Where was the supply of workers who would fill the new, mostly unskilled jobs? Branson was growing so fast that job growth far outstripped the local labor supply. No problem! National publicity about Branson prompted a migration of the unemployed to the Ozark community. The lure of a job and the chance to rub shoulders with the stars provided a powerful incentive to move to Branson, thus demonstrating that labor immobility can be overcome.

Competitive—No Market Power

Like markets for output, labor markets can take several forms. The type of market in which a firm sells its output does not determine the type of market in which it buys its labor inputs. For example, oligopoly firms may purchase labor services in a competitive market.

purely competitive labor market: a labor market in which there are numerous firms and workers, none of which can influence the market wage rate.

A **purely competitive labor market** exists when the demand for labor and the supply of labor establish an equilibrium wage rate and quantity of labor. Characteristics similar to those that apply to pure competition in the output market also apply to pure competition in the labor market, including the following:

- There are many buyers and sellers of labor services in the market.
- The services of labor are homogeneous.
- The market is free of barriers to entry and exit.

The third characteristic means that workers are free to change jobs or move to labor markets that pay higher wages, if they wish to do so. Employers are also free to enter or exit labor markets. In practical terms, employers can freely relocate.

In a purely competitive labor market, employers are *wage takers*, which means that each will be able to hire as much or as little labor as it wishes at the going market wage rate. Figure 8-3 shows the elements of a competitive labor market. The left panel shows the market demand and supply curves in a labor market. The intersection establishes the equilibrium wage rate and the equilibrium market quantity of labor hired. Since the labor market clears, there is neither a shortage nor surplus of labor. In common parlance, a surplus of labor is called *unemployment*.

marginal cost of labor: the additional cost of employing one more unit of labor.

The right panel in Figure 8-3 shows a single, wage-taking employer. In pure competition, the market wage rate equals the marginal cost of labor, the additional cost of employing one more unit of labor, which is also the supply of labor to the firm. Whatever the market structure in the labor market, one rule always holds: **Profit-maximizing firms hire to the point at which the marginal cost of labor equals the marginal value of labor to the firm.** In other words, a firm continues

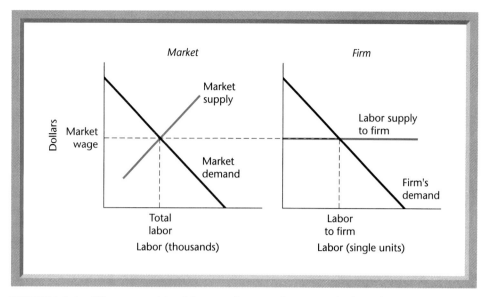

FIGURE 8-3 **The competitive labor market** sets the wage, which implies a horizontal supply of labor to the firm. The firm's demand for labor will determine the quantity of labor it hires at that wage.

adding labor as long as the revenue it receives from the output produced by one more unit of labor is at least sufficient to cover the added cost resulting from employing that unit of labor.

Market Power in the Labor Market—Wages Could Be Driven Up or Down

The model of pure competition assumes that both employers and employees are price takers, meaning that they have no market power. However, market power is often present in the labor market and can drive wage rates either up or down from the competitive level. To the extent that workers gain control of the labor market, the wage rate will increase to more than the competitive level. The wage rate will decrease to less than the competitive level to the extent that employers dominate. These effects are captured in the following labor market models:

- **monopsony**—only one employer of labor;
- **monopoly**—only one seller of labor, a labor union;
- **bilateral monopoly**—only one employer and only one seller of labor.

Fewness of employers creates *monopsony power* for firms. Such firms are able to pay workers less than the competitive wage. The extreme case of monopsony is *pure monopsony*—one buyer of labor's services. The best example of monopsony occurs in geographically isolated mill towns. The mill provides a reason for the town to exist because most of its citizens work there. As the major employer, the mill can offer less than the competitive wage rate to prospective workers. Highly specialized types of labor, such as astronauts or fighter pilots, may also face monopsony in their country's labor market.

Monopolies are said to possess market power because of their ability to raise prices above the level indicated by the intersection of supply and demand. *Labor unions*, discussed in the following section, are analogous to monopolies, in that unions eliminate competition for jobs among workers in order to raise the price of their members' labor. If they are successful in monopolizing the supply of labor's services, unions drive wages higher than would occur in competition.

The Web site for Major League Baseball is located at **http://www. majorleaguebase ball.com**

Under a bilateral monopoly, the wage depends on whether the employer or employee bargains more effectively. Professional sports organizations often approximate bilateral monopoly. In the summer of 1994, for example, major league baseball players went on strike to protect their lucrative wages and benefits. The players union commenced to negotiate with the owners association—one seller and one buyer for players' services. After much acrimony, the two sides resumed playing baseball the following spring. It was not clear which side came out ahead. Because the strike generated ill will among fans, which reduced interest in the sport, it may be that both sides lost.

QuickCheck _____

List the four models that apply to labor markets. In which model(s) are employers wage takers? In which model is it unclear as to whether wages rates will exceed or fall short of the competitive wage?

Answer: The four models are pure competition, monopsony, monopoly, and bilateral monopoly. Employers are wage takers only in the purely competitive model. In the model of bilateral monopoly it is not clear whether wages will be higher or lower than the competitive wage. The outcome depends upon the relative bargaining power of the employer and the union.

Earnings Differentials

Wage differentials among workers sometimes seem intuitive. We expect a heart surgeon to earn more than a janitor. Many wage differentials are not so easy to understand, however. Why should physicians earn more than teachers? Why should star athletes earn more than physicians? Individual earnings differ because of a combination of market and other factors.

Occupational Choice and Change

Modern economies provide numerous occupational choices for workers. The U.S. government catalogs over 750 basic occupations in the publication, *Occupational Employment Statistics*, and over 12,000 highly detailed occupations in the *Dictionary of Occupational Titles*. Occupational choice plays a significant role in earnings power. Generally, the highest-paying occupations are those that require the greatest skills, and the lowest paying are the unskilled occupations.

As economies grow more complex because of technological change, new job opportunities are created as old ones fade away. Just ask the thousands of (mostly) women who earned their living as keypunchers in the 1960s and 1970s how rapidly change can occur. In those days, data were entered into mainframe computers on paper cards that had been pierced with tiny holes by keypunchers sitting at keyboards. Punchcards and keypunch machines are hard to find outside museums today.

The skills required to keypunch were simple typing skills. No knowledge of computers was required. With retraining, many keypunchers were able to master the higher-level skills required by the new personal computers, which became common in the early 1980s. The keypunchers are a paradigm for today's labor market. Today, workers in most occupations are expected to possess more specialized skills and to keep their skills current.

QuickCheck

Can you think of additional occupations that have disappeared or seen their numbers decline because of technological change?

Answer: Elevator operators were supplanted by automatic elevators, switchboard operators by automated systems, longshoremen by mechanized containers, telegraphers by telephones, railway porters by airplanes, blacksmiths by automobiles, . . . the list is endless.

Compensating Wage Differentials

Different jobs have their own advantages and disadvantages. Most people would rather work at safe jobs in air-conditioned comfort rather than at dangerous jobs outside in the extremes of weather. Higher pay in the latter jobs will be necessary in order to equalize their attractiveness relative to the former jobs. Such increases in pay are termed **compensating wage differentials**.

Sanitation workers, coal miners, and others have unpleasant or dangerous jobs. To induce workers to take those jobs, employers must pay a compensating differential. Note that even with compensating differentials included, the pay in such jobs may still be relatively low, because skill requirements in many of these jobs are low.

People choose jobs on the basis of a spectrum of characteristics. Pay, the *pecuniary* attribute, is the most important characteristic for some. For others, job security, status, the likelihood of advancement, safe working conditions, the inherent interest of the work, or the flexibility of employers in matters of dress or hours is most important. Job features unrelated to pay are called the *nonpecuniary* attributes. Positive nonpecuniary features can offset low pay and vice versa.

> **compensating wage differentials:** higher pay that compensates for undesirable aspects of a job.

Unions

Workers join unions to improve their pay and work environments. At the peak of union membership in 1953, 36 percent of U.S. workers belonged to a union. In 1998 that figure stood at 16.2 million members out of the civilian labor force of 138 million, or about 12 percent of the labor force.

> To learn more about unions, visit the Web site of the AFL-CIO at **http://www.aflcio.org/home.htm**

TABLE 8-1	Percentage of Workers Belonging to a Union, by Major Industry, 1998
Agriculture	1.5
Private sector workers, excluding agriculture	9.5
Mining	12.2
Construction	17.8
Manufacturing	15.8
Transportation and public utilities	25.8
Wholesale and retail trade	5.3
Finance, insurance, and real estate	2.0
Services	5.6
Government	37.5

Source: Union Members in 1998, USDL 99-21, Table 3.

The decline in overall union membership masks the concentration of membership in several key industries that are heavily unionized. Indeed, government employee unionism reached record levels in the mid-1990s, with seven million government workers, equal to about 37.5 percent of such workers, belonging to unions. Table 8-1 shows the percentage of workers belonging to a union in major industries.

Possibly the most important factor behind the deterioration in organized labor's strength in the private sector is more global competition in a number of industries where unions have historically been strong. Fewer U.S. workers in these industries mean fewer union members. Examples include steel and autos. Also contributing to the decline in unionism has been the increasing relative importance of white-collar jobs, in which the appeal of unions is relatively weak. Nonetheless, a recent nationwide survey of workers showed one-third of those surveyed who were not union members would like to be.

The NLRB maintains a Web site at **http://www.fedgate.org/fg_nlrb.htm**

collective bargaining: negotiations between labor unions and employers aimed at improving the lot of workers.

In order to survive, unions are facing up to today's economic environment and reaching out for new members. Union organizing efforts culminate in a secret ballot representation election, under the supervision of the National Labor Relations Board (NLRB). When more than half of a firm's employees vote in favor of a union, the NLRB certifies the union as the bargaining agent for the workers. Unions engage in **collective bargaining,** negotiations with employers aimed at improving the lot of workers. Legally, employers must bargain with a union but are not obligated to reach an agreement. Consequently, it sometimes happens that firms resist unionization by refusing to sign a collective bargaining agreement.

When firms balk at union demands, which side will prevail? *Bargaining power* refers to the ability of a union to win an agreement with greater wages and benefits for its members. The primary weapon providing bargaining power to unions is the *strike*, or work stoppage. The ability to shut down an employer is a powerful weapon indeed, although strikers have the incentive to settle a strike because their employer will not pay them while they are on strike. Generally, a strike will be preceded by negotiations between the union and the employer. Thus a strike typically indicates the failure of negotiations. However, there are sometimes *wildcat strikes*, work stoppages that occur spontaneously because of workers' grievances against their employers.

Union bargaining power is reduced in the 21 states with *right-to-work laws*, which permit a unionized firm's workers the option of not joining the union. In these states, union and nonunion workers may work side by side on the job. Hence, workers in right-to-work states are less likely to present a united front when labor disputes arise, which decreases union bargaining power.

Another union weapon is the *boycott*, a campaign to persuade union members and the public to refrain from purchasing the output of a firm with which the union has a disagreement. Boycotts often go hand in hand with strikes.

When an employer faces a strike, its most powerful weapon is the right to hire permanent replacements for striking workers. However, firms will often not exercise that right for fear of violence toward their property or employees. For example, crossing a picket line can be a scary experience for so-called scabs, the disparaging term that union members apply to strike-breaking workers.

Unions have succeeded at winning higher wages for their members. Median usual weekly earnings for union members in 1998 were $659, compared to $499 for those not represented by unions. On the face of it, it seems that unions increase earnings by approximately 32 percent. However, the issue is more complex than a simple comparison of earnings.

Higher pay means fewer jobs in the union sector, which increases the supply of labor to the nonunion sector and drives down wages there. Furthermore, the kinds of jobs held by union members differ from the kinds held by other workers. Some of the higher pay in union jobs is likely to be compensating differentials, which would be paid even in the absence of unions. The consensus of research into this complicated issue, after taking account of all other factors affecting wages, is that **unions do raise wages for their members. However, estimates of the increase vary too widely to know its magnitude with certainty.**

Human Capital and Signaling

The amount of human capital that individuals possess is another important determinant of earnings differentials. Human capital is the knowledge, skills, and other productivity-enhancing attributes embodied within individual workers. Attending college is a prime example of how to increase one's human capital. Sources of human capital include formal schooling, on-the-job training, and skills training in the classroom.

It is costly to build a stock of human capital. There are out-of-pocket, explicit costs, as well as the opportunity costs of forgone earnings. For many college students, opportunity costs far exceed the explicit costs. Is a college degree worth the investment? College graduates are less likely to be unemployed than high school graduates, and earn higher incomes over their adult lives. The $851 median weekly 1998 salary for college graduates exceeds the median of $486 for high school graduates by about 75 percent. The statistics must be interpreted with caution, however, since those going to college may differ in other respects from those who do not.

Several studies indicate that the returns to the investment in a college diploma probably increased during the 1980s and into the 1990s, which helps explain why an increasing fraction of high school graduates attend college. The increase in relative earnings is due to many factors. One is the decline in the power of unions to raise wages above competitive levels for their mostly high school-educated membership. Other contributing factors include (1) the flow of relatively unskilled immigrants into the United States, many of whom compete for jobs against high school graduates; (2) the increased desire of employers to hire college graduates for jobs that have not historically required advanced education; and (3) the high-tech economy, which places a premium on education.

The **signaling** hypothesis provides an alternative to the human capital explanation for the greater earnings of college graduates. Education is seen as providing information to employers about attributes of job applicants. Employers believe that someone with good credentials will quickly be able to learn what is needed to perform a job and will possess the reliability and other qualities necessary to succeed.

This view holds that most college courses do little to increase a person's productivity. In effect, college does not train people for the job market, but instead screens out the winners from the losers. Many economists believe that there is truth in both the human capital and signaling views.

Discrimination, Luck, and Other Market Imperfections

Discrimination in the labor market is the unequal treatment of persons because of their race, gender, religion, or any other characteristic unrelated to the ability to perform the job. Discrimination can take several forms: 1) discrimination in hiring; 2) discrimination in promotions; and 3) wage discrimination. Regardless of the form, discrimination on the basis of race or gender is illegal in the United States, as discussed in Exploration 8-2.

Discrimination in hiring can lead to segregated workplaces. A discriminating employer would hire only the members of one group to do a particular job. Racial and gender stereotyping plays a role in motivating this type of discrimination. The owner of a factory producing clothing would be discriminating if the owner refused to employ males, based upon the belief that women are better sewing machine operators than men. If there is discrimination in hiring in the high-paying occupations, then group differences in earnings will arise.

Promotions into jobs with greater skill requirements and more responsibilities provide workers with the means to improve their earnings. Where the work force is unionized, promotions are often granted on the basis of *seniority*, which refers to a worker's term of employment. To the extent that minorities and women have been discriminated against in employment in the past, their chances for advancement in a seniority-based system of promotions will be impaired. Nonetheless, unless the employer's intent is to discriminate, the practice is generally not illegal.

Many employers are under *affirmative action* plans, which involve a commitment to increase minority and female hiring and promotions. Affirmative action is controversial, with its critics charging that it promotes reverse discrimination. Its advocates respond that the intent of affirmative action is to make up for past discrimination, and that affirmative action plans only level the playing field with white males.

Wage discrimination occurs when a worker who is as productive as other workers is paid less because of race, sex, color, religion, or national origin. This discrimination is illegal in the United States. It is difficult to ascertain what part of wage differences between workers occurs as a result of wage discrimination and what part occurs because of productivity differences.

Evidence accumulated by economists indicates that wage discrimination typically accounts for only a small part of wage differentials among racial and gender groups. An individual's age, ability, health, education, marital status, occupation, and number of years of experience affect his or her productivity and hence earnings. The major part of the lower earnings of minorities and women can be attributed to differences in these attributes, rather than to wage discrimination.

Wage differentials exist even among individuals who are identical in all measurable attributes that may affect earnings, including race and gender. For instance, race and gender discrimination cannot explain the substantial wage differences that exist among 40-year-old, college-educated, married white males who work as managers. Instead, we must acknowledge the effect of difficult-to-measure factors on earnings. Being in the right place at the right time and other forms of luck play a role in wage differences.

Other possible factors creating wage differences include disparities in looks, height, social skills, ambition, selection of marriage partner, and other tangible and intangible attributes. For example, experiments have shown that good-looking people have an advantage in the labor market. When two people with identical credentials have been sent to the same job interview, the good-looking applicant is usually offered the job while the average-looking one is not.

Market imperfections—deviations from the purely competitive labor market model—may also cause wage differentials. Unions and monopsony employers are examples previously mentioned. Additional imperfections include imperfect information, labor market immobility, cronyism, and occupational licensing laws that have the effect of limiting the number of people who pursue a line of work.

Poverty

Low wages or lack of a job can create poverty. Poverty is associated with deprivation, which motivates government transfer programs to aid the poor. Some of these transfers are "cash," such as the well-known welfare check. About two-thirds of government transfers to the poor provide *in-kind benefits*, meaning that valuable services are provided instead of money. In-kind benefits include health care, food stamps, subsidized housing, and subsidized school lunches. These programs seek to preserve a minimum standard of living for the poor and are commonly referred to as the *social safety net*.

Most households in poverty are very close to the **poverty line,** defined by the Social Security Administration as an income that is three times the amount of a nutritionally adequate diet. This income varies by household size and composition. Interpreting "nutritionally adequate" is controversial. A vegetarian diet that emphasizes grains and beans can be nutritionally adequate, for example, and cost far less than one-third of the stated poverty line. Small changes in the definition of this line would result in large changes in the percentage of people classified as poor.

From 1960 to 1973 the number of persons falling below the poverty line decreased from 22 percent to 11 percent of the population, then stayed within the range of 11 to 15 percent over the following 2 decades. Poverty rates for children have been even higher—20.5 percent in 1996. About 44 percent of female-headed families with children fell below the poverty line in 1996. Conversely, with the safety net provided by Social Security, poverty among the elderly has fallen to 11 percent of the elderly population. Overall poverty rates have stayed in a stable range over the last 2 decades, even as spending on poverty programs has increased. One encouraging sign comes from a Census Bureau report that poverty rates have recently declined. Poverty rates fell from 15.1 percent in 1993 to 13.3 percent in 1997.

poverty line: defined by the Social Security Administration as an income that is three times the cost of what it considers to be a nutritionally adequate diet.

To learn more about Social Security programs, visit the Web site at **http://www. ssa.gov/**

To visit the Census Bureau's Web site, go to **http://www. census.gov/**

It would be unreasonable to expect extra spending on in-kind aid for the poor to reduce poverty statistics. The reason is that the official measure of poverty excludes the value of in-kind benefits. As the poor receive more subsidized health care, housing, and other in-kind benefits, it is not surprising that their earnings fail to rise. Higher earnings would cause a loss of eligibility for these valuable programs. If the value of in-kind transfers is included in poverty measures, the percentage of poor Americans drops to approximately 9 percent of the population.

OBSERVATION POINT:
"Cut my Salary. Please!"

Incentives are changed by the existence of government transfer programs. It is not always easy to predict how people will respond to such incentives. Case in point: A few years ago, a professor asked his university's administrators to lower his annual salary by a few hundred dollars. His request was not frivolous. Its purpose was to make his children eligible for subsidized school lunches. The savings from subsidized lunches would have more than made up for his salary reduction. Moral: Those whose earnings are low may have an incentive to reduce their work effort in order to further lower their incomes and qualify for government assistance.

Earnings of Women and Minorities—The Wage Gap Remains

Concern over discrimination in the labor market highlights the significance of earnings differentials between males and females and between whites and minorities. Even though a substantial fraction of earnings differences are explained by factors other than labor market discrimination, these differences have important social implications. The primary focus in this section is on women, although many of the same issues arise concerning the earnings of minorities.

The average full-time female worker in the United States earns about 74 cents for every dollar earned by the average male. This figure is up from 59 cents in 1978. The closing of the earnings gap is explained by women workers developing specialized job skills, thereby allowing women to move into professional and managerial jobs.

Although less so now than in earlier decades, women's earnings are negatively affected by *discontinuous labor force participation*, which occurs when a person leaves and later reenters the labor force. Many women leave their jobs after childbirth and do not return to work for several years in order to care for their children. This in-and-out pattern of labor force participation causes women's human capital to depreciate and reduces their years of labor-market experience relative to men. The result is lower earnings. As increasing numbers of women have stayed in the labor force throughout their lives, their earnings as a group have risen relative to those of men and are expected to rise even more in the future.

Explanations for the remaining earnings gap focus on women's occupational choices. Many occupations are dominated by females. Table 8-2 compares the percentage of males in a select group of traditionally male occupations with the percentage of females in another group containing several traditionally female occupations.

Male-Dominated Occupations (percentage of workers who are males)	Female-Dominated Occupations (percentage of workers who are females)
Engineers (90.4)	Librarians (80.5)
Dentists (82.7)	Registered nurses (93.5)
Clergy (86.4)	Elementary school teachers (83.9)
Firefighters (96.6)	Dental hygienists (98.2)
Mechanics (96.1)	Secretaries (98.6)
Construction workers (97.6)	Telephone operators (83.5)
Truck drivers (94.3)	Child care workers (96.8)

Source: 1998 Statistical Abstract of the U.S., Table No. 672.

Many of these female-dominated occupations pay less than the male-dominated ones that involve comparable education and responsibility.

Occupational segregation, the concentration of women workers in certain jobs, such as nursing and teaching, is commonly cited as evidence that women are discriminated against in hiring. The reasoning is that women are forced into these jobs because other jobs are not open to them. However, many economists deem this view simplistic. Interruptions in women's careers because of childbearing, child rearing, and the need to change jobs because of a husband's job transfer may motivate women to select occupations in which interruptions in labor force participation will be least harmful to their careers. The skills required in these traditionally female occupations are easily transferred from one employer to another and become obsolete only very slowly.

There are other possible explanations for occupational segregation. Gender-based differences in interests may be one factor. In addition, there might be discrimination against women by the educational system, such as school guidance that channels women away from subjects that lead to employment in traditionally male jobs. Employer discrimination in hiring women for some jobs is another explanation. It must be remembered that pay varies from one occupation to another. Unless women work in the various occupations in equal proportions as men and for as long as men, a wage differential will continue to be observed.

One controversial suggestion, which its advocates claim would raise women's earnings to the same level as men's, is called comparable worth. Comparable worth would replace market-determined wages with government-set wages designed to ensure pay equity across different jobs. Several states have passed comparable worth laws, but limit their applicability, such as to government jobs. Its champions propose a federal comparable worth law that would apply to all employers in the United States.

If wages were determined by comparable worth, government would have to decide which occupations involve equal responsibilities and are therefore deserving of equal pay. Government would set higher wages in those female-dominated occupations determined to be equivalent to male-dominated occupations and make it illegal for employers to pay less. Economists' analyses show that the effect would be similar to minimum wage laws—comparable worth would reduce the number of jobs

occupational segregation: the concentration of women workers in certain jobs, such as nursing and teaching.

comparable worth: the idea that government should set wages to ensure pay equity across different jobs, with comparable pay for jobs requiring comparable training effort and responsibility.

Chapter Eight   Income from Labor and Human Capital   **267**

TABLE 8-3 Earnings of Year-Round, Full-Time Workers by Race and Gender, Selected Years, 1979–1997 (percentages are of white male earnings for the same year)

Year	White Males	Black Males	White Females	Black Females
1979	$39,006	$28,111 (72.1)	$23,040 (59.1)	$21,112 (54.1)
1982	37,325	26,509 (71.0)	23,247 (62.3)	20,778 (55.7)
1985	38,325	26,806 (69.9)	24,585 (64.1)	21,763 (56.8)
1988	38,344	28,106 (73.3)	25,538 (66.6)	22,884 (59.7)
1991	36,475	26,665 (73.1)	25,401 (69.6)	22,548 (61.8)
1994	35,132	26,431 (75.2)	25,877 (73.7)	22,340 (63.6)
1997	36,118	26,897 (74.5)	26,470 (73.3)	22,764 (63.0)

Source: 1999 Economic Report of the President, Table B-33. Data are adjusted for inflation and expressed in 1997 dollars.

in female-dominated occupations. Critics of comparable worth also worry that wages would be set in an unfair manner. After all, for comparable wages, would you prefer to introduce yourself as a janitor or secretary? These two occupations are often deemed comparable because subtle points of job status cannot easily be measured.

Table 8-3 compares the earnings of men and women. The earnings data are provided by race; the figures include only full-time, year-round workers. Time series data are provided in order to show the progress that women and blacks have made in closing the wage gap with white males.

The data show a significant earnings gap between black and white males, with the average black male earning just about 75 percent of the amount earned by the average white male in 1997. While narrowing over time, this gap continues to be a source of concern. In contrast, black women earned 86 percent of the earnings of white women in 1997. African-American women show a greater attachment to the labor force than do white women, which increases the earnings of black women relative to white women. On average, black women stay in the job market longer than white women because the proportion of households headed by women is greater among black households than among white.

OBSERVATION POINT:
Homespun—Promoting Family Values?

Is working at home right for you? You can earn an income, be your own boss, eliminate commuting and daycare expenses, and spend time with your children. There is one problem, however: legal barriers. The Fair Labor Standards Act of 1938 outlaws commercial *piecework* sale of women's garments sewn at home. Who would know if child labor laws were violated? What if your hourly earnings fell below the minimum wage? Society has an interest in preventing the abuse of labor, but it also has an interest in promoting family cohesiveness. Sometimes laws promote some values over others.

International Aspects of Labor Markets

Labor issues vary from one country to the next, as the demographic characteristics of the population, customs, culture, and other factors in each country create diversity in labor markets. The International Labour Organization (ILO) devotes considerable resources to monitoring labor issues around the world. At least a few global themes can be identified.

To visit the ILO in cyberspace, go to **http://www. ilo.org/**

First, and perhaps most important, is a worldwide concern with combating child labor. According to the ILO, there are 250 million children who work in dangerous jobs, many of them in the less-developed countries. Robbing children of opportunities to acquire human capital through education, child labor is both a cause and a consequence of poverty. The ILO seeks to have countries pass stronger legislation against child labor.

A second theme is the global challenge facing labor unions. Table 8-4 details the percentage of workers in selected countries who belong to a union. The table illustrates the wide variation in the role of labor unions across countries. An ILO study shows that of 92 countries surveyed, in only 20 did labor union membership increase during the decade from 1985 to 1995. In 48 of the countries surveyed, union membership included less than 20 percent of the workers. Although the benefits and costs of unions are controversial, their defenders see strong labor unions as a force for social justice in less-developed nations.

A third theme, especially in the developed countries where women have traditionally possessed greater rights than in some less-developed countries, is a concern with bringing women's earnings and working conditions up to parity with those of men. The wage gap based upon gender is a worldwide phenomena, not confined just to the United States. For example, women workers in the United Kingdom earn 64 percent of what men earn; in France and Spain the figure is 73 percent; in Sweden, 84 percent. Just as in the United States, there are many reasons why women earn less. In regard to working conditions, maternity leave policies are a focus of ILO efforts to improve the lot of women workers. Currently, only the United States, Australia, and New Zealand, among the industrialized nations, fail to provide for paid maternity leave.

TABLE 8-4 Union Membership in Selected Countries, 1995 (percent of workers)	
Country	**Percent**
Brazil	43.5
Canada	37.4
Mexico*	42.8
Japan	24.0
Denmark	80.1
France	9.1
Germany	28.9
U.K.	32.9

*Mexico, 1991
Source: ILO Press Release, (ILO/97/28)

A final common concern among the countries of the world is fighting unemployment. For example, February 1997 unemployment rates were 3.3 percent in Japan, 5.3 percent in the United States, 7.1 percent in the United Kingdom, 9.7 percent in Canada, 12.5 percent in France, and 21.7 percent in Spain. The exact numbers are not as important as the striking differences in unemployment rates among countries, even the major industrial nations. There is even greater variation in unemployment rates when the less-developed countries are included. Even as some countries succeed in generating sufficient jobs to keep their unemployment rates low, others struggle with excessive unemployment. Individual countries' unemployment rates vary for different reasons, as do policies to combat unemployment.

As diverse efforts to deal with various labor issues are undertaken in different countries, it is well to remember that there are always tradeoffs to be considered. For example, paid maternity leaves increase labor costs and thus have the potential to make a country less competitive in the world marketplace. Balanced against this cost are the benefits to families. Similarly, labor unions can raise wages, but only at the cost of lost jobs. It is up to each country to decide which tradeoffs are desirable.

SUMMARY

- Wages and salaries are augmented by fringe benefits to arrive at total labor costs.
- The fundamental determinant of the wage rate is demand and supply in the labor market. Labor demand varies by occupation, geography, and industry, and is derived from the demand for firms' outputs.
- When the wage rate is less than the individual's reservation wage, a person will choose not to work.
- The backward-bending individual labor supply curve shows that once the wage rate reaches a high enough level, workers may begin cutting back their quantity of labor.
- A personal labor supply curve bends back when the income effect is stronger than the substitution effect.
- Market labor supply curves are upward sloping.
- Models of the labor market include pure competition, monopsony, monopoly, and bilateral monopoly.
- Wages will be lower in a monopsony labor market than in a purely competitive one, but higher in a labor market monopolized by a single union seller of labor services. Wage outcomes cannot be predicted in the case of bilateral monopoly because it depends upon whether the employer or employee is the better negotiator.
- Important factors determining earnings are an individual's choice of occupation, compensating wage differentials, unions, and differences in the amount of human capital.
- Market imperfections include any factors that cause the labor market to deviate from competition. Examples are monopsony, monopoly, unions, and discrimination. Market imperfections contribute to wage differentials.

- The poverty problem is one example of problems created by wage differentials. The wage gap between men and women and between whites and blacks is another. One reason for lower earnings for women is occupational segregation.
- Child labor, the decline in trade union influence, the pay gap between men and women, and unemployment are a few of the international labor issues.

QUESTIONS AND PROBLEMS

1. Why do some employers offer fringe benefits that exceed those required by government mandates? Why do other employers choose not to offer such fringe benefits? Evaluate and state the advantage to an employer who offers the following fringe benefits:

    a. free day care;
    b. flextime—within limits, employees pick their own starting and quitting times;
    c. employee lunchroom with lunches provided to employees at cost;
    d. 2 weeks paid vacation.

2. What is your reservation wage today? What will it be when you graduate from college? What could cause your reservation wage to change?

3. How much monopsony power do you think each of the following employers has? Explain any qualifiers to your answers.

    a. a fast food restaurant in a major city;
    b. the only newspaper in a major city;
    c. one of three television stations in a medium-sized city.

4. Many community colleges pay professors solely on the basis of their educational attainments and their years of experience, which means every professor with the same amount of schooling and experience is paid the same salary. Four-year colleges and universities, on the other hand, usually have merit pay plans, so that professors with identical qualifications may be paid widely disparate amounts.

    a. Why would community colleges reject the merit pay concept, but not 4-year colleges?
    b. "Basing pay raises on seniority rewards mediocrity." Evaluate.
    c. "Merit pay plans allow bosses to reward their favorites and punish those they dislike." Evaluate.

5. Since 1950, the overall labor force participation rate for men has declined slightly while that for women has risen dramatically. What could account for these facts?

6. Discuss the notion of compensating differentials for the following occupations:

    a. nurses;
    b. forest rangers;
    c. movie and TV actors;
    d. the occupation that you would like to pursue.

7. Discuss the income and substitution effects within the context of the backward-bending labor supply curve. Must a person's labor supply curve bend backward? Explain.

8. What factors other than discrimination might explain why women earn less than men? If there were no discrimination against women, would women earn the same as men? Why or why not?

Web Exercises

9. a. Using an Internet search engine such as that provided by Yahoo (located at **http://www.yahoo.com**) or Alta Vista (located at **http://www.altavista.com**), perform a separate search for the following terms: **labor force participation rate, collective bargaining,** and **poverty line**. Visit several of the Web sites that your search reveals for each term and observe the context in which each term is used. Explain whether the manner in which the terms are used is consistent with their use in the text.

b. Repeat the above, but this time use a combination of terms that you select from the chapter. To eliminate Web sites that do not contain all terms, place a plus sign in front of each term you enter, such as +**"civilian labor force"** +**"collective bargaining"**.

10. Visit the Web site maintained by the U.S. Department of Labor at **http://www.dol.gov/**. Explore the government's role in regulating the labor market, such as the enforcement of the minimum wage laws, efforts to eradicate discrimination, and so forth. Summarize what you find by writing a short paper entitled: "Government Regulation of Labor: Purposes and Functions."

Visit the Web site for *Economics by Design* at http://www.prenhall.com/collinge for a Self Quiz over the topics in this chapter.

Exploration 8-1 Income Distribution—A Big Squeeze in the Middle?

This Exploration examines the distribution of income between the rich, the poor, and the middle class. Explanations and possible solutions for income distribution problems are proposed.

What happened to economic security? It seems that most families had to work longer, harder, and smarter in the 1970s and 1980s just to keep from falling behind. Wives joined husbands in the workplace, but even with two incomes combined, median family income (half above and half below) stagnated and barely kept up with inflation. Even the booming economy that characterized the 1992 to 1998 period had only a minor effect. Inflation-adjusted median family incomes, which had been $44,284 in 1989, fluctuated up and down in the 1990s, but consistently stayed below the 1989 figure until 1997. The behavior of median family income over time is documented in Figure 8-4.

Two aspects of the problem of diminishing economic security must be disentangled. One is the slowdown in real income growth over much of the past two decades, which was experienced in the form of stagnant family income. The other is the increase in inequality in the distribution of income. The output of the economy is analogous to a pie. We first want to ensure that the pie keeps getting bigger, especially relative to population growth, and then we worry about the size of our slice of the

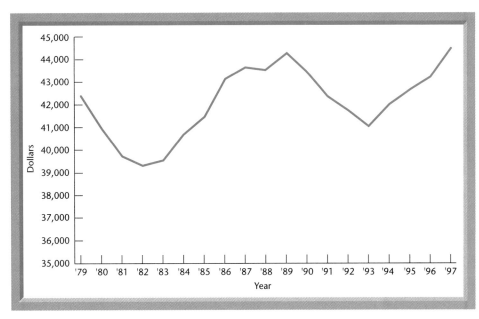

FIGURE 8-4 Inflation-adjusted median money income of families, 1979–1997.

Source: 1999 Economic Report of the President, Table B–33.

pie relative to our neighbor's slice. While the pie grew, the pieces going to those at the top got larger, leaving less for everyone else. These developments put a financial squeeze on the middle class.

The Payoff to Unique Talents

economic rent: earnings in excess of opportunity costs.

Economists have a term, **economic rent,** to describe earnings in excess of opportunity costs. Economic rent is responsible for the incredible earnings reaped by many celebrities. People whose talents and abilities are exceptionally scarce are sometimes able to earn much more than their next best alternative. For example, the talents possessed by every superstar athlete or entertainer are rare and in fixed supply. The combination of fixed supply and high demand for the talents of superstars results in sky-high earnings. Yet their opportunity cost, their best earnings opportunity outside their current employment, is usually not nearly so spectacular.

Wage determination and economic rent for a superstar with unique talents are illustrated in Figure 8-5. The fixed supply of superstar-quality talents results in a vertical supply curve of labor with that talent. A higher wage will not induce a greater quantity supplied, as would be the case if the supply curve were upward sloping, but not vertical. The position of the demand curve for the superstar's talents determines earnings. When demand is large relative to supply, high earnings are the outcome. The portion of earnings representing economic rent is indicated by the blue shaded area in the figure.

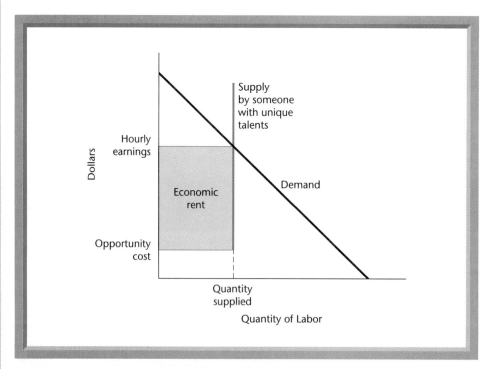

FIGURE 8-5 **Economic rent is determined by demand.** When demand is large relative to the fixed supply, earnings can be far above opportunity costs.

This model applies to a spectrum of workers. Success in many fields requires exceptional skills. The most successful heart surgeons, stockbrokers, economists, attorneys, and business executives, among others, earn economic rents. Some of these people become superstars in their fields. Examples include Bill Gates of Microsoft fame, Nobel-winning economist Paul Samuelson, attorney and Court TV commentator Johnny Cochran, and evangelist Billy Graham.

Not everyone, even those with unique talents, is able to earn significant economic rents. Your favorite club band may possess enormous talent, which is in fixed supply just like Madonna's. Nonetheless, without sufficiently large public demand for that talent, the band members are doomed to work for cover charges until the band's inevitable breakup. Similarly, many minor league athletes are close to major league quality in their talents, but the public is willing to pay high ticket prices only for major leaguers. Hence, a minor leaguer with 95 percent of the talent of a major leaguer may earn only 1 percent or less of the earnings of the major leaguer.

Clearly, the option of becoming a superstar is not open to most people seeking to boost their incomes. The theory of economic rent does, however, explain why some people end up in the group of highest paid workers, at the top of the income distribution. As predicted in 1981 by economist Sherwin Rosen, we increasingly live in a superstar economy, with a reward system of winner take all ever more common.

Slimming Down in the Middle

Downsizing by U.S. companies in response to global competition has been a widespread phenomena of the last 2 decades or so. Hundreds of thousands of American workers who in the past would never have worried about finding themselves unemployed learned the hard way that few jobs are safe. Many of those losing jobs worked in high paying managerial positions that allowed families to live solidly middle-class lives. Others kept their jobs but saw their wages stagnate. Some concepts related to the distribution of income can help clarify the economic effects of this situation.

An *income distribution* reports the proportion of income each segment of the population receives. Since our biggest concern with the distribution of income is inequality, income distribution usually focuses on the fraction of total income received by different *quintiles*, where a quintile contains 20 percent of the population. If everyone's income were equal, each quintile of the population would receive 20 percent of total income. Where inequality exists, the quintiles show variation in the fraction of income received. A simple example will help. Consider a population of five persons, for which the total income received by the whole population is $100. In this example, each person represents a quintile, one-fifth of the population. If each person earned $20, each quintile would show a 20 percent share of income received. There would be perfect equality.

Suppose instead that there is inequality in the incomes received among our population of five. Beginning at the bottom of the distribution and moving up, the first person earns $5, the second $10, the third $15, the fourth $20, and the top earner $50. The total is still $100, but now there is inequality. The lowest quintile receives 5 percent of income, the next quintile 10 percent, and so forth up to the highest quintile, which receives 50 percent of income.

TABLE 8-5 Shares of Income Received by Families in the U.S. (in percent)

Year	Total	Lowest Quintile	Second Quintile	Middle Quintile	Fourth Quintile	Highest Quintile	Top 5 Percent
1977	100	5.2	11.6	17.5	24.2	41.5	15.7
1987	100	4.6	10.7	16.8	24.0	43.8	17.2
1994	100	4.2	10.0	15.7	23.3	46.9	20.1

Source: U.S. Census Bureau, P60-191, Table 1.

In Table 8-5, data on the income distribution for the United States in 1977 is contrasted with similar data for 1987 and 1994. The lowest quintile of the population has seen its share of income fall from 5.2 percent of the total to 4.2 percent. At the same time, those Americans in the top 5 percent of the income distribution have seen their share increase from 15.7 percent to 20.1 percent. Middle America, those in the three middle quintiles, garnered 49.0 percent of the income in 1994 down from 53.3 percent in 1977. Many Americans remain uneasy over the rich getting richer and the poor poorer, as illustrated by changes in the income distribution.

How Equal Should Equal Be?

Is the income distribution in Table 8-5 good or bad? That is unclear. Two important points are not apparent from the data. The first is that in spite of growing inequality, the distribution nonetheless exhibits significant stability. The changes are slight in absolute terms. The second is that there is substantial movement within the distribution. Some people move up and others move down with the passage of time. For example, many younger workers who were at the bottom of the distribution in 1977 had moved up by 1994 after acquiring education and job experience. Meanwhile, many older workers who were at the top in 1977 had moved down because they retired. This dynamic movement in the distribution means that most people are not permanently stuck at the bottom. A final point can also help put inequality in perspective. The average estimated 1996 after-tax income of families in the top 1 percent equaled $438,000; that of families in the bottom quintile was just $8,230. Without upward mobility, such a stark contrast would be hard to justify.

Income distribution is the outcome of a complex process involving numerous forces and depends heavily on what is counted as income. For example, there would be much less inequality apparent if in-kind government assistance to the poor were included in income. Nevertheless, it is reasonable to be concerned about the income distribution. If those who live in poverty come to believe that aspiring to the middle class is an impossible dream, then the frustration created could alienate potentially productive workers, thereby reducing their motivation to obtain schooling and work hard.

The income distribution can be made more equal. Indeed, changes in federal tax policy are capable of reducing the share of the well-to-do. Such policy changes must be tempered, however, by recognition that incentives to acquire human capital and be productive may be reduced by higher taxes. The problem is how to keep the pie growing while ensuring that everyone receives a fair slice.

Equity-A Worldwide Concern

The United States is not alone in being concerned with matters of income distribution. Many countries collect data relating to how rich are the rich and how poor are the poor. Tax policies are often designed to take income from the rich in order to provide benefits to the poor.

In the 13 member countries of the European Union, the poorest 10 percent of the population receives only 2.6 percent of total income, while the richest 10 percent receives 24.0 percent of income. Around this average, there is a significant amount of variation, with the poorest 10 percent being the best off in Denmark, where they receive 4.4 percent of income, and the worst off in Greece and Portugal, where they receive 2.2 percent of income. The share of income going to the richest group ranges from 20.0 percent in the Netherlands to 27.7 percent in Portugal.

Education and Success

Not everyone measures success in terms of money. For those many who do, perhaps the most encouraging fact is that the monetary returns to education have apparently been increasing in recent years. That is part of the reason the rich have been getting richer and the poor poorer. Those with more education have prospered; those without have suffered.

To what do economists attribute the premium placed on skilled labor? The most compelling argument seems to be the impact of technological change on the workplace, best exemplified by computerization during the 1970s and 1980s. Today's workers are forced to work smarter, not harder. Brain power has replaced muscle power as the most important determinant of success in the labor market, which suggests that education and job training could provide the answers to stagnating wages and income inequality.

■ Prospecting for New Insights

1. Is it fair for some people to earn huge economic rents? Should those rents be taxed away? Would taxing rents cause superstars to withhold their talents from the marketplace?

2. If education and job training are the answers to the problems discussed in this Exploration, what could prevent workers from obtaining more education and training? Could government devise policies to overcome those obstacles?

Exploration 8-2 The Price of Prejudice

Markets are seen to play roles in both allowing and correcting racial discrimination. Specifically, although prejudice can sometimes be profitable, it more frequently cuts into profit, the focus of investors. Although government policies of the past have perpetuated discrimination, policy today is intended to eliminate it. There is controversy over whether some current policies have gone too far and become themselves discriminatory.

It was the summer of '64. In colleges throughout the United States, idealistic volunteers mobilized to head south to help register black voters. The cause was civil rights, without regard to the color of a citizen's skin. Faced with the combined courage of both blacks and whites under the leadership of the Reverend Martin Luther King and others, America was forced to take stock of its racial relations. The result was a concerted government effort to both legislate antidiscrimination laws and enforce constitutional protections. Some of the more significant antidiscrimination actions at the federal level, both in regard to race and other types of discrimination, include:

- The Equal Pay Act of 1963, which legislates equal pay for female workers who work in the same jobs as men;
- The Civil Rights Act of 1964, which prohibits employer discrimination based on race, sex, religion, or national origin; established the Equal Employment Opportunity Commission (EEOC) to enforce the act;
- The Age Discrimination Act of 1967, which outlaws age discrimination for workers between the ages of 40 and 65; additional legislation in 1986 was aimed at prohibiting employers from forcing some workers to retire.

In addition, in 1965, President Johnson issued Executive Order No. 11246, which established affirmative action. Many more antidiscrimination laws and policies of various sorts are in place at the federal, state, and local levels.

In spite of this more-than-30-year-old collection of laws and policies, how best to deal with discrimination is an issue that won't go away. Nobel prize winning economist Gary Becker pioneered the application of economic principles to the study of discrimination in his 1957 book *The Economics of Discrimination*. Other economists have followed his lead, with numerous insights that can shed light on this important issue. The following analysis focuses on racial discrimination, but can be applied to other types.

Discrimination in the Workplace

Our jobs are indispensable to our lives and dreams. They afford us the opportunity to get where we want to go. So it is small wonder that discrimination in the workplace is so upsetting individually and has been the focus of much effort in the civil rights movement. Yet pinning discrimination down is often hard to do, because a person's productivity is usually difficult to measure. For example, although most people do not think that the average worker is discriminated against, most people believe that their own productivities at work are underrecognized and underrewarded.

Fortunately, the marketplace helps keep discrimination in check by punishing businesses that discriminate on the basis of anything but workplace productivity. Whether firms discriminate intentionally or through ignorance, their punishment is the same: they lose profits.

To see how the marketplace punishes racial discrimination, consider the market for unskilled labor. Assume that each person in this market is equally productive, and then divide that market into two types: the market for black labor and the market for white labor. Figure 8-6 illustrates this division and the wage differential that would

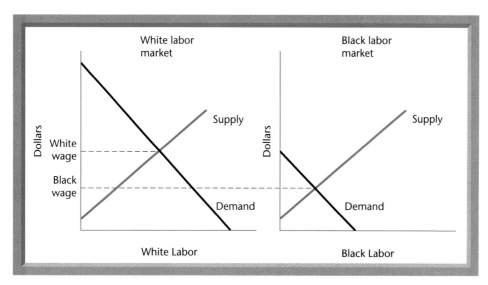

FIGURE 8-6 **Widespread discrimination against blacks in the labor market** would mean a higher wage for white workers than for equivalent black workers, thereby cutting into the profits of discriminating firms. As these firms go out of business or as the owners seek more profit by replacing the discriminating managers, the wage gap between black and white workers would close.

result. Specifically, if the marketplace as a whole exhibits discrimination in favor of whites, then there will be more demand and higher wages in the white labor market.

Since white and black labor are assumed to be identical in this analysis, these two types of labor are perfect substitutes for each other. Given equal productivity for blacks and whites but different wages, firms that hire white workers are placed at a competitive disadvantage to those that hire black workers. Over time, this would tend to drive discriminating firms out of business in favor of those that pay attention only to wages and productivity. As a consequence, black wages would rise and white wages would fall. The invisible hand of the marketplace thus eventually leads to equal wages for white and black labor that are of equal productivity.

Even so, some employers do discriminate and remain in business. This fact can be explained if these firms' prejudicial hirings have no effect on market wages. For example, there would be no effect if the excessive hiring of whites by firms with dis-criminatory hiring policies were offset by extra hiring of blacks by other companies whose hiring policies are color-blind. In other words, if discriminating companies leave more blacks in the labor pool, the color-blind companies would wind up hiring more blacks than they otherwise would. Any time that the discriminating firms' hir-ing of whites raised their wages relative to blacks, nondiscriminating firms would respond to the wage difference by hiring fewer whites and more blacks, which would bring wages between the two groups back to equality.

Alternatively, if widespread discrimination were to push wages up for white workers, discriminating firms that insist on hiring whites would see their profits erode because of the higher costs of hiring whites. Such businesses would continue to discriminate only if the owners of those companies are willing to pay this price. Perhaps some privately held firms would do so. For example, the prejudiced owner-manager of a small business would directly experience satisfaction from practicing discrimination. However, investors almost always seem to have a single-minded focus on profitability.

As proof, stock analysts on Wall Street will quiz companies mercilessly about their profit outlooks. The analysts only seem to care about hiring practices if they are likely to affect those profits. Individual and institutional investors share those priorities. Thus, company managers who choose to sacrifice profits for prejudice might be well advised to start job hunting before stockholders fire them or another company buys theirs and replaces them with managers who will turn the highest profit. It is in this way that, to the extent that black and white productivity is equal but wages are not, the invisible hand of the marketplace drives discriminating firms out of business.

Not all wage differences arise because of employer discrimination. Black and white wages would also differ if there are differences in average productivity between the two groups. The market will tend to pay one worker more than another if the first worker is more productive. Productivity differences among workers often result from differences in human capital, which may reflect differing amounts and quality of schooling. Good schooling requires an investment of time and money, which is hard to come by for poor youths who must eke out livings for themselves or their families.

To the extent that the higher poverty rate among blacks has been caused by systematic discrimination in the past—*premarket discrimination*—the present-day result is poverty that leads to less human capital and lower wages. This situation can also harm blacks with higher-than-average human capital to the extent that employers have imperfect information about individual job applicants and resort to *statistical discrimination*, which is to judge applicants by the average characteristics of their racial or ethnic group.

The Controversy over Affirmative Action

The previous section showed that competition for profit holds down discrimination in the labor market and keeps wages similar for similarly qualified workers. Yet, in part due to differing amounts of human capital, occupational choices, and other factors, we observe that wage gaps remain between whites and blacks, between men and women, between immigrants and native-born citizens, and between various other groups in society. At least some of those differences can themselves be traced back to discrimination in the past, much of which was either promoted or condoned by government policies, such as toward voting and the use of public facilities.

Since government policies supported segregation and other discrimination in the past, should not government policies now make amends? This line of reasoning has led to affirmative action policies that are intended to counter past injustices.

In principle, affirmative action calls for employers that receive government money, such as schools, defense contractors, and so forth, to actively seek out job applicants from *protected classes*, which refer to underrepresented groups in the labor

affirmative action: a policy to increase the number of women and minorities in the U.S. workforce.

force. All job applicants would then be evaluated on the basis of their abilities to best satisfy the job description. Only if there are two equal candidates would affirmative action require the firm to hire the one from the protected class. Although there are some complaints about the increased rigidity of the hiring process inherent in forcing firms to stick to advertised job descriptions, there are relatively few who object to these principles of affirmative action.

In contrast, the practice of affirmative action is the subject of controversy, with charges that it has turned into a form of *reverse discrimination.* Beginning in the late 1960s, the Department of Labor interpreted President Johnson's executive order as something akin to a quota system, forcing employers to fill a certain number of jobs with women and minorities. Furthermore, even if there are no quotas attached to affirmative action, because it is difficult for an employer to prove beyond a doubt that it has hired the best qualified person, affirmative action can bias hiring decisions against white males, who are not covered by its protections. The resulting competition for minority workers tends also to increase their wages relative to those of equally qualified white males.

The wage differentials and minority preferences arise because, if a firm hires a white male instead of a member of a protected class, the employer must potentially justify that decision to the EEOC with a large amount of paperwork that EEOC attorneys might pore over for any slip-ups. The employer would fear that the EEOC could determine that one or more of the rejected applicants was as well qualified as the white male that was selected. If so, the hiring could be delayed or the employer might be subject to serious penalties. On the other hand, if the employer rejects the white male in favor of a member of a protected class, there are few such fears or paperwork requirements. Thus, the balance of prejudice is tilted against white males. Whether this tilt is itself unjustifiable prejudice or merely fair compensation for past societal failings is where the controversy lies.

Discrimination Outside the Workplace

A discussion of discrimination would not be complete without considering discrimination in the output market. Whether such discrimination is possible depends upon market structure and demand. For oil, grains, autos, and the vast majority of products, product differentiation on the basis of discrimination is either not possible or not profitable. This is so because we typically do not know the race of the supplier of the product. However, in some markets, there is a demand for products that involve discrimination.

For example, we see restaurants differentiating their products on the basis of discrimination against smokers, where some allow smoking and some do not. In some situations, laws even force this discrimination on the basis of public health, as in outlawing smoking on commercial airplanes. Until outlawed so as to promote family values, there was discrimination against children in apartments, where some complexes advertised themselves as adults-only and other complexes set adults-only hours for their swimming pools. Most seriously, before the civil rights laws, we saw racial and ethnic discrimination not only in housing, but also in restaurants, movie theaters, and some other commercial establishments. Basically, if there is demand for differentiating a product on the basis of customer discrimination, the marketplace will meet that demand unless laws are enacted to prevent it from doing so.

Which Way Public Policy?

The Civil Rights Act and other legislation sought to prevent state and local governments from exercising their authority to discriminate. Today, the tables are turned, with some states seeking to distance themselves from federal policies that the states consider discriminatory. For example, there is opposition to "set-asides" that favor minority contractors, different academic admission standards for targeted minorities, or any other actions that treat people differently based on race, gender, ethnicity, and so forth. The conflict is between those who claim that affirmative action is necessary to arrive at a society in which race does not matter, and others who view affirmative action as itself discriminatory. Currently, the desirability of affirmative action is being publicly debated, with the Supreme Court likely to settle the debate at some point in the future. In the meantime, however contentious the debate may become, it is well to remember that Americans do share a common pledge—we seek "liberty and justice for all."

■ Prospecting for New Insights

1. Is it fair to allow firms to pay more productive workers more money, even though productivity differences might be caused by poverty? Explain.

2. Some firms suppose that employees work better with others of their own race or ethnicity. For example, a Korean-owned American firm might suppose that Korean-Americans communicate better with other Korean-Americans and thus hire only Korean-Americans in order to enhance productivity. Other firms might hire only Hispanic women, still others only white males. The result would be a lack of diversity in many workplaces. Discuss whether this result is desirable, considering both pros and cons.

Appendix
DERIVED DEMAND—HOW MUCH LABOR WILL THE FIRM EMPLOY?

Consider a firm operating in a purely competitive output market, as shown in Table 8A-1. The first two columns of the table show the relationship between labor and the firm's output. The third column, marginal product, is calculated as the change in output that results from a one-unit change in labor. This price-taking firm sells its output for $2 per unit, as seen in the fourth column. Note that price equals marginal

TABLE 8A-1 Marginal Revenue Product for a Price Taker in the Labor Market

Labor (L)	Output (Q)	Marginal Product	Price (P) (= Marginal Revenue)	Total Revenue (TR = P × Q)	Marginal Revenue Product (ΔTR/ΔL)
0	0	Not defined	$2	$0	Not defined
1	12	12	2	24	$24
2	22	10	2	44	20
3	30	8	2	60	16
4	36	6	2	72	12
5	40	4	2	80	8
6	42	2	2	84	4

revenue for a purely competitive firm. Total revenue is obtained by multiplying price by the quantity of output.

The marginal revenue product of labor is the increase in the firm's revenue arising from the employment of an additional unit of labor, as seen in the last column of the table.

$$\text{Marginal revenue product} = \frac{\Delta \text{total revenue}}{\Delta \text{labor}}$$

marginal revenue product: the increase in the firm's revenue arising from the employment of an additional unit of labor; Δtotal revenue/Δlabor.

Marginal revenue product can also be calculated by multiplying marginal revenue by marginal product. **Marginal revenue product measures the value of an additional unit of labor to the firm.**

If we suppose that the firm operates in a purely competitive labor market, then the firm is a wage taker, purchasing labor's services at the going market wage rate. **The wage rate equals the marginal cost of labor for a wage taker.** For example, if the market wage rate is $16, adding one more unit of labor always increases the firm's total cost by $16. **For a wage-taking firm, the marginal cost of labor is constant and equivalent to the supply curve of labor to the firm.** The reason is that the firm can purchase as many units of labor as it wishes at the market wage rate.

A firm will employ the quantity of labor that maximizes profit. This quantity of labor can be determined by comparing the marginal revenue product of each unit of labor to its marginal cost: **Profit maximization requires a firm to hire labor so long as labor's marginal revenue product exceeds its marginal cost.** If the marginal revenue product is less than the marginal cost of labor, a firm will not hire that worker. For example, the firm in Table 8A-1 would hire three units of labor at the $16 market wage rate. Since the fourth worker's marginal revenue product is less than $16, that worker will not be hired.

The firm in Table 8A-1 is illustrated in Figure 8A-1. The marginal revenue product curve is also the firm's demand curve for labor because it shows how much labor the firm will employ at various wage rates. Observe that the firm's labor demand curve shows an inverse relationship between the wage rate and the quantity demanded of labor.

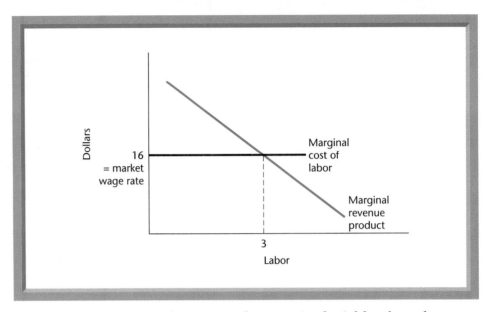

FIGURE 8A-1 **The marginal revenue product curve is a firm's labor demand curve.**
The quantity of labor employed by a profit-maximizing firm is the amount for which the marginal revenue product equals the marginal cost of labor.

The firm's labor demand curve may shift. An increase in labor demand would accompany

- an increase in the market price of the firm's output;
- an increase in the marginal product of labor. Labor's marginal product can increase (1) with technological improvements in production or (2) because labor's skills increase through education or training. Labor demand would decrease if the price of output fell or if the marginal product of labor decreased.

The market demand for labor is the total amount of labor demanded by all firms at each wage rate. This demand can be influenced either by market power in the output market or by market power in the labor market. Consider first the output market.

Imperfectly competitive firms and monopoly firms possess market power over the price of output, which results in higher output prices in these markets compared to the prices that would exist if the markets were purely competitive. Higher prices mean a smaller quantity demanded, which translates into less production and less demand for labor. **Thus, *ceteris paribus*, less labor is employed in markets where firms possess market power than in markets where market power is absent.**

In the labor market, a firm can have market power over the wage rate. In this case, the firm is a wage setter rather than a wage taker. This condition occurs when employers possess monopsony power. Consider a pure monopsony firm—the only employer of labor in a labor market. Data for such a firm are presented in Table 8A-2. As the only employer of labor in this particular labor market, the monopsonist faces

Labor	Wage Rate	Total Cost of Labor	Marginal Cost of Labor	Marginal Revenue Product
0	$5	$0	Undefined	Undefined
1	6	6	$6	$12
2	7	14	8	11
3	8	24	10	10
4	9	36	12	9
5	10	50	14	8
6	11	66	16	7

the market supply curve of labor, which is shown in the first two columns in the table. The firm's total cost of labor for each quantity of labor is obtained by multiplying the wage by the quantity of labor, and is seen in the third column.

In the next-to-last column of the table, the marginal cost of labor is shown. Marginal cost is calculated as the change in the total cost of labor resulting from a one-unit increase in the quantity of labor. Note that, unlike in the purely competitive labor market, the marginal cost of labor exceeds the wage rate in monopsony. The reason is that hiring extra workers increases the wage rate paid to all workers, not just to themselves. The final column of the table shows marginal revenue product data for this firm. The monopsonist will follow the profit-maximizing rule, which says to employ labor to the point where the marginal revenue product equals the marginal cost of labor.

How many units of labor will the monopsonist employ? The answer is 3 units of labor. Up to that point the marginal revenue product of labor is greater than the marginal cost of labor. Beyond that point, the marginal revenue product is less than the marginal cost. At 3 units of labor, the marginal revenue product and marginal cost are equal at $10. However, the monopsonist need not pay a wage rate of $10. Instead, the supply of labor figures in columns one and two show that the firm can attract 3 units of labor by paying a wage rate of only $8. Thus $8 is the wage the monopsonist will pay.

Figure 8A-2 shows the market supply curve of labor, the marginal cost of labor, the demand for labor (marginal revenue product), and the profit-maximizing employment and wage rate. The monopsonist makes its hiring decision in the following two steps:

- Step 1: It employs the amount of labor for which the marginal cost of labor equals marginal revenue product.
- Step 2: It pays as little as possible for that labor, where this wage rate is given by the supply curve of labor at the quantity chosen in step 1.

These choices are shown in Figure 8A-2.

Figure 8A-2 also illustrates a compelling point about monopsony that was raised earlier. If this monopsonized labor market could be transformed into a purely competitive one, the employment of labor would increase to the point where the supply and demand curves for labor intersect. Supply and demand show the competitive

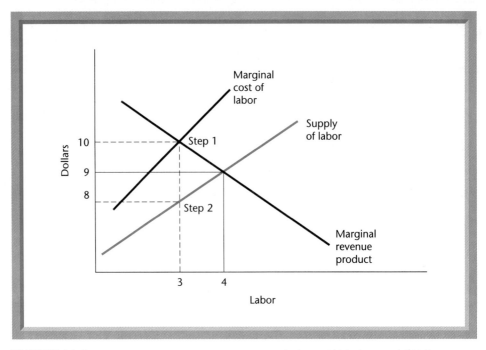

FIGURE 8A-2 **A monopsony firm faces an upward-sloping supply curve of labor.** It chooses to employ 3 units of labor, based on the intersection of the marginal cost of labor and marginal revenue product (step 1). It pays a wage of $8, the minimum needed to attract 3 workers (step 2). This process contrasts with the 4 workers paid a wage of $9 that would arise if the monopsony market behaved in the manner of pure competition.

wage rate to be $9 and the competitive level of employment to be four units of labor. This demonstrates that **monopsony labor markets are characterized by less employment and a lower wage rate than are purely competitive labor markets.**

Applying Concepts

1. Explain in your own words the meaning of marginal revenue product. How does this concept relate to derived demand? Using the data in Table 8A-1, confirm that marginal revenue product can be calculated by multiplying marginal revenue by marginal product.

2. Discuss the shift factors for labor demand. For each shift factor, first explain the circumstances in which labor demand would increase, and then the circumstances in which it would decrease.

PART FOUR

PROBING
THE PUBLIC SECTOR

Public policy can promote efficiency when markets fail to do so, such as in the cases of national defense and pollution. Government also redistributes income to promote equity. This section examines the motivations for government actions and how policies can be designed to achieve their goals. This section also examines the incentives involved both in choosing government actions and in paying the taxes to finance those actions.

9

MARKET FAILURE

A Look Ahead

*Technology tells us what can be done. Economics tells us
what should be done. Politics tells us what will be done.*

THIS OLD SAYING sums up the dilemma facing economists. They are caught in the middle. Economists neither produce goods for consumers nor control public policy. Rather, economists attempt to identify how the intertwining actions of government and markets can offer citizens the best value.

Economists seek to identify when public policy is needed to meet economic goals and the types of government actions that are appropriate. With these goals in mind, this chapter examines both *market failures*—instances in which free markets fail to achieve economic efficiency—and the policy designs that hold the most promise of remedying those failures.

Pointing out when government actions can promote efficiency is an ongoing task. Because subtleties of efficient policy design often get lost in the political process, examining the details of specific policies is equally important. Poorly designed policies can cause unintended problems elsewhere in the economy or even contradict the policies' intended objectives.

When market failures cross national boundaries, governments must work together to solve them. Exploration 9-1 examines such a situation, specifically, the problem of trans-border pollution along the U.S. border with Mexico. Whether in that case or in any other choice of policy action, government must first evaluate alternatives. Cost-benefit analysis provides the means to do so. However, as pointed out in Exploration 9-2, the actual practice of cost-benefit analysis can be complex and subject to error or distortion.

As you are **Surveying Economic Principles** you will arrive at an ability to

- ❑ ascertain why the private marketplace fails to offer valuable public goods;
- ❑ provide an economic justification for some pollution, but not as much as is produced in the unregulated marketplace;
- ❑ discuss how policy instruments that can control pollution can also be used to protect water, fish, wild animals, and other common property resources;
- ❑ identify how private property rights promote conservation of resources;
- ❑ describe why regulations are enacted and why they are resented.

While **Exploring Issues** you will be able to

- ❑ discuss the issue of transborder pollution and the difficulties in finding solutions;
- ❑ identify the principles of cost-benefit analysis and some problems in its application.

Terms along the Way

- ✔ market failure, 290
- ✔ private good, 290
- ✔ public good, 290
- ✔ common property resource, 291
- ✔ externalities, 291
- ✔ external costs or benefits, 291
- ✔ social costs or benefits, 291
- ✔ free-rider problem, 293
- ✔ private costs or benefits, 294
- ✔ Coase theorem, 296

- ✔ user fees, 299
- ✔ moral suasion, 299
- ✔ technology mandates, 300
- ✔ subsidies, 302
- ✔ second-best policies, 303
- ✔ marketable permits, 303
- ✔ specificity principle, 304
- ✔ discount rate, 312
- ✔ present value, 312
- ✔ net social benefits, 312

SURVEYING ECONOMIC PRINCIPLES

Market Failure—What Role Government?

The United States contains over 80,000 separate governments. These range from education, sewer, and water districts through municipal, county, and state governments, on up to the federal government. Each government has its own administrative costs. What can justify so many governments? Should all these governments be abolished so the free market can reign supreme?

The invisible hand of the marketplace leads profit-seeking producers to offer an efficient variety of goods and services. Competition ensures that these goods and services are produced at least cost, and in efficient quantities. However, there are exceptions—instances of market failure in which markets do not lead to efficient levels of production. **Market failures occur frequently when goods are not purely private.**

market failure: when markets fail to achieve efficiency, as in the case of public goods, externalities, and sometimes, market power.

The Spectrum of Goods

private good: consumed by one person only—excludable and rival; most goods and services are private.

A private good is consumed by one person and one person only. Private goods are *excludable* and *rival*, meaning that people can be excluded from consuming the good and that one person's consumption diminishes the amount that is available for everyone else. For example, a swig of Kumquat Delight Fruit Drink would be a private good, because each swig that one person takes leaves that much less for someone else. The goods that we buy are almost always private in nature. However, we consume other goods that are public.

Public goods are just the opposite of private goods. A *pure public good* is both nonexcludable and nonrival. Different people place different values on public goods. However, we have no choice but to each consume the same amount. National defense provides an example of a nearly pure public good. Whether U.S. citizens are pacifists, hawks, rich, or poor, and no matter our race, gender, or ethnicity, we all consume the same amount of national defense.

public good: a good such as national defense or clean air that are nonexcludable and nonrival, meaning that a person's consumption of the good does not reduce its quantity for others; most public goods are impure, meaning that they are not completely nonexcludable and nonrival.

Public goods are usually *impure*. For example, highways represent an impure public good, especially during rush hour when cars slow each other down. Some highways can also be designed for limited access, a means of exclusion. Still, for the most part, highways do offer the characteristics of a public good. Namely, one person's consumption of the services of a highway would not interfere with another person's consumption of those same services, and exclusion would be difficult.

Public goods can extend over a wide or limited area. A city's air quality is an example of a *local public good*. Local public goods provide an economic justification for local and regional governments. For instance, it is better to have local streets and highways under the control of municipal and state governments, respectively, than have decision makers in the nation's capital decide which potholes get repaired and where street lights are installed. The same would hold true for the many other public goods that are primarily local or regional in nature.

In between public and pure private goods are common property resources and private goods with externalities. Sometimes the ownership of something is *common*

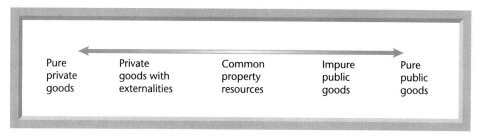

FIGURE 9-1 **The spectrum of goods and resources** is based on the degree of rivalry and excludability, where the left extreme is completely rival and excludable and the right extreme is completely nonrival and nonexcludable.

property, meaning that it is shared. Shared ownership occurs most frequently in connection with natural resources, thus leading to the term common property resource. For example, an oilfield could straddle two separate properties, with each property owner having the right to pump as much oil as the owner desires. A common property resource generates contention over who gets to use it.

Other times, the production or consumption of private goods leads to costs or benefits to third parties—people or businesses who were not party to the transaction. Such spillover effects onto third parties are termed externalities. Externalities can be either negative or positive. Pollution is an example of a negative externality. Negative externalities impose external costs on others. For example, to the extent that air pollution causes health problems or decreases people's enjoyment of outdoor activities, the pollution has imposed external costs on its victims. Conversely, positive externalities confer external benefits, such as when a neighbor kills all the mosquitos on her property, which also results in fewer in your own backyard. The external benefits are the greater enjoyment you derive from your backyard and the money you save on pest control.

Figure 9-1 summarizes the range of goods and resources from the extreme of pure private goods to the other extreme of pure public goods. To reiterate, market failure occurs when goods are not purely private.

Public Goods and the Free-Rider Problem

Public goods are unique in that we all consume them jointly. We share national defense, fresh air, and even access to radio signals. Adding more consumers does not diminish the enjoyment we each get from these goods. This arrangement has repercussions on demand that prevent the marketplace from offering an efficient quantity. Unlike a private good, each unit of a public good is simultaneously consumed by everyone. The value of a public good is thus the sum of its values to all consumers.

Figure 9-2 illustrates this idea, where the public good is worth $9 to Ana, and $12 to Bob, and so forth. It would be efficient to provide this good only if total social benefits exceed total social costs, where social costs or benefits are defined to equal all costs or benefits within the economy.

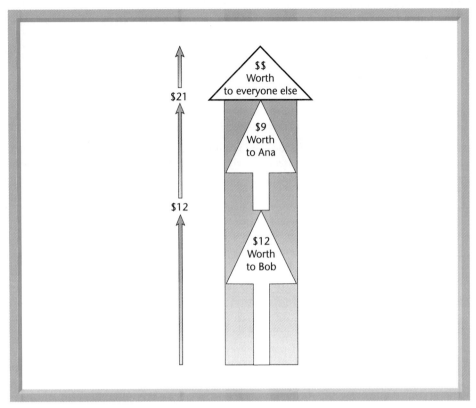

FIGURE 9-2 **The value of a public good is the sum of its value to each person,** because everyone consumes the same amount.

In most applications, the quantity of a public good can vary, which means we must compare the increment to social costs to the increment to social benefits from producing more of the public good. In other words, we must consider not only total benefits and costs, but also marginal social benefit and marginal social cost.

The efficient quantity of a public good is that for which marginal social cost equals marginal social benefit. That quantity maximizes *net social benefit*, which is the difference between social benefit and social cost. Maximum net social benefit is shown as the shaded area in Figure 9-3. Q* represents the efficient quantity of output.

The schedule of marginal social benefits is sometimes referred to as demand for the public good. The law of demand applies as much to public goods as to private goods. The greater is the quantity, the lower is the marginal social benefit from increasing quantity further. This means the marginal social benefit curve is downward sloping. However, this marginal social benefit schedule is demand only in the abstract. In practice, it would be extremely difficult to get people to pay anything voluntarily for a public good.

For private goods, you walk away with something in exchange for your money. With public goods, the amount you consume seems unaffected by how much you spend. Whether you offer a year's wages or nothing at all makes no discernible dif-

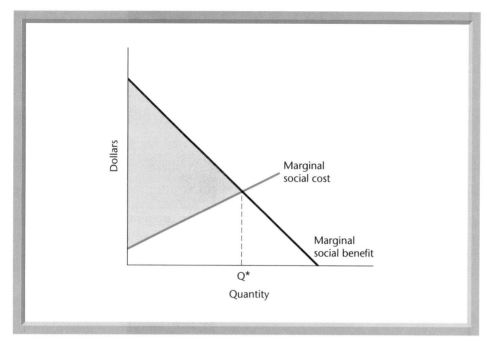

FIGURE 9-3 **The efficient quantity of a public good** occurs when the marginal benefit of another unit just equals its marginal cost. The shaded area is the net social benefit from this quantity.

ference. You can still consume just as much of the public good as everyone else. The result is a free-rider problem, in which everyone has the incentive to let others pay the costs of providing the public good.

free-rider problem: the incentive to avoid paying for a public good, because no one person's payment will have any appreciable effect on the quantity of the public good.

The solution to the free-rider problem ordinarily involves taxation. Government compels everyone to contribute, since everyone shares in consuming public goods. How much money people are forced to contribute is then at the discretion of government rather than the consumer directly. Thus nearly everyone would prefer either more or less government spending on any particular public good.

Sometimes, too, private entrepreneurs find ways to tie public goods to private goods that individuals or firms are willing to buy. For example, broadcast radio and television stations bundle their broadcasts with commercials. Because broadcasts are accessible to all, they are public goods and thus cannot be sold directly. However, commercials are private goods from the standpoint of advertisers. The more valuable is the public good aspect of programming, the more stations can charge advertisers for air time. In this and many other cases, there is at least some private provision of public goods. Unfortunately, there is nothing that compels private markets to produce the most efficient quantity or variety of these goods.

The private marketplace also sometimes offers private alternatives to public goods. For example, if all police forces were to be eliminated, there would be a dramatic increase in sales of firearms, alarm systems, and security guard services. Even so, public safety is likely to be maintained more efficiently through the provision of community-wide police services, a public good.

OBSERVATION POINT:

"What's a Little Snow?"

Buffalo, N.Y. maintains a Web site at **http://www. ci.buffalo.ny.us**

The great blizzard of 1996 paralyzed much of the Northeast. Not Buffalo, New York, though. As one of the snowiest spots in the United States, the people of Buffalo are used to the white stuff. "So what's another foot or two?" they ask as they slog to work, listening to the news reports of prolonged federal government shutdowns and other snow emergencies elsewhere.

True, Buffalonians are battle-hardened veterans of many a winter campaign. But there is more to the story. What's missing is the part about the efficient choice of a local public good—snow removal. Officials in Buffalo know it's going to snow hard, nearly every year. It is thus efficient for them to spend heavily on snow plows and other capital equipment. With snowfalls much less frequent in other parts of the country, officials there find it more efficient to devote that money to other needs. The result is that when the infrequent snowstorm does strike, the Buffalonians drive to work while the Washingtonians wait for a warm, sunny day.

Externalities—When Should There Be Action?

private costs or benefits: costs or benefits that are borne by the decision maker, such as a buyer or seller.

Externalities in the form of external benefits or external costs are all around us, although frequently of minor significance. Externalities occur when the **private costs or benefits** of an action—those borne by the ones taking the action—differ from social costs or benefits, which include both private and external costs and benefits.

$$\text{Social cost} = \text{private cost} + \text{external cost}$$

$$\text{Social benefit} = \text{private benefit} + \text{external benefit}$$

Significant external benefits are not as widespread as significant external costs. For example, constructing a beautiful new house in a shabby neighborhood will increase the value of other homes in that neighborhood. Likewise, people who successfully pull themselves out of poverty or other difficult situations serve as valuable role models for others seeking to escape similar situations. The generation of new academic knowledge also generates external benefits for those who make use of that knowledge. While there are many other examples of external benefits, external costs are more pervasive and worrisome.

The most obvious external cost is from environmental pollution. For example, fumes from the tailpipe of a diesel bus do not bother either the passengers or the bus company. Rather, the cost is external—the fumes bother the drivers behind. Would you wish to follow a gravel truck that drops sand and pebbles that threaten your vehicle? The cost of chipped paint on your Ford Bronco is of no concern to The Pits Gravel Company unless, perhaps, it fears a lawsuit or government reprisal.

Because external costs or benefits are not felt by the person or firm causing the externality, the free market price signal fails to generate efficient outputs. For example, Figure 9-4 shows the supply and demand for a product that is associated with an external cost. The supply curve represents marginal private costs, but fails to reflect

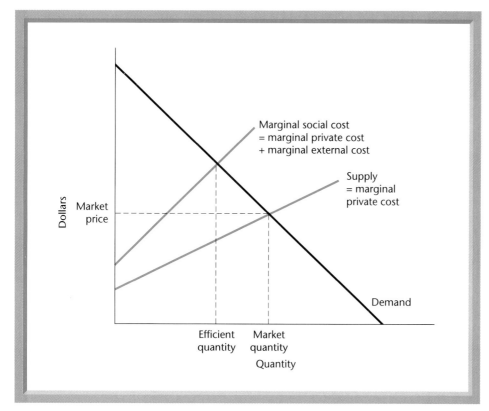

FIGURE 9-4 **When external costs are present,** supply lies below marginal social cost, and the free market produces more than would be efficient.

full marginal social costs. The difference between marginal social cost and marginal private cost is marginal external cost.

Marginal social cost = marginal private cost + marginal external cost

or

Marginal external cost = marginal social cost − marginal private cost

Thus, **when external costs are present, the free market produces too much—** output exceeds that which would be efficient. Conversely, **when there are external benefits, the free market produces too little.**

The presence of external costs does not imply that the externality-generating activity should cease. It is efficient to have some pollution, for example. In the course of a day's living, we are each responsible for pollution, such as from the tailpipe of the vehicles that take us where we want to go. Additional pollution is generated in producing the products we buy.

Are manufacturers evil people, who pollute so that we will be miserable? Actually, pollution results from firms using common-property air or water to remove wastes. The principle of mass balance, a physical law, implies that some waste will always occur when inputs are transformed into outputs. This waste must go somewhere, and water and air provide excellent waste removal services.

Still, lacking government action, polluters pollute too much. The reason is that there is no market for many environmental services. However, there is a market for some. For instance, firms economize on the solid wastes they generate when they must pay the trash collector to have these wastes disposed of. In contrast, in the case of liquid and gaseous waste, firms have no incentive to cut back if they can use the publicly owned environment to remove these wastes for free.

When Markets Are Missing

If environmental services provided by common-property water and air were priced, as they would be if sold in a market, firms would economize and pollute less. They would compute how valuable pollution is to them in terms of the extra output it allows. They would also look for alternate ways to produce their output with less pollution. The upshot is that firms would pollute only when the value of that pollution exceeds its environmental costs. That would be efficient.

Occasionally, firms compete on the basis of how environmentally friendly—how "green"—their products are. For example, consumers may pay extra for recycled paper or nontoxic antifreeze. However, consumers rarely seek information on how much pollution is generated in the production of a product, and are rarely willing to pay much of a premium for green products.

Typically, then, competition forces firms to be environmentally neglectful unless there are public policy incentives to be otherwise. Were a firm to go to the expense of cutting back its pollution, that firm would be at a disadvantage in competing against other firms in its industry. Only the heaviest polluters would survive. This is why pollution externalities represent a market failure, one calling for government action to change the rules of the game. The Clean Air Act was one such action. This Act, amended in 1970, has caused the emission of major air pollutants to fall dramatically as shown in Figure 9-5.

While reliance on public policy is commonplace, it is not the only means to resolve externalities. An alternative would rely upon legal safeguards against damage to the property of others. If pollution damages your property, sue for damages! Polluters will seek to avoid damages if they have to pay.

Coase theorem: holds that parties to an externality would voluntarily negotiate an efficient outcome without government involvement when property rights are clearly defined.

This school of thought is supported by the **Coase theorem,** named after Nobel Laureate Sir Ronald Coase. The Coase theorem holds that parties to an externality would voluntarily negotiate an efficient outcome, without government involvement. Government need merely define and clearly enforce property rights. For example, if the value of changing the amount of an externality exceeds its cost, a mutually beneficial agreement would be struck to accomplish this change. That would be efficient. If the value of change is less than the cost, an agreement would not be reached. That would also be efficient.

Few people believe the Coase theorem offers a general solution to externality problems. For example, imagine your neighbor playing her classic Iron Butterfly album at top volume at 2 a.m. Are you likely to ask how much money that experience is worth to her, and compare the amount with your own willingness to pay to avoid

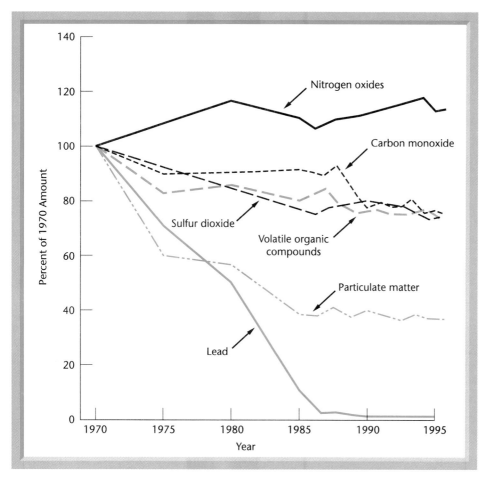

FIGURE 9-5 **Emissions of 5 out of 6 major air pollutants have fallen dramatically** since the passage of the Clean Air Act Amendments of 1970.

Source: 1999 Economic Report of the President, p. 197.

hearing it? Would you offer to pay her enough to get her to turn the volume down? You're a reasonable person, aren't you? "NOT AT 2 a.m.!" you say?

Anyway, if you pay once, you'll wind up paying again, even if your neighbor decides that she no longer likes listening. She likes the money. That exemplifies the problem of *strategic behavior*, which interferes with the practical application of the Coase theorem. That problem becomes significantly worse when the effects of the externality are widespread. In addition, identifying specific culprits and bringing together victims becomes quite difficult when many parties are involved. *Transaction costs*, the expense of coordinating market exchanges, would be high. Thus, the Coase theorem applies only in the absence of transaction costs and strategic behavior. In practice, this means we either resort to public policy to remedy the externality or ignore the problem and let the market fail.

QuickCheck _____

How can it be efficient to ignore the problem of externality?

Answer: Sometimes legal and policy cures are worse than the disease. Many externalities are minor, such as caused by other people's attire, cleanliness, and mannerisms. Imagine the problems of trying to measure these externalities and reward or punish them through either public policy or private lawsuit!

OBSERVATION POINT:
Back in Time to Baker Street

Wouldn't you sometimes like to do away with those stinking internal combustion engines and return to the pristine past of horses and carriages? You could rub Ol' Paint's nose and wouldn't have to deal with smog and ozone alerts.

Dream on, for the reality of life prior to the horseless carriage was anything but pollution free. Witness Old London. Well before the invention of motor cars and lorries, the streets of London were beset with acid rain and choking air pollution. The source of many toxic particulates churned into the air by hooves and carriage wheels was, shall we say, just opposite from Ol' Paint's nose.

The skies over London were also black with sooty smoke from the many coal- and wood-burning fireplaces throughout the city. Now, more than a century later and several million people larger, London offers more breathable air and clearer skies.

Yes, London still sees pollution, because heat, transportation, and nearly every other product cannot be produced without it. The difference is better pollution-control technology spurred on by public policy. Compared with the good old days, then, production is up and pollution is down.

Common Property Resources—No Incentives for Conservation

Common property resources are owned jointly. Examples include groundwater, public lands, wild animals, and fish in the oceans, lakes, and rivers. The problem is that, when many people own the same resource, no one has any personal incentive to conserve it for the future. Owners have rights to take or use the resource, but have no way of ensuring its preservation.

For example, imagine sharing a very large joint checking account with all other students at your college. How much money would be left in the account by the end of the day? Most likely, each student would figure that others would quickly raid the account. The bank would see a stampede of students, each seeking to be the first to transfer the entire balance to a private account. Common property resources face much the same problem.

The Web site for *Science* is located at **http://www.sciencemag.org/**

A classic article entitled "Tragedy of the Commons" by Garrett Hardin in *Science*, 1968, illustrates this problem with reference to the old English commons. The common land accessible to all quickly turned into a desolate expanse of dirt and mud, while private land nearby was lush and green. Grasses on the commons disappeared because shepherds allowed their sheep to overgraze. Shepherds had no reason to graze their flocks lightly, because the grass they saved would in all likelihood get eaten by someone else's flock. In contrast, on private land nearby, owners sought to conserve some grass to provide for future growth. The sheep were herded to fresh pastures before the grass was munched so short as to become endangered.

The common property resource problem is not a thing of the past. For example, overfishing along the coast of Maine and in many other ocean fisheries has caused catches to decline dramatically. Another concern is depletion of the ozone layer in the earth's upper atmosphere, as manufacturers in countries around the globe have little incentive to design ozone-friendly products. Likewise, irrigators and municipalities tapping into groundwater and river water resources have little incentive to practice conservation that would help each other out.

Government can solve common property resource problems by allotting the property to private users, such as through *privatization*. Most often, however, complete transfers would be impractical or politically unacceptable. For example, few would advocate selling rivers, lakes, and oceans to any single owner. The alternative is for government to act as the owners' agent and apportion use of the common property so that overuse is avoided. This is the rationale behind fishing and hunting permits, regulation of mesh size on fishing nets, mandated water-saving toilets, and various other restrictions and user fees—fees for use of a publicly owned good, service, or resource. As we shall see, some policy approaches are more promising than others.

user fees: charges for use of a publicly owned good, service, or resource.

Policy Tools

This section highlights some prominent policy options for the control of externalities and allocation of common property resources. Although several applications will be mentioned, the focus will be upon pollution and water policy. This focus is warranted because pollution is the most prominent externality, and allocation of common-property water promises to become increasingly significant as population grows.

Moral Suasion

"Turn down that thermostat—Don't waste energy!" "Be water tight!" "Don't be a Litter Bug!" "Only YOU can prevent forest fires!"

From U.S. Presidents to Smokey the Bear, we are exhorted to do the right thing. These appeals to our social conscience—called moral suasion—are the easiest and most high-profile form of public policy available to fight problems associated with externalities and common property resources. Moral suasion makes it clear to the public that actions are being taken. Unfortunately, moral suasion is rarely adequate to the task and often has undesirable side effects.

A fundamental drawback to moral suasion is that it has no way of achieving any particular target, efficient or otherwise. Also, moral suasion imposes all costs of cutbacks on the "moral." A third and perhaps most troubling problem is that moral suasion can lead to a self-righteous intrusion on personal privacy.

moral suasion: exhortations to do the right thing, as defined by public policymakers; often associated with public humiliation of those who fail to comply.

Numerous Web sites are devoted to Smokey the Bear. One of them is located at **http://www. smokeybear.com**

OBSERVATION POINT:
Water Waster?—Awarding David Robinson the Scarlet Letter

Remember all those "great books" you were forced to read in school? Perhaps one was *The Scarlet Letter*, by Nathaniel Hawthorne, which depicts life among the Puritans of early New England. The title is taken from a particularly effective technique of moral suasion. Those found guilty of adultery were forced to wear the scarlet letter *A*. Perhaps such a public humiliation would prevent others from engaging in this sinfulness.

Today, mass communication offers alternatives to the ignominious letter. This was brought home to David Robinson, a star on the basketball court and also one of the most charitable people in all of professional sports. "Robinson near top of water-users' list," blared a front-page headline of his hometown's daily newspaper. Also splashed across the front page was a detailed listing of the names and neighborhoods of the ten residential customers paying the highest water bills. Their monthly bills were itemized in the range from $328 to $731, each completely legal.

The modern-day Puritans were proud when David Robinson replaced his lush lawn with a basketball court. Fear of public humiliation can provide a powerful incentive to conserve. No one wants the neighbors to point and whisper. No one wants to wear the shameful tag of water waster.

Standards and Technology Mandates

Have you noticed that toilets installed in recent years don't flush well? The reason is the U.S. Environmental Protection Agency's 1995 nationwide law prohibiting the sale of toilets with tank capacities over 1.6 gallons. This is an example of the administratively popular policy of technology mandates.

technology mandates: occur when government instructs producers as to the exact technology to install to remedy some public problem.

Technology mandates occur when government instructs producers as to the exact technology to install to remedy some public problem. Low-flow showerheads and low-flush toilets are examples of technology mandates designed to avoid wasting water. Catalytic converters on automobiles are mandated to reduce air pollution. Technology mandates are usually chosen because they are easy to observe and enforce, and seem like a very straightforward solution to the problem.

The EPA Web site is located at **http://www.epa.gov/**

Sometimes the mandates are indirect, as with scrubbers on powerplant smokestacks, and other specific pollution control strategies. Here, the Environmental Protection Agency (EPA) specifies emission *standards* that must be met and suggests technologies that will meet these standards. Producers are free to use other technologies, but would be subject to serious penalties if the other approaches fail. If the EPA's suggested technologies fail, the producers avoid liability. There is thus much risk and little incentive to experiment with potentially better ways of pollution control.

Technology mandates are often much more expensive and annoying than other policy options. For instance, it is a waste of money and an annoyance to require high-tech, low-flush toilets in regions where water is plentiful. If external costs can be added directly to the prices of products, the higher prices would induce conservation in ways that regulators might be unable to mandate. A higher price of municipal water might prompt consumers to wash larger loads of laundry and dishes, for example. Using prices avoids the inefficiencies caused by the broad brush of technology mandates.

In the realm of pollution control, economic studies estimate that market-based alternatives to standards and technology mandates and standards can achieve the same amounts of emission cutbacks at roughly one-third the cost. For example, the EPA's bubble plan allows a firm to increase its emissions from some sources if it offsets those increases by decreasing its emissions from other sources. One Ohio utility plant responded by periodically hosing down its piles of coal to prevent wind-blown coal dust, rather than install expensive smokestack technology. The firm's particulate emissions dropped, while the cost of pollution control dropped even more. The EPA's offsets plan extends this flexible concept across firms to capture even more cost savings.

Government planners cannot be expected to foresee all of the options for pollution control. For example, what planner could have mandated that workers reduce pollution and congestion by abandoning their daily auto commute? Could planners in the 1970s have imagined the option of replacing commuters' automobiles with telecommunications? Yet, the recently available technologies of networked home computers and the Internet have led many people to do just that by working at home. Allowing the market to choose this and other less costly strategies of pollution control means that we can have a cleaner environment at a lower cost.

Pollution Taxes—Environmental User Fees

Economists often advocate internalizing the costs of externalities directly into prices. If an activity generates damages, the value of those damages would be estimated, and a tax imposed equal to the amount of the marginal external cost at the efficient level of output. In this way, the tax causes perpetrators of the external cost to pay the full marginal social cost of their activities. This means that externalities become part of the decisions of those who cause them, and efficient choices will be made in the marketplace.

For example, if smoking a pack of cigarettes causes an average of $1 in health damages to others, then a tax of $1 per pack would represent those damages. Such a tax is sometimes referred to as an environmental user fee, since polluters are charged for using the common property environment.

Figure 9-6 illustrates that a corrective tax on cigarettes shifts the supply curve up by the amount of that tax. The reason is that sellers now have to collect that extra payment and pass it along to government. The price would rise from the initial market price of $P_{no\ tax}$ to P_{tax}, but the price increase would not cover the full amount of the tax. The reason is that consumers respond to higher prices by purchasing fewer cigarettes, Q_{tax}, than the initial quantity of $Q_{no\ tax}$. If producers attempt to raise their price by the full amount of the tax, the law of demand would cause quantity demanded to fall, thus resulting in a surplus that would force prices to retreat somewhat. **Although price does not rise by the full amount of the tax, it does rise, which reduces consumption and its external costs.**

Using fees to remedy externalities often encounters difficulties. For example, external damages may depend upon time and place. Smoking at home does not impose the same externality as smoking in a restroom that many people must use. It is not possible to allow for this difference in imposing cigarette taxes. In other applications, such as taxes on water pollution from industrial effluent, fees could vary depending on such factors as season and time of day.

Measurement of pollution is another hurdle in the way of applying pollution taxes. For example, it may be difficult to constantly monitor the emission of pollutants,

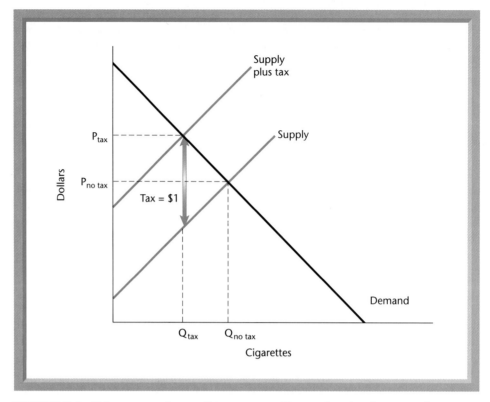

FIGURE 9-6 Using a tax to internalize an externality requires that the tax rate be set equal to marginal external cost at the efficient quantity of output.

especially for autos and other mobile sources. For stationary sources like factories, one can imagine a system of periodic checks and penalties that would punish cheating. Of greater concern, however, is political acceptance of taxing pollution and providing effective penalties to ensure compliance.

Politicians often seek new revenue sources. In contrast to most taxes, those designed to remedy externalities actually promote economic efficiency. Yet, pollution taxes have proven to have little political support. On the one hand, some well-meaning environmentalists will not accept that the environment is an economic resource. They claim that pollution taxes are merely passed along to consumers, and that pollution is not reduced. This line of reasoning ignores the law of demand. It also ignores the role of competition. Competition forces firms to substitute cheaper inputs for the newly priced use of environmental services.

On the other hand, producers usually oppose pollution taxes. The reason is that those taxes result in significant transfers of revenues from polluters to the government, revenues that pay for the firms' ongoing emissions of pollutants. This revenue transfer is in addition to money spent directly on pollution control. Thus, pollution taxes lack powerful constituencies.

subsidies:
payments from government that are intended to promote certain activities.

To overcome political barriers to pollution taxes, policymakers sometimes resort to paying for pollution abatement instead. For example, municipal wastewater treatment plants receive significant federal subsidies. Subsidies are appropriate to encourage actions causing external benefits. Unfortunately, subsidies for abating the external cost of pollution have undesirable side effects. Subsidies drain government revenues. They also reward polluters and can thereby lead to too many polluting firms.

OBSERVATION POINT:
Second-Hand Smoke—To Ban or Not to Ban?

Antismoking laws have cropped up all around the country. Do these laws violate economic principles? After all, if all external costs are represented by cigarette taxes, people make efficient choices. In principle, a tax based upon the external costs of second-hand smoke seems hard to surpass.

Economic theory sometimes justifies **second-best policies,** such as a ban on smoking in certain public places. This justification occurs when the preferred policy has undesirable effects in other areas due to entrenched inefficiencies elsewhere. For example, a high tax on cigarettes would raise the cost of smoking. Some addicted smokers might raid their children's food money or turn to theft to support their habits. If these secondary problems are serious and cannot be resolved directly, they might justify abandoning the tax in favor of smoking bans or other second-best alternatives.

However, it is easy to imagine all sorts of purported secondary effects. Applying these speculations to policy design could lead policymakers down the slippery slope of ever more command-and-control regulations. In the case of restaurant smoking bans, for example, will not diners vote with their feet? If so, they will go to restaurants that best satisfy their wants, including their preferences on smoking. Government intervention in this case would probably reduce efficiency, although some nonsmokers would not mind.

second-best policies: sometimes suggested when the most efficient policy would exacerbate entrenched inefficiencies elsewhere in the economy.

Marketable Permits—Whose Property?

Marketable permits offer the same economic advantages as taxes, but in a way that has much more political appeal. In application to pollution, marketable permits represent property rights to a certain amount of pollutant emissions. Government sets the overall quantity, and then divides up that quantity into a limited number of permits for the various polluters. While these permits could be auctioned, politics causes them more typically to be given away to preexisting polluters without charge.

Because the overall quantity of pollution is controlled directly, environmentalists are usually willing to acknowledge that marketable permits limit total pollution. Polluters prefer this approach to taxes because permits usually require no payment to government. However, polluters do sometimes worry that government might take away those rights or impose supplemental charges in the future.

Marketable permits are valuable property rights. The term *marketable* means that those rights can be bought and sold. This feature has appeal not only to producers, but also to economists. If pollution rights are traded, buyers would be firms with high costs of pollution abatement. Likewise, sellers would be firms with low costs of cutting back emissions. This means that emission reductions are undertaken by firms able to do so at least cost.

Trading in emission rights has mushroomed in recent years, so much so that it has formed an industry of its own. Markets for some pollutants are formal and well

marketable permits: property rights to a specified amount of an activity, such as groundwater pumping or air pollution, where those property rights can be bought and sold; can efficiently achieve quantity targets set by government.

developed. For example, power plants and other emitters can buy and sell rights for sulfur dioxide emissions on the Chicago Board of Trade. Other pollutants have *thin markets*, where trades are few. When markets are thin, environmental consultants facilitate trading by keeping track of firms willing to sell their permits.

Marketable permits also provide a promising alternative in the allocation of common property resources. Here, a central authority determines how much of the resource can be used now, and still leave enough for the future. For example, the authority might estimate how much water can be pumped from a river without irreparable harm to the river's ecosystem. Pumping rights are then distributed among river users, perhaps in proportion to the users' historical levels of pumping. These rights are then good for each period into the indefinite future. Fluctuations in the river's ability to support pumping might cause the same percentage variations in the quantity allowed per permit.

By allowing permits to be marketable, those valuing water most highly would be the ones that would buy or retain the permits. This is just what economic efficiency prescribes. The main issues are distributional. For example, how are the permits to be initially distributed? Should we compensate feed store owners who lose their livelihoods when local farmers and ranchers sell their water rights to big cities? Political questions of this sort have been the largest obstacles to more widespread use of permitting.

Applying Regulation Judiciously

Regulation occurs whenever government acts to influence the specifications of goods and services or the manner in which they are produced. For example, the technology mandates discussed earlier are a type of regulation. Since competitive markets minimize production costs, the effect of regulations is to increase those costs. Regulations increase economic efficiency only if the benefits they provide exceed their social costs.

Speed limits, smoking bans, seat belt requirements, product standards, and workplace safety laws are but some of the many regulations that affect our daily lives. Should businesses be required to allow family leave time that gives workers time to nurture their young and care for sick parents? Should universities be granted public funds if the composition of their faculties, staff, and students fails to reflect that of the surrounding community? Perhaps you will agree—the extent to which various facets of our economy should or should not be regulated is one of the most controversial topics around.

There are market-based alternatives to many command-and-control forms of regulation. For example, this chapter has already discussed situations in which marketable permits can provide an efficient alternative to standards and mandates. In the design of efficient public policy, the specificity principle says to target the problem in as precise and narrow a manner as possible, to hit the nail on the head. Using the specificity principle, the best solution to a market failure is often not to abandon markets altogether by resorting to command and control, but rather to do what is necessary to make markets a success. By following the specificity principle, undesirable side effects of policy actions are kept to a minimum.

specificity principle: the idea that policies should be targeted as narrowly and directly at a problem as possible.

When regulations apply uniformly across the country, they often lead to projects of little value that nonetheless impose heavy costs upon communities. For example,

Great Bend, Kansas, has a population of about 15,000 residents. In 1980, in order to meet federal water quality standards, it upgraded its wastewater treatment plant. Fourteen years later, federal standards changed again. The town finds itself required to spend an additional $5.2 million in order to keep ammonia levels in its wastewater from being toxic to fish in the Arkansas River. The fish? The Arkansas River at that point is little more than a trickle for most of the year. Its fish population consists mainly of minnows, minnows that seem exorbitantly expensive to local residents. Regulators do not bear the costs.

Regulation is sometimes hidden. For example, universities are required to satisfy social criteria pertaining to internal curriculum and policies or lose eligibility for federally funded student aid and other programs. In effect, this requirement places a hefty implicit tax upon deviating from federally sanctioned standards. Because there is punishment for violating these standards, regulation exists, whether it is called that or not.

Many people are concerned about overregulation, especially by the federal government. The more federal programs that are in place, the more weighty would be the consequences to states, municipalities, or private businesses of losing access to federal funding. Regional diversity decreases to the extent that federal funding depends upon conformity with national standards. Since markets operate by allowing consumers a diversity of choice, overregulation represents a threat to market efficiency.

Besides causing changes in the production and selection of goods and services, regulations have real *administrative and compliance costs*. For example, a 1996 survey reported that one- and two-person businesses spent an average of 24 hours per month to comply with local, state, and federal laws. The paperwork and consulting fees spent on compliance with the myriad of government regulations is a daunting hurdle for new and growing businesses. Place yourself in the position of a business seeking to expand without breaking the law. One of your first tasks is to identify the many aspects of hiring, retention, and production that are subject to regulations. It is difficult to find them all. The task may even be so daunting that you choose to avoid expanding altogether.

If you plunge forward and succeed in identifying all areas in which regulation occurs, you still run the risk of unintentionally breaking the law. Table 9-1 provides an example, taken from Equal Employment Opportunity Commission regulations on job interview questions, applicable to employers of 15 or more persons. As you will note, legal and illegal forms of comparable job interview questions are difficult to tell apart.

TABLE 9-1   Regulations Regarding Interview Questions

Legal Interview Questions	Illegal Interview Questions
Do you have 20/20 corrected vision?	What is your corrected vision?
How well can you handle stress?	Does stress ever affect your ability to be productive?
Can you perform this function with or without reasonable accommodation?	Would you need reasonable accommodation in this job?
Do you drink alcohol?	How much alcohol do you drink per week?

Source: EEOC, "Enforcement Guidance on Pre-Employment Disability-Related Inquiries," May 1994.

QuickCheck

Do you think it is legal for an employer to ask either of the following questions at a job interview? "What medications are you currently taking?" or "Are you currently using illegal drugs?" Also, what is the purpose of this exercise?

Answer: It is legal to ask about illegal drug use, but not about medications in general. The exercise illustrates the difficulty of following government regulations.

SUMMARY

- Market failure occurs when goods are not purely private.
- Private goods are excludable and rival, while a pure public good, such as national defense, is nonexcludable and nonrival. Public goods are usually impure, combining to some degree the qualities of a pure public good and a private good.
- Private goods can involve an externality. Externalities can be either positive, conferring benefits upon third parties, or negative, which impose costs upon third parties.
- Market failures can justify government action. This action can involve regulation or government production.
- Direct production by government is often appropriate for public goods, because the free-rider problem causes these goods to be underproduced in the marketplace.
- The efficient quantity of a public good occurs where marginal social benefit equals marginal social cost.
- Regulation is most appropriate for externalities and common property resources.
- Government can choose among various regulatory policy approaches, each of which has different characteristics and implications. Economists usually recommend taxes or marketable permits to control pollution or allocate common property.
- To enhance economic efficiency, policies must equate marginal social costs and marginal social benefits. However, government actions may cause undesirable side effects if not targeted precisely.

QUESTIONS AND PROBLEMS

1. Assuming no market failures, briefly explain why the private marketplace is efficient. What does *efficient* mean in this context?

2. Define and give an example of a public good. How does the condition for an economically efficient output of a public good differ from that for a private good? Explain how the free-rider problem causes private markets to provide too little of the public good.

3. Identify two ways not mentioned in the text in which the private marketplace might compensate for the elimination of all government-run police forces.

4. Suppose three communities would be served by a new sea water desalinization plant that costs $1 billion. Communities A and B each value this plant at $400 million. Community C values the plant at $100 million. Explain whether it is efficient for the plant to be built. Would the plant be constructed if each community shares the cost equally and the decision is made by majority rule? Explain.

5. Affirmative action programs have led to higher salaries for professionals from minority groups. Using the concept of external benefits, explain how this effect might be justified. Explain how the concept of external cost might also apply.

6. Stinkigunco, Inc., has a factory located upstream from a small community which uses the river water for drinking. The plant's emissions of pollutants into the water forces the downstream community to treat the water in order for it to be drinkable. Describe the Coasian solution to this problem of externality and comment on its practicality.

7. a. Explain why, when pollution or common property resource use can be monitored and measured, taxes or marketable permits are preferable to technology mandates and moral suasion.
  b. Using a specific example, explain how to create an efficient marketable permit system.
  c. Would it be efficient for government to distribute permits free of charge each year based upon how much pollution each firm was responsible for the previous year? Explain.

8. It is difficult to get a handle on the costs to firms of identifying and complying with regulations. For this reason, such costs are often ignored. Explain why the costs are difficult to compute and what problems arise when they are ignored.

Web Exercises

9. a. Using an Internet search engine such as that provided by Yahoo (located at **http://www.yahoo.com**) or Alta Vista (located at **http://www.altavista.com**), perform a separate search for the following terms: **public good**, **free rider problem**, and **technology mandates**. Visit several of the Web sites that your search reveals for each term and observe the context in which each term is used. Explain whether the manner in which the terms are used is consistent with their use in the text.
  b. Repeat the above, but this time use a combination of terms that you select from the chapter. To eliminate Web sites that do not contain all terms, place a plus sign in front of each term you enter, such as +**"market failure"** +**subsidies**.

10. Visit the Web site maintained by the Environmental Protection Agency (EPA) at **http://www.epa.gov**. Seek out information about regulation of the environment, such as the enforcement of the antipollution laws. Summarize what you find by writing a series of 10–15 bullet points that describe key government regulations.

Visit the Web site for *Economics by Design* at
http://www.prenhall.com/collinge for a Self Quiz over
the topics in this chapter.

EXPLORING ISSUES

Exploration 9-1 Borderlands of the Southwest—
Whose Pollution? Whose Solution?

Trade between the U.S. and Mexico intensifies preexisting problems of transborder pollution. This
Exploration looks at the very imperfect options available to resolve this issue.

The American Southwest

Wide open spaces, broad vistas, a freshening breeze—our vision of America's Southwest is one of expansiveness and freedom. It is a place to do and be as we please.
The Southwest is part of our psyche; it's a state of mind. It's also a real place with
real problems. As ever more people live in the Southwest, unlimited personal freedom comes into conflict with preservation of the environment that attracts them
there. The environment of the Southwest is ill-suited to accommodate unrestricted
pollution.

As in other parts of the country, citizens of the Southwest must abide by U.S.
environmental laws, which means driving cars or operating factories with emission
controls in place. The special problem of the Southwest, though, is that those controls apply to only a fraction of the sources of pollution. Much of the air and water
pollution has its source in Mexico, an industrializing country with a rapidly growing
population and less stringent control over pollutants. For example, smoke from Mexican forest fires started by burning off cropland—a practice that is restricted in the
United States—blanketed Texas and other states with a cloud of smoke for nearly a
month in mid-1998.

An American Medical Association group depicted parts of the U.S.–Mexican border as "a virtual cesspool and breeding ground for infectious diseases" (Council on
Scientific Affairs). Exemplifying the problem of border air pollution, the city of El
Paso, Texas, is in noncompliance with guidelines set by the U.S. Environmental Protection Agency (EPA). However, the EPA allows this noncompliance to continue
without penalty. There is a reason.

If you were to fly into El Paso and look out the airplane window as you approach
the city, you may have a good idea as to why the EPA makes exceptions for El Paso.
On the south side of the Rio Grande you are likely to see a polluted haze that greatly
restricts visibility. The haze on the north side is much lighter. El Paso is on the north
side and its twin, Ciudad Juárez, is on the south side. Ciudad Juárez has nearly triple
the population and generates proportionally much more pollution than does El Paso.
Unfortunately for El Paso, pollution knows no borders.

Transborder Pollution

Transborder pollution is a problem of growing magnitude around the world. The
problems are worsening for two reasons. On the one hand, economic growth in the
less-developed countries does not emphasize pollution control. Of greater concern to

those countries are such tangibles as food, clothing, and shelter. On the other hand, the increased wealth of the developed countries has allowed them the luxury to focus beyond immediate necessities toward the quality and long-term sustainability of lifestyles. Environmental quality is important to both of those lifestyle goals.

Transborder pollution problems come in many forms. Some are global in nature, such as concerns that emissions of chlorofluorocarbons are depleting the earth's ozone layer. The pollution problem of most concern in America's Southwest is more local in nature. Here we have two countries, each of which feels the effects of the other's pollution. What trouble does this cause?

The problem of localized transborder pollution centers on incentives. There is much more incentive to control pollution that affects your own residents than there is incentive to control pollution absorbed elsewhere. For instance, cities along rivers routinely locate sewage treatment plants downstream and city dumps downwind from the city itself. When cities are all governed by one state or country, there are limits to how much pollution exporting is allowed. For example, while sewage from U.S. cities may be discharged downriver, at least U.S. law requires that it be treated. Given an absence of a world government, is there some other incentive for neighboring countries to be sensitive to each other's concerns?

Pollution Control Policies

It would be very difficult for the United States to apply any particular pollution control strategy to firms in Mexico. Options that work well within a jurisdiction don't work as well across jurisdictions. For example, one option long advocated by economists is for government to impose a tax on emissions of pollutants, such that the *external costs* of pollution are *internalized* into the production process. The idea is to make firms pay for environmental services. In other words, firms would be forced to pay for the waste-removal services of the air above or the river next door in the same way they pay for other types of services. In that case, you can rest assured firms would find ways to economize on smoke emissions and discharges into waterways.

A *second-best*, less desirable, alternative would be to tax the output of the firm. This approach would not give firms any incentive to reduce the amount of pollution per unit of output, but it would at least drive up the price of that output. Higher prices would mean fewer sales and thus less pollution. Could we apply either of these tax ideas to transborder pollution?

The answer is the United States probably could not effectively use pollution taxes on Mexican polluters. The United States could not tax pollution emissions effectively, because it lacks the authority to monitor pollution in Mexico and lacks the authority to impose taxes even if it could monitor that pollution. In principle, the United States could levy a pollution tax on output crossing the border. However, that tax could not effectively differentiate where in Mexico that output was produced. Furthermore, that tax would be politically unpalatable and violate international treaties.

Other policy instruments, such as pollution permits or mandated pollution control technologies, would also be infeasible for the same reasons taxes would not work. Where does that leave us?

Cooperation, Not Contention

The best solution may be voluntary cooperation between the United States and Mexico based on mutual self-interest. While both the United States and Mexico gain from trade between the two countries, the gains to Mexico are proportionally larger because it is the smaller country. This cooperative spirit is attested to by the 1994 implementation of the North American Free Trade Agreement (NAFTA), which incorporated Mexico into a revised and expanded free trade agreement between the United States and Canada.

NAFTA broke new ground in international trade by writing environmental safeguards directly into the treaty and side accords. For example, NAFTA signatories are obligated to maintain effective enforcement of their own environmental laws, even when the affected pollutants spill over the border. While NAFTA does not itself solve the problems of border pollution, it does provide a framework for cooperation on that issue.

What kind of cooperation can the United States legitimately expect from Mexico? Should we expect Mexico to maintain environmental standards equal to our own? Beware of environmental imperialism. The United States cannot expect the world to follow its standards, at least not without granting the rest of the world's citizens voting rights in U.S. elections. Moreover, uniform environmental standards would not make sense across all countries. After all, maintaining those standards is expensive, and incomes in some countries are much lower than incomes in the United States.

Mexico's per capita income is under $5,000 per year. Relative to the average U.S. citizen, the average citizen in Mexico thus consumes less in the way of high-quality food, clothing, shelter, medical care, and so forth. For Mexico to upgrade its control of pollution to match that in the United States would require further reductions in the quality of those goods.

One of the best ways for the United States to see greater control of pollution in Mexico is to see greater per capita income in Mexico. The reason is that environmental quality is a normal good, meaning that people want more as their incomes rise. The growth in income has been occurring in recent years and will be spurred along as NAFTA continues to be phased in. We are already seeing an increased interest in environmental improvement in Mexico. Over time, we can expect this interest to translate into concrete policy action.

In the meantime, there remain pollution problems along the U.S.-Mexican border. For example, sources of air pollution in the El Paso–Juárez air shed include the burning of tires to fuel brick kilns, dusty unpaved streets, and open-air spray painting of automobiles. The citizens of El Paso want action to clean this up sooner rather than later. So too do citizens of Juárez. Is effective action possible?

To answer that question, it must be noted that the environment is a *common property resource*, meaning that we can all use it, but that no one really owns it. This gives us no incentive as individuals to maintain it in the present or invest in its future. The way that government solves pollution problems is, in effect, to lay its own claim to the common property environment. Government then seeks to represent the interests of present and future users of the environment. Policy is implemented via such tools as carefully designed pollution charges, allocation of pollution permits, or mandated pollution controls.

Along the border, local governments have an incentive to cooperate in order to address the common pollution problem jointly. That is exactly what El Paso and Juárez have done. Specifically, those governments have formed a single international air quality management district for their region. This district is empowered with the authority to set air quality goals and employ market mechanisms to meet those goals.

For example, the market mechanism might grant limited emission rights to local polluters, but allow them to buy and sell these rights in the marketplace. In this way, overall pollution would be reduced and the firms that actually undertake pollution reduction would be those who can do so least expensively. The idea is for government to allocate property rights to the quantity of pollution that is permitted, and then let the free market determine which firms actually use those rights. For this approach to work, though, firms must not fear losing future allocations of pollution rights if they do not use those rights in the present. That has been a problem that has bedeviled such programs in the past. Markets function efficiently only when property rights are clear and reliable.

A Big Job, But Who Will Pay?

This Exploration has not dealt with all aspects of the transborder pollution problem. For example, much pollution is left over from the past, especially when it comes to toxins on the land and in the water. Therefore, controlling the flow of new pollutants is not enough; there is the stock of old pollutants to clean up. Who will pay for that cleanup? Part of the answer may be found in the recently established *North American Development Bank*, financed by the governments of Mexico and the United States to fund border cleanup projects. Yes, the hands of government and the pockets of taxpayers are likely to be major parts of any final resolution to the transborder pollution problems of the American Southwest.

More about the work of the North American Development Bank can be found at **http://www. nadbank.org**

■ Prospecting for New Insights

1. The production of many of the goods the U.S. imports from Mexico causes pollution within Mexico. Is this pollution fair to the Mexican people? Alternatively, would it be more equitable for the United States to import only those goods that are not associated with significant pollution or that abide by the pollution standards that U.S. industry is forced to face?

2. When firms in Mexico cause pollution that crosses the border, U.S. residents along the border are damaged. That pollution is an external cost, since the U.S. residents have no way to extract payment from the Mexican polluters. Explain how this sort of pollution raises a different set of issues than that discussed in question 1. What policies should the United States pursue?

Exploration 9-2 Government Cost-Benefit Analysis— Simple in Concept, Contentious in Application

Cost-benefit analysis can help in making better choices. In government, the analysis requires that dollar values be assigned to both monetary and nonmonetary benefits and costs so that alternative policies can be compared. The result is complexity, which can lead to errors and disagreements. Government actions also influence private-sector cost-benefit analysis, with both planned and unplanned results.

Most people have heard of cost-benefit analysis. The term often conjures up a massive report filled with calculations. However, at a basic level, cost-benefit analysis is something everyone does frequently but informally. Should you attend college? You weigh the costs and benefits. Given that you do attend college, should you attend class today? Again, you weigh costs and benefits. Should you read the assigned chapter before coming to class? It's cost-benefit analysis again.

Although cost-benefit analysis is often done more formally in business and government settings, the idea is the same: By weighing the value of benefits and costs, efficient choices can be made. Putting these techniques into practice, though, can lead to contention and unintended results, as will be seen.

Fundamental Techniques of Cost-Benefit Analysis

Businesses use cost-benefit analysis in making decisions. In doing so, marginal revenues and costs must be estimated, taking such factors as quantity and product differentiation into consideration. For example, should a sugar company offer four-pound bags, five-pound bags, or both? Should the sugar be from sugar beets, sugar cane, or both? How should the bags be designed?

Cost-benefit analysis requires choosing a discount rate, which is an interest rate. Benefits and costs are usually stated in terms of present value, which involves *discounting* future costs and benefits to their present-day equivalent. For example, when the discount rate is 10 percent, then one dollar of benefits next year has a value of only about 90 cents today. This valuation is appropriate if 90 cents could be invested in other projects to yield a dollar's worth of benefits next year. In a sense, then, 90 cents today would then be equivalent to a dollar next year. In either the public or private sector, **cost-benefit analysis requires the computation of present values, which usually involve a complex stream of expected costs and benefits over time, and is done with a financial calculator or computer spreadsheet software.**

The guiding principle in business cost-benefit analysis is always to maximize profit, specifically the present value of the expected stream of profits over time. In finance, this is referred to as maximizing the value of the firm. In contrast, when government uses cost-benefit analysis, its goal is to maximize the present value of net social benefits, which are social benefits minus social costs.

In the private sector, firms discount future costs and benefits of a project according to the riskiness of the project and their cost of borrowing. Government undertakes such a large portfolio of diverse projects that, in the aggregate, there is little risk of projects failing. Since government is unlikely to default, borrowing costs are also lower, as can be seen by comparing corporate debt to government debt. The interest rates on corporate bonds are always higher and, depending upon

discount rate: the rate at which future values are reduced to their present value equivalents; the interest rate.

present value: involves discounting future costs and benefits to the present-day equivalent.

net social benefits: social benefits minus social costs.

the stability of the company, sometimes much higher than rates on government bonds.

For this reason, some people argue that government should use a lower discount rate than that used in the private sector. Moreover, many people think that the private sector discounts the future too heavily. According to this line of reasoning, government should be more farsighted and thus employ a lower discount rate. The lower the discount rate, the more valuable benefits far into the future look from the vantage point of today.

This line of reasoning leads to a curious result. Any project with benefits extending into the future is computed to be more valuable if government undertakes it than if it is done in the private sector. This result is nonsensical, since the social value of a project should not depend upon who constructs it. For example, a grocery chain might reject building a new supermarket because population growth in the area is too slow. However, a cost-benefit analysis on that same store built by government might say to go ahead if government uses a lower discount rate.

Government borrows from the same pool of consumer savings as do private companies. If government uses low interest rates to justify undertaking projects that would not pass a cost-benefit test in the private sector, it drives up borrowing costs and competes away projects. Carried to an extreme, all new projects would be undertaken by the public sector, and the private marketplace would wither away. For these reasons, economists usually argue that government should use the same interest (discount) rate that prevails in the private sector.

Valuing Intangibles

Cost-benefit analysis in government is more complex than in the private sector. Like private firms, government has various dimensions to its spectrum of choices. Along each dimension, economic efficiency requires that government seek to equate marginal social benefits and marginal social costs. For example, before determining the optimal size of the military budget, it is necessary to decide how incremental dollars would be spent, which in turn requires the assessment of alternative military strategies. Measuring the social benefits and costs along these dimensions is controversial and imprecise.

Unlike private firms, the government cannot observe the prices that its products sell for in the marketplace. What is the value of saving a wetland? No one offers to purchase public goods of this sort. What is the social cost of hiring workers who would otherwise be receiving unemployment compensation? There is a market price, but it ignores many social costs of unemployment. These are *intangibles*, yet they must be evaluated. To do so, government analysts impute social valuations through sometimes complicated techniques.

Some of the best techniques to reveal social benefits of intangibles involve observing other market prices that relate to the good in question. For example, the cost of noise pollution from airplanes can be estimated by observing how much less homes under takeoff and landing flight paths sell for relative to comparable homes elsewhere.

There are many other techniques that policymakers use, depending upon the specific types of intangibles that need measuring. In all cases, however, it is best to attach dollar values to these intangibles, even if those values have nothing to do with people's consumption directly. It is people that government seeks to represent, and people attach value to preservation and other nonuse attributes of government action. Attaching dollar values provides a common measuring rod by which to measure things that are otherwise seemingly incomparable. Because the economy has scarce resources, such choices must be made.

Government Interaction with Private-Sector Cost-Benefit Analysis

Once costs and benefits are estimated, government is then faced with the challenge of forming public policy that brings about the efficient choice of output. Sometimes, as in the case of highway construction, government selects this output itself. Other times, it merely seeks to influence private-sector choices.

For example, in the case of the aircraft noise discussed previously, officials might have an estimate of the noise cost of an additional landing or takeoff, but not of the private costs and benefits to airlines and their passengers. Thus, it would be inefficient to rigidly restrict the number of takeoffs and landings, ignoring variations in other costs and benefits that occur frequently. Probably the most efficient solution in this case is to charge the airlines for the external cost of the noise that each flight generates and then let them choose the efficient quantity of their own flights. The most efficient takeoff and landing fees would be based on estimates of the size of the payment that would just compensate property owners for the added noise pollution.

When more efficient policies are not feasible, government officials might declare a quantity target, such as a safety standard. Ideally, such a standard approximates government's best estimate of the quantity that maximizes benefits net of costs. For example, food is often declared to be safe with up to a certain percentage of pesticide and bug remnants. Beyond that level, the food is declared as unsafe and banned from sale even though there really is no magical quantity of pesticides and bug remnants, just degrees of riskiness. Private companies must then adjust their processes so that they expect to meet these standards, factoring in a margin for error. Those companies might also factor into their own cost-benefit analyses how likely it would be for violations of the standards to be detected and what the penalty would be if they were.

Government actions can also influence private-sector cost-benefit analysis in unintended ways. For example, for more than a decade air bags were thought to save lives and not take them. But in 1997 evidence surfaced that small adults and children could be killed by the explosive force that was generated as an air bag deployed in an accident. Soon after, in the glare of negative publicity toward air bags, the government began to allow on/off switches for passenger-side air bags to be installed in vehicles. Parents were faced with the dilemma of whether to spend the money to install a switch, banish their children to the back seat where there are no air bags, or do nothing. To maintain the public's faith in air bags the car makers soon began designing a new generation of air bags that would deploy with less force.

Along a different line, we each act in ways that affect others, sometimes for better and sometimes for worse. For example, suppose that Albert answers a question that was puzzling Beulah and Chuck. However, Donde already grasped the concept and resents what she considers the waste of valuable class time. If government were to allow Donde to sue for damages but not allow Albert to collect benefits from Beulah and Chuck, then Albert would be inhibited from speaking even though it might have been efficient for him to do so.

More generally, to the extent that a person may be held liable for unintended external costs but has no claim to external benefits, that person's cost-benefit analysis changes in the direction of having less interaction with others. Thus, rather than construct a sidewalk that might develop a crack that causes an unwitting pedestrian to trip and be injured, a homeowner might choose to skip building the sidewalk altogether.

Cost-Benefit Analysis—Use with Caution

Unfortunately, because of its complexity, cost-benefit analysis by government is often subject to distortion for political purposes. Because assumptions as to the values and significance of its many details are not etched in stone, analysts can often tweak cost-benefit analysis to influence its results. For this reason, it is common practice for consultants to skew cost-benefit analyses in favor of what they think their clients would like to see.

In addition, errors may creep into the analysis, either inadvertently or intentionally. For example, the cost-benefit analysis of a water project might show as a benefit the increased values of nearby farmland. It might also show as a benefit the increased value of crop production. However, this would be the error of double counting because the increase in land values is itself caused by the increase in the value of crop production.

In short, then, government cost-benefit analysis lays the issues on the table and, through careful logic and estimates of costs and benefits, can help government make the best choices. Cost-benefit analysis can also be a minefield, with errors, unintended consequences, and deliberate distortions lying hidden, ready and waiting to destroy attempts at efficiency. Yet while the dangers of cost-benefit analysis are high, the dangers of abandoning its logical analysis are higher still.

■ Prospecting New Insights

1. The presence of intangibles makes it much more difficult to estimate costs and benefits for public-sector projects than for private-sector projects. Give an example of an intangible that might need to be measured in a public-sector cost-benefit analysis, and suggest the lines along which the estimation might be performed.

2. Identify an instance in which the possibility of being sued might change your behavior or that of someone you know. Was this change in behavior efficient? Explain.

10

TAXATION
AND PUBLIC CHOICE

A Look Ahead

"**O**F THE PEOPLE, by the people, for the people,"—that is what we want from our government. That is why government is called the public sector—it is intended to represent the wishes of the public. To finance the many functions of government requires taxation, the types of which can vary widely. This chapter examines some of the array of taxes that exists in the United States and the rest of the world. The chapter also interprets the properties of those taxes and their alternatives.

While markets have their failings, so too does government. There is no invisible hand to guide government toward efficiency as there would be in a competitive market economy. Therefore, along with the many worthwhile programs of government, there come other programs of dubious merit. Even worthwhile projects tend to have inflated costs relative to the competitive ideal. This chapter examines how economic incentives within the public sector can lead to these and other government inefficiencies.

Although the income tax collects more money from U.S. citizens than any other tax, few people understand all of its details. Exploration 10-1 examines some of the reasons why the tax is so complicated and the issue of whether a simple flat-rate tax might not be a better idea. In setting public polices, the self-interest of policymakers is sometimes to have the policy be inefficient, so long as the public does not understand the inefficiency. Exploration 10-2 examines the setting of prices for tap water, which exemplifies this problem.

As you are **Surveying Economic Principles** you will arrive at an ability to

- ❏ list the major revenue sources in the United States;
- ❏ show why workers pay more Social Security tax than they think;
- ❏ distinguish two principles of tax equity, and explain why they conflict;
- ❏ justify why voters may be rationally ignorant of what goes on in government;
- ❏ infer why legislators engage in vote trading that leads to excessive government spending.

While **Exploring Issues** you will be able to

- ❏ interpret why the U.S. income tax is structured as it is, and why critics suggest changing it;
- ❏ identify why some commonplace policies toward water conservation are inefficient, and why the public sector chooses them anyway.

Terms Along the Way

- ✔ transfer payments, 318
- ✔ marginal tax rate, 318
- ✔ consumption tax, 322
- ✔ value-added tax (VAT), 323
- ✔ tax base, 323
- ✔ benefit principle, 324
- ✔ ability-to-pay principle, 324
- ✔ progressive tax, 325
- ✔ regressive tax, 325
- ✔ proportional tax, 325

- ✔ public choice, 327
- ✔ government failure, 327
- ✔ rational ignorance, 328
- ✔ logrolling, 328
- ✔ fiscal illusion, 328
- ✔ rent seeking, 331
- ✔ Washington Monument strategy, 334
- ✔ unfunded mandates, 334
- ✔ marginal-cost pricing, 342

SURVEYING ECONOMIC PRINCIPLES

Taxation: The Price of Government

In this world nothing can be said to be certain, except death and taxes.

—Benjamin Franklin

Few things are less popular than taxes, since *taxes* represent money that is taken from us involuntarily by the government. Taxes go toward financing government activities, including the provision of public goods and the correction of market failures. Taxes are also used for transfer payments that redistribute income to the needy. Transfer payments include unemployment compensation, welfare, and other *safety net* programs that provide economic security. Transfer payments account for approximately 44 percent of total federal spending. Figure 10-1 shows the growth in transfer payments and other components of federal spending over time.

Because taxes take roughly one-third of gross domestic product (GDP), taxpayers are acutely concerned that they not be taken advantage of—that all pay their fair share. This is the goal of *tax equity*. Because taxes can discourage work effort and investment, a second goal is *tax efficiency*. Tax efficiency implies that, unless taxes are targeted to correct an externality, they should be designed to raise revenues in a manner that affects our behavior the least. This approach would offer citizens the greatest possible incentive to be productive. With reference to these goals, this section looks at several types of taxes, with special attention to those used in the United States.

Taxation in the United States and Other Countries

Figure 10-2 on page 320, illustrates the relative importance of revenue sources for the U.S. federal government. The personal income tax is the single largest source, providing 43 percent of all revenues. As U.S. citizens accumulate income over the course of the year, the federal personal income tax claims those earnings at incremental rates starting at 0 percent and increasing to 15 percent, 28 percent, 31 percent, 36 percent, and 39.6 percent as income rises higher and higher. This incremental rate is known as the marginal tax rate, which equals 28 percent for most Americans.

Marginal tax rate = additional taxes owed as a percentage of additional income

In other words, the average citizen pays 28 cents to the IRS on each additional dollar he or she earns. Those taxes are withheld from income on the basis of the taxpayer's estimated *average tax rate*. The average tax rate equals a person's total tax liability divided by total income at the end of the year.

Average tax rate = total taxes owed as a percentage of total income

As seen in Figure 10-2, Social Security taxes, inclusive of the hospitalization portion of Medicare, account for 33 percent of federal revenues, second only to the share of the personal income tax. The Social Security tax is a *payroll tax*, in which the government deducts a flat 7.65 percent from the amount of money the employer pays, plus another 7.65 percent from the amount of money the employee receives.

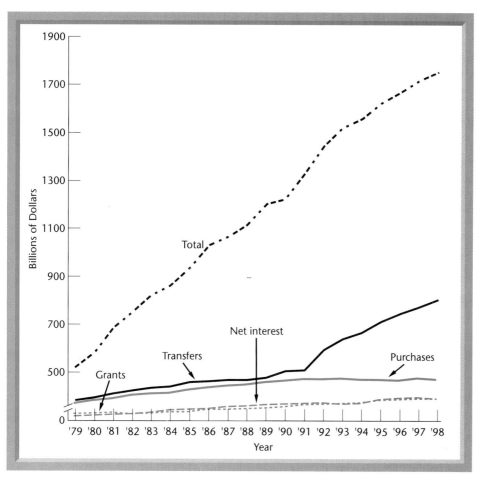

FIGURE 10-1   **Spending by the federal government has grown rapidly in recent years,**
especially spending on transfer payments, interest on the national debt, and grants-in-aid from
the federal to state and local governments. Slightly over half of federal purchases are for
national defense.

Source: 1999 Economic Report of the President, Table B–82.

Taken together, the Social Security tax collects 15.3 percent of payroll income, up to
a maximum individual income of $68,400 in 1998, after which only the 2.9 percent
Medicare hospitalization tax continues to be collected.

Figure 10-3 illustrates the supply and demand for labor in the aggregate. The
sellers are the workers who offer labor; the buyers are the employers. Labor demand
represents the marginal value of additional units of work to the firms. Firms are
unwilling to pay more than this value. Labor supply is shown as a vertical line
because the quantity of labor supplied by primary workers is unresponsive to changes
in the wage rate, as discussed in chapter 8.

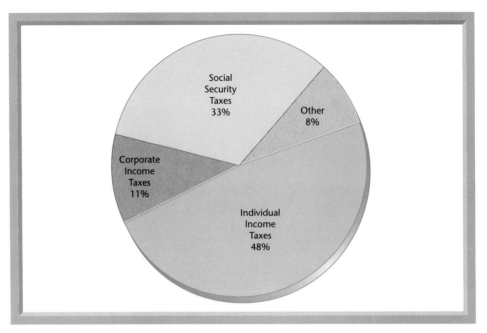

FIGURE 10-2 **Federal Revenue Sources, 1998**
Source: 1999 Economic Report of the President, Table B–80.

The portion of the Social Security tax paid by employers reduces their after-tax demand for labor by the same percentage as the tax, since the value of labor to the firm is reduced by the amount of tax that must be paid for that labor. This reduction is shown in the figure by a downward shift in labor demand, a shift that is just sufficient to cover Social Security taxes. This downward shift is not a constant dollar amount, which would result in a shift that would leave the after-tax demand parallel to the original demand. Rather, it is a constant 7.65 percent of each wage rate, which shifts after-tax demand down more at higher wage rates, and thus causes the after-tax demand to have a lesser slope than the original demand. The effect of requiring firms to pay Social Security taxes for the labor they employ is to reduce the amount they are willing to pay in wages. The portion of the Social Security tax paid by workers effectively reduces workers' take-home pay still more.

As seen in Figure 10-3, requiring the firm to pay Social Security taxes causes the equilibrium wage to be lower by exactly the amount of the tax. In effect, the tax burden has been *shifted* from employers to employees. The result is that workers effectively pay the full 15.3 percent Social Security tax. Many employees are unaware of the true magnitude of the Social Security tax, because only half of the combined 15.3 percent rate appears on their pay stubs.

Social Security tax receipts go into the Social Security trust fund, which provides a buffer between revenue inflows and revenue outflows to Social Security recipients, most of whom are currently retired. The Social Security trust fund contained

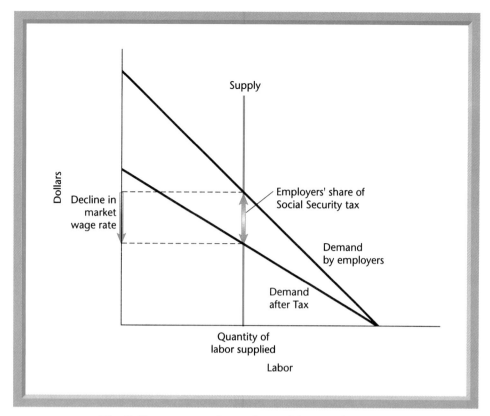

FIGURE 10-3   **The 7.65 percent employer share of the Social Security tax is passed on to workers in the form of lower wages. The employer share of the tax reduces employer after-tax demand for labor by that same 7.65 percent.** To the extent that labor supply is completely inelastic, the market equilibrium wage also falls by 7.65 percent. Workers must then pay another 7.65 percent, which is the part that appears on their pay stubs.

approximately $500 billion as of this writing. However, this amount would only be enough to last less than two years if not supplemented by the Social Security tax. The Social Security trust fund is intended to grow over time to prepare for the increased Social Security outlays expected early in the twenty-first century when the large baby boom generation of the 1950s reaches retirement age. A discussion of the problems afflicting Social Security is found in Exploration 12-1.

The corporation income tax takes approximately 30 percent of corporate profits, and brought in revenues of $188.7 billion in 1998, equaling almost 11 percent of total federal revenues. The corporation income tax has proven to be quite controversial over time because, while it may seem fair to tax corporations as though they are people, the ultimate *incidence*—impact—of the corporation income tax is on the personal incomes of the owners or shareholders of the corporations. Since personal income is taxed by the personal income tax, many economists view the corporate income tax as double taxation of income and wonder what justification it has.

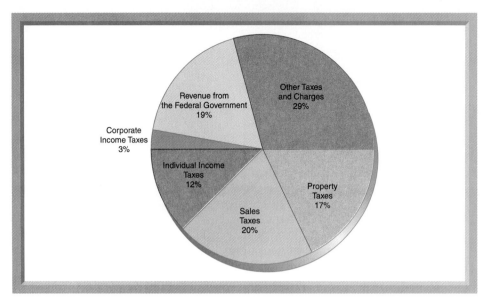

FIGURE 10-4 **Revenue sources for states and localities, 1995–1996.**

Source: 1999 Economic Report of the President, Table B–86.

However, few politicians would dare propose to tax individuals and not tax seemingly wealthy corporations. Thus the corporation income tax lives on.

Figure 10-4 shows state and local revenue sources. Most states rely heavily upon a combination of individual income taxes, sales taxes, revenue from the federal government, and other charges. Major sources of revenue at the local level include property taxes and sales taxes.

Sales taxes collect a percentage of the value of the sale for government. Sales taxes are one form of consumption tax, which takes money as you spend it rather than as you earn it. This tax gives people a greater incentive to save, and may be partly responsible for the higher savings rates in other countries relative to the United States. Most countries of the world, including Canada and countries of Europe and the Far East, rely much more heavily on consumption taxes as a source of public revenues than does the United States.

consumption tax: a tax on spending rather than on income.

Information about taxes in each state is available at **http://kentis. com/siteseeker/ taxusst.html**

States have to be careful not to tax any one source of revenue much more heavily than do other states, or that revenue source will migrate to the less-taxing state. This problem plagued New York State in the 1960s and 1970s, as the poor moved in to receive generous welfare benefits, while many of the wealthy moved away to avoid paying the high income taxes that financed those benefits.

When all the revenues we pay to all units of government are added together, the result is that government collects over one-third of the value of production in the United States. Another way of looking at this is that the average American must work until tax freedom day in early May each year in order to have enough money to pay the government. Beyond that date, the money you earn is yours.

OBSERVATION POINT:
"Don't Tax You, Don't Tax Me—Tax the Fellow Behind that Tree!"

In the abstract, taxes sound great. Higher taxes can eliminate the need for government borrowing and can pay for more of the public services we value. There is only one problem. We want to keep our own money and hence want those taxes to be paid by other people, not by ourselves.

Some localities have found a way to do just that through *tax exporting*, which is getting nonresidents to finance government. For example, speed zones on roads through small towns allow those towns to collect revenue from unsuspecting motorists. The payments on their speeding tickets keep property taxes down. The out-of-towner is never heard from again.

Bigger cities resort to surcharges on hotel and motel bills, since few people will change their travel plans because of a 15 percent tax on their lodging. The tourists and business travelers have probably left town before they know what's hit them. While the travelers grind their teeth and mutter about extortion, the locals can grow their government at a bargain price!

Possibilities for Tax Reform

The most common form of consumption tax in other countries is the value-added tax (VAT). A VAT collects the difference between what companies earn in revenues and what they pay out in previously taxed costs. For example, the wheat farmer would pay a tax on the difference between revenues from the sale of the crop and the costs of fertilizer and other materials used to grow it. Taxing value-added yields the same tax revenues as a retail sales tax, since the price of a final product is nothing more than the sum of the values added.

Government can generally raise revenues more efficiently by broadening the tax base and lowering tax rates. In other words, **it is less disruptive to the workings of the economy to tax as wide a spectrum of income or consumption as possible at a low rate, rather than single out a few things for especially high rates of taxation.** By spreading taxes broadly, people have few ways to escape them and not as much incentive to try; inefficient changes in behavior are kept to a minimum. The Reagan-era income tax cuts put that principle into practice by closing various tax "loopholes" and cutting marginal tax rates to a maximum of 28 percent. However, to generate additional government revenue, those rates were adjusted upward somewhat during the Bush and Clinton administrations.

There are many alternatives to the particular set of taxes chosen in the United States. For example, some have suggested that the United States should adopt a *flat tax*, the topic of Exploration 10-1, in which all income is taxed at the same rate. Others advocate a *consumed-income tax*, in which the value of savings is deducted from income before the tax is applied. The consumed-income tax would remove the bias against saving that is present in a more general income tax, which taxes money when it is earned and also taxes interest on that money when it is saved. The flip side is that, although a consumed-income tax would promote savings, some people view it

value-added tax (VAT): a form of consumption tax that collects the difference between what companies earn in revenues and what they pay out in previously taxed costs.

The Irish tax authorities provide an information sheet discussing how the value-added tax works in Ireland. The location is **http://www. revenue.ie/ vatprint.htm**

tax base: that which is taxed.

A bibliography on the flat tax will be found at **http://www. taxation.org/ taxsite/taxlist. html**

as a tax deduction for the rich and not for the poor, because the ability to save rises sharply with income. That concern leads to the big question: How do we identify taxes that are both efficient and fair?

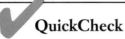

QuickCheck _____

Would it be feasible to eliminate all of the many taxes we pay to different units of government, substituting instead a single, flat-rate tax equal to 16 percent of all consumption or income, without exception?

Answer: No, since governments at all levels currently collect just over one-third of the value of our output, replacing all taxes with a flat-rate tax would call for a rate closer to 34 percent. However, some estimates suggest that a flat-rate income tax of 16 percent would generate about as much revenue as our current multirate personal income tax and could finance most of the federal government.

Income Redistribution—How Much Is Too Much?

> *In general, the art of government consists in taking as much money as possible from one party of the citizens to give to the other.*
>
> —Voltaire

Taxes are intended to do more than collect government revenues efficiently. Taxes also redistribute income from the haves to the have-nots, and are used as a tool of public policy to remedy inequities that arise in a free market economy. Since people's views on equity vary widely, issues of tax equity become a matter of hot debate. Just because equity is difficult to pin down, however, does not mean that equity is not a valid economic objective of taxation and income redistribution.

Monitoring Tax Equity

benefit principle: states that a fair tax is one that taxes people in proportion to the benefits they receive when government spends those tax revenues.

ability-to-pay principle: states that those who can afford to pay more taxes than others should be required to do so.

Information about the food stamp program is provided by the U.S. Department of Agriculture at **http://www.usda. gov/fsp**

There are two primary principles of tax equity, as follows:

- The **benefit principle** states that a fair tax is one that taxes people in proportion to the benefits they receive when government spends those tax revenues.
- The **ability-to-pay principle** states that those who can afford to pay more taxes than others should be required to do so.

The gasoline tax would appear to satisfy the benefit principle of tax equity, because gasoline tax revenues are *earmarked* for highway construction and repair. The more someone drives, the more government-funded highways the person drives on, and the more gasoline tax the person pays. In general, *user fees* are designed to meet the benefit principle of tax equity.

The benefit principle cannot be applied to programs whose purpose is to redistribute income. To see why not, consider food stamps. According to the benefit principle, food stamp recipients should pay for the cost of those food stamps. However, this would have the effect of defeating the fundamental purpose of the food stamp program, which is to help those in need. Food stamps are of no help if you have to pay for them! Thus, to justify redistributional programs, a different principle of tax equity is invoked—the ability-to-pay principle. This principle states that the more a person is able to pay, the more that person should pay.

Many people interpret the ability-to-pay principle to mean that taxes designed for redistributing income should be progressive. A progressive tax collects a higher percentage of high incomes than of low incomes. In contrast, a regressive tax collects a higher percentage of low incomes than of high incomes. A proportional tax collects the same percentage of income, no matter what the income is. The key is percentage. A tax that collects $1,000 from a poor person earning $10,000 and $10,000 dollars from a rich person earning $1 million is regressive, because the poor person pays 10 percent of his or her income, whereas the rich person pays only 1 percent.

Sometimes it is hard to determine whether or not a tax is progressive. For instance, the Social Security tax may be considered either proportional, regressive, or progressive, depending upon which aspects of the system are under scrutiny. Up to $68,400 of payroll income in 1998, the tax is proportional at 15.3 percent. Because the marginal Social Security tax rate beyond that point drops to only 2.9 percent, for Medicare, the average tax rate declines with income and the overall tax is regressive. However, if Social Security benefits are included along with the taxes, the Social Security System as a whole is highly progressive. The reason is that Social Security recipients receive a much higher ratio of benefits to the taxes they paid if their earnings were low during their working years. Social Security thus redistributes income from the wealthy to the poor.

progressive tax: a tax that collects a higher percentage of high incomes than of low incomes.

regressive tax: a tax that collects a lower percentage of high incomes than of low incomes.

proportional tax: a tax that collects the same percentage of high incomes as of low incomes.

OBSERVATION POINT:
Progressive—What's in a Word?

The economist who came up with the terms *progressive* and *regressive* knew which kind of tax he wanted. After all, who could argue against progress? Would you prefer to regress? That would be moving backward, not forward. Bear in mind, though, that there is no magic in the terms.

The ability-to-pay principle of equity says the rich should pay more than the poor to finance government. It does not specify whether the higher taxes should be less than, more than, or exactly in proportion to the higher income. For instance, it would make life simpler if we had one flat-rate income tax, with no exemptions, deductions, exclusions, and so on. Such a tax would be proportional. Would it be fair? That judgment is entirely up to you.

Equity and Efficiency—The Big Trade-off

Economic efficiency involves getting the most valuable output from the inputs available. In effect, efficiency bakes the biggest economic pie. In general, taxes are efficient to the extent that they do not change our behavior. The most efficient tax is one we cannot influence or escape.

To see how taxes cause inefficiency, consider an increase in the income tax. Some workers, especially those who are not heads of households, would cut back their work efforts. Even those who do not cut back would find that getting ahead in the workplace would bring less reward. For this reason, people are less likely to invest their time and money to acquire more human capital. Higher corporate income taxes mean that businesses also don't invest as much, because the corporation income tax cuts down on the return to that investment.

For an efficient tax, we can turn to the *head tax*. In short, if you have a head, you pay the tax! Since head taxes are efficient and require virtually no paperwork, should all of our other taxes be replaced by head taxes? You probably see the problem. While the economic pie would be large, it would be sliced very unfairly. In other words, head taxes would not be equitable.

Not only are tax laws written with an eye toward equity, but government spending is often meant to promote equity directly through provision of a social safety net. This safety net targets the needy with both cash transfers and *in-kind benefits*, which are any benefits other than money. Social Security is far and away the largest cash transfer program, redirecting a significant amount of current earnings to current retirees. The largest in-kind program is Medicaid, which provides health insurance for the impoverished.

A trade-off between efficiency and equity pervades our system of tax and spending programs. Ideally, to provide a broad and generous safety net, government might guarantee good housing, good food, and good health insurance for everyone. The better the guarantees, however, the more the programs will cost and the less will be the incentives to work and invest. There are three reasons for this inefficient reduction in work incentives, as follows:

- There is less need to better yourself to the extent that government guarantees you a comfortable lifestyle. As the saying goes, necessity is the mother of invention.
- If you choose to forge ahead anyway, your greater ability to take care of yourself causes you to lose eligibility for many welfare-type programs. Over some ranges of income, the loss of benefits from Medicaid, AFDC, subsidized housing, food stamps, and other welfare programs more than offsets the value of extra income earned.
- Obtaining the money for safety net programs requires either raising taxes or borrowing, which would require higher taxes in the future. With higher taxes comes less incentive to work and invest.

We could eliminate the second problem if we offer eligibility to everyone, regardless of income. However, that policy would accentuate the third problem.

There is no ready answer to the dilemma of choosing between a generous safety net and incentives for economic productivity. This is an area of seemingly endless political debate and compromise. The fate of the Communist economies in Eastern Europe and the former Soviet Union warns of the dangers of going too far in the direction of the social safety net. We don't want our economy to stagnate. On the other hand, we can afford to provide some economic security for the disadvantaged. Choices of this sort are why policymakers face "the big trade-off" between efficiency and equity in the design of government tax and spending programs. The processes by which they choose are the subject of the next section.

The Public Choice Process

Democracy is the worst form of government . . . except for all the others.

Government policies can correct market failures. For this reason, economists have designed and analyzed numerous techniques to promote the goals of efficiency and equity. However, suggesting policy techniques is not enough. Because government accounts for nearly one-fifth of national output and employment, an understanding of the economy is not complete without an examination of the manner in which government makes its choices. For example, what are the incentives for government to design and implement its policies efficiently? The field of **public choice** examines economic incentives within government, including those that face voters, politicians, and the administrators of government programs.

Incentives within government are often inefficient, because the public sector lacks the guidance of market competition. Correcting market failures through government policy action thus brings up the problem of **government failure**—the inefficiency of government processes. Sometimes government policy action is desirable to remedy market failures. Other times, the cure is worse than the disease. Because there is room for improvement, however, there is no known form of government that can completely do away with inefficiency. Improving incentives within government remains a worthy challenge for us all.

public choice: examines economic incentives within government, including those that face voters, politicians, and the administrators of government programs.

government failure: the inefficiency of government processes.

Why the Discontent?

Survey after survey points to Americans being disenchanted with their government. For example, according to a very large sample survey conducted by the Times Mirror Center, 66 percent of Americans thought that government is almost always wasteful and inefficient. A different 1994 poll found that 68 percent of voters wanted a smaller government, and only 21 percent wanted a bigger one. Still another poll, conducted in mid-1995, found that 76 percent of the respondents rarely or never trust government to do what is right, although by February, 1998, the number trusting government to do the right thing most of the time had risen to 34 percent. In contrast, in 1960, the figure trusting government stood at over 75 percent.* Are there economic reasons for the rise in negative attitudes?

Although more pronounced than in the past, a look back at the last 2 centuries finds that suspicion of government is far from new. Part of the problem is in the nature of government decisions themselves. Because we delegate decisions collectively, none of us gets exactly what we want. Moreover, each candidate represents a *bundled good*, meaning that the voter cannot pick and choose which items on a candidate's agenda to support, and which to oppose—one vote buys all.

The result is a compromise that is not fully satisfying to anyone. In the case of public goods, for example, the quantity that is chosen by public officials must then be consumed by everyone, no matter their personal preferences. However, the culprit is not the public officials, but the nature of the public good itself—public goods are consumed jointly. Where possible, people prefer to make choices for themselves.

---

*Source: Pew Research Center for the People and the Press.

A second source of concern over government action has to do with the *principal-agent problem.* Over 19 million workers in this country are employed by government as public servants. Public servants range from teachers to Marines to, until recently, an official tea taster. No matter the job, they are all *agents* of the public (the *principal*). However, because the public is so large, no individual has direct control. For example, we do not advise informing the traffic officer preparing to give you a ticket that he or she is your servant and should follow your orders. This generalized accountability provides a great deal of leeway on the part of the agents to do as they please.

Although neither of these problems explains directly why antipathy toward government has grown, it might be reasonable to conclude that these concerns increase as government gets progressively larger, as has been the case in most of twentieth-century America. As government grows, choices made at the individual level decline in proportion to choices made collectively. Moreover, as we will see in the next few pages, there is a tendency for government spending to grow more rapidly than is efficient. Historical evidence suggests that the longer a government rules, the more entangling it becomes to a market economy.

Incentives in the Political Process

The size of the populace leads to a dilemma. People want to be involved in their government, but lack the time to do so effectively. Because there are so many voters and so many government policy actions, few voters have much incentive to become fully informed about issues or candidates. Voters delegate decisions to politicians, who in turn delegate to the administrative bureaucracy. The amount of detail involved in governing the country is too overwhelming to do otherwise. Thus citizens maintain what is known as rational ignorance, meaning that voters make the rational choice to remain uninformed on many public choices.

> **rational ignorance:** when voters make the rational choice to remain uninformed on many public issues.

Unfortunately, this **rational ignorance means that politicians and bureaucrats can often safely follow their own personal agendas, even when those agendas conflict with what the public would want them to do.** For example, one item that is high on the personal agendas of most elected officials is to remain in office. Incumbent politicians routinely get reelected, even though *term limitations*—laws that restrict the number of sequential times a politician can hold one public office—are quite popular. How do these politicians do it?

One secret is to engage in logrolling—vote trading—in order to obtain projects of direct benefit to constituents in their districts. Logrolling results in massive spending packages that contain numerous clauses pertaining to local spending projects. These projects (often called *pork*) and other accomplishments are then reported back to constituents through a newsletter. Left out is any focus on cost, however, even though the pork does not come cheaply.

> **logrolling:** when politicians trade votes in order to obtain projects of direct benefit to constituents in their districts.

Remember, to obtain projects for their districts, legislators must vote for all of the other costly items in the legislation, including those of no benefit to their constituents. When voters focus on visible benefits from projects and ignore the less-obvious costs, they are said to suffer from fiscal illusion. Fiscal illusion leads to the Santa/Scrooge syndrome, emphasizing that legislators have incentives to spend more (Santa) and tax less to satisfy miserly voters (Scrooge).

> **fiscal illusion:** when voters focus on visible benefits from projects and ignore the less-obvious costs.

Even when the costs of logrolling are considered, the costs are still likely to be of little concern to the electorate. After all, the costs are in terms of other districts' wasteful projects that are included in an appropriations bill. However, if a majority of other legislators are signing onto the bill, you don't want your district left out. In other words, if you are going to be paying for other districts' pork, you want pork of your own. Thus, constituents rarely hold pork-barrel politics against their own legislators, even though they may disapprove of the practice in general.

There is good reason to disapprove. *Pork-barrel politics* leads to excessive government spending, as the cost of the myriad of relatively small projects gets lost in the general budget. For example, the constituents in most districts would be delighted to accept federally funded projects, such as for highways or drainage. It does not matter whether the project would pass a cost-benefit analysis, because the costs are spread across the country, while the benefits are concentrated in that district. They are grateful to their elected representatives. For voters in other districts, the project is too small to focus on and has no bearing on the reelection of their own representatives. The result is too much government spending.

One check on logrolling can be found in the line-item veto. The *line-item veto* allows a governor to veto parts of appropriations bills, rather than having to accept or reject the bills in their entireties. If the governor were to be a Democrat, for instance, he or she could veto all of the Republicans' pet projects, except projects of Republicans who support the governor's agenda. In turn, because Republicans would know their projects would not survive, they would not go along with voting for the Democrats' pet projects. The result would be much less pork. The governors of 43 states have some form of line-item veto authority. Although Congress voted in 1996 to grant the president line-item veto power, the Supreme Court subsequently ruled it unconstitutional.

Not all vote trading is inefficient. For example, a worthy project might serve only a portion of the country. Consider levees along a river that benefit the residents of only a few states. Without vote trading, the project would not pass through Congress, since a majority of states would perceive no benefits. Such projects could still be undertaken, however, if the affected states join forces and proceed on their own. Payment for the project would then come from the residents of those states instead of from general tax revenues.

 **QuickCheck** _____

Does the line-item veto authority of the president stop logrolling in the federal government?

Answer: Logrolling is reduced but not eliminated. For example, friends of the president would not have their pet projects vetoed. However, the president's friends would have a more difficult time lining up support for those projects in Congress, especially if the president routinely vetoes the pet projects of other legislators.

OBSERVATION POINT:
The Secret to Political Success

A funny thing happens on the road to public office. In U.S. presidential campaigns, for example, Democratic and Republican candidates for president often sound much farther apart on the issues in the primaries than they do when it comes time for the general election. Have they heard each other's arguments and adjusted their opinions accordingly? Don't bet on it.

Rather, the candidates are seeking the decisive *median voter*, the swing voter that can tilt the balance from one candidate to the other. This median voter will be quite different in the general election than the median voter in either the Democratic or Republican primaries. The *median voter model* thus predicts that successful politicians will seek to always follow that median to wherever it moves.

Politicians ignore the median voter model at their peril. In the presidential elections of 1972, for example, George McGovern lost to Richard Nixon by one of the largest margins of all time, winning the electoral votes of only Massachusetts. Sticking to his principles, McGovern's message in the presidential election was nearly identical to the message that won him the Democratic primary. However, the median Democrat in 1972 was significantly to the left of the median voter in the general population. Because McGovern held firm, Nixon was reelected in a landslide.

Interest Groups—Minority Rule?

The United States prides itself on its majority rule. Yet legislation is often influenced by small, well-organized minorities, aligned according to special interests. *Special-interest groups* are characterized by a tightly focused agenda and *lobbyists*—agents who promote that agenda within the political system.

The agendas of the special interests often conflict with the interests of most voters. Special interests are frequently able to get their way, however, by paying close attention to the details of legislators' votes. Legislators who vote against special interests know they lose their votes and campaign contributions. However, legislators who favor the special interests and vote against the wishes of the majority often face no adverse consequences. The reason is that general interest is often more diffuse, with few voters keying their votes around specific issues. In short, **when the benefits of an action are spread broadly and the costs are concentrated, special interests are frequently successful at preventing the action from occurring.**

For example, few people would vote against a legislator because he or she supports sugar import quotas, despite the consequent higher prices for sweeteners, which raises a broad array of food and beverage prices facing the average consumer. However, a legislator who votes to repeal sugar import quotas definitely loses the support of sugar growers, corn sweetener manufacturers, and other allied agricultural interests. While the number of voters who gain from sugar import quotas is minuscule relative to those who lose, the power of the gainers is magnified because they key their votes around this one special interest issue.

You can visit the American Petroleum Institute in cyberspace at **http://www. api/org**

Lobbying by special-interest groups is sometimes efficient in that it provides information that prevents legislative errors. When legislation targets the actions of a particular industry, for example, that industry's lobbyists are in the best position to provide relevant information on the industry's business practices. For example, Congressional staffers attempting to fashion sensible pipeline regulations might obtain information on oil and gas pipeline operations from the American Petroleum Institute, which lobbies for the oil industry. Other interested lobbyists would also submit information. Congressional staffers use this information to design policies that are cost-effective, an advantage to both the oil industry and the economy.

Unfortunately, special interest lobbying is frequently inefficient, because it involves wasteful rent seeking. **Rent seeking** occurs when lobbyists or others expend resources in an effort to come out a winner in the political process. Since economic efficiency looks at the size of the economic pie, not how it is sliced, the time and money lobbyists spend trying to get the pie sliced to their liking is inefficient.

Some observers contend that an emerging trend in Congress reduces the problems of special-interest lobbying and the rent seeking that comes with it. This trend is toward replacing federal programs with *block grants* to states, where the block grants represent sums of money designated to go toward a range of state-administered programs. For example, Congress designates a single block grant to finance many of the welfare programs administered in a state. By leaving the details up to the states, block grants mean that Congress need merely decide on the number of dollars to include in the grant, something that voters will monitor relatively closely. Lobbyists must then compete with each other, state by state, over the allocation of that money.

rent seeking: occurs when lobbyists or others expend resources in an effort to come out a winner in the political process.

OBSERVATION POINT:
Rent Seeking—A National Pastime

There is a big difference between competition in the marketplace and competition for favors from government. In the marketplace, the winner is the one that builds the better mousetrap and thereby increases the well-being of others. Lobbying for political favors is not productive in this way. It is more akin to fighting over a prize. The time and money wasted in fighting over who gets the prize is a form of rent seeking and serves little constructive purpose from the point of view of society at large. The value of government policies is often counteracted by the money that interest groups spend in trying to come out among the winners.

Most of us engage in rent seeking, too. You have done so yourself if you have ever returned a sweepstakes entry, such as in the Publishers Clearing House or American Family Publishers multimillion dollar sweepstakes. At the time, you probably wondered if it was worth the time and postage to apply, because you knew that millions of other people would be sending in their entries. That illustrates the problem of rent seeking—the value of the prize is offset by the cost of seeking it, which is the millions of dollars worth of time and postage spent by all the entrants.

Incentives in Agencies

Administrative agencies face the task of translating general and often vague legislation into detailed programs that are actually implemented. Employees of the many agencies of government are commonly referred to as government *bureaucrats*. The term is not to their liking, however, since it calls up images of stodginess, red tape, and delays associated with bureaucracy. Are the employees of the government agencies unresponsive to the citizens they are supposed to serve?

The employees of government agencies have personal agendas that sometimes conflict with the intent of voters and their elected representatives. Most significantly, for both public-spirited and self-serving reasons, bureaucrats almost always desire budgets for their agencies that exceed what the average citizen and elected official would prefer.

To understand this phenomenon, consider who enters any particular government agency. For example, who joins the armed forces? Most likely, it's people of a military persuasion, who are convinced that the armed forces are more important than most people realize. Likewise, those who join the Environmental Protection Agency have keener interests and greater expertise in environmental matters than do most of the rest of us. They naturally tend to think that environmental protection deserves a higher priority than it gets.

More broadly, who enters government at all? For the most part, it's people who think government is relatively more important than most citizens realize. Thus, employees of government in general and agencies in particular truly believe that their missions are more deserving than the political process acknowledges. For these public-spirited motives, they seek to expand the size of their agencies beyond what is efficient.

There are also self-serving reasons why government employees want larger budgets for their agencies. From the top of the agency to the bottom, a larger budget is seen as good job protection. It opens up promotion opportunities and reduces the threat of layoffs. As a manager, the more budget under you, the more power and prestige you enjoy, and the better your qualifications look should you wish to switch jobs later. Indeed, it is usually considered disloyal for any agency personnel to advocate cutting the agency's budget.

Figure 10-5 shows the marginal net benefit of increasing an agency's budget, where *marginal net benefit* equals marginal social benefit minus marginal social cost. At first, if the agency directs its spending toward its most essential missions, the value of agency spending far exceeds its budgetary cost. As the budget size is increased, however, the agency must fund programs of increasingly less merit. When the value of extra spending is less than the cost of that spending, the agency has spent too much.

To achieve economic efficiency, the agency budget should equal B^* in Figure 10-5, the amount for which marginal net benefit is zero. The total net benefit generated by this spending is given by the triangular area labeled Gain. If the agency spends beyond B^*, total net benefit would decrease. For example, if spending were to equal $B_{too\ much}$, the area labeled Loss would need to be subtracted from this gain.

Turf-Building—Strategies for a Bigger Budget

It is one thing for bureaucrats to want an inefficiently large budget—to expand their turf. Getting that budget is another matter. Unfortunately, the struggle over the size of agency budgets is rather one-sided, because the agency is best positioned to know what its spending options are. If an agency is aware of ways to save money, for exam-

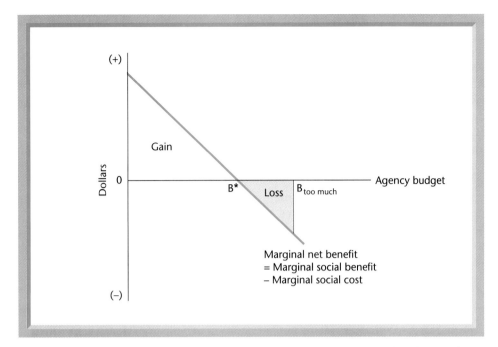

FIGURE 10-5 **Government agencies have the incentive to seek a budget higher than would be efficient.** B* denotes an efficient budget. If the actual budget is B$_{too\ much}$, some of the gain from the agency's existence is offset by a loss from overspending. Gains and losses are shown.

ple, it has little incentive to reveal them. Such *asymmetric information*, in which one party to a transaction knows more than the other, put legislators at a disadvantage in overseeing agencies.

There are various strategies by which government agencies have been known to obtain the budgets they want. For example, agency spending is commonly guided by "use it or lose it." Agencies want to avoid getting caught with extra cash at the end of the fiscal year when the budget expires. Extra cash might indicate to the legislators or public that the agency could accomplish its mission with a smaller budget next time. The response to use-it-or-lose-it incentives is a spending spree near the end of each fiscal year. If you are an agency employee with a pet project, it's a great time to get it funded.

When agencies submit their budgets for review, they are often told to provide a bare-bones alternative budget, perhaps representing a 20 percent reduction from the budget they claim to need. The idea is to give the legislative oversight committee an idea of what services would be sacrificed if the budget were to be reduced. If you are in charge of a government agency and are told to do this, could you manipulate the process to obtain a large budget? Remember, you know more about possibilities for reducing costs in your agency than do the legislators. Would you economize on travel, or on the number of times the trash is collected?

To preserve your budget, you would be better served by suggesting that something more visible and less acceptable be cut. The strategy of selecting widely

Washington Monument strategy: when a government agency offers a bare-bones budget that cuts its most popular functions; intended to increase the chances that a more generous budget will be approved.

The Washington Monument homepage is located at **http://www.nps.gov/wamo/index2.htm**

supported projects for potential cuts has been used so often, it's acquired its own name—the Washington Monument strategy. Using this strategy, the agency offers a bare-bones budget that cuts its most popular functions. For instance, the Park Service might propose to save money by restricting access to the Washington Monument to between 9 A.M. and 5 P.M. on weekdays, with no access at all on weekends. Evenings and weekends are cut because they are the times of peak tourist demand.

The Washington Monument strategy is used at all levels of government, but not always successfully. In 1992, for example, a school district in a major city claimed that it would be forced to eliminate all school crossing guards unless voters approved a tax increase. Surely the school board did not believe that children's lives deserved the lowest priority. This example of the Washington Monument strategy backfired, though, as voters rejected the tax increase. To safeguard the children's lives, a private individual donated the money needed to pay for crossing guards. In following years, the school district quietly appropriated the money needed to fund this essential service.

Addressing Government Failures

Is there anything citizens can do to counter all the incentives within government to spend too much? The options are limited. For example, limiting the number of years legislators can serve might keep representatives more in touch with the voters. However, such term limits deprive government of experienced legislators, and also run the danger of focusing legislators' attentions on personal profit opportunities once they leave office.

A balanced budget amendment to the U.S. constitution has been proposed as a means to restrict excessive spending. The problem is that government itself defines what is counted in the budget. For example, when government sought to accomplish the social goal of providing access for the handicapped, it passed the Americans with Disabilities Act. This act represents billions of dollars in government-mandated spending, paid for by business. It is a large tax and spending program, but never shows up as such in the budget. Were there to be a balanced budget amendment, we could expect an upsurge in such unfunded mandates and other types of off-budget spending.

There is no easy way to provide the proper incentives for efficiency within government. That should come as little surprise. After all, if command and control worked well, there would be little reason to adopt competitive free markets. We resort to government when markets fail. Unfortunately, market failure does not imply government success.

unfunded mandates: occur when government requires the attainment of public policy goals by firms or lower units of government, without providing the funding necessary to carry out those actions needed to achieve those goals; access for the disabled is an example.

OBSERVATION POINT:
Primer for a Bigger Government—How to Hide a Tax

Favorite Recipe: Unfunded Mandates

Unfunded mandates occur when government requires the implementation of public policy actions, without providing the funding necessary to carry out those actions. For example, local telephone customers normally wind up paying a surcharge to fund federally mandated telephone services for the hearing impaired. That cost stays off the federal budget.

Private businesses are favorite targets of unfunded mandates, including family leave requirements for employees, handicapped-accessibility requirements for customers, and many more. While mandated public services have value, it is hard to know whether the benefits are worth the costs. The costs are effectively hidden in the higher costs to firms and higher prices to their customers.

SUMMARY

- Two goals for taxes are equity and efficiency. Tax equity is about fairness. Tax efficiency concerns maintaining incentives to be productive.
- Taxes take about one-third of GDP. The personal income tax raises the largest share of the federal government's revenue.
- The Social Security tax is the second largest source of federal revenue. Although both employees and employers contribute toward Social Security taxes, the burden of employers' contributions is shifted to workers in the form of lower pay.
- State and local governments rely upon individual income taxes, sales taxes, property taxes, and revenue from the federal government to finance their operations.
- A value-added tax (VAT), common in other countries, is based upon the difference between producers' revenues and their costs. A VAT would collect the same amount in taxes as a sales tax since the price of a product is equal to the sum of the values added at each step in the production process. A flat tax and a consumed-income tax are examples of other alternative types of taxes.
- Whatever taxes are imposed, a broader tax base, associated with eliminating tax "loopholes," combined with lower tax rates can reduce the incentive to try to avoid paying taxes.
- The two principles of tax equity are the benefit principle and the ability-to-pay principle. The benefit principle provides the justification for earmarked taxes, such as the gasoline tax. The ability-to-pay principle states that those with the largest incomes should pay more in taxes.
- A tax may be progressive, regressive, or proportional. A progressive tax collects a larger fraction of income as income increases, while a regressive tax collects a smaller fraction of income as income increases. A proportional tax collects the same fraction of income as income changes.
- In pursuing the twin goals of equity and efficiency in the tax system, there are tradeoffs. More equity can mean less efficiency, and vice-versa. In the pursuit of equity, the social safety net provides cash and in-kind benefits.
- Government failure refers to inefficiencies in government itself. The principle-agent problem, rational ignorance, logrolling, and fiscal illusion all contribute to government failure. Pork-barrel politics leads to excessive government spending.
- The line-item veto, available to 43 state governors, allows a governor to veto parts of appropriation bills.

- Government spending is influenced by special-interest groups and their lobbyists. Much lobbying involves wasteful rent seeking. Government agencies employ various strategies to obtain funds. One is the "use it or lose it" strategy. Another is the Washington Monument strategy.

QUESTIONS AND PROBLEMS

1. Using a graph and labeling the axes, curves, and all relevant information, demonstrate how employees wind up paying the employer portion of Social Security taxes.

2. Why it is difficult to design aid to the poor that provides work incentives? Explain with reference to cost and the level of the safety net.

3. We allow people to buy and sell most of what they own, so should we also allow voters to buy and sell their votes? Alternatively, since most potential voters do not vote, should we eliminate voting and replace it with surveys that measure public opinions? Explain.

4. Many governments have term limits to prevent so-called empire building by holders of public office. For example, the president of the United States can serve only two four-year terms. Is this a good idea? Should the idea be extended to other levels of government? What problems are likely to arise?

5. Explain how logrolling can lead to excessive government spending. Would eliminating logrolling cause too little spending?

6. Most people want taxes to be fair. Yet there are strong disagreements over what constitutes tax equity. Using an example and the concepts of equity discussed in this chapter, explain why such disagreement can reasonably persist.

7. Explain why the corporation income tax is often called a form of double taxation. If it is double taxation, why does the political process not abolish it?

8. If you are in charge of rebuilding roads, why might your personal self-interest suggest that you not devote your budget to fixing the worst portions of roads first? If you leave obvious examples of roads in need of repair, what strategy are you following? Is there a danger to this strategy? Explain.

Web Exercises

9. a. Using an Internet search engine such as that provided by Yahoo (located at **http://www.yahoo.com**) or Alta Vista (located at **http://www.altavista. com**), perform a separate search for the following terms: **transfer payments**, **value-added tax**, and **progressive tax**. Visit several of the Web sites that your search reveals for each term and observe the context in which each term is used. Explain whether the manner in which the terms are used is consistent with their use in the text.

b. Repeat the above, but this time use a combination of terms that you select from the chapter. To eliminate Web sites that do not contain all terms, place a plus sign in front of each term you enter, such as +**"public choice"** +**"rent seeking"**.

10. Visit the Web site maintained by the Internal Revenue Service (IRS) at **http://www.irs.ustreas.gov/**. Seek out information about the U.S. tax code. Summarize what you find by writing a series of 10–15 bullet points that would describe key elements of the system of federal taxes to someone who had recently immigrated to the U.S. and had no understanding of U.S. taxes.

Visit the Web site for *Economics by Design* at
http://www.prenhall.com/collinge for a Self Quiz over
the topics in this chapter.

EXPLORING ISSUES

Exploration 10-1 The Tax Man Cometh . . . With a Postcard?

The income tax is complicated by many exemptions, deductions, and other so-called loopholes that lower tax revenues, but often have economic justifications. Replacing the complex tax code with a simple flat-rate tax also has a basis in economics, but would limit government's ability to accomplish social aims.

> ### The Simple Tax
>
> How much money did you make? $____.__
>
> Send it in.

"Too complicated!" We hear that complaint every spring, as Americans once more delve into their financial records to prepare their tax returns. Why is it necessary to compute all the exemptions, deductions, exclusions, alternative minimum taxes, and so forth? Is it just a jobs program for tax accountants, tax lawyers, and Internal Revenue Service agents, or just breaks for special interests wanting to escape paying their fair share? Yes, many people long for a flat and simple tax. Such a tax would have a single rate, applicable to all income. Tax returns could be filled out on a postcard, although not quite the one represented above.

The flat tax has appeal for its simplicity, but there are other considerations that are argued to justify a more complicated system of taxation. These can be seen by asking the most basic question of all: What is the goal of an income tax? The goal is for government to raise revenues for its many programs and to do so in the most equitable and efficient manner possible.

A tax is efficient only if it does not *distort* relative prices within the economy, since price signals are what allocate resources to their highest-valued uses. By taxing all income equally, distortions are minimized. Efficiency thus calls for a *broadly based* tax, meaning one that it is difficult to escape. Much of the complexity of the current income tax code stems from innumerable provisions that remove income from taxation, thus narrowing the tax base.

The ability-to-pay principle of equity suggests that some income should be taxed more than other income, depending on how needy the person is. Exempting low incomes concentrates the tax base and leads to inefficiencies. Thus, the personal income tax is a compromise between efficiency and equity. Unfortunately, the compromise accomplishes neither goal fully and is also complicated.

Taxing Personal Income, with Lots of Exceptions

The concept of income is not altogether easy to pin down, since income is more than money. For example, if you drill a water well in your backyard and inadvertently strike oil, your wealth spikes upward. That change in wealth is income, even if you do not sell any of that newly discovered oil until next year or beyond. A *comprehensive measure of income* would subtract a person's wealth at the beginning of the year from wealth at the end of the year, and then add back in the person's consumption during the course of that year. Consumption is added because it represents income that is spent.

Government does not use this comprehensive measure of income in computing the amount of personal income taxes to collect. It would be too complicated and intrusive for government to attempt assessing how valuable each person's assets are at the end of each year. After all, assets include homes, cars, stocks, stamp collections, and much more. Moreover, even if the government could assess these values, there is the problem of *liquidity*—of converting assets into cash. Liquidity is necessary to pay taxes. The federal government does not want to be responsible for kicking Grandma out of her house, just because property values around her have increased and she does not have the liquidity to pay the taxes on her rising comprehensive income.

The result is that the tax code looks at only a subset of comprehensive income, that which is liquid. If people sell their illiquid assets, they obtain liquidity and are subject to taxation on their *realized capital gains*, the increase in the value of assets between when they were bought and when they were sold. Even here, however, there are exceptions. For example, Grandma would fall under an exemption for the elderly, were she to sell her house. Throughout the tax code, there is special treatment for special-interest groups. Yes, Grandma has a special-interest loophole.

So-called *loopholes* include the various exemptions, deductions, exclusions, and credits that complicate the tax code. Despite their notoriety, there are often economic principles behind these *tax expenditures*, so termed because they sacrifice tax dollars. The basis of tax expenditures often revolves around equity.

For example, the concepts of vertical equity and horizontal equity are two ways to judge whether a tax meets the ability-to-pay principle. *Vertical equity* is hard to pin down, because it concerns the proper tax burden for people of differing abilities to pay. *Horizontal equity*, which suggests that people with equal means should pay equal taxes, is more straightforward. Yet, even ignoring differences in wealth, equal monetary incomes do not necessarily imply an equal ability to pay. Differences in the ability to pay explain why there are tax exemptions for children, major medical expenses, and other facets of life that hit some people harder than others.

The search for equity complicates the tax code and makes it less efficient. This inefficiency hurts us all by reducing our standard of living. Thus, in trying to allocate the tax burden fairly, government winds up increasing it for the average citizen. These efforts to be fair cause price distortions within the economy and waste our labor resources because of the paperwork, accountants, and tax lawyers associated with a tax code that often seems like an imponderable, murky morass to the average citizen. Is it worth it? Has government even accomplished its fairness goals?

The Flat Tax Sounds Appealing

Some people argue that a truly flat tax is not only efficient, but also quite fair. A tax that is truly flat would apply the same tax rate to everyone. As your income rises, you would still pay more taxes. However, as a percentage of income, each person would pay equally. Thus, if the tax rate is 15 percent and your income is $16,000, you would owe $2,400 in taxes. If your income is $160,000, you would owe $24,000 in taxes. A flat tax designed in this way is entirely proportional.

There is still the question of what constitutes income. Proponents of the flat tax often favor exempting income from savings and investment, since such income is generated by other income that has already been taxed. Such an exemption would be efficient, since it avoids penalizing income that is directed to savings and investment relative to that which is directed to consumption.

The biggest appeal of the flat tax is that it is transparent and easy to comply with. *Transparency* means that its operation is easily monitored. We know the rules, and those same rules apply to everyone. Thus we need not worry about clever tax dodges that we suspect others use to avoid paying their fair share of taxes. Moreover, we need not concern ourselves with keeping records and adjusting our behavior in ways that will minimize our own tax burdens. With the flat tax, we pay it when it comes due and ignore it for the rest of the year. That is appealing!

How Flat Is Flat?

In practice, flat tax proposals are not as simple as "Report your earned income, and send in 15 percent." Flat tax proposals usually include some exemptions and deductions. Most prominently, these proposals are made to be progressive by exempting the first many thousands of dollars from taxes altogether. For example, under some proposals, the first $16,000 of income would be exempted. By exempting some income from taxation, the tax rate must be higher because the tax base is smaller. While proposals for flat taxes differ in the amount of income they exclude, some would require rates over 20 percent to bring in as much revenue as the current personal income tax.

There are two reasons that some income is exempted from taxation. One reason concerns equity. For example, since low-income citizens are more needy, many people view it as unfair to take any of their money through taxation. The other reason is politics. Because changing the tax code results in both gainers and losers, care must be taken that more people gain than lose, or the change is not likely to happen. For these reasons, flat tax proposals typically exempt some income and certain popular deductions, such as the deduction for home mortgage interest payments. While there is no obvious economic reason for the tax code to favor homeowners over renters, the idea is to gain the support of special interests that pay attention—in this case, the homeowners.

Low-income citizens comprise another large group of potential voters. Since these people do not provide much tax revenue anyway, why not just promise them a zero tax burden? Exempting income at the low end of the scale has the potential to buy a great deal of public support at a relatively low cost. Of course, the higher up the income ladder those exemptions go, the higher the cost will be.

Not everyone supports the idea of exempting income. Even without exemptions, taking the same percentage of income from the rich and poor alike means that wealthier citizens pay a much higher price for government than is paid by the poor. Moreover, the poor receive benefits from redistributional programs, which are not offered to the more well-to-do. If the poor receive a totally free ride, will they still be responsible citizens? It would be rational for them to support inefficient and excessive government spending, since the costs are borne by others.

There is also a concern over what might be termed psychological issues. If low-income households pay no taxes whatsoever and are on the receiving end of government programs paid for by others, how will they view themselves and their country? Paying taxes denotes participation, being a part of the process.

In contrast, those who receive benefits without paying a dime in taxes may rationalize this situation by viewing themselves as disadvantaged victims of an unfair economy. That way, they can feel good about receiving back from society some part of what was rightfully theirs all along. After all, the powerful people who craft the tax code seem to be saying that those with more money owe amends to the poor, who owe nothing. The message is that the poor are victims and are not responsible for their plight. This message is probably true for some of the poor, but certainly not for all. We might prefer to avoid ensconcing that message in the tax code.

Should the Tax System Be the Tool of Government Policy?

Taxes are the price we pay for living in our country. Government needs the money, so it seems fair to pay. However, because government has a monopoly on the power to tax, it can practice price discrimination. In other words, it can charge some people more than others, irrespective of how much government service they consume. Government can price discriminate on the basis of its citizens' characteristics, such as income or family size, although not by race, color, or creed. Government makes use of this power to vary the prices it charges, just as the theater owner charges higher prices for adults than for children.

A truly flat tax without exclusions takes away from government much of its power to price discriminate. Its hands are tied. Would this loss of a government policy instrument be the country's loss as well? Perhaps the answer comes down to this: When the government adjusts the tax code to right social injustices, does it do a good job? Do the benefits outweigh the costs? If so, the current tax system is justified. If not, perhaps we should order up a flat tax and direct our attention to other matters.

■ Prospecting for New Insights

1. On balance, do you think it is a good idea to adopt a flat tax? If such a tax is adopted, how much income should be exempted? Explain your reasoning.

2. Income taxes provide government with information about your earnings. Information from tax returns has been used to convict bootleggers, narcotics smugglers, and others with large unreported incomes of tax law violations, even when government could not prove that their income was obtained illegally. Some supporters of tax reform would prefer to abandon the income tax altogether and replace it with a value-added tax or other tax that leaves no paperwork trail and keeps individuals' affairs out of the eyes of government. Do you think the information contained in income tax returns should be used by government in prosecuting crime? Should we fear that government will go overboard and misuse tax information to infringe upon civil liberties? Explain.

Exploration 10-2 Drinking Water— Stirring Together Markets and Government

Inclining block rates characterize the provision of municipal water supplies, even though this price structure is inefficient. Unfortunately, public officials are often motivated to prefer inefficient pricing over efficient alternatives, even when those alternatives appear to satisfy goals of equity.

The issue of drinking water is coming ever more to the forefront as populations grow while rainfall does not. Likewise, as we become more aware of the value of free-flowing streams and natural ecosystems, we are less willing to build new dams and reservoirs. For these reasons, municipal water supplies are likely to become increasingly scarce. In an efficiently functioning market, prices would rise to keep supply and demand in balance. Prices would also adjust to provide water of optimal quality, another issue in many areas.

Monopoly Brings in Government

Municipal water markets lack effective competition. Rather, they are characterized by monopoly, which means that customers buy from the one supplier or do without. The market for municipal drinking water is a natural monopoly, in that it occurs without any action of government. The reason arises from the very high cost of installing water lines relative to the cost of the water passing through those lines. The result is usually only one set of water lines into each house or apartment complex.

Suppose that water utilities are to be owned or regulated by government. What price or prices should water sell for? If government follows the lead of the competitive marketplace, it would set a single price that is just high enough to avoid either a surplus or shortage of water. In times or places when water is particularly scarce, however, the market-clearing price could be quite high. Would that be fair? After all, water is one of our most basic necessities of life.

When regulating or setting water rates, politicians respond to voters. Few voters are likely to look favorably on water rates that take in revenue beyond what is needed to cover water's production costs. That suggests some form of *average-cost pricing*. In contrast, the economically efficient market-clearing price of water is based on marginal-cost pricing, given by the intersection of marginal cost with demand. That marginal cost could exceed average cost by quite a bit if the most cost-effective

marginal-cost pricing: an efficient price, determined by the intersection of marginal cost and demand; achieved in a perfectly competitive market; an efficient regulatory objective under conditions of market failure.

water projects are already in place. The newest sources of municipal water are likely to be much more expensive than long-established sources, leading to a low average cost and a high marginal cost.

Political Action: Inclining Block Rates Look Fair

Pricing municipal water creates a political dilemma that policymakers often fail to address in an economic manner. For instance, the most common political solution is to offer *inclining block rates*, which present water customers with ever-higher water rates as their usage goes up. Inclining block rates give the appearance of fairness according to the ability-to-pay principle, since this rate structure punishes high-volume users by increasing their marginal rates, which causes their water bills to go up more than in proportion to their increases in water usage. The problem with inclining block rates is that such rates neither clear the market nor ensure that water goes where it is valued the most.

An inclining block rate structure often proves divisive and ineffective when water scarcity becomes severe. For instance, when Santa Barbara faced a drought a few years ago, the city-owned utility kept adjusting its inclining rate structure until there was a nearly thirtyfold difference between the marginal rates facing high- and low-volume water users—marginal water rates ranged from just about $1 to over $29 per 100 cubic feet. The result was that high-volume users did indeed cut back dramatically to avoid those rates. The problem is that the large majority of customers, those consuming under 500 cubic feet per month, saw no change in their rates and thus did not conserve.

By abandoning the price signal for most residents, Santa Barbara was forced to resort to the command-and-control alternative of telling their residents when and how they would be allowed to use water. Many conservation possibilities could not be brought about in this manner. For instance, it would not be feasible to monitor whether washing machines and dishwashers are full when they are run. Nor would it be feasible to monitor whether toilets are flushed too often or showers taken for too long. Indeed, even though Santa Barbara distributed low-flow showerheads free of charge, they could not monitor the shower to make sure that people truly sacrificed their higher-quality showerheads for the low-flow models. Nor could they monitor how long people stayed in the shower, even with low-flow showerheads.

While many conservation practices could not be mandated, those that were proved quite irritating. The result is that Santa Barbara wound up pouring massive amounts of money into a desalinization plant and other supplemental water sources. Santa Barbara could have saved at least some of that money and much of the irritation if it had chosen a more economical course of action.

Cities facing heightened water scarcity need not choose between onerous expenses for new water supplies or the wrath of the water police. There is a third alternative, one that employs economic incentives to achieve efficient usage of the water that is available. Only when cities are not wasting the water they already have should they shop for new water sources.

Market-Based Alternatives: Big Brother Go Home!

The economic solution is to forgo political prices in favor of market prices, and accomplish equity goals separately. The invisible hand of the free market relies upon a single price to ensure that neither surpluses nor shortages occur and that goods go where they are worth the most. A single market price is unlike inclining block rate water prices, which differ from person to person for purely political reasons. Rather, a genuine market price would present each person with the same marginal cost of using water, equal to that price. We all pay the same price per gallon at gasoline stations—why not per gallon of tap water?

Water utilities can avoid collecting revenues in excess of costs and still maintain an efficient water market. To do so, however, there must be supplemental action. That action could take any of several forms. For example, water utilities could charge an efficient market-clearing price, and then rebate extra revenues to water customers. The rebate must not be tied directly to water usage, since to do so would lower the effective price of water and lead to excessive consumption. Instead, rebates could be based upon which category a customer falls under, such as small-lot residential, two-bedroom apartment, apartment complex, and so on.

Another path is to adopt a trick of the retail trade—coupons. Price discount coupons provide an option to cut down on revenues without affecting market efficiency. Those coupons would offer customers low rates when the coupons are proffered along with payment of their water bills. To ensure efficiency, the coupons must be marketable. This marketability would allow customers to sell the coupons for the market price of the coupon. In this way, coupons would go to those who value the coupons most highly, who would be the same people as those who value water most highly. Corner stores would probably serve as *market makers* for a small margin between the price at which they would buy and sell coupons (the *bid/ask* price), much like currency traders along the U.S. borders.

A third option would employ "feebates" to avoid the transaction costs associated with keeping track of coupons. *Feebates* represent a combination of penalty fees on heavy users, which pay for rebates to light users. Under this option, each user is given a baseline usage amount, above which is assessed a per unit penalty fee or below which is rebated a per unit conservation reward. Baselines would add up to the municipality's water supply. The penalty and rebate rates are to be set equal to each other and adjusted up or down as necessary until the market clears. In this way, water rates could be set to cover average cost only and still achieve an efficient market allocation because each user would face the same opportunity cost of water use.

Implementing any of these options would generate political dickering over the assignment of property rights to entitlements of rebates, feebates, or coupons. The debate would be over defining appropriate usage categories, since defining categories affects the distribution of rebates, feebates, or coupons. However, categories need be established only once. The rebates, feebates, or coupons would continue month after month for as long as desired.

Using any of the market pricing plans would have significant advantages relative to adjusting the prices themselves to achieve equity. For instance, we would not need any heavy-handed government restrictions on how we use our water—no water police. New industry would find no restrictions on its water usage, just the price incentive to conserve. The value of supplementing water supplies would also be revealed.

The Political Barrier to Good Economic Policy

Why then do not more municipalities adopt market-based pricing plans? The answer involves the principal-agent problem, in which public servants (agents) have objectives that differ from those of the public they serve (principals). The public in this case consists of municipal water customers. Few of these customers wish to become experts on water rate possibilities. Instead, they would prefer to leave those things to people they perceive as experts. Unfortunately, they often assume the experts are those with hands-on experience.

Those with hands-on experience at publicly owned or regulated water utilities have little incentive to adopt new, more efficient ways. What's in it for them? Government employees are notorious for being risk averse. After all, if things go wrong, their jobs can be at stake. If things go well, in contrast, they might generate the resentment of other agency employees afraid of upsetting the apple cart. Moreover, public agencies rarely reward public employees for saving the public money, particularly if the savings lead to budget cuts.

The result is little incentive to avoid rate structures that lead to inefficiencies and wasteful new water projects. After all, the less effective is the rate structure at promoting conservation, the more will be spent on other approaches. Is it any wonder, then, that entrenched "experts" commonly reject innovative ideas? This close-mindedness is usually excused on the basis of a myriad of purportedly practical details left unaddressed in alternative proposals. Of course, the other choice would be for the experts to use their practical knowledge to resolve the details themselves.

Rather than adopt a cost-saving rate structure, the water utility is motivated to prefer expensive supplemental water projects or conservation programs. Conservation programs tend to be police- and hardware-oriented, such as programs to provide low-flow showerheads and toilets to public housing projects and other politically chosen recipients.

Separate conservation programs would be unnecessary with an efficient rate structure. Conversely, without efficient incentives to conserve water itself, recipients of low-flow showerheads will most likely remove or drill out the flow restricter to obtain a better feeling shower. After all, why not? Likewise, water-miser toilets will hardly save water if recipients flush them repeatedly for more effective cleaning. Again, where's the incentive not to?

The problem is ultimately one of incentives. We want to provide incentives for water customers to use water efficiently. Unfortunately, the incentives of publicly owned or regulated water utilities are at odds with this principle. The more crisis there is in water allocation, the higher is the profile of the water utility. With a higher profile comes more in the way of size, stature, budget, and job security—all in the self-interest of employees and management, but not of the public.

Still Hurdles to Leap

In the private, unregulated marketplace, competition for profit provides a powerful incentive for firms to provide what their customers want. No corresponding incentive exists in government. Thus, while there are valid reasons to mix government and markets, that mix rarely performs as well as it could. Providing the right incentives within government remains a formidable hurdle in the design of economic policy.

■ **Prospecting for New Insights**

1. Would you object to charging all water customers a single water price? Would you object if this water price brought in extra revenue for the local utility? What if that utility were owned by government? Explain.

2. Studies show that less water is consumed as its price rises. Still, many people do not believe so. Ask yourself—would you change your behavior in any way if you were to see a significant increase in water costs? If so, how? If not, why not?

PART FIVE

AGGREGATES FOR THE BIG PICTURE

Times are good in the United States. By historical standards, inflation and unemployment are low and the value of the economy's output keeps growing. But history and international comparisons show that hard times have existed in the past and still do exist in many countries. What is the secret to the economy's health? There is more than one and this section explores what they are.

11

MEASURING THE MACROECONOMY

A Look Ahead

HOW DO WE live now? How did we live in the past? How will we live in the future? By looking around we can gain impressions of how we're living now. Historians can shed light on the past. Futurists can peer into their crystal balls and tell us their visions of the future. But the keepers of the government's statistics may very well be the ultimate font of knowledge.

This chapter is about economic measurement. Obviously, numbers can never tell the entire story, and so statisticians will never replace social observers, historians, and the like. Nonetheless, economic statistics are quite useful. We have goals as a society: economic growth without inflation, for example. Various macro measures are used to monitor whether we are achieving our goals. Other measures indicate what we can expect in the future, thus allowing us to plan more effectively.

Exploration 11-1 extends the survey of principles by examining why government needs good data in order to take appropriate actions. In particular, issues involving static and dynamic scoring—whether to assume that individuals will or will not change their behavior in response to federal actions—are considered. The second Exploration looks at how things that cannot be measured by government statistics affect the economy. It is seen that market incentives exist for both ethical and unethical behavior.

As you are **Surveying Economic Principles** you will arrive at an ability to

❏ present some widely accepted goals for the macro economy;
❏ delineate the components of GDP;
❏ understand how price indices are used;
❏ explain how the unemployment rate is calculated;
❏ divide unemployment into different types and explain the implications of each.

While **Exploring Issues** you will be able to

❏ identify the advantages and disadvantages of static and dynamic scoring;
❏ discuss the significance of intangibles that are left out of GDP measures.

Terms Along the Way

✔ gross domestic product (GDP), 352
✔ investment, 352
✔ net investment, 353
✔ net domestic product (NDP), 353
✔ value added, 354
✔ potential GDP, 355
✔ underground economy, 355
✔ consumer price index (CPI), 356
✔ producer price index (PPI), 356
✔ GDP deflator, 356

✔ inflation rate, 357
✔ nominal value, 358
✔ real value, 358
✔ unemployment rate, 361
✔ discouraged workers, 361
✔ frictional unemployment, 363
✔ structural unemployment, 363
✔ specific human capital, 364
✔ business cycle, 365
✔ leading indicators, 367
✔ static scoring, 372
✔ dynamic scoring, 372

SURVEYING ECONOMIC PRINCIPLES

Macroeconomic Goals

Macroeconomics deals with the economy as a whole. The performance of the macro-economy thus affects everyone. Government tax policies, spending policies, and monetary policies are aimed at achieving several desirable ends. **Economic growth, full employment, and low inflation are three widely accepted goals of macro policy.** Since these goals may at times conflict with each other, there is sometimes disagreement over which goal should receive first priority in the design of government policies. For example, policies that promote full employment may be inconsistent with low inflation, so one or the other goal must take priority.

Economic growth occurs when the economy's total output of goods and services increases. Higher living standards are a by-product of economic growth. In effect, growth enlarges the economic pie, allowing many people bigger slices. One of the best ways to measure economic progress is through the shrinking amount of time we must spend working to pay for the goods and services we buy. Table 11-1 illustrates

The Federal Reserve Bank of Dallas, which developed the information about living standards, is located on the Web at **http://www. dallasfed.org/**

TABLE 11-1 U.S. Growth: The Decline in the Costs of Selected Products

Product, Years Compared, and Prices	Time Cost
3-pound frying chicken	
1919: $1.23	2 hours, 37 minutes
1997: $3.15	14 minutes
New home	
1956: $14,500	6.5 hours per square foot
1996: $140,000	5.6 hours per square foot
Refrigerator	
1970: $240	72 hours
1997: $338	26 hours
Movie ticket	
1970: $1.55	28 minutes
1997: $4.25	19 minutes
Big Mac	
1940: $0.30	27 minutes
1997: $1.89	9 minutes
Color TV	
1971: $620	174 hours
1997: $299	23 hours
Cellular phone	
1984: $4,194	456 hours
1997: $120	9 hours
Air conditioner	
1970: $150	45 hours
1997: $299	23 hours

Source: Compiled from the *1997 Annual Report of the Federal Reserve Bank of Dallas.*

the decline in the amount of time the average worker spends on the job to earn enough money to pay for a selected group of products. Notice that the price in dollars of the items in the table is higher today than in the past. However, measured in terms of minutes or hours of work, the cost of buying those items is significantly less than previously.

It is generally believed that the economy can sustain a long-term growth rate of 2.5 percent per year. However, some optimists argue that twice that rate is possible. Over the long run, small differences in the growth rate can make a large difference in living standards. It would take 29 years for aggregate output to double at a 2.5 percent growth rate, but only half that time in the more optimistic case.

Doubling times, such as that for aggregate output, can be estimated using the *rule of seventy-two*. Whatever the continuously compounding percentage growth rate of a variable is, dividing that number into 72 will reveal the approximate doubling time. For example, a 5 percent growth rate means that output doubles about every 14.4 years, because 72/5 equals 14.4.

In practice, economic growth does not occur in a smooth fashion. The economy surges and stumbles at periodic intervals. These ups and downs in the growth of output sometimes put the economy above, and other times below, its long-run sustainable growth rate.

When economic growth falls short, unemployment is usually the result. High employment is a major goal of public policy. Concerns over unemployment motivate the development of macro models designed to better understand its causes and identify policies to achieve full employment.

Policymakers also seek to preserve the value of money by keeping the inflation rate low. In practice, the economy has experienced some inflation every year since 1955. Annual inflation reached a peak of 12 percent in the 1970s before declining sharply in the 1980s. By 1999 the inflation rate had fallen to less than 2 percent. With inflation under control, public concern over inflation has subsided. However, even a slightly high inflation rate, say 3 percent, would cause prices to double in about 24 years. If inflation were to reach 10 percent, a level reached during the 1970s, it would take little more than 7 years for prices to double. This explains why increases in the inflation rate merit concern, especially among those living on fixed incomes.

Measuring National Output

From the earliest days of American history, government has kept statistical records. As the economy has grown larger and more complex, the importance of keeping track of the economy has increased. Policymakers rely upon government data to design policies that will improve economic performance.

The value of goods and services produced is the single most important measure of the nation's output. According to the circular flow of income, the value of national output must be identical to the value of national income. This equality occurs because every dollar that buyers spend on output represents income to the sellers of that output.

The economy's output is diverse, running the gamut from A to Z, including the proverbial kitchen sink. One way to measure output is to classify it according to

The U.S. Department of Commerce keeps track of the nation's output. It operates a Government Information Locator Service (GILS) at the following Internet address: **http://www. fedworld.gov/ gils/docgils.htm**

who's doing the purchasing. To this end, purchases are classified by sector: households, businesses, government, and foreigners. Each unit of output finds its way to one of these sectors. The output is valued at *market value*, which is measured by market prices. Apples, oranges, the kitchen sink, and all other goods and services are valued by the common dollar-denominated yardstick of market prices.

Output is measured by tallying the value of *final goods and services*—those which are sold to their final owners. The most widely reported measure of the economy's output is **gross domestic product (GDP)**, the market value of the final goods and services produced in the economy within some time period, usually 1 quarter or 1 year. Spending on *intermediate goods*—goods used to make other goods—is not included so as to avoid double counting, the counting of the same output twice. For instance, a new car purchased by a consumer includes a new battery and tires. Since the total value of the car includes the value of its components, the output and the inputs should not be counted separately. On the other hand, since replacement batteries and tires are purchased by their final user, it is appropriate to count these expenditures in consumer spending.

gross domestic product (GDP): the market value of the final goods and services produced in the economy within some time period, usually one quarter or one year.

Consumption

Consumption spending is purchasing by households. Household spending makes up the majority of spending in the U.S. economy, about 68 percent of total spending in 1998. This spending may be on services or on consumer durable or nondurable goods. Nondurables are goods that are consumed quickly, by definition in 1 year or less. Food is an example. Durables are goods that have an expected lifespan of more than 1 year, such as automobiles.

Investment

investment: spending now in order to increase output or productivity later; can be in either human or physical capital.

Investment—spending now in order to increase output or productivity later—is the most variable component of GDP. Although there are many forms of investment, such as a college student's investment in the human capital provided by an education, GDP statistics record only three measurable types:

- purchases by firms of **capital,** such as new factories and machines
- consumers' purchases of **new housing,** a form of consumer capital
- the market value of the **change in business inventories** of unsold goods

Purchases of capital allow firms the opportunity to increase their future outputs of goods and services. As such, a pickup truck purchased by a firm is counted as investment. If that same truck had been purchased by you for your personal use, it would have been included in consumption. New homes are included under investment because they provide an ongoing stream of housing services over many years.

To see why the change in business inventories is included as investment, consider an increase in business inventories. Inventories increase when firms deliberately produce more than can be immediately sold. Inventories also increase when demand falls short of firms' estimates, as in a recession. Clearly, inventory investment is qualitatively different from investment in capital, in that an increase in inventories may be unintended. Nonetheless, accumulations of inventory represent investment because they allow for increased sales in the future. When goods in inventory are sold, inventory investment shows a decrease and consumer spending an equivalent increase.

Investment may be either gross or net. *Gross investment* is the total amount of investment. Gross investment in the private sector of the economy amounted to about 16 percent of GDP in 1998. **Net investment** is gross investment minus depreciation. Because plants and machines wear out or become technologically obsolete, net investment will be less than gross investment. A positive value for net investment measures the increase in the economy's productive capacity. A negative value for net investment means that depreciation exceeded the total amount of investment, which implies that the productive capacity of the economy declines. When the focus is on net investment, **net domestic product (NDP)** is a more appropriate measure than GDP. NDP equals GDP minus depreciation.

net investment: gross investment minus depreciation.

net domestic product (NDP): gross domestic product minus depreciation.

 QuickCheck _____

What would a value of net investment equal to zero say about the economy's ability to produce goods and services?

Answer: Net investment equal to zero implies that the economy's productive capacity did not grow. The investment that occurred merely replaced depreciated capital. For example, if 100 machines wore out during the year, net investment equal to zero means that the 100 machines were replaced, and the total number of working machines remained constant.

Government

Governments at the federal, state, and local levels account for about 18 percent of total purchasing in the U.S. economy. Governments purchase a wide range of goods and services from businesses. Although estimates differ, perhaps one-tenth of that government spending could be classified as investment, such as in new highways and other infrastructure. Examples include government-owned buildings, such as schools, offices, and airports. Government also pays for social services provided by teachers, social workers, parole officers, and others. These are civilian goods and services. Defense goods, such as tanks and missiles, are also purchased. Defense spending has comprised about two-thirds of federal government purchases in recent years.

Government purchases of goods and services should be distinguished from government transfer payments. *Transfer payments*, such as Social Security and unemployment benefits, are received by individuals who do not provide goods and services in return. Including all levels of government, government transfer payments to persons totaled $1,083 billion in 1997, or 44 percent of total government expenditures. To the extent that transfer payments are used by households to buy goods and services, they are counted as consumption spending.

Foreign Commerce

Some of the output produced by the economy is purchased by foreigners in the form of exports. Because a portion of spending by consumers, businesses, and government is on imports, it is useful to subtract imports from exports.

Exports minus imports defines *net exports*. A negative figure for net exports means that spending on imports is greater than spending on exports; a positive figure means that spending on imports is less than spending on exports. Net exports varies from year to year, with the deficit exceeding 3 percent of GDP in 1987. More recently, the deficit has been closer to 1 percent. For example, in 1998, exports equaled 11.3 percent of GDP and imports equaled 13.0 percent of GDP, leaving exports minus imports equal to about −2 percent of GDP.

OBSERVATION POINT:
Are Disasters Good for the Economy?

Hurricanes, floods, and earthquakes are good for the economy, right? After all, they force people to spend more, which increases output. Isn't an increase in output a reason to rejoice?

Clearly, something is amiss with this reasoning. The key to understanding this faulty logic? Spending on additions to our stock of goods and services increases living standards. However, spending that follows natural disasters merely replaces goods in order to bring living standards back to some semblance of their former levels.

Gross Domestic Product—A Closer Look

GDP is the sum of purchases by the four sectors of the economy. Therefore we can write the following equation for GDP:

$$\text{GDP} = \text{consumption} + \text{gross investment} + \text{government purchases} + \text{net exports}$$

$$(68\%) \qquad\qquad (16\%) \qquad\qquad\qquad (18\%) \qquad\qquad\quad (-2\%)$$

In this equation, government purchases include government investment, so that only private sector investment is counted under gross investment. Gross investment includes U.S. investment undertaken by foreign citizens as well as U.S. citizens. Thus, if a citizen of France purchases a new condominium in New York City, the transaction is entered as investment. However, if this same person purchases U.S.-made business machines and ships them to France, the transaction is entered in net exports.

GDP may also be viewed as the sum of value added in the economy. Each firm takes inputs of materials and intermediate goods and increases their value through the firm's production process. Value added equals the revenue from the sale of output minus the cost of purchased inputs. For example, a farmer who purchases $3,000 worth of seed and fertilizer to grow a crop that is subsequently sold for $10,000 has added value equal to $7,000.

value added: the difference between the price of output and the materials cost of inputs.

Potential GDP is the value of GDP that would exist if all resources in the economy were fully and efficiently employed. When actual GDP is subtracted from potential GDP, the value of lost output due to unemployment and inefficiencies in the economy is revealed. Actual GDP equals potential GDP only if there is no unemployment or underemployment of resources.

Per capita GDP is GDP per person. The total 1998 U.S. GDP of $8.51 trillion ($8,510,700,000,000—a trillion is a million millions or a one followed by twelve zeros) in 1998 is more easily placed into perspective when divided by the population of 270,290,000 persons. Per capita GDP for that year was $31,518. This is the amount of output produced and divided equally among every man, woman, and child living in the United States.

Until 1992, the main measure of the economy's output was *gross national product (GNP)*. GNP differs from GDP in that the value added to production by resources located outside the United States, but owned by U.S. citizens, is counted in GNP. Unlike GDP, GNP excludes value added within the United States by foreign-owned resources. Typically, U.S. GDP and GNP differ by less than 1 percent, so that either can be used to evaluate the performance of the economy.

The nation's statisticians ignore some output, sometimes deliberately. For example, goods and services that we produce for ourselves at home are not counted. So, if you cook your own dinner tonight, the value of that service does not appear in GDP. But if you eat out, those services are counted. That's because there is a market price for a restaurant meal but not for a home-cooked meal.

There are other outputs statisticians would like to measure, but are unable to. These involve economic activity in the underground economy—market transactions that go unreported. Some of these goods and services are illegal and thus not recorded in GDP. Others are not reported so that their producers avoid paying taxes on the output.

potential GDP: the value of GDP that would exist if all resources in the economy were employed efficiently.

underground economy: market transactions that go unreported; associated with black market activity.

 QuickCheck _____

Are each of the following included in computing U.S. GDP?

1. New Corvettes built in Bowling Green, Kentucky?
2. New Honda Accords produced in Marysville, Ohio?
3. New Accords produced in Japan, but purchased by U.S. residents?
4. New Ford cars produced in Ford plants in Great Britain and purchased by residents of Britain?

Answers: (1) Yes, although the value of any imported components would be subtracted. (2) Yes, since the nameplate or ownership of the company does not matter. As in (1), the value of imported engines, transmissions, or other components are not part of U.S. GDP. (3) No. Japanese-built Accords purchased by American consumers are an import. Recall that imports are subtracted from exports in the calculation of GDP. (4) No. U.S. GDP measures U.S. production.

OBSERVATION POINT:
Shhh! Want a Rolex? How about a "Honey Do"?

Interesting stories involving the Rolex watch are at **http://www.w-o-s. com/rolex.html**

While it is obviously difficult to measure illegal activity, estimates place the underground economy at from 3 percent to 15 percent of total economic activity in the United States. Other countries see even higher percentages. As a general rule, the more burdensome are a country's taxes and regulations, the larger will be its underground economy.

Most people think that the underground economy consists of prohibited goods and services, such as drugs and prostitution, along with stolen or counterfeit items. Yes, that Rolex watch being hawked on the street corner is probably fake or stolen. But there is much more. A significant portion of the underground economy consists of legal goods that are sold off the record in order to avoid taxes or regulatory requirements.

Examples of this type of underground activity include toxic wastes illegally dumped, workers illegally employed, goods sold without the collection of sales taxes, and services sold without required paperwork. Yes, the underground economy may include that friendly fellow willing to take on the "honey-do-this, honey-do-that" odd jobs—no license inspected, no credit cards accepted, and no tax collected.

Measuring Inflation

consumer price index (CPI): measures prices of a market basket of purchases made by consumers living in urban areas.

producer price index (PPI): measures wholesale prices, which are prices paid by firms.

GDP deflator: index of prices across the spectrum of GDP.

A fun Web site to visit is maintained by the Federal Reserve Bank of Minneapolis. There you will find the CPI calculation machine. Punch in some numbers and enjoy yourself at **http://woodrow. mpls.frb.fed.us/ economy/calc/ cpihome.html**

GDP can change because the quantities of various outputs in the economy change, or because prices change. Usually, GDP changes in response to a combination of both reasons. Since only increases in output make us better off, we would like to know how much of any change in GDP is due to price changes and how much is due to output changes. A price index can tell us.

Price Indices

A *price index* measures the average level of prices in the economy. There are several price indices, each created for a specific purpose, with a different set of prices measured.

- The **consumer price index (CPI),** the best known index, measures prices of typical purchases made by consumers living in urban areas.
- The **producer price index (PPI)** measures wholesale prices, which are prices paid by firms.
- The **GDP deflator** is the most broadly based price index because it includes prices across the spectrum of GDP.

To understand a price index, the concept of the base period is critical. The *base period* is an arbitrarily selected initial time period against which other time periods are compared. The price index is arbitrarily assigned a value of 100 during the base period. For instance, the base period for the CPI is presently 1982 to 1984, and the CPI has been assigned an average value of 100 over that period of time.

Table 11-2 reproduces selected values for the CPI. The table shows, for example, that the CPI for 1951 equals 26. That value means that a dollar's worth of consumer

TABLE 11-2   Selected Values of the Consumer Price Index

Year	Consumer Price Index
1951	26
1961	29.9
1971	40.6
1981	90.9
1989	124.0
1990	130.7
1991	136.2
1992	140.3
1993	144.5
1994	148.2
1995	152.4
1996	156.9
1997	160.5
1998	163.0

Source: 1999 Economic Report of the President, Table B-60.

purchases in the base period would have cost 26 cents in 1951. The table also shows that the CPI for 1998 equals 163. On average, a consumer would have needed $1.63 to pay for the purchases that cost a dollar during the base period.

If it were possible to count all the prices in the economy, the number of different prices would likely be in the millions. It is unrealistic to expect so many prices to be used in the construction of price indexes. Indeed, the calculation of the CPI is based upon only a few hundred items that consumers purchase. This collection of goods and services used in the calculation of the CPI is called the *market basket*. The market basket represents a sampling of the most important items that consumers buy.

The items included in the market basket are periodically examined, with some items discarded and new items included, as the pattern of consumer spending changes. When this action is taken, a new base period and CPI series are declared, since measuring the prices of different market baskets would literally involve comparing apples to oranges.

Because the CPI has updated the market basket only about once a decade, it has not captured the efforts of consumers to substitute cheaper goods for more expensive ones. Nor does it catch the introduction of new goods. Because of these distortions, it has been estimated that for at least the last decade, the CPI has overstated inflation by 1 percent per year or more. Since Social Security and other payments are adjusted upward with increases in the CPI, the federal budget deficit has been magnified.

When there is a continuing increase in a wide variety of prices, the economy is said to experience ongoing inflation. An **inflation rate** for any year is calculated by taking the percentage change in a price index as follows:

inflation rate: the percentage change in a price index.

$$\text{Inflation rate} = \frac{\text{change in price index}}{\text{initial price index}} \times 100$$

For example, from Table 11-2, the CPI equaled 160.5 in 1997 and equaled 163.0 in 1998. The change in the CPI was 2.5 units, equal to 163.0 minus 160.5. When 2.5 is divided by 160.5, the annual rate is inflation is seen to be 1.6 percent. If the inflation

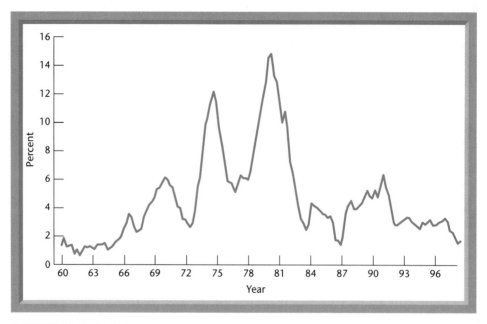

FIGURE 11-1 **Inflation rates in the U.S.** peaked in the late 1970s.

Source: 1999 Economic Report of the President, p. 44.

rate is negative, *deflation* is said to occur. That would happen if the CPI declined in value from one year to the next. Deflation has yet to occur in modern U.S. history.

Disinflation differs from either inflation or deflation. *Disinflation* means that the rate of inflation declines. For instance, if we observed a time series of inflation rates of 7 percent and 2 percent in 2 consecutive years, disinflation would have occurred. The time series of actual inflation rates in the United States since 1960 is shown in Figure 11-1.

Real versus Nominal Values

Increases in economic variables may occur as a consequence of inflation, which "pumps up" the value of macro variables. An increase in GDP due solely to price increases does not increase economic welfare, just as an increase in wages that is completely offset by higher prices leaves workers no better off. We can use a price index to adjust economic measures for the effects of inflation.

nominal value: data that is not adjusted for inflation; for example, the interest rate posted in the bank is the nominal interest rate.

real value: data that is adjusted for inflation; for example, the real interest rate equals the nominal interest rate minus the inflation rate.

The **nominal value** of a variable is expressed in current dollar terms. Nominal values may be considered as "what you see is what you get," because nominal values are not adjusted for inflation. The **real value** of a variable adjusts for inflation. The real value is expressed in terms of the value of the dollar during a selected base period. The time period chosen as the base period is not very important. What is important is that each year's measuring units be the same—dollars with the same purchasing power. A time series of real GDP would reveal how much output actually grows over time.

The distinction between real and nominal values is important to individuals. Consider a worker whose weekly pay increases from $100 to $110. That worker has experienced a 10 percent increase in nominal income. If prices have remained constant, the worker's real income is also 10 percent greater. However, if prices have increased by 10 percent, the $110 of current income will purchase only as much as $100 purchased in the past. That means that the real income has not changed.

The following formula shows how to use a price index:

$$\text{Real value} = \frac{\text{nominal value}}{\text{price index}} \times 100$$

This formula applies to our personal economy. For example, suppose Jack earned $39,000 in the base year and $40,500 in the current year, a 3.8 percent increase. If the price index in the current year equals 105, Jack's real income in the current year is ($40,500/105)×100 which equals $38,571.43. Jack's real income, which measures his purchasing power, has fallen since the base year.

The same formula applies to aggregate economic measures. To calculate the real value of GDP, we would use the price index designed for that purpose, the GDP deflator, as follows:

$$\text{Real GDP} = \frac{\text{nominal GDP}}{\text{GDP deflator}} \times 100$$

For example, as seen in Table 11-3, nominal GDP equaled $8.111 trillion in 1997. The GDP deflator, with 1992 as the base year, equaled 111.57 in 1997. Real GDP thus equaled $7.270 trillion, about 16 percent higher than the $6.244 trillion figure for GDP in the base year. Note that nominal GDP grew more rapidly than real GDP. Nominal GDP will always grow more rapidly than real GDP when inflation pumps up the nominal figure. Thus, the difference of $0.841 trillion between real and nominal GDP in 1997 is due solely to inflation. Table 11-3 shows rounded values for nominal and real GDP for selected years. The real GDP figures have been "deflated" using the GDP deflator.

TABLE 11-3 Nominal and Real Gross Domestic Product

Selected Years	Nominal GDP (in trillions)	GDP Deflation	Real GDP (in trillions of 1992 dollars)
1961	$0.545	23.54	$2.315
1971	1.125	32.06	3.509
1981	3.116	66.01	4.720
1987	4.692	83.06	5.649
1988	5.050	86.09	5.866
1989	5.439	89.72	6.062
1990	5.744	93.60	6.137
1991	5.917	97.32	6.080
1992	6.244	100.00	6.244
1993	6.558	102.64	6.389
1994	6.947	105.09	6.610
1995	7.270	107.51	6.762
1996	7.662	109.53	6.995
1997	8.111	111.57	7.270

Source: Adapted from *1999 Economic Report of the President,* Tables B-1 and B-3.

Measuring Unemployment

An economy with unemployment is wasting resources and producing at a point inside the production possibility frontier. The concept of unemployment applies to any resource that lies idle. In common usage, however, unemployment refers to idle labor rather than idle capital.

The Labor Force

The U.S. *civilian labor force* is composed of persons age 16 and over, excluding those in the military, who are either employed or actively looking for paid work. The labor force typically expands as the population of persons over age 16 increases and as job opportunities improve.

Table 11-4 shows population, civilian labor force, and unemployment data for 1979 to 1998. When the ratio of the civilian labor force to the population age 16 and over is calculated, the result is the *labor force participation rate*. The most notable aspect of the data in the table is the consistent increase in the participation rate. This trend is primarily due to the increase in the participation of women in the U.S. labor force.

Unemployment Rates

To be counted as unemployed, a person must be at least 16 years of age and without work, but actively looking for a job. Separating the employed from the unemployed would seem easy, but there are many details to consider. For example,

TABLE 11-4   Population, Labor Force, and Unemployment 1979–1998

Year	Population Age 16 and Over (millions of persons)	Civilian Labor Force (millions of persons)	Labor Force Participation Rate (in percent)	Number of Unemployed (in millions)	Unemployment Rate (unemployed/ civilian labor force)
1979	164.9	105.0	63.7	6.1	5.8
1980	167.7	106.9	63.8	7.6	7.1
1981	170.1	108.7	63.9	8.3	7.6
1982	172.3	110.2	64.0	10.7	9.7
1983	174.2	111.6	64.0	10.7	9.6
1984	176.4	113.5	64.4	8.5	7.5
1985	178.2	115.5	64.8	8.3	7.2
1986	180.6	117.8	65.3	8.2	7.0
1987	182.8	119.9	65.6	7.4	6.2
1988	184.6	121.7	65.9	6.7	5.5
1989	186.4	123.9	66.5	6.5	5.3
1990	188.0	124.8	66.4	6.9	5.5
1991	189.8	125.3	66.0	8.4	6.7
1992	191.6	127.0	66.3	9.4	7.4
1993	193.6	128.0	66.2	8.7	6.8
1994	196.8	131.1	66.6	8.0	6.1
1995	198.6	132.3	66.6	7.4	5.6
1996	200.6	133.9	66.8	7.2	5.4
1997	203.1	136.3	67.1	6.7	4.9
1998	205.2	137.7	67.1	6.2	4.5

Source: 1999 Economic Report of the President, Table B-35.

- Does an individual who works only an hour per week for pay have a job? Yes, because people are counted as employed regardless of how few hours they work, just so long as it's 1 hour a week or more for pay.

- Can someone who works without pay be counted as employed? Again, yes, just so long as that person is working in a family business for at least 15 hours a week.

- Does going to school count as having a job? No. For students, school may seem to be a full-time job, but it's not considered in that light by government statisticians. Neither are students counted among the unemployed, unless they are looking for jobs.

The BLS Web site is located at **http://stats. bls.gov/**

The unemployment rate is the ratio of the number of unemployed persons to the number of persons in the labor force. The Bureau of Labor Statistics (BLS) estimates the number of employed and unemployed, and hence the unemployment rate, through the results of a monthly survey of households, employers, and a tally of unemployment insurance claims. The last column in Table 11-4 shows yearly average unemployment rates since 1979. Figure 11-2 offers a longer view of unemployment.

unemployment rate: the ratio of the number of unemployed persons to the number of persons in the labor force.

The unemployment rate, while useful, does not tell us all we would like to know about the labor market. Some workers who have part-time jobs would like to have full-time jobs. Those workers are *underemployed*. Other workers would like to have a job, but have tried unsuccessfully to find one in the past and have given up looking. Because they have stopped looking, they are not counted in the unemployment statistics. Such would-be workers are called discouraged workers. **If discouraged**

discouraged workers: people who would like to have a job, but have given up looking; not counted as unemployed because they are not included in the labor force.

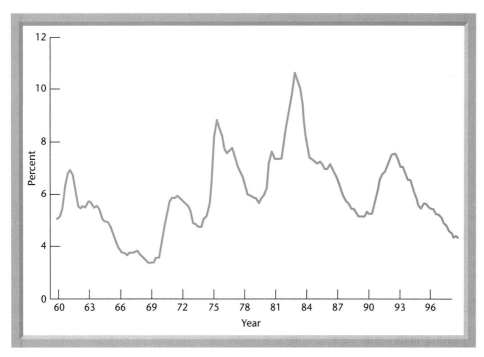

FIGURE 11-2 **The U.S. unemployment rate** has fallen significantly in recent years.
Source: 1999 Economic Report of the President, p. 44.

workers were counted as unemployed, the reported unemployment rate would rise. Estimates put the number of discouraged workers at 300,000 in early 1999.

Concerns over the accuracy and meaning of the unemployment rate have led economists to have a saying about it: "The unemployment rate is like a hot dog. It's hard to tell what's in it." People are unemployed for a variety of reasons, with some reasons of more concern than others. For example, some people are unemployed because they have voluntarily left their jobs. These unemployed persons are of less concern than the unemployed who have been involuntarily laid off. Some other people who are unemployed are actually earning incomes in the underground economy. **The underground economy causes the reported unemployment rate to overstate true unemployment.**

The unemployment rate does not tell us the duration of unemployment—how long people have been unemployed. Short spells of unemployment among workers are of less concern than long-term unemployment. An examination of the unemployed reveals that most unemployment is of short duration; a 1990 survey revealed only 1.3 percent of the unemployed were without work for more than 15 weeks. In 1994 one-third of all cases of unemployment lasted less than 5 weeks.

OBSERVATION POINT:
Demography and the Twenty-First Century Labor Force

A list of links with information on population and demography is located at **http://www.ciesin. org/datasets/ us-demog/ us-demog-home. html**

Demography is the study of population statistics. Demographers offer us small glimpses of the future in which we can have a great deal of confidence. Birthrates and death rates change slowly. Therefore, demographers can predict how many people of various ages will comprise the labor force in 10, 20, even 30 years into the future.

Demographers tell us to expect an aging work force. The large numbers of baby boomers born from 1946 to 1964 were followed by the much smaller number of babies born in the 1970s and 1980s. As the baby boomers grow older, with fewer young workers entering the labor force, the average age of the labor force must rise. That fact has important consequences for labor productivity, Social Security, the health care system, and other aspects of life in the twenty-first century. Demographers warn us that we should begin to plan for those consequences now.

Identifying Various Types of Unemployment

Unemployment can be divided into the following four types:

- *Frictional*—associated with entering the labor market or switching jobs.
- *Seasonal*—unemployment that can be predicted to recur periodically, according to the time of year.
- *Structural*—caused by a mismatch between a person's human capital and that needed in the workplace. This mismatch can be caused by an evolving structure of the economy as some industries rise and others fall. It can also be caused by minimum wage laws or other structural *rigidities* that inhibit job creation or the movement of workers into new jobs.

- *Cyclical*—resulting from a downturn in the business cycle and affecting workers simultaneously in many different industries.

Structural and cyclical unemployment are usually of most concern, because they represent *involuntary unemployment*, meaning that employees have little choice in the matter. In contrast, frictional and seasonal unemployment frequently represent *voluntary unemployment*, which can be planned for and more easily overcome.

Seasonal and Frictional—Waiting for the Old or Switching to the New

Seasonal unemployment affects workers in agriculture, many tourism-related occupations, education, tax accounting, professional sports, and some other industries. There is usually little concern over this unemployment, because it can be planned for—it is part of the job. Workers are not even counted as unemployed if they have labor contracts that restart after the off-season, such as often occurs in teaching and professional sports.

Frictional unemployment occurs when people are between jobs, either because they were fired and have yet to line up new jobs or have quit voluntarily, such as in preparation for moving somewhere else or trying something new. Either way, their stay on the unemployment roles is likely to be brief. Frictional unemployment also includes many young people entering the labor market for the first time and older workers reentering the workforce after an absence, such as for rearing children.

> frictional unemployment: unemployment associated with entering the labor market or switching jobs.

Changing jobs does not imply frictional unemployment. Most voluntary job switching is done without it; people line up new jobs before leaving their old ones. However, involuntary job changes, such as in response to layoffs and firings, commonly do result in frictional unemployment. In the case of involuntary frictional unemployment, publicly provided unemployment compensation acts as a safety net. It allows the job seeker to hold out longer in search of the best job opportunity.

Structural—Human Capital Mismatches and Labor Market Rigidities

Changes in the structure of the economy can give rise to structural unemployment, as demands for some types of goods and services give way to demands for others. This change in structure arises from such factors as technological change, international trade, and changing ways of doing business. For example, computers and telecommunications have opened doors to many types of jobs, but have cost many types of jobs, too.

> structural unemployment: unemployment caused by a mismatch between a person's human capital and that needed in the workplace.

Former telegraph operators exemplify structural unemployment. Once a valuable skill, the ability to speedily send coded messages over telegraph lines now has no market. Telegraph operators who were displaced by the technology of telephones could not easily find other employment at comparable wages. Their skills were not in demand. Until they retrained or found new jobs (usually at much lower wages), the ex–telegraph operators were structurally unemployed.

Rigidities that inhibit labor movement and the creation of new jobs can also cause structural unemployment. For example, the federal minimum wage law introduces a rigidity by making it difficult for workers with little human capital to find a job. Further rigidities arise from the regional nature of many jobs. For example, there may be pockets of unemployment in inner cities and some regions of the country, while there are plenty of job openings in suburbia or other states. If regional migration were without cost, such locational rigidities would vanish.

specific human capital: human capital that is specific to a particular firm or kind of job.

Human capital is often specific to a particular firm or kind of job—specific human capital—and does not apply readily to other firms or in other jobs. As telegraph operators learned the hard way, workers with specific human capital are most prone to structural unemployment. It is a risk that people take voluntarily, since the best-paying jobs usually involve specific human capital. In contrast, *general human capital* involves such skills as communication, reasoning, and math. General human capital is easily transferred from job to job. Those who possess it are less likely to be structurally unemployed. For most students, an economics education represents general human capital. However, graduate training in economics is more specialized, and thus represents specialized human capital.

Structural unemployment is a necessary part of economic evolution. Without structural unemployment, there would be no progress—no industrial revolution, no railroad, no automobile, no computer. Those skilled workers who lose their jobs often find the transition to new jobs difficult, since economic change has depreciated the human capital that supported their incomes. They are usually forced to evaluate their alternatives, and either take a job with lower pay or drop out of the labor force to retire or learn new skills.

Examples of structural unemployment are frequently poignant, involving older workers who have advanced high up career ladders that collapse out from under them. Sometimes the reason involves imports. For example, the U.S. imports much of its steel from countries of Europe and the Far East. Blast furnaces in America's "rust belt" that were built before World War II could not compete with the newer, more technologically advanced facilities in other countries. In response, America's primary steel producers laid off many highly skilled workers. Those skills and a powerful union had combined to increase steelworkers' earnings to levels far above what they could earn in other occupations. Does a 50-year-old ex-steelworker go back to school and start over, compete with teenagers for a minimum-wage job, or retire early and hope the money holds out? The choices are painful.

Structural unemployment is not only in blue-collar jobs. Corporations have eliminated many white-collar managerial jobs in corporate downsizings in recent years. Like their blue-collar counterparts, former managers find that job openings are few and competition is fierce. Their choices are often little better than those of the 50-year-old steelworker just mentioned.

The Employment and Training Administration of the Department of Labor provides information about training opportunities at **http://www. doleta.gov**

Government sometimes offers job-training programs to cushion the blows of structural unemployment. The question arises, though, as to the form of that training. For example, should government train hair stylists? That would take the jobs of other hair stylists or force them to work at lower wages. Such human capital is also so specific that it would not be pertinent for many of the structurally unemployed. The 50-year-old steelworker would probably not enroll.

Cyclical—A Systemic Disorder

A troublesome form of unemployment is caused by downturns in the business cycle, *panics* as they were called in the nineteenth century. In these periodic downturns, people in numerous sectors of the economy lose their jobs simultaneously. As incomes drop, spending drops, and the panics feed on themselves in a vicious cycle.

There just does not seem to be enough spending to go around, at least for awhile. Cyclical unemployment is thus a systemic disorder felt throughout the economy. The question of how to ameliorate the business cycle and the cyclical unemployment it brings has motivated a seemingly endless debate among macroeconomists. Alternative perspectives on this issue will be discussed in chapter 14.

Measuring the Business Cycle

Stages of the Business Cycle

The term **business cycle** refers to the expansions and contractions in economic activity that take place over time. Figure 11-3 shows the stages of a business cycle as a smooth curve. The low point in economic activity is called the *trough*. Following the trough is the *expansion* stage. When the expansion is ready to end, the economy reaches its *peak*, and then falls into *recession*. Officially, recessions are defined as three consecutive quarters of declining GDP. An especially severe recession is termed a *depression*. Subsequently, another trough will mark the point where the process begins repeating itself. The business cycle occurs around an upward trend in real GDP, as shown in the figure.

    In the real world, the ups and downs in the economy do not occur in such a smooth fashion. Expansions typically last much longer and are much stronger than recessions. Thus the business cycle occurs within the context of a rising trend. Figure 11-4 reveals the upward course of GDP over time.

business cycle: the uneven sequence of trough, expansion, peak, and recession that the economy follows over time.

Seasonal Adjustments—Helping to Isolate Cyclical Effects

Many economic variables move either up or down at the same time each year. For example, construction activity slows down during the winter because of bad weather and picks up during the warmer months. Retail sales increase during the Christmas

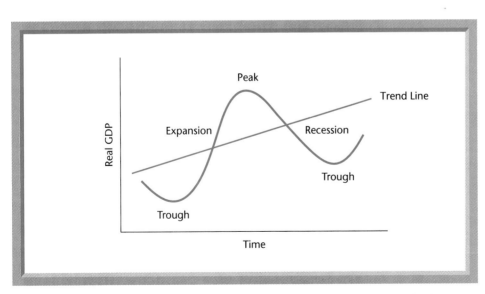

FIGURE 11-3   **The stages of the business cycle** are not smooth in reality. The duration and intensity of stages can differ dramatically over time.

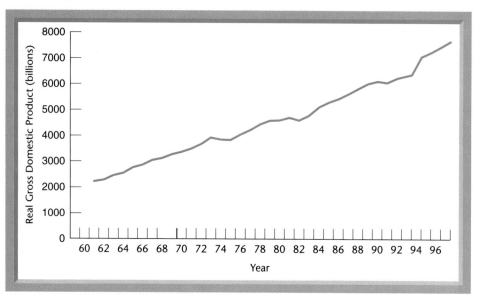

FIGURE 11-4   **The rising trend of GDP** becomes apparent when real GDP is viewed over many years.

Source: 1999 Economic Report of the President, Table B-3.

season. Agriculture follows seasonal patterns. Thus, downswings in economic activity do not always indicate recession, just as upswings do not always signal expansion.

These seasonal effects make it difficult to disentangle actual growth in economic variables from changes due to seasonal volatility. That is why most published data are seasonally adjusted, using statistical models to make the adjustments. Seasonal adjustments to data help reveal the underlying trends. For example, when construction activity drops off in January, the seasonally adjusted data can tell us whether the decline is merely the usual winter slowdown or whether construction is stronger or weaker than usual for that time of year.

Seasonal adjustments can reveal unusual strength or weakness in the economy. For example, if the seasonal adjustment shows that the January decline in construction is not as sharp as usual, and many other economic measures are also above their seasonal norms, we have compelling evidence that the economy is expanding.

Reading the Indicators—Leads and Lags

Who decides when the economy leaves one stage of the business cycle and enters the next stage? Surprisingly, that job is not left to government economists, whose judgment might be swayed by political considerations. Instead, an independent organization, the National Bureau of Economic Research (NBER), is entrusted with the dating of business cycle turning points.

Because important indicators of the economy such as GDP, employment, and industrial production sometimes move opposite to each other, the job of the NBER is a difficult one. In many instances, the NBER will not announce the onset of a recession until it has observed the indicators for months. There are also often delays in dating the beginning of expansions.

There are hundreds of economic indicators capable of illuminating various aspects of the economy. Experience has shown that some of these indicators, called leading indicators, will usually change direction before the economy does. Examples include the index of building permits, housing starts, and manufacturers' new orders for durable goods. These data series and several others are combined to form a composite index of leading indicators, which receives much attention from the media. Other indicators, the *lagging indicators*, usually change direction only after the economy has already done so. The unemployment rate and expenditures on new plants and equipment are examples. Many indicators change direction about the same time the economy changes direction. These are called *coincident indicators*. Examples include the index of industrial production and the prime interest rate charged by banks.

leading indicators: housing starts, manufacturers' orders, and other statistics that are expected to change direction before the economy at large does.

Investors and businesspeople need predictions about the future in order to plan effectively, which motivates an interest in the leading indicators. Unfortunately, the leading indicators do not always give an accurate prediction of the future direction of the economy, and thus must be used with care.

OBSERVATION POINT:
Global Economy, Yes—Global Recession, Who Knows?

A lot of world economic news in 1998 was not good. Indonesia entered a depression. In Japan bad bank loans caused the lengthy recession there to deepen. The Russian economy teetered on the brink of disaster. In the second half of the year, the U.S. stock market reacted negatively to these events, losing enough value to cause investors to wonder if the long-feared "bear market" was upon them. The response by U.S. policymakers was to cut interest rates, although not to the extent that many investors hoped. President Clinton called the situation the most dangerous for the world economy in 50 years.

Would the recessions, depressions, and other crises spread to the United States? For years economists and policymakers touted the benefits of the global economy—less inflation and more economic growth—and suggested that the benefits would spread out like ripples in a pond. Now they were forced to consider the notion that the global economy is a two-way street. Like the flu and other contagious medical conditions that can spread from country to country, the United States began to contemplate that it might not be immune to economic crisis overseas. Is that true? The problem is that no one can perfectly foresee the future. Because of that, what would happen would remain a mystery until it actually happened. In the meantime, the best that investors, workers, and policymakers could do was to watch the leading indicators and worry.

SUMMARY

- In order to know whether the nation is meeting its macro goals, government collects data that measure the aggregate economy.
- The largest component of total spending is consumption-spending by consumers.

- Spending also includes investment, government purchases, and net exports. Investment is spending on capital and on new structures. Net exports equal exports minus imports.
- Gross Domestic Product (GDP) is the most widely reported measure of the aggregate economy. GDP equals the sum of consumption, investment, government purchases, and net exports. For many purposes, per capita GDP is useful. GDP is an imperfect measure of a nation's well-being, because it does not count the value of goods and services produced in underground economy and within households.
- Several price indices, including the Consumer Price Index (CPI), the GDP deflator, and the Producer Price Index (PPI), measure inflation.
- The CPI is calculated using a few hundred items that consumers typically purchase, the so-called market basket of goods and services. The base period is an initial time period, currently 1982 to 1984, to which prices in other time periods are compared. The CPI equals 100 during the base period. As inflation takes place and prices rise, the value of the CPI increases. If there were to be deflation, the CPI would fall.
- A nominal value is expressed without regard to inflation. A real value has been adjusted for inflation. Nominal GDP divided by the GDP deflator equals real GDP. Real GDP is a more appropriate measure of the economy's actual output than nominal GDP. Nominal GDP will rise whenever production increases, but also because of inflation. Real GDP will only rise whenever production increases.
- The civilian labor force equals the number of persons aged 16 and over who have a job or are looking for one.
- The unemployment rate equals the number of unemployed persons divided by the civilian labor force. The unemployment rate must be interpreted carefully, because of the existence of an underground economy and discouraged workers.
- Unemployment of labor comes in four basic types: seasonal, frictional, structural, and cyclical. Cyclical unemployment follows the business cycle, which is the sequence of recession, trough, expansion, and peak. Adjusting data seasonally can help interpret this cycle, and leading indicators can help predict it.

QUESTIONS AND PROBLEMS

1. After obtaining the most recent edition of the *Economic Report of the President* from your library, compare the discussion of macroeconomic goals in this chapter with those discussed in the *Report*. Are all the goals mentioned in the chapter also in the *Report*? What statistics are quoted in the *Report* to buttress the views of its authors?

2. The misery index is defined as the sum of the inflation rate plus the unemployment rate. Some people who are not economists claim that the misery index is a good measure of economic welfare. Evaluate the misery index against per capita GDP as a measure of economic well-being.

3. Explain how, as actual consumption varies from the market basket, the CPI becomes distorted.

4. Can you think of a logical reason for excluding persons under the age of 16 from the labor force statistics, but not excluding persons over age 65 or even age 70 from the statistics?

5. List three instances when you or someone you know has been unemployed. For each, explain the type of unemployment, such as frictional, seasonal, structural, or cyclical.

6. Explain each component of GDP. Include in your explanation answers to the following: a. Is investment gross or net? b. Does the government component include transfer payments? c. How does real GDP differ from nominal GDP?

7. What is *per capita* GDP? Under what circumstances would *per capita* GDP tell us more about the state of the economy than GDP?

8. Go to your library and read at least three articles about the current condition of the economy in magazines such as *Business Week*, *The Economist*, or *Fortune*, or in a business newspaper such as *Investors Business Daily* or *The Wall Street Journal*. What stage of the business cycle is the economy currently in? Which single statistic is the most useful in answering this question? What economic problems are discussed in the articles you have read? Explain.

Web Exercises

9. a. Using an Internet search engine such as that provided by Yahoo (located at **http://www.yahoo.com**) or Alta Vista (located at **http://www.altavista.com**), perform a separate search for the following terms: **inflation rate, discouraged workers,** and **leading indicators**. Visit several of the Web sites that your search reveals for each term and observe the context in which each term is used. Explain whether the manner in which the terms are used is consistent with their use in the text.

   b. Repeat the above, but this time use a combination of terms that you select from the chapter. To eliminate Web sites that do not contain all terms, place a plus sign in front of each term you enter, such as **+GDP +investment**.

10. Visit the Web site of the Philippine Institute for Development Studies at **http://www.pids.gov.ph/**. Using their economic database, seek out information about national income in several countries of your choice. Summarize your findings in a table containing several national income statistics for each country.

Visit the Web site for *Economics by Design* at
http://www.prenhall.com/collinge for a Self Quiz over
the topics in this chapter.

EXPLORING ISSUES

Exploration 11-1 Assessing Economic Performance—
It's Hard to Know the Present, So Dare We Predict the Future?

Measures of economic performance are highly imperfect. Government must use these measures, though, so that it can evaluate its own performance. This raises a concern. If too much weight is attached to economic measures, will the measures themselves become corrupted?

Are You Better Off?

"Are you better off now than you were 4 years ago?" Every presidential election, one candidate or another suggests that we ask ourselves that question. After all, there is no one better positioned to know how we are doing than we are. Nevertheless, as you have seen in this chapter, government does attempt to compute objective measures of economic performance.

Measures of GDP, inflation, unemployment, and other standards of economic performance often seem straightforward. Interpreting them is the tricky part. Consider the CPI, representing the price of a bundle of many different items purchased by consumers. According to the CPI calculation, computers have been subject to deflation, because the price per unit of computing power has declined dramatically over the last quarter century. Thus, computers are responsible for lowering the inflation rate in the overall CPI index below what it otherwise would have been.

Along with the reduction in computer prices, however, has also come a behavioral change. Specifically, more powerful equipment has become a necessity to stay computer literate. In other words, computer users who wish to communicate in the modern world must be proficient on modern equipment running modern software. The money and time needed to keep up with these ever-multiplying changes has risen, not fallen, which is not captured in the CPI.

This situation brings up the question of lifestyle. Microeconomics tells us that both buyers and sellers gain when purchases are made. Thus, our quality of life would seem to have risen dramatically, judging by the huge sales of cars, phones, calculators, computers, and other items embodying modern technology. Yet, the myriad of choices we make as individuals have an effect on the world we must cope with every day. Inventions have changed this world dramatically from what it used to be. Along with greater efficiency have come many more things to know and do. Tasks have gotten simpler, but life has gotten more complex.

Just looking at aggregate economic statistics, it might be hard to fathom how anyone could be nostalgic for the past. After all, GDP is up, and so is the variety of goods and services we can buy. Yet, price indices and GDP measure only goods and services sold in the marketplace, valued at their market prices. There is more to life.

Unmeasured *intangibles* of value include simplicity, love, freedom, harmony, neighborliness, and many other qualities. By the same token economic statistics also ignore intangible "bads," such as pollution, feeling trapped, loneliness, and traffic congestion.

Then there are the things that are measured, but that do not actually indicate that the economy is better off. For example, increases in military spending increase GDP, but do nothing to directly increase a country's welfare if the spending merely offsets that of its enemies. Increased spending on cigarettes could ultimately do harm, yet such spending increases GDP in the same way as increased spending on education and health care. Some spending increases pollution, traffic congestion, and public health problems, or otherwise makes us worse off.

A single *measure of economic welfare (MEW)* that could take into account the effects of spending on the overall standard of living would be an informative adjunct to the GDP statistics. Although economists and social scientists have tried to develop such a measure, their efforts have failed to lead to a widely accepted MEW. The upshot is that, while macro measures are useful handles on the economy, they cannot answer that ultimate question: Are you better off?

Holding the Line on Federal Spending—The Tyranny of the Budget

The federal government must have answers, even if they are not the ultimate answers. It must know whether there are macroeconomic problems. If there are problems, it must know how serious those problems are. Otherwise, government cannot know which actions to take, or even whether to take action at all. Thus, it turns to economic statistics.

Some economists would say that government should ignore the aggregate economy, and just focus on prudent budgetary practices. If the government follows sensible rules, they say, the economy will take care of itself. However, whether or not the government's best macro policy strategy is active or passive, it is still necessary to track economic performance. The reason is that government policies affect the rest of the economy, which in turn affects government revenues and expenses. Without knowing revenues and expenses, government cannot budget effectively.

Of course, just knowing economic data does not mean that government will choose to budget sensibly. The federal budget deficit—a shortfall of federal revenues below expenses—is evidence. The federal government incurred a budget deficit every year between 1969 and 1997. In response to citizen outrage over this, Congress revised its budgetary practices. As we will see, the result has been to give economic statistics a more central role than ever before.

In 1985, in an attempt to lead the federal budget into balance, Congress passed the Gramm-Rudman-Hollings Act. This legislation set specific deficit-reduction targets. Each time targets were not met, the act called for across-the-board budget cuts that would bring spending into line with those targets. According to the Gramm-Rudman targets, the federal deficit was to be eliminated by 1991.

When 1991 rolled around, the federal budget deficit was $267 billion dollars, higher than it had ever been before. What happened? Well before 1991, Congress had modified and then abandoned the Gramm-Rudman-Hollings approach. The across-the-board budget axe was not used. It fell victim to special interests, especially the interests of Social Security recipients. Too much spending was exempted from cuts.

Congress has instead instituted a different set of budgetary procedures to add some integrity to the budget process. Specifically, in the Budget Enforcement Act of

1990, Congress legislated that policy changes should not increase the budget deficit. Thus, policy changes that would add to the budget deficit must be balanced by other changes that would offset that effect. Doing so sounds reasonable, but brings back that basic statistical problem—measuring the effects on government revenues and expenses of alternative public policies. As we will see, these statistics are not immune from politics.

Static Assumptions about a Dynamic Economy

Is government able to forecast the effects of policy changes? In 1990 Congress imposed a surcharge on luxuries, including among other things, new yachts and other luxury boats. Immediately after the so-called luxury tax took effect, orders for new yachts all but disappeared. Although the tax rate was higher, government revenue from boat sales was much lower. Overall the luxury tax did bring in more money, but the amount was about $13 million by 1993, rather than the $76 million over that period that was designated in the Congressional budget.

Although the revenue effect of the luxury tax could have been predicted with much greater accuracy, the Budget Enforcement Act did not allow Congress to do so in its budgetary calculations. Thus, the luxury tax surcharge was assumed to bring in $76 million dollars of extra revenue, which then allowed Congress to pass an additional $76 million of new spending programs.

static scoring: assumes no general change in behavior as a result of government policy changes.

This traditional manner of computing the effects of federal actions is known as static scoring, also termed *static revenue estimation*. Static scoring assumes no general change in behavior as a result of government policy changes. Hence, the effect of the luxury tax on demand was ignored. The alternative is called dynamic scoring, or *dynamic revenue estimation*, which does allow for consideration of all behavioral changes caused by changes in government policy.

dynamic scoring: allows for consideration of all behavioral changes caused by changes in government policy.

Static scoring has led to other serious problems. Prior to its final passage in December 1994, for example, Congress was nearly forced to abandon the internationally negotiated revisions to the General Agreement on Tariffs and Trade (GATT). Negotiations over the GATT had dragged on for over 7 years, as countries around the world sought to retain their special trade protections. The final agreement dramatically lowered trade barriers, thereby promoting free trade, which had been America's objective all along. The problem was those static scoring rules.

Although the entire purpose of reducing trade barriers was to promote trade, static scoring rules assumed that the volume of trade would remain constant. Thus, any tariff cut was automatically scored as a revenue-loser by the same percentage that the tariffs were cut. Budget rules meant that tariffs could not be cut without other policy changes that would add revenues or cut expenditures in other areas to offset the purported revenue loss. It was only through an extraordinary act of juggling user fees and other elements of the budget that the Congressional budgetary rules were finally satisfied.

Static scoring is stupid, you might say. Everyone knows that taxes can change our behavior. For example, anticipating higher taxes after taking office in 1993, President and Hillary Clinton chose to receive Mrs. Clinton's sizable income from her law partnership on December 31, 1992. Conventionally, law firm partners would have received such income the next day, on January 1, 1993. Other Americans also anticipated a tax increase and acted accordingly.

Static scoring has been a budgetary mainstay because it provides an obvious baseline estimate, the baseline being the status quo. Analysts may know that behavior will change, but are unlikely to agree on exactly what forms the changes will take or how significant will be their effects. Because of such disagreement, dynamic scoring must inevitably lead to controversy.

Recognizing Reality, But Whose?

Everyone in the budget process knows that static scoring gives wrong answers. Still, as the saying goes, the devil you know is better than the devil you don't know. If the government were to follow a dynamic scoring standard, who could tell what questionable assumptions would lie buried beneath the surface?

Consider the possibilities. In the early 1980s, *supply siders* sought to cut taxes in order to spur economic growth. Some members of this group, including ex-Congressman and then-current Budget Director David Stockman, based their arguments on the idea that cutting taxes would spur so much investment and extra work effort that tax revenues would go up. Although most economists at the time doubted that tax rates were so high that tax revenues would rise if rates were lowered, the idea that we could have our cake and eat it too was very appealing. Thus, taxes were cut in the hope that economic growth would so increase the size of the *tax base*—that which is taxed—that tax revenues would actually increase. After all, since

$$\text{Tax revenues} = \text{tax rate} \times \text{tax base}$$

a sufficiently large increase in the tax base could more than offset a decline in the tax rate.

After adjusting for inflation, tax revenues from the highest income group did indeed increase following the cut in tax rates. However, from other income groups, real tax revenues fell. In this case, Stockman's speculation was incorrect. More generally, do we wish to incorporate speculation into the budget process? If so, what would be the meaning of budgetary discipline?

The problem of budgetary discipline also arises on the spending side. As debate over static versus dynamic scoring heated up in 1995, advocates of social programs often found themselves attracted to the dynamic standard. For example, the director of an arts project in St. Louis argued vehemently that balancing the federal budget by cutting back social programs could easily have the opposite effect. The idea is that money spent on art programs for inner-city youth fosters self-respect and self-confidence, which leads these youths into lives as productive, taxpaying citizens who give back many times more than they received. Thus, cutting social spending would threaten to increase rather than decrease budget deficits.

The issue of static versus dynamic scoring underscores the old adage that politics makes strange bedfellows. Conservatives seeking to cut taxes find themselves allied with liberals seeking to expand government spending on social programs. Both support dynamic scoring. On the other side are conservatives and liberals who fear political manipulation of the budget process. Whatever the immediate outcome of this tug-of-war, the issue will remain with us.

To Think or Not to Think, That is Government's Question

Is it better to continue with static scoring that we know gives wrong answers or to allow our elected officials the leeway to use their best judgments as to which forecasts to accept? Do we trust them to think well? Is it better to analyze and maybe get it wrong than not to analyze at all? That is the question.

■   Prospecting for New Insights

1. List some of the events in your personal life that have made you particularly happy or unhappy. To what extent were these goods and bads recorded in government statistics on the health of the economy? To the extent that government statistics failed to catch these occurrences, what was the reason?

2. As a taxpayer, do you support static or dynamic scoring? Which do you think is more likely to lead to lower taxes? To higher taxes? Explain your answers.

Exploration 11-2 Virtue—Valuing the Unmeasurable

As individuals, we are taught to choose virtue over vice. As we value the kindness of strangers and resent the road rage of fellow drivers, our quality of life is affected. Yet economic statistics ignore these intangibles because they defy measurement. Nevertheless, it is possible to observe the role of economic incentives in promoting or discouraging such qualities of life.

We each have our own set of virtues and vices. These virtues are developed through nature, nurture, and personal choice. They are also influenced by our opportunities and experiences, which are shaped by economic considerations.

Today we find ourselves bombarded with news reports of reprehensible deeds. We shake our heads and wonder what the world is coming to. At a personal level, we seek to overcome the many hurdles life puts before us. These are issues of morality and personal responsibility.

These are also issues of economics. After all, do we not acknowledge the role of advantages and disadvantages in explaining behavior? For example, some say that children's disadvantages must be offset by public assistance, or we cannot expect those children to grow to productive citizens who are able to shape their own destinies and to provide for themselves and their children. Others point to great men and women from history who built character by overcoming obstacles on their own.

The Market for Virtue

Virtue is a good. We value it in ourselves—virtue is its own reward. We value it in others, too. Unlike a physical good, though, virtue cannot be manufactured and is impossible to trade. We cannot go to the marketplace and offer to buy or sell two units of patience or three units of honesty. In large part, we must produce these things ourselves. However, we do acquire many inputs that assist us in this process. We also acquire inputs that make our job tougher, although we would do without these if we could.

On the positive side, we can purchase good books, tickets to uplifting movies, pleasant restaurant meals, and many other things to brighten our outlooks and dispose us to act virtuously. We can also select our friends, and visit places to get away. Although there is no direct market for friendship, the marketplace does offer places to meet and things to do. Government helps, too, by providing parks and other public goods that allow us to renew our spirits.

Then there is vice. The marketplace also assists us here, if we so desire. Of course, since we have all heard the saying that one man's virtue is another man's vice, who is to say what constitutes virtue and what constitutes vice? Sometimes, though, the vice is not of our own choosing—it is a negative externality. We do not want the vice of fear or of crime against our person or property. We do not want the vices of racism, discrimination, nepotism, or cronyism. We do not want the vice of children lured into pornography. We do not want the vice of mind-numbing noise. Then, too, while a loud rock concert in the park may be vice for some, it is virtue for others.

Just as government provides some inputs that promote virtue, it is also responsible for others that facilitate vice. Sometimes the two go hand in hand. Consider liability laws, for example. These laws are supposed to protect us from carelessness and other vices that do us harm. Yet, *lawsuit abuse* has become a vice in its own right. These days, people are often afraid of doing constructive things, for fear that there might be a slip-up for which they will be sued. Even if they have a valid defense, they know that a lawsuit could easily monopolize their time and other resources.

For example, a few years ago a Texas doctor delivered twins who were 3 months premature. One twin died, and the other lived, but in poor health. The doctor was concerned over the deteriorating condition of the mother, and promptly commenced exploratory surgery. Upon examining the mother, he discovered a rare complication of delivery that had been documented only three times previously. In each case, the mother had died. The doctor performed an emergency operation in time to save the mother's life. He was a hero! He was sued.

The lawsuit alleged that the doctor should have done more, and should have done it sooner. Although the doctor defended himself successfully against these charges, it cost him a great deal of time and stress. It drained his spirit. He had to resist the incentive to work less diligently. After all, if the savings from his many years' worth of work were at risk, and his reward for doing the best he could do was to face charges, why not back off? Those are not the kinds of rewards that promote virtue.

Companies also file lawsuits that are designed to thwart potential competitors. The fairness of these lawsuits is often open to question, especially when large companies with deep pockets direct their litigation against small, upstart companies that may be unable to weather the costs and uncertainties. When faced with potentially devastating lawsuits, such companies often find that their investors pull out, banks withdraw credit, and major customers go with competitors who have a more certain future. Thus, the lawsuit wreaks its damage, no matter the verdict in court.

Anonymity in the Information Age

To excel in the competitive marketplace, firms must provide what customers want. How then can we explain our many experiences with firms that do not? Why do we complain that our homes are shoddily built or our cars poorly serviced? In large part, the answer revolves around a lack of information. This lack is a failure of the free marketplace and promotes vice over virtue.

Take the case of going to a repair shop to have our car's brakes serviced. Since few of us specialize in the details of brake work, we pay attention only when problems arise. When our car's brakes start squeaking, we may ask acquaintances to recommend a repair shop. We may also look for coupons in the newspaper, recall commercials from TV, or merely check the Yellow Pages. None of these procedures provides reliable information.

View brake repair from the perspective of the repair shop. Many customers are only semiliterate when it comes to brakes, and they rely on the shop's expertise. You know that, since brake work is done only occasionally, the odds of any one customer returning are not good. Thus, your actions are not likely either to increase or decrease your future business very much. Is it surprising that "You need new brakes" is almost a cliché for trickery? Telling a customer that the squeak is nothing to worry about and to check again in another 10,000 miles is almost sure to cost you business.

Should you choose virtue or vice? In this case, the economic incentives are to be dishonest, to shade your assessments toward recommending actions that will bring in the most money. True, there is a market niche for firms with reputations for honesty and good quality. The customers of those firms will pay more for the work they have done, though, because that work is not subsidized by a lot of other needless work performed on the cars of the less careful shoppers. This situation leads to another moral dilemma, this one on the part of the shoppers.

In many lines of business, it is possible for the customer to acquire information from one supplier and then make use of that information to actually make the purchase from a different supplier. For example, many service providers offer free estimates as a marketing tool to bring in customers. This offer gives customers the opportunity to get free estimates from dealers with the best reputations for honesty and then get the actual work done at lower-cost, less-reputable establishments.

Along the same lines, customers can go to full-service stores to acquire information about products from furniture to electronics to computer software. Customers who have freely used the full-service store's resources often turn around and make their actual purchases from discount stores and mail-order catalogs. This market failure does not promote virtue. Has it always been this way?

As both population and mobility grow, it becomes ever easier for both people and businesses to escape their reputations. In a way, this ability of people to get away from what they have done is a virtue. America is supposed to be the land in which anyone can leave the past behind and get a fresh start.

In another way, though, being able to escape our reputations makes us less concerned with what we do. The result can be vice. We can honk our horns and make vulgar gestures and not have to live with any consequences. No one recognizes us. Since our reputations provide other people with information about whether and how to deal with us, the lack of that information reduces the incentives for virtue.

For example, would we enter a store carrying a sign that told sales clerks that we intended to buy from a deep-discount catalog-order company? Of course not, because we would get no service. By the same token, if we were known by reputation to be that kind of buyer, we would also get no service. Thus, despite the many information links available in the modern economy, there is also an increase in anonymity that provides incentives that tempt us away from virtue.

What's Different?

There have always been con artists and others who take advantage of imperfections in the flow of information. Still, it seems that society is facing ever more stresses on its virtues. Where are these stresses coming from?

One obvious culprit is population growth and its associated stresses. We have already mentioned the problem of ever more anonymity. Population growth causes other problems, too. For example, population stresses many of the environmental intangibles of life. The world is a noisier and more crowded place. As more people take up ever more space on this planet, we see our natural environment become congested and degraded. It becomes that much harder to find our Walden Pond to sit and contemplate. The result? More stress and less virtue.

Stress can come from freedom itself. Take the increased freedoms that broadcast television, music, and other forms of entertainment enjoy today. The major television networks no longer censor violence, sex, and foul language as they once did. Record companies today promote music that many consider vulgar and irresponsible. Parents who seek to instill other values in their children find themselves pitted against this pervasive music. Does society become coarsened in the process? Entertainment companies argue that they are merely responding to demand.

Stress also comes from restrictions on our freedoms. As both population and government grow, we find our actions increasingly limited by government regulation. This regulation may be necessary to protect us from each others' externalities. However, it also causes us to chafe and yearn for the freer world of the past. At least we can escape to the privacy of our own homes, can't we?

Modern technology makes our homes ever less private. This encroachment upon our privacy comes from a variety of sources. On the one hand, there is government. For example, a Missouri man was recently convicted of growing marijuana in his home. Government was alerted to his illegal acts by modern technology, which picked up the infrared signatures of the grow lamps he was using in his house. Law enforcement officers had become suspicious because he subscribed to *High Times* and was a member of NORML (National Association for the Reform of Marijuana Laws).

On the other hand, private firms have also become adept at using modern technology to invade our homes. Telephone directories that list numbers for people all across the country can be purchased on computer disk for very little money. As a selling point, these directories feature extensive listings of what are supposed to be unlisted numbers. In this world of today, a person cannot safely put a phone number on even the most innocuous of applications or information sheets without risking that the number will be sold for inclusion in such a database. Even greater invasions of our privacy are possible in the future. Proposed new telephone services do much more than simply "ID" a caller. These services are also able to provide name, address, income, marital status, and much more information about callers.

With random and sequential dialing, modern computers allow firms to blanket entire neighborhoods with phone calls. Is it any wonder, then, that we no longer expect a cordial, polite greeting when we call someone. The etiquette has changed. Today, rather than volunteering a friendly hello to whomever may call, people screen their calls with answering machines or Caller ID and only answer the ones they feel like answering. Although the information provided by Caller ID reduces anonymity and thus reduces the vice of harassing phone calls, this impersonal monitoring can be viewed as a vice of its own.

Losing That Which Cannot Be Measured

Economics acknowledges the existence of intangibles. In the case of environmental pollution damages, the value of such intangibles is often measured in dollar terms for inclusion in the cost-benefit analysis of specific government programs. However, there is a wide array of intangibles that escapes measurement altogether. For example, is it a vice to gamble? Gambling can be addictive and difficult for some people to control. Moreover, if parents use their children's milk money to pay gambling bills, most would call that wrong for the sake of the children. However, when no third parties are hurt, is it not a vice to pass judgment on each other's behavior? Is it a vice for state governments to promote and profit from gambling? What if the funds raised will be spent on virtuous goods, such as public education? Evaluating such intangibles can seem mind-boggling.

As a society, we must be cautious. If we focus too much on promoting growth in the output that we measure, we will undoubtedly sacrifice output of intangible goods and services that we do not. We must seek the virtuous middle ground between the vice of being overly judgmental of others and the vice of using no judgment at all.

■ Prospecting for New Insights

1. Do you think virtue is rewarded in the modern world? Are the rewards to virtue now any different than they were in the past? Explain.

2. Some would say that technology promotes virtue. For example, Caller ID makes it less likely that people will make harassing phone calls. Identify some other examples in which technology affects the incentives for virtue or vice.

Appendix
THE NATIONAL INCOME AND
PRODUCT ACCOUNTS

The purpose of national income accounting is to summarize the millions of daily economic transactions in a form that economists, government planners, politicians, and others can easily use and understand. The development of the national income and product accounts began in the 1930s in response to the need to evaluate depressed economic conditions, and the growing realization that the government's existing collection of data meant that it already possessed the primary data that could be used to construct the accounts.

The Bureau of Economic Analysis (BEA), an arm of the U.S. Department of Commerce, is responsible for the preparation of the final reports detailing the national income and product statistics. These reports are prepared using data obtained from other government agencies. Individual tax returns, obtained from the Internal Revenue Service, are an important source of data. Survey data are also extensively employed.

Users of BEA data are familiar with the notion of preliminary and revised data. Preliminary data are estimates that are subject to change. Revised data incorporate changes in data made necessary as more complete information becomes available with the passage of time. Data may be revised several times before the BEA is satisfied with its accuracy. The process of revision can occasionally drag on for years.

Most data are available at quarterly or annual intervals, although some data is available monthly. The monthly Commerce Department publication, the *Survey of Current Business*, is the primary source of national income and product data. BEA-developed data can also be found in other government publications, including the annual *Economic Report of the President*.

In calculating GDP it is useful to recognize that every dollar of production creates an equivalent dollar of spending. **Since every dollar of spending generates a dollar of income for someone, the value of production and income is also equal.** Goods and services are produced and sold, with the dollars spent by purchasers being collected by businesses. These dollars go toward the payment of incomes—wages to workers, for example.

The equality of production and income means that GDP can be calculated in two ways, as seen in Table 11A-1. On the left side of the table, GDP is obtained by measuring the total value of production. The expenditures approach sums spending on consumption, investment, government purchases, and the value of net exports. On the right side of the table, the incomes approach sums various income items plus other charges against GDP. Proprietor's income is received by persons who own unincorporated businesses, such as farmers and physicians. Net interest is interest received by individuals minus individuals' interest payments.

Because of imperfections in data collection, product and income are not exactly equal. This necessitates the inclusion of the statistical discrepancy as part of the "other charges" on the income side. Other complications associated with the income

expenditures approach: computes GDP by summing spending on consumption, investment, government purchases, and the value of net exports.

incomes approach: computes GDP by summing various income items, such as wages and profits.

TABLE 11-A1 Two Approaches to Measuring GDP

Expenditures Approach	Incomes Approach
Personal Consumption Expenditures	Compensation of Employees
Durables	Wages and salaries
Nondurables	Supplements
Services	+
+	Proprietor's Income
Gross Private Domestic Investment	+
Business capital investment	Rental Income of Persons
New housing	+
Inventory change	Corporate Profits
+	+
Government Purchases	Net Interest
Federal	+
State and Local	Other Charges against GDP
+	Capital consumption
Net Exports	Indirect business taxes
	Other items, net
	Statistical discrepancy
=	=
Gross Domestic Product	Gross Domestic Product

Source: Adapted from Federal Reserve Bank of Richmond, "The National Income and Product Accounts," *Macroeconomic Data: A User's Guide*, 3rd ed. 1994.

approach force the inclusion of several additional other charges. Capital consumption measures depreciation in the nation's capital stock. Indirect business taxes are federal excise taxes and state and local sales taxes included in the value of purchases. These complications make the income approach less useful than the more straightforward expenditures approach for most macro analyses.

By making adjustments to GDP, other measures of aggregate economic activity can be calculated, as follows:

- *Gross national product (GNP):* GNP = GDP + income received by U.S. firms and workers outside the United States − income received by foreign firms and workers within the United States
- *Net national product (NNP):* NNP = GNP − capital consumption
- *National income (NI):* NI = NNP − indirect business taxes—business transfer payments—statistical discrepancy + subsidies less surplus of government firms
- *Personal income (PI):* PI = NI − corporate profits − net interest − social security taxes − wage accruals less disbursements + government transfer payments to persons + personal interest income + personal dividend income + business transfer payments to persons
- *Disposable personal income (DPI):* DPI = PI − personal tax and nontax payments

As the adjustments show, national income accounting can be quite complex. Each of the measures defined above is used for a specific purpose, thus justifying the effort. For example, disposable personal income shows how much income people actually have available to spend. Economists who forecast consumer spending find DPI to be useful in making predictions.

A detailed, nontechnical explanation of the national income accounts and subaccounts is contained in the article, "The National Income and Product Accounts" in *Macroeconomic Data: A User's Guide* (1994), published by the Federal Reserve Bank of Richmond. This article contains suggestions for further reading, including sources for detailed definitions of the items comprising the accounts and discussions of the justification and methodology for national income accounting.

Applying Concepts

1. If you manage a major chain of retail stores, and are developing your plans as to how much inventory to stock for the Christmas season, which of the national income and output measures would you be most interested in? Why?
2. GNP rather than GDP was the primary focus of national income accounting until the early 1990s. Under what circumstances would GNP be of more interest to economists than GDP? Given the difference between GNP and GDP, why do you think that attention shifted to GDP?

12

POLICY FOR LONG-RUN GROWTH

Economic growth was once symbolized by new railroads and smokestacks. Now, growth is likely to result from new ways of transmitting and processing information. Either way, growth offers the only means to maintain or improve living standards in the face of an expanding population. Since labor is a resource, an increase in population can itself bring economic growth. However, along with the additional output come additional mouths to feed. Thus, economies turn to capital formation as a way to increase the value of output per capita.

While policymakers have long sought to maintain consistent noninflationary growth, that focus has intensified lately. In a sense, focusing on the long run is a luxury allowed by recent years of relative peace and prosperity. This chapter starts by examining some micro foundations of macro theory that pertain to capital formation. These foundations provide insight into how the marketplace generates the investment needed for economic growth. With this as background, the chapter proceeds to explore the long-run implications of alternative macro policy prescriptions.

Exploration 12-1 examines how Social Security has reduced national savings and could lead to crisis down the road. The Exploration goes on to examine ways in which public policy might be changed to protect Social Security by increasing economic growth. With Russia providing the case in point, Exploration 12-2 looks at the critical role of property rights in bringing about prosperity throughout the world.

As you are **Surveying Economic Principles** you will arrive at an ability to

❏ discuss the concept of the natural rate of unemployment and its significance;

❏ describe the sources of economic growth;

❏ relate the role of savings and investment in the process of capital formation;

❏ explain why incentives are an important determinant of investment;

❏ depict efforts by the World Bank and the International Monetary Fund in promoting growth around the world.

While **Exploring Issues** you will be able to

❏ interpret how taxation and spending associated with Social Security reduce incentives for productivity and capital formation;

❏ draw out the implications of secure property rights in creating a stable climate for growth.

Terms Along the Way

✔ natural rate of unemployment, 384

✔ full employment, 385

✔ capital formation, 387

✔ intended investment, 390

✔ depreciation, 390

✔ crowding-out effect, 390

✔ expected return, 392

✔ capital gains, 394

✔ research, 394

✔ development, 394

✔ new growth theory, 395

✔ supply siders, 396

✔ Social Security trust fund, 405

✔ industrial policy, 407

SURVEYING ECONOMIC PRINCIPLES

In the years during and following the Great Depression of the 1930s, a focus of attention among economists was upon government policies that could resolve problems of unemployment. These days, however, the focus of macroeconomic policy analysis is much more upon how to promote long-run economic growth than upon how to correct short-run unemployment. Some of the reasons include the following:

- yearly unemployment rates in single digits since 1940;
- social safety net programs that reduce the impact of the unemployment that does occur;
- past public policies that offered short-term cures for unemployment, but which ultimately lost their effectiveness and proved inflationary.

This chapter examines the principles, policies, and institutions that underlie economic growth.

The Seeds of Growth

The Long Run—Tendencies toward Full Employment Output

In countries around the globe, unemployment rates average significantly closer to zero than to 100 percent. This is no coincidence. People look for ways to work because work puts food on the table. Even in the Great Depression of the 1930s, unemployment in the United States reached as high as 25 percent of the workforce for only 1 year, 1930, and as high as 20 percent for only 3 years, 1930 to 1932. Given that income is critical to living, however, it does not take many percentage points of unemployment to cause severe human trauma. The Great Depression was proof of the misery that high unemployment can bring. The extent to which government can and should take action to remedy short-run economic fluctuations is an important issue, but one which will be addressed in chapter 14. Here, we ignore short-run economic fluctuations in order to focus on long-run trends.

Even in the long run, the unemployment rate does not tend toward zero, exactly. Rather, the long-run tendency is for unemployment to settle at a few percentage points above zero, due to the inevitable presence of seasonal, frictional, and structural unemployment. The minimum long-run sustainable level of unemployment is termed the natural rate of unemployment, and is thought to be in the vicinity of 4 to 5 percent of the U.S. work force today.

natural rate of unemployment: the minimum long-run sustainable level of unemployment.

The economy would tend toward a lower natural rate in the absence of social *safety net* programs, which include unemployment compensation, Medicaid, food stamps, and additional programs designed to cushion the impact of unemployment, poverty, or other mishaps. Without the safety net, the unemployed would be subject to greater misery, and a correspondingly greater incentive to grasp at any job offer, without regard to its long-term consequences. From an employer's perspective, minimum wage laws, liability laws, and many other policies discourage job formation because of the cost of complying with them. Other government policies, such as employment-related tax breaks, can have the opposite effect. Thus, government policies can and do affect the long-run equilibrium level of employment. Because of government actions, it is likely that the natural rate of unemployment has risen from a little over 2 percent a century ago to 4 or 5 percent today, about the same as it was in the 1960s. In the 1970s, in contrast, the natural rate had climbed to about 7 percent.[1]

The flip side of the natural rate of unemployment is **full employment**, which equals 100 percent minus the natural rate of unemployment. Because the natural rate of unemployment exceeds zero, **full employment occurs when the employment rate is less than 100 percent.** *Full-employment output*, also termed *full-employment GDP*, is the real GDP the economy produces when it fully employs its resources. The economy can temporarily exceed full-employment output if workers accept overtime, work more than one job, or find new jobs exceptionally quickly. Whether actual GDP is above or below its full-employment amount, however, **the existence of a natural rate of unemployment implies that the long-run tendency is for output to move in the direction of full-employment output.**

full employment: occurs when the economy is at the natural rate of unemployment.

QuickCheck _____

What are some reasons that the natural rate of unemployment is higher today than it was a century ago?

Answer: Unlike a century ago, the out-of-work today need not fear starvation or the indignities of seeking private charity. Unemployment compensation, food stamps, and other programs provide a safety net that removes some of the urgency about finding a job right away. Structural unemployment caused by minimum wage laws—laws that did not exist a century ago—is another reason.

OBSERVATION POINT:
Forecasting Jobs Lost to Imports—No Market for the Natural Rate?

We must have an income, and so we work. If many of us are out of work, we offer to work for less pay, which drives the wage level down. As the wage level falls, the price level falls. Our incomes then buy more goods, and more people can work to produce them. The process continues until all but 4 or 5 percent of us have jobs. That is the logic of the natural rate of unemployment.

When it comes to international trade, though, the media has no patience for logic—it wants numbers to drum up interest! How many jobs do we gain from trade? How many do we lose? Reporters eagerly seek out professionals who provide numerical forecasts that international trade cuts down on aggregate employment. Exporters and others with interests in free trade respond with other professionals who provide numerical forecasts that trade increases aggregate employment.

Imports cost jobs in import-competing industries. However, the logic of a natural rate of unemployment leaves no room for international trade to have any long-run

---

[1]We have defined the natural rate of unemployment to include the long-run impact of government policies. Technically, that concept is termed the nonaccelerating inflation rate of unemployment (NAIRU), since government influences are not part of natural market processes.

effect on unemployment in the aggregate. If imports were to cause unemployment, unemployed workers needing an income would pressure wages and prices lower until full employment was reached. Actually, because the dollars spent on imports bounce right back into the United States to buy U.S. exports and investments, full employment can even continue without a drop in wages. Unfortunately, logic lacks the eye-popping magic of numbers, and therein lies the market!

Visit the Web site of the Dallas Federal Reserve Bank to read about the decline in the real cost of living in the United States. The on-line article you are seeking is entitled "Time Well Spent." It can be found by clicking on the link to publications at **http://www. dallasfed.org/**

Sources of Growth—Technology, Capital Formation, and Entrepreneurship

Countries around the world have significant differences in their standards of living and growth rates. For example, Figure 12-1 shows annual life expectancies and per capita gross national product for selected countries, running the gamut from the lowest to the highest outputs. Those countries that currently have high standards of living were not always so fortunate. Perhaps Japan provides the most striking example, having risen to the top ranks of the world's countries out of the ashes of World War II. Economic growth is the fuel that propels countries upward into greater prosperity.

Table 12-1 presents data on the average annual growth rates of selected high-growth countries and, for contrast, a group of selected countries that experienced

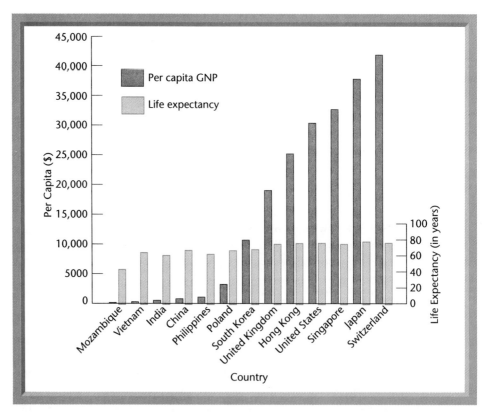

FIGURE 12-1 Annual per capita gross national product (GNP) and life expectancy, selected countries, 1997.

Source: Adapted from *World Development Report 1998/99*, Table 1.

TABLE 12-1 Average Annual Growth Rates in GDP, 1990–1997, Selected Countries

High-Growth Countries	Growth Rate (in percent)	Negative-Growth Countries	Growth Rate (in percent)
China	11.9	Georgia	−26.2
Malaysia	8.7	Armenia	−21.2
Singapore	8.5	Azerbaijan	−15.1
Thailand	7.5	Lithuania	−4.5
South Korea	7.2	Estonia	−4.3
India	5.9		
Hong Kong	5.3		
Pakistan	4.4		
United States	2.3		
Japan	1.4		

Source: World Development Report, 1998/99, Table II and 1999 Economic Report of the President, Table B-4.

negative growth during the period. A careful study of the high-growth countries shows a common factor that accounts for their rapid growth—a significant role for the marketplace. However, even countries that assign markets a significant role have variations in their growth rates and variations in the specific ways in which government influences their economies. Digging deeper into the data can reveal both the features of the economy that are important to growth and how government policies can influence the incentives for the development of those features.

The U.S. economy has probably been studied more extensively than that of any other country. Evidence from the United States reveals quite a bit about what factors are important to growth. The United States has a history of increasing real GDP. However, that GDP growth diminished beginning in the 1970s. For example, from 1947 to 1973, the average GDP growth rate was near 4 percent. From 1973 to 1992, however, that growth rate was only 2.3 percent. The annual U.S. growth rate began to rise in the mid-1990s to between 3 and 4 percent and even higher in some quarters, but it is not clear how long the increase will last or what the average growth rate in the future will be. Why did growth slow down in the 1973–1992 period? Figure 12-2 indicates that most U.S. economic growth is attributable to increases in labor and capital, and to technological change. Both technological change and additional capital increase labor productivity.

Unfortunately, as seen in the figure, the contribution of capital and technology declined over the time interval in question. For example, if technological change had continued at the pace seen in the earlier period, growth would have averaged over 3.5 percent in the later period rather than the actual figure of 2.3 percent. Although there is still some question as to why the U.S. growth rate began turning upward in the mid-1990s, many analysts believe that technological change, embodied in the personal computer and the Internet, played a significant role.

Labor productivity is associated with how much capital—both physical capital and human capital—labor has at its disposal. The labor productivity statistics suggest correctly that the United States has been quite successful at accumulating capital. The creation of new capital is termed **capital formation.** Capital formation requires

capital formation: the creation of new capital.

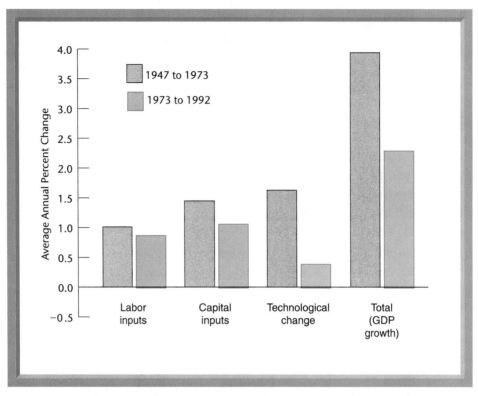

FIGURE 12-2 **Sources of U.S. economic growth, average annual percent change.**
Source: 1994 Economic Report of the President, Table 1–7.

initiative, since to produce capital requires that people identify what additional outputs need to be produced or technologies employed. In market economies, entrepreneurs make these choices based on their best judgements of what is most profitable, meaning of most value to both consumers and producers. The struggle for profit weeds out entrepreneurs who do not make these choices well. Thus, one of the keys to capital formation is to allow this competitive search for profit. Where central planning is practiced, that key is lost. Thus, in Cuba, North Korea, and other economies in which government exercises too heavy a hand, the quantity and quality of capital formation is impaired.

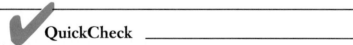 QuickCheck _____

How can entrepreneurship increase labor productivity?

Answer: Improvements in entrepreneurship can hike productivity through organizing resources in superior ways.

Nurturing Growth—Savings and Investment

Capital formation requires investment. Investment can be coordinated centrally, through government. For example, government ordinarily finances the construction of highways, because it would be very difficult for private investors to acquire rights of way or to charge for highway usage. Indeed, rebuilding highways, especially bridges on the U.S. interstate highway system, is thought to be one of the major investment needs in the United States today.

The U.S. Department of Transportation offers a look at investment in transportation at **http://www. dot.gov**

Typically, investment is a decentralized process that responds to supply and demand in the marketplace. Investors finance the capital formation that is necessary to take advantage of market opportunities. For example, investors who expect to profit from the sale of gum balls, livestock feeders, big-screen televisions, or any other product must first finance the capital necessary to produce that product. Firms invest when they wish to do any of the following:

- expand their scale of operations;
- implement better production techniques;
- produce new goods that their old factories are ill-suited to manufacture.

To acquire human capital, individuals invest in themselves. This investment includes the time and money it takes to attend college or otherwise acquire new skills.

Private investors have a strong personal incentive to invest wisely. Because their own resources are on the line, private investors can be relied upon to investigate closely which products are likely to succeed and which are not. While no one can foresee the future with certainty, investors who judge the best are rewarded in the marketplace with additional funds for further investment.

Central to understanding the process of capital formation is the observation that **funds for investment come from savings.** In general, the more savings, the more investment. Sometimes people invest their savings themselves, such as when they buy houses or stocks. Other times, savers deposit their money into financial intermediaries, such as banks and mutual funds, which are then responsible for investing that money.

Savers look to invest for good returns without excessive risk. Without aiming to do so, **government reduces private savings and investment.** This reduction happens in two ways. First, government taxes away income that might be saved. Second, government taxes the returns on investments, thus making them less attractive. In contrast, **government also adds to investment to the extent that it directly invests the tax revenues it receives.** For example, government invests in highways, schools, and the justice system. In turn, these investments are used in the private sector. For example, the production of gum balls, restaurant meals, family vacations, and innumerable other goods and services benefit from an efficient transportation system, educated workers, and the system of laws, all provided by government.

Without government, aggregate savings and investment would be equal. This equality would be true because money saved would either be directly invested or would find its way into investment through banks and other financial institutions. With government, the situation is more complicated because tax dollars can be directed toward government investment or government consumption. Thus, the total amount saved plus the total amount taken in taxes must equal the sum of private investment, government investment, and government spending on consumption items. Lumping together private and government investment, and simply calling the sum investment, we have the following equality:

$$\text{Investment} + \text{government consumption} = \text{savings} + \text{taxation}$$

or, equivalently,

$$\text{Investment} = \text{savings} + \text{taxation} - \text{government consumption}$$

To avoid complexity, the preceding analysis ignores international investment. In reality, some investment funds come from foreigners. The reverse also holds; a country's citizens often invest their savings in other countries in the hope of obtaining a higher return than is available in their own country. Currently in the United States, investment inflows from other countries exceed investment outflows, as discussed in chapter 5.

Not all private investment goes to capital formation. For example, accumulating business inventories for the purpose of selling them in the future is a form of investment. Because it is not possible to forecast sales accurately, businesses often find that they accumulate more or less inventory than they intend. Thus, while actual savings and actual investment are equal, it is not necessarily true that actual investment equals **intended investment**—the amount intended by the investors themselves. These two will differ if there are unexpected changes in consumption spending. In addition, some investment goes to replace existing capital that has depreciated. **Depreciation** occurs when capital wears out, becomes technologically outdated, or otherwise loses some or all of its usefulness. Thus

$$\text{Investment} = \text{new capital} + \text{replacement of depreciated capital} + \text{inventory changes}$$

Investment is a current expense that is made in the expectation of receiving income in the future. When firms borrow to finance new investment, the expected future income must be sufficient to pay off the amount borrowed, plus interest. Higher interest rates raise the cost of investing. Some investments that would be undertaken at low interest rates will not be undertaken when interest rates are high. This result causes the investment demand curve to slope downward, as seen in Figure 12-3.

Investment is also affected by other factors, such as business confidence, which encompasses expectations about the future, current economic growth, and opportunities presented by technological change. Increases in any of these variables would shift the investment demand curve to the right and decreases would shift it to the left.

Government *fiscal policy*—changes in taxes or government spending—can also shift investment demand. An expansionary fiscal policy can stymie the capital formation needed for economic growth. Specifically, when government increases spending or cuts taxes in order to stimulate the economy, it often finances the difference with borrowing. It borrows by selling government bonds to investors. However, government borrowing is in competition with private-sector borrowing, and thus can cause higher interest rates. The resulting reduction in private investment spending is called the **crowding-out effect** of expansionary fiscal policy. In other words, the crowding-out effect represents money that would have gone to private-sector investment, but instead goes to finance government borrowing. However, because so much goes on at once in the macroeconomy, it is difficult to interpret from investment data whether and to what extent the crowding-out effect actually occurs.

---

intended investment: the amount of investment planned by investors; often differs from actual investment due to unplanned inventory changes.

depreciation: a decrease in the value of capital, such as from capital wearing out or becoming technologically obsolete; also, a decline in the purchasing power of a currency when it is exchanged for other currencies, which makes imports more expensive and exports cheaper.

The latest issue of the *Economic Report of the President* can be found on-line at **http://www.gpo. ucop.edu/catalog/ erpxx.html** where the two x's in the address indicate the last two digits of the year. The current issue and last year's issue are available. Fiscal policy is discussed in the chapter on macroeconomic policy.

crowding-out effect: represents money that would have gone to private sector investment, but instead goes to finance government borrowing.

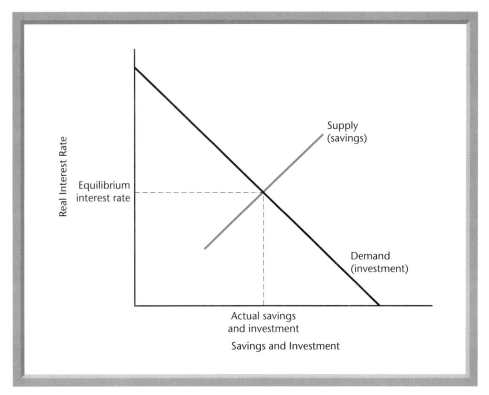

FIGURE 12-3   The interest rate equilibrium occurs at the intersection of investment demand and savings supply. This rate determines the quantity of actual savings and investment. The equilibrium will change if either demand or supply shifts, such as in response to changes in confidence about the future.

Along with investment demand, Figure 12-3 also shows the supply of investment dollars (which comes from savings) and the market equilibrium. *Ceteris paribus*, the higher is the real interest rate, the more savings dollars will be offered to investors through financial markets. However, **the higher the real interest rate, the fewer investment projects will actually be undertaken.** The reason is that the interest rate represents both the price of borrowing and the reward for saving. For the saver, the higher is the reward, the more savings will be offered. For the borrower, the higher interest rate cuts down the quantity of borrowing demanded. The equilibrium interest rate clears the market by equating the quantity of savings supplied to the quantity of investment demanded.

Figure 12-3 highlights how the actual amount of savings and investment depends on market interest rates. Additional real-world detail may be introduced into the model. For example, there are actually many interest rates, including a spread between the interest rate charged to borrowers and paid to savers. This spread is typically included to reward financial intermediaries for their services. For example, banks always pay a lower interest rate on savings accounts than they charge for loans. There are also different interest rates reflecting different degrees of investment risk. This latter complication has some broad-reaching implications, as we shall see in the next section.

Various interest rates can be found on the Internet. By visiting the AltaVista Web site at **http://www. altavista.com** and searching for "interest rates" (within quotation marks), you will find a lengthy list of Web sites providing all manner of interest rate data. More specifically, credit card rates are available at **http://www. bankrate.com/ brm/rate/ cc_home. asp?web=brm**

OBSERVATION POINT:
Japanese Rice for North Korean Rockets

To learn more about Japan, visit the Japan Information Network at **http://jin.jcic.or.jpl**

Was it a test missile or a satellite launch vehicle that North Korea fired in the direction of Japan? Either way, the Japanese were not amused by this unexpected projectile hurtling their way late in the summer of 1998. In response, Japan was quick to cut off its food aid to North Korea. After all, it was the food aid that allowed North Korea the luxury of devoting resources to developing its expertise in rocketry. Food aid from Japan was meant to help the North Koreans survive, not to allow them to reallocate their resources toward financing investment in new, threatening capabilities.

Influencing Growth through Public Policy

The Investment Decision—Risk and Return

To find out what your car is worth, whether it is a Honda or not, visit the Web site maintained by Kelly Blue Book at **http://www.kbb.com**

> *Success represents the 1 percent of your work that results from the 99 percent that is called failure.*
>
> —Soichiro Honda, founder, Honda Motors

expected return: the value of an investment if successful, multiplied by the probability of success.

Private investors do not know with certainty which products will sell and which will not. They accept some risk of failure, in the hopes of getting a return that compensates for that risk. There is always risk ex ante, meaning before the outcome is known. Investors assess the expected return—the value of the investment if successful, multiplied by the probability of success. The *actual return* can be viewed ex post, meaning after the fact. Ex post, an investment might have turned out fabulously, or it might have failed miserably.

Sony's Web site features their current product offerings. Visit it at **http://www.sony.com**

As an example of the difference between expected return and actual return, consider movies. Some low-budget movies reap unexpected success at the box office and prove extremely profitable for their investors. Other movies, some like the latest version of Godzilla with huge budgets and high expectations, bomb at the box office and lose enormous amounts of money for their investors.

Proctor and Gamble offers a Web site at **http://www.pg.com**

The uncertain return on investment has important implications for public policy toward industry. Consider pharmaceuticals. The production cost of many cutting-edge drugs is very low, although their prices are often quite high. Yet if those prices are restricted by government regulation that aims to make drugs more affordable, less investment would occur in the pharmaceutical industry because there would be less expectation of profit. Investors would be unwilling to accept the considerable risk of failure in the hope of only a modest profit from success. The result would be a slower pace of growth in that industry, leading to fewer new drugs. Thus, the trade-off is whether to make current drugs more affordable or to allow the quest for profit to lead to new and improved pharmaceuticals down the road.

The Incentive Effects of Taxation

In addition to regulation, taxes also can affect growth. The U. S. federal government relies upon the personal income tax for the bulk of its revenues. This tax takes a fraction of an individual's income. If the taxpayer uses the remaining income to buy

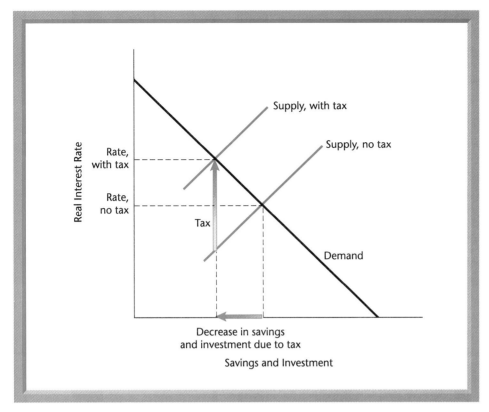

FIGURE 12-4 **Effects of a tax on interest income** This tax shifts the savings supply curve up to cover the amount of the tax, which leads to a higher equilibrium interest rate and less actual savings and investment.

goods and services, no additional income tax is collected from that person. However, if the taxpayer saves some of the remaining income, the government comes back to tax the interest or other return on that savings. The result is that the personal income tax discourages savings. This tax has the effect of driving up interest rates to cover some of that tax cost, thus also discouraging investment.

Figure 12-4 emphasizes the negative effect on private savings and investment when interest income is taxed. Note that tax revenue might be used for investment, although that possibility is ignored in the figure. Savers respond to the amount of interest earnings that they get to keep, which would be all of their earnings if savings were not taxed. This is shown by the "no tax" supply curve in the figure. For any given quantity of savings that is offered, the presence of the tax increases the required before-tax interest rate. The effect of the tax is thus to shift the supply curve upward by the amount of the tax. The result is a higher market equilibrium interest rate, which leads to less savings and investment, as shown in Figure 12-4. In this way, taxation of the return on savings discourages both savings and investment.

Savings are taxed because government wants the revenue. While government does allow tax-deferred retirement accounts, it currently limits how much money can go into these accounts. Debate continues over whether the political focus on short-term revenues is too shortsighted. As of this writing, Congress is considering some proposals that would reduce taxes on savings.

Investment is also discouraged by other taxes, such as the tax on capital gains. **Capital gains** represent the difference between the current market value of an investment and its purchase price. The *capital gains tax* takes a percentage of this difference when the investment is sold. Because investors know about the capital gains tax when making investment decisions, it too has a chilling effect on capital formation. The reduction in investment demand means that banks pay lower interest rates on savings. Likewise, individuals who invest directly in stocks or anything else subject to capital gains taxation also see their expected returns reduced. The upshot is that the capital gains tax leads to less savings and investment.

capital gains: the difference between the current market value of an investment and its purchase price.

 QuickCheck _____

Explain why the capital gains tax discourages investment.

Answer: Investors place their money at risk in the hope of seeing their investments grow. By taking a cut out of that expected return, the capital gains tax reduces the expected payoff and thus makes the investment less attractive.

Subsidizing Research and Development

Even without the inhibiting effects of taxes and regulations, the private sector may not devote an efficient amount of financial capital toward increasing future productivity. This shortfall occurs when there are external benefits from investment in research and development (R & D). Recall that an external benefit occurs when some benefits are received by third parties who are not directly involved in a market transaction. In effect, these third parties siphon off benefits that would otherwise have gone to the firms undertaking the R & D. This reduces the expected benefit to investors, and is thus likely to reduce the amount of resources they devote to R & D.

While often lumped together, there is a significant distinction between research and development. **Research** is aimed at creating new products or otherwise expanding the frontiers of knowledge and technology. **Development** occurs when that technology is embodied into capital or output. For example, research may be aimed at uncovering a superconducting material that allows electricity to flow unimpeded at ordinary temperatures. If the research is successful, many companies could then incorporate the advance in knowledge to design their own products, such as transmission lines, electromagnets, or computers.

research: aimed at creating new products or otherwise expanding the frontiers of knowledge and technology.

development: when technology is embodied into capital.

External benefits are most prominent at the research stage, especially when the research involves creation of knowledge that can be applied to the production of many different products, as in the example just given. It is difficult for any one investor or group of investors to assert property rights over the range of applications from basic advances in knowledge. For this reason, given that the odds of achieving a significant knowledge breakthrough are quite small, private investors usually avoid investments in basic research.

To correct this market failure, and perhaps as a counterweight to the general distortion against investment in the tax code, government subsidizes research. Sometimes government funds research directly, such as cancer research at the National Institutes of Health. Sometimes subsidies are indirect, such as public support of universities that require faculty to conduct research along with their teaching. There is controversy over how generous these subsidies should be, however, since the diffusion of knowledge throughout the economy makes measuring the value of basic research practically impossible.

Much more controversy exists when government subsidizes development. For example, the U.S. Department of Energy funded a variety of alternative energy demonstration projects after the dramatic rise in world oil prices in 1973. However, most of the investments in windmills, solar energy, shale oil, and other forms of alternative energy were never commercially viable. Even gasoline blended with ethanol (alcohol made from corn) survives in the marketplace only because of ongoing government subsidies.

The homepage of the U.S. Department of Energy can be accessed at: **http://www.doe. gov**

Such investments are development rather than basic research. Development by one firm does give other firms ideas about what will be successful and what will not, and thus involves external benefits. However, this situation holds true for airline services, fast-food locations, new toys, and a host of other goods and services offered in the marketplace—competitors learn from each others' successes and mistakes. Such minor external benefits pervade any market economy. For such externalities, it would be inefficient to single out some and not others.

OBSERVATION POINT:
Universities—Advancing the Frontiers of Knowledge

New ideas and information can confer significant external benefits, particularly if businesses can apply the knowledge to develop more valuable goods and services. The trouble is that the value of new ideas and information is often not known until it is produced, and then the applications could be in a variety of industries. Firms that engage in basic research might be unable to claim *intellectual property rights* to this growth in the knowledge base, since patent laws more effectively protect development than research. Firms that advance the knowledge base might even see competitors use that knowledge as well or better than they do themselves. So, where are advances in knowledge to come from? Often it is universities that are the sources.

Government and academia both recognize the role of universities in engaging in valuable research that companies fear to undertake on their own. Government subsidies or grants often provide the funds that make it all possible.

Growth Theory, New and Old

The importance of research and development is a cornerstone of **new growth theory**. New growth theory stresses the association between productivity growth

new growth theory: emphasizes the importance of new ideas in generating economic growth, and of intellectual property rights in providing the profit incentive to generate those ideas.

over time and technological advances that are embodied in new capital. Since no one can know beforehand which lines of research will prove fruitful and which will fail, economies that handsomely reward productive ideas will grow the fastest. Productive ideas can include all sorts of things, including how to make lightweight concrete, how to genetically engineer a healthier potato, how to organize a firm, and any number of other thoughts.

According to new growth theory, the ideas behind new technologies are promoted most effectively by allowing individuals to claim property rights, and the associated monopoly power, over ideas they have. The excess profit associated with monopoly power provides the incentive to create ever better ways of doing things. The idea that private property is the key to growth, however, is far from new.

New growth theory contrasts with mainstream prescriptions for growth in the decades following the Great Depression of the 1930s and World War II. The viewpoint at that time was that government is the centerpiece of economic development. This view of growth was consistent with the high degree of confidence in government that characterized that period in history. For example, the American public works projects and World War II itself were seen as instrumental to moving the economy from the ravages of depression to decades of peace and prosperity. Aid to Europe under the Marshall plan was also credited with getting that continent back on its feet.

Confidence in the ability of government to direct the economy along a pathway of growth rose in the 1930s with the New Deal, and peaked during the period from the 1950s through the early 1970s. Although new in contrast to the prevailing economic wisdom of that period, new growth theory actually taps into themes that have been central to economic analysis for centuries. For example, private property is central to Adam Smith's idea of the invisible hand of the marketplace, discussed in chapter 1, which gives entrepreneurs an incentive to invest and grow the economy in their search for profit. Likewise, private property and the unfettered freedom to use it form a central theme of the *Austrian school* of economic thought, which got its start with the writings of Ludwig von Mises in the early twentieth century. Von Mises emphasized that government rules and regulations that restrict the use of private property impede progress, which "is precisely that which the rules and regulations did not foresee."

Supply-Side Policy

With inflation and unemployment becoming less of an economic threat as the 1980s progressed into the 1990s, the focus in macroeconomic policy turned toward furthering incentives for productivity and economic growth. Economists who emphasize these incentives have become known as **supply siders** because of their focus upon increasing the value of what the economy can produce (the supply side), rather than upon any desire to change consumers' spending behavior (the demand side). **Supply-side analysis focuses on long-run growth, with the idea that the short-run business cycle will sort itself out over time, and will do so better if government does not intrude.**

The objective of supply-side policy is to ensure that the output associated with full employment is as high as possible. Supply-side policies are designed to generate

supply siders: economists who emphasize incentives for productivity and economic growth, such as lower marginal tax rates and less regulation.

capital and increase productivity, which has the effect of increasing the average output per worker and thus increasing full-employment output.

Full-employment output will change in response to changes in structural features of the economy. Structural features include resources, technology, demography, and labor practices. Structural features also include government policies that change how workers and firms behave. Examples include unemployment compensation, minimum-wage laws, and other public policies that affect the natural rate of unemployment.

Supply siders are concerned with any government policies that might cut productivity and lead to structural unemployment. They look with suspicion at the work disincentives embedded in many safety net programs, and at health, safety, and other regulations that make it more costly for firms to hire and fire employees. However, they are most known for their focus on tax policies.

Supply siders recommend keeping marginal tax rates low, so as to leave a higher fraction of incremental earnings in the hands of individuals and investors. In this way, there is more incentive to invest and be productive. The result is that full-employment output is greater. The reason is partly that there will be more work effort provided at the full-employment equilibrium in response to greater marginal rewards for that effort. Mostly, however, output will be greater because investors will have greater incentives to build up the economy's stock of physical and human capital, and thereby increase the productivity of its labor.

Supply-side theory is commonly associated with *Reaganomics*, the economic policies of President Ronald Reagan. Because the concern of the supply siders is with the long run, they have little use for activist fiscal policies designed for short-run goals. Supply siders often see an expansionary fiscal policy as an excuse for a greater government presence in the economy, and worry about the increased regulatory and tax burdens that presence may bring. Most centrally, supply siders wanted to reduce the drag on the economy from high marginal tax rates, which discouraged productivity.

Ronald Reagan knew of these incentives first-hand from his days as a Hollywood actor. He spoke of how he would typically make only one movie per year, which would leave about six months for leisure. The first movie put him in such a high marginal tax bracket that doing a second movie in the year would pay him relatively little after taxes were deducted. Thus, the tax code deterred him from working to his full potential. Doctors, lawyers, and other highly paid professionals often find themselves behaving in a similar manner.

U.S. tax laws passed by Congress in the 1980s largely followed the supply-side agenda of cutting marginal tax rates in order to promote growth. Such growth was intended to provide greater prosperity in the future, as well as a greater tax base over time. The early years of Reagan's first term were marked by the severe recession of 1982. However, beginning in 1983, after the tax cuts took effect, and lasting through the end of that decade, the economy witnessed real economic growth every year along with an inflation rate that was much lower than in the preceding decade. The average growth rate from 1983 through the end of the Reagan presidency in 1988 was 4.1 percent. That growth rate then fell to only 1.6 percent in the 4 years following the Reagan presidency, although it has since spiked to more than 6 percent by the end of 1998.

Concurrently, however, the government ran a large budget deficit, because it did not cut spending proportionally. The budget deficit exceeded 6 percent of GDP in 1983, although it fell to just under 3 percent by 1989. The Reagan-era budget

An interesting Web site devoted to profiling the world of film is the Internet Movie Database. Visit it at **http://www.imdb.com/** and use the search function to learn more about the movies in which Ronald Reagan appeared. The Reagan presidential library can be accessed on-line at **http://www.lbjlib.utexas.edu/reagan/**

deficits look like fiscal policy run amok, with the fiscal stimulus of a tax cut applied to marginal tax rates at the high end of the income spectrum, rather than to rates paid by those struggling to make a good life for themselves. Critics of Reaganomics thus refer to supply-side policies as *trickle-down economics*. This term incorrectly suggests that the policies are intended to make the rich richer so that they might spend a bit more and help the rest of us.

The economy grew, and the rich got disproportionately richer, at least in terms of the income they reported to the IRS. However, while Reagan-era tax cuts reduced real federal tax revenues from most groups in the economy, the tax cuts greatly increased tax revenues from the highest income groups. The top 5 percent of income earners increased their share of total income tax payments from 36 percent in 1980 to 43 percent in 1990. Tax revenues from the wealthy increased for two reasons. Tax cuts gave them: 1) the incentive to skip *tax shelters*, schemes to legally avoid paying taxes, and; 2) incentives to work and invest in economically productive ways since a lower proportion of their incomes would be taken in the form of taxes.

Upward mobility became more commonplace as a result of the lower tax rates. Looking at the lowest fifth of the income distribution in 1980, for example, 86 percent had advanced beyond that by 1988, with 16 percent even making it all the way to the top fifth of the income distribution. Supporters of Reaganomics thus say its critics are motivated by the politics of envy, because the critics ignore the intended purpose of the tax cuts, which is to target growth and opportunity. These supporters blame the increasing government budget deficit witnessed in the 1980s on the political difficulty of cutting entrenched spending programs.

Growing the Global Economy

Issues of Economic Development

One of the most remarkable developments of recent decades was the implosive collapse of Communist economies around the world. The tearing down of the Berlin Wall in 1989 epitomized the failure of the centrally planned Communist countries to even remotely match the living standards in Western economies. At no other time in recent history has the productivity of market economies relative to their centrally planned counterparts been recognized so clearly and by so many people. Market economies have lessons to learn from this event, too, since all countries combine government and market forces. In other words, all countries have mixed economies. Sometimes the mix emphasizes free markets and other times government. The nature of that mix is significant when it comes to growth.

For example, Europe has endured a condition that some have termed *Eurosclerosis*, referring to high unemployment rates and sluggish economic growth in some countries of Western Europe. Economic growth in Europe in the 1950s through the 1970s outstripped growth in the United States. But during the 1980s, that scenario reversed itself. Many economists attribute the problems in Europe to economies rife with bloated bureaucracies and characterized by costly social welfare programs that reduce the incentives of workers to work and of firms to invest. Other analysts also point out the hardships imposed upon Germany, the leading European economy, by the integration of prosperous West Germany with the economically stagnant East Germany.

In recent years, Europe has taken some steps to free up its economies, such as by standardizing regulations from country to country. Trade among European countries is further eased by the adoption of a standard trans-European currency, called the euro. A number of countries have also begun the long march down the road to more market-based economies with less generous benefits for workers, students, and pensioners. The primary focus of these changes is the restoration of incentives in the private sector. While the social safety net has allure, so too do the opportunities offered by a vibrant, growing economy.

The problems in Europe would seem minor in many countries around the world. In the numerous less-developed countries, the most pressing problems are widespread hunger, disease, and other suffering. Thus, promoting economic growth is an especially important goal for these impoverished nations. Often, a major cause of poverty in the less-developed countries is the lack of economic infrastructure. *Infrastructure* is the capital that provides the foundation for development, such as transportation facilities like highways and railroads, power generating facilities, schools, health care facilities, and a telecommunications network.

Development problems are compounded when countries lack markets, either because their governments have policies that discourage markets or because the people are tied to traditional economic systems that discourage the development of markets. For example, tradition in some countries dictates *self-sufficiency*, where people shy away from markets in favor of home production of most goods and services. This is especially true of rural areas when people have little or no money and thus traditionally have grown their own food, built their own shelter, and so forth. Unfortunately, it often seems that the problems are much clearer than the solutions.

Countries Helping Countries

Partly for humanitarian reasons and partly for their own benefit, the developed countries seek to stimulate growth in the less-developed countries. The two most important organizations that channel resources to the poorer countries are the World Bank and the International Monetary Fund, known by its initials, IMF. Although they are often confused with each other, and also often cooperate with each other, the IMF and the World Bank have different missions.

The World Bank does what most people expect banks to do, loan money. **World Bank loans to less-developed member countries are intended to further their economic development.** Since its creation more than 50 years ago, the Bank has loaned more than $400 billion. **The IMF, in contrast, oversees the monetary and exchange rate policies of member countries, with the goal of a stable world monetary and financial system.** The similarities between the World Bank and the IMF include that they are both headquartered in Washington, D.C., that they are both owned by the governments of member countries, that virtually every country is a member of both institutions, and that they were both started in July 1944 through the Bretton Woods agreement that was discussed in chapter 5.

To learn more about the activities of the World Bank, visit the Bank in cyberspace at **http://www. worldbank.org/**

Consider the characteristics of the World Bank's loans in more detail:

- World Bank loans, which only go to developing countries, must be repaid. Unlike aid programs, the World Bank does not provide grants, which are gifts of money. The money for the Bank's loans comes partly from government grants and partly from borrowings from the private sector and governments.

- Lending is of two types. The first is lending to countries that are able to pay near-market interest on the loans they receive. The second involves loans to countries that cannot afford to pay interest. These loans are called credits and are provided through a World Bank affiliate, the International Development Association, for terms of 35 to 40 years. Although interest is not charged, the credits must be repaid. Such credits only go to the very poorest countries and average about $6 billion per year.

- The World Bank can only lend to member governments or under a member government's guarantee.

- To ensure that money is well-invested, the Bank evaluates projects and only lends when a project is expected to earn at least a 10 percent rate of economic return.

A top priority of the World Bank is to stimulate development of the private sector, although direct loans to the private sector are prohibited. The Bank seeks to encourage the private sector by promoting stable, honest government economic policies that focus on expanding the significance of markets. Although the Bank cannot make loans to the private sector, an affiliate called the International Finance Corporation exists for that purpose. It also aids governments in privatizing formerly government-owned businesses.

The World Bank's focus on the private sector is a relatively recent development, one that might surprise economists and government officials who, like Rip van Winkle, had just awakened from a long sleep. From its inception through the 1970s, the Bank tended toward policies that emphasized expanding the government sector in developing countries. It was thought that large-scale government projects were the key to bringing about prosperity, including promoting government-owned industries. However, the Bank changed its policies in response to the successes of the U.S. economy and the failure of central planning in the communist countries in the 1980s, along with the successes of market economies in Hong Kong, Malaysia, and other places.

The homepage of the IMF is located at **http://www.imf.org/**

The goal of the IMF is to encourage confidence in the world financial system. Contrast the characteristics of the World Bank to those of the IMF:

- The IMF aims to tie member countries more closely into world markets, such as by discouraging restrictions on currency exchanges. The IMF also advises members on how to deal with problems that arise from their trade and financial interactions with other countries. Sometimes these problems call for IMF financial assistance, which the IMF offers under the condition that the countries undertake economic reforms that are in accord with IMF advice.

   The reforms can be painful, which leads some countries to complain about IMF arm-twisting. They might even complain of IMF *imperialism*, saying that the IMF seeks to force the values of Western economies upon countries around the world. As of August 1998, the IMF had almost $63 billion in loans outstanding.

- Money to finance IMF operations comes from membership fees that are proportional to the size and economic strength of member countries. All member countries, rich and poor alike, have access to IMF resources.

The IMF is most widely known for the massive loans that it extended to Mexico during the 1994 peso crisis; to the countries of Asia during the 1998 Asian financial crisis; and to Russia in 1998 as that country struggled through multiple economic and social crises. The purpose of these loans was to allow these countries to pay their debts to other countries.

Critics of IMF lending practices term many IMF loans "bailouts" that cause *moral hazard*, whereby countries are tempted to take excessive risks. They say that bailouts lead to more bailouts in either that country or elsewhere, because countries' lenders will not be as careful when they realize the IMF will step in with money when the countries get into trouble. Careless lending practices can impede economic development and sound growth because money will go into projects that are unsound and should not be undertaken. For these reasons, when President Clinton asked Congress in 1998 for $18 billion of U.S. money for the IMF, many in Congress balked and sought to attach safeguards that would prevent future IMF bailouts.

QuickCheck

What is the significance of the World Bank's requirement that a project have at least a 10 percent expected return? What problem is associated with this policy?

Answer: Projects with higher rates of return provide more benefits per dollar invested than do projects with lower rates of return. By seeking to finance only projects that offer the prospect of a relatively high rate of return, the World Bank stretches its budget further and helps more people. The problem is that it cannot know in advance whether a project will actually yield a 10 percent return after the project is completed.

OBSERVATION POINT:
The Best-Laid Plans of Mice and Government

To see why the World Bank now emphasizes markets, consider the outcome of government planning in Nigeria in the 1970s. To bring the nation up to modern standards required roads, bridges, airports, and other infrastructure. This modernization called for massive quantities of cement, much more than the nation could produce domestically. Thus, Nigeria's government planners ordered the needed cement, which was shipped in the holds of freighters from cement-producing nations around the world.

Oops! One slight oversight threw these best-laid plans into disarray. The Nigerian docks were incapable of handling such quantities of cement. In fact, at one point it would have taken nearly 30 years to unload the cement that lay in the holds of ships anchored offshore. Ultimately much of the cement solidified within the ships, thereby providing a concrete example of the dangers inherent in centrally planned development.

SUMMARY

- The economy tends toward the natural rate of unemployment, which means full employment. Today, the U.S. natural rate is estimated to be between 4 and 5 percent.
- Different countries have different living standards and varying growth rates. High-growth economies have in common a significant role for markets and the private sector.
- Labor, capital, technological change, and entrepreneurship are important determinants of growth.
- Economies grow though accumulating resources. They have the most control over capital, which in turn improves labor productivity.
- Together, investment demand and the supply of savings determine the amount of investment.
- Current tax policies discourage savings, which finances the investment necessary for capital formation.
- Some current regulations also discourage investment. Conversely, government promotes technological advancement through subsidies for basic research, such as is conducted at colleges and universities. Otherwise, the existence of external benefits would lead to too little of such research.
- Supply siders seek to minimize structural features of the economy that discourage work effort and capital formation. Reducing regulations and marginal tax rates have been two of their emphases.
- Countries vary greatly in their levels of development, with capital infrastructure often being the key to that development.
- The World Bank and the International Monetary Fund (IMF) are the primary institutions devoted to promoting economic growth and development around the world.

QUESTIONS AND PROBLEMS

1. Discuss the concept of the natural rate of unemployment. Why is its value not the same today as at the turn of the century and as during the 1970s? What role does government play?

2. What factors explain U.S. growth? How did the contribution to growth of these factors change from the 1947–1972 period to the 1973–1992 period?

3. Identify three different opportunities for investment in physical capital. Discuss how a higher real interest rate could make these opportunities less attractive.

4. List three examples of government spending that might be considered investment. Would the private sector have undertaken these projects if government did not? Explain.

5. Using a supply and demand graph, explain how taxation of interest earnings reduces the amount of savings and investment.

6. What is the difference between research and development? Why is the argument for the government subsidizing research stronger than the argument for subsidies to development?

7. Explain the similarities and dissimilarities between new growth theory and supply-side economics.

8. Distinguish the roles played by the World Bank and the International Monetary Fund in promoting growth and development. What criticisms have been aimed at these organizations?

Web Exercises

9. a. Using an Internet search engine such as that provided by Yahoo (located at **http://www.yahoo.com**) or Alta Vista (located at **http://www.altavista.com**), perform a separate search for the following terms: **"capital gains"**, **"supply side policy"**, and **"new growth theory"**. Visit several of the Web sites that your search reveals for each term and observe the context in which each term is used. Explain whether the manner in which the terms are used is consistent with their use in the text.

  b. Repeat the above, but this time use a combination of terms that you select from the chapter. To eliminate Web sites that do not contain all terms, place a plus sign in front of each term you enter, such as +**"property rights"** +**"economic growth"**.

10. Many U.S. states, counties, and communities have an organization called an economic development agency or economic development authority. Create a list of these by using a search engine to search for the term **"economic development"**. Visit at least five of the Web sites revealed by your search. If there is an economic development agency in your area, be sure to include it among the sites you visit. After completing all Internet visits, write a short essay entitled, "Economic Development Agencies: How They Promote Growth."

Visit the Web site for *Economics by Design* at
http://www.prenhall.com/collinge for a Self Quiz over
the topics in this chapter.

Exploration 12-1 Social Security—
Questions of Savings and Investment

Social Security is subject to stresses that bring its future into question. There are likely to be changes that affect national savings and economic growth, as well as individuals' incentives to be productive.

According to a recent survey, college students today are more likely to believe in alien visitors from outer space than in the future of Social Security. What is wrong with Social Security that its very existence is called into question? What does the future really hold? While time will tell, we can nonetheless make some intelligent predictions. We can see the stresses, as well as suggestions on how to relieve those stresses. The consequences are significant, both for individuals and the country. Choices about Social Security will affect productivity for years to come.

The Pay-As-You-Go Puzzle

The fundamental problem with Social Security is that it is *pay-as-you-go*, meaning that current workers pay for people who are currently retired. This arrangement was fine when the program was first established in the 1930s. At that time, the ratio of workers to eligible retirees was quite high. Now that ratio is down to about three workers per retiree. By the year 2030, the ratio is predicted to drop to only about two workers per retiree. Advances in medicine and the aging of the baby boom generation take the blame for these demographic trends. The implications of these developments can be seen by looking at Figure 12-5, which shows that by the year 2028 the Social Security system will be rapidly running out of money. Some other estimates based upon different assumptions put the crisis point off as far as 2045.

If the present structure of Social Security were to be offered by any private business, the owners of that business would be prosecuted for fraud for running an illegal *ponzi scheme*, in which the money from current investors is used to finance paybacks to longer-term investors. Ponzi schemes are very risky; if new investors ever stop coming, the most recent investors lose their money.

Social Security has a significant advantage over the typical ponzi scheme. New investors are forced into the system by government and its power to tax. However, if government changes its mind down the road, investors who have yet to receive a payback could lose out. Even if Social Security were fully financed, though, the low returns it offers would dissuade potential investors. Figure 12-6 on page 406 illustrates these returns. Note that the return to those born before 1945 greatly exceeds the return to those born in later years. For this reason, Social Security is said to be redistributional across generations, in addition to being redistributional within each generation.

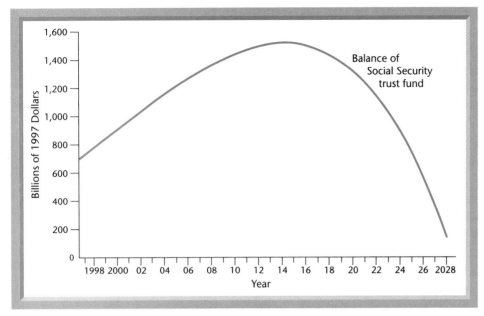

FIGURE 12-5 **Although the Social Security trust fund is predicted to keep growing for well over a decade, predictions are that the trust fund will be nearly used up by 2028** unless actions are taken to significantly change how the system is set up.

Source: Review, Federal Reserve Bank of Saint Louis, March/April 1998, p. 3.

Social Security collects taxes on all payroll income, and allots the proceeds for *OASDHI,* which stands for old age, survivors, disability, and hospitalization insurance. As of this writing, the combined employer and employee Social Security tax rate is 15.3 percent of the first $68,400 of that income, where the threshold is adjusted upward over time for inflation. For income over that threshold, the Social Security tax is eliminated except for the 2.9 percent hospitalization insurance.

If population projections are correct, and if no changes are made in the structure of Social Security itself, the combined payroll tax rate of 15.3 percent would have to rise to over 22 percent in the next 20 years. However, workers might balk at redistributing nearly a quarter of their incomes to the elderly, especially when there is no guarantee that they will see equivalent benefits when they retire. That's why people mistrust the staying power of Social Security.

There is a Social Security trust fund, which collects excess revenue and *earmarks* it for the payment of benefits in the future. However, the approximately $400 billion size of that trust fund is quite small relative to the demands against it. The trust fund would run out in a little over 2 years if not continuously supplemented by the Social Security tax payments of current workers and the firms that employ them. Moreover, if the trust fund is to become a meaningful resource for the future, Social Security tax rates would need to be increased in the present. This action would leave current workers paying not only for current retirees, but also for themselves as well.

Social Security trust fund: Social Security tax receipts in excess of those needed to fund Social Security payments to current retirees; by law, the Social Security trust fund must be held in the form of special government bonds.

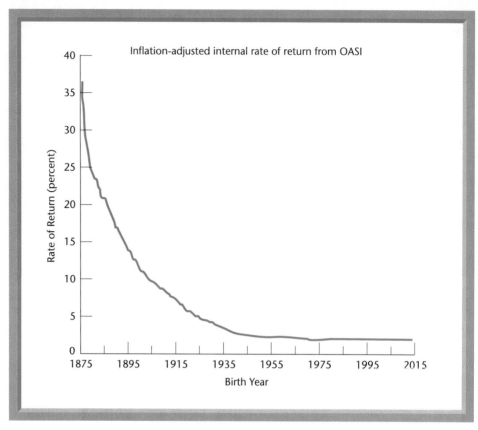

FIGURE 12-6 **The rate of return for Social Security participants** is significantly lower for those born after 1945 than for those born in earlier years.

Source: Economic Trends, Federal Reserve Bank of Cleveland, April 10, 1996, p. 13.

Few workers would support this double taxation. They would rather save their money themselves, instead of entrusting those savings to government.

No Real Savings—No Real Alternative?

The issue of savings is quite troublesome in a macroeconomic sense. As it stands, all savings held in the Social Security trust fund take the form of special government bonds. Since a bond is merely a promise to pay in the future, savings within the Social Security trust fund are nothing more than government IOUs.

To pay those IOUs, government must either create extra money or collect extra tax dollars in the future. Either way, future taxpayers pay. If the government creates new money, taxpayers pay the tax of inflation that eats away the value of their earnings. Otherwise, the trust fund bonds would be redeemed out of general tax revenues, which would require higher personal income taxes or other general taxes. Even if the Social Security trust fund were to stack a warehouse full of its special government bonds, it would still be up to future taxpayers to pay them off. Thus, for the macro-economy, balances in the Social Security trust fund are not real savings.

Not only does the Social Security system fail to augment the country's savings, it actually lowers national savings to the extent that people expect to receive Social Security checks in the future. Workers substitute government's promises for their own savings. Moreover, because the Social Security tax reduces take-home pay, current workers have less money that could be saved. The reduction in the national savings rate because of Social Security implies less money for investment, and thus less capital formation. With less capital, the country's production possibilities grow more slowly. The result is that, when current workers retire, the economic capacity of the country to support them will be smaller than if Social Security never existed in the first place.

For the Social Security trust fund to represent real savings, it must generate real capital that will increase the country's production possibilities in years to come. The amount of savings needed for the Social Security trust fund to be *fully funded*—able to pay off all its future obligations without recourse to future taxation—would be well over a year's worth of GDP. In other words, the buildup of savings in the Social Security trust fund would need to greatly expand the country's current productive capacity.

If government were to invest the Social Security trust fund into the production of real capital, it could take one of two routes. It could produce the necessary capital itself. Government production may be justified to the extent that the needed investment applies to the provision of public goods, such as highway infrastructure needed for smoothly flowing traffic. Beyond this, however, direct government investment would lead the economy in the direction of command and control. Alternatively, government could invest the money in the marketplace, perhaps establishing or designating mutual funds to buy stock in private companies.

If the government were to enter the private marketplace, politics would undoubtedly affect the direction of its investment. Thus, we could expect to see politically correct industries and those with powerful constituencies thrive, while other industries would be denied access to government coffers. The result would be an **industrial policy,** in which government picks the industries in which to stake the country's future. Workers interested in real savings for their retirements might prefer that such investment choices be left to private investors guided by profit rather than by politics.

industrial policy: involves the government promoting certain industries.

Personal Security Accounts—Who Holds the Reins of Investment and Growth?

Individuals do save for their own retirement. *Individual retirement accounts (IRAs)* promote that savings by allowing tax-free or tax-prepaid (for *Roth IRAs*) contributions of up to $2,000 per year. Government has been reluctant to increase that limit, because any increase in tax-free savings would deplete current tax revenues. Government has also been content to accumulate bonds in the Social Security trust fund, because selling those bonds to the trust fund transfers any extra money collected by Social Security taxes into general revenues that can be spent elsewhere.

If government so chooses, it can promote private savings for the future. It can do this in varying degrees. It could start by increasing or eliminating the contribution cap on IRAs. It could go further by eliminating the taxation of all savings. It could even go so far as to require that individuals save some fraction of their earnings for their own retirement. This savings would be placed into *Personal Security Accounts (PSAs)*, which would be financed by a payroll tax but be under the individual's own control and ownership. Because Social Security depends upon current workers to support current retirees, PSAs could only supplement, not replace, Social Security as it now stands. Proposals of this sort have proven to be politically contentious, although one such proposal was made by President Clinton in his 1999 State of the Union address.

Workers who get to keep control of their own savings might be more inclined to accept the double tax of paying for current retirees and also building up savings for their own retirement. Such an approach has the economic advantage of maintaining a free-market allocation of investment. Companies that offer mutual funds and other forms of investment would compete for savings, and the winners would be those companies that offer the best services and investments.

Coming Welfare for the Aged

The strategy of promoting savings and investment by inducing individuals to save for their own retirements does not provide for income redistribution from wealthier workers to poorer ones. As Social Security now stands, it is highly redistributional in this respect. The ratio of payments to retirees relative to the amount they contributed in their working years is much higher for the low income than for the high income. Payments are also adjusted on the basis of need, such as indicated by the number of dependents. Thus, even though the Social Security tax took out the same portion of each person's income when they were working, the percentage that Social Security gives back is much higher for the poor.

On an after-tax basis, Social Security may even pay the retired low-income worker more than he or she earned when working. A worker at the maximum income subject to Social Security tax, in contrast, is likely to receive only about 30 percent as much as when employed. The upshot is that, when Social Security taxes and payments are combined, the Social Security system is highly progressive. Low-income workers have money redistributed their way from the tax dollars paid by higher-income workers.

The redistribution from higher-income workers to lower-income workers is one reason participation in Social Security is required by law. If it were optional, workers with above-average incomes would quit, leaving no money to redistribute. Workers would also be deterred from joining voluntarily by intergenerational redistribution, which gives current retirees a much better deal than can be expected by current workers.

If individuals are poor, suffer financial misfortune, or for any other reason have little savings when they retire, what are they to do? It seems clear that society will demand some safety net to prevent indigent retirees from a life of abject poverty. Thus, there will continue to be redistributional Social Security taxes. However, as people are forced to save for their own retirement, and as Social Security as we know it becomes merely a fallback for those in need, Social Security becomes ever more a welfare program.

In the past, Social Security has been viewed as something that people deserve to have, because they have been forced to pay Social Security taxes all their lives. The more redistributional Social Security becomes, however, the less sense this view makes. If workers see their payroll taxes rise in order to pay for the rising proportion of the elderly, there is likely to be an outcry against paying for those who can afford to pay for themselves. The better-off Social Security recipients will be cut from the roles, and the taxes they paid will not save them. As Social Security advances down this road, it will rightly be perceived as welfare for the aged. The question will be asked: "Why is there a separate tax earmarked for this welfare?" If this scenario is correct, the country will probably see the demise of the Social Security payroll tax, and its replacement by higher income taxes and other taxes.

Whether to Work or Not to Work—That Is the Question

This prediction of the future suggests that workers have some serious thinking to do. Do they struggle to acquire human capital and increase their earnings? If they do, they will face paying for the Social Security welfare of others. The alternative is to live it up and avoid the hard work necessary to earn a high income. After all, living into retirement years is not ensured. Those who live for the moment, acquire little human capital, and save nothing for retirement would have the safety net of Social Security to cushion their fall. If that cushion is too appealing, though, the future of the U.S. economy will not be appealing at all.

■ Prospecting for New Insights

1. This Exploration notes that current workers might not have the incentive to be as productive as they could be. The same has been said of current retirees, who see the value of their Social Security payments fall as the incomes they earn between ages 65 and 69 increase. Why are Social Security payments reduced for those who earn money in their retirement years? Is this fair? How does your answer depend upon whether Social Security is an entitlement that people have earned, or a welfare program?

2. The retirement age, at which a person will become eligible to receive Social Security benefits, is scheduled to rise from 65 to 67 or more. This rise is to be phased in over the next decade. What political reason prevents a more rapid phase-in? What will be the effect of this change on productivity?

Exploration 12-2 Prices and Property Rights— Do Russians Know the Secret to Prosperity?

To develop economically, Russia is transforming itself from the premier example of a centrally planned economy to a market economy. However, private property rights are an important part of this transformation, a part that remains uncertain.

> *If history could teach us anything, it would be that private property is inextricably linked with civilization.*
>
> —Ludwig von Mises

That Was Then

Unlike capitalist countries, the former Communist countries of Eastern Europe and the Soviet Union had no competitive market prices to ensure an efficient allocation of resources. Prices were set for purposes of equity and political expediency, not for efficiency. Soviet planners tried to match resources to outputs and outputs to needs, but faced a difficult problem. To allocate efficiently, planners must know how much value consumers place on alternative outputs. They also must compute the opportunity costs of inputs. In contrast, free markets reveal this information automatically; it is implicit in market prices.

To acquire the information they need, the Soviet planners estimated *shadow prices*, which are what the market prices would have been if there had been free markets. This undertaking is something like trying to answer the old riddle, "How much wood would a woodchuck chuck, if a woodchuck could chuck wood?" Although the planners resorted to complex mathematical models, the estimated shadow prices were still only rough approximations to true market prices. When planners imposed incorrectly estimated prices, people and businesses were led to many wrong decisions about what and how to produce.

Even if the shadow prices were accurate, they would not have been the prices people actually pay. Thus, we saw such strange occurrences as children using loaves of bread as footballs, even though the bread did not last long in that usage, and even though the cost of the ingredients to make the loaves far exceeded their value as footballs.

The problem was that bread was priced very cheaply for political reasons, and customers bought it in much larger quantities than they would have if bread prices reflected the costs of the foodstuffs, labor, and other items used in producing that bread. Still, for political reasons, government attempted to turn out as much of this necessity as consumers would choose to buy.

Politically set prices had one interesting positive effect. They forced Russian authorities to exercise monetary restraint. Too many rubles would just add more purchasing power, which consumers would spend on underpriced goods. The Soviet Union did not have the wherewithal to produce enough of these goods as it was. With the exception of bread and a few other items, shelves were often bare. The only way to prevent even greater shortages was to keep additional money from circulating in the economy. Thus, in the former Soviet Union, price inflation was kept low because government set the prices, and monetary growth was restrained in order to allow the policy of low prices to work. In contrast, when markets are free, the process is reversed. Monetary restraint must be exercised to keep inflation from taking hold in the marketplace.

The policy of holding prices to artificially low levels proved troublesome when it came to foreign trade. The Soviet Union was forced to maintain two sets of prices for each good. One set denominated prices in rubles, the local currency. The other set consisted of prices in dollars or another foreign currency. This second set was intended to correspond to the shadow prices estimated by the Soviet government.

By law, the ruble was *nonconvertible*, meaning that foreigners were not allowed to make purchases in rubles. To have done otherwise would have allowed foreigners to take advantage of the artificially low prices offered to Soviet citizens. The Soviet government would in this way have been subsidizing foreigners, which was not their intent.

The nonconvertibility of the ruble led to many interesting and convoluted barter trades, in which seemingly unrelated items were offered in exchange for each other. For example, in order to do business in the Soviet Union, the Pepsi Company agreed to accept Russian vodka rather than cash. Once Pepsi imported the vodka into the United States, it sold it to liquor wholesalers in exchange for cash. Barter deals were hard to arrange and often fell through. For example, Sikorsky Helicopter opted against accepting children's toys in exchange for helicopters. Children's toys were too far outside Sikorsky's area of expertise.

It was small wonder that the Russian economy spiraled downward over time. The arms buildup of the 1980s hastened that decline and prompted an overthrow of the central planners. First, there was Mikhail Gorbachev, would-be reformer of the communist system. Then came Boris Yeltsin, a free-market revolutionary who extricated Russia from the splinters of the Soviet Union. Many thought that, with markets freed from the central planners, living standards would quickly rise. The statistics said otherwise, and for good reason.

Protecting Russian Property

Russia embraced capitalist ideas, but failed to impose a key ingredient necessary for the success of free markets. That ingredient is certainty over property rights. If individuals and businesses have no confidence that they will be able to keep the fruits of their labors and investments, the profit motive is lost. Sure, we all want to profit, but only if we can keep or spend those profits for our own sakes. Few would seek profit in order to turn it over to the government. Unfortunately, in Russia today, that is a danger.

It is possible to make deals with the Russian government. The problem is, which government? Russia is presently characterized by too many governments, with uncertainty over which governments have jurisdiction over which places and activities. For example, it is possible to buy land in Russia. However, it is nearly impossible to obtain a clear title to it. One government may grant that title, while another government lies in wait to claim the land as its own somewhere down the line. At least one U.S. entrepreneur has seen this situation as a profit opportunity, and seeks to offer title insurance to remedy the problem.

Some Russian entrepreneurs have a different strategy. They specialize in having connections with both legitimate and illegitimate authorities. For example, Ben and Jerry's used these entrepreneurs to establish a network of Russian "scoop shops" to sell its ice cream. Even so, Ben and Jerry's ultimately abandoned its efforts to do business in Russia.

With all the governments come a host of taxes. To some extent, all taxes represent an expropriation of private property. Russian taxes sometimes carry this expropriation to an absurd extreme. Specifically, when taxes from the various jurisdictions are added together, they often sum to over 100 percent. This means that, for every dollar of profit a business makes, it owes more than a dollar to the government.

It would seem that no business would voluntarily choose to operate under these conditions. Yet business does go on in Russia. The reason is twofold. First, many profits are hidden from the tax collector, either through bribery or techniques of accounting. Second, and related to the first, there is a thriving underground economy that is not reported to authorities.

Much of this underground economy is ruled by organized crime. There are thought to be hundreds of criminal organizations in modern Russia. Oftentimes, their leaders are former officials of the communist government, officials who know networks of "enforcers." In a way, these former officials are entrepreneurs. They provide a service for which there is a strong demand. That service is the protection of property rights. For a price, the local crime boss will protect your property from other criminals. Through his connections, he can also offer some protection from excessive government regulation and taxation.

It is thus not surprising to find that statistics from the Russian government show that the transition to free markets caused the Russian economy to shrink. Statistics measure the economy that is reported. Judging from the upbeat attitudes and spending seen on the streets of Russia's cities, the underground economy appears to be thriving.

When economic activity is not reported, government can collect no taxes on it directly. There is a way in which it can be taxed indirectly, however. That way is through inflation. Authorities in Russia's central bank no longer need to worry about sustaining artificially low prices. Rather, by printing money freely, they allow government to spend without collecting taxes. Instead, the tax is inflation that erodes purchasing power in the legitimate and underground economies alike.

There is a danger, though, that Russian central bankers seemed to overlook. Indeed, some say that the Russian central bankers saw the danger and were attempting to sabotage market reforms. The danger is that too much inflation of the ruble could drive the marketplace to forgo using the ruble as its currency. By requiring payment in dollars or barter, for instance, Russia's underground economy can sidestep the tax of inflation.

Not Just in Russia

Around the world, countries have turned to free markets as a means of adding vitality to economies that must support ever more people. Still, free markets are often embraced half-heartedly, with reluctance. In this age of media sound bites, good economics often does not make for good politics. Indeed, for autocratic rulers, free-market economics may be downright threatening.

Free markets promote free thought. To get ahead in the marketplace requires savvy and foresight. It requires that people think about the choices they make. It is but a short step for people used to thinking about their own choices to start also thinking about the choices their country makes. It is only another short step for people to want involvement in decisions affecting their country and its economy. That step can be threatening to the status quo and can invoke increasingly harsh crackdowns in order to intimidate people into submission. The Tienammin Square massacre and subsequent crackdowns in China provide examples.

Although free markets may promote democracy, it is not as obvious that democracy promotes free markets. Participation in making choices collectively is quite different from making choices individually in the marketplace. In the marketplace, individuals live with the consequences of their own personal choices rather than with the consequences of the majority's choice. The property rights that free markets rely upon to function efficiently can be both protected and undermined by a government responding to collective democratic choice.

Taxation and regulation both represent government *takings* of private property. These takings may be a necessary trade-off in obtaining goals of equity, or may promote market efficiency if they correct market failures. Unfortunately, a democratic political process is free to go further and cross the fine line between government actions that correct market failures and government actions that short-circuit market successes.

The Story Unfolds

Russia has undergone a dramatic upheaval, in which the old order of communism was thrown out to make way for the new order of capitalism. However, capitalistic free markets cannot function without the ownership of private property. There has been movement in this direction, such as the privatization of Russian car and truck maker ZIL and other companies. Still, because ownership of private property in Russia is tenuous, its free markets struggle.

The future can take different paths. One path is for an autocratic ruler to take charge, perhaps exploiting the passion of nationalism in the same way that Lenin exploited the passion of communism. Restoring order can add certainty to property rights. However, if the transition is tumultuous, who is to say that more revolution would not be around the corner? Tumultuous change adds uncertainty, which casts the staying power of property rights into doubt.

The other path is less exciting, but might offer more stability and certainty over property rights. That path is to fight the problems of the Russian economy battle by battle, without the upheaval of revolutionary warfare. The question would remain, however, as to which side would come out victorious. Would a democratic Russia battle for sound economic policy? Or would the public be swayed by feel-good sound bites that undermine the principles of private property that support free-market efficiency? We need only wait to see the answer, as the story unfolds before the Russian people and the world.

■ Prospecting for New Insights

1. Consumers like low prices. Yet the transition from government-set prices to free-market prices leads to higher prices of many items, such as bread, milk, and other heavily subsidized products. How can it be in the consumer interest to accept the transition from command-and-control pricing to free-market pricing? Do you think the typical consumer would recognize your reasoning?

2. Free markets rely on private property rights, but those rights are not absolute. In other words, it would not be in the social interest to allow private property to be put to any use whatsoever, without any restriction. What are some examples of legitimate government restrictions on the use of private property? Should the property owners be paid to accept these restrictions?

13

MONEY, BANKING, AND MONETARY POLICY

A Look Ahead

THE LARGE NUMBER of colorful slang words for money suggests that it is never far from peoples' minds. How else can such synonyms as "moolah," "simoleons," "dough," "lettuce," "bucks," and "boodle" be explained? Further evidence is found in the numerous sayings that concern money. You probably recognize these samples: Time is money. Money doesn't grow on trees. Money to burn. Money is the root of all evil. Show me the money.

Money is also at the heart of the macroeconomy. Monetary policy affects interest rates, inflation, unemployment, and economic growth. Because of its broad effects, there is often contention over what monetary policy should be. Monetary policy is established by the Fed, short for the Federal Reserve System. The Fed is the U.S. central bank—the most powerful institution in U.S. money and banking. Commercial banks—those on Main Street—also play a prominent role.

Exploration 13-1 considers the large number of bank failures during the 1980s and contemplates whether a new wave of bank failures could occur. Exploration 13-2 shows how the value of money changes when the economy experiences either inflation, disinflation, or deflation, and how workers try to protect themselves from these effects.

Federal Reserve System: the U.S. central bank, established in 1913; contains three primary components: the Board of Governors, the Open Market Committee, and Regional Federal Reserve Banks; conducts monetary policy and participates in bank regulation.

As you are **Surveying Economic Principles** you will arrive at an ability to

- ❏ identify the types, functions, and liquidity of various money measures;
- ❏ explain the effects of a change in the quantity of money on the macroeconomy;
- ❏ describe the structure, functions, and policy tools of the Federal Reserve System;
- ❏ recite the equation of exchange and explain its role in the conduct of monetary policy;
- ❏ relate the behavior of real and nominal interest rates to the level of inflation.

While **Exploring Issues** you will be able to

- ❏ explain why the banking crisis of the 1980s occurred and whether another banking crisis could happen;
- ❏ discuss the issues of inflation, disinflation, and deflation as they relate to the value of money.

Terms Along the Way

SURVEYING ECONOMIC PRINCIPLES

Money

Money facilitates the exchange of inputs and outputs and is integral to the circular flow of income between households and firms. To put money into perspective, imagine a world in which it did not exist. To fulfill our wants, we would have to either barter or produce on our own all the goods and services we consume. Both alternatives are inefficient. Money provides us with higher living standards. That's why money is no fad and never goes out of style. In one form or another, money has been in continuous use from the earliest days of civilization. Among the important qualities of money are *portability* and *divisibility*. Money should be easily transportable and divisible to make it convenient to spend and receive change.

What Is Money?

Everyone knows what money is. It's the rectangular pieces of paper with pictures of presidents and the shiny metallic coins that we carry with us when we go shopping, right? Not quite. If it has value, is portable, and doesn't turn to mush, it has probably served as money somewhere. In prisoner of war camps during World War II, cigarettes served as money. Among Native Americans, wampum (seashells) was used as money. Tobacco and furs were money at various times in frontier America.

Gold was money for thousands of years. Paradoxically, gold is not money in the United States today. What then performs the role of money? Government-issued currency and coins are money, but they are most assuredly *not* the largest component of the U.S. money supply. The electronic notations of bankers representing checking account money hold that distinction, as will be discussed shortly.

Money performs the following functions:

Interest in gold is widespread on the Internet. To access a Web site that advocates a monetary role for gold, go to "Supply-Side University," an on-line economics tutorial driven by students' questions, at **http://www. polyconomics. com/univ.htm**

- *Medium of exchange.* That is, money is used to make purchases. Money must be acceptable to sellers, who will find it so only if they believe that others will too.
- *Store of value.* Money is a means of holding wealth, but by no means the only one. Real estate, jewelry crafted of precious stones and metals, and stocks and bonds also serve as stores of value, because they are not perishable and are expected to retain their value. Conversely, food and clothing are not used as money.
- *Unit of account.* The market values of goods and services are expressed as prices, which are stated in terms of money. The monetary unit varies from one nation to another. These monetary values are used for a variety of purposes, such as to measure GDP or to make comparisons among goods.

Fiat money is money by government decree. Paper currency and current U.S. coins are examples. Because government accepts fiat money, others do too. Gold and silver coins, once a staple of the U.S. money supply, are examples of *commodity money*. Commodity money was made from precious metals.

Unfortunately, commodity money is subject to *Gresham's law*—bad money drives out good. In other words, people have the incentive to nick, shave, or otherwise reduce the metallic content of coins. Anyone possessing such an altered coin tries to spend it first and hoard the better, unaltered ones. This practice forces recipients of commodity money to examine it carefully, such as by weighing it and even biting it. People do not wish to examine their money this closely, and thus turn to fiat money instead.

The governments of virtually all nations today hold a monopoly on the production of fiat money. The profit from the difference between the value of money and the cost of producing it is called *seigniorage*. For example, if a $100 bill costs 5 cents to print and place into circulation, the government's profit from the issuance of that bill is $99.95.

U.S. paper money is printed by the U.S. Treasury. Twenty-two and one-half million paper notes are printed every day. Visit the Web site at **http://www.treas. gov/** to learn more about the duties of the Treasury.

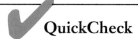

QuickCheck

Many people refer to their credit cards as plastic money. Do credit cards perform any of the functions of money?

Answer: No. Credit cards are not a medium of exchange. Credit card balances must be paid off with the medium of exchange, usually checking account money. Credit cards are also neither a store of wealth nor a unit of account. Credit cards make it more convenient to spend money, but are not themselves money.

The Web site for the Visa credit card includes a discussion of antitrust and the credit card industry, plus information useful to consumers. It can be found at **http://www.visa. com/cgi-bin/vee/ main.html**

OBSERVATION POINT:
Cash In Your Cash

> *The Congress shall have power . . . to coin Money, regulate the value thereof, and of foreign Coin, and fix the standard of Weights and Measures.*
>
> —Constitution of the U.S., Art. 1, Sec. 8

You can bring your "greenbacks" to the U.S. Treasury or the Federal Reserve and redeem them for something of value. Until the 1930s that something was gold. For a while, Silver Certificates circulated as paper money. Silver coins remained a possibility until 1965, when the U.S. Treasury started replacing them with less valuable "sandwiches" of copper covered by nickel. The Treasury still mints a gold coin, the American Eagle, but it is not used as money because its value as gold is too high.

You can still cash in your cash, and receive something valuable in exchange. You can exchange your Federal Reserve Notes for . . . more of the same! A 20 dollar bill will net you two tens, four fives, or twenty ones, at your request.

Liquidity: M1, M2, and M3

When paper money and coins are deposited in banks, money changes form. Deposits into checking accounts create **demand deposits,** also termed *checkable deposits.* More money is held in the form of checkable deposits than in any other form. These deposits are money because checks—orders to a bank to make payment—are generally accepted by sellers. Traveler's checks are also generally accepted by sellers. In addition, currency may be transformed into any of several "near monies," such as balances in savings accounts.

demand deposits: checking account balances.

The Federal Reserve has three definitions of money, termed the *monetary aggregates*, which categorize money according to how liquid it is. Liquidity refers to how easily and quickly something can be converted into spendable form. Something is completely liquid if it is spendable without delay. The monetary aggregates include M1, M2, and M3. M1 is the most liquid of these and totaled $1.1 trillion in 1998. M2 is slightly less liquid and totaled $4.4 trillion in 1998. M3 is much less liquid and totaled $6.0 trillion in 1998. The specific components of each category are as follows:

liquidity: how easy it is to convert an asset into a spendable form; highly liquid assets are often used as money.

- **M1:** The sum of currency and coin in the hands of the public, demand deposits, and traveler's checks. These forms of money are the most easily and immediately spendable. **Currency stored in bank vaults is not counted in the money supply because it is not available to make purchases.**

M1, M2, M3: three measures of the money supply, defined in order of decreasing liquidity.

- **M2:** M1 plus savings deposits and "small" time deposits and money market mutual funds. Time deposits are certificates of deposit (CDs), which can be withdrawn without penalty only after some period of time, such as one or five years. The Fed considers CDs small if they are less than $100,000!

- **M3:** M2 plus large time deposits (at least $100,000), and several other near monies. These additional components of M3 are even less spendable than the items in M2.

time deposits: certificates of deposit (CDs), which can only be cashed in without penalty after a stated period of time, such as one year.

Because currency and coin are immediately spendable, they are completely liquid. Demand deposits are only slightly less liquid, because businesses often require check writers to present some form of identification before the check is accepted. Savings account deposits are slightly less liquid than demand deposits, but can be converted into demand deposits or currency with a trip to the bank.

Financial assets, such as stocks and bonds, are not counted in the money supply figures. They are nonetheless relatively liquid because they can be readily sold in the financial marketplace at fair market value, although brokerage fees reduce their liquidity. In contrast, most nonfinancial assets are not very liquid. For example, automobiles, furniture, and personal belongings are difficult to sell quickly at their market value. Similarly, the sale of real estate usually involves large broker's fees.

To visit the Web site maintained by the New York Stock Exchange, go to **http://www.nyse.com/**

OBSERVATION POINT:
The Euro—Out with the Old and in with the New

U.S. residents take it for granted that the same dollar bills are just as spendable in New York as New Orleans. Europeans, on the other hand, have had to contend with changes in currency and coins even for short trips that cross borders between countries. That is in the process of changing.

January 1, 1999, marked a momentous moment in monetary history. The three-year transition to a new monetary unit began in eleven of the countries making up the European Monetary Union. If all goes well, the German mark, the French franc, the Italian lire, and the other familiar currencies issued by many European countries will begin to disappear in 2002, to be replaced by the euro. More countries may make the jump to the euro as time passes. Monetary union also entails a new European Central Bank to conduct monetary policy, replacing the central banks in individual countries.

The European Commission maintains a Web site devoted to providing details about the conversion to the Euro. The English language entrance is at **http://europa.eu.int/euro/html/home5.html?lang=5**

Why would countries risk confusion by dropping their familiar currencies, not to mention the loss of control over their own money? These changes are all part of a long-term effort to integrate the economies of Europe to make them more competitive with the United States and Japan in the global marketplace. A common currency will also ease the burdens on harried travelers who would rather worry about the price of lodging in the night's ski chalet than about having the right currency to pay that price!

Money and the Macroeconomy

If you've been unemployed, you know the problem—not enough money to spend! If unemployment in the economy is excessive, as in a recession, the problem is the same: Aggregate unemployment stems from spending that is insufficient to purchase the full-employment level of output, given current prices. Thus, to cure the recession, either prices must fall or the quantity of money available to be spent must rise. In general, to maintain full employment, the quantity of money must rise to keep pace with the economy's productive potential.

If the quantity of money rises too much, then the problem is not one of too little spending power to sustain full-employment output. Rather, the problem is that too much money will be chasing the goods and services that the economy is capable of producing, thus driving up their prices and causing a general inflation. **An overwhelming amount of evidence shows excessive growth in money to be the root cause of inflation.** This evidence is from the United States and from many other countries, and covers episodes of inflation throughout history. To see how the quantity of money is determined we turn our attention to U.S. banking and then to the role played by the Federal Reserve.

The Banking System

About 9,000 U.S. commercial banks accept deposits and make loans. Since the mid-1980s the number of banks has plummeted because of bank failures, discussed in Exploration 13-1, and bank mergers. For example, the number of banks fell an astonishing 37 percent between 1984 and the end of 1998. New features on the banking landscape also include the rise of megabanks—large banks that do business in many locations. Megabanks thrive in today's climate of *interstate banking* as legal barriers against branching across state lines have fallen. Electronic banking from home via the Internet is a recent development. The fact is that banks are becoming ever more national and even international institutions.

To learn more about banking, visit the Web site offered by the American Bankers Association at **http://www.aba.com**

Banks are regulated by both state and federal governments. Bank regulation is designed to protect against unsound banking practices that could bankrupt both depositors and government insurance funds. In spite of regulation, unsound lending practices contributed to the multitude of bank failures in the 1980s.

Banking regulation is quite controversial. Since regulations inhibit banks from responding to the demands of their customers, regulations can lead to inefficiencies. For example, under the Glass-Steagall Act of 1933, banks are barred from offering insurance and brokerage services. This act is intended to keep banks away from risky investment activities that could endanger the banking system.

College students who wish to teach young children about bank regulation can direct them to visit the FDIC Learning Bank on the Internet at **http:www.fdic.gov/learning/index.html**

Because consumers value one-stop shopping and because diversification might actually reduce the risk of bank failure, there are continuing efforts to repeal the act.

TABLE 13-1 Major Assets and Liabilities of Banks

Assets (Uses of Funds)	Liabilities (Sources of Funds)
Vault cash	Deposits
Deposits held by the Federal Reserve	Federal funds
Loans	Discount loans
Securities	
Other	

Although these efforts have failed as of this writing, banking regulation has been loosened in recent years. As a result of the loosening of the regulatory knot, banks are currently permitted to own subsidiary companies that supply financial services that the banks themselves are not permitted to supply.

Table 13-1 lists the major assets and liabilities of banks. The assets are things that banks own and show how banks use funds. The liabilities show how banks raise funds.

The most liquid asset is cash. A portion of cash assets are currency and coin held by banks as vault cash. Additional cash assets are held as deposits with the Federal Reserve. The sum of vault cash plus deposits with the Fed is called *bank reserves.* Bank reserves are available immediately to meet depositor withdrawals.

Bank loans go to both the household and business sectors. Banks lend in order to earn income in the form of interest. *Securities,* in the form of *bonds,* are government interest-bearing assets that the government issues when it borrows. Interest payments on securities also provide banks with income.

Bank deposits are liabilities because they are funds owed to depositors. Banks also raise funds by borrowing. Funds borrowed from other banks are called *federal funds.* The interest rate that banks charge on loans to other banks is called the **federal funds rate.** Borrowings from the Federal Reserve are called *discount loans* because the Federal Reserve is said to "discount" its loans. To discount a loan means that banks are required to pay the interest on loans from the Fed when they are made rather than as they are repaid. The rate of interest charged is termed the **discount rate.**

Banks hold some fraction of their deposits on reserve to meet the cash needs of their customers. The remaining reserves are available to make loans and investments. Individual banks are required by law to meet **reserve requirements** imposed by the Fed. The current reserve requirement of approximately 10 percent for demand deposits means that banks must hold at least $10 in reserves for every $100 of deposits. Hence, banks are free to invest most of their reserves, but must hold a relatively small fraction of total deposits in the form of reserves. Reserves in excess of the required amount are called **excess reserves.** Hence, total reserves equal required reserves plus excess reserves.

The possibility that banks might not be able to pay off depositors motivates the *Federal Deposit Insurance Corporation (FDIC)* to insure deposit accounts up to $100,000. This insurance reduces the possibility of bank runs, in which numerous depositors simultaneously seek to withdraw funds because of fears about the financial soundness of a bank. The tradeoff is that FDIC insurance allows banks to make

federal funds rate: the interest rate on reserves banks lend to each other.

discount rate: the interest rate, the rate at which future values are reduced to their present value equivalents; also the rate of interest charged by the Federal Reserve on short-term loans to member banks.

reserve requirements: the percentage of deposits banks must retain as cash in their vaults or as deposits at the Federal Reserve; set by the Federal Reserve.

excess reserves: deposits banks hold as reserves in excess of reserve requirements established by the Federal Reserve.

riskier loans without scaring away their depositors. These depositors know that their funds are secure no matter how many unsound loans a bank may make.

In addition to banks, there are other *financial intermediaries* that raise funds in order to make loans or investments. With minor exceptions, the discussion of banks also applies to credit unions and savings and loans. Insurance companies, mutual funds, pension funds, and finance companies are examples of nonbank financial intermediaries, because, although they are not banks, they invest the funds they raise.

QuickCheck

A bank has $1,000 in deposits and holds $250 in reserves. If the reserve requirement is 20 percent, how much are excess reserves?

Answer: Required reserves equal 0.2 multiplied by $1000, or $200. Since total reserves equal $250, excess reserves must be $50.

OBSERVATION POINT:
Do Banks Discriminate in Making Loans?

"Redlining!" Some banks have been accused of refusing to extend home loans in minority neighborhoods. That would violate the federal Fair Housing Act. Minorities have been turned down for home loans as much as twice as often as whites, evidence in the eyes of bank critics of discrimination. Banks defend themselves by noting that the profit motive prompts banks to make sound loans and reject risky ones. Which argument is most convincing? Some banks—those unable to demonstrate that they applied risk criteria in a color-blind fashion—have been convicted in courts of law of illegal redlining. Other banks, however, have been found to be not guilty. In response, bank regulators now pay much closer attention to the relative number of loan approvals for minorities.

How Banks Create Money

When a bank makes a loan, the quantity of money increases. To see how, suppose you hope to borrow the cost of a new Dodge Neon, $10,000, from your bank, Homestate University National Bank. After discussing your loan request with loan officer Softheart, the loan is approved. Soon you'll be behind the wheel of your first new car.

If you receive the loan as currency, the amount of currency in the hands of the public, which includes you, is greater than before the loan. Recall that this currency, while inside the bank's vault, was not included in the money supply. Once you receive the $10,000, the M1, M2, and M3 money supplies increase by that amount.

You might not feel safe with $10,000 cash on your person. For this reason, you probably received the loan in the form of a $10,000 check deposited in your checking account. Again, the M1, M2, and M3 money supplies increase by $10,000.

When borrowers repay bank loans, the quantity of money falls. If a loan is repaid with currency, the money supply decreases because there is less currency in the hands of the public. If a loan is repaid by writing a check, the money supply falls due to fewer demand deposits.

Meet the Fed

Structure and Functions of the Federal Reserve

In England, it is affectionately known as the "Old Lady of Threadneedle Street," but is officially the Bank of England. In Germany, it is the Bundesbank, in Canada, the Bank of Canada, and in Hong Kong, the Monetary Authority of Hong Kong. What is it? A central bank. The U.S. central bank is called the Fed, short for Federal Reserve System. It was created by the *Federal Reserve Act of 1913* in response to recurring problems of bank failure and the belief that a central bank could contribute to U.S. economic stability. With its creation, Congress sought to provide the banking system with the stabilizing influence of a central bank. To this end, the Fed does the following:

- **Functions as a banker's bank.** The Fed holds reserves for commercial banks.
- **Functions as a lender of last resort.** The Fed lends reserves to sound banks that are temporarily short of reserves. Withdrawals by depositors deplete reserves. If depositors become concerned about a bank's ability to pay, the rush to withdraw funds can create a bank run.
- **Supervises banks.**
- **Conducts monetary policy.** The Fed was established for the purpose of providing an elastic money supply—a quantity of money that responds to the demands of the economy. A tighter monetary policy constrains the quantity of money, perhaps to fight inflation. A looser monetary policy expands the money supply in order to stimulate economic growth or counter an economic slowdown. Fed influence over the money supply is a critical element in the conduct of monetary policy.
- **Issues currency.**
- **Clears checks.**

Congress also sought to keep the Fed *independent*, meaning free from political pressures that might lead it to take actions that would harm the economy in the long run. Because the Fed does not depend upon Congress for its income, but instead earns income from its investments and from providing banking services, the Fed is one of the more independent central banks around the world. This fact is important because evidence shows that countries with independent central banks suffer less inflation. To further insulate the Fed from the political process, the Fed is divided into three components:

- The **Board of Governors,** which is responsible for the overall direction of the Federal Reserve and its policies.
- The **Federal Open Market Committee (FOMC),** which is charged with the conduct of monetary policy.
- The **Federal Reserve Banks,** which regulate and provide a variety of services for banks.

There are seven members of the Board of Governors. They are appointed to 14-year nonrenewable terms by the president, with the advice and consent of the Senate. Terms are staggered so that one term expires every 2 years, which minimizes political influence over the Fed. One of the seven is named by the president to chair the Board. The chairperson serves a 4-year renewable term. The chairperson is the most powerful individual in the Fed and one of the most powerful people in the country. As of 1999, economist Alan Greenspan held the position.

The FOMC consists of twelve members, the seven members of the Board plus four rotating district bank presidents, and the president of the New York District Bank. The president of the New York Fed is always a member of the Committee because New York City is the hub of the nation's financial markets. The FOMC usually meets at intervals of approximately four to six weeks, making adjustments in the conduct of monetary policy in accordance with its assessment of economic conditions.

There are twelve regional Federal Reserve Banks, as shown in Figure 13-1. Together with their branches, these Banks perform the routine functions of the Fed. Chances are that you have benefitted from their services today. Federal Reserve

The Minneapolis Federal Reserve Bank provides addresses and Internet links to other Fed entities at **http://woodrow. mpls.frb.fed.us/ info/sys/banks. html**

The New York Fed's Web site is chock full of material. Among other interesting information is an explanation of how you can save brokers fees by investing in U.S. Treasury bonds through the TreasuryDirect program. This site is located at **http://www.ny. frb.org**

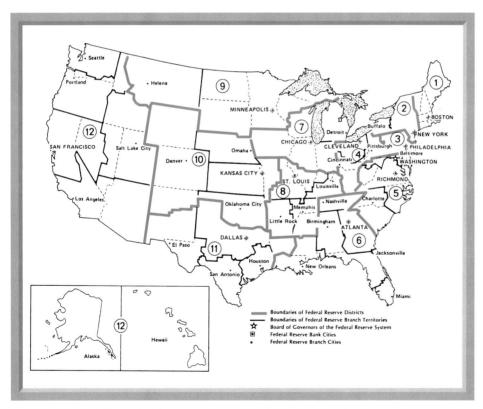

FIGURE 13-1 **The Federal Reserve System** is divided into 12 districts.

Banks issue currency, which bears the location of the issuing bank. Commercial banks within a district make deposits of reserves into their district's Federal Reserve Bank. Federal Reserve Banks also operate the Fed's check-clearing operations, which allow funds to be expeditiously transferred from check writers' accounts to the accounts of the banks that cash the checks. These banks also participate in the supervision of commercial banks in their districts.

National banks—those chartered by the federal government—are automatically members of the Federal Reserve. Banks with state charters may join at their option. Whether or not they are members of the Federal Reserve System, however, all banks have nearly equal access to the Fed's services and are subject to its regulations. Thus, although only about 4,000 banks are formal members, in practical terms all banks fall under the purview of the Federal Reserve.

Open Market Operations

open market operations: when the Federal Reserve enters the financial marketplace to buy or sell government securities, such as Treasury bonds.

The principal method used by the Fed to influence the money supply is open market operations. **Open market operations** occur when the Fed enters the financial marketplace to buy or sell government securities, such as Treasury bonds. The Fed does not itself issue government securities; the U.S. Department of the Treasury issues Treasury bonds, for example. The Fed can only obtain them in the open market, hence the name. Open market operations allow currency, in the form of Federal Reserve Notes, to make its way into circulation.

For example, suppose your Aunt Elvira sells a bond to the Fed for $10,000. The Fed issues a check written on itself, payable to Aunt Elvira. When she deposits the check in her checking account at Investors' National Bank, demand deposits in the banking system increase by the amount of the check. Thus, the money supply increases. If she had cashed the check instead, currency in the hands of the public would have increased. Either way, the money supply rises.

When an individual buys a bond sold by the Fed, the money supply decreases. Suppose the buyer pays for the bond by writing a check. When the buyer's bank pays the Fed, the buyer's checking account is reduced by the amount of the check. Thus, demand deposits decrease, as does the money supply.

The bulk of the Fed's open market operations involve banks directly. An open market sale to a bank by the Fed decreases bank reserves. Fewer reserves mean that the bank is able to do less lending. Thus, open market sales tend to reduce the money supply. A greater volume of open market sales is consistent with a tighter policy.

An open market purchase by the Fed from a bank increases bank reserves, which in turn tends to increase the money supply, as banks have more money to loan. A greater volume of open market purchases is consistent with a looser monetary policy. However, whether loans are actually made and the money supply actually increased depends upon the willingness of banks to make loans and upon the desire of the public to borrow. **Thus, the Fed influences but does not control the money supply.**

monetary base: the sum of currency held by the public plus bank reserves; can be controlled by the Federal Reserve.

However, by conducting open market operations, **the Fed controls the monetary base.** The **monetary base** is the sum of currency held by the public plus bank reserves. **An open market purchase by the Fed always increases the monetary base by the amount of the purchase; an open market sale always decreases the monetary base by the amount of the sale.**

QuickCheck _____

If Aunt Elvira deposited the Fed's check into her savings account, would the money supply increase?

Answer: The M1 money supply would remain unchanged. However, M2 and M3 would rise, because these measures include savings accounts.

The Money Multiplier and the Monetary Base

The effects of open market operations do not stop with the initial purchase or sale. Secondary effects magnify changes in the money supply. For example, an open market purchase from an individual increases the money supply once when the seller receives the proceeds of the sale. If those funds are deposited in a bank, and then loaned to someone, the money supply increases again. This process can continue over and over.

The money multiplier shows the total effect on the money supply of each dollar of open market operations. To see how the money multiplier works, return to Aunt Elvira's sale of a bond to the Fed. When her checking account increased with the deposit of the Fed's check, we saw that demand deposits in the banking system increased.

money multiplier: the amount by which a new deposit is multiplied to arrive at the actual increase in the money supply; maximum value is given by the deposit mutliplier.

If we assume for simplicity that Investors' National Bank was just meeting a 10-percent reserve requirement prior to the $10,000 deposit, then the bank will find itself holding excess reserves of $9,000. Actual reserves have increased by $10,000, but the bank is only required to hold 10 percent of that amount, equal to $1,000, as required reserves. The bank is thus able to make loans up to the amount of excess reserves and still meet the reserve requirement.

As it happens, your best friend wishes to borrow $9,000 to finance the purchase of a used Saturn automobile. After speaking with loan officer Pushover at Investors' National Bank, your friend's loan is approved. That loan increases the money supply by $9,000. When the dealer is paid, your friend's check will be deposited into the dealer's bank. That bank will then have excess reserves to lend. The amount of required reserves equals $900, so excess reserves equal $8,100, the amount that can be loaned.

This lending-depositing-lending sequence could continue. Someone can borrow $8,100. When the loan is spent, and someone else deposits the $8,100 in their bank, that bank will have excess reserves, which it is able to lend. At each succeeding step in the process, the sum of money loaned, which is new money, grows smaller because each succeeding bank in the sequence must hold a portion as required reserves. Thus the process is eventually exhausted when the last bank in the sequence has essentially nothing left to lend.

What is the total of new money created when the expansion of the money supply is complete? The answer depends on the money multiplier.

$$\text{Money supply} = \text{money multiplier} \times \text{monetary base}$$

The money multiplier can vary according to loan prospects and people's behavior, and is thus hard to calculate with precision. However, an upper bound can be found by calculating the deposit multiplier—**the maximum possible value of the money multiplier.** The deposit multiplier is calculated by assuming that all money is held as demand deposits and that banks do not hold excess reserves. In practice, the true value of the money multiplier will be less than the deposit multiplier.

The deposit multiplier is the reciprocal of the percentage reserve requirement, meaning

$$\text{Deposit multiplier} = \frac{1}{\text{reserve requirement}}$$

For example, if the reserve requirement equals 10 percent, then 1 divided by 10 percent equals 1/0.1, which gives a deposit multiplier of 10. To use this multiplier, multiply the Fed's original open market purchase of $10,000 by the multiplier, 10. The total of new money in that case is $100,000.

The following three factors affect the money multiplier, and thus the actual expansion of the money supply:

- **The reserve requirement:** Changes in the reserve requirement would change the deposit multiplier, and thus the maximum value of the money multiplier. A lower reserve requirement means that banks are able to lend a greater fraction of deposits; a higher reserve requirement has the opposite effect.

- **The public's desire to hold currency instead of deposits:** If people hold more of their money as currency and less as deposits, banks will have fewer dollars to lend. If Aunt Elvira had taken the original $10,000 from the sale of her bond as currency and buried it in her backyard, the multiple expansion of the money supply would not have taken place.

- **The desire of banks to hold excess reserves:** Excess reserves may be held in order to meet unexpected depositor withdrawals, or because lending opportunities seem poor. Reserves that are not loaned out do not add to the money supply.

Other Tools of the Fed

In response to unexpected customer withdrawals or other reasons, banks may wish to borrow from the Fed in order to maintain their required reserves. Recall that loans from the Fed to banks are called discount loans, and the rate of interest charged is called the discount rate. An increase in the discount rate makes it more costly for banks to borrow; a decrease makes it less costly.

Increases in the discount rate tend to decrease the quantity of money by prompting banks to borrow less from the Fed. Conversely, a decrease in the discount rate leads banks to borrow more from the Fed, which tends to increase the amount of money in circulation. Thus, **a change in the discount rate tends to cause the money supply to change in the opposite direction.**

Changes in the discount rate are typically front-page news because they are an easily understood signal of the Fed's policy intentions. A decrease in the discount rate signals a looser monetary policy. The Fed may wish to see the money supply grow faster

TABLE 13-2	The Fed's Monetary Policy Options	
Tighter Monetary Policy	**Looser Monetary Policy**	
Open market sale of securities	Open market purchase of securities	
Increase in discount rate	Decrease in discount rate	
Increase in reserve requirement	Decrease in reserve requirement	

to stimulate growth and employment. An increase in the discount rate signals a tighter policy. Perhaps the Fed would like to slow down monetary growth to fight inflation.

The Fed could change the money supply dramatically by altering the reserve requirement. A decrease in required reserves would increase the money multiplier and spur monetary growth. An increase in the reserve requirement would reduce the money multiplier and thus decrease the money supply. Excess reserves, which banks are able to loan out, would become required reserves, which cannot be loaned out.

The Fed is reluctant to increase reserve requirements because banks without sufficient excess reserves would be forced to sell securities or call in loans—actions that could prove disruptive to the bank and its customers. Thus, while potent, changes in reserve requirements are rarely used as an instrument of monetary policy. Table 13-2 summarizes the Fed's options in setting monetary policy.

 QuickCheck _____

When the Fed lowers the discount rate, why does it become more likely that the money supply will increase?

Answer: A lower discount rate lowers the cost to banks of borrowing reserves from the Fed. Banks that are short of reserves are more likely to borrow reserves from the Fed and less likely to borrow from other banks. Thus, more funds are available in the banking system to lend to the public.

Guiding Monetary Policy

The goals of Federal Reserve monetary policy are high employment, low inflation (price stability), and economic growth. Successful monetary policy must steer a course that keeps inflation in check without creating an unacceptably high level of unemployment. The Fed maintains some secrecy over exactly how it strives to reach these goals. In recent years, observers of the Fed speculate that the Fed has followed a *price rule*, by which it adjusts the money supply up or down in order to keep the prices of certain basic commodities, perhaps including gold, within a target range.

The Fed also designates *monetary targets*, which are acceptable ranges for the growth rates for the M2 and M3 money supplies. In practice, the Fed often misses its targets because it has no direct control over the money supply; it controls only the monetary base. Moreover, monetary targets may sometimes conflict with the Fed's price rule or other objectives.

Between 1993 and 1998 the range of target growth for M2 was 1 percent to 5 percent. This target represents the Fed's best guess about the amount of monetary growth that is best for the economy. When economic conditions change, the Fed can change the targets. Such adjustments are made bearing in mind that too much growth in the money supply has the potential to set off higher inflation; too little, a slowdown in total spending.

The Equation of Exchange—Money and Prices

equation of exchange: an identity that shows that the amount of money people spend must equal the market value of what they purchase; money supply multiplied by velocity of money equals the average price of output multiplied by aggregate output (MV = PQ).

The equation of exchange was originally proposed in the nineteenth century as a means of explaining the link between money, prices, and output. The equation of exchange reveals that the amount of money people spend must equal the market value of what they purchase, as follows:

$$M \times V = P \times Q$$

The left side of the equation represents total spending in the economy. What is spent? Money (M in the equation). But the dollar you spend today was spent by someone else earlier, and will be spent again later. The typical dollar will change hands more than once as the economy's output is purchased. The average number of times money changes hands in a year is called the **velocity of money** (V), which was 1.9 in 1994 for the M2 definition of money. Total spending is calculated by multiplying the money supply by velocity.

velocity of money: the average number of times money changes hands per year.

On the right side of the equation, P is a price index showing the average level of prices. The aggregate output of goods and services is represented by Q. When P and Q are multiplied, the result is the dollar value of purchases, which is equivalent to nominal GDP. Because the value of what is bought must equal the value of what is sold, the equation of exchange is always true.

quantity theory of money: contends that velocity and aggregate output are unaffected in the long run by a change in the money supply, implying that a change in the quantity of money causes a proportional change in the price level; based on the equation of exchange.

The equation of exchange forms the basis for the **quantity theory of money.** The quantity theory contends that velocity and aggregate output are unaffected in the long run by a change in the money supply. Thus, the effect of a change in the quantity of money must be a proportional change in the price level. An increase in the money supply brings a higher price level. Conversely, a decrease in the money supply lowers the price level. Except for determining the price level, the quantity theory suggests that money does not matter, because the economy will always operate at the full-employment level of real GDP. For this reason, the quantity theory cannot explain recessions.

 **QuickCheck** _____

If the money supply doubles, what does the quantity theory predict?

Answer: The quantity theory predicts the price level would double. If the money supply tripled, prices would triple, and so forth.

OBSERVATION POINT:
Taxation through Inflation—What a Money Maker!

The Fed's ability to affect the money supply provides the federal government with opportunities to collect an "inflation tax," which occurs when the Fed escalates its purchases of government bonds. Because fewer bonds are in circulation, government debt to the public decreases, just as it would if government collected more taxes.

This way to reduce federal debt is appealing, except for one thing. The Fed's purchases of government bonds increase the money supply and may lead to inflation. This inflation further reduces the real burden of federal debt, because it allows government to repay its remaining debt with cheaper dollars—dollars that have less purchasing power than those originally borrowed. In effect the government would have tricked the buyers of bonds, and those buyers will not forget. Future government borrowings would become much more expensive, meaning that future government bonds would be forced to pay much higher interest rates.

The Monetarist Prescription

Monetarism is a school of economic thought, founded by Nobel-winner Milton Friedman (1912–), that offers a modern version of the quantity theory. Monetarists readily agree with one contention of the original quantity theory: Velocity and aggregate output are independent of the quantity of money in the long run. However, unlike the quantity theory, monetarism acknowledges the existence of a short run.

According to the monetarist view, the quantity of money may indeed affect velocity and aggregate output in the short run. For example, a reduction in the growth rate of the money supply may cause a reduction in aggregate output. This effect could occur if people cut their purchases of goods and services because bank loans become more costly or difficult to obtain. If that happens, the economy slows down. Thus, monetarism offers an explanation of how too little money can lead to a recession.

To avoid the recession that could result from too little money, or the inflation that could result from too much money, the monetarist policy recommendation is for the Fed to increase the money supply at a steady rate, equal to or slightly greater than the long-run growth in aggregate output. Because long-run growth of output tends to be about 2.5 to 3 percent, a steady annual monetary increase of about 3 percent or slightly higher is called for. The idea is to provide sufficient money so that the economy's additional output could be purchased without setting off significant inflation.

monetarism: view that the Federal Reserve should maintain a slow and steady growth of the money supply, because monetary policy cannot effectively counter short-run economic fluctuations.

Milton Friedman is currently associated with the Hoover Institute at Stanford University. Visit his homepage at the Institute's Web site at **http://www-hoover.stanford.edu/bios/friedman.html**

Implementing Monetarism—Some Practical Impediments

The Fed announces a range of monetary targets that are adjusted infrequently, which is consistent with monetarism. However, the Fed also makes ongoing adjustments in monetary policy that cause the actual growth in the money supply to deviate from its targets, at least temporarily. Thus, the Fed is accused by monetarists of being too quick to increase or decrease the growth rate of the money supply. Monetarists claim that this activist policy accentuates economic instability; they have compared the Fed to a driver who jerks a car's steering wheel first one way, and then the other, before accidentally steering the car off the road.

There are some practical problems in implementing monetarism. The basic problem is that the Fed does not control the money supply. The Fed only controls the monetary base. Growing the monetary base at a slow and steady rate does not mean that the money supply will do likewise. Spirits of pessimism or optimism can greatly affect the money multiplier, which relates the monetary base to the money supply.

For example, the federal government partially shut down in November, 1995, laying off 60 percent of its employees. That shutdown lasted only one week. Had it continued, it would probably have generated widespread economic uncertainties, which would have prompted bankers to hold off on making many loans. The reduction in loans would have reduced the money multiplier, and thus the money supply. It is likely that the economy would have entered a recession, even if the monetary base remained the same. The Fed could counter such a drop in the money supply with an increase in the monetary base. However, that action would require the Fed to predict consumer confidence in the economy, which is beyond its abilities. Consumer confidence is dampened by wars, stock market crashes, and economic troubles in other countries, which can occur without warning.

Another factor also complicates the Fed's search for stable prices. One is that changes in the money supply affect inflation with, as Milton Friedman put it, a "long and variable lag." Today's change in monetary policy may not take effect for months or even years, at which time economic conditions may be quite different from what they were at the moment the policy was implemented. Therefore, the effects of monetary policy are hard to predict.

Interest Rates

interest rate: represents the cost of borrowing and the reward for saving or lending.

Interest rates represent the cost of borrowing and the reward for saving or lending. Conventionally, interest rates are expressed as annual percentages. For example, a bank depositor who receives a 10 percent interest rate on deposits will receive $10 per year in interest payments for each $100 deposited; a borrower who borrows at 10 percent would pay $10 per year in interest for each $100 borrowed. Interest rates commonly encountered by consumers include interest rates on credit cards, car loans, bank accounts, and mortgage loans.

Real versus Nominal Rates

Inflation affects the reward for saving and the true cost of borrowing. To see how, suppose that Lydia has agreed to lend Jon $100 at 10 percent interest, with a loan maturity of 1 year. Jon will thus repay Lydia $110 one year after the loan is made. If inflation increases prices by 10 percent during the year, the $110 that Lydia receives from Jon will buy only as much as the original $100. If effect, Lydia's true reward for giving up the use of her dollars is zero. If Lydia had expected a 10 percent rise in prices, she would not have accepted a 10 percent interest rate on the loan. Only a higher interest rate would have increased her purchasing power at maturity relative to its original value and given her a real reward for making the loan.

A *nominal interest rate* is an interest rate that is stated without reference to the inflation rate. The nominal rate on Lydia's loan to Jon is 10 percent. A *real interest rate* adjusts a nominal rate for inflation in order to show the true cost of borrowing

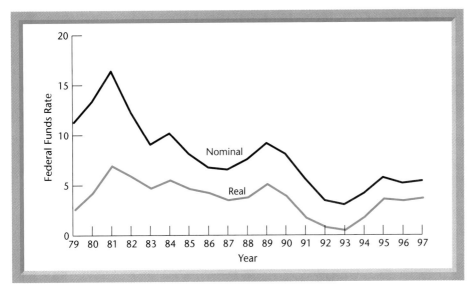

FIGURE 13-2 **The nominal and real federal funds rate, 1979–1997.** Real federal funds rate is calculated as the nominal rate minus the change in the GDP implicit price deflator.
Source: 1999 Economic Report of the President, Tables B-3 and B-73.

and the true reward for lending. If inflation is 10 percent, the real rate on Lydia's loan is 0 percent. The following equation sums up this relationship:

$$\text{Nominal interest rate} = \text{real interest rate} + \text{inflation rate}$$

Before deciding upon the interest rate on her loan to Jon, Lydia should have used this equation. If she expected 10 percent inflation, and she was only willing to make the loan in exchange for a real return of 5 percent, then she should have set a 15 percent rate on the loan. Upon being charged 15 percent by Lydia, Jon should use the equation to calculate the real rate. The real rate would tell Jon the true cost of the loan. Jon would algebraically manipulate the equation to read as follows:

$$\text{Real interest rate} = \text{nominal interest rate} - \text{inflation rate}$$

Figure 13-2 shows the nominal and real federal funds rate since 1979.

✔ **QuickCheck** _____

(A) What is the real interest rate if 30-year government bonds pay 8 percent interest, and bond investors expect inflation to average 3 percent over the next 30 years? (B) What is the real rate on $100 kept in a bank account that pays 2 percent interest, and expected inflation is 3 percent?

Answers: (A) Use the real interest rate equation: 8 percent is substituted for the nominal rate and 3 percent for inflation. The real rate equals 5 percent. (B) Substituting in the real rate equation, the real interest rate is −1 percent. A negative real interest rate shows a loss of purchasing power.

Monetary Policy toward Interest Rates

To a degree, monetary policy works through interest rates. **A key interest rate is the federal funds rate, the interest rate on reserves banks lend to each other.** The Fed does not directly set the federal funds rate, but can influence it by changing the quantity of bank reserves through the conduct of open market operations. Open market sales by the Fed reduce the quantity of bank reserves, and thus increase their price, which is the federal funds rate. The higher price of reserves is likely to be passed along to borrowers in the form of higher interest rates on bank loans. Conversely, open market purchases by the Fed tend to reduce the federal funds rate, and can thus lead to lower interest rates on consumer and business loans.

Monetary policy often targets short-term interest rates. A tight policy causes real interest rates in the economy to rise, with the goal of keeping inflation in check. If successful, then, a tight monetary policy would lead to nominal interest rates that are not much higher than the real rates. For example, if the inflation rate equaled zero, real interest rates would equal nominal interest rates. A loose monetary policy causes real short-term interest rates to fall, which leads to more lending. A loose monetary policy is usually advocated when the economy is weak and inflation is not a problem.

Because interest rates are an expense to businesses and many households, some politicians and businesspeople argue that the Fed should aim to keep them low. Although the Fed could try to keep real rates low by expanding the money supply, the result would likely be inflation that causes nominal interest rates to soar as time passes. The reason is that in the long run, the Fed's open market purchases used to drive down interest rates will increase the money supply and thus inflation. **Monetary policy cannot lower interest rates in the long run, except through lower inflation.** A Fed policy that ignored this principle is often held responsible for the upsurge of inflation in the 1970s.

OBSERVATION POINT:
Fed Watching—From Wall Street to Main Street

Because the Fed is so powerful its actions directly affect people's lives. The stock market, mortgage interest rates, returns on investments in bonds—all these and more are subject to the Fed's influence. The consequence is that Fed watching is something of a national sport. Economists, stock market analysts, and policymakers follow the money supply figures closely. The general public is more likely to have a greater interest in how Fed actions affect interest rates. The monthly payment on that new house or car depends not only on how good a deal the consumer is able to find, but also on monetary policy! Hints as to the future direction of monetary policy can be found when the chair of the Fed testifies before Congress each February and July.

SUMMARY

- The quantity of money affects the macroeconomy through its effects on spending.
- The M1, M2, and M3 money supplies are defined according to decreasing liquidity, respectively.
- The Federal Reserve controls the monetary base and thereby influences the quantity of money.
- The bulk of the money supply is created by banks when they make loans.
- An initial deposit of new money into a bank results in an expansion of money through the money multiplier effect.
- The Federal Reserve is composed of three primary parts: the Board of Governors, the Federal Open Market Committee, and twelve regional Federal Reserve District Banks.
- The tools of monetary policy are open market operations, changes in the discount rate, and changes in the reserve requirement. Most monetary policy is conducted through open market operations.
- Monetarists argue that the Fed should target a slow and steady growth path for the money supply, so as to provide enough money for economic growth, but not so much as to cause an unacceptable level of inflation.
- The Fed also influences interest rates, which in turn affect other aspects of the economy. If the Fed is successful at controlling inflation, real and nominal interest rates will be close together.

QUESTIONS AND PROBLEMS

1. Suppose it became lawful for anyone to issue money without any government restrictions of any kind. What factors would influence an individual to either accept or reject privately issued money?

2. List the components of M1, M2, and M3. Explain why the additional items in M3 make it a less liquid measure of the money supply than M1.

3. On your personal balance sheet, what is the ratio of liquid assets to illiquid assets? Since illiquid assets often pay higher rates of return than liquid ones, why bother to hold liquid assets? Explain.

4. What Fed actions are consistent with a looser monetary policy? Which are in accord with a tighter policy?

5. Suppose M = the money supply = $200, V = velocity = 2, and Q = quantity of output = 100 units. What is the price level? According to the quantity theory of money, what happens to the price level if the money supply triples to $600?

6. What is monetarism? How does it relate to the quantity theory of money?

7. What is your bank's current nominal interest rate on savings deposits? What is the real interest rate on savings deposits? If the real rate is negative, would people continue to hold dollars in savings accounts? Why?

8. Some people urge the Fed to aim to keep interest rates in the economy very low, both in the short run and the long run. Yet the policies that keep interest low in the long run might sometimes require high interest rates in the short run. Explain, making reference to the distinction between real and nominal interest rates.

Web Exercises

9. a. Using an Internet search engine such as that provided by Yahoo (located at **http://www.yahoo.com**) or Alta Vista (located at **http://www.altavista.com**), perform a separate search for the following terms: **"federal funds rate,"** **"monetary base"**, and **"interest rate"**. Visit several of the Web sites that your search reveals for each term and observe the context in which each term is used. Explain whether the manner in which the terms are used is consistent with their use in the text.

b. Repeat the above, but this time use a combination of terms that you select from the chapter. To eliminate Web sites that do not contain all terms, place a plus sign in front of each term you enter, such as **+"equation of exchange" +"velocity of money"**.

10. Visit the Web site of the Federal Reserve System at **http://www.bog.frb.fed.us/** Browse items in the contents. Then select at least two items that relate to each of the functions of the Fed listed in this chapter. Write a short essay that extends the text's discussion of those items.

Visit the Web site for *Economics by Design* at http://www.prenhall.com/collinge for a Self Quiz over the topics in this chapter.

EXPLORING ISSUES

Exploration 13-1 The Banking Crisis of the 1980s—
Could It Happen Again?

Much of the blame for the failure of banks and savings and loans in the 1980s is traced to federal
deposit insurance combined with bank deregulation. The role of moral hazard is highlighted.

Fifty years is a long time. Yet two rounds of legislation, 50 years apart, set the stage
for the banking crisis of the 1980s. Between 1980 and 1994, nearly 3,000 federally
insured savings and loan associations went out of business. This Exploration focuses
on bank failures, without mention of savings and loans, because these institutions and
what can lead them to fail are very similar.

Round one of the structuring of the U.S. banking system that led to today's banking system occurred in the 1930s. Following upon the heels of the closure of banks
and the "bank holiday" declared by President Roosevelt, that decade witnessed New
Deal legislation that created the Federal Deposit Insurance Corporation (FDIC) to
insure funds deposited in banks and the passage of the Glass-Steagall law to restrict
the investment-related activities of banks. The purpose of the FDIC insurance was to
restore public confidence in the banking system; that of Glass-Steagall was to prevent bank failures by keeping banks away from risky investments.

For many years afterward, bankers lived on Easy Street. Bank failures were rare,
as shown in Figure 13-3. Bankers could pay depositors low interest rates because of
the FDIC insurance and because depositors had few alternatives. The financial climate was also salutary, with low inflation and stable interest rates the norm. In the
1960s, though, things started to change. Inflation was no longer quite so low and
the public intuitively understood that a 3 percent interest rate on deposits meant that
the real interest rate was minuscule or even negative. Bankers had to start competing
for deposits with more than a free toaster for every new account.

Deregulating Banking

Round two of the legislation that shaped today's banking system occurred with the
passage of the *Depository Institutions Deregulation and Monetary Control Act of 1980
(DIDMCA).* This legislation loosened the regulatory knot that was holding back the
banks. Regulation Q, which limited the interest rates banks could pay, was also rolled
back. Now banks were freer to compete for depositors' money. But how could they
pay the higher interest rates that they needed in order to compete, and yet still maintain their profitability? The answer is that in the competition for deposits that came
to characterize the latter 1970s and the 1980s, banks had to take on a large volume of
what proved to be high-risk loans and investments. The alternative was to keep their
rates on deposits low and see depositors flee to other banks, savings and loans,
money market mutual funds, or even the bond market, all of which offered higher

An overview of the
mission of the
FDIC can be had
by clicking on the
icons displayed
at the FDIC's
homepage at
**http://www.
fdic.gov**

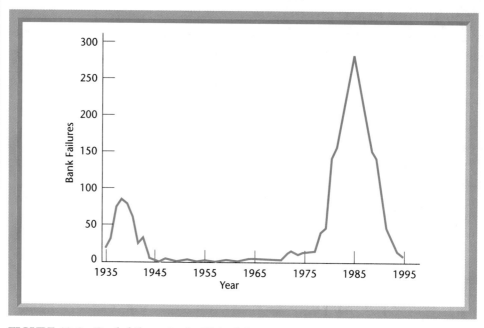

FIGURE 13-3 **Bank failures in the United States** soared in the 1980s and did not return to normal until the mid-1990s. The number of bank failures in this period far exceeded those during the Great Depression of the 1930s.

Source: Federal Deposit Insurance Corporation, *History of the Eighties*, 1998, p. 5.

returns. After all, with the FDIC insurance, the only thing depositors cared about was high interest rates.

If it hadn't been for the FDIC insurance, depositors would likely have shopped for banks that invested wisely. They would have had to pay attention to the ratings in *Consumer Reports* magazine, or other publications that would have found it informative to their readership to profile the safety ratings of banks. Such actions by depositors would have been the only way to ensure that their money was safe.

Moral Hazard and "Too Big to Fail"

The problem of *moral hazard* occurs when people change their behavior because of insurance. When the price of risk goes down, people will do riskier things. It is clear that the moral hazard problem led both depositors and bankers to take on more risk than they otherwise would have accepted. For the bankers' part, they could seek out lending opportunities with higher returns but greater risk without experiencing howls of protest from depositors worried about the safety of their deposits. Depositors could sleep soundly as long as their deposits did not exceed the $100,000 FDIC limit.

In practice, the government even guaranteed deposits above the $100,000 level by adopting a policy of "too big to fail," and by encouraging the merger of insolvent banks—those whose asset values fell below the value of their liabilities—with sound banks. Both of these government policies were equivalent to insurance. A large bank that was deemed too big to fail because its failure might diminish public confidence in the banking system was allowed by bank regulators to continue to operate. Some other troubled banks were forced to merge with sound banks. In these cases the sound banks acquired only the good loans of the merged bank. The government took over ownership of the bad loans.

The market also found a way to extend deposit insurance to those with deposits of more than $100,000. The business of deposit brokering was invented. Deposit brokers could guarantee that any amount of deposits was insured by breaking up large deposits into blocks of amounts less than $100,000 and then placing these blocks with different banks. For example, a $1,000,000 deposit could be placed into ten different banks in $100,000 blocks. With this innovation, the FDIC limits became meaningless.

A Cloudy Future

Could another massive wave of bank failures occur? The healthier economy of the 1990s did much to restore bank profitability and cut bank failures. Some fine-tuning of bank regulation also probably helped. However, people still have the same incentives to change behavior whenever insurance is present. Perhaps for this reason, numerous reports of diminished loan quality and easy credit have again surfaced, as evidenced by how easily students with no credit history can obtain credit cards. Some banking experts worry that the good times of the 1990s have produced a sense of complacency among bankers and their regulators that is not justified. So, unless regulators continue to be on guard in monitoring the quality of bank loans, the combination of deposit insurance and competitive banking could lead to a repeat of the banking crisis of the 1980s.

■ Prospecting for New Insights

1. a. To prevent bank failures should there be more or less regulation of banks?
   b. Make a case for the position you take. For example, if you believe that more regulation is called for, explain what regulations you would want to see enacted. If you believe in less regulation, explain why.
   c. Critique the position you took in part a. For example, if you favored more regulation, for what reasons might that be a bad idea. If you favored less regulation, what are the dangers?

2. Should another wave of bank failures occur in the future, what response should government take? Specifically, should the government try to keep banks going or should it let them fail? What would be the consequences of each policy for the economy?

Exploration 13-2 Inflation, Disinflation, and Deflation— Changes in the Value of Money

Money can lose or gain value . What causes changes in the value of money? Who is harmed by changes in the value of money? Does anyone benefit? In this Exploration we examine the issue of inflation, and an issue that has for the most part been ignored since the 1930s—deflation.

> *Inflation is the process of making addition to currencies not based on a commensurate increase in the production of goods.*
>
> —*Federal Reserve Bulletin* (1919)

Monetary systems today are based upon fiat money, which has no intrinsic value. Such money is vulnerable to losses in value due to inflation, because governments may be tempted to finance expenditures through the issuance of more printing-press money, rather than through borrowing or taxation.

Hyperinflation

Hyperinflation is inflation out of control. With hyperinflation, money loses its value quickly. Take an annual inflation rate of 10,000 percent, for example. What would a dollar be worth after just 1 year of such continuous hyperinflation? The answer: less than a penny. To put it another way, it would take over $100 at the end of a year of such hyperinflation to purchase what $1 would have purchased at the beginning of the year.

The most widely documented episode of hyperinflation occurred in post-World War I Germany in the years 1922–1923. Germany had been held responsible by the victorious allies for the payment of war reparations. That responsibility overburdened the government's ability to tax and borrow. The only avenue of escape left for the German government was the printing press. Before the presses stopped and currency reform occurred, prices had increased by a factor of 1.5 trillion (a trillion equals one followed by 12 zeros). If the U.S. suffered an inflation of similar magnitude, a $50 textbook would rise in price to $75 trillion.

Imagine a hyperinflated world. Your purse or wallet would not be large enough to transport enough money to make a simple purchase. You might demand that your boss pay your wages at the end of every workday, or even more often than that. A dollar received now would have more purchasing power than a dollar received later. You would also want to budget enough time to spend that money. During hyperinflation, money is like a hot potato. Everyone wants to get rid of money as quickly as possible, thus increasing the velocity of money.

Hyperinflation is much more than pages out of a history book. Many modern countries have gone through the same problems. For example, imagine yourself peering from your apartment window in Buenos Aries, Argentina, in 1989. You spy an armored car pulling up to La Dora Restaurant down the street, and carting away sacks of money. It is midnight. You recall seeing the same event the previous midnight and the midnight before that. Come to think of it, you'd seen bags of money carted away from that same restaurant every day at noon. Are you alarmed? Should you call the police to report a money laundering operation? Actually, these events were real, but represented nothing more than the restaurant seeking to get its money into an interest-earning bank account as quickly as possible. At a 1989 inflation rate of 100 percent per month, it did not take long for the Argentine currency to lose its value.

With prices changing so rapidly, imagine the effort that would have to be devoted to keeping track of price changes in supermarkets, restaurants, and other retail establishments. Some people would wish to opt out of the monetary economy as completely as possible by arranging to participate in barter arrangements with others. Others would seek out foreign currencies that were stable in value, as Mexicans and Russians have done with the dollar during recent bouts of inflation in their countries. Overall, hyperinflation would be a giant headache to deal with. The efforts of people to cope with hyperinflation would reduce labor productivity, thus resulting in real reductions in the standard of living.

Inflation and the Rule of 72

In recent decades, hyperinflation has occurred only in less-developed economies. Why, then, is a certain nervousness over inflation detectable in most advanced industrialized nations? One insight can be gained by applying the rule of 72 to various inflation rates. The rule of 72 allows an estimate of how many years it would take prices to double for any rate of inflation. The calculation involved in the rule of 72 is simple: Take an inflation rate and divide it into 72. Table 13-3 shows the outcome of applying the rule of 72 to selected annual inflation rates between 1 percent and 16 percent.

The calculations in Table 13-3 show that an increase in the inflation rate from levels that are initially low can have dramatic long-term effects. For instance, a sustained 2 percent inflation rate, such as was the approximate norm in the United States during the 1950s, would mean that it would take almost half of the average person's lifetime for prices to double. At a 4 percent inflation rate, a figure in line with recent U.S. experience, prices would double about four times over a lifetime. At a 10 percent inflation rate, prices would double over and over a total of ten times. At that inflation rate, newborns had better not become used to the idea of a $2 loaf of bread. In their golden years, bread would be expected to cost $20 a loaf.

TABLE 13-3   Applying the Rule of 72

Annual Inflation Rate	Estimated Number of Years for Price Level to Double
1%	72
2%	36
4%	18
8%	9
10%	7.2
16%	4.5

Unanticipated Inflation and Indexing

By making the distinction between *anticipated inflation* and *unanticipated inflation*, we can more easily discuss the gains and losses produced by inflation. Anticipated inflation is expected by the public. Unanticipated inflation is inflation that catches the public by surprise.

Anticipated inflation, when everyone's crystal balls are working properly, can be taken into account in wage negotiations, mortgage loans, the tax system, and a variety of other contractual agreements. In theory at least, everyone is thus able to defend against losses imposed by anticipated inflation.

When inflation is unanticipated, the story changes. An increase in inflation, which makes inflation higher than expected, provides borrowers with a windfall resulting from a lower-than-expected real interest rate. Because borrowers win, lenders lose. To see this relationship, suppose I borrowed $1,000 from you to be repaid in 1 year. We both anticipate an inflation rate of 2 percent over the year, and agree that a 3 percent real return on your loan is fair. Thus, we strike a deal that I will repay you $1,050, the original sum I borrowed, plus $20 to make you whole for the loss of purchasing power you suffer because of inflation, plus another $30 for giving up the use of your money for the year.

Now suppose inflation proves greater than we anticipated. For example, suppose inflation rises to 5 percent. The real interest rate on the loan drops to zero. The $1,050 I repay you provides you with no reward for giving up the use of your money. You lose. I win, because I was able to use your money without having to pay you a real return. In other words, I used your purchasing power, and returned the same purchasing power to you. If inflation had risen to a rate greater than 5 percent, I would have returned less purchasing power to you than you had before. You would be an even bigger loser.

A solution to the problem just discussed is called indexing—automatically adjusting the terms of the agreement to account for inflation. If we indexed our loan agreement, we would agree to adjust the amount I repaid you according to some price index, say the consumer price index (CPI). If the CPI showed an inflation rate of 5 percent over the year of our loan agreement, I would be required to repay you $1,080, equal to the $1,000 I borrowed, plus the 3 percent real return you wanted, or $30, plus the 5 percent, or $50, to make up for the reduction in purchasing power caused by inflation.

A number of high-inflation countries, such as Brazil and Israel, have resorted to indexation to deal with inflation. In the United States, variable-rate home mortgages are a form of indexing. When market interest rates rise because of inflation, home buyers find their monthly payments also rising because the interest rate built into their mortgage agreement rises accordingly. Traditional fixed-rate home mortgages are not indexed. Lenders who make fixed-rate loans take the risk of inflation-induced losses in exchange for a higher interest rate than is initially attached to a variable-rate mortgage of the same duration and risk.

Since January 1997 the U.S. Treasury has financed a portion of its borrowing by issuing Treasury Inflation-Protected Securities (TIPS). Investors who own TIPS will find their interest earnings rising as inflation rises and falling as inflation falls.

In the 1970s, when U.S. inflation was relatively high and rising, cost of living adjustment (COLA) clauses in labor agreements were a popular form of wage indexing. COLAs call for periodic upward adjustments in the wages of covered workers to match increases in the CPI. With unions losing power and inflation losing steam during the 1980s, COLAs lost popularity. Social Security payments, however, are still indexed to the CPI.

Indexing can lead to problems. One is that indexing attaches extraordinary importance to the index numbers used. As noted in Chapter 11, indexes are approximations that can easily overstate the true inflation rate. The CPI's overstatement of inflation partly explains why Social Security benefits have become more generous in real terms over time. Indexing is also criticized for feeding the very inflation it is intended to fight because indexing may weaken the will of the monetary authorities to fight inflation and cause the public to expect more inflation. In 1995, for example, Brazil began a deindexation program that outlawed indexation in a variety of scenarios. Brazil recognized that indexation contributes to a vicious cycle of ever-rising inflation.

Why Not Zero Inflation?

If hyperinflation is potentially destructive, and even a little inflation might require adjustments in the form of indexing, why do not governments pursue policies of zero inflation? If inflation is, in the widely-quoted words of Milton Friedman, "always and everywhere a monetary phenomenon," then why can't inflation be eliminated?

One answer is political—it takes willpower to endure the disruptive effects, including perhaps a recession, of limiting monetary growth. The other is operational—central banks can influence, but not control, the rate of inflation. Figure 13-4 plots the inflation rate and money growth in the U.S. for 1959 to 1998. The figure shows that lower money growth is not always associated with lower inflation. A portion of the inflation rate is outside the control of monetary policy, at least in the short run.

Disinflation or Deflation?

Referring again to Figure 13-4 we see that the rate of inflation began to fall in 1981. Thus, began a long period of *disinflation*—declines in the rate of inflation—that continues as of this writing. By 1998, with the CPI increasing at the surprisingly low rate of barely more than 1 percent a year, the buzz among policymakers turned to whether the economy might be experiencing a transition from disinflation to deflation. *Deflation* is falling prices. Policymakers speculated that deflation could be happening because the CPI typically overstates inflation. They pointed to price declines in key products during 1998, including the prices of gold, farm commodities, and many other goods. The price of services was an exception to falling prices, thus offering contradictory evidence to the hypothesis of deflation, and room for disagreement among policymakers.

With deflation, money increases in purchasing power. While consumers benefit, policymakers fret over the possibility. If people expect lower prices, they will often

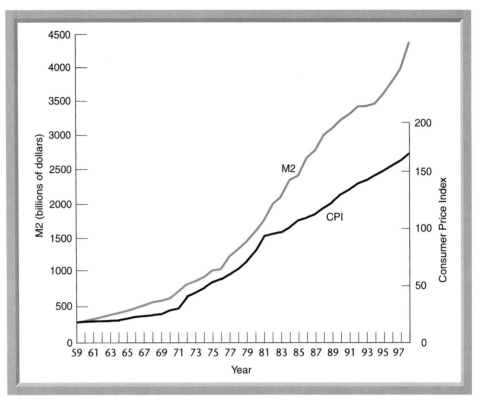

FIGURE 13-4 **Monetary growth and inflation** are closely tied, but not identical, as is illustrated by the growth rate of the CPI and of M2.

Source: 1999 Economic Report of the President, Tables B-60 and B-69.

wait for those lower prices to appear before making purchases. If enough people stop spending, unemployment can result. Thus, policymakers fear that deflation could lead to recession, which might lead to more deflation, and an even deeper recession. Such a downward economic spiral might not be easy to turn around. Historical episodes of U.S. deflation include the 1875–1900 period, when economic growth was strong, and the Great Depression, when deflation was associated with a sharp decrease in output. Because of the mixed historical evidence, economists debate the significance of deflation to the economy.

To conclude, economists recognize the possible problems associated with both inflation and deflation. It is also recognized that zero inflation is difficult to achieve. For these reasons, a concern over the value of money will most likely continue in the future.

1. Why do you think the United States has not experienced hyperinflation in your lifetime? If the United States did experience hyperinflation, what changes in money and banking do you think the voters would demand?

2. Would you prefer to see the Fed adopt the goal of zero inflation or have it accept a little inflation? If there is a trade-off between inflation and unemployment, should the goal of low inflation or low unemployment carry more weight? Explain.

14

EMPLOYMENT, OUTPUT, AND FISCAL POLICY

A Look Ahead

YOU'VE PROBABLY HEARD the joke, "If you line up all the economists in the world, end to end, you still won't reach a conclusion!" It sometimes seems that there are as many perspectives on the macroeconomy as there are economists. Perhaps this lack of agreement is not surprising. After all, because all kinds of things happen at once in the economy as a whole, what causes what is often not obvious. Value judgements will also differ about how much weight to attach to alternative policy goals. This said, macroeconomists actually share a great deal of common ground, especially within two broadly defined schools of thought—Keynesian and classical.

This chapter looks at the interplay between expenditures, output, employment, and the price level in the short run, en route to a long-run equilibrium. This look involves first considering the nature of fluctuations in economic activity, and then considering what, if anything, to do about them.

Exploration 14-1 recollects the days in the late 1970s during which unemployment and inflation were both high. We see that some current economic policies could lead the economy in this direction again, although those ill effects have thus far been averted by the dynamics of the marketplace in adopting technological changes. Exploration 14-2 considers the issue of whether excessive consumption in the United States puts its economy at risk. Neither the trade deficit nor the national debt are found to threaten U.S. economic security, although current accounting practices do not give an accurate picture of future federal obligations.

As you are **Surveying Economic Principles** you will arrive at an ability to

❑ contrast the perspectives of classical economists to those of Keynesians;

❑ interpret and apply the aggregate demand-aggregate supply model;

❑ relate the difference between demand-pull and cost-push inflation;

❑ describe how new spending can have a ripple effect throughout the economy because of the expenditure multiplier;

❑ identify the automatic stabilizers and the lags associated with fiscal policy.

While **Exploring Issues** you will be able to

❑ interpret how government regulations and lawsuits can cause long-run cost-push inflation, and how this effect may be masked by technological change;

❑ describe how foreign ownership of U.S. land and capital can add to national security.

Terms Along the Way

✔ Keynesian, 446
✔ classical, 446
✔ long-run aggregate supply, 447
✔ aggregate demand, 448
✔ sticky wages and prices, 450
✔ unemployment equilibrium, 450
✔ fiscal policy, 451
✔ demand-pull inflation, 454
✔ inflationary expectations, 454
✔ cost-push inflation, 454
✔ autonomous spending, 457
✔ induced spending, 457

✔ expenditure equilibrium, 457
✔ marginal propensity to save (mps), 458
✔ marginal propensity to consume (mpc), 458
✔ expenditure multiplier, 459
✔ balanced budget multiplier, 461
✔ fiscal policy lags, 462
✔ automatic stabilizers, 462
✔ national debt, 471
✔ budget deficit, 471
✔ budget surplus, 471

SURVEYING ECONOMIC PRINCIPLES

If you find a job you love, it won't be work at all.

People derive sustenance, both material and spiritual, from the work they do. It is of great concern, then, when jobs are hard to come by. Economists are quite aware of the suffering associated with unemployment and the loss of productivity that goes with it. Yet, when it comes to choosing the proper public policy toward aggregate employment and output, well-meaning economists disagree sharply. The differences commonly revolve around economists' different perspectives on the trade-off between short-run and long-run goals. It is because the issues are so important that the controversy becomes so intense.

The 1936 publication of *The General Theory of Employment, Interest, and Money* by British economist John Maynard Keynes (1883–1946) revolutionized the study of the macroeconomy. Keynes sparked the emergence of macroeconomics as a field of analysis separate from microeconomics. In response to the pressing problems of the Great Depression, Keynes offered a new, short-run perspective that came to be termed **Keynesian** economics. Prior to that time, economists emphasized long-run economic tendencies, viewing short-run fluctuations around the long-run trends as transitory problems that would correct themselves. That way of looking at the macroeconomy became known as **classical** economics. Both classical and Keynesian perspectives are used today. However, the two viewpoints suggest very different roles for government in its quest to keep the economy fully employed.

The Route to Full-Employment Output

The Classical Perspective

According to the classical view, unemployment is nothing more than a transitory *disequilibrium* in the marketplace—a time markets take to adjust to their market-clearing equilibriums. Specifically, there is a surplus of workers in the labor market. The market response is for wage rates to fall until the surplus is absorbed. In response to lower labor costs, competition forces output prices to fall, too. These wage and price adjustments reflect supply and demand in action in the many markets that make up the economy as a whole.

Today classical economics includes Monetarism, supply side theory, new growth theory, and some other schools of thought that each emphasize different forces that affect long-run economic objectives. One of the earliest expressions of the classical viewpoint was by the French economist, Jean Baptiste Say (1767–1832). According to Say, the aggregate value of what is produced will provide the income with which to buy it. Periods of unemployment are thus disequilibriums that will be corrected when the marketplace figures out the profit-maximizing mix of goods and services to produce. Put another way, *Say's law* states that supply creates its own demand. The logic of Say's law is much the same as that of the natural rate of unemployment, discussed in chapter 12.

Modern-day classical economists point out that periods of relatively high unemployment, such as occurred in the Great Depression, are the exception rather than the rule. In the last 80 years, U.S. unemployment has averaged just over 6 percent of the work force. Most episodes of relatively high unemployment in the United States

Keynesian: any economist subscribing to the macroeconomic perspective of John Maynard Keynes; emphasizes the short run and the importance of fiscal policy.

classical: a macroeconomic school of thought that emphasizes the long run; relies upon market forces to achieve full employment.

To learn more about the Great Depression, through both text and pictures, go to the National Archives and Records Administration at **http://hoover. nara.gov/gallery/ gallery06.html**

and around the world have been associated with a breakdown of the monetary system. In the United States, the Great Depression was precipitated by a banking system collapse that shattered people's confidence in the security of their bank deposits. *Hyperinflation*, in which governments print so much money that its value seems to diminish daily, has been the culprit in other countries. For example, hyperinflation was a central component of the disarray in the German economy in 1922 and 1923.

Other reasons for upward spikes in unemployment also revolve around systemic collapses. For example, recent threats to the security of property rights in Russia have led to relatively high unemployment in that country. However, these are exceptions. More generally, **the desire of people to receive income pushes unemployment down toward its natural rate and leads to full-employment output in the long run.**

Recall that full employment occurs when the economy is at its natural rate of unemployment. Recall also that the amount of output that is produced when the economy is at full employment is termed either full-employment output or full-employment GDP. The economy supplies full-employment output in the long run, no matter the price level, as shown by the vertical long-run aggregate supply in Figure 14-1. Long-run aggregate supply would shift to the right if the economy's productive capacity increased, such as through more resources or better technology. Long-run aggregate supply would shift to the left if productive capacity were to decrease.

As evidence that the price level does not matter in the long run, consider that the price level today is quadruple that of the late 1960s. However, market wages have

long-run aggregate supply: the idea that, in the long run, the price level does not affect the amount of GDP the economy produces; graphically, long-run aggregate supply is vertical at full-employment GDP.

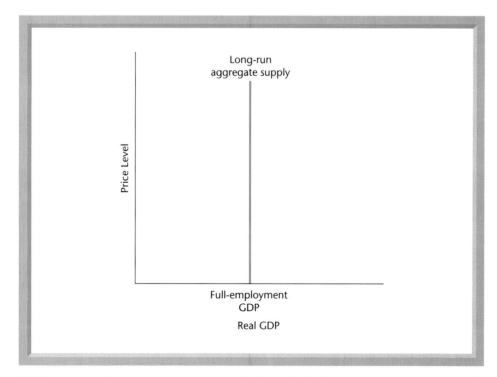

FIGURE 14-1 **Long-run aggregate supply** shows that full-employment output, measured by real GDP, does not depend on the price level.

also adjusted upward. Other than requiring that we earn and spend about three times as much to obtain the same goods and services, the rise in wages and prices has had little long-run significance for the aggregate economy. Thus, we must look elsewhere for an explanation of fluctuations in economic activity around the level of full employment output. Classical economists do so by pointing to the role of workers' and firms' expectations about the price level and about wages and prices in their market segments. Specifically, when consumers and producers are surprised by changes in market conditions, their plans are thrown into disarray. There is temporary unemployment as workers and firms sort out the new realities and as some workers find new jobs to replace their old ones.

OBSERVATION POINT:
The Real Business Cycle—Some Shocking Surprises

Cars, wars, oil cartels, and computers may not seem to have much in common, but they do. They have all shocked the economy one way or another. How could ordinary citizens have foreseen the potential of the auto or the carnage of World War II? We did not know of the oil crisis of the 1970s before it happened, and we did not forecast its disappearance in the 1980s. Nor did businesses predict the Asian financial crisis of 1998. As for the future, who knows what new technologies will lead to, or when catastrophe will strike?

All of these things and more jolt the economy, either to make it more productive, or to knock it back a notch. They represent real changes in countries' production or trade possibilities to which businesses and their employees must adjust. Put another way, the economic shocks cause a *real business cycle*. Policymakers can predict these events no better than the rest of us, and so can do little to avert these unexpected economic disruptions to the smooth path of economic growth. When it comes to the real business cycle, then, it is best to expect the unexpected!

Aggregate Supply Meets Aggregate Demand

Aggregate supply reveals how much real GDP the economy will offer at various price levels. But what determines what that price level will be? To answer this question, we must turn to aggregate demand. **Aggregate demand** relates how much real GDP consumers, businesses, and government will purchase at each price level.

A conventional demand curve tells the quantity of a good or service that will be purchased at each of various possible prices. For example, as the price of Pepsi rises, the quantity demanded falls because consumers substitute Coca-Cola and other beverages. In the event of a general inflation in the prices of all goods and services, though, consumers can no longer merely substitute away from products whose prices have risen. Yet, consumers can no longer buy as much as before, either, because the inflation has eroded their wealth and the purchasing power of their income. Thus, *ceteris paribus*, an increase in the price level will cut back the aggregate quantities that consumers purchase.

Likewise, a decrease in the price level will increase aggregate purchases. The reason is twofold. First, at a lower price level, money buys more goods and services. In other words, even if all of us continue to spend the same amount of money, a lower

aggregate demand: relates how much real GDP consumers, businesses, and government will purchase at each price level; graphically, aggregate demand slopes downward.

A cool, refreshing Web site will be found at the official Coca-Cola Internet address at **http://www. cocacola.com/ home.html**

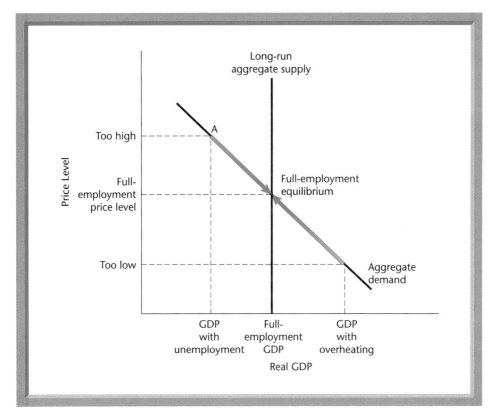

FIGURE 14-2 **The long-run macro equilibrium occurs where aggregate demand intersects long-run aggregate supply.** Competition prevents the price level from remaining either too high or too low.

price level causes the real GDP we purchase to be greater. Second, a lower price level increases the real, inflation-adjusted value of money that has been saved, and thus increases the fraction of current income that goes toward spending. In other words, a lower price level means that: 1) consumers get more goods and services for each dollar that they spend; and 2) consumers spend more money out of their current incomes because the lower price level increases the real value of their savings. For both reasons, **aggregate demand has a downward slope.**[1]

Figure 14-2 shows a downward-sloping aggregate demand curve, along with long-run aggregate supply. The long-run equilibrium price level occurs where the

---

[1]Some authors contend that there is also an "international substitution effect" that accentuates the downward slope of aggregate demand to the extent that a lower price level reduces imports and increases exports. However, the increasingly accepted view among economists is that trade deficits do not affect aggregate purchasing power. The reason, as discussed more fully in chapter 5, is that foreign exchange markets ensure that most currencies quickly bounce back to their respective countries, and that those which do not can be replaced by monetary authorities. Thus the international substitution effect boils down to an issue of how much money is in the domestic economy. Since aggregate demand assumes that the money supply is held constant, no international substitution arises.

two curves intersect. At any higher price level, aggregate spending will be insufficient to support full employment. Unemployed workers will compete for jobs, which will drive down wages. Competition in the output market will force firms to lower prices in response to these lower wages. The lower price level this brings means that spending will buy more output and thus lead to greater employment. The process continues until the economy reaches full employment and the corresponding full-employment GDP, as shown in Figure 14-2.

If the actual price level were below the equilibrium shown in Figure 14-2, the economy would "overheat," with aggregate purchasing power exceeding the economy's ability to produce. Firms would compete for workers, thus driving their wages up. Competitive firms would pass on these higher wages to consumers by raising their prices. The resulting increase in the price level would soak up the excess purchasing power, thus leading the economy back to its long-run equilibrium.

In the Long Run, We Are All Dead

"In the long run, we are all dead" is perhaps the most famous saying of John Maynard Keynes. What is the significance of his oft-quoted observation? If you have ever been involuntarily out of a job, perhaps you know. Long-run trends toward full employment are little consolation to someone struggling to find enough work to keep body and soul together.

The macroeconomic views of John Maynard Keynes came to prominence during the Great Depression of the 1930s. That decade was characterized by both stubbornly high unemployment rates and a meager safety net of social programs to assist those who found themselves without any means of support. This combination lends itself to a short-term view of the world. Economic policies that are merely long-term tendencies cannot match the allure of public policy action to correct problems in the here and now. If short-term fixes are expected to have long-term costs, so what? "In the long run, we are all dead." Keynes thus chose to ignore long-run tendencies toward full employment.

To learn more about Keynes, visit **http://www. wam.umd.edu/ ~mglondon/ London/Keynes/ keynes.htm** or **http://www. jobsletter.org.nz/ jbl04611.htm**

sticky wages and prices: wages and prices that are inflexible in a downward direction, possibly caused by labor contracts or inflationary expectations.

unemployment equilibrium: a short-run equilibrium GDP that is less than full-employment GDP; the amount of real GDP that occurs when aggregate demand intersects short-run aggregate supply at a price level above the price level at which aggregate demand intersects long-run aggregate supply.

In contrast to classical economists, Keynesians dismiss the significance of waiting for wage and price adjustments to cure a recession. Their rationale is the existence of sticky wages and prices, where *sticky* refers to an inflexibility in a downward direction. If wages are very sticky, the downward movement in wages required to reach a long-run equilibrium could take so many years that it becomes irrelevant. This downward stickiness could be due to labor contracts between unions and employees. It could also be due to human psychology—when firms cut wages, their workers resent it. The result is lower quality and lower productivity. Firms thus hesitate to cut wages.

If aggregate demand is insufficient to bring about full employment at the current price level, Keynes assumed that neither wages nor prices could fall. The result would be an unemployment equilibrium **at which the economy continues to produce less than full-employment GDP. In Figure 14-2, for example, sticky wages and prices would block any downward movement along aggregate demand from a price level that is too high, such as at point A. Rather, Keynesians would say that point A would persist as an unemployment equilibrium. In contrast, if the price level is too low, both classical and Keynesian economists agree that inflation would soon cool off an overheating GDP.**

If the price level cannot fall to correct an unemployment equilibrium, the only solution is to shift aggregate demand rightward by increasing spending power. To accomplish this shift, Keynesians look to fiscal policy, which is government policy toward taxation and spending. Keynesians commonly advocate using *expansionary fiscal policy*—increased government spending or reduced taxation—to *stimulate* aggregate demand. The Works Progress Administration and other New Deal programs of President Franklin Roosevelt are examples of stimulative fiscal policies. Indeed, World War II seemed to prove the validity of Keynesian economics, since the massive amount of government spending it involved paved the way from the Depression of the 1930s to the prosperity of the 1950s.

fiscal policy: government tax and spending policy; can be either expansionary, such as through lower taxes and higher spending, or contractionary, such as through higher taxes and reduced spending.

Another way to shift aggregate demand to the right is through an expansionary monetary policy. An increase in the money supply shifts the entire aggregate demand curve to the right, while a decrease would shift it to the left. This abstract concept makes sense at the personal level. After all, if you've been unemployed, you know the problem—not enough money to spend! If unemployment in the macroeconomy exceeds the natural rate, the problem is the same: aggregate unemployment stems from too little money being spent to sustain the full-employment output, given the current price level.

Rather than try to fine-tune the money supply, classical economists usually prefer to wait for the price level to fall, so that the money in circulation can buy more real output. In this view, the problem is not one of too little money, nor of insufficient aggregate demand, but of too high a price level. In the Keynesian view, in contrast, unemployment is a present-tense event. There should be no waiting; rather, there should be action taken right away to shift aggregate demand to the right. Keynesians recognize that increasing the money supply can shift aggregate demand to the right, but doubt that monetary authorities have the ability to accomplish this goal in times of severe economic crisis.

Specifically, although the Federal Reserve can add liquidity to the banking system such that banks are better able to lend out money, banks must in fact make those loans before the money supply in the economy increases. The problem is that banks are likely to be extra cautious about making loans in times of economic crisis, which puts the Fed in the position of "pushing on a string." In other words, the Fed can keep adding to the monetary base but cannot force banks to pass the extra dollars along to consumers and businesses. This situation is known as a *liquidity trap*.

According to Keynesians, the key to bringing the economy out of a depression is not merely to increase the quantity of money in the hands of consumers, because consumers cannot be relied upon to spend it. Instead, Keynesians advocate government spending on goods and services as the way to directly increase the amount of money in circulation. With more government spending, aggregate demand shifts to the right, as shown in Figure 14-3. **Note that the position of aggregate supply is independent of the quantity of money. Only aggregate demand is directly affected by money.**

Keynes' assumption that wages and prices cannot fall at all in the short run is too extreme. These days, wage cuts are reported in a variety of industries. Labor unions are not as powerful as they were in the 1930s. Indeed, it is often unionized employees who see the most dramatic wage cuts. In the late 1980s, for example, President Frank Lorenzo of Continental Airlines succeeded in slashing the pay of Continental's pilots, mechanics, and other workers drastically, sometimes to less than half of their previous salaries.

Travel to the Continental Airlines site on the World Wide Web at the following Internet address: **http://www.continental.com/**

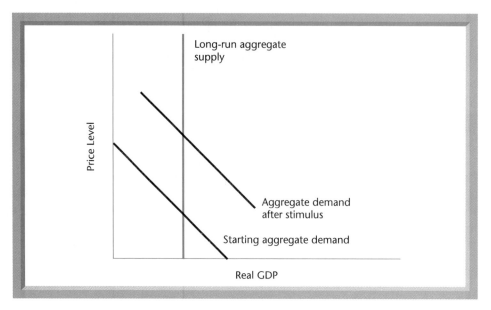

FIGURE 14-3 **Aggregate demand will shift to the right in response to a fiscal or monetary stimulus.** This shift in aggregate demand has no effect on long-run aggregate supply.

However, wage cuts do not come easily. In the case of Continental, its actions precipitated several years of confrontations with organized labor and the ultimate departure of Frank Lorenzo. Thus, while wage cuts do happen, downward stickiness also occurs. It should be noted that classical economists disagree with the contention that wages and prices are sticky, particularly if there are also competitive sectors of the economy that offer other job opportunities to those who would otherwise be unemployed.

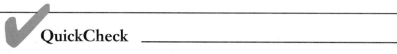 **QuickCheck** _____

Does the amount of money affect aggregate demand, aggregate supply, or both?

Answer: Aggregate supply is determined by the productive capacity of the economy, and is thus not affected by money. Aggregate demand shifts outward when the amount of money increases.

Macro Adjustment—The Short and the Long of It

When aggregate demand is increased through monetary or fiscal policy, there is likely to be inflation. If the economy is at full employment before the stimulative policy takes effect, the reason for inflation is clear—the economy would move vertically up its long-run aggregate supply curve to a new long-run equilibrium at a higher price level.

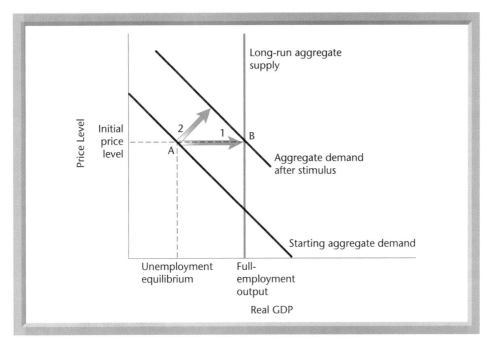

FIGURE 14-4   **In shifting aggregate demand to remedy an unemployment equilib-rium,** the idea is to move the economy from an unemployment equilibrium (A) to a full-employment equilibrium (B) without causing inflation, such as shown by the arrow labeled 1. Unfortunately, in practice, there is likely to be inflation that limits the effectiveness of the stimulative policy, such as shown by the arrow labeled 2.

In contrast, suppose the economy starts at an unemployment equilibrium. In principle, aggregate demand could shift to the right until full employment is reached without precipitating a higher price level as was indicated by arrow 1 in Figure 14-4. However, in practice, new spending power that is added to the economy tends to raise wages and prices where it first hits before eventually diffusing throughout the economy. Thus, an increase in spending cannot move the economy in the direction of full-employment output without bidding up wages and prices in some sectors. This process in turn leads to a higher overall price level along with higher output, as was shown by arrow 2 in Figure 14-4.

For example, suppose the economy starts at the unemployment equilibrium. To combat unemployment, government policymakers decide to spend an extra $1 billion to buy a new Poseidon-class destroyer. The additional spending shifts aggregate demand to the right and increases employment. However, the fiscal stimulus is also inflationary because the spending does not diffuse rapidly throughout the economy. Rather, the added demand for jobs is concentrated in the defense industry. Industries that compete for workers with the human capital used in defense contracting find that their costs rise and that they must in turn raise the prices of their outputs. Job seekers without the required skills remain unemployed.

demand-pull inflation: occurs when a rightward shift in aggregate demand moves the economy up short-run aggregate supply; associated with greater employment and output.

inflationary expectations: predictions about future inflation that people factor into their current behavior.

cost-push inflation: occurs when the economy moves up the aggregate demand curve; associated with less output.

The sequence of events described in the previous paragraph causes demand-pull inflation. Demand-pull inflation **occurs when a rightward shift in aggregate demand moves the economy to both a higher output and a higher price level.**

Past experience with inflation can also cause inflation in the future. This phenomenon occurs when workers and firms form inflationary expectations, and so demand higher wages and prices over time to compensate for the inflation that they expect. The problem is that aggregate demand does not shift to the right in response to inflationary expectations. Without a rightward shift in aggregate demand, there is insufficient purchasing power to allow both a higher price level and full-employment output. Until workers and firms adjust their inflationary expectations downward, then, the result is that the economy moves up the aggregate demand curve to a point of higher prices and lower output. Inflation that is caused in this way is called cost-push inflation. **Cost push inflation reduces output and increases the price level.** This result is sometimes called *stagflation*—the simultaneous occurrence of inflation and economic stagnation.

Demand-pull and cost-push inflation can feed upon each other. Cost-push inflation is caused by past experiences with inflation, which was most likely caused by policies that had allowed aggregate demand to increase in the past. To counter cost-push inflation and keep the economy near full employment, policymakers might choose to expand aggregate demand again. That would reinforce inflationary expectations in future periods, causing another round of cost-push inflation. Thus, if government responds to cost-push inflation by stimulating aggregate demand, the result is likely to be an "inflationary spiral" of demand-pull inflation followed by more cost-push inflation, leading to a cycle that goes on and on. Figure 14-5 illustrates this process.

To avoid the inflationary spiral, classical economists advocate a hands-off policy to let inflationary expectations subside. That policy was followed in the United States in the early 1980s, after a decade in which inflation had risen to the double-digit range. The result was a short-lived recession during which people adjusted their inflationary expectations downward. Afterward, the economy returned to full employment, but at a much lower rate of inflation.

Table 14-1 summarizes the differences between the classical and Keynesian approaches. Bear in mind that both schools of thought have the same goal, which is to reach full employment output without inflation. The essential difference is that the Keynesians will set aside long-run goals to combat the short-run suffering of the unemployed, while classical economists "keep their eyes on the horizon" to get as quickly as possible to a sustainable long-run equilibrium of stable prices and full employment.

 QuickCheck _____

What is the difference between cost-push inflation and demand-pull inflation?

Answer: Cost-push inflation involves a movement up the aggregate demand curve as prices rise. It is caused by the inflationary expectations of workers and firms that drive up production and output costs. Demand-pull inflation occurs when the aggregate demand curve shifts outward, as when more money is placed into circulation, either through monetary or fiscal policy.

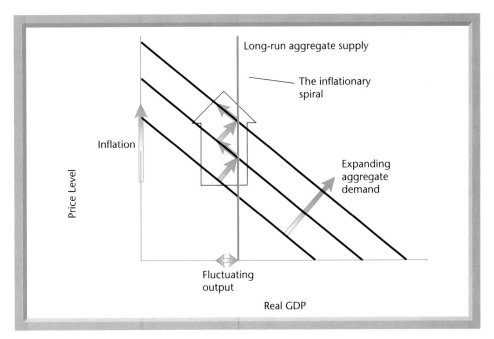

FIGURE 14-5 **When aggregate demand is increased in order to correct an unemployment equilibrium, the result can be an inflationary spiral,** which is an ongoing sequence of demand-pull inflation (arrow pointing upward to the right) followed by cost-push inflation (arrow pointing upward to the left).

TABLE 14-1 Summary of Classical and Keynesian Views

Classical	Keynesian
The focus is on the long run.	The focus is on the short run.
Prices and wages will adjust upward or downward as needed to reach a full-employment equilibrium.	Prices and wages adjust upward without difficulty, but are downwardly sticky and thus unable to lead the economy from an unemployment equilibrium to full employment.
Government should not attempt to manage aggregate demand.	Government should actively adjust taxes and spending in order to manage aggregate demand.
Shortcoming: Remedying unemployment requires patience.	Shortcoming: Remedying unemployment can lead to demand-pull inflation and possibly an inflationary spiral.

OBSERVATION POINT:

The Ephemeral Phillips Curve—Battling Unemployment with Inflation

Upon examining British data from the 1950s shortly before that decade ended, British economist A. W. Phillips found a striking result—the *Phillips curve* revealed a tight, curvilinear relationship between inflation and unemployment. It appeared that unemployment could be lowered by allowing greater inflation. U.S. economists and policymakers were intrigued to find that U.S. unemployment in the 1960s also shrank as inflation was allowed to rise, as seen in Figure 14-6. With so much data to support it, the tradeoff between inflation and unemployment came to be accepted as a given—some sort of fundamental economic truth.

Then came the combination of rising unemployment and rising inflation in the 1970s and the falling unemployment and falling inflation in the 1980s. Oops, no more Phillips curve in sight! Looking back, the Phillips curve experience of the 1950s and 1960s looks like an aberration around the fundamental truth—in the long run, inflation has no bearing on unemployment.

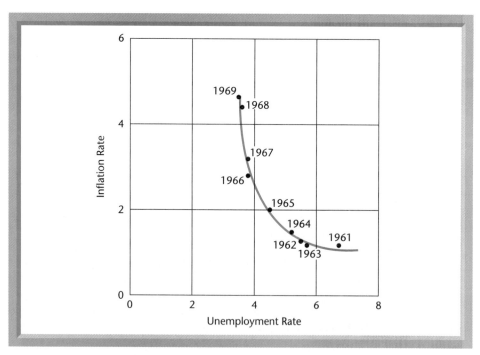

FIGURE 14-6 The Phillips curve showed a tight, inverse relationship between inflation and unemployment in Britain in the 1950s. U.S. data in the 1960s appeared to confirm this relationship, as shown above. In later decades, however, the relationship no longer held true.

Source: 1999 Economic Report of the President, Tables B-3 and B-43.

Keynes' Call to Action

Although classical analysis is respectable today, it fell into disrepute during the Great Depression of the 1930s and remained that way for the next quarter-century. During the Depression era, people did not understand why high unemployment persisted year after year despite falling prices. The public wanted government action to correct the problem. Keynesian macroeconomic theory provided the intellectual basis for such action. Keynesian economics focuses on the demand side of the economy, and is thus sometimes referred to as *demand-side economics*. Economists today are likely to say that aggregate demand is only part of the picture. However, nearly all will agree that it is an essential part.

Behind Aggregate Demand: The Expenditure Equilibrium

Behind the aggregate demand curve lies spending by consumers, government, and investors. We will focus initially on consumer spending, since consumption accounts for almost 70 percent of GDP. To determine how much this spending will be at any given price level, Keynes examined what motivates people to spend and the amount of spending these motivations lead to. Keynesian analysis focuses on spending, because one person's spending is another person's income—the two go hand in hand. Likewise, the circular flow model tells us that aggregate income and output must be equal.

Aggregate national income = aggregate national output

Money spent on a cheeseburger, for example, is split into income to the employees and owners of the restaurant, as well as to the suppliers of the cheese and other inputs that go into the burger. Thus, gross domestic product can be viewed as a measure of both output and income.

Spending can be divided into the following two types:

1. Autonomous spending: spending that would occur even if people had no incomes.
2. Induced spending: spending that depends upon income.

Autonomous spending includes investments people make and goods and services that people buy, irrespective of their incomes. For example, if it became necessary, people would draw upon their accumulated wealth to buy such necessities of life as food and shelter. Even college students without any earnings have been known to draw down their parents' bank accounts in order to pay for room and board at school!

Autonomous spending causes induced spending, because money that one person spends autonomously adds to the income of others, which in turn induces them to buy more output. This process generates an ongoing cycle of greater income and greater output. At each stage in this cycle, however, some income is likely to be saved, thus eventually bringing the cycle to a halt.

For example, suppose that Dawn spends her wages to buy boots at Bubba's Bargain Basement. Dawn's spending in turn provides Bubba with income that he spends at J-Mart, which in turn, well, you get the story! This process is termed the *multiplier effect* of spending. Through this multiplier effect, autonomous and induced spending add up to **an expenditure equilibrium, which is the level of real GDP that the economy tends toward in the short run, at a given price level.**

autonomous spending: spending that would occur even if people had no incomes.

induced spending: spending that depends upon income

expenditure equilibrium: the level of GDP that the economy tends towards in the short run, at a given price level.

At the expenditure equilibrium, actual spending equals *intended spending*—how much consumers, businesses, and government desire to spend. For businesses, actual and intended spending often differ. The reason is that businesses intend to spend enough to maintain their inventories at desired levels, but cannot predict exactly how much of their products consumers will buy. For example, toy sellers cannot predict exactly how many Mighty Warriors, Nintendo games, and other toys consumers will buy at Christmas.

An expenditure equilibrium implies that there are no unintended inventory buildups or drawdowns that would prompt a change in business plans. Thus, all businesses must correctly forecast demands for their products. The world is not that precise. Because there will always be some forecasting errors, the economy will achieve an equilibrium only approximately.

Keynes saw investment as playing an especially important role in determining the expenditure equilibrium. He regarded investment as particularly significant because it is the most likely component to fluctuate suddenly. He saw the behavior of investors as unstable because the future cannot be known with certainty, and thus investing is risky business. Keynes judged investors as easily swayed by slight changes in the perceived risks involved in investing. If business conditions were poor, he regarded investment as being unlikely to occur even if the monetary authorities pushed interest rates low. A small change in investment could cause a large change in income because of the multiplier effect upon investment spending.

The strength of the multiplier effect depends upon the proportion of income that is devoted to spending. To the extent that people save their incomes, those savings represent a *leakage* out of the multiplier process. The fraction of additional income **marginal** that people save is termed the **marginal propensity to save (mps)**. Likewise, the **propensity to save** fraction of additional income that people spend is called the **marginal propensity to** **(mps):** the fraction **consume (mpc)**. Together, of additional income that people save.

$$mpc + mps = 1$$

marginal The mpc and mps must sum to one because consumption and saving are the only **propensity to** possible uses for an extra dollar of after-tax income. Of course, taxation itself would **consume (mpc):** be another leakage from the spending stream. the fraction of additional income Table 14-2 illustrates how the value of the mpc determines the increase in spendthat people spend. ing as income rises from zero to $5,000. The table assumes that autonomous spending is $1,000. Although actual values of mpc and mps depend upon consumer confidence,

TABLE 14-2 Spending Depends Upon the Marginal Propensity to Consume (mpc) (Assume autonomous spending = $1,000, mpc = 0.6, mps = 0.4)

Income	Spending	Savings
$0	$1,000	−$1,000
$1,000	$1,600	−$600
$2,000	$2,200	−$200
$3,000	$2,800	$200
$4,000	$3,400	$600
$5,000	$4,000	$1,000

the table will for simplicity assume that the mpc is a constant 0.6, meaning people spend 60 cents out of each additional dollar of income. Savings are also shown in the table, because income not spent is saved. Thus, the mpc of 0.6 implies an mps of 0.4. A negative value for savings, which occurs at lower income values in the table, means that there is *dissaving*—spending out of existing saving. The leakage from taxation is ignored for the sake of simplicity by assuming that the tax rate equals zero.

If autonomous spending rises, **the expenditure equilibrium will rise by the increase in autonomous spending multiplied by the expenditure multiplier.** The expenditure multiplier is the amount by which equilibrium real GDP grows as a result of an increase—an *injection*—of new autonomous spending. For example, if investors gain confidence in the economy and so increase their autonomous investment spending, equilibrium GDP would rise by more than that amount. Specifically, the equilibrium GDP would equal the increase in autonomous investment multiplied by the multiplier. Conversely, if autonomous spending were to decrease, the expenditure multiplier would reveal how much real GDP would fall.

If people always spend every penny of income they receive, the multiplier process would never stop. For example, if Ann were to receive $1,000 in income, she would spend $1,000. That would provide others with $1,000 in income, which they would spend, thus providing others with $1,000 in income, and so forth. In practice, however, there are leakages, such as savings and taxes, that eventually bring this process to a halt. For example, if the mps were to equal 0.2, Ann would only spend $800, and 20 percent of that $800 would be saved by those receiving it, so that the next round of spending would amount to only $640. Most centrally, considering only the leakage of savings, the expenditure multiplier is the reciprocal of the marginal propensity to save, as follows:

$$\text{Expenditure multiplier} = \frac{1}{\text{mps}}$$

The expenditure process is summarized as follows:

$$\Delta \text{Autonomous spending} \times \frac{1}{\text{mps}} = \Delta \text{expenditure equilibrium}$$

where Δ denotes "change in."

The change in autonomous spending could be undertaken by government, businesses, or consumers. If autonomous spending changes, **the change in autonomous spending multiplied by the expenditure multiplier gives the change in equilibrium expenditures.** For example, if government spending rises by $1 billion, and the marginal propensity to save is 0.2, the expenditure equilibrium will rise by (1/0.2) multiplied by $1 billion, which equals 5 multiplied by $1 billion, or $5 billion.

Note that there is nothing here to indicate whether the expenditure equilibrium occurs at full employment. However, **there must be some idle resources for the multiplier effect to occur.** If an injection of new spending occurs when the economy is already at full employment, consumers and others bid up prices by seeking to buy more output than the economy is capable of sustaining. The result is inflation, implying a rising price level that offsets the multiplier effect by making money not go as far in real terms. Thus, rising prices thwart the multiplier effect, even to the extent that extra spending might cause no increase at all in real GDP.

expenditure multiplier: the reciprocal of the marginal propensity to save in the simple Keynesian model; when multiplied by a change in autonomous spending, gives the change in equilibrium GDP.

If the expenditure equilibrium occurs below full-employment GDP, there will be unemployment, and thus downward pressure on prices until full-employment GDP is achieved. However, this point is where Keynes draws the line from his classical predecessors. Regarding the expenditure equilibrium, Keynes wrote, "There is no reason for expecting it to be *equal* to full employment." What justification did Keynes offer for this break with the past? As discussed earlier, Keynesians view prices as downwardly sticky. Keynes went so far as to dismiss any possibility for prices to fall, because that process would only occur in the long run. As you have heard before, "In the long run, we are all dead." Thus, **the expenditure multiplier assumes a constant price level.**

QuickCheck

Suppose the marginal propensity to consume is .75. Using the expenditure multiplier, what is the effect on equilibrium GDP of an extra $10 billion federal spending program?

Answer: If the economy is below full employment, and the price level remains constant, the effect equals $40 billion. This result is obtained by multiplying $10 billion by the expenditure multiplier. Because the mpc equals .75, and because the sum of mpc and mps must equal 1, the mps must equal .25. The multiplier thus equals $1/.25 = 4$.

The Role of Multipliers in Fiscal Policy Design

To prevent an unemployment equilibrium, in which the economy is stuck in recession, Keynesians argue that either autonomous spending or the multiplier itself must be increased. The multiplier will increase to the extent that people decrease their marginal propensity to save. Because savings represent a leakage out of the multiplier process, Keynesians emphasize the value of consumption. If people consume a greater fraction of their income, the multiplier increases and equilibrium occurs at a higher GDP.

For example, if the marginal propensity to save were to equal 1, that would mean that people save every dollar they receive. In that case, the expenditure multiplier would equal $1/1 = 1$, meaning that the effect of an extra dollar of spending is that dollar and no more. If the mps equals 0.2, in contrast, people save only twenty cents per dollar of additional income. In that case, an extra dollar of spending would generate $1 multiplied by (1/0.2), giving a result of $1 multiplied by 5, which equals a $5 increase in equilibrium spending and output. Thus, a decrease in the marginal propensity to save means that equilibrium income will be a greater multiple of autonomous spending.

How can the multiplier be increased or autonomous spending be stimulated? According to Keynes, when business conditions are bad, the private sector is unlikely to make it better! Because he doubted increases in private-sector spending, Keynes was a strong advocate of increasing government spending during recessions. Keynesians argue that the most powerful force for achieving and maintaining a full employment equilibrium is government fiscal policy.

Keynesian analysis also suggests that the economy could be stimulated through tax cuts. However, Keynesians note that people might save some of their tax refunds rather than spend them to stimulate the economy. In other words, the *tax multiplier*—the expansionary effect of a tax cut or contractionary effect of a tax increase—would be less than the expenditure multiplier. Thus, **Keynes viewed extra government spending as the most effective policy to cure a recession.**

According to Keynesian analysis, financing extra government spending with an equivalent increase in taxation would have an expansionary effect, because the expenditure multiplier exceeds the tax multiplier. The balanced budget multiplier combines the expenditure multiplier for an increase in government spending and the tax multiplier for the increase in taxes to finance that spending. It can be shown that the balanced budget multiplier equals 1, meaning that, when financed by a tax increase, an increase in government spending increases equilibrium GDP by the amount of that extra spending and no more.[2]

Critics of Keynesian analysis contend that Keynesian multiplier analysis is flawed because it ignores the impact of financing government spending. Specifically, the tax multiplier and balanced budget multiplier assume that higher taxes have no effect on incentives to work or invest. The critics disagree. For example, since higher taxes reduce the expected return on investments, tax increases are likely to reduce investment, and thus impede the growth of worker productivity and output over time. If government spending is financed by borrowing, critics contend that the borrowing is likely to drive up interest rates, thus causing *crowding out*—reduced borrowing in the private sector—which reduces investment and consumption spending, but is not factored into multiplier analysis.

> **balanced budget multiplier:** the effect on equilibrium GDP per dollar of additional government spending, when that spending is paid for by additional taxation; equals 1 in the simple Keynesian model.

OBSERVATION POINT:
The Paradox of Thrift—Does Saving More Save Less?

The baby boomers are aging. Retirement looms, and their lifestyles are threatened. Guess what? Now they all want to start saving their money! Watch the national savings rate rise and the economy grow! More savings means more investment, you know, . . . or does it?

According to Keynes, investors are unimpressed with the increased availability of investment monies and the consequent lower interest rates. Rather, investors are dismayed to see the demand for goods and services shrinking. They will invest no more than before, and maybe even less. That heightened urge to save merely reduces the multiplier and lowers equilibrium GDP. The country winds up saving a higher fraction of a smaller national income. Although the fraction of income that people save may be higher, national income could possibly drop so much that total savings will be the same or lower—that's the *paradox of thrift*. In this Keynesian model, the baby boomers should keep on spending!

Although the paradox of thrift has become entrenched in many people's minds, few economists today believe it. The reason is that the paradox of thrift ignores a key

---

[2]The tax multiplier formula equals −mpc/mps. When combined with the autonomous expenditure multiplier formula of 1/mps, the result is (1 − mpc)/mps = mps/mps = 1.

concept, which is the long-run trend toward full employment. Thus, rather than being a determinant of where the unemployment equilibrium will be, the amount saved in the economy is now seen as determining the amount invested in new capital, which is critical to economic growth. The difference between now and the time Keynes formed his model is partly one of perspective. With people begging for jobs in the 1930s, who can blame Keynes urging everyone to unstuff their mattresses and spend their money instead of sleeping on it!

Implementing Fiscal Policy

When the economy overheats, Keynesians call for *contractionary fiscal policy* to slow it down. When unemployment is the problem, Keynesians suggest expansionary policy to reach the full employment equilibrium. Unfortunately, even the best intentioned *discretionary* public policy—policy adjusted at the discretion of lawmakers—is unlikely to follow the Keynesian policy prescription. The reason has to do with the three fiscal policy lags:

fiscal policy lags: the time it takes between when a macroeconomic problem occurs and fiscal policy action takes effect to correct it; consists of a recognition lag, action lag, and implementation lag.

- The *recognition lag*—It takes time to know that a recession is at hand. Officially, it takes three consecutive quarters of declining GDP before a recession is declared.
- The *action lag*—Tax and spending bills are not passed overnight.
- The *implementation lag*—It's great to build a highway, but most people expect to have it planned out before crews are sent to lay asphalt! Planning government spending takes time. It also takes time before tax changes can take effect.

Because of fiscal policy lags, the business cycle may have turned by the time the money starts flowing. The spending may be more likely to cause inflation than to reduce unemployment. Policy lags make it very difficult, if not impossible, to *fine-tune* the economy to even out the ups and downs of the business cycle.

automatic stabilizers: features embedded within existing fiscal policies that act as a stimulant when the economy is sluggish and act as a drag when it is in danger of inflation.

Instead of discretionary policy, lawmakers can rely upon automatic stabilizers, which are features embedded within existing fiscal policies that act as a stimulant when the economy is sluggish and act as a drag when it overheats (grows so fast that inflation threatens). The U.S. economy has automatic stabilizers imbedded within its system of taxation and spending. On the tax side, government tax revenues decline when output slows, because tax revenues are a percentage of that output's value. When tax revenues decline, the effect is expansionary, because the lower tax bill somewhat offsets the economy's loss of purchasing power. Likewise, if the economy overheats, the same percentage tax collects more revenues, which is contractionary because it serves to soak up some of the excess purchasing power. No policy action is necessary.

On the spending side, payments for welfare, unemployment compensation, and other public programs rise as the economy slows and more people seek these safety net services. Conversely, this spending falls when the economy heats up, just as Keynesian policy prescribes. Again, the action to stabilize the economy is automatic; no policy adjustments are needed.

Taken as a whole, the automatic stabilizers should be expansionary when the expenditure equilibrium is less than full employment and contractionary when the reverse is true. In practice, however, there is a significant tilt toward the expansionary side. For example, the economy has been in the vicinity of full employment for much of the past two decades. Even so, there have been substantial annual budget deficits in almost all of those years. If the automatic stabilizers were designed to match the Keynesian policy prescription, government would run neither a surplus nor a deficit when the economy is at full employment.

QuickCheck

(A) Once federal spending is approved, why is there an implementation lag? Use a new highway as an example. (B) Must all fiscal policies have a long implementation lag? Explain.

Answer: (A) Projects must first be planned. A new highway requires a considerable amount of surveying before the specifics of its route and features are established. Land must then be acquired. There continues to be a sequence of employing different types of labor and other inputs for different phases of the construction. The final product may not be completed for several years. (B) Projects that require little planning will have a shorter implementation lag.

OBSERVATION POINT:
Spend, Spend, Spend

Keynesian policy is often seen as providing politicians with an excuse to justify doing what is closest to their hearts—spend! Unfortunately, putting the brakes on an overheating economy is another matter altogether—politicians do not like to raise taxes and cut the "pork." So, while politicians talk of balancing the budget over the business cycle, it rarely happens. The federal budget did not record a surplus between 1969 and 1998!

Ideology and Policy Perspectives

The Great Depression was ended by World War II, which involved a massive amount of government spending. Thus, in the prosperous decades following the War, Keynesian analysis was thought to have been proven correct. As President Richard Nixon phrased it, "We are all Keynesians, now." However, the 1960s proved to be the last decade in which Keynesian economics was widely held in such high esteem.

In the decades that followed the 1960s, macroeconomics has moved in the direction of emphasizing its microeconomic foundations, such as the incentives facing individuals and firms that, when looked at collectively, can influence the performance of the overall economy. This orientation has led *new Keynesians* to offer evidence from the labor market that suggests Keynesian analysis is valid in the short run. However, new Keynesians are more willing than traditional Keynesians to acknowledge the importance of long-run tendencies toward full employment.

New classical economists, in contrast, emphasize that free markets will lead to a full-employment equilibrium, but acknowledge factors that may cause short-run disequilibriums. With lines between Keynesians and classical economists blurring,

The Nixon library and birthplace provides perspectives on the Nixon presidency at **http://nixonfoundation.org**

economists frequently term themselves as eclectic, agnostic, or another term of that sort, meaning that they prefer not to pigeonhole themselves into any single category.

Economic analysis influences people's politics and vice versa. For example, Keynesian policy prescriptions are often adopted by people whose politics are liberal, as the term is commonly used today. The reason is presumably not because most liberals have studied the economy in detail and are convinced of the validity of the Keynesian economic model. More likely, political liberals tend to believe that an activist government can be a powerful force for good in the world. Keynesian economics calls for government to be just such a force. It provides justification for a large government, but leaves open specific categories of spending.

A similar analysis applies to political conservatives who tend to adhere to a classical perspective on the role of government. Conservatives usually distrust big government, preferring instead a more laissez-faire approach. Classical analysis suggests that much government action does more harm than good to the macroeconomy, which is in keeping with the conservative perspective.

While some controversy in macroeconomics is positive, concerning factual issues of cause and effect, most disagreement among macroeconomists is normative. For example, modern Keynesian models incorporate classical analysis of the long run. What makes these economists and their models Keynesian is that they discount the significance of the long run, preferring instead to emphasize wage and price stickiness and other short-run phenomena. Thus, the disagreement between modern Keynesians and classical economists often boils down to the degrees to which they are willing to trade off short- and long-run objectives.

SUMMARY

- Keynesian economics takes a short-run perspective, whereas the older classical economics emphasizes long-run tendencies. Say's law that supply creates its own demand is within the classical tradition, which views unemployment as a temporary phenomenon that will be corrected by market forces.

- The long-run tendency in the marketplace is toward the natural rate of unemployment and its associated output. That is the classical focus, but the process takes time.

- In the short run, unemployment could be higher or lower than the natural rate.

- The determination of real GDP, and hence unemployment, is modeled through aggregate demand/aggregate supply.

- The long-run aggregate supply curve is vertical at full employment. It will only shift as the economy's productive capacity changes. That shift will be outward as productive capacity increases.

- The aggregate demand curve is downward sloping because a lower price level will increase the purchasing power of money and prompt people to spend more.

- Keynes suggested that sticky wages and prices might hinder the economy's adjustment to full-employment output, if the economy starts at a short-run unemployment equilibrium. To remedy this situation, Keynesians focus on stimulating aggregate demand through expansionary fiscal policy. Keynesian analysis suggests that monetary policy might be ineffective, as in the case of the liquidity trap.

- More money in circulation will shift the aggregate demand curve, but leave aggregate supply unchanged. An outward shift in aggregate demand could lead to demand-pull inflation.

- Aggregate demand is underlaid by intended spending, which can be autonomous or induced.

- Induced spending multiplies autonomous spending to reach an expenditure equilibrium, which is a point on aggregate demand associated with the current price level. The expenditure multiplier equals 1/mps.

- If the expenditure equilibrium is at less than full employment, Keynesians advocate additional government spending until the economy reaches a full employment equilibrium. The resulting stimulus to aggregate demand could lead to inflation and develop inflationary expectations that are hard to break. Various lags make the application of fiscal policy a tricky proposition.

QUESTIONS AND PROBLEMS

1. Explain how the natural rate of unemployment relates to long-run aggregate supply.

2. State the essential difference between classical and Keynesian schools of thought. If you were a public policymaker and received conflicting advice from a classical and a Keynesian economist, how would you choose? Explain.

3. Illustrate graphically and explain the long-run macro equilibrium.

4. On separate graphs, show demand-pull and cost-push inflation, labeling the axes, curves, and changes in output and the price level. Explain how cost-push inflation might prompt policymakers to cause demand-pull inflation. Then explain how this demand-pull inflation could lead to another round of cost-push inflation.

5. Explain why the sum of the marginal propensity to consume (mpc) and the marginal propensity to save (mps) must equal one. What is your personal value for the mpc?

6. a. Suppose the marginal propensity to save is 0.4 and autonomous spending is $1 trillion. Identify the expenditure equilibrium.
  b. To increase the expenditure equilibrium by $1 trillion, what change in autonomous spending would be needed? Why is this amount less than $1 trillion?

7. What are the three kinds of lags? Explain each. Why do lags make it harder to implement fiscal policy?

8. Identify some federal programs that act as automatic stabilizers. In each case, explain why.

Web Exercises

9. a. Using an Internet search engine such as that provided by Yahoo (located at **http://www.yahoo.com**) or Alta Vista (located at **http://www.altavista. com**), perform a separate search for the following terms: **unemployment equilibrium, fiscal policy,** and **marginal propensity to consume.** Visit several of the Web sites that your search reveals for each term and observe the context in which each term is used. Explain whether the manner in which the terms are used is consistent with their use in the text.

b. Repeat the above, but this time use a combination of terms that you select from the chapter. To eliminate Web sites that do not contain all terms, place a plus sign in front of each term you enter, such as **+"aggregate supply"** and **+"aggregate demand"**.

10. Visit the Web site of the U.S. Senate Joint Economic Committee at **http://www.senate.gov/**. Use the search feature (type in the word macroeconomics) to obtain a list of links to committee documents pertaining to macroeconomics. View five or more of these documents and briefly summarize each. Then write a short essay that explains how and why macroeconomics is a political concern.

 Visit the Web site for *Economics by Design* at
http://www.prenhall.com/collinge for a Self Quiz over
the topics in this chapter.

Exploration 14-1 Stagflation and Malaise: Ghost from the Past or Specter of the Future?

Firms face expenses associated with government mandates regarding employment and production. These expenses increase the real opportunity costs of production, thus providing an impetus for cost-push inflation. However, other forces are also at work in the macroeconomy. Specifically, innovations in production techniques reduce real production costs, thereby keeping output growing and inflation at bay.

In 1980 inflation in the United States exceeded 14 percent, and unemployment hovered over 7 percent. OPEC had succeeded in shocking the U.S. economy with another round of oil price increases. Something was wrong with the country. As President Jimmy Carter put it, there was a malaise across the land.

Since those days, technological progress has put downward pressure on *real production costs*, meaning that the opportunity cost of producing outputs has gone down. This, along with monetary restraint, led to an expanding economy with low inflation throughout the 1980s and into the 1990s.

All is not rosy, however. Leaving aside productivity-enhancing technological improvements, recent years have witnessed a number of worrisome increases in real production costs. Most notably, firms have seen their real production costs increase in response to higher indirect employee costs, higher costs of complying with government regulations, and higher legal costs. The result could easily be cost-push inflation in which real GDP and per capita living standards drop, even as inflation takes root. To see this, consider the macro forces at work in the labor market.

The Carter presidential library offers a look at President Carter's presidency at **http://carter library.galileo. peachnet.edu/ index.htm**

Costly Changes in the Labor Market

Firms across America have been hit with increases in the payroll costs that lead to neither greater output nor to higher real incomes for their employees. Rather, the costs are associated with hiring new employees, matching these employees to the right job, accommodating existing employees, and, when necessary, terminating employment.

Hiring new employees is no longer as simple as advertising a job, interviewing the applicants, checking the references, and making the best choice. Great care must now be taken to avoid lawsuits in this process. The lawsuits could come from the federal government, perhaps guarding against discrimination. Lawsuits could also come from some of the many people involved, such as someone who was not hired. Such a lawsuit might allege an unfair hiring process.

Jobs nowadays must be advertised exactly. Whereas in the past, if a particularly appealing applicant came along, the job could be tailored to suit that applicant's unique abilities, such actions today would wave the red flag of lawsuit over discriminatory treatment of those who were not hired. Hiring exactly according to the written advertisement avoids this problem, but also lowers the expected payoff to the firm from advertising a new opening. This caution increases the cost of producing the firm's output. These costs are not measured in official statistics.

Information about prospective employees is increasingly hard to come by. The Equal Employment Opportunity Commission (EEOC) issues detailed guidelines about questions that are or are not appropriate to ask of job candidates. The same questions must be asked of each candidate. The employer cannot revise the list once interviewing has started, even if it becomes obvious that some pertinent questions have been overlooked. This very formal process makes it difficult for an employer to get a feel for whether an employee will fit into the organization.

Little help is obtained from letters of recommendation. These letters are often nearly devoid of meaningful information. The threat of lawsuits bears much of the blame. After all, previous employers or others who know of reasons why someone should not be hired have no incentive to reveal it. Even if their information is true, they might still be sued for slander, defamation of character, or some other charge. There could even be dangers of lawsuits from future employers if letters of recommendation are misleadingly glowing.

Since the certain expense and uncertain outcome of a lawsuit is something few letter writers wish to face, letters of recommendation are often little more than reports on such dry, objective facts as a job applicant's previous position and duration of employment. The upshot is that, when hiring, firms face an increasingly risky process, and are less likely to find the best-qualified person for the job. This process increases per unit production costs. It also affects the marginal decision about whether to hire. The result is fewer employees per unit of output.

Government regulations and mandates have also increased employment costs. For example, the Americans with Disabilities Act mandates that firms accommodate a variety of employee disabilities. Thus, a firm cannot simply fire a worker for showing up to work inebriated, since that might be a symptom of alcoholism. Alcoholism is a covered disability. Health and safety regulations, antidiscrimination laws, family leave requirements, and other government actions are intended to make the workplace better. They are also inflationary because they increase per unit real production costs.

Such cost increases even arise from government-mandated protections for employees about to lose their jobs. For example, consider the requirement that firms notify their employees at least 60 days prior to closing a production facility and laying off employees that work there. In those 60 days, firms can expect to see both productivity and quality drop, perhaps precipitously. After all, employees are not usually motivated to do their best if they know that they will be out of work shortly. If they choose to produce at all, firms must be prepared for high absenteeism, low productivity, and even sabotage. In these ways, legislation designed to cushion the blow of unemployment has the unintended side effect of increasing firms' real production costs.

The Cost-Push Specter—Not a Short-Term Visitor?

The previous section focused on the increasingly costly process of creating and maintaining jobs. The many items mentioned tell only a small fraction of the story of how government legislation and private litigation have combined to raise the real

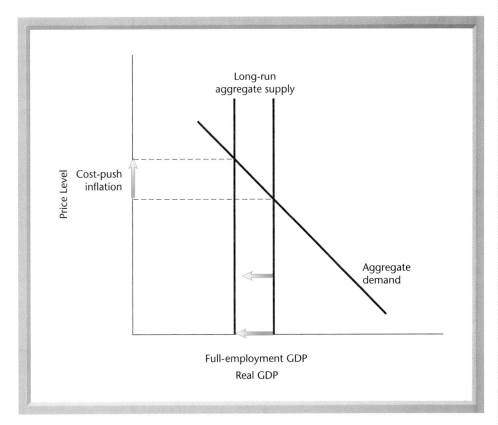

FIGURE 14-7   **Long-run cost-push inflation** can arise from changes in employment practices that lead to higher real production costs.

cost of doing business. The result is a reduction in real GDP, as we measure it. However, to the extent that the legislation and litigation are worth doing, then it has
countered that loss of measured GDP with unmeasured intangible benefits. The idea
is to make the workplace safer, fairer, and less disruptive to private lives. In the
process, however, purchasing power falls and prices rise.

Figure 14-7 illustrates the effect of higher real production costs on the macroeconomy. Because the changes are structural, they shift the long-run aggregate supply curve to the left. Long-run aggregate supply shifts to the left because the
combination of legislation and litigation has increased structural rigidities in the
employment process, thereby increasing the natural rate of unemployment. Mostly,
however, it is that resources are taken away from the production of goods and services measured in GDP.

The leftward shift in long-run aggregate supply causes *long-run cost-push inflation*,
as shown by the increase in the price level in Figure 14-7. The result of the long-run
cost-push inflation is that the same amount of money buys fewer goods at higher
prices.

Job Stress and the Elusive 40-Hour Workweek

Despite all the government presence in the employment process, it often does not seem that life on the job is any easier. This is not surprising. The same incentives that reduce the number of employees firms wish to hire also motivate firms to obtain more productivity from the employees they already have. From the employees' perspective, finding new jobs is more difficult. Because all employers face similar incentives to increase productivity, employees have little recourse but to bear down and be more productive. Thus, we see the rise of workweeks that are much longer than the traditional 40 hours.

Incongruously, we also see more temporary and part-time positions. The reasons for both trends are similar. Part-time and temporary workers are easier to hire and fire and require fewer federally mandated benefits. For example, firms will go to extraordinary lengths to stay below 50 full-time employees. Firms that exceed that threshold find themselves subject to an array of costly mandates and regulations. Part-time and temporary workers often provide the flexibility to avoid that threshold.

Taken as a whole, then, the increasing presence of well-meaning laws pertaining to the workplace is threatening that mainstay of middle-class American existence, the 40-hour workweek. Part-time and overtime work is on the rise. Whether or not these changes are for the long-term good, is it any wonder that jobs seem stressful? Employment statistics measure the quantity of employment. We have no federal measure of its quality. The increasingly common reports of violence in the workplace give reason to wonder.

Doom and Gloom or a Technology Boom?

Inflation arising from the cost-push inflationary forces described so far would lower the purchasing power of our incomes. Real GDP would fall. Government would be reluctant to fight this inflation too vigorously, because that would require it to shift aggregate demand leftward, which would compound that falling GDP. We are thus left with stagflation and the malaise of more stressful jobs. This is a gloomy prognosis, indeed.

We can take comfort, however, in observing that many of the cost-push forces described in this Exploration have been growing stronger for many years, whereas inflation and unemployment remained modest for most of those years. One prominent reason might be that, even as firms are faced with higher costs per employee, they are also incorporating more efficient technologies and modes of operation. Technological progress has been an ongoing process that tends to reduce real production costs and thereby lower the price level and increase output. The result is just the opposite of stagflation. Ongoing technological improvements offer the prospect of offsetting the costly structural changes in the workplace.

Technology can even help defeat malaise, because it can make work more invigorating and rewarding. Thus, there is hope that the forces of doom and gloom will be kept in check by a technology boom.

1. The macroeconomic orientation of this Exploration is best characterized as classical with a focus on the supply side, because the Exploration highlights the effects of legislation and litigation on productivity and notes that technological change might counter these effects. Keynesian economists might choose to highlight other features of the macroeconomy. Identify some additional forces at work in the macroeconomy. Would they support or counter concerns over stagflation and malaise?

2. This Exploration notes that laws and regulations are enacted in order to accomplish some worthy end. However, because these benefits are not elaborated upon, the reader might get the impression that legislation and litigation have imposed costs in excess of their benefits. Have they? Justify your answer with some specific examples.

Exploration 14-2 The National Debt and Trade Deficit— Is the United States on a Dangerous Consumption Binge?

The justification for the U.S. federal debt is that the United States offers future taxpayers valuable assets that the debt has helped pay for. Foreign ownership of that debt also poses little threat to, and may actually enhance, the security of the United States. However, there are few safeguards within government to ensure that sound decisions are made as to additions to or subtractions from the national debt.

> *I place economy among the first and most important virtues, and public debt as the greatest of dangers.*
>
> —Thomas Jefferson

Why do babies cry? You would cry, too, if you were born nearly $20,300 in debt. That is how much debt Uncle Sam has already rung up for each new baby born as a United States citizen. The federal government adds to that national debt each year in which it runs a budget deficit, that is, a shortfall of revenues below expenditures. The 1998 budget surplus—the opposite of the budget deficit—represented the first time in nearly three decades that the debt actually shrank a little.

The national debt can be thought of as the *stock* of accumulated past budgetary imbalances, and the deficit or surplus as a *flow* that, respectively, adds to or subtracts from that debt. By 1998 the budget surplus was $69 billion, and the national debt stood at over $5.5 trillion. That debt represents about 70 percent of the annual value of U.S. output. Interest payments alone account for about 14 percent of total federal government spending.

Is this situation fair? Is our government doing the right thing by spending our next generation's money, without them having any voice in the matter? After all, the colonists of Massachusetts rebelled against unjust English taxes in the 1773 Boston Tea Party. Their rallying cry, "Taxation without representation is tyranny!" provided one more spark to the fire that formed the United States of America. Is our government engaging in tyranny against future American citizens?

national debt: how much money the government owes; in recent years, has been about two-thirds of U.S. GDP.

budget deficit: a situation in which government collects less revenue than it spends.

budget surplus: a situation in which government collects more revenue than it spends.

Why Borrow?

To answer these questions, ask yourself when debt is justified. You may run up debt to pay for a college education. If you expect a payback in the form of a better income down the road, some debt while in college seems justifiable. What if you "own" a home? Few people own their homes outright. Yet most homeowners, even those with hefty mortgages to pay off, do not consider themselves debtors. Government statisticians count them as debtors, though.

Most people are willing to take on debt when that debt allows the purchase of assets of greater value. The homeowner who takes on a mortgage and the lender who offers that mortgage figure that the value of the house is more than enough to cover the balance due on the mortgage. Indeed, most homeowners with mortgages view the difference between the value of their homes and what they still owe as a primary source of their savings.

Government statisticians take a different view. When the government measures how much Americans save, it subtracts from that savings figure the amount that is owed on mortgages. The value of the homes is left out because it is difficult to measure. Because there are so many homeowners with mortgages in the United States, America's savings rate then appears artificially low when compared with that of other countries.

Likewise, when the government reports its own debt, it does not offset this debt with the value of the assets it owns. After all, how do you value assets of the government? Those assets include such things as parks, highways, military bases, military equipment, a judicial system, and much more. Taken as a whole, we know the value is quite high. We also know that new babies born as U.S. citizens will obtain benefits from these assets for years to come. From this perspective, expecting future citizens to bear some of the costs does not seem so bad.

Would the next generation accept this deal—to be born with both the privileges and obligations of being a U.S. citizen? While we cannot ask them, we can observe their parents answering that question with their actions. It would be most unusual to find an expectant mother seeking to leave the United States so that her baby would be born elsewhere. In contrast, many expectant parents from other countries attempt to enter the United States so their babies can become U.S. citizens.

Just because most people believe that, on balance, there is a positive value to living in the United States does not tell us that the United States has the right amount of debt. If the accumulation of debt exceeds the accumulation of assets, the value of our country diminishes over time. If the United States holds down debt by cutting back on public investments, the country runs the risk of missing out on investment opportunities that would look good in hindsight. U.S. opportunities for economic growth would diminish, meaning that long-run aggregate supply would not shift rightward as rapidly as it could.

The Overstated Dangers of Foreign Debt

As a country, we often accuse ourselves of being on a spending binge, one we will have to pay for later. As evidence, we point to both the federal debt and the U.S. *trade deficit*. The trade deficit is the amount by which the value of goods we import exceeds the value of goods we export. Because we spend more of our dollars on foreign goods than foreigners return in exchange for American goods, foreigners have extra dollars left over to invest in the United States. Those investments represent future obligations of this country to other countries. Yet, while it is the collection of our individual actions that leads us to a trade deficit, we don't usually consider ourselves to engage personally in irresponsible spending.

Over 80 percent of government debt is owed to U.S. citizens. Nevertheless, as the federal government adds to its debt, so too do U.S. citizens. Attracting additional foreign investment accumulates obligations to repay that debt in the future, even if the debt is in the form of foreign ownership of land, buildings, and factories. After all, it becomes their assets that we hold in this country. Is that dangerous? The problems many third-world countries had in repaying their debts are legendary. Is that problem in store for the United States?

Third-world countries ran into problems repaying their debt because that debt was denominated in U.S. dollars. They had to acquire those dollars. To the extent that the United States owes financial debt to citizens of other countries, that debt is also denominated in dollars. The critical difference is that those are our dollars; we control the presses that print the money.

Some people worry over a sudden exodus of foreign investment, possibly as a means to exert political pressure. Such worries are unfounded. If foreigners for some reason wish to stampede out of the United States, they would have to leave behind all but a small fraction of their assets. Likewise, foreign holdings of our currency pose no threat to us, because that currency will either be spent in the United States or could be replaced by newly minted bills. The United States is thus largely immune to the problems that plagued third-world debtor countries.

The other worry is whether, by borrowing and spending so much, we are selling out our heritage. Indeed, some wonder if we are somehow in another world war, this time one we are losing to the Japanese and other countries of the Far East. Are we about to lose our country to their money instead of their guns? Should we protect ourselves by not allowing foreigners to buy so many investments here?

To answer those questions, we must recognize that when foreigners invest in the United States, they are allowing us political and economic control over things of great value to them. In that way, foreigners acquire a strong interest in having our economy perform well and in maintaining good political relations.

Also, unlike in a military defeat, all investment transactions are voluntary. For instance, when Japanese investors purchase golf courses in the United States, the U.S. sellers of those golf courses think that they benefit, or they would not sell. In fact, so far, Japanese investors have not proven very astute at making real estate investments in the United States.

We have seen that the federal debt can be justifiable and that the consequences of those increases are not as worrisome as many people think. Just how much debt is the right amount, however, remains an open question.

No Clear Route to Fiscal Discipline

Suppose the public decides that government should reduce the national debt. How is it done? Should taxes be raised? Taxes take away our personal control over the money we earn. Raising taxes also tends to cut into productivity because it reduces the rewards for work effort and taking business risks. Then there is that other problem:

Those in favor of higher taxes rarely think that the extra tax burden should be borne by themselves.

The other alternative is to cut spending. Which spending? After all, everyone has their pet projects, especially when it comes to Congress. The problem is that, in the abstract, everyone wants to cut the budget because no one likes to pay. When it comes to particulars, though, the public can't agree.

There is no easy way out. Meat cleaver approaches, such as legislation or a constitutional amendment to balance the budget, are unlikely to live up to the hopes of their supporters. The problem is that Congress can hide its taxes and spending, because it has no accounting firm overseeing its budget.

For example, without the excess of Social Security tax revenues over expenditures, the federal budget deficits would have continued uninterrupted since the late 1960s. Yet including the Social Security surplus in the federal budget is highly misleading, since the reason to build up extra revenue is to meet Social Security's obligations in the future. Such future obligations would be recorded by firms in the private sector on their quarterly and annual reports, in accordance with generally accepted accounting principles. In contrast, the budget of the United States is a long way from meeting generally accepted accounting standards. There are reasons.

The U.S. budget contains a current accounting of revenue inflows and outflows, along with an accounting for debt. Missing, however, is any capital account, listing the value of assets and liabilities. For example, taxpayers faced huge liabilities from federal insurance of bank and savings and loan deposits in the 1980s, but the potential for those liabilities was never recorded in the federal budget when the insurance was granted. How many more such liabilities lie in wait for us?

Conversely, the vast wealth of land and capital owned by the federal government is also not accounted for. Thus, should it wish to do so, Congress could reduce the budget deficit by selling federal land and capital to whoever would pay the most. There is no ledger of the value lost when these sales occur. Thus, it would be tough to force Congress to adhere to a budget, when it has so much leeway over what that budget contains.

Hush-a-Bye Little Baby

In summary, the newborn baby need not cry over the bill from Uncle Sam. After all, Uncle Sam is handing over a lot of valuable assets along with that bill. Nor need the baby lose a great deal of sleep over international debt, as the dangers are overstated. Giving government the incentive to economize, however, will continue to be a challenge in the years ahead.

■ Prospecting for New Insights

1. JUAN: It makes me mad sometimes to realize that so many U.S. workers are working for foreign-owned companies. We are becoming a country of servants who won't ever have much chance of making it to the top of those foreign firms.

TERRI: What's the alternative? Should we refuse to buy foreign products unless they are made abroad?

What do you think? Are we becoming a nation of servants because of increased foreign investment? Is this a consequence of our choice to borrow and spend so much?

2. Keynesian economics suggests that deficit spending can be justified to pull the economy out of an unemployment equilibrium. Yet deficit spending has occurred every year in recent memory, despite the economy being at or near full employment in the large majority of those years. What are some likely explanations for this expansionary fiscal policy? Should Keynesian economics take any blame?

Appendix
SHORT-RUN PATHS TO A LONG-RUN EQUILIBRIUM

THE INCOME-EXPENDITURE MODEL BEHIND AGGREGATE DEMAND

Keynesian analysis of the demand side of the macroeconomy can be understood with the help of the *Keynesian cross* model, also called the income-expenditure model, which relates intended spending to actual GDP. This model, illustrated in Figure 14A-1, has two components: the 45-degree line and the aggregate expenditure function, to be discussed in the following paragraphs.

The 45-degree line shows how much spending can be sustained by any given amount of production. If intended spending and production are equal, then the economy must be at some point on that 45-degree line.

The aggregate expenditure function shows how much is intended to be spent at each possible level of real GDP. Actual GDP will always be the same as aggregate expenditures, except for unintended changes in business inventories. Unintended inventory changes show up as the difference between intended and actual investment, as follows:

Aggregate expenditures = consumption + intended investment
+ government + net exports

Actual GDP = consumption + actual investment + government + net exports

Because of autonomous spending, the aggregate expenditure function has a positive vertical intercept, as shown in Figure 14A–1. The autonomous spending leads to production, which leads to induced spending through the expenditure multiplier effect described earlier. The result is an expenditure equilibrium, in which the values of spending and production are equal. This equilibrium occurs at the intersection of the aggregate expenditure function and the 45-degree line.

To see why this intersection represents an equilibrium, consider what would happen if real GDP were either above or below it. If the economy produced less than the equilibrium, intended spending would exceed output and inventories would be drawn down. Firms would then increase output in order to replace those inventories. Likewise, if production exceeded the equilibrium, intended spending would not keep pace with production and inventories would build up. Firms would cut back output

income-expenditure model: used to show how the economy arrives at an expenditure equilibrium, which is determined by the point at which actual GDP and intended expenditures are equal.

aggregate expenditure function: shows how much is intended to be spent at each possible level of real GDP.

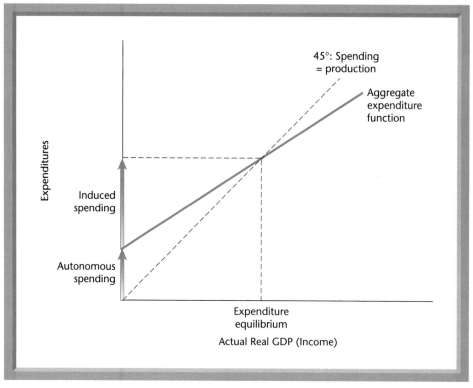

FIGURE 14-A1 **The Keynesian cross.** When the value of autonomous and induced spending just equals the value of actual production, the economy is at an expenditure equilibrium.

until the equilibrium was reached. When intended spending and actual output are identical, inventories are neither drawn down nor built up, and thus the economy is in an expenditure equilibrium.

The Keynesian model is now thought to tell only part of the story, however, because it omits any mention of supply-side features. The modern tool of aggregate supply and aggregate demand analysis incorporates the Keynesian cross implicitly. The Keynesian cross lies hidden behind the aggregate demand curve. To see how, consider Figure 14A-2.

The top portion of Figure 14A–2 shows that an increase in the price level shifts the aggregate expenditure function downward. This shift occurs because the higher price level represents inflation that erodes the purchasing power of both autonomous and induced spending. For example, consumers without income will spend less if inflation has diminished the value of their savings. There is then less of a multiplier effect, and the expenditure equilibrium drops to a lower GDP, such as from GDP_1 to GDP_2 in Figure 14A–2.

The bottom part of that figure merely notes that the higher price level, P_2, is associated with the lower expenditure equilibrium, GDP_2. By the same token, the lower price level, P_1, is associated with the higher expenditure equilibrium, GDP_1. This relationship between the price level and the expenditure equilibrium is nothing more or less than aggregate demand.

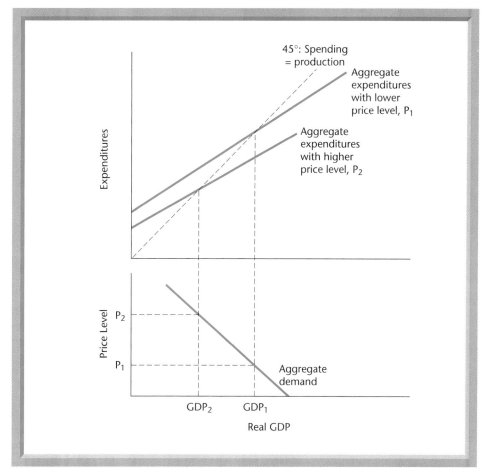

FIGURE 14-A2 **From the Keynesian cross to aggregate demand.** As the price level rises, the real purchasing power of both autonomous and induced spending falls, thus lowering the expenditure equilibrium from GDP_1 to GDP_2. Aggregate demand shows the expenditure equilibrium for each price level.

SHORT-RUN AGGREGATE SUPPLY

The movement from an unemployment equilibrium to a long-run equilibrium at full employment can be understood more fully with the help of short-run aggregate supply. **Short-run aggregate supply** tells how much output the economy will offer in the short run, at each possible price level. Short-run aggregate supply holds all labor supply curves of individual workers constant, meaning that worker expectations about wage opportunities are also constant.

Short-run aggregate supply slopes upward, as shown in Figure 14A-3. Two reasons for its upward slope are as follows:

- *Structural rigidities*—as new spending power is added to the economy, it tends to raise wages and prices where it first hits, before eventually diffusing throughout

short-run aggregate supply: tells how much output the economy will offer in the short run, at each possible price level.

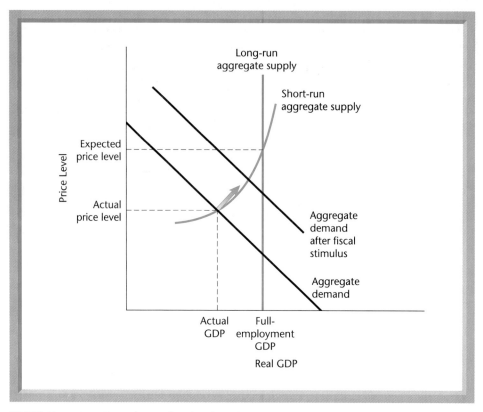

FIGURE 14-A3 **Stimulative fiscal policy shifts aggregate demand, moving the economy up the short-run aggregate supply curve.** The result is an increase in output along with demand-pull inflation.

the economy. Although not named, this effect was discussed in the main body of the chapter in the section entitled "Macro Adjustment: The Short and the Long of It."

- *The production effect*—when the price level rises and labor supply curves remain fixed, firms can profit by increasing output and employment. If the economy is already at full employment, they will employ workers overtime, thus allowing the economy to exceed full-employment output temporarily.

The production effect relies upon workers being fooled by inflation or deflation. After all, if the price level changes, workers should adjust their own labor supply curves accordingly. In the event of inflation, for example, individual wage requirements should rise, thus shifting each worker's labor supply curve upward. However, while it is easy for workers to know past rates of inflation, it is much more difficult to recognize contemporaneous price-level changes. For the economy to be in long-run equilibrium, workers must have accurate wage and price expectations. For this reason, **short-run aggregate supply always intersects long-run aggregate supply at the expected price level.**

Because the short-run aggregate supply curve intersects long-run aggregate supply at the expected price level, a change in that price level will shift short-run aggregate supply vertically. For example, if the expected price level increases, short-run aggregate supply shifts vertically upward until its intersection with long-run aggregate supply occurs at the new expected price level. Likewise, if the expected price level decreases, short-run aggregate supply shifts downward.

Such shifts are likely because workers revise their expectations over time. For example, as inflation rose significantly from 2 percent in 1960 to 6 percent in the early 1970s, most people commenced to factor inflation into their labor supply decisions—they developed **inflationary expectations,** and could be fooled only by actual inflation that turned out differently from what they came to expect. Thus, stimulative fiscal policies that shifted aggregate demand to the right were offset by upward shifts in the short-run aggregate supply curve.

When aggregate supply shifts up and to the left, the result is **short-run cost-push inflation,** as shown in Figure 14A–4. The shifting short-run aggregate supply becomes a moving target for government policymakers. If government chases an upwardly shifting aggregate supply with ever more stimulative policies that shift out

inflationary expectations: predictions about future inflation that people factor into their current behavior.

short-run cost-push inflation: occurs when an upward shift in short-run aggregate supply moves the economy up aggregate demand; associated with less output.

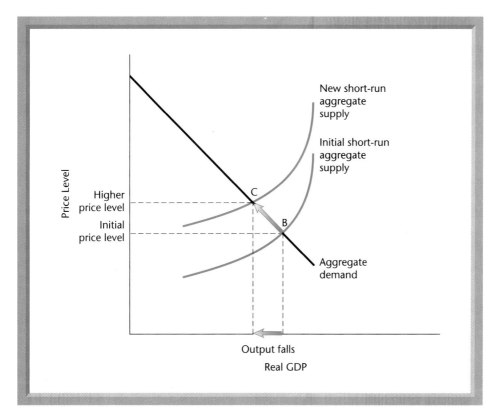

FIGURE 14-A4   An increase in inflationary expectations causes an upward shift in short-run aggregate supply. The result is short-run cost-push inflation, in which output falls and the price level rises, as illustrated by the movement from point B to point C.

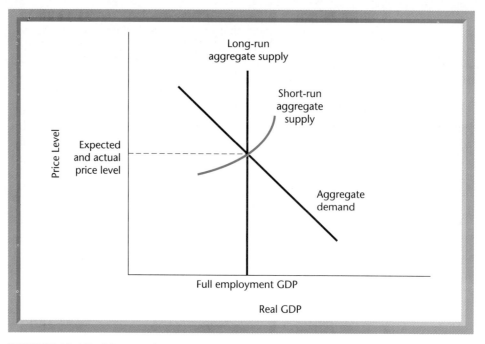

FIGURE 14-A5   Macro policy aims to achieve the full-employment output and a stable price level, which occurs when the actual price level equals that which is expected. The actual price level is given by the intersection of short-run aggregate supply and aggregate demand. The expected price level is given by the intersection of short-run supply and long-run aggregate supply.

aggregate demand, the result would be the reinforcement of inflationary expectations. As inflationary expectations rise, short-run aggregate supply shifts up and output falls, which prompts more fiscal stimuli in an ever-repeating cycle. The result is an ongoing inflationary spiral of rising and falling output along with continually accelerating inflation.

Figure 14A-5 depicts a sustainable long-run macro equilibrium, in which the expected and actual price level are equal. The expected price level is given by the intersection of short- and long-run aggregate supply. The actual price level is given by the intersection of short-run aggregate supply and aggregate demand. Because these intersections both occur at the same point, a point on long-run aggregate supply, the economy is at full employment.

In the absence of inflationary expectations or anything else that would shift short-run aggregate supply upwards, the economy will remain at full employment without inflation. Whether achieved through government policy intended to manage aggregate demand, or through a hands-off policy of giving short-run aggregate supply time to adjust on its own, this long-run macro equilibrium is usually considered to be the ideal outcome of macro policy.

Applying Concepts

1. Apply the income-expenditure model to illustrate a situation in which business inventories are being unintentionally depleted. Explain the effects of this inventory depletion within the context of that model.

2. Using two possible price levels, show how aggregate demand can be derived from the income-expenditure diagram. Label the axes and all curves and equilibrium points on both the income expenditure graph and the aggregate demand graph.

GLOSSARY

ability-to-pay principle states that those who can afford to pay more taxes than others should be required to do so.

absolute advantage the ability to produce a good with fewer resources than other producers.

adverse selection those who seek out insurance coverage are the most likely to need it; makes it difficult for individuals to get affordable health insurance and thus promotes employer group insurance.

aggregate demand relates how much real GDP consumers, businesses, and government will purchase at each price level; graphically, aggregate demand slopes downward.

aggregate expenditure function shows how much is intended to be spent at each possible level of real GDP.

allocative efficiency involves choosing the most valuable mix of outputs to produce.

appreciation when a currency buys more of other currencies than previously; makes imports cheaper and exports more expensive.

asymmetric information occurs when one person has access to more information than another on a subject of mutual interest.

automatic stabilizers features embedded within existing fiscal policies that act as a stimulant when the economy is sluggish and act as a drag when it is in danger of inflation.

autonomous spending expenditures that do not depend on income.

average cost per-unit cost; total cost/output.

average revenue revenue per unit of output; total revenue/quantity; equals price for firms that charge a single price.

balance of trade the monetary value of exported goods minus the monetary value of imported goods.

balanced-budget multiplier the effect on equilibrium GDP per dollar of additional government spending, when that spending is paid for by additional taxation; equals 1 in the simple Keynesian model.

barriers to entry   when investors or entrepreneurs find obstacles to joining a profitable industry.

barter   the exchange of goods and services directly for one another, without the use of money.

benefit principle   states that a fair tax is one that taxes people in proportion to the benefits they receive when government spends those tax revenues.

bilateral monopoly   a market with only one buyer and only one seller; usually refers to a labor market.

black market   an illegal market, which could be for illegal goods or for legal goods when buyers and sellers seek to avoid government taxes or regulations.

bonds   promises to repay borrowed funds with interest at a specified future date.

budget deficit   an annual shortfall of government revenues below government expenditures.

budget surplus   an annual excess of government revenues above government expenditures.

business cycle   the uneven sequence of trough, expansion, peak, and recession that the economy follows over time.

capital   anything that is produced in order to increase productivity in the future; includes human capital and physical capital.

capital account   component of U.S. balance of payment accounts that records the monetary value of foreign investment in the U.S. and U.S. investment abroad.

capital formation   the creation of new capital.

capital gains   the difference between the current market value of an investment and its purchase price.

cartel   a form of oligopoly characterized by collusion; intended to increase profits, but illegal in the United States.

ceteris paribus   holding all else equal.

charter schools   public schools in which a non-profit group receives a contract called a charter to operate a school for a limited period of time, usually 5 years, after which time the charter is renewed if the school meets educational standards.

circular flow   a model of the economy that depicts how the flow of money facilitates a counterflow of resources, goods, and services in the input and output markets.

civilian labor force   the population age 16 or over who are either employed or actively seeking employment.

classical   a macroeconomic school of thought that emphasizes the long run; relies upon market forces to achieve full employment.

Coase theorem   holds that parties to an externality would voluntarily negotiate an efficient outcome without government involvement when property rights are clearly defined.

collective bargaining   negotiations between labor unions and employers aimed at improving the lot of workers.

command and control   government decrees that direct economic activity.

common property resource   a jointly owned resource, such as groundwater; people have little incentive to conserve common property resources, but rather seek to capture them for their own private use.

comparable worth   the idea that government should set wages to ensure pay equity across different jobs, with comparable pay for jobs requiring comparable training effort and responsibility.

comparative advantage   the ability to produce a good at a lower opportunity cost (other goods forgone) than others could do.

compensating wage differentials   higher pay that compensates for undesirable aspects of a job.

complement   something that goes with something else, such as cream with coffee; the cross elasticity of demand is negative.

conglomerate merger   brings together firms whose lines of business have no obvious relationship to each other.

constant returns to scale   when the long-run average cost remains constant as the firm proportionally expands its use of all its inputs.

consumer price index (CPI)   measures prices of a market basket of purchases made by consumers living in urban areas.

consumer surplus   the difference between the maximum amount that a good or service is worth to consumers and what they actually pay for it; in brief, demand minus market price.

consumption tax   a tax on spending rather than on income.

contestable markets   when new rivals can enter or exit the market quickly and cheaply; could characterize either oligopoly or monopoly.

corporation   a type of firm that is a legal entity separate from the people who own, manage, and otherwise direct its affairs.

cost-push inflation   occurs when a leftward shift in either short-run or long-run aggregate supply moves the economy up aggregate demand; associated with less output.

cross-subsidization   when prices on some goods or services are set high enough to offset losses on other goods or services; may be required by government, such as for postal services.

crowding-out effect   represents money that would have gone to private sector investment, but instead goes to finance government borrowing.

current account   records the monetary value of imports and exports of goods and services.

demand   relates the quantity of a good that consumers will purchase at each of various possible prices, over some period of time, *ceteris paribus*.

demand deposits   checking account balances.

demand-pull inflation   occurs when a rightward shift in aggregate demand moves the economy up short-run aggregate supply; associated with greater employment and output.

deposit multiplier   the maximum possible value of the money multiplier; equals the reciprocal of the reserve requirement.

depreciation   a decrease in the value of capital, such as from capital wearing out or becoming technologically obsolete; also, a decline in the purchasing power of a currency when it is exchanged for other currencies, which makes imports more expensive and exports cheaper.

deregulation   the scaling back of government regulation of industry.

derived demand   the demand for labor; exists only because there is a demand for the firm's output.

development   when technology is embodied into capital.

discount rate   the interest rate; the rate at which future values are reduced to their present value equivalents; also the rate of interest charged by the Federal Reserve on short-term loans to member banks.

discouraged workers   people who would like to have a job, but have given up looking; not counted as unemployed because they are not included in the labor force.

diseconomies of scale   when the long-run average cost rises as the firm proportionally expands its use of all its inputs.

dumping   the selling of a good for less than its cost of production; prohibited by the General Agreement on Tariffs and Trade.

dynamic scoring   allows for consideration of all behavioral changes caused by changes in government policy.

economic growth   the ability of the economy to produce more output.

economic rent   earnings in excess of opportunity costs.

economics   studies the allocation of scarce resources in response to unlimited wants.

economies of scale   when the long-run average cost declines as the firm proportionally expands its use of all its inputs.

efficiency   means that resources are used in ways that provide the most value, that maximize the size of the economic pie; economic efficiency implies that no one can be made better off without someone else becoming worse off. Economic efficiency is divided into two types: allocative efficiency and technological efficiency.

egalitarianism   the idea that an economy's output should be divided equally among all its citizens.

elastic   refers to either demand or supply, where the value of the elasticity exceeds 1.

elasticity   measures the responsiveness of one thing (Y) to another (X), specifically, the percentage change in Y divided by the percentage change in X.

elasticity of demand measures the responsiveness of quantity demanded to price, specifically, the percentage change in quantity demanded divided by the percentage change in price, expressed as an absolute value.

elasticity of supply measures the responsiveness of quantity supplied to price, specifically, the percentage change in quantity supplied divided by the percentage change in price.

entrepreneurship personal initiative to combine resources in productive ways; involves risk.

equation of exchange an identity that shows that the amount of money people spend must equal the market value of what they purchase. Money supply multiplied by velocity of money equals the average price of output multiplied by aggregate output (MV = PQ).

equilibrium see market equilibrium.

equity fairness.

excess reserves deposits banks hold as reserves in excess of reserve requirements established by the Federal Reserve.

exchange rate price of one currency in terms of another.

exit when a firm goes out of business; the firm no longer has either fixed or variable costs.

expected return the value of an investment if successful, multiplied by the probability of success.

expenditure equilibrium the level of GDP that the economy tends toward in the short run, at a given price level.

expenditure multiplier the reciprocal of the marginal propensity to save in the simple Keynesian model; when multiplied by a change in autonomous spending, gives the change in equilibrium GDP.

expenditures approach computes GDP by summing spending on consumption, investment, government purchases, and the value of net exports.

exports goods and services a country sells to other countries.

external costs value lost to third parties that is not included in market supply and demand, such as the costs of pollution.

externalities side effects of production or consumption that affect third parties who have no say in the matter; these can involve either external costs, such as from pollution, or external benefits, such as from a neighbor maintaining an attractive yard.

federal funds rate the interest rate on reserves banks lend to each other.

Federal Reserve System the U.S. central bank, established in 1913; contains three primary components: the Board of Governors, the Open Market Committee, and Regional Federal Reserve Banks; conducts monetary policy and participates in bank regulation.

fiscal illusion   when voters focus on visible benefits from projects and ignore the less-obvious costs.

fiscal policy   government tax and spending policy; can be either expansionary, such as through lower taxes and higher spending, or contractionary, such as through higher taxes and reduced spending.

fiscal policy lags   the time it takes between when a macroeconomic problem occurs and fiscal policy action takes effect to correct it; consists of a recognition lag, action lag, and implementation lag.

fixed cost   the cost of fixed inputs, which are those that cannot be changed in the short run.

floating exchange rates   when currency prices are determined by market forces, without much intervention by governments.

free markets   the collective decisions of individual buyers and sellers that, taken together, determine what outputs are produced, how those outputs are produced, and who receives the outputs; free markets depend on private property and free choice.

frictional unemployment   unemployment associated with entering the labor market or switching jobs.

full employment   occurs when the economy is at the natural rate of unemployment.

game theory   the notion that market participants use strategies to play economic "games," similar to strategies used in winning at bridge, poker, chess, and other games.

GDP deflator   index of representative prices across the spectrum of GDP; used to compute real GDP.

General Agreement on Tariffs and Trade (GATT)   an agreement signed by most of the major trading countries of the world, which limits the use of protectionist policies; enforced by the World Trade Organization.

government failure   the inefficiency of government processes.

gross domestic product (GDP)   the market value of the final goods and services produced in the economy within some time period, usually 1 quarter or 1 year.

horizontal integration   when a firm merges with another in the same line of business.

housing vouchers   government grants that the recipient can spend only on housing.

human capital   acquired skills and abilities that increase the productivity of labor.

implicit opportunity costs   the monetary value that capital investments and the entrepreneur's time would have in their best alternative uses; also, the value of any best forgone alternative.

imports   goods and services a country buys from other countries.

incentive pay   a pay structure in which workers profit if their actions add to the profit of their employer; intended to counter the principal-agent problem.

income-expenditure model used to show how the economy arrives at an expenditure equilibrium, which is determined by the point at which actual GDP and intended expenditures are equal.

incomes approach computes GDP by summing various income items, such as wages and profits.

indexing automatically adjusting the terms of an agreement to account for inflation.

induced spending expenditures that depend on income; rises if income rises, and falls if income falls.

inelastic refers to either demand or supply, where the value of the elasticity is less than 1.

infant industries start-up industries that might be unable to survive the rigors of competition in their formative years.

inferior goods demand for these goods varies inversely with income; their income elasticities of demand are negative.

inflation rate the percentage change in a price index.

inflationary expectations predictions about future inflation that people factor into their current behavior.

intended investment the amount of investment planned by investors; often differs from actual investment due to unplanned inventory changes.

interest rate represents the cost of borrowing and the reward for saving or lending.

investment spending now in order to increase output or productivity later; can be in either human or physical capital.

invisible hand the idea that self-interest leads the economy to produce an efficient variety of goods and services, with efficient production methods as well. As described by Adam Smith in *The Wealth of Nations* (1776), the invisible hand of the marketplace motivates producers in search of profit to provide consumers with greater value than even the most well-intentioned of governments could do.

Keynesian any economist subscribing to the macroeconomic perspective of John Maynard Keynes; emphasizes the short run and the importance of fiscal policy.

labor people's capacity to work, exclusive of any human capital they possess.

labor force participation rate the ratio of the civilian labor force to the population age 16 and over.

land all natural resources, in their natural states; gifts of nature.

law of diminishing returns when additional units of labor or any other variable input are added to the production process in the short run, the marginal product of the variable input must eventually decrease.

leading indicators housing starts, manufacturers' orders, and other statistics that are expected to change direction before the economy at large does.

limit pricing charging the highest price customers will pay, subject to the limit that the price not be so high that potential competitors enter the industry.

liquidity   how easy it is to convert an asset into a spendable form; highly liquid assets are often used as money.

logrolling   when politicians trade votes in order to obtain projects of direct benefit to constituents in their districts.

long run   period of time sufficiently long that all inputs are variable.

long-run aggregate supply   the idea that, in the long run, the price level does not affect the amount of GDP the economy produces; graphically, long-run aggregate supply is vertical at full-employment GDP.

long-run average cost   cost per unit of output when all inputs are variable.

M1, M2, M3   three measures of the money supply, defined in order of decreasing liquidity.

managed care   patient care with an emphasis upon cost control, such as provided by a HMO.

marginal benefit   the value obtained by consuming one additional unit of a good.

marginal cost   the cost of producing one more unit of output; Δtotal cost/Δoutput, or, equivalently, Δtotal variable cost/Δoutput.

marginal cost of labor   the additional cost of employing one more unit of labor.

marginal cost pricing   an efficient price, determined by the intersection of marginal cost and demand; achieved in a perfectly competitive market; an efficient regulatory objective under conditions of market failure.

marginal product (of labor)   additional output produced by the addition of one more unit of labor; Δoutput/Δlabor.

marginal propensity to consume (mpc)   the fraction of additional income that people spend.

marginal propensity to save (mps)   the fraction of additional income that people save.

marginal revenue   the increase in revenue to the firm from selling one more unit of output; Δtotal revenue/Δoutput.

marginal revenue product (of labor)   the increase in revenue to the firm from selling labor's marginal product; Δtotal revenue/Δoutput.

marginal tax rate   tax rate on additional income; Δtax payment/Δincome.

market equilibrium   a situation in which there is no tendency for either price or quantity to change.

market failures   when markets fail to achieve efficiency, as in the case of public goods, externalities, and sometimes, market power.

market power   when individual sellers have at least a bit of control over the prices of their outputs; arises from barriers to entry.

marketable permits   property rights to a specified amount of an activity, such as groundwater pumping or air pollution, where those property rights can be bought and sold; can efficiently achieve quantity targets set by government.

microeconomics   concerns the individual components of the economy.

mixed economies   the mixture of free-market and command-and-control methods of resource allocation that characterize modern economies.

models   simplified versions of reality that emphasize features central to answering the questions we ask of them.

monetarism   view that the Federal Reserve should maintain a slow and steady growth of the money supply, because monetary policy cannot effectively counter short-run economic fluctuations.

monetary base   the sum of currency held by the public plus bank reserves; can be controlled by the Federal Reserve.

money   a medium of exchange that removes the need for barter; also a measure of value and a way to store value over time; defined by the Federal Reserve as M1, M2, and M3.

monopolistic competition   a market with numerous firms selling slightly differentiated outputs.

monopoly   a market with only one seller of a good without close substitutes.

monopsony   a market with only one buyer; usually a labor market with a local or highly specialized employer.

moral hazard   the temptation for consumers to increase their consumption of an insured good or service, such as healthcare, if insurance covers part of the cost; more generally, a distortion of price signals under insurance plans, resulting in inefficient behavior.

moral suasion   exhortations to do the right thing, as defined by public policymakers; often associated with public humiliation of those who fail to comply.

mutually interdependent   when the individual actions of firms in an industry have direct effects on market conditions facing other firms in that industry.

national debt   how much money the government owes; in recent years, has been about two-thirds of U.S. GDP.

natural monopoly   when one firm can supply the entire market at a lower per-unit cost than could two or more separate firms; associated with economies of scale.

natural rate of unemployment   the minimum long-run sustainable level of unemployment.

net domestic product (NDP)   gross domestic product minus depreciation.

net social benefits   social benefits minus social costs.

new growth theory   emphasizes the importance of new ideas in generating economic growth, and of intellectual property rights in providing the profit incentive to generate those ideas.

nominal values   data that are not adjusted for inflation; for example, the interest rate posted in the bank is the nominal interest rate.

nontariff barriers   any of a variety of actions other than tariffs that make importing more expensive or difficult.

normal goods   demand for these goods varies directly with income; the income elasticity of demand is positive.

normal profit   the accounting profit just sufficient to cover implicit opportunity costs.

normative statements   statements having to do with behavioral norms, which are judgments as to what is good or bad.

North American Free Trade Agreement (NAFTA)   trading bloc that includes the United States, Canada, and Mexico.

occupational segregation   the concentration of women workers in certain jobs, such as nursing and teaching.

Occam's razor   the idea that all nonessential elements should be stripped away from a model.

oligopoly   a market with more than one seller, where at least one of those sellers can significantly influence price; usually characterized by a few significant sellers.

open market operations   when the Federal Reserve enters the financial marketplace to buy or sell government securities, such as Treasury bonds.

opportunity cost   the value of the best alternative opportunity forgone.

original position   occurs prior to when we have assumed identities as separate people—we do not know who we will become; attributable to philosopher John Rawls.

positive statements   statements having to do with fact, concerning what is, was, or will be. In principle, the accuracy of positive statements can be checked against facts.

potential GDP   the value of GDP that would exist if all resources in the economy were employed efficiently.

poverty line   defined by the Social Security Administration as an income that is three times the cost of what it considers to be a nutritionally adequate diet.

present value   involves discounting future costs and benefits to the present-day equivalent.

price ceiling   a law that restricts price from rising above a certain level.

price discrimination   the selling of a good or service at different prices to various buyers when such differences are not justified by cost differences.

price floor   the lowest legal price; most commonly associated with farm price supports or minimum wage laws.

price freeze   a law that restricts a wide array of prices from rising above their current levels.

price gouging   the practice of raising prices to exploit temporary surges in demand; often illegal.

price searcher   a firm that is able to influence the price at which it sells its product; faces a downward-sloping demand curve.

price taker   an individual, firm, or country with no influence over the market price.

principal-agent problem the difficulty of making agents, such as managers or public servants, act in the interests of principals, such as shareholders or voters.

private costs or benefits costs or benefits that are borne by the decision maker, such as a buyer or seller.

private good consumed by one person only—excludable and rival; most goods and services are private.

producer price index (PPI) measures wholesale prices, which are prices paid by firms.

production function the relationship between the amounts of inputs and the quantities of output a firm produces.

production possibility frontier model that shows the various combinations of two goods the economy is capable of producing.

profit total revenue minus total cost; unlike accounting profit, economic profit defines cost to include implicit opportunity costs.

progressive tax a tax that collects a higher percentage of high incomes than of low incomes.

proportional tax a tax that collects the same percentage of high incomes as of low incomes.

public choice examines economic incentives within government, including those that face voters, politicians, and the administrators of government programs.

public goods goods such as national defense or clean air that are nonexcludable and nonrival, meaning that a person's consumption of the good does not reduce its quantity for others; most public goods are impure, meaning that they are not completely nonexcludable and nonrival.

pure competition a market in which there are numerous firms, all of which are price takers, although not all of which are otherwise identical.

purely competitive labor market a market in which the intersection of market supply and market demand determine the wage rate; no firm or worker possesses market power.

quantity demanded the quantity that consumers will purchase at a given price.

quantity supplied the quantity that will be offered for sale at a given price.

quantity theory of money contends that velocity and aggregate output are unaffected in the long run by a change in the money supply, implying that a change in the quantity of money causes a proportional change in the price level; based on the equation of exchange.

quota quantity limit on imports.

rational ignorance when voters make the rational choice to remain uninformed on many public issues.

real values data that are adjusted for inflation; for example, the real interest rate equals the nominal interest rate minus the inflation rate.

regressive tax   a tax that collects a lower percentage of high incomes than of low incomes.

rent controls   a price ceiling on apartment rents.

rent-seeking behavior   occurs when lobbyists or others expend resources in an effort to come out a winner in the political process.

research   aimed at creating new products or otherwise expanding the frontiers of knowledge and technology.

reservation wage   the lowest wage at which an individual will offer labor services.

reserve requirements   the percentage of deposits banks must retain as cash in their vaults or as deposits at the Federal Reserve; set by the Federal Reserve.

scarcity   a situation in which there are too few resources to meet all human needs.

second-best policies   policies to achieve the most efficient outcome possible, given that there is some inefficient policy or situation that will not be changed.

shift factors   anything that would move an entire curve on a graph.

short run   period of time in which at least one input is fixed.

short-run aggregate supply   tells how much output the economy will offer in the short run, at each possible price level.

short-run cost-push inflation   occurs when an upward shift in short-run aggregate supply moves the economy up aggregate demand; associated with less output.

shortage   the excess of quantity demanded over quantity supplied, which occurs when price is below equilibrium.

shutdown   when a firm ceases operations in the short run, but still incurs fixed costs; occurs when price is less than average variable cost.

signaling   sending a message, such as a college degree signaling that the recipient is an achiever.

social costs or benefits   the sum of all costs or all benefits to all members of society, usually associated with the production of a specific good.

Social Security trust fund   Social Security tax receipts in excess of those needed to fund Social Security payments to current retirees; by law, the Social Security trust fund must be held in the form of special government bonds.

specific human capital   human capital that is specific to a particular firm or kind of job.

specificity principle   the idea that policies should be targeted as narrowly and directly at a problem as possible.

static scoring   assumes no general change in behavior as a result of government policy changes.

sticky wages and prices   wages and prices that are inflexible in a downward direction, possibly caused by labor contracts or inflationary expectations.

structural unemployment   unemployment caused by a mismatch between a person's human capital and that needed in the workplace.

subsidies payments from government that are intended to promote certain activities.

substitutes something that takes the place of something else, such as one brand of cola for another; the cross elasticity of demand is positive.

substitution effect (of a wage increase) when wage rates rise, the opportunity cost of leisure rises, thus causing the quantity of labor supplied to rise, *ceteris paribus*; the actual change in the quantity of labor supplied will also depend on the substitution effect.

supply relates the quantity of a good that will be offered for sale at each of various possible prices, over some period of time, *ceteris paribus*.

supply siders economists who emphasize incentives for productivity and economic growth, such as lower marginal tax rates and less regulation.

surplus the excess of quantity supplied over quantity demanded, which occurs when price is above equilibrium.

tariff tax on imports.

tax base that which is taxed.

technological efficiency implies getting the greatest quantity of output for the resources that are being used; for any given output, then, a least-cost production technique must be chosen.

technology possible techniques of production.

technology mandates occur when government instructs producers as to the exact technology to install to remedy some public problem.

"the dismal science" economics, viewed from the perspective of Thomas Robert Malthus, in which population growth must eventually reduce us all to no more than a subsistence existence.

the margin the cutoff point; decision making at the margin refers to deciding on one more or one less of something.

time deposits certificates of deposit (CDs), which can only be cashed in without penalty after a stated period of time, such as 1 year.

total product the total quantity of output produced by a firm's labor.

trade creation efficient specialization and trade caused by lower trade barriers among members of a trading bloc; implies a greater amount of world trade.

trade diversion trade among members of a trading bloc that would more efficiently be conducted between trading bloc countries and other countries outside of the bloc.

trading blocs agreement among a group of countries that provides for lower trade barriers among its members than to the rest of the world.

transfer payment the redistribution of income from one group to another.

underground economy market transactions that go unreported; associated with black market activity.

unemployment rate the ratio of the number of unemployed persons to the number of persons in the labor force.

unemployment equilibrium a short-run equilibrium GDP that is less than full-employment GDP; the amount of real GDP that occurs when aggregate demand intersects short-run aggregate supply at a price level above the price level at which aggregate demand intersects long-run aggregate supply.

unfunded mandates occur when government requires the attainment of public policy goals by firms or lower units of government, without providing the funding necessary to carry out those actions needed to achieve those goals; access for the disabled is an example.

unit elastic refers to either demand or supply, where the value of the elasticity equals 1.

universal access the requirement that all citizens face the same prices and access to services, regardless of the cost of serving them; most commonly associated with the provision of postal services.

universal coverage a situation in which everyone has equal access to health insurance; eliminates the problem of adverse selection.

user fees charges for use of a publicly owned good, service, or resource.

value added the difference between the price of output and the materials cost of inputs.

value-added tax (VAT) a form of consumption tax that collects the difference between what companies earn in revenues and what they pay out in previously taxed costs.

variable cost the cost of variable inputs; in the long run, all costs are variable.

velocity of money the average number of times money changes hands per year.

vertical integration when a firm acquires another firm that supplies it with an input, or acquires another firm which can sell the first firm's output.

voluntary export restraints an alternative to import quotas in which exporting countries agree voluntarily to limit their exports to the target country; has an effect similar to an export cartel, such as OPEC.

vouchers provide spending power, but only on certain categories of goods or services, such as food or housing.

Washington Monument strategy when a government agency offers a bare-bones budget that cuts its most popular functions; intended to increase the chances that a more generous budget will be approved.

World Trade Organization (WTO) international organization formed to administer the General Agreement on Tariffs and Trade.

zero-sum game a situation in which the winner wins only what the loser loses; in contrast to voluntary economic transactions, in which both parties gain.

INDEX

Efficiency
  of market equilibrium, 90–92
  market failures and, 11–12
  of taxes, 318, 338
  tradeoff with equity, 9–10, 325–326
Egalitarianism, 21–22
Einstein, Albert, 17
Elastic demand, 123
Elasticity, 121–127
  of demand. *See* Demand elasticity
  of supply, 127
Electrical products, safety of, 101
El Paso, Texas, 308–311
Emission standards, 300
Employment
  domestic, international trade and,
    55–56, 160–161, 385–386
  full, 385
  increasing workweek and, 470
  Social Security and. *See* Social
    Security program
Employment discrimination, 264–265,
    277–282. *See also* Wage
    discrimination
  affirmative action and, 264, 280–281
  premarket, 280
  public policy and, 282
  reverse, 281
  statistical, 280
Energy prices
  alternative energy sources and, 395
  OPEC and, 110
Engels, Friedrich, 21
Entrepreneurship, 41, 202
Entry into industry, 196
  barriers to, 220, 223–224, 240–241
  in pure competition, 221, 223
Environment
  externalities and, 296
  pollution of. *See* Market failure;
    Pollution *entries*
  standards for, as argument against
    free trade, 172–173
  technology mandates and, 300
Environmental Protection Agency
    (EPA), 300, 301, 308
Epcot Center, 231
Equal Employment Opportunity
    Commission (EEOC), 468
Equal Pay Act (1963), 278
Equation of exchange, 428
Equilibrium, 83–92
  expenditure, 457–460
  long-run. *See* Long-run equilibrium

market. *See* Market equilibrium
  market demand and supply and, 83
  unemployment, 450
Equity
  of global income distribution, 277
  of taxes. *See* Tax equity
  tradeoff with efficiency, 9–10,
    325–326
Escobar, Pablo, 137
Espionage, industrial, 205
Ethics, of business, 204–205
Euro, 418–419
Eurobond market, 184–185
European Economic Community,
    148, 167
European Monetary Union, 418–419
Eurosclerosis, 398–399
Excess reserves, 420
Exchange
  equation of, 428
  money as medium of, 416
Exchange rates, 148–153
  currency appreciation and
    depreciation and, 150–152
  fixed, 151
  floating, 151–152
  target zones for, 150
Exclusive franchises, 226
Executive Order No. 11246, 278
Existence, perpetual, of
    corporations, 183
Exit from industry, 196
  in pure competition, 221, 223
Expansional fiscal policy, 451
Expansion stage of business cycle, 365
Expectations
  demand shifts and, 78, 79
  inflationary, 454, 479
Expected benefits, 98
Expected prices
  demand shifts and, 78, 79
  supply shifts and, 81
Expected return, 392
Expenditure equilibrium, 457–460
Expenditure multiplier, 459
Expenditures approach to GDP, 379
Experience goods, 97
Exports, 53, 153–155. *See also*
    International trade
  net, in GDP, 354
  voluntary restraint of, 164
External benefits, 65, 290–291
External costs, 64, 290–291
  externalities and, 294–296

External funds, 184
Externalities, 11, 290–291, 294–296.
    See also Market failure

F

Fair Labor Standards Act (1938),
    252, 268
Fallacy of composition, 15
Family farms, 206–210
Farm Aid, 206
Farming
  corporations and, 207–209
  family farms and, 206–210
  price supports and, 116–118
  subsidies and, 166
Federal budget deficits, 371–372, 471
Federal Deposit Insurance Corporation
    (FDIC), 420–421, 435, 436
Federal funds, 420
Federal funds rate, 420, 432
Federal Open Market Committee
    (FOMC), 422
Federal Reserve Act (1913), 422
Federal Reserve Banks, 422, 423–424
Federal Reserve Bulletin, 37
Federal Reserve System (Fed), 414,
    422–430
  fed watching and, 432
  monetary policy and, 427–430
  money multiplier and monetary base
    and, 425–426
  open market operations of, 424
  structure and functions of, 422–424
  tools of, 425–427
Federal Trade Commission
    (FTC), 245
Federal Trade Commission Act
    (1914), 245
FedEx, 42, 241, 242
Feebates, 344
Fiat money, 51, 416
Final goods and services, 352
Financial capital, 41
Financial intermediaries, 184, 421
Financial investments, foreign, 158
Financial markets, global, 184–185
Financing, of firms, 183–185
Firms, 180–217. *See also specific firms*
  competitive. *See* Competition; Pure
    competition
  dominant, with competitive
    fringe, 234
  downsizing of, 275